Principles
of Counseling and
Psychotherapy

Principles
of **Counseling** and
Psychotherapy

Learning the Essential Domains and
Nonlinear Thinking of Master Practitioners

Gerald J. Mozdzierz,
Paul R. Peluso, &
Joseph Lisiecki

Routledge
Taylor & Francis Group
New York   London

Routledge
Taylor & Francis Group
711 Third Avenue
New York, NY 10017

Routledge
Taylor & Francis Group
2 Park Square
Milton Park, Abingdon
Oxon OX14 4RN

International Standard Book Number-13: 978-0-415-99752-2 (Softcover) 978-0-415-99751-5 (Hardcover)

Visit the Taylor & Francis Web site at
http://www.taylorandfrancis.com

and the Routledge Web site at
http://www.routledge.com

GJM—This book is dedicated specifically to Felix and Genevieve Mozdzierz, whose devotion to parenting, guidance, and support provided the foundations for learning, hard work, and contributing; it is in general dedicated to those teachers and supervisors who served as mentors of great humanity, wisdom, and patience.

PRP—To Roy M. Kern and Augustus Y. Napier, my teachers, my mentors, and my friends. Many thanks for all the lessons I have learned.

JL—To Jack Cowen, Kurt Adler, and all of our other mentors, colleagues, clients, friends, and family who inspired us.

Contents

Foreword

About this book: In 1960, in his preface to his collection of essays on personality titled *Personality and Social Encounter* (Allport, 1960), Gordon W. Allport, one of the wisest men ever to come to grips with the issue of personality, asked, "What is human personality?" He found he could offer no definitive answer. Instead, he gave voice and recognition to the truth that lay in all those positions that honestly sought the answer to that question, even though they provided responses to it that he termed *paradoxical*. He wrote,

> Some would say that it [personality] is an ineffable mystery—a shaft of creation, an incarnation. Since no man can transcend his own humanity, he cannot hold the full design of personality under a lens. The radical secret will ever elude us.
>
> Others would say that personality is a product of nature. It is a nervous-mental organization, which changes and grows, while at the same time remaining relatively steadfast and consistent. The task of science is to explain both the stability and the change.
>
> Those who would hold either of those views—or both—are right. ...
>
> Some say that personality is a self-enclosed totality, a solitary system, a span pressed between two oblivions. It is not only separated in space from other living systems, but also marked by internal urges, hopes, fears, and beliefs. Each person has its own pattern, his own unique conflicts, he runs his own course, and dies alone. This point of view is correct.
>
> But others say that personality is social in nature, wide open to the surrounding world. It owes its existence to the love of two mortals for each other and is maintained through love and nurture freely given by others. Personality is affiliative, symbiotic, sociable. Culture cooperates with family in molding its course. 'No man is an island.' This view, too, is right. (p. v)

And, of course, Allport recognized that other frames also merited consideration.

Instead of quailing at the metaphysical paradoxes posed by these seemingly veridical yet competing views of what it is to be a person—either by retreating to the ideological security provided by one of the part views of human existence generated by a "great man's" theory, and in so doing blind himself to that which is also true, or by restricting his descriptions of human nature exclusively to "facts" gleaned by an army of social insects following well-marked, approved trails, and thereby miss the larger picture or leave the field in abject surrender—Allport (1960) chose to bravely soldier on, much, I believe, to his advantage and ours. His approach, he wrote,

> is naturalistic, but open-ended. Naturalism, as I see it, is too often a closed system of thought that utters premature and trivial pronouncements on the nature of man. But it can and should be a mode of approach that deliberately leaves unsolved the ultimate metaphysical questions concerning the nature of man, without prejudging the solution. My essays are all psychological and therefore naturalistic, but they have one feature in common—a refusal to place premature limits upon our conception of man and his capacities for growth and development. (Allport, pp. v–vi)

Given that, explicitly or implicitly, therapeutic interventions are based wholly or in part (sometimes one just repeats that which one perceives to have worked, with no other reason for doing so) upon one's conceptualization of personality, one would expect, if Allport's analysis of the state of personality theory were correct, that a proliferation of psychotherapies would ensue, a goodly number containing a kernel of actuality in addition to their other constituents. This is indeed the case, I believe.

Today we stand not 10 years past the midpoint of the previous century, but 10 years into a new century. Although I have little doubt that our understanding of the human condition has improved somewhat in these 50 intervening years, I believe it has done so in detail. The larger picture, that divined by Allport, remains basically unchanged. And although there seems to be increased agreement that the efficacy of a subset of the panoply of interventions labeled psychotherapeutic has been reasonably established, and that these work effectively to reduce human misery and some specific miseries more so than others, how and why they do so are still moot in spite of, I believe, sectarian claims to the contrary.

That you are reading this foreword at all, I take as evidence that you, as well as Allport and the authors of this excellent book, have not yielded to the seductive enticements of nihilism, be it represented by a retreat to ideology, "factism," or "burnout." What, then, to do? What other course provides a good-faith alternative, one that, again to quote Allport (1960), can "open doors and clear windows so that our chance of glimpsing ultimate philosophical and religious truth may not be blocked?" (p. v). To my mind, the authors of this work, Gerald Mozdzierz, Paul Peluso, and Joseph Lisiecki, provide one. The overarching aim of psychological treatment, as they envision it, is to foster clients' *disengagement* from preoccupation with symptoms, pathology, dysfunctional frames, and defective action patterns so that engagement with healthier beliefs and behaviors can occur. The tack they employ is to teach how master therapists think across the essential domains of competence that are necessary if a therapist—whether a beginning, advanced, or established therapist—is to be effective with patients. These are (a) connecting with and engaging clients; (b) assessing the clients' readiness for change and their strengths and goals; (c) building and maintaining a therapeutic alliance; (d) understanding, empathizing into, and working respectfully with the clients' cognitive schemata; (e) addressing the clients' emotional states and traits; (f) understanding and working with clients' ambivalences about change; and (g) using insight-generating nonlinear thinking and interventions to communicate more effectively with clients and to help clients communicate more effectively with themselves. The authors emphasize and demonstrate cogently, clearly, and to good effect that master practitioners do not think exclusively in conventional, linear ways, but at crucial times in the process of intervening in the lives of their clients distinguish themselves by a recourse to nonlinear thinking and communications in the service of engendering positive changes in their clients.

Befitting a text that takes such pains to distinguish degrees of therapeutic sophistication, the authors give considerable attention to the "stages of development" that would-be therapists traverse on their path to mastering the science and art of intervening for the better in the lives of those who come to them for help. The model the authors adopt to schematize that journey is that proffered by Stoltenberg (1997). Using this flexible, three-level, integrated, developmental schematization of counselor development, the authors define and describe the personal preoccupations of therapists at each level that may interfere with their growth as therapists and offer workable suggestions as to how they might get back on track should they be detoured.

Just as I have, I trust that you, regardless of where you place yourself on the ladder of psychotherapist development, will find this book useful and enlightening, for its authors have done an excellent job of summarizing and synthesizing the relevant literature, empirical and theoretical, on how psychotherapy when it is psychotherapy proceeds and works. Their presentation on training and developing psychotherapists is also state of the art. Their prose is lucid, straightforward, and nuanced. Just as I have, you will, I trust, appreciate the breadth and depth of knowledge that they express so clearly. Although that is all well and good and cannot be gainsaid, the exceptional worth of this book inheres in the insights it conveys into how master therapists function with their clients. And, make no mistake about it, the authors[1] give every indication that they are indeed master therapists. Their clinical illustrations are apt, pithy, and illuminating. They write of their clients with warmth, respect, and empathetic and insightful understanding. Their examples of nonlinear intervention are well-chosen, witty, enlivening, and perspicacious.

To sum up, to my mind, little has changed since Allport (1960) fully 50 years ago concluded that no one veridical, comprehensive view of personality had yet emerged. Instead, he believed that the human sciences created numerous descriptions of human nature and action, many of which represented an aspect of truth, but none the total picture. Although one could hope to build an accurate whole out of analyzing and synthesizing these part pictures, Allport (1960) surmised that it was impossible to harmonize their fundamentally conflicting elements. His response to this state of affairs was not to leave the field or proceed to study it in "bad faith." His alternative: to continue on, while refusing to prematurely limit the conception of what it is to be human, and to work toward a valid naturalistic approach to human nature that, as he put it, "must have open doors and clear windows, so that our chances of glimpsing ultimate philosophical and religious truth may not be blocked" (Allport, p. v).

Because our understanding of psychotherapy and counseling is inherently linked to our understanding of human personality, those who wish to rightly alter for the better the state of those who present themselves as clients are faced with the same choice that Allport confronted. The authors of the text before you, Mozdzierz, Peluso, and Lisiecki, have provided, I believe, an appropriate response to that challenge. Train oneself and train others in the strategies and thinking that master therapists employ to engage and assist their clients in living better. Mozdzierz, Peluso, and Lisiecki's text is admirably designed to assist in that task. It is up-to-date and factual. Its principles of intervention are applicable to a diverse clientele experiencing diverse difficulties. It enables therapists of differing theoretical orientations to employ the frameworks provided by the theories they adhere to while applying the schemas that master therapists use in treating their clients. And, it teaches them admirably well, for not only are its authors master therapists, but they are also master teachers.

Herbert H. Krauss, Ph.D.
Pace University
September 29, 2008

ENDNOTE

1. In the interest of full disclosure, I ought to indicate that I have had a close professional and personal friendship with the first author, G. J. M., for over 40 years. On my part, it was based on my respect for him as an exceptionally able psychologist and a fine and decent man of unquestionable integrity. I have met J. L. and have had no contact with P. P.

Preface

> If I have seen further it is by standing on [the] shoulders of Giants.
>
> Sir Isaac Newton, 1676

As odd as it may seem, this text has a "story" to tell—it contains a narrative of sorts. The theme of the narrative concerns evolution, and as such it represents the growth in our collective understanding of how counseling and therapy work—their effective ingredients and how they work together in a sequence of sorts. As our understanding has evolved, it is clear that there has always been much to be learned from what master practitioners *do* when they interact with their clients, but there is even more to learn from *how they think about things therapeutic.* That revelation is a major part of the backdrop in our narrative.

Following that major understanding about our "narrative," in each of the four major sections of our text, which obviously succeed one another, we first describe more fundamental and foundational thinking (and therapeutic understandings) that must precede more advanced concerns. It's just like telling a "story"— here is where our story begins, and as a consequence of that, here is how it evolves in the next section, and so on. The evolution of the thinking that we describe is not absolute—few things seem to be. Rather, it is heuristic, and meant to help counselors and therapists develop *their* thinking to evolve further.

Like all good narratives, we believe that our story has a rather unique, timeless, and sparkling introduction and a somewhat surprising ending. Although we would hope that our story is a "page turner" that will leave the reader breathless, it is after all a textbook that will be inspiring to some and mind-numbing to others.

Like some stories, we also have a "prequel" to tell. We give a hint regarding the nature of our prequel in the quote at the beginning of this preface by Sir Isaac Newton. That is, our narrative has precursors to whatever contributions that we may be making to an understanding of the nature and processes of counseling and psychotherapy. The coming together of this text reflects a combination of several things: a love for the field of counseling and psychotherapy, decades of study, practicing our craft, writing, teaching, and supervising. We collectively share amazement at the potential for healing that counseling and psychotherapy have in settings too numerable to mention. Our text and its prequel also reveal a deep respect and amazement for those master practitioners who seem to practice effectively and effortlessly. Those practitioners' efforts in concert with the creative, disciplined, and methodical work of countless researchers are the "shoulders" upon which we have stood to make our observations and write our "story."

Our narrative is an effort to take the seemingly therapeutically mysterious (i.e., the apparent magical results that master practitioners obtain) and demystify it. In doing so and revealing their "secrets" (i.e., *how* they think), we can hopefully put the "magic" we are unveiling to use in training practitioners and benefiting their clients. The historic classical giants of our field deserve recognition in our "prequel" (e.g., Freud, Adler, Jung, Horney, Rogers, and Sullivan). We note sadly that other, more modern masters passed away during the preparation of our manuscript. These include Paul Watzlawick, Insoo Kim Berg, Steve de Shazer, Michael White, Albert Ellis, and Jay Haley, just to name a few. Their passing punctuates the fact that if the best elements of their diverse (yet similar) ways of mastery were not preserved, they would pass into legend and be forgotten. That would be an unnecessary loss to the field and to coming generations of practitioners (as well as their clients). We are grateful for all their precursor contributions. It is our fondest hope that this text continues the evolution in thinking and understanding about psychotherapy and counseling that they nurtured.

There is a somewhat muted but nevertheless ominous reality underlying our narrative as well. It is our fear that the best ideas and methods of teaching are in danger of becoming lost in the training of new practitioners. This may very well be due to the fact that although demands for more training are being imposed, some aspects of training have become curtailed. To add further intrigue to our "plot," emphasis seems to have moved more toward the technical and mechanical aspects of *what* to say and *how* to say it, pinpoint pigeonhole diagnoses, psychopathology, risk management, and so on, rather than a more acute focus on developing and shaping the critical and reflective thinking that enables a practitioner to *know* how to provide clients what they need. We do not believe that this needs be the case and offer our work as a way of conceptualizing *how to think like a counselor and therapist.*

Gerald J. Mozdzierz

Paul R. Peluso

Joe Lisiecki

Acknowledgments

A project like this requires dedication and support in order for it to get through the process to publication. There have been many people who have helped us keep our dedication, and have supported us throughout. One person in particular who was instrumental in making this work was Dana Bliss and everyone from Routledge. We would be remiss if we did not also acknowledge those friends and colleagues who have encouraged us along the way, most especially Jon Carlson, Jim Bitter, Richard Watts, and Bernard Shulman.

We are also indebted to the countless clients and families with whom we have worked who sparked our imaginations, stimulated our thinking, and in the end promoted our development as better clinicians. These nameless individuals were the inspiration for the clinical case examples contained in the book.

Last, and most heartfelt, we could not have devoted the time, energy, and effort that a work such as this requires without the love and support of our families, especially our spouses, Charlene Mozdzierz, Jennifer Peluso, and Mary Ann Lisiecki. We also extend a specific loving acknowledgment to our children (Kimberly, Krista, Pamela, and Andrea Mozdzierz; Helen and Lucy Peluso; and Ann Marie, Joseph, Teresa, and Paul Lisiecki).

PART ONE

Introduction

Introduction to Part 1

About This Book

CONTENTS

This book has been written with students, beginning therapists, and more seasoned practitioners in mind, professionals who are feeling stuck, slightly burned out, and concerned that they are "missing" some training, skill, or awareness of how to practice effective therapy. The latter practitioner may be working too hard at the wrong things. This book is designed to provide the experiences recommended above, and help developing therapists to learn about the processes that underlie effective outcomes with a wide variety of clients. This goal is guided and supported by several recurring themes:

1. *Highly effective (i.e., "expert") therapists think in a different way from novices that allows them to connect and intervene with clients successfully and efficiently.* Readers are introduced to the thinking processes of those practitioners (i.e., therapists with consistently good therapeutic outcomes) as they pertain to clinical assessment and intervention, which we believe will increase their knowledge and skill as therapists as well as reduce feelings of loss, confusion, frustration, inadequacy, and burnout.

2. *Empirical research has revealed a "convergence of understanding" about a common set of factors that very effective master practitioners attend to and utilize in treatment that are*

3

repeatedly associated with good outcomes. Convergence of these factors, or domains of competence, does not force a therapist to adopt a certain theoretical orientation, but rather allows a therapist to operate within her or his own unique philosophical framework. By exposing the reader to the seven domains of competence (see below), which must be attended to in addressing individual patient concerns, therapists can target their strengths or weaknesses, and begin to increase their effectiveness.

3. *Therapists' abilities seem to mature according to a progressive model of development.* As a certain set of domains are mastered, therapists are able to advance to levels of greater complexity and ambiguity, which allow them to be able to work with clients that present with multifaceted psychological problems. By placing the aforementioned domains of competence within a model of therapist development, readers can understand the logical progression toward mastery that will decrease feelings of being lost, confused, and stuck.

Given these guiding philosophies, it becomes clear that this is *not* just another "basic counseling skills" textbook. Rather, it represents the first major attempt to help beginning therapists and established practitioners learn about the essential domains of competence and thinking processes that are required in order to be effective with a broad spectrum of clients, rather than having to rely on a series of disconnected "techniques" or theories of personality. We address each of these themes below.

LEARNING TO *THINK* LIKE A THERAPIST: THE CHARACTERISTICS OF EXPERT THERAPIST THINKING, AND WHY IT IS IMPORTANT TO LEARN *HOW* TO THINK LIKE A THERAPIST

All professions share a certain "common rule" in training and educating new professionals. Whether it is medicine, law, journalism, nursing, physical therapy, or financial investing, students are taught to *think* in a particular way, that is, how to go about achieving the stated goals of their particular profession. This kind of thinking customarily consists of appraising a particular "problem," deciding what *not* to do, and choosing the best way of professionally dealing with the particular unique set of circumstances that are the current focus of attention from within their given discipline. For example, from the beginning of their training, physicians are taught to think in a certain way beginning with the first rule of medicine, namely, "Do no harm!" Doctors are taught that *not doing* can be as important as—if not more important than, in many instances—doing the wrong thing or doing something too quickly and needlessly aggravating a condition.

Successful stockbrokers and stock analysts also demonstrate *a way of thinking* that is distinct from that of the uninitiated. John Q. Public will not want to buy stocks when they are depressed in price or out of favor. Professional stockbrokers and mutual fund managers, however, see such circumstances as potential opportunities to buy underappreciated stock assets. In other words, "The time to buy is when blood is running in the streets!" Unknowledgeable people are selling in panic at the bottom of stock market cycles (i.e., "when blood is running in the streets") in order not to "lose everything" and are buying at the peak in order not to miss out (i.e., greed) on "making a fortune" like everyone else. They are caught buying high and selling low—an impossible way to make money. Among other things, professional stockbrokers and traders don't care what a stock has done in the past; they care where it is going. They *think differently.*

Likewise, law students are taught a *process of thinking*: not only how to construct the side of an issue they are defending, but also how to construct their opponent's side of the issue. They learn that knowing the other side of the issue will help them to see the arguments that they will encounter and thus how to derive counterarguments.

The same principle of learning *how to think* ought to hold true for psychotherapists and counselors. Training today does not appear to emphasize an awareness of thinking processes or to help therapists explicitly learn how to think like therapists. Instead, training programs continue to teach antiquated methods designed to train students how to mimic "experts," but not how to think like them. Although many of these experts have acquired the ability to think in nonlinear ways over many years of study and practice, we do not believe that one must necessarily wait for 5, 10, or 20 years of experience (i.e., trial, error, and clinical failure) in therapy to begin to cultivate this way of working effectively with clients. In fact, this text develops, in depth, not only what those nonlinear thinking processes are, but also how to apply them from the beginning of one's career. We define *nonlinear* processes as being at the heart of master therapist thinking.

Linear Versus Nonlinear Thinking

Linear thinking is essentially defined graphically by a straight line from a simple problem to a simple solution (a simple case example is illustrated in Clinical Case Example S1.1). "Common sense" is an example of the usefulness of linear thinking. Most people can agree on what constitutes a commonsense approach across typical human experiences: It is best not to smoke because tobacco has proven to be carcinogenic. Eat healthy food, drink alcohol moderately, don't use illicit drugs, and get a moderate amount of exercise.

However, life is often not that simple, and many people violate all of these commonsense principles everyday. The simple reason for this is that we are actually one step removed from reality and must make decisions based on our *perceptions* of reality. In turn, our perceptions are influenced by a highly engrained schematic representation of ourselves, others, and the world around us. For example, clients who are anorexic or bulimic may know that their eating disorder and weight loss are potentially killing them and that they should just eat (linear thinking, simple solution), but they often continue to restrict their dietary intake to dangerous levels because they fear getting fat (distorted perception of themselves).

The term *nonlinear* appears to be the best poetic metaphor that we can conjure to describe the sort of thinking we envision. It is frequently defined as being disproportional to its inputs (like an equation), or, to put it in more generic terms, "The sum is greater than the whole of its parts." A nonlinear way of thinking does not resemble a straightforward, characteristic, one-dimensional, logical approach to human problem solving but rather the sort of thinking that turns things upside down and inside out—it departs from the linear way of thinking about things. In other words, it is a distortion, just like the perceptions of the client with an eating disorder presented above. De Bono (1994) discussed what he calls "lateral thinking," which is similar to nonlinear thinking, as follows:

> Lateral thinking is both *an attitude of mind* and also a number of defined methods. The attitude of mind involves the willingness to try to look at things in different ways. It involves an appreciation that any way of looking at things is only one among many possible ways. It involves an understanding of how the mind uses patterns and the need to escape from an established pattern in order to switch into a better one. (pp. 59–60; emphasis added)

Lateral thinking "involves escaping from a pattern that has been satisfactory in the past" (de Bono, 1994, p. 70) but that may not be working anymore: "We switch to a new pattern and suddenly see that something is reasonable and obvious" (de Bono, p. 57). Linear thinking is the process of looking at a problem along one dimension, a familiar, habitual, and perhaps previously successful way of approaching a problem or even life itself. At its core, linear thinking represents the characteristic and traditional way in which a particular personality approaches life and problem solving. By contrast, nonlinear (or lateral) thinking is "out-of-the-box" thinking. It requires therapists to see and understand the client's characteristic, old, "personally" linear pattern; envision a new, alternative way (or pattern) of seeing and behaving; and communicate that new way to the client. Thus, it may appear to be mysterious, seemingly askew, perhaps risky, and not logically following from what the client presents. However, when nonlinear interventions are presented to the client, the thinking is revealed to be dynamic, energizing, and deeply understanding of the client's concerns on a profound level. A simple case is illustrated in Clinical Case Example S1.1.

Clinical Case Example S1.1: A Serious Heart Condition and Obsessing

A man with a serious cardiac condition entered counseling complaining of being unable to stop thinking about his ex-wife. To stay preoccupied and "obsessed" with his ex-wife would appear to be for all practical purposes nonproductive and certainly disruptive to his daily functioning. She is gone, and typically the prospects of repairing divorced marriages are dismal. A client may know that but "can't control" it. For the therapist to tell the client to "stop" thinking about his ex-wife (i.e., linear thinking, which is direct and straightforward and common sense) is futile because if he could heed such counsel, he would have stopped doing it and not needed counseling in the first place. Hence, when confronted with the rigid pattern of the client's mal-adaptive behaviors (i.e., obsessing about one's ex-wife), the expert practitioner considers ways of understanding the client's pattern and suggests a new, larger pattern that the client's obsessing behavior may be a part of. This is demonstrated when the therapist points out how useful and helpful it may be for a man to keep thinking about his "ex." What frequently follows such an unexpected intervention is an unconventional (i.e., quite different from the characteristic manner in which a person has been thinking) response; a changed and enriched reality follows as the client sees how the new or enlarged pattern encompasses his old behavior. At this point, the client must make a choice about what to do next. Thinking about one's ex-wife may very well serve a protective function—an individual "obsessed" with what happened in the past, by exclusion, can't be thinking about what he needs to do to get on with his life. He simply may not be ready to begin thinking about life and making decisions about what to do without his former wife. In fact, thinking about his ex-wife may even be presented to him as a useful barometer of how prepared or unprepared he is at that particular moment to actually think about much more frightening matters such as the seriousness of his cardiac condition. As such, letting the man know that it may very well be useful to him to "*not* get your ex-wife out of your mind right now" simultaneously has an unexpected as well as a distinctly emotional impact. It has become axiomatic in the therapy literature that shifts in an individual's thinking are more likely to occur when there are elevated levels of affect or arousal. An unexpected (i.e., nonlinear) response from a therapist triggers just such an unexpected response and elevated affect or arousal from a client.

As de Bono (1994) has suggested, nonlinear, or lateral, thinking is in part an "attitude of mind" that involves a willingness to look at things in different ways (i.e., think nonlinearly). One of the strategies for challenging irrational thoughts in cognitive therapy is to ask the client, "Are there any other possible explanations for what you concluded?" or "What might a friend tell you about your conclusions?"

It can be quite risky to begin looking at things in a different way! As such, for maximum efficacy, a nonlinear way of thinking must be incorporated with—and integrated into—one's philosophy along with other salient aspects of psychotherapy (e.g., assessing the client's readiness for change; assessing and accessing the client's strengths; aligning properly with the client's motivations, goals, and strengths; creating a strong therapeutic relationship; showing respect for the client; appropriately confronting inconsistency; understanding his or her schematic representations of the world; and handling emotional content).

Learning How to Think in Nonlinear Ways

How does someone learn about "nonlinear thinking" and how to use it in therapy? Generally, therapists learn the thinking exemplified in Clinical Case Example S1.1 only slowly and gradually through a sometimes painful trial-and-error process, or if they are referred to certain literature, if at all. Again, we do not believe that this *has* to be the case! In fact, we believe that individuals should learn these *nonlinear thinking processes* from the earliest points of their training. Of course, learning *how to think like a therapist* (i.e., astute assessment; the process of formulating what this particular case is all about, the purpose being served by symptomatic behavior, what a client is seeking, and what is needed; and devising a coherent plan about how to proceed that encompasses the relevant clinical findings and social circumstances of the person) is vastly different from telling someone *what* to think. Such "how" thinking maximizes therapist flexibility in dealing with the infinite variety that clients bring to the treatment setting. Teaching *what to think* would involve, for example, insisting that others learn a particular orientation (e.g., Freudian, Adlerian, or Jungian) framework and work only from that framework as the "truth." Traditionally, psychotherapists are exposed to a particular theory of personality, a theory of therapy, specific protocols on how to treat particular conditions (e.g., anxiety, obsessive-compulsive disorder, or depression), or a set of micro skills that they then adopt as an operational model. It is our hypothesis that each novice adopts a particular theory (of personality or therapy) because of its "fit" with his or her own worldview (see Information Box S1.1, "Theory Is for the Clinician; Therapy Is for the Client!"). The therapist then learns "how to think" from that particular frame of reference.

The amazing thing is that the research literature demonstrates that the particular theory or model of therapy (e.g., object relations, Adlerian, or Jungian) makes absolutely no difference in treatment outcome (see Duncan, Hubble, & Miller, 2000; Hubble, Duncan, & Miller, 1999; Lambert & Barley, 2002; Miller, Duncan, & Hubble, 1997a; Norcross, 2002b; Walt, 2005). In fact, it was suggested more than half a century ago (i.e., in Fiedler, 1950) that experts with different theoretical orientations are much more similar than different in what they actually do with clients. Hence, to learn about therapist nonlinear thinking, in combination with the factors that are known to increase a therapist's effectiveness, from the earliest point of development seems to be the most appropriate way to train clinicians.

Information Box S1.1: Theory Is for the Clinician; Therapy Is for the Client!

Clinicians who think in nonlinear ways and understand how to effectively utilize the common convergence factors (i.e., domains of competence) can have a greater likelihood of achieving maximally effective therapeutic outcomes. At the same time, those clinicians who have a firm grasp on their *own* theory of counseling or personality have a roadmap *for themselves* whereby they can understand and interpret the client and the problem, the process of therapy, and their own role in the change process. Consider the following metaphor to understand this point more fully.

Suppose you are putting together a jigsaw puzzle that has a picture on it. The box has the completed puzzle picture on it to give you an idea of what the puzzle will look like when finished. The client gives you information about him or herself (the pieces), but you don't know in what order to place them. You know that there is a picture that the puzzle should make. Having a good grasp of theory is like having a completed puzzle box picture to let you know where the pieces should generally fit, and what the picture (i.e., the collection of all of the client's pieces) should look like. Although you can try to put together a 500- or 1,000-piece puzzle without the box, it will probably take a lot longer. The same is true with conducting therapy without a solid theoretical grounding. You may get a lot of the client's "pieces," but to fully understand and appreciate what they mean and what to do about them will take longer.

THE RESEARCH LITERATURE AND CONVERGENCE OF UNDERSTANDING: LEARNING AND UNDERSTANDING THE SEVEN DOMAINS OF COMPETENCE

The second defining characteristic of this book is drawn from the research on "common factors" (or what we term *convergence factors*). These factors are the basic ingredients that consistently appear to be identified in the literature as vital to all effective therapy, regardless of a practitioner's theoretical orientation. Several authors have tried to identify and quantify these factors. Lambert and Barley (2002) cited and summarized numerous studies over the last 40 years that have provided interesting consistent clues regarding *therapists'* contributions to successful therapeutic outcomes. In particular, they not surprisingly concluded that therapists who exhibit more *positive* behaviors—warmth, understanding, and affirmation—and fewer *negative* behaviors—belittling, neglecting, ignoring, and attacking—were consistent predictors of positive outcome. Furthermore, they emphasized the *vital* importance of having a strong therapeutic alliance, focusing on the therapeutic relationship and making discussions about it a regular part of dialogue in therapy, and being willing to spend time on complicated issues with a sense of optimism, which are all positive characteristics of successful therapies. Last, they concluded,

> Therapist credibility, skill, empathic understanding and affirmation of the patient, along with the ability to engage with the patient to focus on the patient's problems, and to direct the patient's attention to the patient's affective experience, were more highly related to successful treatment. (Lambert & Barley, p. 22)

The critical and technically complex areas of focus are assessing readiness for change, successful problem solving and goal alignment, fostering a solid therapeutic relationship, dealing *appropriately* with client defensiveness, understanding complex cognitive schemas, a willingness to focus on the therapeutic relationship, and navigating with clients through their emotional landscape. As a result, these factors can be more challenging to learn than "techniques." But, once one learns how to think like a therapist, the process of providing treatment becomes thoroughly enjoyable. Nevertheless, for the present purposes, these factors are all integrally related to the crucial domains for which beginning therapists need training.

What Are Domains?

A *domain* can be defined as the scope of a particular subject or a broad area or field of knowledge (Skovholt & Rivers, 2004). In other words, it encompasses all aspects (the breadth and depth) of a particular topic. Regardless of the field of knowledge, mastery of essential domains is what accounts for the differences between the *abilities and results* of novices *and* experts. Novices can learn the basics of the domain (the breadth) and, over time, develop a richer understanding of the subtleties of it (the depth). As a result, it is worth stressing that domains are *not* the same as skills or techniques—skills are applied within the context of a domain of knowledge (or field). As such, they represent a *refinement of one's thinking within a certain area* rather than an application of mechanical skills. The refinement of one's thinking within particular domains includes the thought processes behind skills, explanations, and theories regarding the topic, and research about the subject area. It represents an *understanding and discernment*. The skilled surgeon knows *how to operate*, whereas the wise surgeon knows not only *how* to operate but also *whether or not to operate* in a given instance.

To further illustrate the difference between being trained to do something and knowing how and when to use it in therapy, consider the use of hypnosis or systematic desensitization. Learning the techniques of hypnosis or systematic desensitization is significantly different from understanding the circumstances of when *and how* it is (or is not) appropriate to use them. *That* is an example of being competent within a particular domain (i.e., fostering a therapeutic alliance). A practitioner may be gifted in the ability to induce a hypnotic trance or construct an anxiety hierarchy (skill competence). But if he or she tries to use them in the initial session or with every client (domain incompetence), the result is likely to be more therapeutic failures and discouragement for both the client and the therapist than successes. In fact, this is indicative of *linear thinking* within a given domain (i.e., this technique has worked in the past, so it will or should work now), whereas knowing when *not* to use the particular skill is a type of *nonlinear* approach to the domain.

When researchers looked at different practitioners' use of these "domain-specific" concepts compared to "procedural" concepts (i.e., skills), they found that "experienced counselors displayed greater consistency in the concepts they used than novices" (Skovholt & Rivers, 2004, p. 25). In other words, these experts seemed to be more familiar with the multifaceted and multidimensional aspects of the client's problem behavior (social, interpersonal, etc.) without having to rely on technical aspects of therapy (i.e., techniques) as the novices did. According to Skovholt and Rivers, this familiarity with domain-specific concepts (e.g., client readiness, treatment goals, the therapeutic alliance, cognitive schemas, and emotional underpinnings) gave them a greater sense of optimism and encouragement about making progress with the client. By contrast, novices tended to focus more on the procedural aspects of a given client problem (i.e., "How do I work with a …") rather than focus on the client's concerns. Therefore, it is important to be thoroughly familiar with a domain in order to work within it efficiently (i.e., apply the skill, use the concepts, maximize the result, etc.) and be able to apply nonlinear thinking within the domain to work with a client effectively. In this text, we will draw distinctions between linear and nonlinear thinking within each of the domains.

What Domains Are Not!

We do not recapitulate domains into a therapeutic system that forces a therapist to adopt a certain theoretical orientation. Rather, domains of competence enable the therapist to operate within his or her own, unique philosophical framework (Horvath, 2001; Miller & Moyers, 2004). As a result, the domains of competence are the common "active" ingredients that are a part of all successful therapy, but that offer multiple perspectives within them for counselors to explore and develop lifelong understanding and appreciation (Frank & Frank, 1991).

The reader is cautioned not to look at these domains as rigid constructs that run parallel to one another and never intersect. Rather, they merge seamlessly within the therapeutic endeavor so that almost every interaction between therapist and client encompasses all of the domains together.

Although a therapist could learn all of the basic (and even advanced) skills of psychotherapy, without an understanding of the broader picture of how the seven domains of competence converge and interact with their nonlinear thought processes, many developing and practicing therapists wind up wandering from client to client, becoming frustrated that an intervention or given skill set works with one client, but fails to work with another. However, with sound training and opportunities to develop these elements (i.e., nonlinear thought processes within the seven domains of competence), beginning and more advanced practitioners can develop deeper, more meaningful conceptualizations of their clients' presenting concerns. *That* is what allows for a clearer understanding of *how* to proceed in an efficient and effective manner (Skovholt & Rivers, 2004).

Introducing the Seven Domains of Competence

1. *The domain of connecting with and engaging the client—Part 1: listening; and Part 2: responding.* This domain includes both linear and nonlinear listening and responding to clients as primary vehicles for "connecting with and engaging" the client in the work of therapy. By understanding linear and nonlinear aspects of "connecting with and engaging" clients— especially in the initial interview—clinicians will be able to increase the probability of clients becoming invested in the therapeutic process in the crucial first sessions.

2. *The domain of assessment—Part 1: clients' symptoms, stages of change, needs, strengths, and resources; and Part 2: the theme behind a client's narrative, therapeutic goals, and client input about goal achievement.* This domain describes the linear and nonlinear methods of assessing clients' presenting problems and concerns at multiple levels. That includes attending to clients' readiness for change and their symptom patterns, diagnoses, strengths, and (untapped) resources that can be used in overcoming problems. The domain of assessment also includes actively eliciting client cooperation in the treatment-planning process and developing appropriate preliminary goals for treatment, which are especially important in the early stages of therapy and represent another dimension of connecting with and engaging the client in the treatment process.

3. *The domain of establishing and maintaining the therapeutic relationship and the therapeutic alliance—Part 1: relationship building; and Part 2: the care and feeding of the therapeutic alliance.* This domain encompasses perhaps the central aspect of psychotherapy: developing a therapeutic alliance. An integral part of this domain concerns developing an understanding of what factors contribute toward building a trusting therapeutic relationship with a client in the service of establishing and maintaining the therapeutic alliance. It includes such elements as listening empathically, demonstrating respect, and providing hope and ongoing goal alignment. In addition, clinicians must learn to be constantly alert to possible ruptures in the therapeutic alliance and how to repair them.

4. *The domain of understanding clients' cognitive schemas—Part 1: foundations; and Part 2: assessment and clinical conceptualization.* This domain requires a clinician to have both linear and nonlinear understandings of clients' schematized view-of-self, view-of-others, and view-of-world around them. This domain deals with global concepts such as clients' internal response sets and belief systems that guide attitudes, thoughts, and behavior that can impact treatment. As such, it is important for clinicians to understand the nonlinear components of clients' schematized belief systems. It includes becoming proficient in working with the effects of clients' developmental (family-of-origin) dynamics on their perceptions. In addition, utilizing this domain includes skills for helping clients challenge and alter distorted perceptions of the world around them.

5. *The domain of addressing and managing clients' emotional states—Part 1: basic understandings; and Part 2: managing common negative emotions in therapy.* This domain defines the nature of emotions in all of their complexity. In addition, it requires the clinician to have an understanding of the relationship between affective expressions, internal feelings, and emotional states, and their role in treatment progress (or lack thereof). Clinicians must learn the art of managing overwhelming emotions (e.g., grief and anger) that clients may express, allowing them to feel emotion in appropriate and productive ways. Likewise, in this domain clinicians must learn how to access clients' affective states—especially when no emotion appears to be expressed and there ought to be.

6. *The domain of addressing and resolving client ambivalence—Part 1: understanding and identifying client ambivalence; and Part 2: working with and resolving client ambivalence.* This domain deals with understanding the process of client "ambivalence" in its multiple dimensions as well as developing effective strategies for dealing with it, appropriately holding clients accountable, and successfully helping clients maintain therapeutic focus.

7. *The domain of understanding nonlinear thought processes and utilizing paradoxical interventions.* This domain is the pinnacle of the therapeutic endeavor. It is not a trick or technique, but a sophisticated method of nonlinear thinking that can be used to quickly and efficiently help to facilitate clients' progress toward their therapeutic goals by neutralizing, energizing, tranquilizing, or challenging dysfunctional thought and behavioral patterns. It crystallizes the direct relationship between nonlinear thinking and the previous six domains.

There is one last piece of the puzzle to complete a therapist's journey from novice to master. That is a roadmap or guide to his or her own professional growth and development.

A DEVELOPMENTAL MODEL OF THERAPIST GROWTH: GUIDING THE READER THROUGH THE LEARNING PROCESS TO HELP SPEED UNDERSTANDING OF THE SEVEN DOMAINS OF COMPETENCE AND NONLINEAR THINKING

It is not enough to simply know about the content areas of the domains (linear thinking); one must also apply them and appreciate the richness, depth, and utility of each (nonlinear thinking). That is the essence of competence, or the ability to do something well. George Leonard, former president of the Esalen Institute in California, eloquently defined mastery as "the mysterious processes during which what is at first difficult becomes progressively easier and more pleasurable through practice" (1992, p. xi). Therapists who can operate within each of the domains competently and have an appreciation for all the factors mentioned above characterize masters in the field (e.g., appreciation of complexity, personal growth, and valuing depth and breadth). It is not something that happens overnight; it is a process of development. We do not want to imply in this text that mastery happens quickly just because a practitioner thinks nonlinearly, and can utilize the seven domains. We believe that these are the elements that—when competently employed—make clinicians more effective. However, according to Skovholt and Jennings (2004), in order to achieve *mastery*, certain things have to take place. In particular,

> It is important for developing practitioners to work within a structure that provides opportunities for innovation and support when facing complexities and challenges. In addition, the structures most conducive to growth offer the developing therapist of counselor balanced opportunities for, to use Piaget's terms, assimilating and accommodating new knowledge. Ultimately, this is all part of the "support/challenge balance," where counselors are not only provided experiences that stretch and even exceed the confines of what they know, but are supported while navigating through what they do not know. (Skovholt and Jennings, p. 22)

In other words, the keys to successful growth for clinicians are good learning atmospheres that allow for divergent (i.e., nonlinear) thinking to occur, and supportive experiences that provide the developing therapist opportunities to explore the essential elements that comprise successful therapy (i.e., the seven domains). Ideally, this should all take place within a predictable arc of development. Other fields, like medicine, have predictable arcs of development for beginners. There are milestones and benchmarks that trainees hit along the way to mark their progression toward mastery. Until recently, however, models that tracked counselor development throughout their career did not exist (Skovholt & Rivers, 2004). Indeed, this lack of a roadmap has often contributed to the problem of therapists feeling lost, confused, frustrated, and ill prepared to help clients in the real world. The real problem was that many practitioners felt that it might never get better, which typically leads to burnout, or worse (Miller, 2004).

No matter how diverse a "community" of skilled practitioners may *appear* in their work, their *practices*—what they do, and what processes they attend to and emphasize in working with clients—represent a convergence of what is effective! This convergence reflects the thinking of Lave (1988) and Lave and Wenger (1991) and what they have called "situated learning"—the idea that novices gradually acquire expertise from their association and collaboration with a "community" of experts. Lave assumed the position that a case can be made for learning being social and stemming in large measure from experiences of actually participating in the community of daily activities of what is being learned.

A community of practice involves much more than the technical knowledge or skill associated with undertaking some task. Members are involved in a set of relationships over time … communities develop around things that matter to people. … *For a community of practice to function it needs to generate and appropriate a shared repertoire of ideas, commitments and memories. It also needs to develop various resources such as tools, documents, routines, vocabulary, and symbols that in some way carry the accumulated knowledge of the community … it involves practice … ways of doing and approaching things that are shared to some significant extent among members.* (Situated Learning, n.d.; emphasis added)

Lave and Wenger (1991) indicated that novices begin as "peripheral" participants in a "community," but as they improve in their skill level, they move toward "learn(ing) *from* talk as a substitute for legitimate peripheral participation … to learn(ing) *to* talk as a key to legitimate peripheral participation" (pp. 108–109).

Stoltenberg's Developmental Model

Stoltenberg (Stoltenberg & Delworth, 1987; 1997), in recognizing this deficit, proposed a three-level integrated-developmental model of counselor development. These three levels are meant to facilitate a sense of the *typical* personal and professional issues confronted by clinicians at various stages of growth and development. As therapists are able to locate and gauge their sense of progress, they can determine which professional areas (domains) need improvement. Development and growth in professional skill and judgment are not rigid concepts.

According to Stoltenberg, "Level I" counselors are characterized by focusing primarily on themselves, feeling highly anxious, and requiring structure. They may not be particularly insightful, and often look for specific techniques (i.e., "How do you …?") to utilize with clients. "Level II" counselors tend to have more confidence in their own ability and seem ready to concentrate on the cognitive and emotional experience of the client. There are, however, some shortcomings in therapists at this stage of development, as they may become overconfident in their abilities, oversimplify issues, or become emotionally overinvolved with their clients and lose professional objectivity. Last, "Level III" counselors demonstrate an awareness of the cognitive, emotional, and relational aspects of the interaction between the client *and themselves.* These therapists can listen reflectively with the "third ear," calculate the impact of particular interventions on a client, and see the client completely within his or her context without losing sight of the empathic, therapeutic alliance that is necessary to be effective.

Integrating Stoltenberg's Developmental Model With the Seven Domains

Within each of these levels of development, we insert the corresponding domains of competence that every therapist needs to acquire in order to be effective. Figure S1.1 graphically illustrates this. It is in the shape of a cone in which each level represents a greater refinement and appreciation of increased complexity, on the way toward mastery. Because Level I counselors are new and focused on more concrete, performance-based aspects of the therapeutic process, the domains of competence that must be mastered at this stage of development include effectively connecting with and engaging the client, performing an accurate assessment, determining the client's readiness for change, setting achievable treatment goals, and building a strong therapeutic alliance.

As therapists mature and develop some mastery in these domains, they begin to realize that there is more to doing therapy effectively than these particular skill sets. It is at this plateau point (between Level I and Level II) that most beginning practitioners are likely to feel lost if they do not know about the normal developmental arc of therapists' abilities. Quite paradoxically (i.e., nonlinearly), such a plateau does not necessarily signify a frustrating conclusion to the learning process, but rather can be a sign of a period of

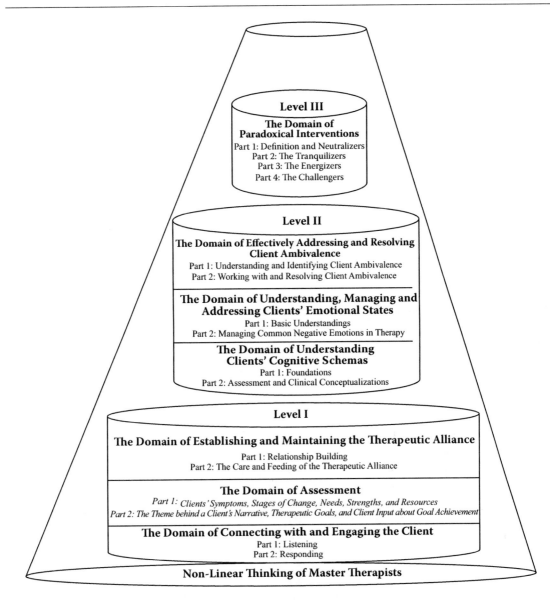

FIGURE S1.1   The Seven Domains That Master Practitioners Attend to and Emphasize.

consolidating what has been learned. Those therapists who work through the frustrations of such a period of consolidation (usually through effective supervision) begin to develop mastery of the Level II domains of competence.

At Level II, therapists are better able to focus on more complex client issues and are not as preoccupied with their own performance. These issues include understanding the client's underlying schemas (or personality) dynamics, managing and working with the client's emotional states, understanding client ambivalence, and being able to comfortably confront client resistance in a nonthreatening manner. These clinicians often feel a sense of pride in their development as they master the various domains. However, just as with the transition from Level I to Level II, if clinicians are not aware of or able to move to the next level, they are likely to eventually become discouraged and impatient with the pace and results of treatment. Likewise, Level II counselors can become impatient with the process of supervision and demonstrate their own sense of autonomy by challenging their supervisors directly or "acting out" (e.g., displaying inappropriate behavior with clients), all of which can lead to burnout.

If therapists are able to move past this transitional frustration, however, they proceed to the third level of development and begin to synthesize all the domains of competence and development. There is a flexibility and a seamlessness between the cognitive, emotional, and relational elements of the therapeutic process, as well as an ability to be able to be fully present with the client while at the same time be able to critically reflect on the content and process levels of the session. In effect, there is a maturity in their *thinking*. All of these processes are part of the advanced, nonlinear thought processes of the master therapist. The ultimate demonstration of such nonlinear thought processes is the ability to use appropriate paradoxical interventions to strengthen the therapeutic alliance, increase rapport, orchestrate symptom disengagement (by neutralizing, tranquilizing, energizing, or challenging the client), and facilitate personal growth more quickly and efficiently.

Although this process of mastery does take time, we don't believe that it must necessarily be a painful or mysterious journey. Coexistent with the educational purpose of this text, we also hope to demystify the seemingly unfathomable. We do not believe that the lengthy process of mastery should be an excuse for providing substandard therapy to clients. It is our contention that if one masters the linear and nonlinear thinking aspects of each of the domains for a particular level of development, the end result will be a more effective and personally satisfied clinician compared with those who do not undertake this. Furthermore, as a therapist progresses from level to level and masters the domains of each successive level, he or she will be able to be more effective with a greater versatility in the same way that "master therapists" are.

In order to accomplish this, this book does the following:

- Targets the training and development of a therapist's *thinking* ultimately and specifically converging on the use of nonlinear thinking in general and specifically paradoxical interventions (a complex therapeutic task).
- Helps students to learn the essential factors (the seven domains of competence) necessary for any and all effective therapists *regardless* of their theoretical orientation or individual personality characteristics based on empirical and clinical research as well as clinical experience. This is derived from Skovholt and Jennings' (2004) research on the skilled therapist.
- Places each of the seven domains of competence within the context of Stoltenberg's model.
- Applies a developmental approach utilizing Stoltenberg's well-researched three-level model of therapist development.
- Places not only the tools but also the *thinking* behind the use of these tools solidly in the hands of readers so they can begin incorporating and utilizing them in practice settings or field placements.
- Discusses how current neuroscience research findings relate to the psychotherapy process.
- Discusses how issues of diversity, culture, and context relate to the psychotherapy process.

In addition, we feel that this text is highly innovative in what it *does not* purport to do, such as the following:

- Claim that you will "be a miracle-working therapist in seven easy steps!" Becoming a therapist takes training, experience, supervision, and time. What this book *does* hope to do is accelerate the natural development of many individuals by introducing the seven domains of competence in a way that is demystified.
- Propose any of the seven domains of competence (especially paradoxical interventions) as a "trick," "gimmick," or "technique" that is *used to "put something over"* on clients. Rather, we take a relational approach that a therapist must collaborate with clients and be able to gain their cooperation in order to be effective.
- Indoctrinate readers into any particular theoretical orientation, or rigid way of conducting therapy. Rather, we help the student to learn the thought processes underlying successful therapy that can be utilized as a part of any school of psychotherapy.

In closing, Miller, Mee-Lee, Plum, and Hubble (2005) have cautioned that decades of research have shown "that 'who' the therapist is accounts for six to nine times as much variance in outcome as 'what' treatment approach is employed" (p. 50). This book is written for you and your development as a practitioner with that very idea in mind.

The Basic Skills of Counseling and Psychotherapy

A New Look

1

CONTENTS

THE PROBLEM OF THE SORCERER'S APPRENTICE

In the Disney movie *Fantasia*, Mickey Mouse takes the role of the sorcerer's apprentice. It is a story that dates back 2,000 years to a Middle Eastern tale of a powerful sorcerer and his apprentice who watches the master's great feats and wants to learn the secrets of the magic. The apprentice (Mickey Mouse) is consigned to perform menial tasks, including getting water from a well. But the apprentice aspires to be a great sorcerer himself (of course), and borrowing the sorcerer's magic hat one night, he casts a spell to animate a broom and get it to fetch water for the household. At first he's successful, and soon he begins to dream of becoming a great sorcerer and commanding the stars, the clouds, and the waves. The problem is, he can't make the broom stop fetching water, and it begins to flood the house! In a panic, the apprentice tries to hack the broom to pieces with an ax. But each fragment becomes a whole broom, and the army of brooms brings a deluge of water that floods the entire house. Just when it seems that there is no hope of controlling the spreading deluge, the sorcerer appears as a *deus ex machina*, takes his hat back from the apprentice, magically dries up the flood, and restores order. The sorcerer chastises the apprentice for mistaking technique for mastery and overestimating his powers.

In many ways, beginning a career and developing expertise as a psychotherapist resemble the story of the sorcerer's apprentice. In our training, we watch tapes of legendary masters of the craft, or perhaps witness a live demonstration at a workshop or conference. Masters seem to resolve the most complex of problems with penetrating insight or exacting skill. Often, it is our first clinical supervisors who seem so skilled and so knowledgeable at a time when we are finding our way through the maze of what there is to learn.

All of these individuals have one thing in common: They all seem to be "sorcerer like" in their ability to illuminate cases and develop treatment strategies, especially as compared to our own abilities as beginners. When new therapists begin to work with their first clients, there is generally very little therapeutic movement or success. Anyone who remembers treating their first Axis II personality-disordered client, unrepentant perpetrator, or entrenched substance abuser can recall having an overwhelming feeling of utter futility or failure. Sometimes, we may even try to mimic a master or supervisor, and unintentionally overreach ourselves, creating more havoc than help.

Often the beginning therapist becomes frustrated, and either acts out or emotionally withdraws from the client, which makes a complex situation still more complex. Later, the supervisor easily brings the client's issue into its proper therapeutic context. The supervisor demonstrates that what was needed was something simple and well within the beginner's reach. Just like the sorcerer, the master practitioner brings order from chaos and reinstalls normalcy. And are we beginners happy? Rarely. Such skilled supervision more often than not leaves the novice feeling foolish, inept, and in awe of the supervisor's expertise.

As a result the beginning therapist will go through the motions and use the same techniques as his or her supervisor, but not necessarily with the same results. In fact, successfully mastering the craft is about something beyond going through the motions or using techniques that have worked with another therapist. We believe that these initial disastrous results occur because novices do not know *the thought processes* behind the craft. They do not understand or know how and why certain therapist behaviors are effective and others are not effective.

We believe that novices' misguided therapeutic activities in which they mimic their supervisors are universal and that all developing therapists experience them. But, depending on the complexity of the client's problems, novice therapists may not easily recover from early failures. Instead of learning from these early experiences, they risk lapsing into a career of uneventful "routine" sessions, that is, endlessly doing the same therapy with every client. Ronnestad and Skovholt (1993) discussed the consequences for students of improper training and early clinical failures. Specifically, these students become increasingly anxious for "fixes" and look to supervisors to teach them "how to." Inexperienced supervisors often make the mistake of responding too quickly to these students, and "may easily and quickly resort to giving suggestions as to how to act, instead of engaging in the more difficult task of dwelling on understanding and unraveling the complexity that is being expressed" (Ronnestad & Skovholt, p. 398). This only compounds the problem because students develop a limited therapeutic flexibility, fail to fully appreciate complex clinical situations, eventually stagnate, and perhaps burn out rather than evolve into competent therapists. As a result, treatment outcomes for clients in therapy are often inconsistent and call into question for the therapist (and others) the effectiveness of counseling and psychotherapy as a whole (Miller, 2004).

The "problem" of the sorcerer's apprentice and learning to be a competent therapist is summarized thus: *What* apprentices are learning in schools (e.g., applying "techniques," or attempting to mimic masters) is the way that they come to *believe* what is important (e.g., "Say these words...." or "Do these gestures...."). The problem is that this is simply *not* adequate preparation for becoming an effective master therapist!

THE CURRENT STATE OF PSYCHOTHERAPY

Before further discussion, there are four core facts about counseling and psychotherapy worth noting.

Therapy Is Effective in Helping People With Mental Disorders, Adjustment Problems, and Relational Difficulties in Life

Despite many shadowy claims to the contrary, the facts are irrefutable: Many people have been helped by therapy. Miller, Mee-Lee, Plum, and Hubble (2005) summed up the findings of over 4 decades of research on the effectiveness of psychotherapy:

> Research leaves little doubt about the overall effectiveness of therapy, once it is obtained. Regardless of the type of treatment, the measures of success included, the duration of the study or follow up period, study after study, and studies of studies, document improvements in physical, mental, family, and social functioning. (pp. 42–43)

Indeed, as we will detail below, many aspects of therapy and the therapeutic process have been put to the test and found to be scientifically valid over a number of studies. Even when groups of studies are evaluated together (a meta-analysis), there are robust and replicable results (Asay & Lambert, 1999; Hubble, Duncan, & Miller, 1999; Miller et al., 2005; Norcross, 2002a). According to DiAngelis (2008), "Research shows fairly consistent results: For most nonpsychotic disorders, behavioral interventions (i.e., psychotherapy) are just as effective as medications and they hold up better over time" (p. 49). Additionally, it seems that these effects are noted (with a few specific exceptions) regardless of the particular theory of counseling (Norcross, 2002a).

Therapy Can Be Effective Quickly and Is a Cost-Effective Treatment

In fact, about 75% of clients improve during the first 6 months of therapy; about half of all clients show improvement in as few as 8 to 10 sessions (Asay & Lambert, 1999). This is particularly important when viewed in light of the high personal, financial, and societal costs of mental disorders. According to Prochaska (1999), "Mental health and behavioral health problems, such as depression and the addictions, are among the most costly of contemporary conditions—costly to the individuals afflicted, their families and friends, their employers, their communities, and their health care systems" (p. 233). In other words, the economic impact in terms of lost productivity and time (for both themselves and their loved ones) for those with mental illness or trouble adjusting to life circumstances can be substantial (U.S. Department of Health and Human Services, 2000), and helping those people function more effectively has a significant economic benefit. These facts led John C. Norcross (a nationally recognized leading researcher and writer on psychotherapy effectiveness) to conclude, "In a climate of accountability, psychotherapy stands up to empirical scrutiny with the best of health care interventions" (2002a, p. 4).

Despite These Potential Benefits, It Is Still Difficult to Get Treatment for Those Who Need It and Retain Them as Clients so That They Get the Help They Need

According to some estimates, less than one fourth of individuals with a diagnosable DSM-IV-TR[1] (*Diagnostic and Statistical Manual of the American Psychiatric Association*, 4th ed., text revision; American Psychiatric Association, 2000) disorder will ever seek therapy, and of those who do, roughly half drop out of treatment before there is significant improvement (Prochaska, 1999), even though research shows that treated patients are far better off than untreated patients (Asay & Lambert, 1999). In previous generations, the stigma of therapy might have been blamed for this situation. Over the last 30 years, however, therapy has become more and more acceptable. Why, then, do patients either never seek treatment or leave it prematurely?

The answer may lie in the result of focus groups conducted by the American Psychological Association (hereafter, APA) in 1998 of potential consumers of psychotherapy. In these groups, 76% of participants reported that they did not have confidence in the outcome of therapy, and that was the main reason why they were not seeking treatment (APA, 1998). In fact, the percentage of individuals who lacked confidence in the outcome of therapy was far greater than that of individuals who reported that therapy had a stigma attached (53%). This constitutes a vote of no confidence in psychotherapy itself despite its demonstrated benefits (Miller et al., 2005).

Finally, as the Above Suggests, the Truth Is That Effective Therapy Is Not Being Provided on a Consistent Basis

This is a serious problem. As Brown, Dries, and Nace (1999) reported, if clients do not begin to improve by the third visit, they are not likely to improve at all *and* are twice as likely to terminate therapy as those who are improving. Thus, the people who need therapy the most are the ones who are not being helped. Why is this the case?

According to Ogles, Anderson, and Lunnen (1999), new professionals are being trained in ways that primarily emphasize specific techniques and treatment approaches, and, although these are useful, "with few exceptions, *existing research evidence on both training and treatment suggests that individual therapist techniques contribute very little to client outcome*" (p. 216; emphasis added). In other words, techniques bring a very small return on investment, accounting for only 15% of the variance attributable to outcomes (Lambert and Ogles, 2002).

PROPOSED SOLUTIONS AND THEIR LIMITATIONS

1. There has been a search for empirically supported or manualized treatments (evidence-based psychological practices, or EBPPs) that are applied to a given problem and have expected results (much like the physician and the prescription).
2. There has been a search for a unified approach to therapy that all practitioners can use to be effective, called *integration* (much like a medical protocol).

Both of these movements are guided by the best of intentions (to improve the practice of psychotherapy and the results obtained from it), and both have made contributions to the field. But neither approach has been sufficient to answer the challenge of how to help *developing therapists* become more proficient or how to have a better understanding of the therapeutic processes. As national concern over burgeoning health care costs has continued to escalate, the impetus behind these movements has received momentum from other sources, as Kazdin (2008) noted,

> State legislators and third-party payers ... are drawing on research to decide what is appropriate to do in practice, what is reimbursed, and what the rates of reimbursement will be ... the merits of this or that treatment or set of studies and the generalizability of findings now have a larger audience. (p. 156)

Suggested Solutions to Improve the Process of Learning How to Become an Effective Therapist: The Movement Toward "Manualization"

Practitioners and theorists in the 1950s and 1960s who were frustrated by the apparent (and, in some respects, actual) lack of rigor in the field were inspired by Gordon Paul's (1967) call to find "what treatment by whom is most effective for this individual with that specific problem, and under what specific set of circumstances" (p. 111). As a result, a line of research was built on the belief that effective therapies must have similar steps that, if identified, quantified, and replicated, would reliably produce the same effective results, regardless of who the client or the therapist was. These researchers felt that the way to accomplish this was to break down a particular therapeutic approach into its constituent parts, so that any practitioner could learn it and faithfully reproduce the treatment with a client. And so we saw the birth of treatment "manuals," providing a "how-to" methodology for clinicians to follow, and establishing guidelines for specific treatments and techniques, and their implementation. These manuals are typically derived from studies that carefully select patients who meet rigid criteria for the establishment of the particular diagnosis from the DSM-IV-TR for the treatment that is under study. Patients are evaluated periodically, and if there is sufficient (i.e., statistically significant) improvement with a majority of the clients, then the treatment is considered "empirically supported" (i.e., evidenced based). The pinnacle of this search was the development of *empirically supported treatment* (EST; also called *empirically validated treatment* [EVT] or EBPP).[2]

How did such efforts fare? According to Hubble, Duncan, and Miller (1999), "As it turned out, the underlying premise of the comparative studies, that one (or more) therapy would prove superior to others, received virtually no support" (p. 6). Researchers found evidence (as mentioned above) that psychotherapy in general was beneficial and effective. Research even demonstrated that there were some therapeutic approaches that seemed to work better with certain diagnoses (e.g., behavior therapy with phobias, and cognitive therapy with depression). But the search for one therapy that might prove superior to others in all cases of a particular diagnosis has not been the unqualified success for which researchers had hoped. For example, according to Hollon, Stewart, and Strunk (2006), the "enduring" effects of cognitive and behavioral therapies are clear in treating depression and anxiety, but the mechanisms for their effectiveness may be less clear.

To a larger extent, Wampold (2001), following a review of EVT research, cautioned that "adherence to a protocol is misguided" (p. 201), and Whipple, Lambert et al. (2003) pointed out that overreliance on EVT research is risky because it is based on small treatment effects. In fact, other researchers (e.g., Castonguay, Goldfried, Wiser, Raue, & Hayes, 1996; Henry, Strupp, Butler, Schacht, & Binder, 1993) suggested that overadherence to a "manualized" approach to treatment can actually produce negative effects (e.g., client dissatisfaction with therapy, or premature termination) and be harmful to clients (Ogles et al., 1999). Finally, Kazdin (2008) noted that "an EBT may have support for its effects, but within individual studies and among multiple studies, the results often are mixed (i.e., show different effects or no effects)" (p. 148).

Where do these attempts to create manualized treatment go awry? One problem is that people do not fit neatly into diagnostic categories, as Kazdin (2008) noted:

[P]atients in controlled trials have been characterized as having less severe disorders and fewer cormorbid disorders that patients who routinely come to treatment ... recruiting, selecting, and enrolling cases for research (e.g., soliciting and obtaining informed consent, conveying that the treatment provided will be determined randomly) differ considerably from the processes leading individuals to come ... for their treatment (Westen & Morrison, 2001). Another concern about research on psychotherapy pertains to the focus on symptoms and disorders as the primary ways of identifying participants and evaluating treatment outcomes. In clinical practice, much of psychotherapy is not about reaching a destination (eliminating symptoms) as it is about the ride (the process of coping with life). Psychotherapy research rarely addresses the broader focus of coping with multiple stressors and negotiating the difficult shoals of life, both of which are aided by speaking with a trained professional. In clinical practice, sometimes symptoms are the focus; even when they are the focus, over half of patients seen in therapy add new target complaints or change their complaints over the course of treatment (see, e.g., Sorenson, Gorsuch, & Mintz, 1985). Outcomes that seem loose and fuzzy (e.g., angst, quality of life, coping) or that are moving targets are rarely addressed in controlled therapy trials. (pp. 147–148)

A second cautionary factor regarding EVT efforts is that researchers appear to take the person of the therapist out of the equation. In some studies, researchers were so preoccupied with training the therapists to adhere to the treatment manual that they did not pay attention to *basic, effective counseling skills*. In other cases, therapist skill level was more likely to predict the positive treatment effects than the treatment itself—a result that is tantamount to the empirical validation of quality therapists, rather than techniques or theories (Brown et al., 1999; Hubble et al., 1999; Norcross, 2002; Wampold, 2001). Norcross (2002) perhaps best summarized the failure of EVT research to take into account therapist considerations:

EST lists and other practice guidelines depict disembodied therapists performing procedures on Axis I disorders. This stands in marked contrast to the clinician's experience of psychotherapy as an intensely interpersonal and deeply emotional experience. Although efficacy research has gone to considerable lengths to eliminate the therapist as a variable that might account for patient improvement, the inescapable fact is that the therapist as a person is a central agent of change. (p. 4)

Miller and Rollnick (2002) noted that treatment outcomes, even at 6-month follow-up interviews, can be attributed to the therapist's style: high empathy and low confrontation in the first few sessions. This style is associated with retention of clients in treatment and positive outcomes. This finding suggests that therapists demonstrating such behaviors are crucial elements of the change process; hence, it is beneficial, and even essential, to begin to understand these therapist factors (Brown et al., 1999).

Nevertheless, controversy remains. Perhaps the most cogent counsel we can provide regarding the debate between clinicians' concerns about EBTs and researchers' case for greater empiricism is that provided by Kazdin (2008): "[T]here are avenues where critical issues of concern to both researchers and practitioners come together and where advances in research and practice can build bridges between science and practice" (p. 150). More specifically, Kazdin (2008) noted that researchers perhaps need to focus on "mechanisms of change" (i.e., "not correlates of change alone but explanations of how therapy works"; p. 157), "moderators of treatment and how they work" (i.e., across all treatments or only one treatment), and qualitative research. In turn, he suggested that regardless of whether an EBT or EBPP is being used, clinicians need to monitor treatment progress in a systematic way.

EBPPs are an important development in the ongoing evolution of providing mental health treatments. When a therapist is considering a "manualized" treatment for a particular client, it is nevertheless important to assume a *sense of balance and context* in applying such an approach because *treatments cannot be applied in a strictly linear way*, as research from wide-ranging treatments for a variety of human problems informs us. For example, Miller et al. (2005) noted the importance of this in their treatment of problem drinkers: *"The movement of the field (is) away from diagnosis and program-driven treatment towards 'individualized assessment-driven treatment'. Research has made clear that, regardless of type or intensity of approach, client engagement is the single best predictor of outcome"* (p. 42; emphasis added). Another example comes from a controlled clinical trial[3] conducted by Kaptchuk et al. (2008) on how a placebo contributes to outcomes in the treatment of irritable bowel syndrome.[4] They concluded that the placebo effect has different components and that those components can be added one upon the other so that the power of the placebo is significantly increased but that *the patient–practitioner relationship is the most robust component*" (Kaptchuk et al., p. 999).

Hunsley (2007b) provided sound guidance regarding EBPPs:

> Within psychology, it would be erroneous to equate EBP with any particular set of psychological services or lists of empirically supported assessments or treatments, as the full range of relevant research must be considered and utilized, not just treatment outcome studies and psychometric evaluations of assessment instruments. (p. 33)

The Search for an Integrated Approach to Therapy

Long before the results of EVT studies demonstrated it, there were those practitioners and researchers who maintained that the therapist was the chief catalyst for change in the therapeutic process. They noted that when investigators observed research findings on effectiveness across vastly different settings and with vastly different populations, they found that clients seemed to improve at roughly the same rate (Miller, 2004; Prochaska, 1999). This ran counter to conventional wisdom, because the approaches were so widely varied, ranging from psychodynamic, to behavioral, to systems theory. Furthermore, they concluded that the way to best achieve (and later train others to achieve) effectiveness in therapy was to see what factors comprised effective therapeutic responses and integrate them into a single coherent approach. The hope was that this work would equip clinicians with everything that they needed in order to be more effective with a broad variety of clients, using the best from all theories of counseling.

Although they did not do so specifically in response to the EVT–EVB research, several practitioners and theorists turned from a focus on external behaviors or procedures toward a focus on the internal features of the therapist and on the elements that make up effective therapy. This quest created three levels or types of integration (or eclecticism): technical, theoretical, and common factors (Messer & Warren, 1995).

Technical eclecticism (or *technical integration*) refers to the pulling together of techniques or interventions that come from two or more different systems or schools of therapy, but that are used with a given client because of their perceived usefulness in helping with a specific client problem (Hansen, 2002). For example, a client may seek help to stop smoking. The therapist might not be a behaviorist, but he or she may choose to use principles of reinforcement or perhaps implosion techniques to break the smoker's habit. Unfortunately, this form of integration is a hit-or-miss approach that focuses on specific techniques to instill change—and a technique-driven approach is a fundamentally unsound strategy on which to base client treatment (Asay & Lambert, 1999; Miller et al., 2004).

The *theoretical integration* movement in psychotherapy sought to find commonalities among approaches to psychotherapy from a transtheoretical (one-theory-fits-all) approach. Hence, the promise of integration was to translate valuable concepts from one "language" to another and to enhance prospects of learning what is effective. How did the theoretical integrationists do? Norcross (1997) put it bluntly, stating that "psychotherapy integration has stalled. ... [T]he meaning ... remains diffuse, its commitment typically philosophical rather than empirical, and its training idiosyncratic and unreliable" (p. 86, as cited in Miller et al., 2005, p. 2).

At the turn of the 21st century, some 500 different theoretical approaches to psychotherapy could be identified, with the majority representing attempts at some kind of integration (Miller et al., 2005; Norcross, 2002). Different "models" of psychotherapy have been derived from a synthesis of theories, techniques, and formats, all in the name of simplicity of theory. Clearly, this is a mind-boggling number! It would paralyze even seasoned practitioners, let alone developing therapists, who are trying to make sense of how to be effective with clients. According to Hansen (2002), "Integration is tantamount to crossbreeding animal and plant life: The underlying genetic structures that determine the life forms are so completely different that it is impossible to develop a hybrid that retains the essence of each" (p. 317).

The attempt to create a single unified or integrated theoretical approach to psychotherapy, like the attempt to create a manual of treatment strategies, fails to take into account the therapist's personal talents, personality traits, personal styles, and theoretical-philosophical preferences. Though the one-size-fits-all approach of integration may tantalize developing practitioners with the idea that a grand unified theory can be adopted and easily implemented, the result is that the clinician then has very little freedom to adopt a perspective that is in harmony with his or her view of the world. Instead, with theoretical integration, every therapist must adhere to an a priori way of looking at the world of psychotherapy.

The *common factors* or *convergence* approach (Messer & Warren, 1995) also suggests that there is considerable overlap among the various theories and systems of psychotherapy. But rather than seeking to combine theories, those who subscribe to the convergence movement seek to identify the universal elements of the change process that are common to all effective systems of psychotherapy regardless of the different languages they use to describe what they do.

Frank and Frank (1991) described these common or convergence factors with the metaphor of shared "therapeutically active" ingredients. These ingredients are contained in all therapeutic approaches and can be thought of like the ingredients of painkillers, which comprise a variety of products under different names. There may be subtle and unique differences that make each one ideally suited for different conditions (e.g., migraine headaches versus muscle pain versus arthritis), but all have common core elements. Perhaps the most widely known study of common factors (Lambert & Barley, 2002) identifies four elements that seem to be present in all effective psychotherapy and the relative contribution of each to overall client improvement:

1. Extratherapeutic factors (client factors)[5] were the most important, accounting for 40% of the total change.
2. Expectancy, or the placebo effect, accounted for 15% of the improvement.
3. Therapeutic techniques accounted for an additional 15%.
4. "Common factors" (i.e., the variables that contribute to the therapeutic relationship that can be considered "common" to most therapies) accounted for 30% of the overall improvement.

The common factors that Lambert and Barley (2002) identified comprise a variety of variables including therapist warmth, empathy, acceptance, and encouragement of risk taking (Lambert, 1992). These effects are seen regardless of theoretical orientation, and no particular school of psychotherapy seems to be more effective than another (aspects of Lambert's common factors will be discussed in greater detail in Chapters 2, 3, and 4).

Are these four factors—warmth, empathy, acceptance, and encouragement of risk taking—all that any clinician needs to be successful? The reality is that, although these factors make up the core elements (and 30% of the effectiveness) of any successful therapeutic endeavor, they are not finally sufficient in guiding a clinician in *how* to conduct therapy. In fact, researchers have shown that training that emphasizes the therapeutic alliance is *not* sufficient to produce client change (Horvath, 2001). According to Miller et al. (2004), "[L]ogically, there is and can never be a 'common factors' model of therapy because all models by definition already include the factors. Even the usefulness of the factors as general organizing principles for clinical practice is uncertain" (p. 3).

It would nevertheless appear that "establishing these common content factors of counseling approaches would be a significant step," but "speculations about common content factors of counseling approaches are seldom mentioned in the counseling literature" (Hansen, 2002, p. 315). This makes it difficult to create a clinically useful approach to training or conducting therapy without becoming merely a technical eclectic or theoretical integrationist. We think understanding common factors is critical to becoming an expert therapist, and the rest of this chapter—and this book—will suggest what we hope is an understanding of the common content factors of effective psychotherapy approaches that is clinically useful enough to enhance overall effectiveness, while preserving the poetic individualism and integrity of each individual approach.

The literature from expert clinicians, theoreticians, and researchers has repeatedly reinforced the development, importance, use, and efficacy of the common or convergence factors we talk about above. In their essence, they represent "commonalities" between and amongst all theoretical orientations. As such, a convergence factor represents an aspect of the therapy process that is recognized as salient and critical in understanding and facilitating the process of change across a broad spectrum of theoretical diversity. In fact, we believe that there are a number of "convergence factors" in psychotherapy that have emerged to provide greater clarity regarding the process of learning how to help others to make changes in their lives. These convergence factors can be found at the heart of all successful therapy and represent what master practitioners pay attention to. They are as follows:

1. Connecting with and engaging the client
2. Assessing and accessing the client's motivations, goals, and strengths
3. Building and maintaining the therapeutic relationship—an "alliance" with the client
4. Understanding a client's cognitive schemas
5. Addressing and managing a client's emotional states
6. Understanding and addressing client ambivalence about change
7. Understanding and using nonlinear-paradoxical thought processes and intervention in treatment

LEARNING FROM EXPERTS—THOSE WHO DEMONSTRATE THEIR EFFECTIVENESS

One way that some researchers have tried to answer the problems posed above is to look at those therapists who seemed to have successfully mastered the therapeutic process. Research findings of "expertise" in therapy have potentially shed light on the processes of highly effective practitioners. Understanding the processes and practices of highly effective practitioners, in turn, may provide valuable clues as to how to solve the problem of the sorcerer's apprentice. According to Lambert and Barley (2002),

> We know from both research and experience that certain therapists are better than others at promoting positive client outcome, and that some therapists do better with some types of clients than others. For example, Orlinsky and Howard (1980) reported the outcome ratings of 143 female cases treated by 23 therapists who offered a range of traditional verbal psychotherapy. As would be expected, some therapists' clients experienced better outcome than others. Few factors predicted better outcome, although having a therapist with experience beyond six years was associated with better results in this study. … Those (therapists) with poor average outcomes did not perform poorly across all cases, but did well with some clients. (p. 21)

Thus, it is not simply a matter that there are naturally gifted therapists and (conversely) naturally dreadful therapists. If it were so, then the therapists with poor outcomes would do poorly *all the time*. But, they did not do poorly all of the time. In fact, they were able to have a positive impact with some clients.

What, then, makes an expert? Do such therapists become masterful as a function of time spent doing therapy? Does each have innate abilities that are unique to that individual, or are there some common traits that each of these therapists share that make them experts? Some researchers have studied the *problem-solving methods* of novices and compared them with those of experts. Skovholt and Jennings (2004) reported that, when novices in the physical sciences are given complex problems and asked to solve them, they tended to apply a particular formula and solve backward from the formula. Experts, on the other hand, tended to reason forward from the problem, "as if cues or signposts for potential problems are embedded in the problem itself" (Skovholt & Jennings, p. 4). In other words, they find the solution within the problem itself, which allows them to "see deeper, faster, further, and better than the novice" (p. 4). Experts *think* differently!

In psychotherapy, this is analogous to beginning therapists who rely on a particular *theory* or *technique* of counseling without fully accounting for the uniqueness of a client's perspective or circumstances. According to Skovholt and Jennings (2004), this is primarily due to the difficulty that novices have in dealing with the ambiguous nature of client problems, and the therapeutic process itself. As a result, novices tend to move quickly toward "premature closure," or the "tendency to latch on to one simplistic solution, theory, or frame of reference with which to view clients in order to avoid being cognitively or emotionally overwhelmed" (Skovholt & Jennings, p. 20). The vulnerability of novices, who feel overwhelmed and hence *less than adequate* to the complex and ambiguous task at hand, may very well be central to their gravitating toward more simplistic solutions. This cognitive or emotional feeling of inadequacy is what frequently leads to problems such as premature termination and other manifestations of client resistance. Such developments can leave the beginning therapist feeling lost, confused, frustrated, and ill prepared in addition to feeling inadequate to help clients.

By contrast, experts' performance "requires basically the same thing: vast amounts of knowledge and a pattern-based memory system acquired over many years of experience" (Skovholt & Jennings, 2004, p. 3). In other words, experts *think* differently because they have a broad perspective that derives from having considerable experience that they have built on over many years.

Experts have a vast database of both client experiences and psychotherapeutic practice in general to call upon when faced with the inherent ambiguities of client issues or responses (Martin et al., 1989, as cited in Skovholt & Jennings, 2004). They are able to "draw upon this knowledge efficiently and parsimoniously to determine the best course of action regarding specific client problems" (Skovholt & Jennings, p. 25). Experts recognize that although clients' complaints may be similar (e.g., complaints of anxiety or depression), they don't focus on that solely; they attend to the uniqueness, subtleties, ambiguities, and nuances that each client offers that distinguish them from another client with similar complaints. Furthermore, the more experience, knowledge, and sense of comfort that experts have with *the processes* of psychotherapy, the less vulnerable they become to the ambiguities and stresses that their clients bring to treatment.

They do not have to prematurely foreclose on a single solution, but rather understand that therapy is a process of exploring multiple solutions that can be generated by the therapist, the client, or jointly. In contrast, as we noted earlier, novices *seek closure* too soon, before the client is ready, falling back on techniques they have learned or mimicking something they saw an experienced therapist do in the hopes of "making something happen" with the client without knowing whether it will happen or, if it does, *why*. Experts, on the other hand, know, understand, and *trust the processes* underlying therapeutic effectiveness.

Personal Characteristics of "Master Therapists"

Skovholt and Jennings (2004) pursued the question of expertise by qualitatively researching the traits of expert therapists. Through extensive interviews with 10 master therapists, they defined the personal characteristics that were common to these practitioners and created a model of characteristics that may be useful in solving the problem of the sorcerer's apprentice. The researchers found that there were specific *personal characteristics* that allowed certain therapists to "use both experience and intelligence to increase their confidence and comfort when dealing with complexity and ambiguity" (Jennings & Skovholt, 1999, p. 9). Their model of these characteristics has three broad domains—cognitive, emotional, and relational—and nine specific categories (see Table 1.1).

The Cognitive Domain

Skovholt and Jennings (2004) identified these cognitive characteristics of master therapists:

- They are voracious learners.
- Accumulated experience has become a continually accessed, major resource for them.
- They value cognitive complexity and the ambiguity of the human condition.

TABLE 1.1   The cognitive, emotional, and relational characteristics of expert therapists

DOMAINS	CATEGORIES	DESCRIPTION
Cognitive	1. Expert therapists are voracious learners.	Demonstrate a love for learning, and continuously seek out professional development.
	2. Accumulated experiences have become a major resource for master therapists.	Experience is reflected upon and enriches the practice of therapy.
	3. Expert therapists value cognitive complexity and the ambiguity of the human condition.	Complexity is welcomed as a part of the dynamic makeup of clients' thinking and of therapy itself.
Emotional	1. Master therapists appear to have emotional receptivity defined as being self-aware, reflective, nondefensive, and open to feedback.	Need for continuous self-reflection and feedback in order to learn more about themselves and their work.
	2. Master therapists seem to be mentally healthy and mature individuals who attend to their own emotional well-being.	See themselves as congruent, authentic, and honest, and strive to act in congruence with their personal and professional lives.
	3. Master therapists are aware of how their emotional health affects the quality of their work.	See the benefit of appropriately utilizing transference and countertransference reactions in session.
Relational	1. Master therapists possess strong relationship skills.	Developed, many times, out of family-of-origin dynamics, caring for the welfare of others, or a wounded past.
	2. Master therapists believe that the foundation for therapeutic change is a strong working alliance.	Have a deep respect for client's right to self-determination, and power of self-directed change. Value the client's struggle to discover answers over supplying the solution.
	3. Master therapists appear to be experts at using their exceptional relationship skills in therapy.	Therapeutic relationship provides the safe environment where challenges can be issued and accepted, and where tough issues can be brought up.

Source: From Jennings and Skovholt (1999).

In other words, master therapists delight in the pursuit of knowledge, have a healthy sense of curiosity, have the intellectual sophistication to handle complex situations, and understand that ambiguity in human problem solving is normative, not aberrant.

The Emotional Domain

According to Jennings and Skovholt (1999), expert therapists access and use the following behaviors:

- They appear to have *emotional receptivity*, defined as being self-aware, reflective, nondefensive, and open to feedback.
- They seem to be mentally healthy and mature individuals who attend to their own emotional well-being.
- They are aware of how their emotional health affects the quality of their work.

Hence, master therapists are nonreactive (e.g., non-defensive, calm, etc.) in the face of a client's strong emotional reactions, can appropriately use their emotional impulses to illuminate the therapeutic discourse, and have sufficient capacity to soothe themselves in the moment when their emotions are stirred up.

The Relational Domain

Last, in terms of how they relate to others, expert therapists are characterized as follows:

- They possess strong relationship skills.
- They believe that the foundation for therapeutic change is a strong working alliance.
- They appear to be experts at using their exceptional relationship skills in therapy. Briefly, this means that master therapists are keenly attuned to the relationship dimension with a client, and have the ability to perceive how much change they can expect the client to tolerate before there is a rupture in the therapeutic alliance. Clearly, all of these are crucial in employing the convergence factors and being effective with clients.

The road to expertise may not be easy, but overall, research supports our contention that those therapists who do not at first appear to have these abilities can be taught how to *think* about clients and therapy like a master practitioner does.

THE PURPOSE OF THIS BOOK: LEARNING TO THINK LIKE A THERAPIST

New knowledge, like the kind that has been generated by the last 2 decades of research presented above, requires new approaches to training beginning therapists. Without these new approaches to training, the field of psychotherapy runs the risk of repeating the same errors (i.e., focusing exclusively on learning formulaic techniques, micro skills, and theories of therapy) that will perpetuate the problems outlined above. That simply prolongs the "problem of the sorcerer's apprentice."

Unfortunately, training methods do not appear to have kept pace with advances in understanding how to be more effective in treating our clients. Again, the recent trend in the instruction of beginning therapists is to teach them how to act like therapists—that is, to follow one's particular interpretation of a theory of therapy, rely upon micro skills, utilize a technique-based practice, or implement a somewhat formulaic evidence-based practice. There are several reasons for this, including reduced time for training, increased training demands, expanded requirements for credentialing (accreditation and licensure), demands for increased productivity, and pressures from third-party payers. As a result, in their training programs today, beginning practitioners often do not explicitly learn how to think like therapists.

The disparity between coursework knowledge and competent application in clinical settings creates a significant "theory–practice" gap. Students who have the most difficulty and the most to overcome are also those who experience the widest gulf between what they have learned and what they are called upon to do in the field (Ronnestad & Skovholt, 1993). Hence, if the necessary processes aren't properly instilled during formal training, the beginning therapist has few opportunities to effectively correct them. If they are fortunate, they slowly pick it up through trial and error or through good prelicensure supervision. The sad part, however, is that the majority of practitioners never get exposed to the thought processes that belie clinical expertise and mastery, and thus never reach their full potential. Like birds born in captivity, if they don't learn the songs of their species at the critical moments, they are permanently impaired and often do not survive burnout in the wilds of clinical practice.

The easy and obvious solution to this dilemma is to institute training that is effective, focuses on therapist development, emphasizes effective common (i.e., "convergence") factors, assesses outcomes in practice, fosters strong therapeutic relationships, and teaches students how to tailor treatment for each individual client, while placing less emphasis on "fad" treatment approaches, outdated modalities, or formulaic protocols (Hubble et al., 1999; Miller et al., 2005; Norcross, 2002; Ogles et al., 1999). In addition, Skovholt and Jennings (2004) recommended training that focuses on providing corrective feedback to trainees about *how* they conceived the problem and derived their intervention(s). This feedback would increase the trainees' flexibility and increase their tolerance for complexity. In other words, they recommended training that gives attention to *the thought process behind interventions and techniques* in order for trainees to achieve mastery. Taken altogether, this kind of training would decrease the likelihood of "premature foreclosure," instead "setting the stage where one can continuously strive toward mastery of the highly ambiguous, difficult to understand phenomena" (Skovholt & Jennings, p. 21). These are the strategies that will increase effectiveness and solve the problem of the sorcerer's apprentice.

In conclusion, Gordon Paul's (1967) call seems logical on the surface, namely, to find what treatment and by whom is most effective for this individual with that specific problem, and under what specific set of circumstances. The problem is not the question, but how the field has tried to answer it. The field has searched for an answer that seeks to fill in all of the blanks of the type of client, the type of problem, the types of treatment, and the types of circumstances. Clearly, it is an impossible task to research each of these variables, and every possible combination of them. Frankly, we think that this is the wrong way to address Paul's question. As Miller et al. (2005) have cautioned, and as we mentioned earlier, decades of research have shown "that 'who' the therapist is accounts for six to nine times as much variance in outcome as 'what' treatment approach is employed" (p. 50). Hence, the only way to properly answer the question is to focus on the therapist and how he or she is trained. It is our assertion that if they are taught the ways that therapists think along with the domains of competence that are couched in a model that facilitates proper development, then they should be able to work effectively within their own theoretical orientation, with most clients, and under almost any circumstances. As Hubble et al. (1999) concluded, "The survival of the mental health professions, in other words, will be better ensured by identifying empirically valid treat*ers* rather than empirically validated treat*ments*" (p. 439). The aim of this book is to help the development of such practitioners.

ENDNOTES

1. We will discuss the DSM-IV-TR (American Psychiatric Association, 2000) further in Chapter 3.
2. In August, 2005, the American Psychological Association's Council of Representatives passed a proposal entitled "Evidence-Based Practice in Psychology" (EBPP), as reported by Gill (2005): "The proposal presented to Council stated that the goals of evidence-based practice initiatives are aimed at improving quality and cost-effectiveness and to enhance accountability. Just as importantly, however, it speaks with one voice about what APA stands for to legislators and third-party entities" (p. 4). For a thorough discussion of the multitude of issues that arise regarding evidenced-based treatments, see Norcross, Beutler, and Levant (2005); Hunsley (2007a); and Kazdin (2008).
3. A controlled clinical trial is a powerful type of research that is taken as a "gold standard" for results that scientists can accept as valid.
4. Irritable bowel syndrome (IBS) is a condition accompanied by cramps, diarrhea, and abdominal pain, but often no physical findings.
5. Variables such as the emotional support of others, reading self-help books, and attending religious services.

PART TWO

The Level I
Practitioner Profile

Introduction to Part 2
The Level I Practitioner Profile

CONTENTS

This section introduces the reader to the Level I Practitioner Profile.

Each of the three levels that we address represents somewhat of a milestone of practitioner development with certain domains of competence that realistically and typically require understanding and mastery before the practitioner is able to undertake more complex domains. As Stoltenberg (1993; Stoltenberg & Delworth, 1987; Stoltenberg, McNeill, & Delworth, 1998) suggested, Level I practitioners are obviously new to the treatment setting. Although they may have experiences in other helping professions, they most likely are new to the experience of specifically being a therapist or counselor. Having acquired the theoretical academic exposure that is a prerequisite for becoming a practitioner, Level I therapists must now begin to translate what it is that they have learned in the classroom into the practical realm of relating to *real* people with *real* problems; classroom exercises are no longer the focus of attention. Clearly, the transition from the academic to the clinical world is a daunting task for the Level I clinician. Although Level I practitioners may vary considerably in age and life experience (from the new baccalaureate graduate to the midlife career changer), one of their most prominent characteristics is their skewed understanding (or lack of it) of what it is to be a novice practitioner. Both in the literature on training, and in our experiences teaching in courses, conferences, seminars, and workshops throughout the United States, Canada, and Europe, we have observed students at Level I demonstrate many of the *same* preoccupations and concerns.

SELF-VERSUS-OTHER FOCUS

One of the signature psychological features of Level I therapists is an understandable but excessive preoccupation with their performance and ability, rather than focusing on the task or client. The *self-focus* has four different basic elements or components: anxiety, the quest for perfection, insecurity, and an underdeveloped sense of clinical judgment. We will outline these briefly here.

Anxiety

The first manifestation of *self-focus* is the feeling of anxiety about being inadequate to fulfill the role of a therapist. The difference between the level of self-expectation and perceived level of performance can be viewed as the approximate degree of anxiety experienced by the Level I practitioner. If counselors' personal expectations are unreasonably high (and they generally *are* in the beginning) while they simultaneously doubt their ability, then the anxiety level can be *high* to the point of near immobilization! For some beginning therapists with more realistic appraisals of their abilities, the feeling is more muted. Thus, the more personally mature and life experienced the Level I person is, the more attenuated the feeling of inadequacy may be than in those individuals who have yet to establish a mature personal identity.

The Quest for Perfection

The second manifestation of *self-focus* found in the Level I practitioner is the muted and implicit search for "performance perfection" in one form or another. This search for perfection is most typically demonstrated in questions such as "How do you …?" "What do you say when the client …?" or "What does it mean when a client …?" The motivation for performance perfection is generally a genuine desire to do "good" work, "help" clients, develop expertise, *and* enhance self-esteem through one's work. However, the sort of questions above represent a reflection of underlying anxiety about being inadequate, doing harm, doing something "wrong," being "good" at what one does, and not doing the "right" thing. As mentioned above, in this stage of development such blocks are most likely precipitated by an implied striving to be the "ideal" or "perfect" therapist rather than oneself. Such therapists seek comfort in trying to "do the right thing" and learn "techniques" as solutions to addressing clients' concerns and problems. Those techniques serve as substitutes for relating to clients in an authentic way. Again, such preoccupations are indicative of focusing on the counselor's ability, rather than on the client's issues and experiences. These preoccupations can cause the counselor to feel blocked or at a loss as to how to help the client, which amplifies the feelings of inadequacy.

Insecurity

The third manifestation of self-preoccupation is a feeling of uncertainty, insecurity, and lack of confidence. Experiencing a lack of confidence prompts Level I therapists to engage in invidious comparison of their own performance with what they perceive the performance of others to be. This has been aptly expressed by a noted clinician and psychotherapy researcher, Scott Miller:

> [T]he first major crisis in my career was at the outset! Others seemed much more certain of their ability and skills than I did. I'd watch my supervisors or fellow students work and was surprised, and secretly envious,

of the confidence with which they stated their diagnostic opinions and offered their technical expertise. I, on the other hand, was plagued by doubt. (Quoted in Walt, 2005, p. 1)

Again, this is a common experience for new therapists. Because of the general lack of confidence and uncertainty in a new role, perhaps the biggest manifestation of this is an implied concern with one's *performance* (i.e., "How well am I doing?"). Obviously, such concern reflects *self*-preoccupation about one's performance and not a focus on how *the client* is doing. As an illustration, an aging famous clinician who had developed a life-threatening illness was teaching a course to advanced practitioners, all of whom were licensed and quite experienced in their particular professions—psychiatrists, counselors, psychologists, and clinical social workers. The class was well attended because it was clear that the revered clinician-teacher might not have long to live.

The clinician was notorious for being a demanding taskmaster and very much interested in classroom demonstrations of the clinical interviewing process. Actual clients would be solicited to be interviewed in front of the class in consideration of a waived fee in order to receive feedback from the revered clinician. He also typically asked for volunteers from the class to serve as clinician-interviewers. When the clinician asked for a "volunteer" to interview a client in front of the class, not a single hand went up. The renowned clinician turned to the class and said, "If you are going to be so preoccupied with your performance and 'How well am I doing in front of the class?' you won't be able to do your job!" Under the stated set of conditions, it is clear that even this group of mature clinicians was reflecting a concern with prestige (or loss of it) and how they might be evaluated by their teacher in front of colleagues.

Underdeveloped Sense of Clinical Judgment

The fourth manifestation of *self-focus* in Level I counselors is the underdeveloped sense of *clinical judgment*. Besides a very real concern with becoming a therapist in order to earn a living—in most cases, that is—therapists at this level of training often express a desire to "help" others as their motivation for their choice of counseling as a profession. Although such motivation is well intended, before the basics are learned, the desire to help may be guided by preconceived, ill-formed, and poorly conceptualized ideas about *how* to help others in counseling as well as exactly what constitutes *helping*. Thus, although eager, Level I practitioners are more likely to gravitate toward "helping" based on giving advice, persuasion, mandates, or perhaps even scare tactics if the problem continues (e.g., "Your wife will divorce you if you don't stop drinking"). As Miller and Rollnick (2002) pointed out, helping in the form of advice giving and persuasion only tends to increase client resistance and result in poorer clinical outcomes. Sound principles of therapy need to be understood and cultivated regarding the processes of change and what constitutes "helping" others.

At Level I functioning, because of a dearth of clinical experience and a lack of clinical judgment that inexperience fosters, the counselor-in-training can be prone to developing an overidentification with the client. "Identification with the client" should be in the service of developing empathy with the *plight and feelings of the person* and not the person him or herself. There is a substantial difference between these two positions of identification. The former expresses, "It's just awful to feel taken advantage of!" The latter expresses, "I feel just like Suzy, who *is* being taken advantage of."

Empathizing with the *feelings* of the client (if appropriately understood) provides the clinician with a therapeutically valuable sense of the client's *frame of reference* (see Chapter 2) while simultaneously maintaining an essential objectivity toward one's client. To understand clients' frames of reference is an enormous advantage in comprehending the basis for their behavior (i.e., what leads them to impasses, immobilization, etc.). However, if a practitioner identifies with the *client* (rather than the client's frame of reference), such a response can result in overidentification and problematic *countertransference* (see Chapters 6 and 7) issues in treatment. In such instances, clients' difficulties become compounded by the practitioner's failure to keep *her or his* personal issues from interfering with clients getting the benefits for which they came to therapy. The Level I practitioner is vulnerable to such misjudgments, which can lead to practitioner burnout.

LIMITED AWARENESS OF PROFESSIONAL IDENTITY

As Stoltenberg (1993) has indicated, awareness of a professional identity is still low at this stage of development. Consciously or unconsciously, given exposure to supervisors, students invariably begin to model their supervisors. Sometimes such modeling is positive, and sometimes it is ill conceived. At Level I and even beyond, practitioners are prone to developing misconceptions of what modeling is all about.

Milton Erickson[1] was a brilliant clinician who died in 1980. He left behind an incredibly rich legacy (e.g., see Haley, 1973, 1993) of healing that included successful cases, practitioners who he had trained, and masterful, mysterious, and adroitly crafted interventions that could eventually be unraveled for others to learn from. A mythology developed around Erickson and his work along with a cult following. Hammond (1984) pointed out how misguided imitation can be, especially among uninformed therapists:

> Amid all the emphasis on magic, metaphors and indirect techniques (among cultists that is), it also seems that Erickson's fundamental beliefs about the vital importance of establishing rapport are often neglected. Framed in terms of Rogerian constructs (Rogers, 1957; Truax & Carkhkuff, 1967), Erickson listened very attentively, summarized empathically, and stressed respectfully accepting the patient and his perceptions. However, concentrating primarily on techniques, a naïve therapist might deliver confusion techniques with more of an air of secret superiority and an attitude of smugly putting something over on the patient, rather than with an "interested" and earnest manner (Erickson, 1980, Vol. 1, p. 259). We need to be cautious about becoming so enamored with the esoterica of … techniques … so that we do not neglect the fundamentals of caring and establishing a relationship. If we hope to emulate Erickson's success, we must mirror his humanity and genuine caring for patients. (p. 243)

If emulation and cultism are *not* the answer, then what might be instructional for the Level I practitioner regarding emulation, modeling, and the linear application of the techniques of any number of master practitioners? Again, Hammond (1984) made a suggestion:

> Haley studied intensively with Erickson, acknowledged very openly Erickson's influence on his thinking, but then went on in his own way beyond Erickson to make his own contribution. He did not just worshipfully cite Erickson as the fount of all wisdom. He credited Erickson, and then built on Erickson's ideas in the way that suited his individuality. (p. 244)

Level I practitioners need to be aware of the fact that no matter how famous or effective Dr. X may be, only they as individuals can do what they do with clients. Students trying to *be* Dr. X by applying techniques in a linear manner would appear to be substituting mimicry for thinking. In contrast, learning about what Dr. X has to say, how Dr. X thinks, and then possibly adapting it in keeping with their own personality and thinking would appear to be a first step toward development to another level of mastery (see Hammond, 1984; Mozdzierz & Greenblatt, 1994; Mozdzierz, Lisiecki, & Macchitelli, 1989). Given these fundamental considerations, learning to concentrate on the three basic domains of competence that are discussed in section 1 of this text and mastering specific ways of thinking within each domain establish a firm foundation for a Level I person's professional development.

LEARNING TO THINK LIKE A MASTER PRACTITIONER

It is clear that master practitioners demonstrate enormous respect for their clients as a fundamental operating principle. It is also clear that such masters do not think in conventional ways. From the very beginning of the journey to become a master practitioner, it is necessary to learn how to *think* like a therapist. Such a task is daunting but doable, and in the process of its development an entire world of new understanding about human behavior, problems, and the process of change can emerge. Thinking in conventional, linear, and commonsense terms is always helpful, but it is far from being the major therapeutic tool in stimulating and promoting change. Throughout the text, we elaborate on the therapeutic *nonlinear-thinking* activities that new and more advanced practitioners can begin to absorb, integrate, and utilize.

As discussed in the introduction, we have called the specific therapeutic activities and areas of content that are universal throughout all therapies *domains of competence*. It is within each of these domains of competence that Level I practitioners need to learn to think in nonlinear ways. Each of these most basic of therapeutic activities must be engaged *simultaneously*, which is something challenging but ultimately achievable. In many respects, they are overlapping and yet separate and distinct.

Given the above considerations, the Level I practitioner requires several essential things to develop the ability to think in nonlinear ways and grow professionally. The first is reading and study, both of which will eventually become lifelong habits of the most satisfying and enjoyable sort. The next essential is experience and exposure to clients appropriate for the practitioner's level of development. The third factor is attentive clinical supervision, encouragement, and reassurance well tailored to individual needs. Such positive reinforcements are essential at the Level I stage of development. The fourth factor requires reflection about what has transpired in treatment, what is to be learned from each client and each session, and how it relates to what has been learned academically and in self-study. The final requirement is an understanding of the content areas of therapy that need to be mastered so that they become second nature.

WHERE TO BEGIN?

"In the Beginning ...": The First Session and Level I Practitioners

Given these basic Level I challenges, cautions, and concerns, where to begin? This is a question with several different meanings. First, where do we begin in presenting the entirety of the field of psychotherapy? The truth is that although, in this text, the Level I domains are presented serially—(a) connecting with and engaging the client; (b) assessing the client, accessing strengths, and goal setting; and (c) establishing a therapeutic relationship and the therapeutic alliance—they are interwoven during the therapeutic encounter. The reader is cautioned about thinking, "OK, I have to master all of domain 1, then all of domain 2 ..." In fact, that would be a perfect example of *linear* thinking.

So how does one do this? How should a clinician approach clients in the initial session? Should a clinician adopt a skeptical posture with the client and question every statement? Researchers have demonstrated that this kind of combative, adversarial position is not productive (Lambert & Barley, 2002). As we have said, in order to effectively work with these contradictory elements, the initial therapy session requires the development of *nonlinear thinking* as a means of accomplishing multiple goals such as

- Establishing rapport
- Connecting with and engaging the client in the therapeutic process
- Empathically understanding the client *and* her or his unique situation
- Understanding the unconscious factors operating in the patient's life
- Instilling hope in a client that he or she can experience relief from symptoms that are disruptive and emotionally painful

The clinician must do all of this without alienating the client, too! Although this may appear to be a very tall order, we believe that even the Level I therapist, with the proper training, can accomplish these beginning tasks. This represents the beginning of effective psychotherapy, and can offer much-needed help to clients, even if they come to therapy with complex and difficult issues. The first very important task for Level I practitioners to understand and become familiar with is "connecting with and engaging" the client for treatment—it is the first domain of competence to which we turn our attention.

ENDNOTE

1. See Haley (1973) for a vivid description of some of Erickson's most brilliant therapeutic accomplishments.

The Domain of Connecting With and Engaging the Client

2

Part 1: Listening

CONTENTS

INTRODUCTION

The first session can be daunting for Level I counselors. Entire books have been devoted to the topic of how to conduct this crucial, initial meeting. There are multiple tasks that must be accomplished: informed consent, orientation to the therapeutic process, the collection of essential demographics, mandated intake forms, issues of payment, cancellation policies, satisfaction surveys, privacy policy, and more. Unfortunately, with so many different tasks requiring attention, the client and his reason for coming for therapy are almost afterthoughts! In recognizing the many demands impinging on the Level I counselor, it is relatively easy to understand why it is tempting for such a beginning practitioner to take a default position that is *linear* in its emphasis.

One of the characteristics of *linear thinking* is its expediency—after all, the fastest way to get from one place to another is in a straight line. The initial interview guided by *linear* thinking then becomes a series of checklists and a sprint to find the correct answer for the question "Does this client fit the criteria for this particular DSM-IV-TR diagnostic category?" The answer to such a linear question (i.e., simple question, easy answer) accomplishes many purposes simultaneously. It helps to focus a practitioner's attention by looking for symptoms that cluster logically (e.g., depressed mood, weight loss, insomnia, lack of pleasure in most things, and suicidal thoughts). It also decreases a Level I practitioner's level of anxiety about *what to do* (e.g., things required by a clinical supervisor, clinic procedures, quality assurance, insurance companies, and government regulations) and *how to do it* (e.g., ask the questions that get the "facts" to fill out the required forms). Each of these boosts feelings of confidence (e.g., "I got all the right information and the diagnosis!"). Thus, a linear approach can facilitate rapport building simply by decreasing the therapist's anxiety (Note: More on the assessment of symptoms will be covered in Chapter 4, and rapport building will be covered in Chapter 6.)

However, such *linear thinking* alone does not necessarily do the *client* much good in the long term. The majority of clients don't necessarily derive much benefit from knowing their DSM-IV-TR (American Psychiatric Association, 2000) diagnosis, unless, that is, they have come for treatment wanting to know, "What's wrong with me?" Most times, clients *know* what is wrong with them (e.g., they're anxious, depressed, or can't sleep) and really just want the clinician to *help them get better* (Miller, Mee-Lee, Plum, & Hubble, 2005).

The first step toward helping a client is by making a positive *connection* with her. When a therapist successfully *connects* with a client and *engages* a client, the therapist can also simultaneously accomplish the task of collecting the necessary linear information required for diagnosis, billing purposes, and so on, as well as begin to address the client's question (i.e., "Can I be helped?"). Decades of psychotherapy research overwhelmingly reveal that the best way of making such a therapeutic connection is by *listening and responding to* a client in very particular ways.

LISTENING

Listening. At the heart of all counseling and psychotherapy, listening is the one common activity required by all therapists in every session. But, *how* individual therapists listen and *what* they listen for are important to distinguish. Master practitioners use listening effectively to identify those client statements that are more clinically significant. This allows the therapist to respond more effectively, as well as help the client to feel validated, affirmed, and significant. Knowing how to listen *nonlinearly* is especially important because it helps to shape *what* to listen for, which in turn helps to shape the questions therapists will want to ask as well as the comments they make. Such listening also helps clients move along the change process. Listening in both linear and nonlinear ways facilitates the identification, clarification, and development of strategic goals that a client would like to accomplish. Yet, this is often overlooked or given short shrift in training programs. We will distinguish between *linear* and *nonlinear* listening, provide guidance on how to effectively listen both ways, and delineate how both are essential to the domain of connecting with, engaging, and assessing.

How Do You Listen in a Linear Way?

Listening effectively in psychotherapy as well as in other areas of life requires both linear and nonlinear awareness. In fact, it is the true master practitioner who realizes that she is listening both linearly and nonlinearly at the same time! No matter how disjointed, evasive, "quirky," exaggerated, or hesitant a "story" may *appear*, what a client has to say gives therapists their first glimpse into a client's world. It is a mistake to gloss over and dismiss what a client says and how he says it on the surface. As a result, we will touch on *what it is* to listen in a linear manner and *how to* listen linearly. *That* is the starting point of *all* psychotherapy. The two basic elements of linear listening are *listening for content or information* and *listening for feelings*.

Listening for Content or Information

Listening for content or information is the most basic aspect of communication. It represents one person simply transmitting information to another person. It is the *what* that is being said (Carkhuff, 2000). To use the cliché from the old TV show *Dragnet*, when you listen for content or information, you are listening for "Just the facts, ma'am." Content is *factual* or *observational* in nature, and can be about the *past*, *present*, or *future*. Content represents the "what" we are talking about. For example: "I had pancakes for breakfast this morning." The content is factual (pancakes for breakfast) and about the past (this morning). Being factual means that there was little or no interpretation necessary (i.e., there is not that much to interpret when it comes to pancakes!). *Observational* comments, however, may contain ambiguity and require some interpretation. For example, consider the statement "I think my husband is cheating on me." It is a statement about the present and about what a client has been thinking, and the content is observational because the person *believes* this is happening, but is not sure. Hence, it is open to interpretation and is ambiguous. That is, does "cheating" mean a torrid sexual affair, an emotional entanglement, or innocent flirtation? In addition, because it is observational, there is no proof but rather only suspicion of cheating. In Exercise 2.1, we present an exercise regarding various patient comments that are made that require judgments about the nature of listening for content or information.

Exercise 2.1: Listening for Content or Information

Directions: Read each statement and determine if the information or content is factual or observational, and if it is about the past, present, or future.

1. "I made a betrayal decision and was messing around with another woman; I had feelings of guilt and told my wife about what had been going on!"
2. "I developed migraine headaches in my third year of medical school."
3. "I've seen lots of therapists in the past. I've been through a lot of trauma, so I'm not unfamiliar with therapy. I need a neutral resource and some tools to get through a crisis."
4. "There are some 'demons' that I need to deal with—personal traits. For the first time in my life, I'm seeing things for what they are."
5. "I have feelings of being bisexual. In the past I'd push 'em away, and then I'd accept 'em and they would disappear. Then, I'd feel like I was heterosexual, and the feelings of being bisexual would come back."

Why is "content" important? Listening for content provides basic information about what the client believes to be her problem, where it stems from, potential goals for treatment, and client assets that may be used to address the problem. Content also reveals what *area* of a client's life needs to be the focus of attention. For the Level I therapist, consciously paying attention to content is a way of slowing down one's thinking, and not getting too far ahead of the client. This determination to slow down on the therapist's part decreases the likelihood that the therapist will "foreclose" (or decide) on a strategy or conclusion before a client has told her full story. In addition, listening for content and information can also help a therapist know how to respond in a way that solidly engages the client and facilitates an assessment of her situation (Carkhuff, 2000).

Listening for Feelings

If listening for content and information provides "the facts" in black and white, then listening for feelings gives therapists all of the colors that enrich a client's story. Clients universally have multiple wide-ranging feelings of varied intensity about the content that they are relating. The *type and intensity of feelings* provide crucial additional information about the importance of the statements that they are making or the stories that they are telling (Carkhuff, 2000; Skovholt & Rivers, 2004). That is, *what is it* about given facts and circumstances that a client is relating that gives rise to such intensity of feelings that, in turn, often become a focal point for the work of therapy? There are three basic methods for determining what a client is feeling: by what the client says, by the client's demeanor, and by the counselor's own feelings in reaction to the client's story (see Table 2.1).

The first, *listening for feelings based on what a client says,* is the most linear and straightforward. When a client says, "My boss makes me so angry," the *stated* feeling that is associated with the boss is anger. Of course, listening for feelings isn't as simple as that (as we will discuss below). There are elements of uncertainty to the expression of feelings such as anger (e.g., what exactly does a client mean by *angry*: annoyed, irritated, mad, enraged, or something else?). But, generally speaking, when feelings are expressed, it is a fairly accurate place for counselors to begin understanding their client.

The second method for determining, assessing, and understanding a client's feelings is *"listening" for feelings based on a client's demeanor*. This type of *listening* involves detecting what emotion a client is conveying with his comments and behavior. For example, if a client is talking about someone or some event and begins to cry, his *demeanor* suggests that he is sad. Likewise, if a client is describing an accomplishment that she is proud of, and is smiling broadly, it suggests that she is feeling happy. Or, if a client's eyes begin to well up with tears even slightly while discussing something, it suggests very sad and strong feelings that require follow-up. Such *behaviors* are a genuine expression of feeling, particularly because clients are usually unaware of them until they are pointed out.

Listening for feelings based on a client's *demeanor* requires *observation* or "reading" of the client— what a client *looks like* when speaking. What is it that can be seen on a client's face?[1] What are the qualities of her speech? Is it loud, soft, subdued, or the like? What is the tone of voice? Calm? Excited? Agitated? All of these, if accurately read, yield clues for astute clinicians to gather. Equally valid observations can be made when therapists are confused by what they are "reading" in a client's voice and demeanor and simply ask the client for clarification of what they have observed. Many of these same elements are a part of sound assessment, which will be discussed in Chapters 4 and 5.

Sometimes, a therapist can determine what a client is feeling by using her or his own feelings as an "emotional barometer." But when a counselor *uses her or his own feelings* in order to listen for client feelings, this is a less straightforward (i.e., *nonlinear*) process. Thus, there is a greater possibility for error (i.e., "misreading" a client). Such *nonlinear listening*, which we discuss later in this chapter, requires some degree of intuiting or "guessing" (Carkhuff, 2000; Egan, 2002).

There are two tiers to listening for feelings: the *cognitive tier* and the *emotional tier*. Only one, the cognitive tier, is linear and better suited for Level I counselors. Becoming at ease with using this type of listening, however, allows a person to deal with the *emotional tier* more easily (these topics will be discussed in the chapters related to the therapeutic alliance and client emotions: Chapters 6, 7, 10, and 11).

In *listening for feelings using a counselor's own feeling-cognitive tier*, a counselor listens to a client's story and asks, "If I were in this person's shoes, how might I feel?" Another way of putting this is to ask, "What would it be like to be in this person's shoes?" This approach is particularly helpful when a

TABLE 2.1   Methods of Listening for Feelings

Listening for feelings based on what the client says
Listening for feelings based on the client's demeanor (i.e., behavior, or what the client is doing)
Listening for feelings based on the counselor's feelings in reaction to the client (cognitive tier)
Listening for feelings based on the counselor's feelings in reaction to the client (emotional tier)

client may have a more constricted emotional range and is unable or unwilling (for whatever reason such as lack of trust, resistance, stage of change, or personal emotional disposition) to share much information with the counselor. For example, a client may come for treatment and describe in a dispassionate tone of voice how he got into an automobile accident in which his car was hit and spun into oncoming traffic, and faced a tractor-trailer truck barreling down on him. But, if neither the client's words nor demeanor shows the slightest hint of feeling, something is amiss. Thus, a counselor must ask, "If I were in this situation, how might I feel—what would that experience be like?" The answer would probably be some variation of "That would be terrifying!" Having this information can help a counselor to decide how to best respond to the client, and can also provide important clues as to a client's problems, state of mind, and readiness for change, which are all crucial to the process of connecting with, engaging, and assessing the client. We present Exercise 2.2 to illustrate this further.

Exercise 2.2: Listening for Feelings

Directions: Find a classmate or partner, and practice listening for feelings. Have each person in the dyad recall and record a recent event that evoked particular feelings (positive or negative). After writing down what was felt *without* sharing it with your partner, take turns *listening* to each other's story. When the person verbally sharing his story has finished, the listener should record what the storyteller was feeling, and what method of *listening for feeling* (e.g., what was said, demeanor, or feeling reaction in the counselor) was used to draw that conclusion. Switch roles, and have the first listener share her story while the partner listens. Repeat the step of writing down the storyteller's feeling(s) and what *listening for feeling* method was used. Once both partners have taken turns, compare the original feeling(s) written down by the storyteller with the feeling(s) recorded by the listener and method used for identifying the feeling. How accurate were the written responses? What methods did you use?

Variation: In a public place (e.g., a store, restaurant, or mall "food court"), do some "people watching." Pick out individuals who are engaging in conversations, and try to determine what they are feeling and what emotions they are expressing. Positive or negative? Which method of *listening for feeling* did you use to determine it?

How to Listen in a Nonlinear Way

Listening in a *linear* manner is an important but limited basic tool for *all* therapists. The therapeutic information that is derived by training oneself to listen for content and information as well as listen for feelings *is* important. But it does not necessarily provide important details about clients' lives such as information that a client is unprepared to disclose to a clinician. Thus, for a fuller picture of a client, it is important to learn to listen in *nonlinear* ways. Exercise 2.3 may help to begin to demonstrate this.

Exercise 2.3: Beginning the Use of Nonlinear Thinking

Because human beings have become more and more "civilized," they have become increasingly reliant upon formal language as a means of communicating with one another. At the same time, it soon becomes obvious that important aspects of communication have very little to do with *verbal language*. It has long been known that the *manner* in which someone says something is as important as, if not more important than, the particular words that are said. Lederer and Jackson (1968) elaborated on this in a more elemental way:

Every message has at least three aspects—the report aspect, the command aspect, and the context aspect. The *report* aspect consists of what is said or written, the actual meaning of the words, the content of the message—what is literally asked for, reported. The *command* aspect helps define the nature and meaning of the message, indicating how it is supposed to be heard, how the sender is attempting to influence the nature of his relationship with the receiver. ... When "Go to hell" is said with a snarl and a menacing glance, the report and command aspects reinforce each other. A very different message is conveyed by "Go to hell" said with a smile. ... The *context* aspect is determined by the cultural implications of the situation of the communicants. ... *There are many instances when the message received is not the message sent.* (pp. 100–101, emphasis added)

As a brief example of this, consider the following identical sentences. But, as you read them to yourself, accent the particular words that are italicized, and ask yourself how the meaning of the sentence is changed slightly by emphasis on a different word. A different version of this same exercise would be to say these six sentences out loud with your voice inflection emphasizing the italicized words in each sentence:

I don't want to go with you.
I *don't* want to go with you.
I don't *want* to go with you.
I don't want to *go* with *you*.
I don't want to go *with* you.
I don't want to go with *you*.

- What were the *linear aspects* of these sentences (information and feelings)?
- When speaking the sentences (or hearing them spoken), what differences in meaning did you detect when emphasis changed to a different word?
- How did the sentences differ when you heard the different inflections?
- Do some of the sentences with different inflections signify potentially more noteworthy meanings?
- What noteworthy meanings can you detect that would most likely be conveyed to someone?

This enjoyable little exercise illustrates the fact that we are influenced not by words alone (i.e., all six sentences are identical in the words used) but by the various ways in which human beings can qualify the meaning of the words they use to express themselves through tonal inflection. Now imagine, as Lederer and Jackson (1968) noted above, how the interpretation changes if the person says this with a wry, playful smile—or an angry scowl. Does the meaning change substantially? This is but one example of the complex phenomenon of human communication, and the need to listen nonlinearly.

As the above exercise demonstrates, there is more to listening than just the information contained in what a person is saying (i.e., "I don't want to go with you") and the emotion. In fact, *nonlinear listening* requires that a therapist does several things when hearing a client's story, including the following:

1. *Listening* not only with one's ears but also with one's eyes, feelings, and intuitions, and a generally open mind
2. *Hearing* things that aren't spoken or are conspicuous by their absence

3. *Identifying* certain things that clients may spend too much time discussing (i.e., "red herrings")

4. *Understanding* the subtleties of language, and what the words, expressions, images, behaviors, and feelings a client expresses *really* signify

In order to demonstrate this kind of listening more clearly, we have organized the typical examples of *nonlinear* listening into the following categories:

1. Listening for congruence (i.e., correspondence—or lack of correspondence—between what is said and what is meant)
2. Listening for absence (i.e., what is *not* said—either by silence or information overload)
3. Listening for inference (i.e., the purpose behind "I don't want ..." statements)
4. Listening for presence (i.e., nonverbal behaviors that add meaning)
5. Listening for resistance (i.e., the desire *not* to change)

We describe each of these categories below.

Congruence (i.e., Correspondence—or Lack of Correspondence—Between What Is Said and What Is Meant)

Listening for correspondence between *what* someone says and *how* it is said is called *congruence*, and it is an important part of *nonlinear listening*. At its most fundamental level, *incongruence* (or the dissimilarity between what someone says and how she says it) represents a discontinuity between processes: When a client's story or messages are *incongruent*, what she is experiencing *inside* and what she is expressing *outside* simply do not match. A discussion of congruence and its importance in therapy must make several distinctions.

Although it may not come as a surprise, most human beings do distort, exaggerate, withhold information, and even lie. Some people may do such things "better" than others. There are any number of reasons why a client might do this, but one of the most prominent is because he is not prepared to accept the consequences of telling the truth (e.g., out of embarrassment, shame, guilt, or fear of loss of prestige). Another prominent reason that someone might lie is because it can provide him with some benefit (e.g., rewards, putting others at a disadvantage, and getting "off the hook"). How do you know if a client's narrative is truthful?[2] Sometimes it is impossible to tell, and sometimes not. What a therapist is *more* interested in determining is whether or not there is *correspondence* between the *conscious story and the unconscious story* being told in therapy. The way that human beings commonly sense if someone is being congruent is by determining whether *what a person says* matches with *what they do* (their behavior) or how they appear (demeanor). When therapists listen for congruence, they are listening in a *nonlinear* way to determine if two stories (i.e., conscious and unconscious) match. It is essential for integrity to rule the psychotherapeutic process.

Part of that integrity depends on an honest exchange taking place between client and therapist and between the client and herself. For example, if a woman describes a "bad" marriage at considerable length, but then states half-heartedly (with a heavy sigh), "I guess I should get a divorce," it obviously lacks conviction. The words don't necessarily match the deep sigh or any conviction. It is at that moment in time that the therapist can state, "It doesn't *sound* as though you are terribly convinced of your own conclusion." When the therapist notes the discrepancy, it can help the client to become familiar with her *ambivalence* (see Chapters 12 and 13) as represented between her conscious story (i.e., "I guess I should get a divorce") and her unconscious story (i.e., the deep sigh and lowered tone of voice). Detecting such a disconnect can potentially be the gateway to understanding the core of such a client's dilemma: "I want to get a divorce, but I can't do so without feeling like a failure, facing great uncertainty, losing face, and becoming just another *divorcée*!"

Sometimes, the discrepancies detected are a matter of *therapist interpretation* or a matter of *miscommunication between the therapist and the client.* At times, however, inconsistencies are a matter of *deception* (i.e., either self-deception or deceiving the therapist). Whatever the underlying reason, inconsistency provides information for a therapist that may not be present on the surface, but that is crucial to being effective. When these inconsistencies happen, therapists can respond in ways that foster a client's engagement. Pointing out inconsistencies *should never be conducted in an aggressive or accusatory manner,* but rather in a friendly way as if the therapist is confused or looking for clarification, as will be described below.

Nonlinear listening for congruence involves using all of one's senses, including a sense of curiosity and empathy. Taking a client's words *only* at face value is a *linear* approach to therapy that can be counterproductive. As a result, one thing that is integral to the process of nonlinear listening is a counselor's sense of *curiosity.* The curiosity of nonlinear listening must *always* be finely tuned, and begins with sensitizing oneself to the words that a client uses. Words expressing emotions and feelings such as *hate, hurt, fear, love, sad,* and *lost* have vastly different meanings from one person to another and must be elaborated upon for their specific meaning to a particular client. If they are not, a therapist runs the risk of proceeding with a client from a faulty set of assumptions. Consider the following example. Because of his adult only son's long history of disappointments, arguments, incidents of drug abuse, and hospitalizations for mental illness, a client stated, "I think I hate my son! I'm ashamed to say that!" In actuality, despite the overt power of the statement, the man's expression of feeling hatred for his son is somewhat ambiguous, as is *the way* in which he said it. Exactly what does the word *hate* mean to him? It may pass through his lips in one way, but what passes through his lips, what we hear, and what he actually means upon closer scrutiny may have entirely different meanings. Does he mean he *hates* (i.e., detests) his son? Or, does he perhaps mean that he *hates his son's behavior?* Hating his son and hating his son's behavior contain two vastly different meanings. Separating the son's *behaviors* from the *personhood of the son* is an important distinction to make. The first step in *nonlinear listening* is to make sure that you listen for such distinctions. They can have vastly different implications for the direction of therapy.

When a lack of congruence is due to some deception on the client's part, it is important to understand the circumstance surrounding it (e.g., is the client trying to "save face" versus trying to evade being "caught" doing something wrong?). For example, you see Bob drop a bowling ball on his foot, yell out in pain, grimace, and start hopping around on one foot. You would use your powers of observation and (correctly) conclude that he was in pain. However, when you go over to help him, Bob dismisses you and says, "I'm OK! I'm OK!" while he is still wincing. This is not consistent (or congruent) because you know it isn't true! Bob is deceiving himself, when it is obvious that he is in pain. Inconsistencies in what and how clients express something reveal that they are unsettled about something. Pursuing such unsettled discrepancies between conscious and unconscious processes is one of the major avenues through which therapeutic movement occurs. Returning to poor Bob, why would he want to deny what is obvious? Maybe he feels embarrassed at his carelessness, or perhaps he feels that to acknowledge pain is a personal failing (i.e., weakness). In that case, he is clearly unsettled about it and chooses to deny physical pain to avoid emotional embarrassment.

There are certain psychological processes, however, that by their nature are *incongruent.* One of those processes is psychological "numbing." This refers to the general lack of emotional responsiveness that an individual can demonstrate subsequent to being exposed to very traumatic circumstances that are not part of typical human experience. A "flattened affect" is also one of the conditions that demonstrates a disconnect between unconscious and conscious processes. In and of themselves, such signs are *symptoms* and indicative of a particular underlying psychological condition. "Stonewalling" (Gottman, 1993, 1995; Gottman & Silver, 1999) is another such process in which one spouse *says* that she (or he) understands her partner while her behavior actually "tunes out" the other, is not responsive, and pays little meaningful attention to her mate, all of which has a profound effect on the vibrancy of the relationship.

If clients are congruent in their statements, the process of therapy (most notably, connecting with the client) becomes much more straightforward. When they are not congruent, the process of therapy (*especially* engagement) becomes more complex. But there are ways to understand and work with incongruence that can actually foster rapport and encourage a client to engage in treatment. It is the *nonlinear-listening* and *nonlinear-thinking* therapist who is attuned to the potential meaning of such behaviors and pursues them when they are in evidence. We will discuss how to respond to these below.

Listening for "Absence" (i.e., What Is Not Said—by Silence, Avoidance, or Information Overload)

"Absence" can take two forms: what is not said or when *too much* is said! Though they may seem to be on opposite ends of the spectrum, the underlying thread binding such communications is *the lack of information* provided to the therapist. We address both below.

What Clients Do Not Discuss: Omissions

At times, what clients *do not discuss* can be as important as what it is that they *are* discussing, if not more so. Sometimes, a client not discussing an issue simply may be because he or she does not believe or experience it to be problematic. Although that may be true at times, at other times such omissions may not be the case. On the other hand, particularly painful experiences, events, circumstances, failures, and issues for which a client does not want to be held responsible for fear of being found lacking at times are conspicuous by the client's avoidance of them. *Nonlinear listening* requires patience and the development of the ability to be attuned for such things. For example, if a person with two children enters therapy but talks about only her older child as problematic and never mentions the younger child, a therapist may become curious. A therapist "wondering" and asking herself *why something is not being discussed* may very well be a clue that something is amiss and *conspicuous by its absence*. It will be important to explore this curiosity, even if there *really* is nothing wrong with the younger child.

When Clients Talk Too Much: Land Mines, Rabbit Holes, and Other Red Herrings

At times, a client may wish to bring up material that one might discuss for a lifetime without any hope of resolution. This type of material can be classified as *land mines*, *rabbit holes*, or *red herrings*. A landmine is just that: a topic that is so emotionally explosive that a therapist will never want to step on it twice! For example, a client came for treatment because his stepdaughter had called the police and accused him of fondling her. Every time she came up in session, the client would become enraged, call her a "bitch" and a "whore," and make other unpleasant comments. Even though she was central to the presenting concern that brought the client for treatment, it was almost impossible to approach the subject without enduring an abusive tirade. As a result, many beginning (and even experienced) therapists might want to avoid such a topic so as not to incur the client's anger. In doing so, however, the relationship with the stepdaughter can't be explored. The conversation gets directed to "safe," emotionally neutral topics. This is precisely what the client wants, though it spells certain doom for any therapeutic progress to be made.

Some clients will want to "war story"—repeatedly talk about what they did or what happened without forward movement or resolution. This is an example of a therapeutic *Alice in Wonderland* rabbit hole,[3] material that has the potential to lead treatment in an unfruitful direction. Clients in substance abuse treatment or some victims of abuse may repetitively review details of their experiences over and over, but are unable to utilize the discussion to make any progress. As therapists engage such clients in these stories (either as part of an intake session, or in later sessions in the hope of gaining some useful information), the stories become more powerful for the client and dominate the therapy, to the exclusion of anything else. As a result, other aspects of the client's story (e.g., his or her strengths, potential, hopes, and alternatives) can't be explored.

Red herrings are the scrumptious "tidbits" that clients throw out. They *seem* like real issues, but don't necessarily have anything to do with a client's needs (much like rabbit holes). However, although rabbit holes may have some therapeutic benefit, red herrings usually do not. At times, clients will talk about sensational issues (e.g., past overindulgences, or fantastic insights about themselves) or want to explore hidden dimensions of themselves (via hypnosis or dream work). These can be "false leads" used to deflect a therapist from focusing on the client. As an example, a client entered therapy complaining about symptoms of depression that were interfering with her work. During the initial interview, however, she went into extreme detail about episodes of past sexual abuse. In subsequent sessions, the topic of the past abuse dominated the conversation, and any discussion about present-day concerns was avoided. When *listening for absence*, it is essential for a therapist to remember that he or she is listening to a client's story: "What is it that I am *not* hearing in this client's story that may be very important?"

Listening for Inference (The Purpose Behind "I Don't Want ..." Statements)

As incredible as it may seem, clients typically enter therapy with vague ideas about what they want to accomplish—indeed, many times they actually have poorly formulated specific goals for treatment. Instead, what clients almost universally *do* come to therapy with is a formulation of *what they don't want*. In other words, they *infer* what their goals are, without making them explicit.

Common examples of how clients vaguely describe their "goals" are "I don't want to lose control of myself," "I don't want to fight with my wife anymore," "I don't want to be depressed," "I don't want to be anxious," "I don't want to smoke," "I don't want to drink anymore," "I don't want to be fat," and "I don't want to be a loser." When clients frame their problem by telling you what they don't want, in most instances they are acknowledging that actually they *do* have a problem. They do not know what would be occurring if they weren't fighting with a spouse, drinking excessively, or being depressed. This is an important consideration because *disengaging* from symptomatic behavior is required *before* one can embrace more constructive pursuits. But, a client must have specific goals and objectives if he is to disengage from what he doesn't want!

Other clients claim that *someone else* is the problem. They frame *their* problems in similar negative terms: "*I don't want* my husband (or wife, boss, parents, children, etc., as the case may be) to treat me that way!" Such expressions only serve to *prompt and promote* a client's *grappling* with the problematic or symptomatic behavior and remaining stuck with it. That is, the client struggles with it, tries to overcome it, and generally fails. The *linear-thinking* client's *focus of attention* typically is the struggle to stop or get rid of something. But, the more that a person wrestles with *getting rid of* something, the more she is actually engaged with that "something," much like "trying hard *not* to think of alligators." The more someone repeats, "I'm not going to think of alligators," the more she *is* actually thinking of alligators. It is important for clinicians to remember this because clients so preoccupied with what they *don't want* most often have no specific idea of what they *do want*. It is the clinician who must first listen for these implicit or inferred goals and then present them to the client.

It is also important to remember that clients generally seek treatment only after they have repeatedly struggled with a problem or symptom without success. Thus, a client may have built up a problem-centric view of himself and can't see alternative views. Clinical Case Example 2.1 may help to illustrate this point.

Clinical Case Example 2.1: Nervous in Cars

A young, attractive, and successful businesswoman sought help after many years of suffering from anxiety. When asked why she was seeking help for her anxiety at this particular point in time, she indicated, "It's particularly noticeable when I'm in cars and someone else is driving. I realized that this wasn't normal. I want this fixed! It would be nice *to not have to worry about what could happen*! It would be nice *to not be so nervous in the car*." The reader will notice that this young woman has expressed what she *doesn't want*—to be nervous when riding in a car. But, an expression of what she *doesn't want* gives no indication of what she *does want*. What *would* she be doing and how would she be acting if she *wasn't* fretting while riding in a car as a passenger? Does her anxious fretting represent more of a fundamental approach to life— namely, "Life, in general, makes me nervous"? Or, might her anxiety be related to something traumatic that occurred while she was a passenger in a car accident?

This phenomenon of inference spans the entire scope of clinical practice. A couple that complains of marital strife may have no clear idea of how they should or would interact with each other if they were *not arguing and distant* from one another. Substance abusers, particularly problem drinkers, have no clear idea what they would be doing if they were sober during the multiple hours previously spent drinking daily. How would the chronic marijuana user or abuser "relax" if *not* using cannabis to do so? Most obese people have no clear idea of what they would do in their lives and how their lives would change substantially (e.g., the broad implications of normal weight) if, indeed, they were to adopt sensible eating habits, modest regular exercise, and increased general activity, and lose their excess weight—perhaps that is why so many individuals with major weight loss (an estimated 95%) gain back the lost weight and then some.

In part, therapy uncovers *inferred goals*, and translates them back to a client so treatment can move toward addressing problems, meeting client needs, and achieving more clearly defined and reasonable goals.

Listening for Presence (Nonverbal Behaviors That Add Meaning)

Nonlinear listening necessitates developing a capacity for understanding the *potential implied meaning of messages*. These messages may be conveyed through a client's tone of voice or bodily expressions (e.g., facial expressions, body posture, blushing, nervous giggles, a rolling of the eyes, changing posture, and deep sighing). The *nonlinear*-thinking therapist will follow up with a client on these subtle body messages (i.e., "body language") in order to clarify what is being said. Such body messages are *qualifiers* of what a client is saying verbally. To put it another way:

> It is first of all necessary to remember that the scope of "communication" is by no means limited to verbal productions. Communications are exchanged through many channels and combinations of these channels, and certainly also through the *context* [emphasis added] in which an interaction takes place. Indeed, it can be summarily stated that *all* behavior, not only the use of words, is communication (which is not the same as saying that behavior is *only* communication), and since there is no such thing as non-behavior, it is impossible *not* to communicate. (Watzlawick & Beavin, 1977, p. 58)

In other words, even if a client is defiantly refusing to speak, or is limiting responses to one-word answers, he is still communicating messages through his nonverbal behavior.

Pioneers in family therapy can be credited with recognizing the importance of all behavior in communicating meaning. Specifically, classical communication theorists such as Haley (1963), Lederer and Jackson (1968), Satir (1964), and Watzlawick and Beavin (1977) all highlighted the importance of nonverbal communication. Classic powerful research by Mehrabian and Ferris (1967) provides empirical support for the assertion that in human communication, the *transmission of meaning* tends to come from three important sources. Actual words spoken may account for as little as 7% of meaning expressed. Interestingly, the *tonal characteristics* of the speaker's voice may account for as much as 38% of meaning conveyed. Significantly, Mehrabian and Ferris (1967) found that facial expression accounts for up to 55% of the messages communicated. Some practitioners prefer the term *body communication*, rather than *body language*, to convey the fact that there are important messages contained in this nonverbal behavior: "Body communication … is the communication made through bodily movements and changes. It's the communication given by a person's physical bearing, facial expressions and physiology" (Emerick, 1997, p. 89).

It is essential to grasp the importance of nonverbal messages that are conveyed by clients. What a client *does* during a therapy session (i.e., behaviors demonstrated) is as important as what he or she is saying. Gottman (1995, 1997) has reported epic research and powerful conclusions on the communication between spouses in troubled marriages:

> *Body Language.* In its most subtle form, contempt is communicated with a few swift changes of the facial muscles. Signs of contempt of disgust include sneering, rolling your eyes, and curling you upper lip. At times in our research, facial expressions offered the clearest clue that something was amiss between a couple. For example, a wife may sit quietly and offer her husband an occasional "go on, I'm listening"

while he airs his grievances. But at the same time, she is picking lint off her skirt and rolling her eyes. Her true feelings—contempt—are written in body language. (1995, p. 81)

Listening for the *presence* of *nonverbal behaviors* means that a therapist takes into consideration not just words spoken but also voice tone and body language (Hill, 2004). Such *nonlinear listening* is a fundamental part of *nonlinear thinking*. In the example provided by Gottman (1995) above, if the husband irately proclaims, "HEY! You're not listening to me!!" The wife may retort, "What do you mean—I *told* you I was listening." *Linear thinking* ignores anything beyond spoken words (and agrees with the wife). *Nonlinear thinking*, however, makes note of the *presence* of the behavior that the wife is demonstrating in rolling her eyes with a dismissive and contemptuous attitude. Learning to be sensitive to behaviors that qualify words being articulated (e.g., tone of voice, facial expression, body posture, rolling of the eyes, clucking of the tongue, and finger drumming) is without a doubt a vital part of therapist development that is best addressed early and often by a Level I practitioner.

Listening for Resistance: The Desire Not to Change

Clients may come to therapy but, for many reasons, are not ready to make the essential and substantial changes necessary to resolve their problems. Many times, they may express good intentions but soon fail to show the commitment that is necessary for change to take place. In such instances, it is the therapist's role to help clients to not only remain in therapy but also benefit from it. At other times, clients may enter therapy stating that someone else is the problem or someone else *made* them come, and that they are *not* happy to be there! Chapter 4 will present a method for classifying a client's *readiness* for change, which is crucial for the initial assessment of the client.

However, the first warnings about a client's level of readiness for a commitment to change come from clients' verbal expressions. Therapists must be attuned to these overt or covert signals and be able to react in a manner that helps clients to overcome their resistance and engage in the therapy. Although a more thorough discussion of the concept of client resistance will be presented in Chapters 3 and 5, there are some basic verbalizations clients frequently use that *can* betray signs of resistance. Several common verbalizations that clients use, especially in the initial stages of counseling, to express resistance are "I'll *try*. ..." "I know that I *should*. ..." "*Yes, but* ..." "I've already *done that, and it didn't work*. ..." and "I can't *because* ...."

On the other hand, clients may complain that they are incapable of doing something routine (e.g., paying bills on time, or cleaning the house) but claim that they are able to do other extraordinary things (e.g., play music professionally, or program computers) that most other people can't do easily. The question then becomes, is this something that the person is *unwilling* to do, *unprepared* to do, or *unable* to do? If they are unwilling to do something, then that is not congruent with the statement that they *cannot* do something. If they are unprepared to do something, they are likely to face failure if they attempt it. The important thing is to listen for additional instances of this behavior that would indicate a pattern, which would be suggestive of an area to work on.

Perhaps the most common of all statements that clients use to express little expectation for change is some variation of the statement "I'll try." Expressing good intentions, or "trying," may also express some lingering doubt about their ability to change or an underlying ambivalence about making a change. For example, a client may say, "I've tried everything else, and nothing has worked, so I thought I'd give therapy *a try*." Embedded in that statement is the *unspoken* sentiment "... but I am pretty sure it will not work." This statement acts as a *covert* expression that the client has little or no expectation of success.

A close linguistic and psychological "relative" of the statement "I'll try" is "I should. ..." This expression suggests that a client knows what it is she is *supposed to do* but not what it is that she *wants* or intends to do (hence, *resistance*; see Chapter 12). The client may describe her unacceptable problem behavior as a "habit" or use the phrase "I can't help myself." This can also reflect a self-image of being a victim who can't change these strong habits (Mosak & Gushurst, 1971). For example, a client who complains of a compulsive gambling habit, saying, "I've destroyed my finances because of gambling! I should stop; it shouldn't be that hard, but it is!" already has the seeds of doubt as to his ability to stop gambling, with failure the most likely result.

Finally, practitioners like Berne (1964), Gottman (1995), as well as others (e.g., Adler, 1956) have observed one of the most potent verbalizations of resistance, called the "Yes, but ..." statement. Simply put, the initial "yes" that the client says in response to a therapeutic comment or suggestion is instantly negated by a "but" asserted after it. Superficially, a client appears to be agreeing with what the therapist is saying. On closer inspection, however, it reveals a socially polite way of saying, "I disagree with everything you just said and don't propose to do anything different!" In a similar vein, a parent may lecture a teenage child about the need to call when he is out late to tell the parent that he is safe. Often, children know that this makes sense and agree with their parents: "Yes, I know that it is important to call you, *but* what if I can't get a cell (or it is too late, or ...)?" The simple fact that the person is conceiving of an instance in which he might not be able to comply with what was agreed to (via the "yes" part) suggests that there is some resistance (i.e., disagreement) to it in the first place. Such expressions bear taking note of because therapists can fall into the trap of thinking that the client is "on board" when he or she is not. Exercise 2.4 is meant to enhance sensitivity to nonlinear listening.

Exercise 2.4: Clinical Nonlinear Listening

Directions: Read each vignette, and answer the following questions. (Answers will be provided at the end of the chapter).

1. Listening for content or information. What are the "facts" that the client is reporting?
2. Listening for feelings. What is the client feeling?
3. What type of nonlinear listening is required by the client's story?
4. What do you hear from the client based on these nonlinear approaches to listening?
5. How does the *nonlinear* approach to listening change your understanding of the client based on the linear approaches (Questions 1 and 2)?

A. A client states that she wants help for her son, whose grades are "poor." She further complains that he doesn't do any studying at home. When asked what his grades are, she replies, "B's, but he *should* be getting A's with all the money I am paying for his private school!" The client goes on to add, "I just don't want him ending up like his father!"

B. A 40-year-old gentleman comes to an initial session of therapy stating that he wants counseling for issues related to "life management." He reports that he has seen counselors on and off for the last 15 years, but never stays long. Presently, he lives with his mother, is still in college, and complains that he cannot seem to "finish things" in his life. When pressed for details, he is vague and evasive.

C. An in-patient being treated for substance abuse comes for an individual session stating that the staff is "abusive" to her: "They were abusive to me first, so I slapped at one of them. Now they won't let me go to outside AA meetings! I need them for my recovery." The client then states, "I'm not sure why I am even here; I don't have a problem." A few minutes later, she adds, "I slapped at the staff so that they would discharge me!"

D. A client reports being in an abusive relationship with her husband. She relates an incident about her husband getting angry, yelling at her, and pushing her into a crowd while they were in public. She coolly states that she really doesn't believe that he will do her harm, although she noticeably fidgets and has a tremble in her voice whenever she talks about her husband.

E. A busy executive comes into an initial session stating that he wants to make more time for his family. As you start to make some suggestions about how he might strive to achieve his goals, he begins to discuss his work obligations and how he must "work around" them. Finally, he says, "All right, I will give some of these suggestions a try."

Listening in a nonlinear way requires sensitizing oneself to a variety of possible meanings implied in client verbalizations and behavior. It is implied meanings that provide opportunities for clarification, understanding, and interventions that foster engagement (Carkhuff, 2000; Hill, 2004). In fact, *nonlinear listening* becomes an avenue to all of the *nonlinear* interventions in the subsequent portions of this text. It is to the other half of the domain of connecting with and engaging the client, namely, responding, that we now turn our attention.

ENDNOTES

1. A major development in "reading" others comes from the "recognition of facial affect" and pioneering research done in this area by Ekman, Levenson, and Friesen (1983) and Ekman (1992, 1995). Research on the recognition of facial affect involves identifying specific facial muscles that human beings cross-culturally use in expressing different basic emotions.
2. For an elaborate discussion of research about human beings being able to detect when someone is not telling the truth, we recommend the work of Ekman (1995) and Gladwell (2005).
3. *Rabbit hole* is a reference to Lewis Carroll's *Alice in Wonderland*, in which Alice followed the rabbit down into a "wonderland" of the bizarre.

Answers to Exercise 2.4: (A) inference; (B) absence; (C) congruence; (D) presence; and (E) resistance.

The Domain of Connecting With and Engaging the Client

Part 2: Responding

3

CONTENTS

INTRODUCTION

Second only to listening, responding is perhaps the most important thing that a therapist does. It is wise for Level I therapists to be aware of the subtleties and implications of language and the influences—intended or not—that responses can have on their clients. Words from a person in a position of power and influence (e.g., a psychiatrist, psychologist, counselor, or social worker) must be chosen carefully, because clients are vulnerable and suggestible (see Acosta & Prager, 2002; Peluso, 2006a).

Just as there are differences between linear and nonlinear listening, there are also differences in responding linearly and nonlinearly. These logically follow from the categories of linear and nonlinear listening described in Chapter 2. This chapter focuses on responding *linearly* and *nonlinearly* to a wide variety of client statements. In subsequent chapters, we will expand on how to respond to clients in effective ways that address increasingly complex aspects of therapy.

LINEAR RESPONDING

Linear responding follows from linear listening—from the statements a client makes. If done well, *linear responding* facilitates the engagement process, signaling to a client that someone understands her story at a basic level without judgment or blame. In turn, *linear responding* encourages a client to reveal more of her story because it is safe to do so. The two types of linear responding we will discuss are *responding to content or information*, and *responding to feeling*.

Responding to Content or Information

Carkhuff (2000) has detailed the importance of responding to content. It provides the conversational "space" for a client to know that he is being heard and understood by the therapist, and can continue with his story. Just as listening to content is about the facts of a client's statement, responding to content is a therapist's reflection of the facts of the client's statement. This type of responding represents the lowest level of intensity or threat that a therapist can utilize. Carkhuff recommended starting sentences with "You're saying ..." and then reflecting back to the client a summary of what he has been saying. Others recommend posing a question like "So what I hear you saying is ...?" The main purpose of such linear responding is twofold: gaining clarification, and the therapist conveying an understanding of what a client is saying. Such clarification invites a client to proceed further with his story or the theme of what is being discussed. But, clients aren't always direct in what they are saying or implying—their meanings can be obscure and unclear.

As a clinical example, after much debate a client may state that she has resolved to quit her job. A response to the content or information may take the form of "So you've made a decision to resign." When therapists respond to content or information, they should do so in a way that conveys a neutral stance (i.e., neither agreeing nor disagreeing) and that they are genuinely interested in hearing more factual information about a client's story. Typically, other avenues for discussion begin to follow. In the example above, a client may decide to talk about future plans (e.g., "I'm going to open my own business!") or discuss her concerns (e.g., "Yeah, it was hard to do, and I'm nervous about what is going to happen."). Responding in a linear manner is ultimately limited, and responding at a deeper level is necessary to gain greater depth of understanding and rapport with a client. It is important to note that the more robotic and mechanical that therapists are (i.e., like a parrot) in feeding back what a client is expressing, the less effective they will be in connecting with and engaging a client.

Responding to Feelings

A therapist's verbal statements of empathy and understanding that are congruent (i.e., in harmony) with the way in which such statements are made play an important role in a client feeling valued, validated, understood, and accepted (Carkhuff, 2000). In turn, such harmonious expressions of empathy are an essential component of building a strong therapeutic alliance—the foundation for all work that is accomplished in therapy. Responding to clients' feelings communicates that you understand and can connect with them on a deeper, more intimate level—beyond understanding the linear facts they present. Again, following listening for feeling, these responses usually take the simple form of "You feel ... (insert a feeling word here or another word, phrase, metaphor, etc)." For example, suppose a client says, "I just wish that my mother would stop treating me like a child! It infuriates me when she tells me what to do with my life. It's like she doesn't think that I can take care of myself!" As a therapist listens to the client, it is important to listen for the feelings being expressed by (a) what the client says ("infuriates me"), (b) the client's demeanor (e.g., face contorted in an angry expression), or (c) reference to a therapist's own feeling (i.e., recall the distinctions between these categories described in Chapter 2).

The next step, before responding, is to simply ask oneself, "What is it that this client is feeling?" The answer to that question becomes the basis for a response. So in the previous example, the answer to what a client may be feeling could be "angry," "upset," "distressed," or "frustrated" (amongst others). The response could be "So—you *really* feel upset with your mother for treating you like you were 5 years old." This communicates an understanding of *the emotional impact of the client's story*. This is especially true and very important when a therapist's response matches the level of a client's feeling. As a result, a further question that therapists need to ask themselves before they respond is "*To what degree* does the client feel this way? A mild, medium, or large degree?" The therapist must match her or his response in proportion to the client's expression in order to be effective in fostering a sense of understanding, engagement, and connectedness. Again, utilizing the example above, if a therapist used feeling words that were too severe and didn't match clients' feelings (e.g., "You feel *enraged* at your mother") or not strong enough (e.g., "You feel uneasy about your mother"), a client may feel *emotionally* misunderstood or perhaps that the clinician did not care about him.

Another pitfall for clinicians when responding to a client's feeling is using the client's *exact phrasing* (commonly referred to as *parroting*). Just like inaccurately responding to feelings, parroting makes the processes of connecting with and engaging a client more difficult, if not impossible. Thus, it is important to understand a client's particular feeling and the level of the feeling, and then summarize it accurately, but not just "spit back" clients' words to them. Clinical Exercise 3.1 provides some information on increasing your feeling vocabulary.

Clinical Exercise 3.1: Increasing Your Feeling Vocabulary

Accurately responding to feelings or getting a "recognition reflex" requires a therapist to have a wide vocabulary of feeling words. As human beings, we have a rich and wide-ranging palette of feelings (much like an elaborate color palette with all the shades of various colors). As children grow and develop, they begin experiencing the full range of these feelings and must look to their parents and other adults to help them interpret and label what they are feeling (Gottman, 1997). Many times, adults do not have a rich vocabulary to guide children in identifying their feelings. As a result, they are taught basic feelings of happy, sad, mad, and scared. When these limited words are applied to the broad and subtle variations of feelings that human beings experience, confusion can result, and many people report that they do not feel many things at all. In addition, they may use nonfeeling words like *good, bad, fine,* and *I don't know*. It is as if parents brought their child to the ocean, gazed upon a crystal aquamarine sea framed by an icy azure sky, and called them both "blue." Although this is true, it does not accurately convey the breadth and impact of the encounter, and, as a result, something of the experience is lost. It is the same with feelings. For example, a person may have ended a long-term relationship and is feeling devastated. Meanwhile, another person could have ended a weeklong relationship and feel mildly upset. If both of these people describe themselves simply as "sad," would it tell the whole story? What would be missing? Clearly, it is technically accurate, but it does not tell the entire story. Instead, good, useful information comes with the subtle shading. As a result, therapists must have a repertoire of feeling words for each of the major feelings (happy, sad, angry, afraid, and hurt). They also need words of low intensity, medium intensity, and high intensity in order to help clients label their own feeling state. The more feeling words at your disposal, the more likely you will hit a client's "emotional solar plexus."

Instructions: Develop a repertoire of feeling expressions by filling in low-, medium-, and high-intensity words for each of the basic emotions. Share your words with class members to develop a larger list of feeling words for each.

PRIMARY FEELING	LOW INTENSITY	MEDIUM INTENSITY	HIGH INTENSITY
Happy			
Sad			
Angry			
Afraid			
Hurt			

Variation: Form small groups, and pick one of the basic feelings. Then, create case scenarios that match each of the categories (low, medium, and high). Present the case scenarios to the other groups, and ask them to assign a feeling word that best matches the case scenario.

Accurately responding to feeling fosters greater engagement, whereas inaccurately responding to feeling can create a "rupture" (i.e., break) in the therapeutic relationship (this will be covered in more detail in Chapter 7). How do you know if you have responded to a client's feelings accurately? Again, sometimes therapists will know that they have correctly responded to what a client is feeling when they hear a client say, "That's it!" "That's exactly how I feel!" or "You hit the nail on the head!" In some instances, a client will actually tell the therapist if he or she is correct or not.

Many times, however, clients will not necessarily tell therapists verbally that they are correct. But, there is an automatic response that people have when they hear what they are feeling reflected back to them. Called a *recognition reflex*, it usually takes the form of a smile, eyes brightening, or some form of head nodding (Driekurs, Grunewald, & Pepper, 1982). It can also take the form of tears welling in a client's eyes. In fact, it is almost impossible to *not* have a recognition reflex *if* a therapist accurately reflects back the exact emotion that a client is feeling. It is as if a client says, "How did you know that?" Some people indicate that they feel warmth radiating from their stomach (sometimes called *hitting the emotional solar plexus*).[1] Hence, accurately listening for and responding to feelings afford clinicians another opportunity to connect with clients on a deeper, more intimate level and facilitate their engaging in the therapeutic process.

Advanced Linear Responding

In addition, combining a response to content or information with a response to feelings can foster a very deep level of exploration and engagement. Carkhuff (2000) referred to this as a "response to meaning," which takes the general form of "You feel ... (fill in the feeling word) because (fill in the content) ..." Using the earlier example, a therapist may respond to the client who was in conflict with his mother by saying, "You really feel upset with your mother because she treats you like a baby and doesn't respect you." These linear responses, however, are limited—they often do not go to the core of a client's concerns. Research has shown that clients who don't feel that their problems are understood by a therapist in the early sessions do not stay in therapy very long and do not get the help they need (e.g., Brogan, Prochaska, & Prochaska, 1999; Hubble, Duncan, & Miller, 1999; Miller, Duncan, & Hubble, 1997a).

A final note about the strategic use of linear responses, particularly when a client is overemotional: At such times, a therapist may choose to respond to content (i.e., information) as a way of helping clients to disengage from unproductive ruminating about feelings and have them concentrate on more rational elements (thinking, logic, problem solving, etc.). Likewise, there are times when responding to feelings can be used to help clients to evaluate their own emotional states (i.e., being too emotionally rigid or "robotic") when they are unable. By strategically using these linear responses, therapists help such clients to focus on internal processes that they are not accessing.

To summarize linear listening and responding, in essence, it is the therapist's job to (a) detect as closely and exactly as possible what core meanings, sentiments, emotions, and feelings a client is expressing by her or his verbal and nonverbal expressions; and (b) succinctly reflect those core meanings, sentiments, emotions, and feelings back to the client in an empathetic way so as to elicit the client saying the equivalent of "Yes! That's it exactly!" Although at first this may seem like a daunting task, mastery of it requires less "technical" skill than a way of thinking. Once a novice "gets" the notion, the rest is practice that ultimately morphs into a natural way of attending to clients. As a result, although reflecting accurate empathy back to a client and congruence on the part of the therapist have been called "facilitative conditions to therapy," they are not enough (Lambert & Barley, 2002). Instead, clients require a level of response that gets to the heart of their problem or concern. This necessitates responses that are *nonlinear* in their approach.

NONLINEAR RESPONDING

Responding nonlinearly is clearly different from responding in a linear manner. Remember that by *nonlinear*, we mean things that are askew, that may not logically follow from what has been presented, but that ultimately do begin to shed new light on a given issue for a client. Therapists' *nonlinear responses* are motivated by several factors, including client ambivalence about making changes and therapist curiosity about elements of the client's story that may be vague. Nonlinear responses often break the linear flow of a client's story and can alienate a client if done poorly. On the other hand, if nonlinear responding is done well, it can foster quicker rapport as well as facilitate therapeutic progress.

Underlying all of the nonlinear-listening categories listed above (i.e., congruence, absence, presence, inference, and resistance) is some level of client confusion or ambivalence. A therapist's job entails (a) detecting the ambivalence a client is expressing and presenting it appropriately to the client, and (b) responding to the ambivalence in a way that facilitates a client engaging in therapy to sufficiently explore problems and arrive at an acceptable solution. In addition to the aspects of nonlinear listening identified above, responding in a nonlinear way also includes the following:

- *Asking well-formed questions* that elicit more information
- *Translating* what it is that a client is saying
- *Relating* what a client says to his or her past statements, one's past clinical experiences, and one's theoretical frame of reference
- *Forming* and *testing* hypotheses

The elements of nonlinear responding to be discussed are as follows:

- *Responding to incongruence* (i.e., "I hear that there is more than one side to this")
- *Responding to absence* (i.e., "I see what you are not showing me")
- *Responding to inference* (i.e., "I hear what you are not saying")
- *Responding to presence* (i.e., "I see what your body is saying, even if you may not")
- *Responding to resistance* (i.e., "I understand that you might not be ready for this")

A key element in the domain of connecting with and engaging a client in treatment is conveying that therapy can sometimes be a daunting and scary experience and a person may not be entirely ready to deal effectively with such a threat. At the same time, a therapist must communicate a sense of optimism, namely, that if a client perseveres with treatment, improvements can be made.

Nonlinear Responding to Incongruence (i.e., "I Hear That There Is More Than One Side to This")

Recall that incongruent statements made by clients generally occur for one of two basic reasons: It is either *misunderstanding or miscommunication* between counselor and client, or because of unintentional *deception* on the client's part. *Responding to incongruence* is an attempt to understand the ambiguous meaning of what a client is saying. Because this is quite common, it is little wonder that Carl Rogers and researchers who followed him emphasized *congruence* (i.e., agreement between what is expressed and the *manner* in which it is said) as one of the basic principles of the therapeutic process[2] (Truax & Carkhuff, 1967). The important thing is, *what does the client mean by what he or she says*? If the answer is unclear, the therapist may want to respond in the following way:[3] "I know what I mean when I say ____, but I'm not sure what you mean by ____. Can you tell me what that means to you?" Clinical Case Example 3.1 might be helpful in illustrating this.

Clinical Case Example 3.1: A Man With a Drinking Problem and a History of "Bumps"

A man with an admitted drinking problem—who sought help on his own—came to therapy after voluntarily acknowledging to his wife that he could not handle alcohol and wanted to go to a hospital for detox. After detox, he accepted participation in a structured 4-week program in recovery and sought psychotherapy to learn more about why he gravitated to drinking and eventually became addicted to the use of alcohol. In the second session of treatment, during the process of describing his early family life, he indicated that there were "bumps" while growing up in a "good" family atmosphere. The therapist heard this comment and became *curious* about the word *bumps*. He decided to follow up on this and responded, "I know that I had a few 'bumps' as a kid growing up and what that means to me. But, I'm not sure what having some 'bumps' means to you. Can you tell me what you mean?" Although everyone has encountered some "bumps" growing up, not everyone likely describes them in that particular manner. To this question, the client responded that his mother had become paralyzed when he was only a toddler and that he had to live with his grandparents many miles from his family home for a number of years.

Obviously, the "bumps" described by the client in Clinical Case Example 3.1 were of a significant nature and indeed much different from the "bumps" that the therapist envisioned in his own life. These events were significant in the early life of the client, and became a significant issue in therapy. But, consider what might have happened if the therapist had responded in a linear way (i.e., to content and information or to feeling). Imagine the vast amount of information that would have been missed. *Nonlinear responding* not only requires a client to slow down and elaborate on his story, but also closes the gap in understanding between client and therapist.

Sometimes, incongruence or discrepancies are a matter of *deception* (either self-deception or deceiving the therapist). Remember the example in Chapter 2 of the man who said that he "hated" his son and his son's drug abuse? His statement was "I think I hate my son! I'm ashamed to say that!" The question that lingered was "Does he really *hate* his son, or is he expressing his pain and anger over what has become of his son?" If he literally hates his son, then there are different issues to deal with than if he merely hates what is happening to his son. One meaning—that he hates his son's behavior—perhaps offers the man hope and a sense of redemption from the guilt and embarrassment he is feeling. The other offers him a bad feeling about himself for "hating" his son and a sense of unredeemed guilt. Furthermore, the man states that he "think(s)" he hates his son. Such an expression suggests that he isn't certain, or is *deceiving* himself in a way that doesn't allow him to reach out to his son. So, how might one respond to him? Rather than accept his comment at face value, the therapist can ask, "I know what I mean when I say, 'I hate someone or something,' but I'm wondering how *you mean* that you hate your son?" By both *listening and responding to incongruence*, the therapist can be encouraging to a man who is obviously discouraged and embarrassed by his self-disclosure. The therapist can *compliment* the man on his *honesty* in expressing feelings and his *integrity* in saying something that must be incredibly difficult to divulge! Inquiries stated in that way say to the client, "I hear that there is more than one side to this." It communicates a level of interest in the client, and can foster a positive, deeper measure of engagement.

Nonlinear Responding to Absence (i.e., "I See What You Are Not Showing Me")

Listening for and responding to absence make up one of the hallmarks of a *nonlinear* approach to counseling. It is the process of seeing *beyond* what is present to what is absent. It is stimulated by therapist curiosity about what a client *isn't* saying or discussing. A therapist "wondering" and asking herself why something is *not* being discussed may very well be the clue that something is amiss and conspicuous by its absence. How does a therapist respond to this type of absence in a nonlinear way? Sometimes *not* responding is the appropriate response, whereas other times stopping the client in the moment is the best thing to do; it is a matter of timing.[4] Nevertheless, when a therapist interprets or brings up the topic of avoidance, it should always be done tactfully, affably, and perhaps "contritely" (see Information Box 3.1: "The Colombo Approach").

Information Box 3.1: "The Colombo Approach"

The detective character developed by the actor Peter Falk in the nationally acclaimed TV series *Colombo* can be seen as a caricature of a manner that partly resembles the way in which the topic of interpretation or avoidance can be advanced. In psychotherapeutic terms, the "Colombo approach" is similar to adopting a "not-knowing" stance (common in family therapy). Such an approach requires therapists to thoroughly understand a client's perspective by not taking for granted that they understand what clients mean in telling their story. Instead, they must listen deeply and stimulate clients to make the meaning of their statements very clear. If this is done well, it helps to maintain the therapeutic alliance by saying, "I may not be clear on this point— can you help me?" or "I'm confused. Could you help me to understand how it is that …?" Another version of this is to use words such as "I noticed …" "I'm curious …" "I couldn't help but notice that …" and "That's the third time I've heard you take such a big sigh when we talk about …" This stance communicates the following messages simultaneously: (a) "I seem to have noticed something that for whatever reason you are not showing me"; and (b) "I could be wrong, but this is my observation." Such nonlinear responding gives a client a certain amount of "space" either to acknowledge what is conspicuously missing, or to correct an oversight or misperception. For example, in the section on *listening for absence* in Chapter 2, regarding the woman who talked about only one child but not the other: A *nonlinear* response to that may be "I noticed that when you talk about your children, you only seem to talk about your older child but not your younger child. I was curious about that." The client may acknowledge that the younger child either is or is not her favorite, that the younger child is a "perfect" child, or that the client didn't think to mention the younger child because the problem didn't affect him. Regardless, responding to this absence communicates that the therapist is sensitive to things about which the client may not be cognizant.

There are clients who appear to talk incessantly about certain topics (e.g., *land mines, rabbit holes,* and *red herrings,* discussed in Chapter 2), which is another aspect of *nonlinear listening and responding to absence* concerns. Recall that these may be more active attempts to distract a therapist from addressing underlying issues. Perhaps the least effective way to respond to such behaviors is to make an effort to tackle them head-on (i.e., in a linear way) and attempt to "work" on that issue. Such an approach is likely to result in devoting time to topics that are unproductive. An example of this is the client (described in Chapter 2) with the "land mine" explosive temper that was triggered by the topic of his stepdaughter. A therapist who attempts to "work" on the issue by forcing the client to talk about the stepdaughter runs the risk of forcing the client out of therapy. A linear approach to such a land mine tends to feed the client's desire to *not* talk about the stepdaughter. A nonlinear response to this client would be to talk about the *process* that is going on in therapy at that moment (see Information Box 3.2). For example, a counselor may say,

> I can't help but notice that although she is a key reason for why you are here, whenever we try to talk about your stepdaughter you get *very* angry and I change the subject. Now, I know that her behavior has hurt you in the past, and that you're not eager to discuss your relationship with her, but we are going to have to talk about it civilly at some point. Let's see if we can figure out how and when to do that.

The conversation and the therapeutic challenge have shifted from (a) the topic of the stepdaughter to being about the *dynamic process* represented by the client and counselor, and (b) avoiding a difficult subject altogether to discussing *when* and *how* to talk about the relationship with the stepdaughter.

The same principles of using the "Colombo approach," namely, "I noticed ..." statements, and talking about the process rather than the content apply to *rabbit holes* and *red herrings* where the conversation does not move the therapy forward. Too often, Level I counselors either want to follow clients on these detours or create new detours (i.e., talk mindlessly about distracting subjects like "how the week was")[5] rather than get more to the heart of the matter. *Responding to absence* does just that.

Information Box 3.2: Content Versus Process in Therapy

At every moment in counseling, there are two distinct levels that are occurring simultaneously: the *content* level and the *process* level. Should the reader ask, "Exactly what does the term *process* mean?" we offer the following brief explanation. Dialogue between two individuals (or in a group of individuals) can focus on the *content* of what is being discussed (e.g., family of origin, marriage, health status, money, and parents), or it can focus on *process* (e.g., what manner of transactions are occurring between the participants, which means *how* transactions are being conducted—friendly, competitive, antagonistic, hostile, avoidant, blaming, humorously, etc.).

A therapist who *thinks* in a nonlinear manner is aware of both of these levels and is able to operate on both levels. At Level I, however, although this may appear daunting and unfamiliar, it is suggested that most people have been aware of these two levels in a relationship they have had at some time in the past. Being aware of the *content and process levels* of interactions does require some conscious effort or discussion with a supervisor. There are many dimensions to examining the processes that go on between the participants in a dialogue. They will be detailed further in Chapter 4. As therapists move toward greater mastery (i.e., Levels II and III), they find that their interventions work on the content and process levels *simultaneously*. It is helpful for the Level I therapist to know that *nonlinear thinking* is useful in determining a better understanding of what is being transacted in therapy, so he or she should ask, "Is this process or content? Do we need to be discussing this content or this process?"

Nonlinear Responding to Inference (i.e., "I Hear What You Are Not Saying")

When clients tell therapists what they *don't want*, or *what they don't want someone else to do*, in a sense, they *are* indicating what they want. They are doing so, however, in a way that fundamentally limits a counselor's ability to help clients achieve change. This is because clients are asking a counselor to either (a) prevent something from happening or stop something that is currently happening (e.g., "I don't want to be depressed" or "I don't want to end up like my mother"), or (b) stop someone else (or "life") from doing something to them (e.g., "I don't want my wife to work such long hours"). These are limiting because counselors are powerless to influence things outside of the therapy session. Instead, what *a therapist can do* is help clients to shift their focus from struggling with their problem to the solution—that is, shifting from what other people are doing to the empowerment of what the client can do (e.g., accepting something, or calming down), and from what the client doesn't want to what the client wants and how to achieve it.

By *responding to inference*, counselors can provide the impetus for clients to look at these issues from another point of view. Oftentimes, this can take the form of statements like "You know, a lot of times people don't know what they want. You at least have half the battle won; you know what you *don't* want! However, I am not sure how I can help you until I know what you *do* want." Or (responding to absence), "I can't help but wonder, I hear what you don't want other people to do, but I don't know what you want to do. ... I haven't heard you say what you are going to do or can do about it?" Another response, called the "miracle question," is also a way to help clients focus on goals, or what would happen if they got what they wanted. (The "miracle question" will be discussed in greater detail in Chapter 5.)

All of these *nonlinear* responses help clients to *disengage* from what they are obviously preoccupied with (despite being phrased as a "negative"; e.g., "I *don't want to* ...") when describing their problem. Recall the case of the woman in Chapter 2 who gets anxious, particularly when riding in cars. Her statements of "It would be nice *to not have to worry about what could happen*! It would be nice *to not be so nervous in the car*" told what she didn't want. A response to the *absence* of what she does want might be to invite her to look at the other side, namely, "I hear that you don't want to be anxious all the time, but I wonder what you do want?" On the other hand, a response may be more direct, such as "What would you do with yourself if you didn't worry all the time?" In answering these questions, she might be inclined to give information about what it is that she is avoiding (or gaining, such as others' attention) by worrying all the time, or that she likes control, or that life makes her nervous. Each of these answers would be a stepping stone to formulating treatment goals for her (discussed in Chapter 5), once she has fully engaged in treatment.

Nonlinear Responding to Presence (i.e., "I See What Your Body Is Saying, Even if You Don't")

Much like the other nonlinear responses outlined above, *responding to presence* requires that the therapist go beyond what is being spoken to what is being communicated. Therapists must reflect on what they have heard, interpret a client's implied meanings, and express that in a way that neither insults nor assaults. When therapists *respond to presence*, they must make accurate observations of both a client's verbal and nonverbal behaviors and "give voice" to what a client does not actually verbalize. Clients have to bring up material that is often difficult to discuss with the therapist (i.e., someone who is a stranger), especially early in the therapy relationship. There may be a "disconnect" between what a client says verbally and his or her body language. For example, when a client discusses a painful subject (e.g., rape, torture, other horrific abuse, a perceived failure, or a painful divorce) in a monotonous, matter-of-fact tone, punctuated with deep sighs, eyes welling up with tears, and significant pauses, it undoubtedly suggests the presence of something deeper. A therapist, observing such subtle behaviors, can empathically comment, "Those deep sighs (or tears welling up, etc.) as you describe this suggest how really painful and difficult this was for you, and still is. Can you tell me about those tears?" Such *emotional punctuation marks* are behaviors worth noting and commenting on. They can be a significant source of building both rapport and the therapeutic alliance.

Other behaviors such as facial gestures that occur whenever a certain topic is discussed can also be addressed. Again, using "I noticed …" statements can be particularly useful in these circumstances. For example, "I notice the way you wrinkle your nose every time that the topic of your mother comes up. I'm not sure what it means when you do that." Clients can then either admit that there is something underlying the noted behavior or express amazement and claim that they were unaware that this occurs! However, the next time that it happens, and it is tactfully pointed out to them, it will be harder to deny. This amounts to a variation on a wise theme that advises watching others' feet, not their words, as the most reliable indication of what their *actual* intentions and meanings are.

As mentioned above, as the work of therapy proceeds, it is necessary for clients to describe painful, embarrassing, and clearly difficult personal circumstances, catastrophic events, failures, and mistakes. Discussion of such material often stimulates associative thoughts not necessarily shared with the therapist immediately. Not sharing such thoughts is not necessarily an indication of resistant or uncooperative behavior in therapy. When dialogue is interrupted for some reason, clients can sometimes be found to be staring away, defocusing, focusing upward, or staring down. Just like the emotional punctuation marks noted above, such staring behaviors can also be very revealing. No matter what the therapist had intended to say, it is generally much more profitable therapeutically to ask the client, "What were you thinking just then?" This is referred to as "using (the process of) immediacy" (Egan, 2002), meaning that whatever is happening now becomes the topic of discussion (in this case, the staring). The staring, defocusing, and other behaviors are typically indicative of ongoing thinking processes. The *nonlinear-thinking* therapist is quick to detect these therapeutic jewels and utilize them for the client's benefit. Responding to the presence of such thinking processes can be pursued as opportunities to further therapeutic connecting and engagement and later movement through the stages of change.

Nonlinear Responding to Resistance (i.e., "I Understand That You Might Not Be Ready for This")

Like the other nonlinear responses, *responding to resistance* requires that a therapist be aware that clients may be feeling ambivalent about making changes in their lives. Being ambivalent, clients will *resist* attempts to move them too quickly to make decisions when they feel ill prepared. At other times, a client may be more direct in verbalizations that indicate resistance, such as those discussed above (e.g., "I'll try. ..." "I should. ..." and "Yes, but ..."). Often, a therapist may be aware of her or his own feelings of confusion regarding a client's behavior, or perhaps irritation at a client's lack of commitment.

When responding to these various statements of resistance, it is appropriate for counselors to gently probe for more information, but not to challenge too early in the therapeutic relationship, because it is counterproductive to the essential process of connecting with and engaging the client. The *nonlinear-*responding strategies presented above, such as the "Colombo approach," clarifying ("I know what I mean when I say ___, and I wonder what it means for you?"), or responding to the nonverbal behavior ("I can't help noticing that this is difficult for you. ..."), can help. More sophisticated examples of responding to resistance will be discussed in Chapters 4, 5, 12, and 13, and handling ruptures to the therapeutic relationship will be discussed in Chapter 4.

Clinical Exercise 3.2: Counselor's Experience of Connecting With and Engaging Others

Think of a time when you had to start something new that involved interacting with people who you didn't know (such as the beginning of a class, or the start of a new job).

- How did you feel when you started?
- What made you feel more comfortable?
- How did you begin to engage with the other people?
- What helped you to begin to connect with others?
- Or, if this did not happen, what prevented you from feeling connected with or engaged in the group?

In class: Form dyads or small groups, and discuss these experiences. Were there experiences in common that helped (or hindered) your ability to engage or connect? How can you apply this to working with clients?

CONCLUSION

What is the purpose of emphasizing linear and nonlinear listening and responding? The answer is as follows: to connect with and engage a client, encourage him to tell his story, and become involved in the process of therapy. In order for someone to *tell* his story, he needs an appropriate atmosphere (i.e., a set of circumstances) that is conducive to doing so. In turn, such connecting *with* and engaging can be greatly facilitated if a therapist is aware of the many subtleties of both *linear and nonlinear listening and responding* that influence those processes.

The purpose of this chapter has been to discuss the elements of the domain of connecting with and engaging the client for treatment. This domain is the foundation of establishing a strong "therapeutic relationship and alliance" with a client (discussed in Chapter 7). Connecting with and engaging a client through listening and responding are *the major ways of creating that atmosphere*. In turn, once that story begins to unfold, a therapist is in a better position to understand the dynamics underlying a client's story and arrive at a starting point for treatment. In turn, that is the purpose of the interview, which has both *linear* and *nonlinear* aspects to it. From here, once the client's story has begun to unfold, and she is participating in therapy, the next step is for assessment and goal setting to take place.

Issues in Diversity Box 3.1: "Contextually Cultural"

There is a growing professional literature on developing multicultural competencies (e.g., Delphin & Rowe, 2008; Sue, Arrendondo, & McDavis, 1992; Sue et al., 1982, 1998) in the therapy and counseling profession to enhance effectiveness in therapists' work with clients from diverse cultures with diverse ethnicity. With so many diverse cultures, what is a Level I therapist to make of such issues in meeting with clients who may have not only diverse backgrounds but also equally diverse problems? To discuss this question, we cite the following.

In the science fiction television series of the 1980s and 1990s, *Star Trek: The Next Generation*, one of the main characters was an android, Lt. Commander Data. He was a benign figure who, though he possessed superior cognitive and physical capabilities, yearned to be more human. In one particular episode, Data discovers after having an accident that he has a "Dream Subroutine" written into his programming. The "Dream Subroutine" was programmed to be activated when Data had reached a certain level of development.

As he explored his "dream programs," like many of us, he encountered bizarre images that didn't make sense to him. In an effort to understand these disjointed and often puzzling visions, he sought out the computer's database filled with information from *thousands* of cultures for help. He discovered that certain images meant different (and often conflicting) things in different cultures, which brought him no closer to the truth about the messages that his dream metaphors were telling him.

Frustrated by this lack of progress, he sought out his captain's input. The captain sized up Data's approach to the problem and asked, "Why are you looking at all these other cultures?"

Data replied, "The interpretation of visions and other metaphysical experiences are almost always culturally derived. … And I have no culture of my own."

The captain then seized on the moment and said, "Yes you do. You are a culture of one. And that's no less valid than a culture of one billion." He then encouraged Data to explore what the meanings of his dreams are for *him*, rather than fitting them into a context that isn't his own.

In many ways, the practice of culturally sensitive or multicultural counseling presents the same dilemma for counselors. In fact, there are both *linear-* and *nonlinear-thinking* aspects to incorporating cultural sensitivity in the practice of psychotherapy, and care must be taken to successfully traverse what can be a confusing issue.

Many times, Level I or *linear*-thinking therapists adopt the same strategy as Data for understanding clients of a different culture by absorbing *as much* information about *as many* different cultures as they can. The thinking demonstrated in such an approach is that knowing about a culture will translate directly into a linear way of knowing how and what to say to an individual because she is from a particular culture. Part of the difficulty of this linear approach is that there are literally *hundreds* (if not *thousands*) of human cultures and subcultures. It is impossible to be familiar with all cultures. This leads to a thornier dilemma, namely, overgeneralization.

Consider for a moment some of the broad categories that we use for ethnicity: African American, Asian American, Asian, Caucasian, Hispanic/Latino, and so on. Now consider the following: Are all the members of these groups the *same*? Are all Asians the same? Are *individuals* of Chinese descent the same culturally as those of Japanese, Korean, Laotian, or Vietnamese descent? What about their cultures? Are they interchangeable? Clearly, the answer to these questions is an emphatic *no*! Although many texts relate somewhat broad generalizations about people from different cultures, care must be exercised in *applying* those generalizations without determining if they are relevant to the *individual* client.

Nonlinear thinking about *cultural sensitivity* extends to other areas of human beliefs and values, such as religion, ethnicity, race, and gender. The *nonlinear-thinking* therapist asks, "How important is *this particular client* making the issue of his culture (or religion, ethnicity, race, or gender) in describing the troublesome issues for which he is seeking treatment?" Culture (or religion, ethnicity, etc.) may play a great role, a small role, or no role for *this particular individual* seeking treatment for this particular issue.

Instead, we tend to endorse a *nonlinear-thinking* approach much like the captain's. When clients from a different cultural (or ethnic, racial, religious, etc.) background seek treatment, it is preferable to start with the *flexible* position that this is an individual who is a *culture of one*. As a clinician, it is incumbent upon a therapist to explore how a client's cultural (religious, ethnic, etc.) heritage potentially *relates to her and the problem for which she is seeking help.*

Clinically, this not only suggests considering the client's *heritages* (because many individuals come from family backgrounds with multiple cultural influences) but also means taking his *developmental stage* as well as the *time (era) in which he has lived* into consideration as well. The therapist must *ask such questions as and listen nonlinearly for the following*:

"What does it mean to be who you are?"

"What does it mean to you to be where you came from?"

"What does it mean to you to have grown up and developed during particular periods of time (e.g., childhood, preteen, adolescence, and early adulthood) in your life?"

"Are these experiences (e.g., cultural, religious, and ethnic) a source of pride or embarrassment?"

"Is this heritage a source of strength that you can draw from?"

"What role does your heritage play in your thinking about the problem for which you are seeking help?"

By adopting *a nonlinear-wondering stance* (or not-knowing stance), both the client and counselor are invited to jointly explore the issue of heritage and derive a richer meaning of it from the client's perspective rather than a preconceived perspective being imposed by the counselor. This is what we mean by being "contextually cultural." It does not mean that the counselor is *blind* to cultural differences, but rather expands upon them and embraces them as valuable client resources (or, at the very least, artifacts). There are applications of this in each of the seven domains that we will present that will demonstrate this perspective and challenge the reader to consider some of his or her own cultural dynamics.

ENDNOTES

1. The solar plexus is a group of nerves and nerve endings in the abdomen that create radiating sensations throughout the body that many people associate with positive and negative emotions.

2. A basic element of good mental health is for the client to express truthfully and accurately what he or she felt and meant. Thus, to help a client accomplish this, it is important for a counselor to model congruence in his or her statements to a client (Carkhuff, 2000; Rogers, 1951; Truax & Carkhuff, 1967).

3. Please note that these statements are not meant to be rigidly copied by the reader, but are meant as general guides for formulating your own responses that fit the situation, and reflect your own style of speaking.

4. "Timing" is the art of knowing *when and how* to interpret or bring up something that a therapist believes a client may be avoiding. It is a difficult and sensitive expertise to develop and is nurtured by the development of what is called *clinical judgment*, which we discuss later in this book.

5. Please note that there are many times when this is a legitimate topic for a therapy session, especially in the first few minutes of the session to discuss any recent developments in the client's life. However, when it is used to fill up time, then it becomes "mindless."

The Domain of Assessment

Part 1: Clients' Symptoms, Stages of Change, Needs, Strengths, and Resources

4

CONTENTS

INTRODUCTION

As discussed in Chapters 2 and 3, a therapist who uses both *linear* and *nonlinear* methods of listening and responding substantially increases the likelihood of connecting with and engaging a client. Engaging a client in the treatment process overcomes potential reluctance about telling "a complete stranger" the intimate details of his or her story. A client's "story" provides a wealth of information for a clinician to work with, but most often the information initially presented is not enough to begin to work toward definable goals. Sometimes, more detailed information is missing (e.g., "How long have you felt this depressed? Have you ever felt this way before? If so, what did you do about it back then? How did you get yourself out of that depression?"). Sometimes, there may be substantial gaps in a client's story (e.g., "You told me a lot about your childhood, but I'm not clear on how you see that affecting you today"). In other words, a client tells only the *conscious* part of a story. Thus, a master practitioner of necessity conducts a very thorough *assessment* of a client's history, needs, strengths, and goals before more definable therapeutic interventions can be considered and implemented.

When conducting an assessment, a master practitioner looks for connections, hypotheses, themes, patterns, resources, and so on to guide his understanding of and work with a client. In fact, a therapist uses the assessment process to understand and connect with a client's unconscious themes. A therapist can then be more responsive to the needs that the client's themes represent and for therapy to proceed in a positive way. When this is accomplished, the probabilities significantly decrease that a client will develop feelings of being disconnected from the therapist and the therapy process.

Thus, the basic elements of the assessment domain are as follows: (a) An inventory of a client's story must be made to allow for a thorough accounting of her history and needs (both known and unknown), as well as a reckoning of the strengths and resources that the client brings to the therapy; (b) therapists who use *nonlinear thinking* (even at Level I) understand that not all clients seek treatment with the same motivation or readiness for change, and every client's level of readiness for change *must* be taken into account before setting goals and initiating treatment, no matter how convincing her conscious narrative may be; and (c) therapists assess for *themes* in a client's narration to greatly facilitate an understanding of the meaning behind the more conscious story. Once these elements are put in place (in conjunction with the domain of connecting with and engaging the client), a client and counselor can arrive at mutually agreed upon preliminary goals for treatment (i.e., the particular direction that their collaborative efforts will take). At the same time that *preliminary goals* for therapy are established, there is an explicit understanding of the fact that those goals might be changed in the future. But, at least the initial goals provide a direction for the course of the treatment. This maximizes the potential benefits of and satisfaction with treatment. Another exceptionally important variable in achieving agreed upon goals is to elicit client feedback. The first step in this process is to assess the client's symptoms, diagnoses, strengths, and untapped resources.

ASSESSING THE CLIENT: SYMPTOMS, DIAGNOSES, STRENGTHS, AND (UNTAPPED) RESOURCES

Recall from Chapter 1 Lambert and Barley's (2002) analysis of effective therapy—40% of what accounts for successful treatment comes from "client factors." Chief amongst these are personal resources, strengths, and social supports. Too often in a client's life, these factors are downplayed or not actively utilized. Likewise, in therapies that focus solely on the problems, symptoms, and diagnosis of the client (i.e., a *linear* approach), strengths and resources are not featured prominently. *Nonlinear-thinking* therapists, however, recognize the value of these strengths and resources, and utilize several methods for including them in the therapeutic dialogue. There are several ways that therapists assess these untapped resources (both *linear* and *nonlinear*). We will begin with the linear assessment of a client's symptoms, problems, strengths, and resources.

Linear Methods of Assessment: Looking for Symptoms and Diagnoses

Whether it is conflict with loved ones, earning a living, perceived failure, coping with substance abuse, dealing with life-threatening or chronic illness, disordered brain chemistry, or managing their own lives and well-being, human beings encounter problems in living.[1] It is individuals' inability to find constructive solutions for those problems that prompts the development of symptoms. One straightforward (i.e., *linear*) aspect of a clinical interview is evaluation: making an assessment of a client's "clinical" symptoms. It is akin to the following:

Physician: "What is it that prompts you to come and see me today?"
Client: "I have been having night sweats, a fever, chills, a feeling of being weak all over, and I have no energy."

The client's job is to report what he is experiencing and what is troubling for him. It is the doctor or therapist's job to make sense out of what is troubling the client. In order to make sense out of symptoms that a client reports, the clinician first develops a *linear understanding* of what the client reports as being the problem. In order to reach a *linear understanding* of a client's problem, a great deal of *factual information* must generally be collected. This is accomplished through what is referred to as a traditional diagnostic or psychosocial interview. A diagnostic interview is typically a *structured* (or *semistructured*)[2] process that addresses numerous areas of a client's present life (e.g., biological health, and psychological and social functioning), as well as the person's history (e.g., family of origin, education, employment, previous illness, and prior treatment). In addition, the psychosocial interview includes specific questions related to a client's present cognitive and emotional functioning, along with symptoms and the etiology (development) of his "presenting" concern.

The psychosocial assessment, also referred to as an *initial assessment* or an *intake assessment*, provides essential broad-spectrum information that is useful in arriving at both a *formal DSM-IV-TR diagnosis* (American Psychiatric Association, 2000) and what is called a brief *dynamic formulation*. The dynamic formulation relates to information discovered in the psychosocial assessment regarding the development of the client's problem. A simple example might be a man in his mid-60s whose wife accompanies him to a clinic setting. They are interviewed together, and the wife reveals that since her husband retired from the job he held for 40 years, he has become increasingly sullen, withdrawn, and uncommunicative; he has lost weight, sleeps a lot, and so on. Clearly, after ruling out other possible factors (e.g., he has had a recent physical exam that revealed he is healthy), the loss of his job potentially looms as *the* significant factor in the development of his symptoms of depression. Until a thorough psychosocial assessment is done, however, this cannot be determined. Information Box 5.1 details traditional areas that are assessed as a part of a psychosocial interview. The reader will note the extensive nature of the topics that are covered. A *linear* approach to the psychosocial assessment collects information in a rapid, staccato firing of questions and a simple collection of answers. In some settings, much basic information is collected via a computer terminal or a form. Gathering information in a conversational manner is a *nonlinear* approach that encourages a sense of relationship.

Information Box 4.1: Sample Information Collected in a Biopsychosocial Assessment

Demographic Data
>   Date of Assessment
>   Name
>   Address
>   Date of birth
>   Social Security number

General Information
>   Clinic information
>   Insurance information
>   Requisite insurance information
>   Referral source
>   Required signatures

General Assessment
>   Current living situation
>   Employment
>>   Present
>>   History
>   Family background
>   Educational background
>   Cultural factors
>   Military experience
>   Religious preference

History of Present Illness
>   Stated purpose of visit
>   How problem developed
>   Previous history of similar problem
>   How was that problem resolved?

Previous History of Problems
>   If no previous history, does client mention anyone who had a similar problem and how *that person resolved* it?
>   Does client have expectations about how he or she thinks the problem will be resolved (i.e., the client's model of change)?
>   Past use of psychiatric (and other) medications?
>   History of abuse (physical, mental, or sexual)

At Risk For
>   Self-injury?
>>   Suicidal thoughts?
>>   Suicide plan?
>>   Adequate controls?
>   Injury to others?
>>   Homicidal thoughts?
>>   Homicide plan?
>>   Adequate controls?
>   Previous history of risk for injury to self or others?
>   Vulnerable (e.g., handicapped, or elderly)?

Abuse by others?

Substance Abuse
Present use
Past history of use or abuse
Past treatment for substance abuse
Past participation in self-help (e.g., AA)

Medical-Physical Health
Current health or health problems
Has or has not obtained a physical exam by a physician?
Need for immediate medical attention?
Need for hospitalization?

Mental Status
Memory
Judgment
Orientation
Intellectual ability
Affect
Mood

General Appearance
Neat and well-groomed
Careless and indifferent
Disheveled or unkempt
Bizarre and eccentric
Appears to be stated age
Need for medical attention
Under the influence: alcohol and/or drugs?

General Attitude
Attitude toward appointment
Attitude toward therapist
Attitude toward problem

Behavioral Observations
Normal behavior
Peculiar behaviors
Agitation
Tremors
Depression
Anxiety
Signs of neurological dysfunction
Gait

Spontaneous Speech
Fluency
Syntax
Grammar
Awareness
Dysarthria
Repetition
Difficulty naming objects
Comprehension
Expression

Goals of Treatment
  "I'd feel better!"
  What *concrete*, visualizable goals does the client have (i.e., something behavioral)?
Thought Processes
  Intact
  Circumstantial
  Flight of ideas
  Clang associations
  Thought blocking
  Looseness of associations
  Obsessive thinking
  Speed of thoughts
Thought Content
  No abnormal thoughts
  Delusions of persecution
  Delusions of guilt
  Delusions of disease
  Delusions of religiosity
  Delusions of poverty
  Ideas of reference
  Paranoid thoughts
Emotions
  Anxious
  Fearful
  Depressed
  Manic
  Angry
  Jealous
  Affect
  Normal affect
  La Belle indifference
  Euphoric
  Inappropriate
  Labile
  Flat affect
  Depressed
Dynamic Formulation (see Chapter 9)

When evaluating a client's symptoms, it is important to understand their duration and intensity. This understanding can be reached by means of *linear* responses to content and information and to feelings. For example, if a client announces that he no longer feels comfortable going out to places where there are a lot of people for fear of being a victim of terrorism, a linear response to explore these symptoms might be "I understand that you have been feeling anxious about going to public spaces—that's an awful feeling to have. When did this begin? Has anything similar ever happened before in your life?"

Collecting this information in an efficient way can certainly be daunting for the Level I counselor—especially when considering that *the most important goals* that need to be accomplished are *connecting with and engaging* the client. We would offer the Level I counselor the following guidance regarding this potential conflict of interests, so to speak, between collecting linear information and connecting with the client. Connecting with the client is essential, and if done well, information can be collected to fulfill the required documentation. As therapists gain experience collecting information, these two important tasks (connecting and engaging, and assessing) will merge together and feel more seamless.[3]

A useful way of viewing the biopsychosocial assessment is to understand that it has both a "formal" and an "informal" goal. The informal goal (i.e., *nonlinear* in nature) is to *connect* with a client by collecting the necessary "diagnostic" information. This is especially important if the person conducting the initial psychosocial assessment will also become the person's therapist. If, however, that is not to be the case, it is still important to *connect* with clients during the initial assessment process because it can both calm clients and prompt them to be more receptive to the idea of receiving help even if their treatment is to be conducted by someone else.

The ultimate formal goal (i.e., *linear* in nature) of the psychosocial interview is to arrive at a diagnosis. Because symptoms can be grouped into certain categories such as anxiety, depression, or psychosis, it becomes the clinician's task to determine the specific kind of disorder in question. The ability to recognize the patterns of such groupings is obviously helpful and useful (e.g., different kinds of depressions, anxiety disorders, adjustment disorders, and personality disorders). A formal diagnosis is defined as the process of identifying a client's signs, symptoms, and syndromes (i.e., the grouping of symptoms or signs that tend to be found together) and determining what criteria for a particular category of pathology they match as expressed in the DSM-IV-TR (American Psychiatric Association, 2000). The purpose of the DSM-IV-TR is "to provide clear descriptions of diagnostic categories in order to enable clinicians and investigators to diagnose, communicate about, study, and treat people with various mental disorders" (American Psychiatric Association, 2000, p. xi). The DSM-IV-TR is a complex, detailed, and empirically derived method of classifying mental, developmental, and behavioral disorders. In any given diagnostic category of the DSM-IV-TR, numerous criteria are required for a client to be accorded a particular diagnosis. This is necessary for a variety of reasons, such as the need for a common medical terminology, third-party reimbursement, government regulations, procedural requirements, the need for clinic documentation, and conducting research, among others. In fact, the DSM-IV-TR is not only a standard compendium of psychiatric conditions but also a means of establishing a common, mutually understood language among practitioners and agencies, clinics, regulatory bodies, and insurance companies via its multiaxial system.[4] Although the DSM-IV-TR has many benefits and establishes a uniform way of talking about different disorders and decreasing the frequency of misunderstanding, when it comes down to the treatment of a single unique individual, Norcross (2002a) has adroitly pointed out,

> In the behavioral medicine vernacular, *it is frequently more important to know what kind of patient has the disorder than what kind of disorder the patient has.* ... Research studies problematically collapse numerous patients under a single diagnosis. It is a false and, at times, misleading presupposition in randomized clinical trials that the patient sample is homogeneous. Perhaps the clients are diagnostically homogeneous, but nondiagnostic variability is the rule, as every clinician knows. It is precisely the unique individual and singular context that many psychotherapists attempt to treat. (p. 6; emphasis added)

Bolstering this point of view, Beutler, Moleiro, and Talebi (2002) indicated,

> While it is certainly advantageous to cluster patients into homogeneous groups in order to better observe the effects of treatment, sharing a diagnostic label is probably a poor indicator of how similar or different patients are from one another especially as pertains to predicting the effects of psychological treatments. (p. 129)

In other words, DSM-IV-TR criteria are useful in the aggregate for diagnoses, but those criteria have somewhat less dynamic relevance for *individual treatment*. This is due to the fact that DSM-IV-TR criteria alone cannot fully describe the unique nature of individuals and the particular circumstances that have led to the development of their disorders. At the same time, it is very easy to see how the Level I practitioner may be tempted to revert to *linear thinking* in this regard. *Linear thinking* is reflected in simply collecting DSM-IV-TR criteria as an antidote to feeling overwhelmed by having to do so many things at one time in the clinical situation. That especially includes times when the Level I practitioner is also focused on (a) making the therapeutic experience as beneficial as possible to a client (i.e., establishing rapport, being empathic, connecting with and engaging a client, etc.), (b) minimizing the likelihood of premature drop-out, and (c) obtaining information from a client that maximizes therapeutic impact. Thus, overreliance on the linear-thinking methods of the psychosocial interview and fixating on making the "right" diagnosis, at the expense of *nonlinear-thinking methods* of working to connect with a client and establish a therapeutic alliance, are precisely the *wrong* (i.e., least therapeutically effective) things to do.

Linear Methods of Assessment: Looking for Strengths and Resources

For the linear-thinking Level I counselor, once a diagnosis is determined, the next logical step is set-ting goals (usually a straightforward reduction of symptoms and the discomfort that accompanies them) with treatment immediately commencing along a logical trajectory toward a "cure." In reality, however, this is seldom the case with clients. A beginning counselor might wonder, "Why is this? Shouldn't a 'good' psychosocial evaluation contain all relevant client information that a therapist needs?" There is more to a unique human being than a collection of facts and a diagnostic assessment—even though these are useful and fundamental. Nonlinear-thinking therapists recognize that there is other informa-tion that may be even more important to successful treatment than a client's symptoms or diagnosis. Hence, whereas a linear-thinking therapist sees a client in a single dimension only (i.e., problem, symp-toms, and diagnosis), it is the therapist who utilizes nonlinear thinking that integrates both a client's problem and symptoms as well as her strengths and resources when forming a multidimensional picture of a client.

The most common linear way to look for client strengths and resources actually derives from a basic intake interview, as described above. In reality, a client doesn't know that he is telling you about his resources and strengths—he is simply providing basic linear information, which for the most part is straightforward and psychologically nonthreatening. That linear information, however, can also translate into a *nonlinear* understanding of a client that we elaborate upon below.

The intake interview is a historical narrative: what a client has been *doing* in his life. What a client has accomplished and experienced in such areas as education (e.g., how many years of formal education), employment (e.g., a steady work history that demonstrates growth, or an irregular one that could have a number of different causes), marriage (e.g., a successful marriage or numerous divorces), and health his-tory (e.g., relatively healthy, major illnesses, or catastrophic illness) can be an indication of what the client can perhaps realistically accomplish in the future.

The intake evaluation also reveals very important information about a client's *current functioning*— mental status, marital status, income, employment status, physical health, friends, and other resources. All of these have been shown to be correlated with health, wellness, and level of functioning (Sperry, Carlson, & Peluso, 2006). Directly asking a client questions about her successes, what makes her happy, who she gets support from (friends, family, fellow church members, coworkers, etc.), and what she does to relax or have fun are all good examples of ways of getting information about strengths and resources. The question is, *why* keep all of these things in mind?

The simplest answer is that *all strengths and resources* become assets that can *directly or obliquely* be called upon to help a client to overcome a particular problem. Resources and strengths reside within a client or are within her purview. However, they are perhaps not psychologically available to the client at a particular time because she is currently overwhelmed and preoccupied by difficulties. Clients may also not be particularly aware of strengths and resources. Therapy always builds on strengths.

A vignette may illustrate.

John Lennon—the much loved, multitalented, and legendary leader of the Beatles—was actually very depressed from time to time. On one occasion, Lennon was miserably and very seriously depressed when experiencing the aftereffects of LSD. Derek Taylor, a longtime friend, came along and noted some of his strengths. Lennon's reaction to Taylor's encouragement was phenomenal:

> I destroyed myself. ... I had destroyed me ego. I didn't believe I could do anything ... I just was nothing. I was shit. Derek [Taylor] ... sort of said "You're all right," and pointed out which songs I had written. "You wrote this," and "You said this" and 'You are intelligent, don't be frightened. ..." Derek did a good job building me ego one weekend at his house reminding me who I am and what I had done and what I could do, and he and a couple of friends did that for me. They sort of said, "You're great! You are what you are!" and all that and then the next week Yoko came down to Derek's and that was it then. I just blew out! It all came back to me like I was back to age 16. All the rest of it had been wiped out. (Quoted in Miles, Marchbank, & Neville, 1978, pp. 117–119)

Although oversimplified, Lennon is an example of how a friend can positively affect someone by gently understanding him and reminding him of accomplishments, strengths, and resources. Lennon was *moved* by his friend's sincerity, words, and encouragement. Perhaps if more people had friends in their lives as endorsing of them as Taylor was of Lennon, there might be less need for counseling and psychotherapy. For a depressed client (like Lennon) to believe what is being said (and not dismiss it as "Oh, you're just *saying* that"), the key is to be honest and accurate with the observation of strengths and resources.

Other *linear methods* of assessing strengths and resources include listening to a client during the natural course of dialogue in which she reveals different things she has accomplished, is skilled at, or is qualified for, such as musical talent, athletic ability, academic achievements, or competitiveness. *Connecting a client* to such resources is a method of stimulating her courage so that the client can make small changes.

Nonlinear Methods of Assessing for Strengths and Resources

By contrast, one of the things that makes for a *nonlinear-thinking* therapist is to constantly look for the opposite of what seems logical. For example, to find client strengths, *linear thinking* might not prompt one to ask a client about the most painful or traumatic moments of a person's life. But, that may be exactly what is called for. The most common nonlinear methods are *looking for unused or misused power* and *connecting with untapped social supports.*

Looking for Unused or Misused Power

An old expression states that everyone has power and everyone uses power. From a child throwing a temper tantrum in a checkout line at a local supermarket, to a tycoon who is about to acquire another corporation, everyone has some form of power. The issue is more a matter of individuals' awareness and appreciation of the power that they have to influence their circumstances in life (i.e., *empowerment*). Some individuals know how to use their power (i.e., they feel empowered and aware of their choices, resources, strengths, understanding, and ability to influence others and the world) to sway the direction of their lives.

As the saying goes, choosing not to decide is still making a choice. Hence, even when someone gives up power, it is a choice. This can often be the first, most basic step in working with someone who feels so discouraged, demoralized, or victimized that he no longer believes that he has a choice. Perhaps Victor Frankl[5] (1963) summed up best the power that everyone inherently has: "Everything can be taken from a man but ... *the last of the human freedoms—to choose one's attitude in any given set of circumstances, to choose one's own way*" (p. 104; emphasis added). Stimulating awareness of empowerment can help clients recapture their "attitude in any given set of circumstances."

Creativity in solving life's problems is another form of power. Many times, however, the "solutions" that individuals find for their problems are not constructive and may even seem to be eccentric or downright "crazy." Such "solutions" are called symptoms, misguided behaviors, inappropriate or unregulated emotional responses, defense mechanisms, and the like.[6] Nevertheless, these maladaptive solutions are assets that enable clients to get things done—they excuse; absolve from responsibility; save face; achieve privately useful goals (but not goals useful to others); allow an individual to function, albeit to her own (as well as others') detriment in a less than optimum way; and so on.

These maladaptive "solutions" are nevertheless based in the resources that all people need to accomplish the tasks of life. Among others, they include such things as personal attributes, intellectual ability, education, emotional sensitivity, a work ethic, honesty, a sense of humor, religious faith, a positive moral sense, not giving up, a sense of responsibility, and enjoyment of people. The list of potential assets is limited only by the nonlinear-thinking therapist's sensitivity and imagination. However, a nonlinear-thinking therapist recognizes the power that is bound up in negative client "solutions." Therapists can encourage clients to see that their "neurotic" behaviors are actually misapplied or misguided *strengths* (i.e., attempts to problem solve but not in the most constructive way). Some of the *nonlinear*-listening and -responding methods (from Chapters 2 and 3) of *absence* ("What is it you are not telling me?"), *inference* ("What am I supposed to read into this behavior?"), and *presence* ("What is it that you are demonstrating or showing me?") are useful in getting at these unused or misused sources of client power.

Passive-aggressive behavior is also a demonstration of power, as anyone who has been victimized by it can attest. People acting in a passive-aggressive manner do not directly confront anyone if they disagree, but rather disagree by behaving poorly, "forgetting," or being late when you are counting on them. Many times, such behaviors are done "unconsciously" (i.e., the perpetrator is unaware). Therapists at all levels of development are vulnerable to being manipulated in the course of treating passive-aggressive clients. Being alert for this emotional manipulation and knowing how to deal with it effectively are the mark of a master therapist (and will be discussed further in the Level II and III sections).

Linear thinking is mostly ineffective with such clients and, more often than not, perpetuates the behavior. If such individuals are asked directly about their behavior or motives, they will deny them and even feel offended. Nonlinear methods of listening for and responding to congruence, presence, and resistance can be useful in working with such individuals. This will be discussed further in Part 4.

Personal strengths and deficiencies are not absolute in nature. Nonlinear thinking reveals that strength can be a weakness and weakness can be a strength, given the appropriate circumstances. It falls to the therapist to be able to identify those characteristics in the client's particular circumstances that may serve as assets. Likewise, positive attributes can serve as liabilities. For example, above-average intelligence can lead to intellectual pride that doesn't allow a client to accept another person's point of view. She believes that she is "right" and others are just plain "wrong." Likewise, a generally perceived negative characteristic such as passivity can be seen as containing a gentleness that does not threaten others. *Nonlinear listening* suggests that a therapist be aware of the general resources, strengths, and assets that a client brings with her to treatment. It also suggests listening with a sense of *opposites* in which strengths contain weaknesses and weaknesses contain strengths—a great deal more will be discussed about the topic of dialectics in Part 4.

Connecting With Untapped Social Supports

Human beings are social and communal in nature—we live in groups organized in a variety of different ways (e.g., family, church, town, city, state, and country). As such, human beings seek to affiliate—that is, they want to *belong*. The social dimension in human personality (McAdams & Pals, 2006) and the need to belong are primary factors in understanding human needs (Peluso, 2006). At times, clients become isolated through their own misbehaviors, and estranged from family members and coworkers. It is absolutely essential for therapists to develop a sense of the extent to which the clients they serve feel connected to "groups" that are important to them such as family, friends, and church, synagogue, or mosque. Feeling connected in a meaningful way to a group or groups is important to a client; it is a fundamental human need and a distinct asset that helps them in their efforts to feel valued, functional, and optimistic.

Most clients have meaningful support systems in their lives; the problem is that they are frequently underutilized. At times, some clients (e.g., substance abusers) may feel that they have "burned their bridges" to others that they formerly could have counted on. Nevertheless, it is all too common for clients to fail to recognize that there are vast people resources that surround them. This might be due to personal feelings, attitudes, or beliefs such as the following: To ask for help is somehow "weak"; people have to "pull themselves up by their own bootstraps"; "All is lost, and there is no one"; or "I've done something just too terrible for others to accept me." Such views represent "schemas," a topic to be discussed in Chapters 8 and 9. Another reason may be a lack of trust, particularly if the client has been significantly disappointed by others or is characterologically averse to placing trust in another human being.

One method for helping clients identify and activate a myriad of resources is the genogram. A genogram is a powerful tool used by family therapists for both understanding the influence of a client's family of origin as well as providing feedback about family dynamics (McGoldrick, Gerson, & Shellenberger, 1999). Genograms are "a simple, graphic way to trace the multi-generational influences on an individual or family's present-day functioning" (Sperry et al., 2006, p. 251). They can also provide a picture of people surrounding the individual, which might make it easier for a client to reconnect with them. McGoldrick et al. (1999) provided the most comprehensive discussion of genograms and their application.

Although having people in our lives to provide emotional support is generally an asset, there are individuals who can be "toxic." Such individuals are a net drain on our general sense of well-being and felt ability to cope. A clinical assessment *must* contain an evaluation of the client's social support and whether or not it is available. Clinical Case Example 4.1 might prove useful.

Clinical Case Example: 4.1: A Mother With Preschool Children

A talented and professionally successful young woman with three preschool children sought help from a specialist regarding her youngest child's behavior. Although the woman obtained expert counsel from her family physician, a neurologist, and learning specialists regarding her child's developmental disabilities, she wanted specific advice regarding discipline. As part of the assessment process, the counselor wisely asked the woman if her husband was supportive (i.e., social support) and involved regarding the general rearing and disciplining of their child. When the woman replied that for the most part her husband was not, the counselor sagely commented, "It's best if you are clear about some things. In this instance, it appears that you need to know that you are for the most part alone in disciplining your child." Although such counsel might appear unjust and even harsh, it is nevertheless direct and sets realistic expectations. To this feedback, the woman replied, "I've come to realize that."

Sometimes, it is difficult for a client to acknowledge strengths, especially if this entails reliving traumatic or painful events. A nonlinear-thinking therapist, however, can find it extremely advantageous to operate from a "not-knowing" stance in helping clients identifying strengths. Expressing confusion and asking for clarification can help clients to become clearer in what they are expressing and feeling, thus moving along the therapeutic process. When progress has been made and a client has been able to cope quite well with circumstances that previously might have been considered problematic, a therapist can ask in a "confused" way (e.g., "Can you help me to understand how you managed to …?"). This can help clarify how *the client was instrumental* in bringing about improved circumstances. Still another way of presenting the same therapeutic challenge can be seen in the following: "*How on earth* did you manage to …?" Again, this stimulates a client's thinking to make clear his own instrumentality in bringing about desired changes. Just as clients bear a responsibility for maintaining self-defeating attitud_ of behavior, so too must they become aware of and get credit for having improved their ´ the way, they may discover strengths and supports that they didn't know they had. It therapist's expertise as someone who is supposed to have "all the answers."

Clinical Case Example: 4.2: Putting It All Together

A recently married and now pregnant woman in her mid-30s called for an appointment with her therapist. They had a therapy relationship going back 8 years, during which time the therapist saw the client a total of 41 times. Half of all the therapy visits occurred within the first 2 years. During the early part of the treatment, she was hospitalized for an acute episode of anxiety that would not subside and was accompanied by thoughts of suicide. She recovered and resumed her career and a fully productive life.

The number of therapy visits she felt she needed steadily declined as the client achieved a greater sense of effectiveness in coping with chronically nagging issues. She carried a diagnosis of a generalized anxiety disorder. She presented herself for the latest episode of treatment because, as she stated, "There's so much going on. … Our lives have been constantly changing since I met my husband." Among other things that had changed, the client had not been working for the past year after being a stellar career woman who began as an 18-year-old high school graduate who moved out of her family's home and put herself through undergraduate and graduate school as well. Working full-time, she not only put herself through college without incurring debt but also managed to buy her own home. She had spent the last year making a major move, selling two properties that she owned, and preparing for motherhood. Her husband had also changed jobs, and at times she felt that they didn't "communicate" very well.

From her previous treatment, the therapist has condensed a major cognitive theme in the client's life as being "Life makes me nervous." Several weeks before calling to make an appointment, she "caught" herself "spiraling down" (i.e., became aware of being "depressed"), not sleeping well, not eating, being fearful as well as "paranoid" (i.e., easily feeling attacked and criticized, and very insecure due to losing an attractive figure while pregnant), and battling with what she called "panic attacks."

She summarized her current position by stating, "There are so many things I'm afraid of. … I realized that I couldn't take any medication like in the past because of the baby. … I was in that mode of everything falling apart and that triggered, 'It (i.e., being anxious) is a state of mind, like I learned about in therapy.' One day I got so mad! I was sick of this being anxious, being afraid, sick of the negativity, and I refused to feed it. I just woke up and said, 'That's it!' I was *catching myself*, being more proactive versus allowing this stuff to take over and snowball. I *decided* to call you and set up an appointment. I think it's taken a lot of effort to confront it. It's like a creeping vine that's starting to grow. It's something that's said or that I see, and if I don't chop it off it takes over!" When asked to evaluate what was to be a single session of therapy at this time, she responded, "This relationship has always been a *safe* place for me!"

Exercise

1. What would you say this client's problems or needs are?
2. What are the client's strengths and resources that can be determined linearly?
3. What are the client's strengths and resources that can be identified nonlinearly? Any unused or misused power? Any unused social supports?
4. How might you help this client see her "problem" in a more positive light?
5. What form(s) of encouragement do you believe that the clinician might best utilize with this client?

It is clear that the woman in Clinical Case 4.2 is feeling anxious *and* overwhelmed by so many recent changes. *Linear thinking* might suggest *getting to the bottom* of her difficulty with anxiety and "curing" it. On the other hand, *nonlinear thinking* suggests emphasizing the positive and helping her to reevaluate: She has done a wonderful job of "catching" herself beginning to engage in a characteristic pattern (i.e., "Life makes me nervous"). Furthermore, she called for an appointment to reinforce her own efforts with those of the therapist whom she trusts and has known for a long time. The origins of her long-term (i.e., chronic) anxious disposition are less important *in the present context* than reinforcing what she has already done and continues to do to help calm herself down—not only now but also on a more consistent basis in the future. This could have a "carry-over" effect to her physical health as well (i.e., during her pregnancy). Hence, this strengths-based positive focus for therapy is likely to produce more satisfying results for this client in gaining perspective regarding recent events.

Once the therapist has the data about the client's symptoms and strengths, there is another level of assessment that master therapists pay close attention to. Enhancing such understandings, Fisch, Weakland, and Segal (1982) described the difference between a "client" and a "patient," although many times the terms are used interchangeably:

> A "client" ... is an individual actively seeking help ... a complaintant ... "patient" here refers to the individual the complaintant defines as the deviant or troubled person, either himself or another. Defining oneself as a client means that one is seriously interested in change and relief from the complaint, whether that complaint is about oneself or about another. In its essence, such a definition includes three elements: (1) "I have been struggling with a problem that significantly bothers me." (2) "I have failed to resolve it with my own efforts." (3) "I need your help in resolving it." One cannot expect most clients to state it that clearly and succinctly, however. Usually, it is conveyed in the narration of the problem and of the efforts fruitlessly made to resolve it, or in response to comments made by the therapist. (p. 97)

Determining whether an individual is a "client" or a "patient" is an important step in the therapeutic process. A critical, empirically derived approach to this level of assessment is determining the client's readiness to change.[7]

ASSESSING A CLIENT'S READINESS FOR CHANGE: THE STAGES OF CHANGE MODEL

For many years, clients have been described in the psychotherapy literature as if they all had the same level of motivation, and were equally prepared for making changes. As a result, therapists would typically proceed from the assumption that anyone with a given problem wanted it solved and was prepared to do what it takes to solve it. When a client did not "get with the program" (i.e., do what the *therapist* thought was best), he would be labeled as resistant (which will be discussed in greater detail in Chapter 12). This represents a *linear* view of clients and therapy. Real and lasting change does not necessarily come easily for human beings.

In the last few decades, a more comprehensive model for understanding the change process has emerged, primarily from the work of Prochaska, DiClemente, and their associates (Prochaska & DiClemente, 1982, 1984, 2005; Prochaska, DiClemente, & Norcross, 1992). They derived an understanding of *how* people change (i.e., *the processes*) via development of a transtheoretical model called the "stages of change" (SOC) model. Table 4.1 outlines the five stages of change (precontemplation, contemplation, preparation for action, action, and maintenance) as described by Prochaska and DiClemente (2005). The SOC model suggests that people are *not uniform* in their understanding of problematic behavior and the need for change, or their motivation to make changes.

In our estimation, the SOC model represents a *nonlinear-thinking* approach to assessing a client's motivation for therapy. As such, the SOC model proposes that treatment interventions are not necessarily *linear and straightforward* but rather must correspond to and be in harmony with a particular person's phase of preparedness to embrace change. Many failures in difficult areas to treat (e.g., obesity, smoking,

TABLE 4.1   Transtheoretical Stage Model of Client Readiness for Change

STAGE	DESCRIPTION
1. Precontemplation	The client has no intention to change behavior in the foreseeable future. Many individuals in this stage are unaware of their problems, or greatly minimize the severity of the problem.
2. Contemplation	Clients are aware that a problem exists and are seriously thinking about overcoming it in the future, but have not yet made a commitment to take action.
3. Preparation for action	Clients in this stage intend to take action in the next month and/or have unsuccessfully taken action in the past year.
4. Action	Clients modify their behavior, experiences, or environment in order to overcome their problems in this stage.
5. Maintenance, or relapse or reversal	Clients work to consolidate the gains attained during the action stage and prevent the relapse of problem behavior.

Source: From Prochaska, DiClemente, and Norcross (1992).

alcohol, safe sex, and cocaine use) can be attributed to a mismatch between a client's stage of change and a therapist's set of interventions. An often-cited illustration of this is in the area of substance abuse treatment. For many reasons, perhaps 90% of treatment programs in existence today are appropriate for clients in the action stage. But, of the clients seeking treatment in such programs, 90% are most likely in the precontemplation or contemplation stage of change. Hubble, Duncan, and Miller (1999) cited that the SOC model outpredicts other variables such as demographics, type of problem, and severity of problem in determining who stays in treatment and who drops out early.

Brogan, Prochaska, and Prochaska (1999) compared standard psychotherapy client characteristic variables with variables derived from the SOC model to determine which of the two more accurately predicted clients who would terminate prematurely, stay in therapy, and terminate appropriately. In fact, the SOC variables correctly classified and predicted 92% of the clients, an astounding percentage in which other studies have indicated that more than 40% of clients terminate prematurely. In addition, clinical research (Prochaska & DiClemente, 2005) using the SOC to determine initial readiness for change has shown a direct link between a client's stage prior to treatment and the amount of progress made after treatment (i.e., does the change last?). In fact, according to Prochaska and DiClemente (2005),

> During an 18 month follow-up, smokers who were in the precontemplation stage initially were least likely to progress to the action or maintenance stages following intervention. Those in the contemplation stage were more likely to make such progress, and those in the preparation stage made the most progress. (p. 164)

Such findings are powerful research-based testament to the efficacy of the SOC model. Complementing data derived from the SOC model, Fisch et al. (1982), de Shazer (1985b, 1991), and Johnson (1995) distinguished between "visitors" to treatment (i.e., those who are mandated to go for treatment), "window shoppers" (i.e., those expressing significant ambivalence about whether or not they have a substance abuse or other problem), and "customers" (i.e., those seriously interested in and preparing themselves for action). We turn our discussion to a description of the five stages of change, followed by a discussion of how to utilize elements of linear and nonlinear thinking to begin to work with clients in the various stages.

Precontemplation

Precontemplation represents a stage of change in which clients are essentially blind to having a problem. According to Prochaska (1999), clients in this stage "underestimate the benefits of changing and overestimate the costs" of continuing their behavior (p. 229). These clients may or may not be consciously aware that they are engaging in problematic behaviors, that is, behaviors that *they* see as causing them a problem. This lack of awareness makes treatment difficult (if not impossible) and *significantly interferes* with a person making changes. In turn, that allows for more damage to be done to themselves and others around them. Such clients may have been mandated (e.g., court-ordered) to come for treatment, feel coerced (e.g., were told by their lawyer to go for treatment because it will "look good" in front of a judge, were told by a spouse that they either go for treatment "or else," or warned by a physician that they had better go for help "or else"), or believe that it is someone else in their life who needs to change (e.g., a boss who is "impossible" to get along with, a spouse who is "miserable" or difficult to live with, or a fiancée who won't listen). The person in this particular stage of change has most likely encountered someone of significance in his life who has told him, "*You* have a problem, and I insist that you go and do something to fix it!" A client in the precontemplation stage of change clearly demonstrates that he is *not seeing* a problem or, as Prochaska has suggested, is overestimating the costs of change and underestimating the benefits. Some might call this stage of change *denial*, as reflected in the general attitude "It's not me—it's someone else. … I don't have a problem. … It's 'them.'" According to DiClemente and Velasquez (2002), there are four types of precontemplators: *reluctant*, *rebellious*, *resigned*, and *rationalizing*.

Reluctant precontemplators "are those who, through lack of knowledge or perhaps inertia, do not want to consider change … the effect of their problem behavior has not become fully conscious" (DiClemente & Velasquez, 2002, p. 205). *Reluctant* precontemplators tend to be comfortable where they are, fearful of change, and more likely to be passive in their reluctance, and they either tend to repeat "Yes, but …" in responses to their therapist or blame someone else for their problem.

Rebellious precontemplators are the opposite from *reluctant* precontemplators because they "often have a great deal of knowledge about the problem behavior. In fact, they often have a heavy investment in their behavior. They are also invested in making their own decisions" (DiClemente & Velasquez, 2002, pp. 205–206). The *rebellious* precontemplator is perhaps the easiest to recognize. Such an individual will often argue with the therapist, disagree with many comments a therapist makes no matter how innocuous, make it obvious (verbally or nonverbally) that she doesn't want to be in treatment, and generally provide reasons why she is not going to change (e.g., "I have a high-stress job, and pot relaxes me," or "Getting that driving under the influence (DUI) was a fluke; I didn't have that much to drink"). In addition, they don't like being told what to do, and clinicians who try to be "heavy-handed" or confrontational will find such clients to be hostile, argumentative and in disagreement, and highly resistant to change.

On the other hand, *resigned precontemplators* have "given up on the possibility of change and seem overwhelmed by the problem" (DiClemente & Velasquez, 2002, p. 206). Such individuals come to treatment with an overwhelming sense of hopelessness, the feeling that they are caught in the grip of the habit or behavior (which "controls" them), and the belief that it is far too late for them to change (e.g., "I have tried to control my weight for years, and I can't keep it off. It's only a matter of time before I have a heart attack or a stroke!"). These clients may have tried to change several times, but became demoralized after several "failed attempts" (Prochaska, 1999).

Rationalizing precontemplators are different from resigned precontemplators: They seem to have an answer to every challenge to their behavior. "These clients are not considering change because they often think that they have figured out the odds of personal risk or believe that their behavior is the result of another's problem, not theirs" (DiClemente & Velasquez, 2002, p. 207). These clients tend to debate therapists on a cognitive level, often dismissing facts, common sense, or their own feelings of ambivalence in order to make their point and "carry the day." Despite differences among these precontemplators, what links them are the unmistakable facts that they are not interested in, prepared for, or willing to change, as demonstrated in Clinical Case Examples 4.3. and 4.4.

Clinical Case Example 4.3: A Case of Stopping Smoking!

An elderly man consulted a therapist who uses hypnosis. He described his purpose in coming and requested help as follows: "*I want you to make me want to stop smoking* because my wife wants me to quit." For many beginning therapists, this might seem to be a straightforward and sensible client request for any number of reasons (e.g., the client has come to a therapist's office, smoking is bad for one's health, and the man is listening to his wife and requesting hypnosis to help him quit). It is easy enough to believe that the client is motivated to follow through with the treatment. This, however, would be an example of a *linear-thinking* approach to the problem (i.e., "The client said he wanted to stop; therefore, he wants to stop"). On the other hand, if the therapist utilizes nonlinear listening (i.e., listening for congruence, absence, or resistance), she may begin to believe that the client is a *reluctant precontemplator*. She may try to respond to this client in a nonlinear way (e.g., "I can't help but notice that it is your *wife* who wants you to stop smoking, but I am not sure *what it is that you want*"). By asking that question, the counselor would learn that this gentleman actually enjoyed smoking immensely and was well aware of the health hazards, which he had (up to now) never experienced. As a result, it might very well prove to be quite futile to recommend that the person undergo hypnosis, use the nicotine patch, or undergo some other standard treatment. The SOC model would recommend addressing issues at the precontemplation level by supportively helping a client begin to address how he felt about the many health factors associated with stopping smoking, what he thinks about his own smoking (e.g., what he believes that it does for him), what he thinks and feels about his wife telling him to stop smoking, and so on. Specific strategies for doing this will be discussed later in the text (see Chapters 8–13).

Clinical Case Example 4.4: A Case of DUI

A client came for therapy after being charged with his third arrest for DUI within a 12-month period. He didn't think that he had a problem with drinking, and the only reason why he came to therapy is because his lawyer thought it would be a good idea. The therapist asked the client to reflect on what he thought about someone who has been arrested three times in a short span. He replied, "I have never missed a day of work. I take care of my family. I don't beat my wife. So, I am not an alcoholic, and I am not going to stop drinking."

When the therapist began a traditional substance abuse inventory, which includes such questions as "How much do you drink?" "How often do you drink?" and "How does drinking affect others in your life?" it became clear that the client did have a significant drinking problem according to standard criteria. When the counselor tried to delicately bring this to the client's attention, the latter immediately retorted, "You're just trying to convince me that I'm a drunk. You're like the lawyers and judges: You want me to wind up paying more money. It's a scam! Besides, what about all the health benefits of alcohol, huh? Do you ever drink? Have you ever drunk too much? Does that make you an alcoholic?"

Clearly, Clinical Case Example 4.4 is a *rebellious precontemplator*. The client's verbalizations betray the fact that he does not agree with the determination of others (i.e., his family, the court, his attorney, etc.) that he has a problem. If the therapist tries to "fight" the client and coerce him to acknowledge that he is an alcoholic, it will quickly lead to a therapeutic impasse and a failure to build and maintain a therapeutic alliance. Obviously, under such conditions, it is difficult to "connect with and engage" the client.

Such impasses result from a therapist's linear thinking (i.e., "Don't question me! You're the problem; you need to get help and fix it"). Instead, a therapist may consider the explosive nature of the client's rebellion (i.e., a *land mine*, discussed in Chapter 2) and utilize the methods of nonlinear listening and *responding for absence*. For example, the clinician may wish to adopt the "Colombo" approach of "I'm confused. ... Tell me some more about how that works for you" or "I'm confused. ... How did a nice guy like you ever get into such a mess with lawyers, courts, and psychologists telling you that 'you're this,' 'you're that.'" Another approach might be for the therapist to comment on the *process* that is going on between the client and the counselor. For example, "You know, I'm not sure what we are supposed to accomplish here. Every time I ask you about drinking, you get very upset. Perhaps you feel that this is a quick way to get me off your back? There really is nothing in it for me to make you upset!" This allows the client to vent his frustration in a more constructive way, and gives the therapist an opportunity to "win over" the client to at least continue the conversation in a less combative way.

In each of these examples, once a practitioner grasps the general thrust of what the client's *precontemplation* is about, it is easier to resist the *linear-thinking* temptation to exhort, admonish, subtly threaten, or otherwise coerce clients into owning (or at least exploring) problems that at the present moment they are not prepared to own. Coercive comments simply do not match *the client's view* of self, life, or circumstances and do not facilitate ownership of whatever problem he may actually have. If the clinician continues to "push" a client into adopting a problem that he refuses to see, this will only lead to further resistance and premature termination. When the therapist recognizes this stage of change, however, it allows her or him to avoid the trap of trying to make the client own the problem, just as the client's significant others have attempted to do but to no avail. In the frame of reference proposed here, identifying the fact that the client sees no problem and responding to the client accordingly represent nonlinear thinking. It is nonlinear because it is counterintuitive to what "everyone" (i.e., an important person(s) or authority figure) has told the client. It allows for an opportunity to connect with and engage the client, as discussed in Chapters 2 and 3, and facilitates development of a working alliance between client and therapist (to be discussed in Chapter 7). One particular method that is used to discuss issues and help a client move out of a precontemplation stage is motivational interviewing (see Chapter 13).

Contemplation

Contemplation is the stage of change in which an individual recognizes that a distressing set of life circumstances exists; she is interested in exploring whether or not her "problems" are resolvable, and *perhaps* counseling could be useful to her in that regard (DiClemente & Velasquez, 2002). At this stage of change, a client is assuming greater awareness of and perhaps a need for work on a particular aspect of life. As such, she may be expending considerable time and energy thinking about her "problem." The thinking may show itself by increased consciousness raising and attempts at decision making (DiClemente & Hughes, 1990). At this stage, for practical purposes a person is acknowledging that a problem exists. Although not exactly certain what to do about it, the individual is demonstrating a marked shift from precontemplation. However, clinicians should not be lured into a feeling of complacency that change will automatically follow just because a client has acknowledged that she has a problem. Clients in the contemplation stage are reminiscent of St. Augustine's famous quote, "Oh Lord make me chaste ... but not yet!"[8]

A clinician can recognize the contemplation stage in many instances when a client is expressing great "ambivalence" regarding the issue(s) at hand (Prochaska, 1999). Ambivalence is reflected in client sentiments such as "I *may* have a problem, and *if* I do, I'm not quite certain that I am prepared to tackle it." Or, a client may feel that solving a problem in a direct fashion might result in failure of one sort or another. Such unconscious recognition may prompt considerable anxiety because it puts a client in a "double bind": "If I address this problem directly, the way I should, it could result in failure.[9] If I don't address this problem, I'm going to have continued difficulty in this area of my life!" It is as if he is in a love–hate relationship with his dilemma. This level of ambivalence, or double bind, can keep a client stuck in the contemplation stage for a long time, becoming what Prochaska called "chronic contemplation or behavioral procrastination" (p. 230).

A *linear-thinking* therapist may grow impatient as a client vacillates between feelings of changing and remaining the same, and may attempt to put undue pressure on the client (e.g., "What do you mean you are going to stay with your wife? Just last week, you were convinced that you were going to leave. Make up your mind!"). On the other hand, a nonlinear-thinking clinician recognizes and utilizes the listening and responding to incongruence and resistance methods discussed in Chapters 2 and 3 to help draw out different options and guide a client toward making a decision that he is prepared to see to completion.

As such, the type of questions and interaction that a clinician utilizes will be quite different from those used with a client who does not accept the idea that she has a problem (i.e., is in the precontemplation stage). Such a client may feel that he lacks the resources (e.g., courage and skills) to deal with the problem, does not know how to go about addressing it, simply wishes to "explore," or may simply need to talk about the problem with a professional. Frequently, a client will express the contemplation stage of change by stating, "I'm sorry for being so scattered in my thoughts … I don't know if I'm making any sense … I don't know if I have a problem or not." Most often because of the *feelings involved in coming to see a therapist* (e.g., embarrassment, anxiety, confusion, defensiveness, or failure), it is difficult for a client to present what he believes is a coherent narrative regarding his particular problem. Although this is perhaps true of a client, the story being told will make a great deal more sense to a *nonlinear-thinking* practitioner.

Preparation for Action

Preparation for action represents a decision-making stage of change. The client is literally "gearing up" for action. The gearing-up process is demonstrated by decisions actually being implemented to take constructive steps, make inquiries, check things, and incorporate a need to do something about one's life situation *in the near future* (e.g., within the next month). Clients in this stage may also have taken some concrete positive steps toward change in the last year, and in the process they have most likely learned lessons for the upcoming change (DiClemente & Velasquez, 2002; Prochaska, 1999). DiClemente and Velasquez noted, "Individuals in this stage of change need to develop a plan that will work for them" (p. 210).

The most significant feature of the preparation for action SOC is that change is contemplated *in the near future*, and *often a specific target date is set*. In Western culture, it is commonplace to make "New Year's resolutions." This phenomenon dictates that in early December, a person commits to quit smoking, stop drinking, go on a diet, and begin exercising on New Year's Day. Couples in marital conflict may not say that they will stop arguing on New Year's Day, but they may express the intention to call for a therapy appointment the day after the holiday. Individuals with self-defeating patterns of behavior that involve chemicals (i.e., alcohol or drugs) or habits or addictions (e.g., gambling, eating disorders, spending, shopping, or some kind of sexual behavior) may decide to take steps to demonstrate that they are preparing for action (e.g., setting a target date to change their behavior and taking preparatory steps toward that end). Clients may practice self-management techniques to reduce the frequency of the self-defeating behavior in preparation for actually stopping it completely on the target date. They may also take deliberate steps to rearrange their environment, thus making unwanted behaviors more inconvenient (e.g., not smoking with a cup of coffee or while driving). Some individuals may put in place concrete steps such as depositing notes in key locations of the house, car, or work area to remind them of the advantages of making a change in their behavior to ensure ambivalence resolution. They may "go public," announcing their intention to change and thus enlisting significant others' cooperation and support but without the benefit of some sort of counseling from a practitioner. A commitment to consult a professional is not necessarily part of their resolution. Such "resolvers" may start out well on New Year's Day, but without sufficient preparation or professional help, they soon fall prey to human nature and typically fail to successfully implement their resolutions. Individuals who never even take the first step other than making a declaration are simply expressing "good intentions."

Work with clients in this stage must be supportive as well as provide them with guidance or skill building. But DiClemente and Velasquez (2002) cautioned, "Commitment to change does not necessarily mean that change is automatic, that change methods used will be efficient, or that the attempt will be successful in the long term" (pp. 10–11). Practicing self-management techniques and environmental management strategies strengthens *confidence* in the desire to change. "Going public" with the intended change strengthens *commitment* because a plan shared with others is more likely to be kept by the person. Clients who make good use of "preparation" time, and don't leap into the action stage prematurely, are more likely to be successful with their change[10] (DiClemente & Velasquez).

Action

In the "action" phase of the SOC model, a client demonstrates active steps toward changing something that he deems pertinent to the defined "problem" and seeks help to accomplish implementing his action strategies. According to DiClemente and Velasquez (2002), clients in this stage "overtly modify their behavior. They stop smoking … pour the last beer down the drain. … In short, they make the move and implement the plan for which they have been planning" (p. 211).

The action stage is the most active and obvious stage of change. Everyone in a client's immediate circle knows that some sort of change has been made. As a result, during the action stage, a client generally receives recognition and support, though not always. Sometimes, friends and family members subtly tell clients that their change is too radical for them to handle. Not infrequently, clients will hear such things as "I liked you better when you were stoned," or "(Sigh) I wish you would have a cigarette and lighten up already!" When clients hear these "change-back"[11] messages, therapists must be supportive to help a client gain perspective on what he is hearing from loved ones (DiClemente & Velasquez, 2002; Prochaska, 1999). Clinical Case Example 4.5 is an example of a client in the action stage of change.

Clinical Case Example 4.5: Action in Dealing With Anxiety

A woman in her early 30s sought help from a psychologist. When asked what sort of difficulty prompted her to come for help, she replied, "I've been thinking about going and talking to someone for quite a while (*contemplation*). I mentioned that I've been thinking about going to see someone (*preparation for action*) to my boyfriend, and he gave me your name as someone that he could recommend. I had talked to several other therapists (*preparation for action*) on the phone, but they either didn't appeal to me, didn't call me back, or were not on my insurance list of preferred providers. I called you, and you were so nice to talk to, so I scheduled an appointment."

Then the woman began talking about her "suffering from anxiety." Her anxiety was especially pronounced when driving in her car and being preoccupied with potential dangers. Furthermore, she noted that the problem can *increase* in intensity when someone whom she does not know well is driving.

When asked how it came to pass that she decided to come to therapy now, she indicated that she became more comfortable in discussing her nervousness with her family members. Those discussions led her to conclude that experiencing anxiety wasn't normal. She then said, "I want this to be fixed!"

Further along, the therapist asked what sort of things she had done to deal with the problem of being anxious while driving or being a passenger in someone else's car. She responded, "I play this game and say, 'OK Monica, *you're not going to get concerned* about the person driving.' I also try to look at the road, and if there is something scary, I look away. At other times, I won't look at the road at all. I also concentrate on breathing, and finally I concentrate on staying calm."

The young woman spontaneously added, "I don't like to take medications. I just don't want someone to say, 'Take pills.' I want to find out why I am this way."

Clinical Case Example 4.5 is *very instructional*, as are the client's attempts at managing her anxiety herself. In fact, the vignette makes several important points to be noted for the Level I practitioner. To begin with, the young woman *is* attempting to do something to help herself—she takes action, albeit inconsistent in its effects at ameliorating her anxiety (i.e., *action stage of change*). The therapist lauded her efforts at what she had been *doing* and noted that perhaps therapy could help make her *own efforts* more consistently effective. This represents an attempt to encourage her, build on her assets (i.e., the coping she was already familiar with), and strengthen a sense of therapeutic alliance—"I'm on your side; you're doing some positive things. Let's work together on this!" Finally, this woman is telling the therapist what she is uncomfortable with and *does not want* to hear (listening for *inference*). To paraphrase it, she said, "Don't tell me to take pills to make this go away!" After hearing such a declaration, it would be extremely imprudent of anyone to tell the client that she needs and must take medication. It would have the impact of saying, "I really don't care what it is that you want; you have to take medications." At the same time, if a practitioner believes that a client is in need of a medication evaluation, there is *a professional obligation* to tactfully point out that medication is an option. The prudent practitioner does not know what this apparently well-motivated and courageous young woman can do to manage her anxiety without medication.

Maintenance

An individual must consolidate and integrate changes once they have been made (the action stage can be up to 6 months of active changing or more). At this stage, according to DiClemente and Velasquez (2002) and Prochaska (1999), clients realize that they no longer have to be *as* active or conscious in their change behavior, but they do have to pay attention to it. Even a "recovering" problem drinker participating in AA *with years of sobriety* will refer to maintaining sobriety as "one day at a time." They are "mindful" of the need to keep an eye on their sobriety but also get on with the business of life. As time passes (between 6 months and 5 years), the positive behavioral habits take hold, and clients become more confident that they are being successful in implementing long-term changes.

Perhaps the easiest way to appreciate the maintenance stage of change is to ask yourself (or someone you know) if you have ever lost a significant amount of weight. It takes as much as a year and longer after the weight loss for the permanent sense of a "new me" to emerge with more sensible nutritional habits, activity patterns, and mental attitudes toward food than were previously held. Perhaps that is one of the major reasons why, as we mentioned in Chapter 2, 95% of those who have lost a significant amount of weight gain it all back and then some.

At times, clients who have attained their treatment goals are reluctant to terminate therapy. In effect, they believe that therapy and the therapeutic relationship serve as a sort of "rabbit's foot," and they are hesitant to relinquish it. For some clients, this dilemma is easily resolvable by a therapist suggesting less frequent visits to see how things go. Thus, a client can continue holding his "rabbit's foot" until he is more confident and comfortable in getting on with life without the therapy relationship.

Relapse

Once an individual has made substantive changes, it is clear that it is not always a simple matter to maintain the gains made regarding a problem, a problematic behavior, or difficult relationships. According to Prochaska (1999), the main reason for relapse in the early action stage is because the client did not prepare well for change in previous stages. Such clients tend to *underestimate the effort* that will be needed or *overestimate their own capabilities* for coping with the stresses associated with real and lasting change. As a result, they give up easily at the first sight of trouble and head toward relapse. Anyone who has stopped smoking, lost weight, done something about overcoming anxiety or depression, or reengaged in an on-again/off-again relationship that is going nowhere knows that life does not necessarily cooperate in helping one to maintain resolve and preserve the gains that have been made. Sometimes, the "cravings," "urges," "old habits," or other self-depictions of "falling off the wagon" are difficult to eliminate permanently. Other times, a client's support network fails to accept the change in a client (i.e., change-back messages). In some instances, a client becomes complacent about maintaining her gains and "backslides" into her old behaviors.

Linear-thinking therapists might see relapses as nothing but treatment failures, because a client was not able to "permanently" maintain treatment gains. Because it often takes clients several instances of reaching therapeutic goals and relapsing before finally arresting problem behavior, nonlinear-thinking therapists will often view "slips" as sometimes necessary steps backward toward the longer term goal (DiClemente & Velasquez, 2002).

Linear-thinking therapists might also see a client's "plateau" (i.e., a period of no apparent *further* therapeutic gains) as a sign of resistance. A nonlinear-thinking therapist is not only likely to consider viewing such a plateau as a period of *consolidation of gains made* but also likely to convey such a suggestion to the client in order to be encouraging.

It is the nonlinear-thinking therapist who also views instances of *relapse as opportunities for the client to delineate lessons learned*. Instead of giving up on a client, it is at this time that the client most needs a therapist as a trusted person to provide support, reenergize him, and motivate him once again. Another nonlinear-thinking "strategy" to implement with a client who has relapsed is to point out that "no one can take away what you were able to do—and hopefully what you will be able to do again." Clinical Case Example 4.6 illustrates movement between stages of change.

Clinical Case Example 4.6: A Woman Making Movement

An attractive, divorced woman in her early 50s became involved with an unsavory, manipulative, and emotionally abusive man with an equally unsavory, manipulative, and self-indulgent past. After several sessions of therapy, she stated that she understood the man's original seemingly hypnotic-like appeal. It was a tearful and painful acknowledgment to make to herself and the therapist. But, her acknowledgment of what she had previously been unwilling or unable to admit precipitated a number of declarations about no longer wanting him in her life. Despite these declarations, however, she felt manipulated by his friends and family, who lived less than a mile from her, to maintain contact with him and help him when he became ill with a virulent, long-lasting winter virus. She began taking friends' advice, resolving to "get out of any contact with him." As a result, at the conclusion of one session she stated, "If I have to move [i.e., change residences] to get out of harm's way, that's what I'll do!"

The following session was spent in discussing past experiences in which she had difficulty in setting limits and establishing boundaries as well as an episode of involvement with the man currently the focus of her concern to which she said, "I don't know how to set boundaries." But during the following session, she indicated, "It's not over, but I feel stronger!" In subsequent months, she took concrete steps of removing some of the man's possessions that he had been storing at her home as well as other concrete demonstrations of movement to permanently end the abusive relationship.

The therapist, mindful of the stages of change, indicated to the woman that relationships such as she had been struggling with seldom end in a precipitous, well-defined manner. Rather, they end over time with greater resolve, further concrete steps taken, setbacks and self-recrimination about felt failure, more resolve, still further concrete steps, and planning for the future. Verbalizations in different sessions included, "I've been scammed by him one too many times (preparation for action). ..." "I haven't given myself permission to say, 'I don't want to talk to you' (preparation for action). ..." "I'm sick of all this. ... I think I'm starting to put my self-respect back together again (action). ..." and "I'm learning how to set boundaries (action). ..."

After several months, the woman successfully rebuffed several attempts by the man to reenter her life. To reinforce the changes she had made, the therapist asked her how she thought that she had been able to accomplish her stated objective. Although she gave credit to God, friends, and the therapist, the therapist stressed her efficacy, strengths, hard work, resolve, and willingness to take risks in bringing about the change.

HOW TO IDENTIFY A CLIENT'S STAGE OF CHANGE

There are linear and nonlinear methods of listening, responding, and interviewing in order to determine "where" a client is currently along the SOC continuum. Linear methods include listening and responding to content and information and to feeling, as well as an assessment tool (see Information Box 5.1). As mentioned above, nonlinear methods of listening and responding (described in Chapters 2 and 3) are also powerful means for determining a client's stage of change.

Although a stage of change is easily described, identifying it often is not (particularly for the Level I therapist). Clients do not move in a neat, orderly, and linear fashion from one SOC to the next, but may move back and forth on the "readiness to change" continuum. Clients well into the "maintenance" SOC for months may have fleeting episodes of "ambivalence" from time to time that may or may not be recognized by a clinician. It is clinically vital to use both linear and nonlinear listening to monitor and be sensitive to a client's struggles with the particular stage of change *at that time*. For example, although relapse is (strictly speaking) not a stage of change, it is unfortunately a common occurrence in treatment, regardless of the particular problem. It is not unusual for someone to be doing well in treatment for months (i.e., being well in the "maintenance" stage of change) and then to encounter a highly emotionally charged and perhaps unexpected life circumstance (e.g., a death in the family, or a threatened job loss). Such circumstances may precipitate treatment reversals and noncompliance for weeks or even months. If a client has successfully completed treatment, it may be necessary for her to reenter therapy. A client abstinent of alcohol for many months or even several years could relapse and enter a detox program with plans to return to a specific AA meeting on the day of discharge from that program. Such behavior is seen as a sign of the "preparation for action" or even the "action" stage of change. Some clients in therapy for the first time may still be struggling with "ambivalence" and "contemplation." As with any client, assuming that each individual in detox is in the same place regarding his stage of change represents linear thinking. And, in addition, it is clinically unwarranted.

Moving Through the Stages of Change

What motivates a client to move from one SOC to another? According to Prochaska (1999), no *inherent motivation* exists for people to progress from one stage of change to the next, but Prochaska and his colleagues identified two dynamisms that seem to be a part of such motivation. The first concerns *developmental events* (i.e., turning a certain age, or passing a certain milestone). The second dynamism concerns *environmental factors* (i.e., an event occurs—9/11, a friend dies, a divorce, an anniversary, a significant accident, an unexpected bout of severe illness, or any event that impinges upon a client in a significant way). A therapist's task is to constantly monitor a client's SOC and capitalize on environmental factors to direct therapeutic interventions and assist his or her client in moving to the next SOC.

Both identifying a client's stage of change and identifying movement (or lack of it) between stages require linear and nonlinear listening and responding. The following are indications of change being underway to which a therapist can direct comments:

- Verbalizations that small initiatives have been undertaken
- Client expressions of failure to take bigger steps to change
- Comments that steps taken were discouraging or aborted
- Feelings of taking "two steps forward and one step back" (or "one step forward and two steps back")
- Expressions of having undertaken something new or different
- Avoidance of, or declining, opportunities to regress

Listening for and attending to such client verbalizations, complaints, feelings, sentiments, and self-assessment can be fruitful for the client and the therapy.

Information Box 4.2: Research on the Stages of Change Model

How effective has the SOC model been? Over several decades, Prochaska, DiClemente, and their associates (1982; 2005) have conducted dozens of studies on the SOC. Prochaska et al. (1994) were very specific on their findings regarding the SOC model:

> To date, *we have found that processes of change that have their theoretical origins in such variable and supposedly incompatible approaches as behavioral, cognitive, experiential, humanistic, and psychoanalytic therapies can be integrated empirically within the stage dimension of change*[12] (Prochaska & DiClemente, 1982). We have also found evidence suggesting that self-efficacy theory can be integrated within the same stage dimension (Velicer et al., 1999). The present results add substantial evidence that core constructs from a decision-making model can also be integrated within the stage (of change) dimension. We hope that such results can advance us beyond the all-too-common form of either-or thinking (either this model is correct or the competing one is better), and we anticipate the possibility of integrating alternative perspectives into more comprehensive approaches to behavior change. (p. 45; emphasis added)

Since those comments were made, the SOC model has continued to receive support in the literature regarding its efficacy in helping to structure how to approach individuals with almost any problem. We cite the following as illustrative of how the concept of stages of change and how people change can be useful in any number of areas: self-management and self-reported recommendations as a means of dealing with diabetes (Ruggiero et al., 1997); smoking cessation in adolescents (Pallonen et al., 1998); regular exercise (Laforge et al., 1999); immoderate drinking in college students (Migneault, Velicer, Prochaska, & Stevenson, 1999); health risk behaviors in older adults (Nigg et al., 1999); and 12 problem behaviors comprising smoking cessation, quitting cocaine, weight control, high-fat diets, adolescent delinquent behaviors, safer sex, condom use, sunscreen use, radon gas exposure, exercise acquisition, mammography screening, and physicians' preventive practices with smokers (Prochaska et al., 1994). In addition, Velicer, Norman, Fava, and Prochaska (1999) have demonstrated that the SOC model has a high degree of sensitivity and predictive validity across an entire spectrum of behaviors and problems. Finally, Brogan et al. (1999) compared standard psychotherapy client characteristic variables with variables derived from the SOC model to determine which of the two more accurately predicted clients who would terminate therapy prematurely, those who would stay in therapy, and those who would terminate therapy appropriately. The outcome: The SOC model did much better than other standard measurements of client characteristics.

The University of Rhode Island Change Assessment (URICA; McConnaughy, Prochaska, & Velicer, 1983) was devised to measure which stage of change the client has reached. The URICA is a 32-item Likert-type survey that is available for research purposes only (see http://www.uri.edu/research/cprc/Measures/urica.htm). The instrument contains items related to all of the stages of change except preparation for action. In addition, the items can be combined to create an overall measure of client readiness. Although the instrument is still in development, it provides a valuable tool for clinicians and researchers interested in the SOC model.

Knowing clients' symptoms, strengths, and resources as well as their stage of change gives the therapist a lot of information. It guides a therapist's initial interventions so that they are in keeping with a client's current "position" (i.e., stage of change, and client, patient, or complainant status) relative to achieving therapeutic goals. That is, if a therapist is dealing with a "client," that person is at least past the "precontemplation" stage and perhaps at either the contemplation or preparation for action stage. Accordingly, a therapist will want to employ certain strategies to specifically engage such a person. It is at this point, however, that master therapists find ways to pull together the client's narrative into a coherent whole, or *theme*. Once all of this information is gathered, the client and counselor can begin to move from assessment toward setting some goals for treatment. It is to these topics that we turn our attention.

ENDNOTES

1. The reader should note that these subjects (symptoms, psychosocial evaluations, mental status exam, and diagnosis) are each topics for *entire* texts that are beyond the scope of the present text. We present them briefly here as they pertain to the domain of assessment, though more formal and thorough training in these areas is necessary. For example, for a delineation of how to conduct a "clinical interview," see Othmer and Othmer (1994).

2. The terms *structured* or *semistructured* refer to required or essential categories of information or topics that need to be surveyed and questions that need to be asked in order to fulfill the professional obligations that clinicians have to their clients. As an analogous example, a physician conducting a physical examination has certain required categories or systems (e.g., heart, lungs, kidneys, liver, senses, glands, and history of illnesses and surgeries) that must be evaluated because they can have a bearing on what it is that the patient is complaining of at the time of the evaluation. For a physician *not* to listen to a patient's heart when the patient is complaining of chest pains or shortness of breath would be irresponsible.

3. We encourage students to find a standard biopsychosocial assessment tool and practice collecting information in a conversational way with fellow students in class in order to feel more comfortable with the process.

4. Again, a thorough treatment of the multiaxial diagnostic system of the *DSM-IV-TR* is outside the scope of this text. The reader is encouraged to consult the *DSM-IV-TR* (American Psychiatric Association, 2000).

5. Dr. Frankl's expertise in this area stems from his personal experience in the Nazi concentration camps. His book *Man's Search for Meaning* (Frankl, 1963) remains a classic for any therapist to read.

6. Some symptoms are decidedly the result of disordered biology and not the creation of the individual. Discerning the difference between symptoms of chest pain motivated by someone having "a lot on their chest" and someone experiencing cardiac insufficiency, angina, or a heart attack at times can be challenging to discern.

7. We use the term "client" throughout this text to refer to that person who presents him or herself in the therapist's office.

8. From St. Augustine's *Confessions* (397/1909–1914), Augustine's famous prayer when he begins to realize that he has been living a sinful life, but doesn't want to abandon it yet!

9. Failure is defined as a set of circumstances that might result in a client's efforts falling significantly short of the ideal or expected at some venture, thus losing prestige, "losing face," being embarrassed, feeling rejected, and so on.

10. This may also account for the abysmal failure of New Year's Day resolutions. Although a target day is set to initiate change, there may be little preparation to build confidence or strengthen commitment to change.

11. Developed from family systems theory, these are subtle messages sent by friends and family members that are the product of their anxiety over the changes that the client has made. It is as if these people are saying, "We are unsure about this 'new you.' We felt more comfortable the way you were, so please change back now."

12. As noted in Chapters 1 and 2, the model of universal domains being proposed in the present text finds support in the research of Prochaska and his colleagues (1982; 2005).

The Domain of Assessment

5

Part 2: The Theme Behind a Client's Narrative, Therapeutic Goals, and Client Input About Goal Achievement

CONTENTS

INTRODUCTION

A client's "story" has two basic elements to it that therapists must assess. There is the linear element consisting of the facts of the story, and the nonlinear element consisting of the theme or meaning behind the story. Awareness of an underlying theme can be enormously useful in appreciating what a client really wants (or needs) from therapy. In turn, knowing what areas may be more important and what areas are less important to a client is helpful to a therapist. We will describe each below, along with examples and suggestions for how linear and nonlinear listening (and responding) may be helpful in working with such a pattern.

ASSESSMENT: THE THEME BEHIND A CLIENT'S NARRATIVE

A master practitioner automatically listens for a client's narrative theme—much like being intimately involved in absorbing and understanding the plot in a movie or a novel. At Level I, the common themes are focused on the problem itself. As a therapist progresses to Levels II and III, assessment delves into deeper patterns in the client's life (i.e., schemas, to be presented in Chapters 8 and 9). However, it is important for the beginning therapist to begin to rapidly assess for some of the more common themes that are present when a client tells her story. Although we have attempted to arrange them in a descending order from the most obvious to the most subtle, human ingenuity demands that we caution the following: These are not the only way to look at themes. They are as follows:

1. Theme of desperation: *"I have a problem that I need to work on!"*
2. Theme of helplessness: *The symptom is out of control ("I can't help myself").*
3. Theme of hopelessness: *"I have a chronic problem."*
4. Theme of defensiveness: *"Who or what is the problem? ('Cause it's not me!)"*
5. Theme of exhaustion: *Being overwhelmed (physically, emotionally, and/or psychologically).*
6. Theme of despair: *The experience of loss.*
7. Theme of fear and confusion: *Double binds.*

In order to assess for these themes, it is important to use both *linear* and *nonlinear* listening and responding (i.e., congruence, absence, inference, presence, and resistance). A client may not even realize what the underlying theme is, but an effective (i.e., *nonlinear*-thinking) therapist soon discovers it.

Theme of Desperation: "I Have a Problem That I Need to Work On!"

Many times, clients will come into therapy in a state of crisis. These clients are often clear (initially) about what the problem is that they need help with ("I have a problem that I need to work on!"), and they are often desperate to have the problem "cured." Clients with extreme phobias that prohibit them from engaging in their routine tasks are one example. People addicted to alcohol or drugs who have "hit bottom" are another. This level of desperation often gives beginning therapists hope that the client is sufficiently motivated for change, and will be responsive to treatment.

On the one hand, it is obvious from such a client's statement that what he is pointing to *is* the problem. If the therapist helps him with that problem, the client will be able to live life happily. Sometimes that is the case, and treatment is straightforward. But to treat everyone in that way is a *linear* way of thinking. Many times, things are never quite as simple as they seem, and generally require a therapist to probe a little deeper. The starting point, however, is right at the surface. Clinical Case Example 5.1 illustrates.

Clinical Case Example 5.1: A "Fragile" Man

A talented man (a carpenter, electrician, etc.) in his late 40s came to therapy complaining that he was unable to sleep, had a poor appetite, and was "not feeling well" in general. He further reported that he went to see his family doctor, who prescribed an antidepressant and anxiolytic (i.e., antianxiety) medications. He knows that he is depressed and anxious, then adds, "My doctor says that I'm 'fragile' right now and that he doesn't want me returning to work for at least another 3 weeks."

In Clinical Case Example 5.1, several things are obvious even with the very brief description of the client's circumstances. On the surface, the client admitted that he was having problems, and wanted to sleep better and not suffer from depression and anxiety. His situation was desperate. From a linear perspective, if a therapist could help him sleep, get his appetite back, and help him feel stronger and not so "fragile," then therapy would be a success. Nonlinear listening for *absence* (what the client isn't saying) and *inference* (what the client doesn't want) reveals more to the story, and perhaps points to an underlying theme. The theme of desperation was accurate, and his problems were real, but the nonlinear question that the therapist has to ask is, what is he "desperate" about?

The answer lies in the client's story: Of all the things that the client's doctor told him, why would he bother to mention the doctor's comment about *not returning to work for 3 weeks* if it wasn't important to him at this particular time? Such a comment might also raise the counselor's curiosity about the client's workplace (which seems to be a focus of his attention regarding his "problem"). In fact, when he was asked about his work, the client replied,

> I work for a transportation company—for 22 years, and the stress on the job is very high. There's no let up—it's a 365-day-a-year operation. Last year I had more physical illnesses and had to take a lot of time off—I couldn't get above it. Last week, I got sick, and I *couldn't think* (emphasis added to reflect the client's different tone of voice) about going to work without having a panic attack! I had a hard time breathing, and I was kind of incoherent.

In the example above, the client tells the therapist *what he does want* (*inference*): not returning to work, because it's *too stressful*. Hence, the therapist is subtly told *not to try to encourage* him to return to work. Also, the client *doesn't* tell the therapist anything about the other areas of his life, or times when his work *wasn't* stressful (*absence*). This is a classic example of listening for things that the client is *not* telling you. Although clients may not necessarily be conscious of an underlying theme, it is crucial for assessment as well as the setting of treatment goals to first understand both the story (i.e., "I have a problem that I need to work on!") and the underlying themes that can either expedite or derail therapy.

Theme of Helplessness: The Symptom Is Out of Control ("I Can't Help Myself")

Another common theme is one in which a client, directly or indirectly, acknowledges feeling "out of control." Verbal expressions that tend to signify such difficulty are often represented by comments such as "I can't help myself," "I don't know what comes over me," "I feel out of control," "Something comes over me," "It comes out of nowhere," "This is all pretty scary to me," and "I don't know what's going on." One particular client, feeling particularly out of control, described his work environment as follows: "I feel like I'm behind the controls of a 747 and I know it's going to crash and there's nothing I can do about it!" Of course, clients don't always necessarily express themselves quite so clearly, but sentiments of being out of control can be discerned in the narrative story that a client relates. From compulsive shopping, to obsessive thoughts, to an inability to stop drinking, the underlying theme is that a client feels helpless in the face of her compulsion, illness, or symptom. Consider Clinical Case Example 5.2.

Clinical Case Example 5.2: Pregnant and Anxious

A 34-year-old recently married woman who is 6 months pregnant called for an appointment with a psychologist because she has developed a paralyzing fear of needles. When she appeared for her appointment, the therapist asked how he might specifically be of assistance to her. The young woman replied, "I've been under a great deal of stress! Everything imploded at once. When we were preparing for the wedding, I had the perfect wedding dress, the perfect invitations, and the perfect reception hall. Everything was going along just perfectly. Then, 3 weeks before the wedding, I found out that I was pregnant. I had just changed jobs for advancement in my career and found out that I would unfortunately be let go because the person who was supposed to be leaving was now intending to stay. I had to temporarily go on public aid until my husband's insurance covered me. And now I'm feeling every symptom from the pregnancy that you can imagine!"

The therapist noted that she said absolutely nothing about needles, which she had discussed in their conversation on the telephone! This represented a significant disconnect (or *incongruity*) between what her *original* statement was and what she was *now* "complaining" of. When specifically asked about the fear of needles discussed on the phone, she revealed that as a very young child, she had been quite ill and required hospitalization with numerous IVs, injections, and blood tests. She summed up her childhood reactions to all of that as "It never fazed me. I was a little squeamish but never afraid. They even drew blood twice a day and did a spinal tap."

More recently, in a routine blood draw regarding pregnancy health, a nurse collapsed a vein. Until that time, she had not contemplated any inherent difficulty (i.e., "no problem") with giving her obstetrician permission for the use of an epidural[2] anesthetic for delivery, or any other medical procedures to assist in the delivery. But the client stated when her sister-in-law delivered a baby several months earlier, she had serious panic feelings. "When they said they were sewing her up, I lost it!"

In dealing with all of these many things, she stated powerfully that "the biggest mistake I made was to go for my blood test by myself. I've always been someone who says, 'I might as well do it myself.' I'm used to getting what I want not because I'm spoiled but because I go out and work for something and can usually get it. My parents always said, 'If you want something, work for it and you can have it. Don't expect anyone to give it to you.' I like to be prepared along the way, but *when I expect things to go one way and they go another way, it bothers me.* I don't like surprises. I then think to myself, 'What happens if I'm all positive and I'm having trouble?'"

When asked what she would like to realistically accomplish through treatment, she indicated that she would like to get through her labor, have a healthy child, and not hurt her baby. *"My goal is not just to get blood samples or vaccinations. ... I'd like someone to see me through a successful delivery ... and go through the delivery like an adult!"*

In Clinical Case Example 5.2, the obvious problem the client presents is that she needs to have regular blood tests as part of her prenatal care, but this is seriously distressing to her. At first glance, there appears to be a straightforward complaint and a reasonable request for a particular treatment (i.e., using therapy to deal with fears). Despite this, an assessment of the underlying *themes* is perhaps one of the most important things a clinician can do, even in the most straightforward linear cases. In this case, it makes a major difference in the effectiveness of her treatment.

The therapist allowed her to tell her story, and the way that it unfolded pointed to the underlying theme. On the surface, the client's fear of needles placed her in such a state of anxiety that she felt unable to control it. She felt helpless. But, initially she did not seem to place much importance on her fear of needles. Even though the fear of needles was not in the forefront, the theme of helplessness remained throughout her story.

The bottom line for this client is that she feels out of control about her situation, and helpless to do anything about it. She clearly had *beliefs* about the way "things ought to go," but her life circumstances took her another way. Such clients are accustomed to having control (as she did when she was employed and planning her "perfect" wedding), but the control has since been lost (once the pregnancy began). In addition, she has lost her identity (from a single, employed, self-reliant woman to an unemployed, pregnant newlywed). Although she does have her husband's support, it is limited by his preoccupation with a new job and being tired after working long hours. She feels alone and helpless. Her symptomatic "fear of needles" becomes a metaphor for her helplessness and sense of loss of control (i.e., "I have no choice in the matter"). Hence, it is clear from her statements that she will be disappointed if she is treated *linearly* (i.e., the therapist-hypnotist deals strictly with her announced "fear of needles") and sent on her way. She will not be satisfied, and her problem will probably not go away.

Nonlinear listening for inference informs the therapist about what the client does not want. In addition, there are some statements that reflect *incongruence* (e.g., wanting to go through the labor as an adult, but depending on her husband and family that are not "there" for her). As a result of this underlying context, the client focused on scaring herself through a fear of needles to bring her into therapy. Thus, the woman has treatment objectives (i.e., "I will find someone to help me go through this and not feel helpless"), even if she is not consciously aware of it. Once goals and expectations are clarified, collaboration between the client and therapist can work out the specific details of how they will accomplish them. Notice how nonlinear listening for inference also can help a therapist to identify where along the stages of change spectrum the client seems to be stuck. Setting goals and expectations for treatment will be discussed later in the chapter.

Theme of Hopelessness: "I Have a Chronic Problem"

Some individuals come for treatment with what is obviously a "chronic" problem—something they have struggled with (e.g., a chronic mental health issue such as depression or anxiety) for many years, sometimes more successfully and sometimes less so. On the surface (linear), the condition may be either exotic or routine, and it may be tempting for the counselor to try to address or even treat the condition by giving the client advice.[3] However, with chronic conditions (especially ones that the client has dealt with for years), very often a therapist is much more constrained in what can be done to alleviate the condition. But when therapists use nonlinear listening for the theme that underlies a client's chronic complaint, they can offer support. When the client's chronic condition is making her life difficult, there is usually a theme of hopelessness that is below the surface. The therapist will likely listen for and respond to themes of chronic complaints with all the nonlinear elements (congruence, absence, inference, presence, and resistance). If a therapist can assess and intervene with the client to revive her or his own sense of hopefulness, then the client will generally get "back on track" and manage the condition more successfully. Clinical Case Example 5.3 may be helpful as an illustration.

Because the woman in Clinical Case Example 5.3 is someone who has a chronic problem does not mean that she is not doing some things that are positive and adaptive. In fact, she is not describing that she is in crisis but simply feels the need for someone to be supportive, point out some of her positive attributes,

---

Clinical Case Example 5.3: On-and-Off Treatment for Years

A widow in her 60s with a long history of "on-and-off" treatment with several therapists was transferred from one therapist who was retiring to another. She dressed in somewhat plain clothing, wore no makeup, was mildly overweight, and appeared older than her stated age. Nevertheless, she was neat in her appearance and well groomed.

When presenting her story, she is articulate and logical, and demonstrates an impish "off-the-wall" sense of humor of which she seems quite proud. Although she has little income, she works part-time and is adamant that she always pays her bills. In her first interview, she described herself as "semiretired," and about to quit her latest part-time job because it was "not working out." She also described herself as very sensitive, chronically depressed, angry, chronically annoyed, and wanting to stay in bed, but "I'm not suicidal."

She described childhood as being laden with criticism of her, with high parental expectations but little demonstrable love, affection, or positive reinforcement, especially when compared to her siblings.

---

and thus stimulate her sense of hopefulness. Often, this can take the form of assessing for strengths (discussed below). In this case, the client might be asked in a *nonlinear* way how she has done so well (e.g., manages to work, financially keeps herself in her own home after becoming a widow even though she realistically has little money, looks after an aging parent, contributes as a volunteer in her local community, and maintains her sense of humor) despite life and family circumstances having been so unkind to her. Reminding clients of their constructive and adaptive behaviors that support healthy coping with their condition is often a crucial first step in helping them regain their sense of equilibrium and hope—even with a chronic mental health complaint.

Theme of Defensiveness: "Who or What Is the Problem? ('Cause It's Not Me!)"

It is tempting to think that just because someone comes to see a therapist that he is acknowledging that he has a problem. The fact is that many people come to therapists because they believe that *someone* or *something else* is the cause of their problems. Parents who bring their children to a therapist in order to be "fixed" represent a vivid example of this (see Peck, 1983). The child may be exhibiting behaviors that create discipline problems in school, or is constantly seeking (negative) attention. Some children brought for consultation to therapists may have legitimate problems of autism, or some other pervasive developmental disorder. However, it is not uncommon for children brought in (usually against their will) to therapy to get "fixed" to have *parents* who are abusive, addicted, or lack effective parenting skills. Yet, to suggest any role or part in the child's behavior to the parents usually results in anger and defensiveness. In these circumstances, it is important for the therapist to be listening for and responding to *congruence*, *absence*, *inference*, and *resistance* in order to determine who the client really is: Clinical Case Example 5.4 may be helpful.

Clinical Case Example 5.4: Abandoned by a Daughter

An elderly woman with no previous psychiatric history consulted a psychologist because of a series of events that had recently culminated in an adult daughter no longer wanting very much to do with her with no explanation of any sort. Accompanied by her husband, the woman looked her stated age and was pleasant but mildly depressed and clearly distressed by the lack of contact with her daughter. She was also greatly distressed because access to her grandchildren was now tightly controlled by her daughter. Her husband had "washed his hands" of the matter and refused to talk to the client about their daughter. As far as he was concerned, the issue was dead. Furthermore, the woman did not want to bring up this issue with her daughter for fear of further limitations being placed on her access to her grandchildren.

At the time of treatment, the client was incredulous regarding her daughter's behavior. She declared her daughter's complaints were vague and untrue. According to the client, her daughter would say, "Mom, you didn't support me!" The client perceived herself as making many sacrifices on behalf of her daughter (e.g., giving up her job to be a caretaker for her grandchildren, keeping accurate diaries of their development, moving closer, etc.). The client proclaimed innocence regarding having wronged her daughter. Her purpose in presenting herself for treatment is to figure out, "What's wrong with our daughter? Why is *she* doing this?"

In Clinical Case Example 5.4, if using just linear listening for content, the therapist will be led to the same conclusion as the client: The daughter is the problem—something is wrong with her daughter, but no one seems to know exactly what. According to the client, she had curtailed her own career to be the primary caretaker for her grandchildren without any recompense while the daughter worked. However, now the daughter is claiming that the client was unsupportive and is unworthy of having access to the grandchildren. Hence, the purpose of therapy would be to help the client change her daughter. But at this point, it is important to ask oneself: Exactly who is the client and who is the problem?

Nonlinear listening reveals *incongruence* between the client's story (i.e., "I am a good mother and grandmother") and the reality of the situation (i.e., her daughter didn't feel supported and doesn't want anything to do with the client). In addition, listening for inference reveals the client's indignation at being marginalized by her daughter. Furthermore, *listening for resistance* indicates that the client feels that she has done "all of the work" and that it is her daughter's responsibility to act (not hers). In terms of the stages of change, she would be a precontemplator. All of this points to a theme of defensiveness regarding her relationship with her daughter.

The therapist must pay careful attention to the client's defensiveness, and not enter into a *linear-based* discussion of what the mother and father did or didn't do. Such a discussion would begin to ascribe responsibility for the breach in the relationship with their daughter to the mother and father. This would likely result in a power struggle with the client, the *therapist* would be alienated from the client, and there would be a likely premature termination.

The type of nonlinear therapeutic intervention needed in such instances requires that the therapist acknowledge the client's hurt and simultaneously provide the parents with an acceptable rationale that potentially "explains" the other person's seemingly irrational behavior, which can help them change their stance toward their daughter. Such an intervention can only be provided through nonlinear-thinking processes, which are described in the latter portions of this book (see Chapters 14–18). At this stage, however, accurately assessing the clients' themes and understanding that they are in the precontemplation stage comprise the most important thing in building a therapeutic alliance.

Theme of Exhaustion: Being Overwhelmed (Physically, Emotionally, and/or Psychologically)

There is no question that life is extremely demanding at times. In fact, at times it can be brutally cruel, overwhelming, and randomly tragic. The trauma of experiencing war as a combatant or as a civilian victim, surviving a natural disaster and being dispossessed of one's home and possessions, being a traumatized "first responder" to a disaster, and being a victim of physical, verbal, and sexual abuse are all examples of this. When such events transpire, the psychological aftermath can be as disabling and immobilizing as the "theme of hopelessness" presented earlier. Such individuals are different, however, because the underlying theme is exhaustion, rather than hopelessness. Clinical Case Example 5.5 may be helpful.

Clinical Case Example 5.5: A Rare Medical Illness

A beautiful, pleasant, soft-spoken, and accomplished woman contracted a rare cardiac condition. She was a woman in the prime of life, with a brilliant career as a university professor, financially doing well, and dating a man whom she cared for dearly. She exercised vigorously on a daily basis, ate healthy foods, maintained an ideal body weight for her height, and generally led a moderate lifestyle. Nevertheless, she was suddenly struck by a random and whimsical illness whose origin is unknown. Her condition is a rare chronic disease that can be fatal and thus must be monitored closely and treated aggressively with exotic medication is for life, or she will die.

After being close to death, the woman recovered sufficiently to return to work. But emotionally and psychologically she felt defeated, frightened, vulnerable, and metaphorically "constantly looking over my shoulder," monitoring whether or not the illness was going to return unabated in the same stealthy manner that it had first overtaken her. Clearly, in such a case, a therapist must acknowledge and validate the linear aspects of her condition (e.g., "This is a serious condition, you are *right* to pay attention to it, and you have a right to be overwhelmed"). At the same time, when dealing with a client's feelings of being overwhelmed, the therapist must look for the nonlinear elements of *absence* (what is the client *not* doing as a result of being overwhelmed?) and *congruence* (is the client *truly* overwhelmed, or possibly exaggerating?).

The client in Clinical Case Example 5.5 has weathered the storm of her illness and fought her way back to a sense of normalcy, and as a result she has some hope. But her fight with such a terrible illness has left her exhausted. In such cases in which there is no secondary gain (e.g., workman's compensation, seeking disability retirement, or gaining attention or service from others; see Chapter 12), it becomes important for a clinician to be highly supportive and alert for positive and healthy things that a client is doing in order to cope with her condition. It is also important to inquire *how* the client was able to accomplish certain things to emphasize the fact that *she* was instrumental in such accomplishments. It is important to assess clients for strengths and help them see that their efforts are *not* routine but (often) extraordinary. This level of assessment can motivate them to move into the action stage of change.

Theme of Despair: The Experience of Loss

Unquestionably, human beings are extraordinarily vulnerable to grief subsequent to the loss of a loved one. Deep affection, intensely interwoven lives, interdependence, and shared experiences are all part of the things that an individual loses when he or she experiences the death of a loved one. Human beings can also experience grief, uncertainty, and a sense of loss upon retirement, being "let go" from a long-held job, the breakup of a romantic relationship, profound changes in a company's employment philosophy, the death of a dearly loved family pet, an extreme reversal in health status, or financial loss. The point is that individuals react with grief when they experience an important loss, and very frequently they do not recognize what they are experiencing. Although they may realize that they are depressed, blue, or down, they may not understand that they are *grieving*.

Because deeply felt losses are not necessarily a daily occurrence, individuals often have no comparable experience to which they can relate their current loss. They lack a template of understanding for what they are experiencing and how to deal with it. A therapist will want to look for nonlinear aspects such as *absence* (i.e., what part of your life has not been touched by the loss?), *inference* (i.e., when the client says, "I don't want to let go"), *presence* (i.e., subtle body language that betrays emotion), and *resistance* (i.e., not wanting to move forward with life).

Long ago, Kübler-Ross (1969, 1975, 1981) identified four stages often found in individuals who are dying, namely, denial, anger, bargaining, and acceptance. Worden (1982) discussed the stages of grief that individuals experience after a significant loss, namely, accepting the reality of the loss, experiencing the pain of the grief associated with the loss, adjusting to a world and an environment in which the deceased is absent, and disinvesting "emotional energy" from the lost person and reinvesting it in another relationship. These processes represent approximate templates. The processes are similar for everyone but at the same time distinctly different for each individual. Each individual's grief lasts according to her own time frame, the different stages are unique for each individual, some find one stage harder to deal with than others, and so on, but all individuals go through all the stages to a greater or lesser extent when "successfully" recovering from losses and moving on with their lives (a more thorough description of how to work with complex emotions will be discussed in Chapters 10 and 11).

It can be useful to the Level I clinician to understand that linear empathizing with the client's loss is both essential and helpful. Giving "advice" about what to do to "get over" one's grief represents *linear thinking*. Instead, helping the client to understand that he will have to live with the loss for the rest of his life, and validating the client's despair without trying to "make it all better" or helping him "get over it," can be the most therapeutic thing that a therapist can do. It helps to focus the client on his real fear: not being able (or willing) to go on in the face of his loss. Therefore, it is sometimes necessary to counsel people dealing with loss *not* to move too fast. Clinical Case Example 5.6 is illustrative.

Clinical Case Example 5.6: Loss of Spouse *and* Career!

A professional man with a distinguished career sought counseling after the death of his wife, whom he loved dearly. Shortly after his wife died, company policy "forced" him to accept retirement at a specified age from a career that he also loved. In effect, he lost his wife and his career within the span of several months. Nevertheless, by all measures he was going through the stages of the grieving process and found himself going to the cemetery almost daily to visit his wife's grave. Although still visiting his wife's grave daily, he had also begun casually keeping company with a never-married coworker whom he had known on a friendly basis for many years. Within a period of about a year, they found their mutual interests, enjoyment of each other's company, and mutual fondness to be sufficiently developed to talk about getting married. It was approximately at that time that he sought counseling.

The man explained that he felt he was gradually "getting over" the loss of his wife but that he just didn't know if getting married was the right thing to do *at this time*. At the same time, he didn't want to lose this woman who comforted him regarding the loss of his wife and understood his grief. She was also fun to be with and a good companion, and they had a mutual interest in their profession. His loyalties appeared divided to him because he was still going to the cemetery to visit his wife's grave. The woman was strongly signaling that if he didn't know what he wanted, she needed to move on with her life because of her advancing age and desire to be married as she moved closer to retirement.

In Clinical Case Example 5.6, it appeared clear that the theme of this counseling was "loss" and the fear of its aftermath. Listening for *presence* (client's physical reactions) and listening for *absence* (what is not being said) can help to assess for this theme. The client was ambivalent and "stuck" regarding the possibility of moving forward with his life and investing in a new relationship. At the same time, he was still investing in his relationship with his wife by visiting her grave almost daily, and was in despair that he would not be able to move forward.

Theme of Fear and Confusion: Double Binds

A *double bind* is an expression used to describe a client's experience of being stuck between two unpleasant choices ("I'm damned if I do, and I'm damned if I don't"). Although double binds are a clinically significant dynamic, they are not always easily discernible. In fact, it can often take a while for beginning therapists to discover that the client is exhibiting characteristic signs of double binds. Because of their complexity, therapists generally are required to utilize all of the nonlinear forms of listening and responding (i.e., congruence, absence, inference, presence, and resistance) to assess for double binds. It is important to remember, however, that the theme underlying a double bind is fear and confusion—fear of change or making a mistake, and confusion from an inability to commit to a decision. These clients are often in the contemplation or preparation for action stage of change. This can lead to a frustrating sense of lack of progress in therapy. Clinical Case Example 5.7 illustrates.

Clinical Case Example 5.7: The Aftermath of an Affair

A woman who caught her husband participating in an extramarital emotional-non-physical affair became literally enraged and threw him out of the house. She sought therapy to help herself determine what she should do—divorce him or "try to work things out." Over a period of several months, she managed to calm down significantly. Nevertheless, it was clear that she occasionally had difficulty coping with the reality that her husband had "cheated." She kept vacillating: On the one hand, she would experience harmonious and intimate moments with her husband motivated by desperately believing in marriage and wanting to keep hers going. Equally profoundly, upon exposure to any references to infidelity, divorce, prostitution, and the like in *any* media, she would impulsively become enraged, scream obscenities at her husband, and make unfounded accusations.

During one session, the therapist asked her what she had learned about herself in the process of doing her "homework" (i.e., thinking about her uncontrolled swings of mood and behavior). She replied, "It's not like I've had a huge revelation, but there are two things that I've figured out. One is that I've always said I would never put up with infidelity—if it happened, I'd get divorced. The second thing I figured out is that I *totally* believe in marriage and in always working things out. These two things are in conflict. I always try to do the right thing."

In Clinical Case Example 5.7, it is clear that the client's uncontrolled bouts of rage and moments of working things out are reflections of her belief system and values. Staying in the marriage represents one side of the double bind (i.e., "totally believ[ing] in marriage" and "always working things out"), and screaming and raging represent the other side of the double bind (i.e., "I would never put up with infidelity"). Her behavior can be seen as "wanting to have her cake and eat it too." She wants to stay married (i.e., she views divorcées as "losers"), and at the same time she is totally intolerant of the fact that her spouse had "cheated" (i.e., she has long maintained that she would get divorced if her husband was unfaithful). She is afraid to make a mistake by leaving, and she is equally afraid to stay. This leads to her apparently confusing behaviors. From a nonlinear perspective, however, the behavior does make sense.

In terms of the nonlinear listening involved, her vacillation was a sign of *incongruence* and some *resistance* to dealing with the subject. Also there is an *absence* of her own part in the marital dyad that may have contributed to the infidelity, plus her strong emotions are clearly a *presence* in the therapy that contradicts many of her incongruent statements. In addition, her declarations of what she "would not tolerate" allow the clinician to *infer* her goals for therapy. Clearly, for her to move into the action stage would mean that she would have to make a decision. Therefore, by vacillating she is able to put off making a decision (though at a price!). We will discuss the important subject of schemes, double binds, the ambivalences they generate, and nonlinear ways of dealing with them in greater detail in the later chapters of the book (Chapters 12–17). Next, we discuss assessing client symptoms, diagnoses, strengths, and resources.

Brain in a Box 5.1: Visualizing Goals

As discussed in Chapters 2 and 3, most typically, when a client is asked what she might like the outcome (i.e., goal) of treatment to be, she replies, "I want to *feel* better … more relaxed.… I *don't* want to argue with my husband.… I want to be happier in life.… I don't want to be depressed.… I don't know.… I don't want to have these urges.… I want all of it to go away.…" All such articulations are understandable when someone is in the throes of suffering. But, in terms of how the brain actually operates, it becomes difficult for a client to pursue *feelings* as an objective. Feeling good is the *result* of achieving a particular desired goal. On the other hand, *pursuing a goal* that is concretely visualizable is much more in keeping with how the brain actually works. For individuals to aspire to therapeutic goals, it is *valuable and perhaps essential* that they specify in concrete and clear—preferably visualizable—terms what it is that they *do want* or *how they want to be*, to the extent that it could be seen on a TV monitor.

Pinker (1999) illustrated creative thinkers' use of imagination to solve complex problems:

> Many creative people claim to "see" the solution to a problem in an image. Faraday and Maxwell visualized electromagnetic fields as tiny tubes filled with fluid. Kekulé saw the benzene ring in a reverie of snakes biting their tails. Watson and Crick mentally rotated models of what was to become the double helix. Einstein imagined what it would be like to ride on a beam of light or drop a penny in a plummeting elevator. He once wrote, "My particular ability does not lie in mathematical calculation, but rather in visualizing effects, possibilities, and consequences. Painters and sculptors try out ideas in their minds, and even novelists visualize scenes and plots in their mind's eye before putting pen to paper.… Images drive the emotions as well as the intellect.… Ambition, anxiety, sexual arousal, and jealous rage can all be triggered by images of what isn't there." (p. 285)

Research in neurobiology is revealing that "thinking in images engages the visual parts of the brain" and "images really do seem to be laid across the cortical surface" (Pinker, 1999, pp. 287, 289). Clinical hypnosis has historically utilized the "subconscious'" relationship to visualization as a major factor in helping clients to achieve therapeutic successes: "There is a tendency on the part of the subconscious to carry out any prolonged and repeated visual image" (Cheek & Le Cron, 1968, p. 60). Kroger and Fezler (1976) and Hammond (1984) have compiled a series of images and metaphors designed to enhance clients' success in overcoming a wide range of human problems.

We propose that the mind–brain must form *images* that concretize what it is that clients would like to accomplish in treatment, which, in turn, is what makes it possible to pursue goals.

THERAPEUTIC GOALS

Establishing treatment goals is critically important if a client is going to be "successful" in therapy. As a result, it is vital that the therapist's and client's goals for treatment are in alignment. Otherwise, client and therapist work at cross-purposes. Clinical Case Example 5.8 may prove useful.

Clinical Case Example 5.8: Art, Not Sex!

A handsome, middle-aged, well-educated, never-married retired man in excellent physical condition was participating in supportive psychotherapy on a monthly basis. He was well aware and accepting of his need for help in dealing with his propensity for overreacting to and obsessing about many of life's ordinary difficult circumstances. At the same time, he was taking a psychotropic medication designed to help calm him and manage his mood; this was prescribed by a physician who had known the man and his history for several years. Although the client was a multitalented individual who had casually dated attractive women for many years, he had never engaged in sexual relations. Consciously, he explained the reason for this as being because of "religious hang-ups." When asked what these hang-ups might be, he explained that having sex outside of marriage was a sin and he never felt prepared to accept (i.e., he felt "overwhelmed" by) the financial and psychological responsibility of being married with a family to support. His doctor told him off-handedly, "You should get laid!"

In Clinical Case Example 5.8, the client saw his therapist after an appointment with his doctor and confided that he was very upset. He began discussing what his doctor had told him and knew that he was obsessing about it. When asked if he felt prepared to pursue having a sexual relationship with a woman, he decisively indicated, "Definitely not!" He explained that pursuing such a goal would cause him no end of "guilt" and obsessive preoccupation at the expense of what *he* was interested in pursuing, namely, perfecting his considerable artistic abilities. With a strong therapeutic alliance, the therapist perceived the myriad problems that would result from this action, and agreed with the client that he had other preoccupations and that seeking a sexual encounter was not very high on his list of life priorities. In addition, as the client stated, the therapist supported the client's contention that having a sexual encounter with a woman was likely to generate further problems with "guilt."

Obviously, a misalignment between a practitioner's goals (in this case, the client's physician) and the client's goals can easily cause significant problems. An active and clear discussion must take place of what issues are to be worked on and what are *reasonably achievable goals*. Such a discussion clearly lays out agreed upon expectations for and steps of therapy—that is, what will be discussed, what won't be discussed, identifying and evaluating signs of progress, identifying signs of regression, and finally the proper end point to the therapy itself (see Skovholt & Rivers, 2004). Without such goals, the course of therapeutic encounters can wander.

The question remains, what makes for good therapeutic goals? In addition to the factors listed above, effective goals should result from a careful examination of a client's needs and wishes. This does not mean, however, "Whatever the client says, goes." This is because sometimes clients do not know what they want, or feel "coerced" into therapy when they are neither ready nor willing to make changes (e.g., they are precontemplators). Still other clients come to therapy with unrealistic goals and expectations. Thus, a therapist has an important role to play in helping the client set appropriate goals. She must take into account the resources (e.g., strengths, use of power, and social supports) that a client brings into therapy, and then focus the client on goals that are reasonable and realistic. Last, a therapist must also help to set an appropriate and reasonable time frame for the change to occur that encourages working toward desired changes, rather than failure (Skovholt & Rivers, 2004).

Although a therapist's role is important, a client's role in the goal-setting process is equally valuable. Clients must be willing to challenge themselves, commit to the change process, and confront whatever core issues may arise as a result. They must recognize and identify a significant life issue that they want to change. In addition, both therapist and client, when setting goals, need to focus on *positive*, not negative, change and provide for the necessary "checks" along the way (i.e., short-term and midrange goals on the way to longer term goals). Whatever goals that client and counselor agree upon, such goals must be consistent with the client's needs and the counselor's capabilities to help (Skovholt & Rivers, 2004). Last, goals should be open to change, revision, and evolution, as the therapeutic process moves forward, therapeutic milestones are reached, and new elements emerge. Perhaps Hoyt and Berg (1998), in discussing the development of solution-focused goals, put it most succinctly, stating that the best goals:

> are small rather than large; salient to clients; articulated in specific, concrete behavioral terms; achievable within the practical contexts of clients' lives; perceived by clients as involving their own hard work; seen as the 'start of something' and not as the 'end of something'; and treated as involving new behavior rather than the absence or cessation of existing behavior. (p. 316)

Information Box 5.2: Questions for Client and Counselor in Considering Goal Setting

QUESTIONS TO ASK CLIENTS FOR SETTING GOALS

- How would you like for things to be different?
- What would you like to change in your life?
- What would you like to accomplish? How would you know that you had achieved what it is that you came to therapy for?
- How would you know that therapy was successful?
- If your problems were resolved and you were living the life you wanted, what would be different in your life (miracle question)?

QUESTIONS TO ASK ONESELF (AS A COUNSELOR) FOR SETTING GOALS

- Does the goal address the client's symptoms or problems?
- Does the goal match the client's readiness level for change?
- Is there a good *purpose* for the goal? Is it *reasonable* and *measurable, with a time frame* for completion? Is it *achievable* in the time frame with specifically defined *action steps*?
- Will treatment goals address core issues underlying the problem?

Exercise: Return to Clinical Case Example 4.2 in Chapter 4, and apply the questions above. Answer using case material that was given. Form dyads (or group of students), and discuss possible treatment goals.

CLIENT INPUT: AN ESSENTIAL INGREDIENT TO SUCCESSFUL THERAPEUTIC OUTCOME

Historically, therapy has been regarded as a procedure that has been *done to* or *done for* a client—rather than something *done with* a client. Such misplaced emphasis appears to be a holdover from and a direct result of the historical origins of contemporary therapy in psychoanalysis. Even the name *psycho*therapy is an enduring holdover from the historic days of Freud. The analyst *psychoanalyzed* the client (or patient, as they were known in psychoanalysis). It was the analyst who held the key to successful treatment through conducting an analysis of the client's "free associations," interpreting the client's dreams, working through the client's resistance, and analyzing the transference relationship. The client, or rather patient, came to the therapist, who analyzed his or her condition. Earlier, we discussed the significance of the *patient* being "done to," that is, being put in a somewhat passive relationship to the therapist, as opposed to the *client*, who takes an active role in her or his own life and difficulties. Indeed, the patient's participation in psychoanalysis was limited to producing "free associations"!

Freud, originally trained as a physician, had conducted significant research on cocaine. Medicine at the turn of the 20th century was based on what is called *medical paternalism*. Contemporary therapy grew from that *traditional paternalistic medical model*. Even as late as the 1960s, paternalism was the state of the art in the practice of medicine—a philosophy of "The doctor knows best—don't ask questions—follow my directions—it's doctor's orders—everything will be OK. …" This phenomenon was so profound that it led Cummings[4] (1986) to note,

> It is a propensity of psychotherapy that every patient who walks into a therapist's office receives the type of therapy the psychotherapist has to offer. If the therapist is a Freudian analyst, he or she does not care what the patient has—alcoholism, marital problems, or job problems—that patient is going to get the couch. If the therapist is a Jungian analyst, the patient is going to paint pictures. If the therapist is a behaviorist, the patient is going to get desensitization. (p. 429)

In the past 40 years, researchers like Norcross; Lambert; Miller, Duncan, and Hubble; and their colleagues have conducted revolutionary outcomes therapy research. The central thread running through their research findings has been that it is the *client* rather than the *therapist* who is the primary agent of change in therapy. Although this might seem to be a commonsense statement, it flies in the face of over 80 years of tradition and training that emphasized therapist "techniques" and "skill" as the conditions for *eliciting* client change. Most outcome research, however, has revealed that a client's experience of and participation in the therapeutic endeavor are significant predictors of successful outcome in therapy (Duncan, Miller, & Sparks, 2004; Miller, Mee-Lee, Plum, & Hubble, 2005). Accordingly, as we have advocated, much of the thinking about and informed understanding of the practice of therapy have shifted toward connecting with, engaging, involving, and collaborating with rather than doing something *to* a client that would supposedly produce (i.e., elicit) cognitive and emotional change.[5] Yet, despite this (as mentioned in Chapter 1), the training of therapists has continued to emphasize specific fragmented approaches and techniques, and has pretty much ignored the value of seeking and using feedback from clients to guide the therapeutic process (Miller et al., 2005).

As an indication of the importance of eliciting feedback from a client, consider the therapeutic task of goal setting. In addition to providing an appropriate collaborative structure to the therapy, setting goals that match *a client's needs* also leads to better therapeutic outcomes. According to Miller et al. (2005), "Congruence between a person's beliefs about the causes of his or her problems and the treatment approach results in stronger therapeutic relationships, increased duration in treatment, and improved rates of success" (p. 46). Orlinsky, Grave, and Parks (1994) found that positive client outcomes were associated with how clear the goals of treatment were and the level of counselor–client agreement about treatment goals. Mutually agreed upon goals are more likely to keep clients engaged in the process of therapy

(Miller et al., 2005). We believe this is a function of the convergence of several elements: nonlinear listening and responding, understanding the underlying dynamics of client concerns (i.e., those things a client can't articulate directly such as the double bind she feels or the ambivalence she expresses but doesn't recognize), ascertaining a client's readiness for change, and appreciating particular strengths and resources.

In this chapter, we have demonstrated several ways to elicit client feedback in the assessment of strengths and resources, as well as in the setting of treatment goals. Miller and his colleagues (Miller, Duncan, & Hubble, 1997a), however, have placed the active solicitation of client feedback as a central component of *each and every* therapeutic session. They have found, "Clients whose therapists had access to outcome and alliance information were less likely to deteriorate, more likely to stay longer (e.g., remain engaged) and twice as likely to achieve clinically significant change" (Miller et al., 2005, p. 45). As a result, they have focused on and developed a "client-directed, outcome-informed approach" that actively engages the client as the director of the therapeutic process. Treatment is based on and tailored to a client's needs and wishes for therapy, rather than a fixed, "one-size-fits-all" approach to treatment. In order to accomplish this, a therapist must not only involve a client in the assessment and goal development process, but also conduct an *ongoing* assessment of client perception of and satisfaction with the therapeutic process.

The client-directed, outcome-informed approach is both linear *and* nonlinear in its underlying conceptualization. It is linear in that the *methods* that are used to solicit the client's feedback are, for the most part, straightforward (i.e., a client fills out the instruments, and the results are clear). On the other hand, it is nonlinear in its emphasis of a client's role as not just the primary agent of change but also *the primary source* of treatment effectiveness. This places a client's perceptions of change as the sine qua non of therapy. And yet, even clients who are ambivalent about therapy or are in a precontemplation or contemplation stage of change may not have the same perceptions of (and, hence, goals for) treatment as a therapist or other entities (family members, the justice system, the workplace, etc.). As a result, establishing workable goals for a client, regardless of his stage of change, must focus on his perceptions of change. Even the most chronic psychiatric patients recently released from a long-term care facility can participate in the development of a goal such as "doing whatever it takes to stay out of the hospital." Although such a global goal can be refined (e.g., take medication regularly, develop methods to insure adherence to a medication regimen, and attend supportive aftercare meetings) and may not appear very dynamic, it can be extremely effective.

Hence, learning ways to connect with and engage a client in therapy (Chapters 2 and 3) becomes crucial; and developing a therapeutic relationship (Chapters 6 and 7) and addressing and managing a client's ambivalence for treatment (Chapters 12 and 13) all play important roles in working with a client's perceptions of therapy and developing healthy change.

TREATMENT PLANS

A treatment plan is an overview of the understanding between therapist and client as to the more *formal* agreement that they have. As a *plan*, it is an outline of what both parties can expect: goals, objectives, steps to be taken, time frames, and mechanisms for review. Clinics, inpatient psychiatric hospitals, outpatient treatment centers, substance abuse programs, and so on all require that a *treatment plan* is properly entered in the medical record and updated periodically. In fact, in some settings *multidisciplinary* input is required, for example the Joint Commission on the Accreditation of Healthcare Organizations (JCAHO) or the Commission on Accreditation of Rehabilitation Facilities (CARF).

Specifically, treatment plans cover what type of mental health procedures will be provided (e.g., marital therapy, cognitive behavioral therapy, or group therapy), for what problem, by whom, how often, and the desired goal (e.g., criteria). Formal treatment plans need to be signed and dated by the therapist, and reviewed and updated periodically to make certain they reflect changing client needs.

Treatment plans are meant to keep what happens in treatment on track.[6] As such, a formal treatment plan is a complement to such procedures as eliciting client feedback on therapeutic progress.

WHAT HAPPENS WHEN GOALS DON'T ALIGN?

Despite the best efforts, there are times when a client's goals simply don't align with what the therapist believes the stated goals of treatment to be. When this occurs, it is usually because one or more of the elements presented over the last two chapters have been missed. Consider the following:

- Did the counselor connect with the client (i.e., listen and respond effectively to the client)?
- Did the counselor understand the underlying client dynamics and take into consideration the client's stage of change?
- Were strengths or resources overlooked or underutilized?
- Did the client's goals change during the course of the therapy without the therapist being aware of it?

Answers to such questions are important. For example, if a therapist was too eager to move a client toward a solution when the client demonstrated signs of being a reluctant precontemplator, then that therapist is contributing to the client's resistance. Likewise, if part of a treatment plan requires a client to use undeveloped skills or needs to rely on the support of other unavailable people, then the treatment plan will likely fail. When this happens, a therapist must review the treatment plan and look at the elements within it. Perhaps, the counselor missed an element, or perhaps the client was simply not ready to move forward. Slowing down treatment to review the treatment plan signals to a client that such things are valued—which can strengthen the therapeutic relationship.

Issues in Diversity Box 5.1: "Contextually Cultural"

Developing the expertise of a master practitioner for connecting with and engaging clients in treatment is an art. It is the master practitioner who engages in a lifelong process of learning about human nature, the world we live in, and how to be oneself while relating to a wide spectrum of different individuals. In that process, they learn that all individuals share much in common by virtue of the fact that human beings are social[7] creatures by nature. At the same time, living in different regions of the world, in different climates, and with different geographical conditions, customs, languages, and values, human beings have clustered themselves into racial, ethnic, nationalistic, religious, and tribal groups. These "clusters" make for the development of different customs, values, and cultures (i.e., ways of seeing and doing things) between groups. Given human beings' felt sense of inferiority and natural competitive strivings, ultimately, perceived differences in one's position *above* others (i.e., feeling included and superior) or *below* them (i.e., feeling excluded and inferior) make fertile ground for the development of barriers, discriminations, tensions, and aggressions between groups.

The master practitioner has trained herself to be sensitive to the differences between her own cultural underpinnings and those of the clients she sees in treatment. It is incumbent upon clinicians to keep in check their own biases and simultaneously be open to different values that are represented by different ethnic, racial, cultural, and religious groups. A clinician's own biases can undermine her capacity to connect with and engage a client in treatment. Therapists' fiduciary responsibility to put the interests of their clients above their own interests demands this. The extent to which practitioners can relate to clients from a group different from their own is a function of their flexibility, exposure to different groups, and willingness to learn about others with diverse origins.

Beyond the above fundamental considerations, contemporary research is determining that cognitive processes are affected by people's cultural backgrounds in such areas as "categorization, learning, causal reasoning, and even attention and perception" (Winerman, 2006, p. 64). More specifically, Winerman related,

> Another difference between Westerners and Asians regards the fundamental attribution error—a mainstay of psychological therapy for the last 30 years that, it turns out, may not be so fundamental after all. The theory posits that people generally overemphasize personality-related explanations for others' behavior, while underemphasizing or ignoring contextual factors. So, for example, a man may believe he tripped and fell because of a crack in the side-walk, but assume that someone else fell because of clumsiness. But … most East Asians do not fall prey to this error—they are much more likely to consider contextual factors when trying to explain other people's behavior. In a 1994 study … psychologist Kaiping Peng, PhD analyzed American and Chinese newspaper accounts of recent murders. He found that American reporters emphasized the personal attributes of the murderers, while Chinese reporters focused more on situational factors. (p. 65)

Understanding such enormous subtleties helps therapists connect to clients from backgrounds different from their own. Master practitioners have trained themselves to be exquisitely sensitive to human individuality and its potential for impacting the therapeutic encounter.

SUMMARY

This chapter has outlined the elements of the domain of assessment regarding client needs, strengths, and goals. In many respects, this has become a standard practice in therapy because of the contemporary requirements that managed care insurance companies and other regulatory bodies impose on clinicians and the treatment process. As we have noted, however, there are both linear and nonlinear methods for assessing clients. The master therapist is able to utilize both in order to get the most complete picture of a client and focus for treatment. We contend that practitioners at Level I can become adept at using these methods in order to increase their effectiveness. The key is to remember that the focus must be on and proceed from the client. Perhaps Tallman and Bohart (1999) put it best:

> Clients then are the "magicians" with the special healing powers. Therapists set the stage and serve as assistants who provide the conditions under which this magic can operate. They do not provide the magic, although they may provide means for mobilizing, channeling, and focusing the clients' magic. (p. 95)

Among *the most important means* that master practitioners have for eliciting the healing powers that reside within clients is their *ability to establish a meaningful relationship* with them. Although "connecting with and engaging" a client in the beginning stages of treatment is essential for limiting the chances of a premature termination, establishing and maintaining a positive working therapeutic relationship—*the therapeutic alliance*—are essential for successfully conducting and completing the work of therapy. It is to a discussion of the *therapeutic relationship* that we now turn our attention.

ENDNOTES

1. The reader should note that these subjects (symptoms, psychosocial evaluations, mental status exam, and diagnosis) are each topics for *entire* texts that are beyond the scope of this present text. We present them briefly here as they pertain to the domain of engagement, though more formal and thorough training in these areas is recommended. For example, for a delineation of how to conduct a "clinical interview," see Othmer and Othmer (1994).

2. An "epidural," as it is called, is a regional anesthetic (i.e., it produces numbness to an entire region of the body) and consists of an anesthetic agent being injected into the peridural space of the spine.

3. Please note: It is *never* a good idea to give medical advice if you are not medically trained.

4. Former president of the American Psychological Association.

5. Of course, this does not exclude therapists from the therapeutic endeavor. In fact, they play a crucial role and use the domains of competence and nonlinear thinking to create the conditions for collaboration with the client toward improved functioning or personal change.

6. For more information on treatment planning, see Adams and Grieder (2005).

7. The term *social* when used in this context refers to the fact that human beings live and work in groups and are interdependent upon one another for survival. It also means that human behavior must always be interpreted within its *social context*.

The Domain of Establishing and Maintaining the Therapeutic Relationship and the Therapeutic Alliance

6

Part 1: Relationship Building

CONTENTS

INTRODUCTION

It may seem that the initial domains, connecting with and engaging a client and assessment, are the "basics" of the professional therapist's work. This does not mean that they are not important, or should be overlooked! In fact, mastering the linear and nonlinear elements of these basic domains is crucial to understanding and mastering the domain subject matter of this chapter and the following chapter: establishing a therapeutic relationship and maintaining the therapeutic alliance, respectively.

Although there are many subtle and complex issues related to this topic (e.g., the differences between establishing rapport, developing a therapeutic relationship, and creating a therapeutic alliance), decades of psychotherapy research have identified the *therapeutic alliance*—a therapeutic relationship with specific characteristics—as the significant ingredient of therapy that contributes the most to a successful treatment outcome. As such, the therapeutic alliance, once established, cannot be taken for granted and is vulnerable to rupture. As a result, it is the therapist's responsibility to constantly monitor and maintain the alliance. Throughout this chapter, we discuss how nonlinear thinking is used in order to facilitate rapport, the initiation and maintenance of successful therapeutic relationships, and the therapeutic alliance itself. To set the stage for the *clinical* dimensions of a therapeutic relationship, we first highlight what the research literature says about this domain.

RESEARCH FINDINGS: THE THERAPEUTIC RELATIONSHIP AND THE THERAPEUTIC ALLIANCE

As previously mentioned, Lambert and Barley (2002) summarized available research and concluded that certain variables contributed significantly different percentages[1] to successful outcomes. These factors (and their percentages) are as follows: Expectancy contributes 15%, technique contributes 15%, extratherapeutic change contributes 40%, and common factors contribute 30%. Lambert and Barley carefully pointed out that the data accumulated from psychotherapy research demonstrate that "specific techniques contribute much less to outcome than do important interpersonal factors common to all therapies" (p. 21), such as empathy, warmth, and acceptance. These conclusions are *highly instructional* for the Level I practitioner but also apply to all levels of practitioner. In the absence of confidence and experience, the Level I practitioner is more likely to gravitate toward such things as the use of "techniques" or honing "micro skills" in psychotherapy as an approach to treatment. "Techniques" typically provide an illusion of expertise and control (i.e., "If I do the 'techniques' the 'right way,' then I'll get a positive outcome"), which comforts the Level I practitioner's anxiety. By comparison, developing *a way of thinking* about what is required for effective therapy can be more unfamiliar and uncomfortable. Thus, Level I clinicians may feel less certain that *merely* developing a therapeutic alliance with a client will be effective, *despite* the evidence that those relationship factors contribute twice as much to successful therapy outcomes as techniques. As a result, we will briefly outline the research that has been conducted on this critical domain (i.e., building and maintaining the therapeutic relationship) before discussing its clinical elements.

The literature has traditionally tried to describe the salient qualities of the "common factors" in therapy by referring to the *therapeutic relationship*. Indeed, without a positive therapeutic relationship between client and counselor, nothing significant would be accomplished in therapy. Even though it is a professional engagement between a client and a practitioner, at the core, the therapy relationship is a human encounter. As Orlinsky and Howard (1977) stated, "The inescapable fact of the matter is that the therapist is a *person*, however much he may strive to make himself an instrument of his patient's treatment" (p. 567; emphasis added). It is the personhood of the therapist that the client experiences, evaluates, and reacts to in treatment, seemingly no matter what sort of treatment, theory, or technique the therapist espouses to practice.

As it turns out, perhaps the most powerful predictor of a successful therapeutic outcome is the *client's appraisal* of the therapist's qualities. Lambert and Barley (2002) put it this way:

> In their comprehensive review of more than 2000 process-outcome studies since 1950, Orlinsky, Grave, and Parks (1994) identified several therapist variables that have consistently been shown to have a positive impact on treatment outcome. *"Therapist credibility, skill, empathic understanding, and affirmation of the patient, along with the ability to engage with the patient, to focus on the patient's problems, and to direct the patient's attention to the patient's affective experience, were highly related to successful treatment."*[2] (p. 22; emphasis added)

Hence, it is the *human encounter* with these qualities in the therapist described by Orlinsky, Grave, and Parks (1994) that is exceptionally important in building a therapeutic relationship, as well as determining success in psychotherapy (Hubble, Duncan, & Miller, 1999; Lambert & Okiishi, 1997; Luborsky et al., 1986).

Centorrino et al. (2001) demonstrated how important the therapy relationship is in determining successful treatment outcomes. They investigated factors associated with outpatient mental health treatment compliance (e.g., keeping scheduled clinic appointments) versus noncompliance (e.g., failure to keep appointments, and treatment dropouts). Only three factors contributed to treatment compliance: (a) the perceived warmth and friendliness of the therapist, (b) talking to the client about something that was of importance to the client, and (c) talking to the client in a structured manner. These three (relational) factors were shown to be more important in determining outcome than client diagnosis or demographics. Last, clients who felt that they were going to be *listened* to by a therapist, rather than merely *treated* by a medical professional with medications, were more likely to be compliant (a prerequisite for eventual success in therapy). Lambert and Barley (2002) summarized what this study and others demonstrate:

> 1) Psychotherapy is a successful therapeutic endeavor as determined by an average of 80% of clients [that] are better off than individuals not treated. 2) Studies that compare different therapies support the conclusion that they are relatively equivalent in promoting change in clients. 3) The therapeutic relationship *consistently* is more highly correlated with successful client outcomes than any specialized therapy techniques. Associations between the therapeutic relationship and client outcome are strongest when measured by client ratings of both constructs. (p. 26)

Although the therapeutic relationship has been held up as the *sine qua non* of therapy, what does the literature suggest that the *therapeutic alliance* (i.e., the relationship *in action*, so to speak) contributes to successful outcomes in therapy?

RESEARCH ON THE THERAPEUTIC ALLIANCE

Researchers primarily study the overall effects of particular variables across numerous studies through meta-analysis,[3] which produces an effect size[4] (ES; see Lipsey & Wilson, 1993).[5] As a result, several meta-analyses (and their resulting effect sizes)[6] have been conducted recently on several psychotherapy variables, particularly the therapeutic alliance.

In their meta-analysis of 79 studies of psychotherapy outcome, Martin, Garske, and Davis (2000) determined that the relationship between alliance and outcome is consistent no matter what variables have been proposed as possibly influencing it.[7] They also concluded that the relationship between alliance and outcome seems to represent "a single population of effects." That suggests that there likely aren't any moderator variables[8] that might explain the relationship between alliance and outcome. Furthermore, Martin et al. (2000) suggested that there is a therapeutic and healing effect in the alliance itself, and that if an appropriate alliance is established, a client will experience the relationship as therapeutic *regardless of other psychological interventions.*

Another powerful conclusion from Martin et al. (2000) is that *the strength of the therapeutic alliance* predicts outcome whatever the psychological component underlying the relationship between alliance and outcome. In other words, other variables do not seem to influence the relationship between outcome and alliance. Variables that don't affect the relationship between the outcome and the strength and quality of the therapeutic alliance include the type of measure that is used to evaluate outcome, when during the course of treatment the alliance assessment is taken, the rater making the estimate of the strength of the alliance, and the type of treatment provided. More recently, Horvath and Bedi (2002) summarized 90 outcome (ES) studies conducted between 1976 and 2000 and concluded,

> [I]n the opening phase [of treatment,] the therapist faces the challenge of becoming attuned to the phenomenological experience of the client. It seems clear and well supported by evidence that the client's experience of being allied with the person of the therapist, the ritual of therapy, and with the goals of the therapy process plays not only a statistically but also a clinically significant role in helping the client stay in treatment and in accomplishing positive outcomes … in medium- to long-term therapies, effective treatment [seems] accompanied by a convergence of the client's and therapist's assessment of the alliance … if the therapist has reason to believe that such convergence has failed to occur, it may be a helpful indicator that the therapeutic relation needs more attention … while building a "good enough relation" early in therapy is important, a therapist should not assume that the strength of the relationship will hold throughout treatment. (p. 61)

Horvath and Bedi (2002) made some very important points:

- The alliance is important in facilitating a client staying in treatment and in determining a positive outcome.
- There has to be clear agreement between the client and the therapist about the strength of the alliance.
- The strength of the relationship early on shouldn't be taken for granted.
- Finally, therapists have to pay close attention to the alliance throughout therapy (despite the strength in the beginning).

Finally, Horvath and Bedi provided cautions and limitations regarding the use of techniques in therapy and the linear thinking they imply:

> Meta-analytic investigations of between-therapy effects suggest that the differences due to the kind of treatment offered across different client dysfunctions are modest. In contrast, across a broad variety of treatment approaches and client concerns, the quality of the therapeutic alliance seems to be linked to therapy outcome. (p. 61)

Thus, though the therapeutic alliance has overall moderate statistical support,[9] of the many variables that have been hypothesized to affect therapy outcome, it appears to be a stable and irreducible factor.

In summary, the therapy literature is strongly and consistently suggestive of the following:

- Therapy is effective.
- Supposedly different types of therapy or different theoretical orientations demonstrate no difference in effectiveness between them.
- It is the therapeutic alliance, and not particular therapeutic techniques, that consistently and strongly correlates with successful outcomes.

These results have been consistently reported in various degrees of refinement and span over a considerable span of years (e.g., Bordin, 1979; Fiedler, 1950; Horvath, 2001, 2006; Norcross, 2002b; Rosenzweig, 1936) of empirical and clinical research.

FACTORS THAT CONTRIBUTE TO THE THERAPEUTIC RELATIONSHIP

It is clear from the empirical evidence that a strong relationship resulting in a consistent therapeutic alliance is an important vehicle in determining successful treatment outcomes. But the essentials of *how* to create this alliance are not easily described.

Primarily, a therapeutic alliance is built on a professional therapeutic relationship between a counselor and a client that is created by and imbued with essential human considerations such as trust, mutual respect, optimism, and empathy, to name a few—very much like other relationships in life. No one in the counseling profession has been more directly linked to the importance of the therapeutic relationship than Carl Rogers. He famously proposed that certain conditions were necessary for growth and change to occur in therapy: unconditional positive regard, accurate empathy, and congruence of the therapist (Rogers, 1957). These qualities facilitated removing obstacles that interfered with clients' ability to resolve their problems:

> The most impressive fact about the individual human being seems to be the directional tendency towards wholeness, toward actualization of potentialities. I have *not* found that psychotherapy … [is] effective when I have tried to create in another individual something that is not there, but I have found that if I can provide the conditions that make for growth, that this positive directional tendency brings about constructive results. (Rogers, 1957, quoted in Bien, 2004, p. 493)

Rogers suggested that the way to achieve this is through the *therapeutic relationship*. Indeed, without a relationship between client and counselor, nothing would be accomplished in therapy. Since Carl Rogers, theorists, researchers, practitioners, and Rogers himself have stated that the conditions of therapy and therapists that he articulated (i.e., congruence, accurate empathy, and unconditional positive regard) were necessary but insufficient conditions for change. Yalom (1995) elaborated on conditions necessary for change to include

- the perceived warmth and friendliness of the therapist;
- respect for the client;
- nonjudgmental listening;
- expressed empathy;
- validation;
- self-disclosure;
- confrontation;
- immediacy;
- instilling hope;
- optimism;
- caring; and
- catharsis coupled with insight.

Norcross (2002a), reporting on Division 29 of the American Psychological Association's Task Force on Empirically Supported Therapy Relationships,[10] defined the psychotherapy relationship as "the feelings and attitudes that therapist and client have toward one another, *and the manner in which these are expressed*" (p. 7; emphasis added). These general characteristics have come to be identified under a more global theme as components of the *therapeutic relationship*.

In the following sections, we discuss the salient factors that contribute to a clinical understanding of the therapeutic relationship. Understanding what makes up a therapeutic relationship sets the stage for grasping what a therapeutic alliance is and how it works. We propose to elaborate subtle and discrete distinctions in terms and processes (e.g., rapport, empathy, creating trust, and creating a relationship) that make up a therapeutic relationship and a therapeutic alliance. They are amazingly intertwined, continuous, fluid, and accomplished in a seemingly effortless manner by the master practitioner. Identifying more discrete processes as part of their larger context will facilitate the Level I practitioner's understanding of the domain of establishing and maintaining a therapeutic alliance. We will present exercises designed to have readers reflect on their personal experiences related to relationship building. Furthermore, we believe that no two therapists will create or maintain a therapeutic relationship in the same way. Instead, we present guidelines that readers can practice on their own, with classmates or clients. As with the other domains, there are both linear and nonlinear ways to work within this domain. We begin with a discussion of the precursor to a relationship, namely, *establishing rapport*.

RESONATING TOGETHER: NONLINEAR METHODS OF ESTABLISHING RAPPORT

Before a therapeutic alliance can be formed, a positive working relationship must be formed. In turn, when therapist and client first meet, they have not yet formed a relationship. Although it may appear quite arbitrary, rapport is seen as a precursor to establishing a therapeutic relationship. What is rapport?

An example of a master practitioner demonstrating the art of establishing rapport taken from a popular film may be helpful. In the film *Don Juan DeMarco* (Leven, 1995), Marlon Brando plays an aging psychiatrist who is consulted about a young man wearing a mask, dressed as an 18th-century Spanish nobleman, brandishing a sword atop a billboard, and threatening to jump to his death! The young man, played by Johnny Depp, claims to be the great fictional lover, Don Juan DeMarco. He further declares that he is awaiting the return of another nobleman whom he intends to challenge in order to win back the lost love of his life. Brando introduces himself as Don Octavio De Flores, another Spanish nobleman, and invites Don Juan to come to his "villa" and "await" the return of the nobleman. Don Juan accepts this gentlemanly gesture and agrees to accompany "Don Octavio" to his "villa." The villa, of course, is the state psychiatric hospital where Brando works.

For the remainder of the film, Brando works with Don Juan by having him tell his story, never doubting that Don Juan is who he says he is. In fact, Brando even begins to entertain the possibility that, in some strange way, Depp *could be* Don Juan himself! The result of the accepting relationship that is built between the two is that Don Juan is slowly able to tell Brando the true story of his life, without having to sacrifice his persona. Meanwhile, Brando is able to convince a psychiatric board that Don Juan is not insane and should not be committed.

What does this enchanting film have to do with building rapport and nonlinear thinking? Actually, a great deal! Brando's character is able to use what we have designated as nonlinear thinking to establish rapport with and respond to Depp's Don Juan persona and the nonlinear thinking that the character demonstrates. Although *logical* to Don Juan, the thinking he demonstrates is only *privately logical* (i.e., that he *is* Don Juan, the famous lover from the 18th century, and is awaiting an adversary to fight him for a fair maiden's hand—all the while perched on a modern-day billboard). To the rest of the world, the thinking he demonstrates is not rational or logical. Thus, Don Juan's thinking is nonlinear: not based on straightforward commonsense (i.e., consensually validated) thinking, and rigidly adhered to. As a result, Brando as the therapist must choose between either (a) staying within his own perceptual frame, using consensually validated linear thinking to persuade Don Juan out of his "delusion" and to come down from the billboard; or (b) finding a way to engage, connect with, and meet Don Juan where he is, thus perceiving the world through *his* eyes in order to establish rapport with him. By presenting himself to Don Juan as a Spanish nobleman himself, he chooses the latter path. In choosing to accept Don Juan's frame of reference, Brando has engaged and connected with his client by responding to him in a nonlinear way, as described in Chapter 3.

As a result of choosing to enter Don Juan's perceptual frame, Brando also poses a double bind: If Don Juan says, "Oh come on, you are not Don Octavio, there is no such person, and you do not have a villa. This is the 21st century!" then he has "broken character" and must admit that maintaining he is Don Juan is just an act. If, however, Don Juan accepts that Brando is a nobleman, then he must treat Brando with respect and courtesy as a gentleman. He must listen as well as be heard. By posing the double bind (see Chapter 5), Brando has created conditions that *establish rapport* with Don Juan. Such rapport can lead to a *therapeutic relationship* with him *on terms* acceptable to Don Juan, thus successfully bypassing much potential "resistance."[11] That is, a power struggle could easily erupt over the Don Juan persona issue, resulting in such dialogue as "You are not Don Juan; he doesn't exist." "Oh yeah, I *am* Don Juan, and you can't tell me otherwise." That is, Brando uses nonlinear-thinking processes that mirror Don Juan's exceptionally idiosyncratic nonlinear thinking as a vehicle for achieving therapeutic goals and progress.

What is abundantly clear in the film is that Brando's use of nonlinear thinking renders him eminently more successful than other therapists in the psychiatric hospital who use more linear approaches with Don Juan to no avail. He gave his "permission" for Don Juan to have the symptom (nonlinear thinking) rather than struggle with his client to eradicate it (i.e., linear thinking).

Clinical Exercise 6.1: *Don Juan DeMarco*

1. After reading this entire chapter, rent the film *Don Juan DeMarco*, and note the various ways in which Marlon Brando demonstrates nonlinear thinking in the service of establishing rapport with a man who appears to be "mentally disturbed."
2. Distinguish between the traditional psychiatrists' linear thinking and Brando's nonlinear thinking.
3. Do an analysis of what you believe to be the benefits and shortcomings of both methods of thinking.

The example of *Don Juan* may seem to be an extreme illustration of the use of nonlinear thinking in building rapport. The film is very instructional, however, about ways that nonlinear thinking can be used to quickly and effectively build rapport with clients in a way that encourages a greater likelihood of success in therapy. Horvath and Bedi (2002) reported research that demonstrates one of the major reasons for premature termination is a failure in the therapeutic alliance. That is, on some level (cognitively, emotionally, or relationally), the therapist who failed to connect with and engage the client in the collaborative work of therapy has "lost" a connection with the client (i.e., suffered some form of therapeutic rupture; see Chapter 7). From our perspective, such therapeutic failures can be avoided by appreciating clients' nonlinear thought processes, and working through such thinking and helping clients prepare for change.[12] As we discussed in Chapter 4, the result of misjudging clients' "stage of change" is that therapists use interventions that are essentially more appropriate for another stage of change. Such interactions with clients are likely to result in poor therapeutic outcomes.

BUILDING RAPPORT: VIBRATING TOGETHER

A simple "experiment" from an elementary school science class may also demonstrate what *rapport* is about. If a tuning fork is struck, it vibrates. If the vibrating tuning fork is then moved close to a nonvibrating fork of the same (or similar) frequency, the nonvibrating fork will begin to "resonate" with the frequency of the vibrating fork (without ever directly contacting the vibrating fork). In other words, the vibrations in the air are picked up by the second tuning fork, causing it to vibrate in synch. Consider also the opposite situation, as when a vibrating fork is brought near another tuning fork that does not have a similar frequency—the second fork will barely vibrate or will not vibrate at all.

Clients frequently come for therapy feeling defensive about their circumstances, and a little wary about the therapist or therapeutic process. They may be alert for any indication that the therapist understands them on a deeper level. Procedurally, in order to accomplish this, the therapist must use the linear and nonlinear listening and responding methods outlined in Chapters 2 and 3. A therapist using both linear and nonlinear thought processes acts like a tuning fork that sympathetically vibrates in response to a client and communicates a sense of connection and understanding. Listening for and responding to information or content, feelings, congruence, absence, presence, inference, and resistance all combine to help a client feel more at ease and establish a connection. A therapist who can follow the nonlinear (i.e., privately logical) aspects of a client's thinking processes is more likely to stimulate a client to feel connected and understood.: "You get it. You understand!" Also, the feeling of connectedness occurs simultaneously on the cognitive, relational, and emotional levels. Clients want to know that you are in tune with them!

Rapport in therapy refers to being in synch, harmony, alignment, and accord with one's client. Even a telephone conversation prior to scheduling a first session of therapy is very important in establishing rapport with a client. A pleasant voice and manner, providing appropriate answers to requests for information, being as accommodative as possible to a client's limited availability for an appointment, and patience all contribute to establishing a harmony and alignment between therapist and client. Clinical Case Example 6.1 might help to illustrate the sensitivities related to establishing rapport (i.e., being in synch) that can arise before therapy begins.

Clinical Case Example 6.1: Telephone Contact

An established practitioner returned the phone call of a woman seeking counseling. She left no information about herself or her situation other than stating her *potential* interest in scheduling an appointment. Upon returning her call, the woman indicated that she had Googled the therapist's name on the Internet and discovered his curriculum vitae, which she described as "very impressive." The therapist responded by saying that the publications, presentations, and honorifics noted in the vita were the product of many rewarding years spent in a career. But, he also noted in all honesty and humility that, as impressive as those publications, presentations, and so on may seem, unfortunately, they have nothing at all to do with how one relates to clients or how effective someone is in his or her clinical work.

Unknown to the therapist at that time, the woman turned out to be a physician with many years of experience. She subsequently noted that many physicians have impressive vitae but that she would not refer clients to them because of their manner of relating to and effectiveness with clients. The therapist's acceptance of the woman's compliments while at the same time temporizing them with modesty was "in synch" with her experience—an impressive vita is not necessarily correlated with compassion, acumen, ability to relate to others, or overall effectiveness.[13]

In Clinical Case Example 6.1, the therapist built rapport with the client by linearly listening for the content of what she was saying (i.e., "Your credentials are impressive!") and nonlinearly listening for the *inference* behind her message (i.e., "You *look* competent on paper, but are you competent to relate to me as a person and help me with my problem?"). Many times, in order to establish rapport and an effective therapeutic relationship, a therapist must look beyond the surface meaning of a client's words and statements, even when they seem to be a harmless compliment. Consider for a moment if the therapist, upon hearing that the client was a physician who was familiar with his work, had begun to discuss the latest article or book that he was writing. How might such therapist behavior have affected the development of rapport and the relationship?

FOSTERING RAPPORT AND BUILDING THE THERAPEUTIC RELATIONSHIP

There are numerous dimensions to being therapeutically in synch with one's client. For example, having pleasant surroundings can help a client to feel welcome and comfortable and contribute to the *context* in which rapport can be established. Rapport is not, however, simply a matter of comfortable surroundings and the intuitive "touchy-feely." In fact, there are specific behaviors that facilitate establishing rapport at a very subtle level such as maintaining eye contact; matching one's posture with that of the client; accurately paraphrasing what a client is saying; speaking in easy, natural vocal tones; relating empathically; and even breathing in synch with a client.

Rapport actually has three very specific components—*mutual attention, mutual empathy,* and *coordination or synchrony*—as described by Goleman (2006) from meta-analytic research by Tickle-Degnan and Rosenthal (1990). The first essential correlate of developing the rapport necessary as a precursor for beginning a therapeutic (or any) relationship is *mutual attention*. According to Goleman (2006), "As two people attend to what the other says and does, they generate a sense of mutual interest, a joint focus that amounts to perceptual glue. Such two-way attention spurs shared feelings" (p. 29). The second research-based factor of rapport is *mutual empathy*, which involves a sense of being emotionally present and emotionally responsive. Goleman (2006) differentiated such empathy as different from "social ease"; in the latter, one may be comfortable, but "we do not have the sense of the other person tuning in to our feelings" (p. 29). The third essential factor necessary for rapport is *coordination or synchrony*. Such coordination occurs via the utmost subtlety: Pacing, timing, free flow, and feeling expression are all markers of such subtleties.

Such rapport is a precursor to forming a therapeutic relationship, and an attempt to ensure that the parties are in harmony with one another. It addresses the fundamental question "Can we work together in harmony?" An example of being in synch and connecting with a client can be seen in Clinical Case Example 6.2.

Clinical Case Example 6.2: A Bad Case of Anxiety

A middle-aged woman called for an appointment to see a therapist for a long-standing problem with anxiety. She related that the problem had become so "bad" that she was having an increasingly difficult time leaving her home. Strangely, she arrived for her appointment on time, having driven herself! The therapist's office was rather small but comfortable, well lit, and tastefully decorated. Approximately 15 minutes into the session and apparently not discussing content of any particularly obvious threat, the woman quite suddenly proclaimed that she didn't think she would be able to continue with the session because her anxiety was mounting and becoming intolerable.

Exercise: Before reading on, think about what you might do in this situation. Is what you are thinking indicative of linear or nonlinear thinking? Compare it with the description below.

A linear-thinking approach to Clinical Case Example 6.2 might suggest that the therapist try to calm the woman and talk her out of her anxiety. The therapist instead used nonlinear thinking and suggested a number of options that the two of them could exercise given her sudden and unexplained burst of near panic. The first option that the therapist suggested was that they could abruptly end the session at that moment and reschedule it for the following week.

The nonlinear rationale behind such a suggestion is simple but requires taking the woman's complaint in context and listening for inference and presence. Listening for presence reveals that she is complaining of physical symptoms of anxiety; listening for inference reveals a simple conclusion—that the process of being in the therapist's office and talking about herself "is difficult for me." She has already described that she generally has difficulty in leaving her home, and it is easy to conclude that she expended great effort in driving herself for the therapy appointment alone. At this point, the therapist responded nonlinearly by suggesting that they *could* end the therapy session immediately after only 15 minutes. This would be in keeping with her immediate needs and complaint. By making such a suggestion, the therapist would be in synch with her immediate needs. That would help establish rapport by honoring her present set of circumstances, namely, feeling overwhelmed with anxiety and near panic, and feeling unable to continue with the session. If she chose this route, it means that she would have expended enormous effort (i.e., leaving home, driving herself to the appointment, having to drive back home alone, having to return to the office next week, etc.) with much anxiety and little to show for it, with the prospects of having to repeat the ordeal the following week! In addition, there was the expense of having to reimburse the therapist for the entire session and the next session.

The next alternative suggested by the therapist was to take a few minutes' "break" from the session, perhaps make a trip to the restroom and see how she felt after the break. A third alternative proposed was to open the door to the office so that there might be some exposure to the hallway and "let some air into the room."[14]

There was a brief pause after the client heard the therapist's suggestions, and the woman said she thought she could make it through the remainder of the session. The rest of the session was largely uneventful. In subsequent weeks, the woman made improvements in her condition and changed from needing weekly sessions to biweekly and then monthly visits. In several months, she was symptom free.

Was the woman unconsciously "testing" the therapist to determine if he would be intolerant of her demanding symptomatic behavior as her family members had become? Or, was the therapist respecting her personhood by offering her several choices regarding how she might cope with her anxiety at the moment? Providing her with choices stimulated a sense of control and freedom, rather than linearly prescribing a "textbook" relaxation exercise.[15] The answer will never be certain, but it is clear that the therapist kept himself in synch with the woman's immediate needs while simultaneously understanding the context in which they arose. Being respectful of her and honoring her need to perhaps end the session prematurely comprised an important step in establishing rapport, empathy, and acceptance. That respect facilitates the development of a strong therapeutic relationship so that the woman and her therapist could collaborate well together to help resolve her anxiety.

Specifically *listening* for the issues that relate to a client's theme or "underlying dynamics" (e.g., "None of these problems I'm having are my fault") and stage of change (SOC; see Chapter 5, Clinical Example 5.4)—for example, "I'm not really sure why I'm here," "I might have a problem," and "I've had issues like this before, and I want to nip this in the bud"—provides an enormous advantage to the practitioner in establishing rapport. As previously discussed (see Chapters 2 and 3), *where* a client is at in the stages of change process helps to guide comments: "So, if I understand you correctly, I can see how you *really feel* that you haven't done anything to be getting all of this flack" or "I can see how really *blameless* you feel about this situation while others are definitely pointing the finger at you!" Such verbalizations in response to a client's specific dynamics or SOC demonstrated (e.g., the client does not believe that he has a problem—and thus is in the precontemplation stage) is very effective in establishing rapport and validating the client. Notice that the client feels validated as a person (i.e., feels valued even though troubled). The therapist, as a person, is validating the client. It is an exchange that says, "I see your point of view!" It also says, "I, as a therapist and authority figure, am not going to impose *my* point of view on you." Such validation is fundamental to the process of establishing rapport, a therapeutic relationship, and ultimately an alliance that allow the work of therapy to be accomplished successfully.

Clinical Exercise 6.2: Building Rapport

Building rapport and the therapeutic relationship is dependent on a person's individual style or preferences when confronted with new situations and people. Preferred style determines the methods that someone uses most often to establish rapport with others. Examining *your* preferences may be helpful in discovering how you might try to make other people feel at ease. Take a moment to think about some situations recently when you have had to interact with people who you didn't know.

1. Did you feel comfortable or uncomfortable? Why?
2. What did you do to reduce any discomfort? What did others do to reduce your discomfort?
3. Can you identify some specific aspects of *rapport* in which you engaged as a vehicle for establishing a meaningful relationship?
4. Identify a specific encounter with someone in which you felt decidedly "not in synch."
5. What elements of that encounter can you now identify as prompting you to feel "out of synch"?

Because it is the client who is consulting and paying for the therapist's services, it is professionally incumbent and obligatory upon the therapist to adapt her behavior to make certain that she is in synch with the client. Rapport, however, is a precursor to change, and a preliminary element of the domain of establishing and maintaining the therapeutic relationship. In Chapters 2 and 3, we briefly introduced the concept of empathically *listening* and *responding to feelings* for the purposes of establishing rapport as a foundation for a therapeutic relationship. We now elaborate on empathy, both the concept and how it relates to establishing a relationship and the therapeutic alliance at different levels of therapist development.

EMPATHY

The term *empathy* is used a lot when discussing the processes of counseling; however, little time is typically taken to thoroughly examine its complexities. In fact, Level I of counselor development is an ideal time to learn that the essence of empathy is multidimensional. It may be relatively easy to intuitively understand the importance of being empathic and expressing it sensitively in establishing and maintaining the therapeutic relationship. On the other hand, a master practitioner understands that it is the level of empathy perceived by the *client* that is the deciding factor, regardless of how the therapist thinks he may be expressing it. Several authors (Johnson, 1995; Miller, Mee-Lee, Plum, & Hubble, 2005) recommend that client perceptions of counselor empathy should be frequently evaluated, even as often as at the end of each session.

Clinical Exercise 6.3: A Lesson in Empathy!

- Generate your own definition of *empathy*. In your definition, describe its importance in therapy (if any).
- In a small group, discuss the different definitions of *empathy*, and develop a common definition.
- Brainstorm ideas for discussion and the design of a perceived empathy or relationship scale of 5 to 10 items that could be administered to a client after a therapy session.
- Last, share your group's definition and instrument with the rest of the class.

A *linear expression of empathy* would be to tell someone in a monotone, "I understand what you are going through," or to merely verbatim repeat or parrot feelings that the client had just expressed with no further imaginative texture.[16] But such an expression would be devoid of genuine feelings. It would result in the client *not* feeling the sense that "this person knows what I've been experiencing" (i.e., the client does not feel *in synch* with the therapist). Master practitioners understand that empathy is an art. They transform mere client facts, experiences, and expressions into the transmission of a common bond by conveying truly shared *meaning*. Telling someone, "I understand," can, in fact, at times be countertherapeutic! Some narratives told in therapy defy understanding, such as experiences of the horrors of war, childhood sexual abuse, rape, or the loss of a child.

When clients relate their incredibly tragic experiences, double binds (such as in *Sophie's Choice*),[17] losses, and the like, comments such as "I can't imagine what it was like for you to discover ..." "You must have been totally overwhelmed and exhausted when ..." "It must have seemed as though it would never end. ..." and "It's as though a bomb has gone off in your life. ..." *can be helpful*. They convey in a non-linear way (i.e., the opposite of saying, "I know how you feel") a sense that the therapist is sensitive to and grasps as closely as possible the essence and substance of the terrible nature of what the client experienced without the therapist having gone through the very same experience. When the therapist relates in such a manner, the client's unconscious reckoning is "Yes! That's it! That's how I feel—like no one could know what it was like to go through such a horrible thing."

Ultimately, as a master practitioner, the therapist's goal in empathy is to use nonlinear processes to *see* things that aren't said, *hear* things that aren't seen, and *feel* things that are ethereal (e.g., *listening* and *responding to absence*). Sometimes, however, the best response that a therapist has to convey is to say, "I *couldn't possibly know* how you feel. ..." On the surface, this seems like the *opposite* of empathy, but from a nonlinear perspective it conveys that you understand a client has experienced something so profound and tragic that it is something beyond the counselor's ability to grasp.

Nonlinear thinking provides still another way of understanding *empathy*, namely, by looking at its opposite. Challenges to a client's sense of being worthwhile, disbelieving the client, negating her feelings, and relating to the client in a "plastic" manner (i.e., with little feeling or personal regard) are all manifestations of a lack of *empathy*, or (at the very least) of rapport that is being eroded. When this happens, the foundation for the development of resistance or premature termination (both evidence of poor therapeutic outcomes) is set. To treat a client's experience casually or to assume an understanding of what a client is feeling can be devastating to the relationship. We cite Clinical Case Example 6.3 to illustrate.

Clinical Case Example 6.3: A Mother in Distress

A mother in her 50s was attending to her critically ill, unconscious son in an intensive care unit. Her son, a formerly brilliant, vibrant, and successful man in his mid-20s, had been reduced to clinging to life by a rare illness. Multiple surgeries, innumerable instances of being placed on a ventilator, and exotic and powerful steroidal medications with profound side effects were all part of his daily routine only to be succeeded by the next life-threatening crisis. This had gone on for *several years*. An experienced mental health practitioner[18] was called to evaluate the client for a possible change in the young man's anticonvulsive medication. Not knowing the background of the client, the psychiatrist asked the client's mother about her unconscious son's history. She related a gut-wrenching, condensed version of the "facts" as tears welled in her eyes. She then expressed how helpless and frustrated she felt at not being able to help her son, especially with the very real prospects of death looming daily for 3 indescribably long years. At that point, the well-meaning practitioner replied, "I know how you feel."

Later, as the mother related the experience to her therapist, she stated her reaction to the psychiatrist's comment as "How *dare* he tell me after 5 minutes of listening that he knows how I feel!"

The vignette in Clinical Case Example 6.3 conveys a powerful example of how important it is to be cautious when putting oneself in the shoes and skin of another human being who is experiencing unimaginable circumstances. Can we *really imagine* what it would be like to have one's adult child suffering over a period of years and routinely facing death? Obviously, the mother felt her experience had been trivialized. The professional made an attempt at *linear* empathy, and it turned the mother away from the practitioner rather than toward him. One of the authors has worked extensively with family members who have had a loved one killed by homicide or suicide. The tremendously painful emotions such clients felt and experienced are extreme, to say the least (working through emotional issues like this will be discussed in Chapters 10 and 11). But, despite having specialized training in complicated, traumatic grief, the therapist did not have the personal experience of having a direct family member die by suicide or homicide. The therapist could either attempt to empathize linearly by drawing on the experience of losing loved ones to illness and old age, or acknowledge that he did not have these experiences, but would be guided by the client's experiences. In every instance, when disclosing that he had not had that experience, family members would express gratitude that the therapist would not try to tell them that he "knew how they felt." A seemingly counterintuitive nonlinear approach to empathy actually fosters a therapeutic relationship.

Nonlinear thinking also reveals empathy to be something other than one-dimensional. Bachelor (1988) noted that empathy is perceived and experienced in different ways. For certain clients, a therapist expressing what the client "felt" was experienced (i.e., "received") as empathy. On the other hand, other clients believed that the therapist feeling what the client was relating was most meaningful and empathic. Still other clients experienced a nurturing response or the therapist disclosing some personal information as empathic. Specifically what constitutes an empathic response for a client is as yet unknown. But, it is clear that empathy is best understood in nonlinear ways rather than the linear understanding of "one size (i.e., type) of empathy fits all."

Brain in a Box 6.1: The Brain, Empathy, and Culture

There is no question that functional magnetic resonance imaging (fMRI) technology has made diagnosis in medicine much more precise. Use of fMRI has made it possible to unravel more and more secrets of brain functioning more quickly than the more traditional methods of neuroscientists in the past (e.g., LeDoux, 1998). Literally no area of brain functioning has eluded study, including human empathy.

Gibson (2006) described empathy as not only a "basic human impulse" that has affected "the course of history, culture and personal connections" but also a "neurological fact" (p. 34) whose secrets are being divulged through the focused study of neuroscience. As an example, Jackson, Meltzoff, and Decety (2005) studied one component of human empathy, namely, the "interpersonal sharing of affect" (p. 771). Subjects in their study were shown a series of still pictures "of hands and feet in situations likely to cause pain" and a matched set of control pictures devoid of any discernible painful events. They were then requested to evaluate online what they believed to be the pain level of the person in the pictures. Jackson et al. (2005) found that there were significant bilateral changes in the brain's electrical and metabolic activity in a number of areas, including the anterior cingulate, the anterior insula, the cerebellum, and to a somewhat lesser degree the thalamus when subjects were asked to evaluate (from pictures) the pain level of people whose hands and feet were in situations likely to cause pain. From previous research, it is known that these same regions of the brain participate significantly in pain processing. They also observed that the subjects' ratings of others' pain was strongly correlated with activity in the anterior cingulate. They concluded that there is *an overlapping of areas in the brain that process perceptions of pain in others and experiences of our own pain.* The brain is inherently sensitive to the differences between our own and someone else's pain.

In another study, Jackson, Brunet, Meltzoff, and Decety (2006) proposed, "When empathizing with another individual, one can imagine how the other perceives the situation and feels as a result. To what extent does imagining the other differ from imagining oneself in similar painful situations" (p. 752). Once again, participants were given pictures of people with their hands or feet in painful or nonpainful circumstances with directions to "imagine and rate the level of pain perceived from different perspectives," namely, those of both the self and other. Both perspectives yielded the activation of portions of the neural network that have been demonstrated in pain processing, including the parietal operculum, anterior cingulated cortex, and anterior insula. But, the self-perception of being in painful circumstances versus the other person being in pain also yielded differences in the areas of the brain that were activated. Jackson et al. (2006) concluded not only that there are similarities between the self's and others' pain but also that there are distinct and "crucial" differences: "It may be what allows us to distinguish empathic responses to others versus our own personal distress. These findings are consistent with the view that the empathy does not involve a complete 'Self-Other' merging" (p. 752).

Lydialyle Gibson (2006) did an extensive interview of Jean Decety, one of the neuroscientist coinvestigators of the studies cited above, who said that the implications of these findings for therapists are not casual:

> [E]mpathy requires emotional control—the capacity to distinguish self from other. People who lose themselves in other people's pain … experience "personal distress." While empathy is "other-oriented," personal distress turns inward. It drowns the impulse to assist. "If you are in the same state of distress, I don't know how you can help the other person," Decety says. "But if you are able to separate yourself, then *the non-overlap in the neural response frees up processing capacity in the brain for formulating an appropriate action.*" (p. 36; emphasis added)

Other questions still abound regarding the neuroscience of empathy, as suggested by Gibson (2006). For example, does it correlate with age? Are there sex differences? Does empathy transcend the boundaries of one's race, ethnicity, or culture? As Peng and Nisbett (1999) have demonstrated, human beings from Chinese versus European and American cultures *reason* differently about such things as "contradiction": The former culture tends to be accepting of polarities, whereas the latter cultures tend to take one side or the other. By extrapolation, do cultures differ regarding the processing of emotions?

Empathy requires the discipline of separating oneself from another person's pain in order to be maximally effective. Perhaps an effective mechanism for realizing this separation is as we have noted in this text—it is important to empathize with the plight of the person, that is, what would it be like to be in their given set of circumstances? But it becomes equally important not to identify with them according to a self-statement that proclaims, "I feel just like Jane does in *my* marriage!"

TRUST, VULNERABILITY, AND FIDUCIARY OBLIGATIONS

Trust is at the core of *any* relationship—especially a treatment relationship. In our culture, however, few people appear to trust car dealers, politicians, lobbyists, or lawyers. Indeed, the proliferation of affairs in marriage and the erosion of trust in leaders of all sorts have led many individuals to feel far from trusting.

A *professional relationship* is based upon the concept of a professional person having a specialized knowledge and set of skills to perform particular services. The consumer *trusts* (i.e., has faith) that the professional person they consult has the education, training, requisite skills, knowledge, and judgment to effectively provide the services desired. In turn, *moral obligations* develop from the relationship a professional person has with a client due to the responsibilities incurred on behalf of a client. The professional individual acts in a *fiduciary* capacity in which the *client's interests* are her primary concern. That is the essence of the word *fiduciary*—the obligation to put a *client's interests* before one's own interests. The client has *confidence* (i.e., trusts) that *the client's interests* will be *the primary concern* of the professional person, and *not the professional person's personal interests*. This is certainly the case regarding the client–practitioner relationship in therapy.

It is essential to note that therapy clients represent a vulnerable group. They are vulnerable because of multiple factors. Among other things, clients come to therapy anxious, dejected, depressed, feeling hopeless, sleep deprived, immobilized, unable to make decisions, confused, unable to think clearly, suicidal, homicidal, and on and on. Such states of mind in many instances have a biological (i.e., brain-based) component that compounds clients' vulnerability. Given this, a vast power imbalance exists between client and therapist that renders a client *vulnerable to exploitation*. Credentialing (i.e., the processes of schools, professions, professional organizations, and state regulations for certification and licensure) represents attempts to protect the unsuspecting and vulnerable public from exploitation by unqualified, unscrupulous, and predatory others.

One of the most important ways for a therapist to make certain that he or she maintains ethical and fiduciary obligations to a client is by honoring the implicit and explicit *boundaries* of the therapy relationship.

Clinical Exercise 6.4: Violations of Trust

1. Can you identify a violation of trust that you (or someone that you know) experienced in a professional relationship?
2. What was the emotional impact of that violation?
3. What criteria do you use to guide whether or not you can trust someone?
4. How accurate is your barometer of trust?

> 5. What course of action(s) did the violations of trust prompt?
> 6. What are the processes and mechanisms by which trust is reestablished?

RESPECT, CARING, POSITIVE REGARD, AND LIKING

As noted in Chapters 4 and 5, therapists are required to "assess" (i.e., evaluate) clients. But, it is important to note that therapists must be aware of and carefully distinguish between assessing a client's symptoms, complaints, and clinical and life circumstances and the *personhood* of a client. Regardless of the bizarreness, peculiarity, or severity of clinical and symptomatic features that a client presents, it is incumbent upon the therapist to convey a sense of *respect for a client's personhood*. There are three reasons for such respect: Human beings inherently deserve respect; respect for *personhood* is a core element in building a therapeutic relationship and a nonnegotiable expectation that therapists must fulfill; and we note emphatically that if therapists presume to evaluate clients, clients are also indisputably evaluating their therapists.

The evaluations a client makes of his therapist are generally of two kinds. The first has to do with the therapist's competence. Competence has to do not only with a therapist's professional qualifications but also with a client's belief in the therapist's ability to be helpful. That is, a therapist may have wonderful professional credentials and "look good on paper," but if a client doesn't believe in the person with those credentials, a credibility gap exists that can significantly impinge upon the ultimate effectiveness of a therapeutic relationship. The work of Miller et al. (2005) on the importance of clients providing feedback to therapists about satisfaction with their therapy is precisely the sort of evaluation clients make with or without formal feedback.

The second evaluation that a client makes of the therapist has to do with respect, caring, and liking. That is, a client "reads" the therapist and asks herself, "Does this therapist *really* respect, care about, and like me—or is this therapist judging me?" People "reading" one another and situations are an inescapable part of human functioning and reflective of how the brain works in making its intuitive emotional appraisals. LeDoux (1998) has described this well:

> The concept of appraisal was crystallized by Magda Arnold in an influential book on emotion. … She defined appraisal as the mental assessment of the potential harm or benefit of a situation and argued that emotion is the "felt tendency" toward anything appraised as good or away from anything appraised as bad. *Although the appraisal process itself occurs unconsciously*, its effects are registered in consciousness as an emotional feeling … once the appraisal outcome is registered in consciousness as a feeling, it becomes possible to reflect back on the experience and describe what went on during the appraisal process. This is possible because … people have introspective access to [conscious awareness of] the inner workings of their mental life, and in particular access to the causes of their emotions. … Appraisal remains the cornerstone of contemporary cognitive approaches to emotion. (pp. 50–51; emphasis added)

This is exactly what a client does in the setting with a therapist. He is reading or appraising unconsciously whether or not he feels a tendency toward his therapist as "good" or away from his therapist as "bad." The "good" and "bad" referred to are not moral judgments but elemental intuitive appraisals made by the inner workings of the limbic system in the midbrain.

Respecting, caring about, and liking someone are conveyed as part of a significant body of information that is exchanged between client and therapist at a nonverbal level. What does it mean to "care" about another human being? It means that a therapist is concerned for his or her welfare and above all is respectful. Sincerity in caring about clients is essential and achieved via the congruence discussed in Chapter 2. Sincerity and caring cannot be "faked." If they are, sooner or later they will be exposed. The foundations for sincerity and genuine caring are found in empathy, that sense of asking oneself, "What would it be like to be in this client's shoes?" Caring about clients, however, does not suggest that the cautions regarding boundaries and dual roles be disregarded for the sake of caring. It is possible to convey a genuine sense of caring for one's clients *and* be a guardian of appropriate boundaries.

It thus is incumbent upon therapists to act in accord with clients' interests. But, can an egalitarian relationship exist between client and therapist? The answer is, of course, that client and therapist are of *equal worth* and each is deserving of equal respect from the other. The power, prestige, status, and success of a therapist's position, however, can distort and erode that sense of equal worth. Therapists must disavow exercising any "power" of their office such as superior authority, superior knowledge, "correct" decision making, and knowing "what's best," which can easily render a client feeling arbitrarily diminished.

Liking a client may in some instances be difficult because clients can engage in very disagreeable behaviors. One way of helping Level I therapists to deal with the issue of liking a client who demonstrates such disagreeable behaviors is to understand the difference between a client's behavior and his or her personhood. Some therapists may find it difficult to work with certain types of clients (e.g., antisocial personality, borderline, or narcissistic personality disorders), and yet other therapists not only treat and enjoy working with such clients but also specialize in treating them.

OPTIMISM AND HOPE

Perhaps one of the most famous and ominous phrases from all classical literature comes from *The Divine Comedy of Dante Alighieri* (1321/1805). As Dante and his guide, the poet Virgil, are about to traverse the gates of hell and begin their journey, Dante notes a sign over the gates that reads, "All hope abandon, ye who enter here." The tenor of this brief sentence is indeed truly menacing. In the final analysis, therapists offer their clients, many of whom face overwhelming life circumstances, a sense of hope. However, although a therapist may offer a sense of hope that a client's condition and circumstances can be improved, a therapist must also be careful to avoid making outrageous and irresponsible promises or "guarantees" of success. Such "guarantees" not only are prohibited by codes of ethics but also defy sound principles of therapy.

Although clients are often very modest in terms of what they expect from therapy, Kirsch and Lynn (1999) have pointed out,

> [I]t has long been recognized that positive expectancies about treatment outcome play an important role in stimulating behavioral change in psychotherapy ... virtually all schools of psychotherapy acknowledge the importance of bolstering positive expectancies to maximize treatment gains and minimize noncompliance ... behavior therapists have been most explicit with regard to specifying tactics and strategies for enhancing and shaping clients' positive expectancies. ... Goldfried and Davison (1976) catalogue a variety of expectancy-enhancing maneuvers. These include alluding to similar clients who have achieved success, assigning relevant literature, encouraging clients to recognize that pessimistic attitudes are unrealistic, and singling out a readily changeable behavior to maximize optimism about positive therapeutic outcomes. (p. 511)

Therapist encouragement can reasonably convey and instill belief that a client's condition and circumstances *can* improve. Even under dire clinical circumstances, a therapist's attitude that conveys, "Let's put our heads together and see what we can work out," goes a long way toward instilling hope without making outrageous predictions of client success. Conveying hope must also take into consideration the particular SOC in which a client enters treatment. For example, if a client is in a precontemplation SOC and thus isn't certain that she has a problem, care must be exercised in the messages conveyed. With a client who doesn't believe that she has a problem—or *any* client—a message that states, "You have a problem, but it's OK—I can fix it," is hardly warranted.

Perhaps Kirsch and Lynn (1999) summarized the role of optimism and hope best: "A variety of different therapeutic approaches, either implicitly or explicitly, harness the power of expectancies to establish, shape, and fulfill treatment goals" (p. 513). The Level I practitioner is well advised to heed such an observation, which implies the clinical utility of *all* therapies regardless of theory or technique.

CONCLUSION

Thus far in this domain, we have discussed the basic ingredients for building a therapeutic relationship, as well as their demonstrated importance in achieving effective therapy. We next turn to a discussion of how the therapeutic relationship becomes a working alliance between the client and the counselor, and how this alliance is used to bring about therapeutic change.

ENDNOTES

1. The percentages derived *were not* formally derived as a result of meta-analytic techniques but "characterize the research of a wide range of treatments, patient disorders, dependent variables representing multiple perspectives of patient change, and ways of measuring patient and therapist characteristics as applied over the years. These percentages are based on research findings that span extremes in research designs, and are especially representative of studies that allow the greatest divergence in the variables that determine outcome. The percentages were derived by taking a subset of more than 100 studies that provided statistical analyses of the predictors of outcome and averaging the size of the contribution each predictor made to final outcome" (Lambert & Barley, 2002, p. 18).

2. It is noteworthy that these are similar to several of the domains common to all effective therapies presented in this text.

3. Meta-analysis is a research procedure that examines all (or many) *research studies* conducted on a particular topic (e.g., psychotherapy outcomes). Thus, the different studies serve as the "subjects" to be sampled in the investigation, and the data from these studies are analyzed similarly to data in other quantitative studies.

4. *Effect size* is the term used to describe a class of indices *whose function is to calculate the magnitude of a particular treatment effect*. It differs from a test of significance in that ES indices are statistically independent of the size of the sample studied. In today's psychotherapy outcome studies, ESs are the measures derived from the meta-analysis of studies to describe *how much* influence a particular treatment variable (e.g., the therapeutic alliance) under investigation has on outcome.

5. See Lipsey and Wilson (1993) for a thorough discussion of the use of meta-analysis in psychological research.

6. There are a number of different formulas for determining effect size.

7. They found an overall ES of .22, which is generally considered to be a modest, though significant, effect.

8. A moderator variable is any variable that can affect the strength of the relationship between two variables. For example, if the therapeutic relationship was stronger for women than men, then sex would be a moderator variable (see Baron & Kenny, 1986, for a more thorough discussion).

9. Horvath and Bedi (2002) reported a median ES of .25, similar to Martin et al.'s (2000) finding. Again, this is a modest, though significant, effect.

10. In doing so, they adopted Gelso and Carter's (1985, 1994) definition of the therapeutic relationship.

11. This is the sort of nonlinear thinking and intervention that will be discussed in Chapter 7. Such interventions set the stage for good therapeutic work to be done (instead of writing off the client as "difficult" or untreatable).

12. Working through, processing, and learning about *nonlinear-thinking* ways of dealing with *clients'* nonlinear-thinking processes and other issues will be discussed in Parts 3 and 4.

13. More about the topics of compliments and criticism of a therapist will be addressed at Parts 3 and 4.

14. The therapist's office was in a very low-traffic end corridor of the building, and few people ever came that way at that particular time of day except for a scheduled appointment with the therapist.
15. This is not to say that relaxation techniques are not useful interventions, but in this case it would have been linear and ineffective.
16. This is perhaps what had allegedly led Carl Rogers to say that he would never be a Rogerian (source unknown).
17. A novel written by William Stryon (1979) and produced as a movie of the same name. The lead character (played in the movie by Meryl Streep, who won an Academy Award for her performance) requests clemency from a certain death sentence from a Nazi concentration camp officer for her son and her daughter. She is granted the clemency and is then told she must instantly choose which of the two that she wishes to save! If she doesn't choose instantly, they will all die in the gas chamber.
18. Not one of the authors.

The Domain of Establishing and Maintaining the Therapeutic Relationship and the Therapeutic Alliance

7

Part 2: *The Therapeutic Alliance*

CONTENTS

INTRODUCTION

As described in Chapter 6, establishing rapport, trust, caring, congruence, warmth, and so on are all important characteristics of a therapeutic relationship. Admittedly, they are also linked, overlapping, and sometimes indistinguishable from one another. But, differentiating these qualities provides a refined way of looking at components that comprise the complexity and richness inherent in a therapy relationship. These qualities are always in the service of establishing and maintaining a *therapeutic alliance*, and that is *the* key variable leading to successful treatment outcomes as defined by clients. But exactly what is a *therapeutic alliance*?

THE THERAPEUTIC ALLIANCE

Like many concepts in psychotherapy, it is difficult to arrive at a consensus definition of a therapeutic alliance. Drawing on 20th-century history, during World War II, Britain and the United States formed an *alliance* to defeat the Axis powers. In this alliance, they agreed to share their strengths and ally their efforts toward the goal of winning the war. They planned their troop movements and battle strikes as joint enterprises. As a result of working together cooperatively (though not always harmoniously), they were able to fight a war on several continents throughout the world and gain total victory. Martin, Garske, and Davis (2000) approached their study of the *therapeutic alliance* by acknowledging the diversity of "alliance conceptualizations" (which seems to match our historical exemplar) and concluded that:

> most theoretical definitions of the alliance have three themes in common: (a) the collaborative nature of the relationship, (b) the affective bond between patient and therapist, and (c) the patient's and therapist's ability to agree on treatment goals and tasks. (p. 439)

Although the concept of a therapeutic alliance (working alliance or helping alliance) appears to loom large as an important variable in determining successful outcomes across different forms of treatment, Horvath and Bedi (2002) carefully pointed out that the term still seems to lack a universally accepted definition. In an attempt to encapsulate prior theoretical work (e.g., Barber, Connolly, Crits-Christoph, Gladis, & Siqueland, 2000; Bordin, 1979, 1994; Horvath, 2001; Martin et al., 2000) and convey what appears to be a consensus clinical definition of the term *therapeutic alliance* emerging in the literature, Horvath and Bedi proposed the following definition:

> The alliance refers to the quality and strength of the collaborative relationship between client and therapist in therapy. This concept is inclusive of: the positive affective bonds between client and therapist, such as mutual trust, liking, respect, and caring. Alliance also encompasses the more cognitive aspects of the therapy relationship; consensus about, and active commitment to, the goals of therapy and to the means by which these goals can be reached. Alliance involves a sense of partnership in therapy between therapist and client, in which each participant is actively committed to their specific and appropriate responsibilities in therapy, and believes that the other is likewise enthusiastically engaged in the process. The alliance is a conscious and purposeful aspect of the relation between therapist and client: It is conscious in the sense

that the quality of the alliance is within ready grasp of the participants, and it is purposeful in that it is specific to a context in which there is a therapist or helper who accepts some responsibility for providing psychological assistance to a client or clients. (p. 41)

This definition for a therapeutic alliance can serve as a useful template and clinical guide for the Level I therapist—a conceptually useful starting point for understanding and working with a client to develop a therapeutic alliance. With experience, understanding of the sentiment of the definition hopefully becomes an automatic disposition that is expressed in the art and science that is therapy. The definition is not formulaic and must ultimately be integrated into one's thinking (both linear and nonlinear) about therapy and behavior. Clinical Case Example 7.1 illustrates the challenges of establishing a therapeutic alliance.

Clinical Case Example 7.1: Husband Versus Wife Over Internet Porn

A middle-aged man and his wife entered couples therapy after the wife discovered him seeking pornography on the Internet. He complied with her request that he leave the family home due to how intolerably upset she was with his behavior after many years of marriage. While living alone, the man spent many lonely hours in a tiny apartment committed to writing a diary of his thoughts, his feelings, and things that he apparently wanted to talk about with his wife. Keeping a diary had been recommended to him by another therapist. When the husband brought the notebook to therapy to discuss its issues with his wife, she expressed considerable trepidation regarding whether or not she wanted to do so.

In discussing the contents of the notebook, the husband revealed that there were many sexual fantasies that he wanted to present to his wife. It was abundantly clear that the wife cringed at any such discussion because she had been sexually abused in childhood. In terms of the stages of change, the wife was between the contemplation and preparing for action phases, whereas the husband was in the action stage. They appeared stalemated.

Questions: Before reading further, consider the following questions.

1. What are the issues presented in this case?
2. How can the therapist intervene in a way that preserves the therapeutic alliance?

In Clinical Case Example 7.1, the therapist suggested that perhaps he could look at the diary and then offer a suggestion as to whether or not discussion of the material was presently relevant to what they had described originally as their problem. Upon reviewing the manuscript before their next therapy session, the therapist determined that a discussion of the material had the potential to lead treatment in an unfruitful direction—a therapeutic "rabbit hole."[1] The diary was largely filled with very pornographic, titillating, and very explicitly lewd fantasies. A frank discussion of such material would not have been very productive, especially in the light of the wife's stage of change (i.e., felt sense of unpreparedness).

On the other hand, the therapist reviewing the diary accomplished several therapeutic objectives: (a) He legitimized and honored *the husband's* desire to introduce the material into the therapy, and by reviewing it, the therapist was acknowledging, validating, and respecting the husband's wishes that the material be introduced into the therapy; (b) it honored the wife's felt sense of unpreparedness to deal with such issues and her sensitivities about them as a victim of childhood sexual abuse; and (c) it provided the therapist with an understanding of the husband as an excitement-seeking individual whose lifelong pursuit of exciting adventures (e.g., sky diving, scuba diving, drugs, alcohol, a high-"stress" and fast-paced professional career, and pornography) had often exposed him to very dangerous situations sought for the "rush" they produced. That understanding of the husband proved advantageous for both him and his wife in the treatment that followed. Many of the husband's other "exciting" pursuits became much more understandable to him and his wife. At the same time, introducing the material in the diary into the therapy did not prove to be a distraction from the larger issue at hand, namely, helping the couple to reconnect and once again build on the positive and successful relationship that they had had for many years. Refraining from a frank discussion of the fantasy material also helped the alliance with the wife, who was clearly not prepared for any such discussion. In the meantime, with the help of the therapist, the couple demonstrated an ability to talk about talking about a problem in a nonconflictual way—a desirable therapeutic outcome.

This is a couple that had problems talking to one another about other issues, let alone discussing sexual fantasies. But, both spouses felt that the therapist had not taken sides. The husband had the material introduced and respected by the therapist as potentially valuable in providing a greater understanding of some of his concerns; the wife felt respected by not having to discuss material that she was far from prepared to discuss. Hence, the alliance with both was preserved.

THE THERAPEUTIC ALLIANCE IN ACTION

What specific clinical suggestions can we make regarding the strengthening of the therapeutic alliance? Using Horvath and Bedi's (2002) definition—(a) positive affective bond, (b) cognitive factors, (c) a consensus on goals, (d) collaborative in nature, and (e) conscious and purposeful—we suggest the following.

Positive Affective Bond

A positive outcome for therapy is contingent upon the "quality and strength" of the alliance. In more human terms, this means that there is a "positive affective bond" between therapist and client. In turn, that positive affective bond is composed of the qualities discussed previously about establishing a working relationship—mutual trust, positive regard, liking, respect, and caring. It is an attachment relationship between the client and counselor that has depth and feeling. At the same time, it is a professional relationship that is governed by rules, ethics, and so on (we will discuss these aspects below). Because it is an attachment relationship, the therapist brings her personal style to it. This includes her personality characteristics and personal history. As a result, no two therapists display caring, respect, or other responses in identical ways, nor will any two clients perceive a therapist's efforts in this regard in the same way.

It becomes essential that Level I therapists thus learn early in their training to be themselves in conveying these characteristics rather than trying to be like a mentor or a master practitioner viewed in a video work sample. Thus, what is conveyed to clients is "What you see is what you get"—an authentic, real person. Especially in this regard, it is important that therapists disabuse themselves of "trying to change" a client. Although a therapist is a "change agent," being such means that he develops the conditions under which it becomes possible for a client to make positive decisions and alter behaviors, attitudes, and emotions.

Cognitive Factors

A second factor that Horvath and Bedi (2002) included in their definition of a therapeutic alliance is "cognitive factors." This refers to a *mutual understanding and agreement* on the goals that therapist and client are striving for. Perhaps the most cogent way to arrive at this is to help a client develop more concrete (i.e., behavioral and visualizable) indications that she either is approximating or has actually arrived at what it is that she wants to accomplish. Oftentimes, a simple question can greatly help facilitate a client's development of specific goals, such as "How would you know that you had gotten what it is that you have come to counseling for?" Although it is quite human, all too often clients seek *relief* from suffering but have no clear idea of what specific behavior(s) to engage in (e.g., thoughts or actions) that would provide them with that sense of relief.

"Cognitive factors" also include *commonly agreed upon means* of achieving particular goals as part of the therapeutic alliance. In Chapter 5, we discussed the importance of setting realistic and achievable goals. Once the goals are agreed upon, then the client and therapist must consciously work toward achieving them. We have encountered innumerable instances of therapists of all levels of experience attempting to impose a particular treatment method on their clients. One example can be seen in a client coming for treatment for a phobia that the clinician believes would best be treated by hypnosis. Some clients are ill disposed to the use of hypnosis due to fear of not being in control of themselves if they were to be hypnotized. Insistence on the use of hypnosis would be imprudent.

Partnership

A third characteristic of a therapeutic alliance as proposed by Horvath and Bedi (2002) is that it represents *a partnership*. As such, each "partner" in the therapeutic venture incurs "specific" and "appropriate" responsibilities and is "enthusiastically engaged" in the process of treatment. In the preceding case, the therapist had successfully established rapport, had built a therapeutic relationship with the client, and was in an alliance with her to meet her goals. When this is in place, a therapist can help move a client forward toward achieving her goals. Even when there is a discrepancy in the best way to proceed, if a therapist has built and maintained a strong therapeutic alliance, a client can usually tolerate hearing unpleasant or uncomfortable things from a therapist.

Conscious and Purposeful

In proposing their definition, Horvath and Bedi (2002) referred to the therapeutic alliance as having a "conscious" component. That is, the participants must realize that their relationship can be influenced by past relationships that each has had (i.e., transference and countertransference feelings). When these arise, they must be dealt with appropriately or else the alliance will suffer (see "Ruptures to the Therapeutic Alliance," below). In addition, this conscious component requires that both therapist and client recognize that there is a "purpose" to the therapeutic endeavor. Although some clients *do* come to therapy purely to "find themselves" and explore their life's experiences, it is more often the case that clients have a specific agenda to pursue.

Last, Horvath and Bedi (2002) indicated that a therapeutic alliance is "purposeful." As a result, a client must be the one to "do the work" of making changes. A therapist is also accountable in that he or she accepts responsibility for being a helper to a client, and holding the client accountable for making changes. All of these obligations indicate that there will be some inevitable friction, even to the best built therapeutic alliances. When these frictions occur, a therapist must understand either how to maintain positive momentum in therapy (if the friction is minor) or how to repair the alliance (if the friction is major). We now turn our attention to that element of the domain of maintaining the therapeutic alliance.

MAINTAINING THE THERAPEUTIC ALLIANCE

Creating a therapeutic alliance is a crucial skill that therapists of all developmental levels—and all theoretical persuasions—must achieve in order to be effective with clients. Although this is a formidable task requiring the skills discussed above, there is an equally important element to the relationship domain that is often overlooked in the training of Level I therapists—*maintaining* a therapeutic alliance.

Too often, beginning (and some advanced) therapists feel that merely creating the therapeutic alliance is sufficient for moving a client forward in accomplishing the therapeutic goals. This linear view implies that the alliance, once established, is a static (or unchanging) entity that does not need attention. The therapeutic alliance, however, is a dynamic (and often nonlinear) function of the therapeutic endeavor that requires a therapist's constant monitoring and attention. It is akin to the carnival act that has a row of five plates spinning at the top of broomstick handles. As long as the performer pays attention to the plates and keeps them spinning, they will not fall off the broomsticks. Similarly, a therapist must be aware of the state of the therapeutic alliance, understand what issues threaten it, and be skilled in how to repair ruptures to its fabric. Although there are literally *thousands* of ways that an alliance can be threatened, we will address several of the more common issues that Level I therapists confront that can jeopardize the therapeutic alliance: boundary issues, multiple relationships, transference, countertransference, and self-disclosure (in subsequent chapters, we will discuss further threats to the therapeutic alliance and ways to maintain it relative to Level II and Level III domains). Last, we will discuss the development and repair of therapeutic ruptures.

Boundary and Role Management I: Boundaries

All relationships are guided by boundaries. That is, within a given type of relationship (e.g., parent–child, husband–wife, teacher–pupil, doctor–patient, and supervisor–supervisee), there are certain behaviors and actions that are *prescribed* (i.e., must take place) and certain behaviors and limits that are *proscribed* (i.e., must not take place). When these boundaries are maintained, the function and the purpose of the relationship can take place more or less smoothly. Violations of prescribed and proscribed behaviors, on the other hand, represent *boundary crossings*, which can disrupt the normal "flow" of the therapeutic alliance. Although such boundary crossings can occur on the part of *either* individual, Poon et al. (2007) indicated that in a *professional relationship* such as between counselor and client, it is *always* the professional individual who has responsibility for making certain that appropriate boundaries are maintained. Sommers-Flanagan, Elliott, and Sommers-Flanagan (1998) put it this way: "The challenge to the professional and, we argue the moral obligation of the more powerful person in any relationship, is to be conscious of all boundaries and willing to extend or hold firm, depending on circumstances" (p. 39).

Take for example the following scenario. After several successful sessions, a client suggests that you and she should go into business together because "We make such a great team." This is clearly a boundary crossing that is prohibited—a therapist cannot maintain a therapeutic relationship and a business interest with a client. Such a "dual relationship" has the potential to damage a therapeutic alliance because (a) it misunderstands the essence of the therapeutic relationship—"We make such a great team because it is a professional relationship that is governed by rules, not because of our compatibility"; and (b) to introduce the dynamic of business partner into the therapeutic endeavor would create confusion about a number of issues. Consider the following.

In any business venture, disagreements between partners are inevitable. How would a therapist and client *ever* be certain about whom they were relating to in such a disagreement? Would a client be disagreeing with her therapist or her business associate? Would a therapist be disagreeing with his business associate or with his client? In addition, a therapist's motives come into question. As a therapist, one's fiduciary responsibility is to put a client's interests first, before one's own interests. When a therapist's business and financial interests are involved, such interests are likely at some point to come into conflict with a client's best interests, thus prompting *self-interest* to take precedence over a therapist's fiduciary responsibilities. Hence, *linear thinking* about boundary crossings would suggest that any boundary crossing is an ethical *violation*. This is primarily true of the Level I practitioner, who is concerned about jeopardizing the therapeutic alliance, or violating any ethical standard.[2]

Nonlinear thinking, on the other hand, gives rise to the question as to whether all boundary crossings actually represent ethical violations. Although the answer is "no," such boundary crossings nevertheless have the *potential* to be ethical violations, and hence in a therapy relationship boundaries must be carefully monitored. Peluso (2007) described this issue particularly well as it pertains to Level I counselors:

> Any alteration, extension, or crossing of the relationship boundary either may temporarily or permanently change the nature of the therapeutic relationship positively or negatively. This can occur even if the violation or crossing is inadvertent. Even if the therapist's intentions are good, she cannot know how the client will react to a particular crossing, which will necessarily cause a shift in their perception of the client. This may affect the amount and type of information that is shared in therapy, and even how the client feels about the therapeutic process itself. Of course, this does not mean these changes cannot be incorporated into the relationship, nor does it mean the boundary violation or crossing is automatically damaging to the therapeutic relationship. (p. 36)

Ethics and Boundaries

To help guide therapists in maintaining appropriate boundaries, various professional organizations, including the American Counseling Association, the American Psychological Association, and the National Association of Social Workers, have developed codes of ethical conduct to help define the therapy relationship and thus protect *both* client and counselor. As Sommers-Flanagan et al. (1998) argued, by helping to define this relationship, the ethical codes protect both the counselor and client:

> Professional ethics codes formally articulate professional relationship boundaries. As such, boundaries guide a host of potential interactions, some of which are more central to defining professional relationships, whereas other interactions are less specific, less impermeable, or less damaging to change. In professional relationships in which there is a clear power differential, there are boundaries of such clarity and precision that to violate them essentially redefines the relationship (i.e., sexual contact). (p. 38)

Concretely, what are some of the boundary issues that therapists should be concerned about? Obviously, a sexual relationship with a client is forbidden. A therapist who claims that he was "seduced" is not using a valid argument regarding such behavior. The harms accruing to a client from a sexual relationship with his or her therapist are numerous and significant. To begin with, given the intrinsic nature of client vulnerability, a sexual encounter is heinously exploitive. Individuals engaging in such boundary violations are hard-pressed to rationalize such encounters with clients as being "for the client's benefit." Sexual encounters add confusion to client *feelings* about the nature of the relationship (i.e., from that of a helper and helped to one of romance). Furthermore, sexual involvement with a client clearly can aggravate psychosexual issues already patent within an individual.

Gift giving is another area with the *potential* for boundary violations. The question arises as to exactly *when* a gift from a client represents a boundary violation. A therapist accepting home-baked cookies by a grateful client during the holidays is a case in point. Poon et al. (2006) suggested that the operational criteria to apply in determining if a boundary violation has occurred are several—are the client's interests being served, and what is the potential for harm accruing to a client if the therapist accepts the gift of home-baked cookies? Acceptance of tickets to a playoff sporting event may be an ethical violation if the client harbors an expectation of a quid pro quo such as a preferred appointment time or an extended therapy session. Making relevant distinctions between small tokens of gratitude and expectation of a quid pro quo is not always easy, and the Level I clinician is well advised to seek consultation regarding gift giving if uncertainty arises in a particular situation.

Maintaining appropriate boundaries is essential in the service of a therapeutic relationship. An important bit of guiding wisdom says that therapists are not here to judge, punish, or be entertained by our clients but to assist them in figuring out how they are making themselves unhappy.

Clear boundaries guide transactions and can deepen the therapeutic relationship, leading to positive treatment outcomes—even when it is a client who acts inappropriately. Johnson (1995) has noted that a therapist has to be "disengaged from the emotional demands of the situation" (p. 75). Although this is difficult and at times impossible given the suffering that many clients experience when seeking help for traumatic experiences, losses, bouts of life-threatening illness, or end-of-life-issues, it is most useful for therapists to monitor their emotions. This does not mean that a therapist is not empathic, however. It does mean that therapists do not respond to clients in the same way that clients' suffering, symptomatic, inappropriate, irritating, or manipulative behaviors typically precipitate in others. Johnson presented an example of an attractive female client had who suggested that she and her therapist have a sexual relationship so that she could resolve her sexual hang-ups with men like him. The therapist, with warmth and empathy, refused. Because the therapist's response made the client feel safe in the relationship, she "felt emboldened by his boundaries" (Johnson, p. 70) and pursued issues that she had previously avoided in treatment. It has been noted, "The only unique thing that therapists have to offer is that we don't try to meet our own needs in therapy. Everything we do should be with the intention of helping the client" (Johnson, p. 79).

The Level I therapist will note that the example cited by Johnson (1995) is demonstrative of nonlinear thinking regarding transference (discussed above). That is, a client's sexual advances and outright proposition might suggest that the therapist provide a linear response to be more careful about *not provoking* such behavior in the client (i.e., "I have to be more careful because this client might misinterpret some of my behavior as a sign of wanting sex with her"). Instead, the therapist declined the invitation *with warmth and empathy*. He did not change his behavior toward the client in the least. One could easily make the case that the therapist provided a safe place (i.e., one in which her usual behaviors would not provoke the response that they typically did). At this point, he could invite the client to explore what elements of the therapeutic relationship she found satisfying, and find ways to get this level of satisfaction from her romantic relationships (i.e., redirecting the client's extratherapeutic feelings back into the therapeutic endeavor). Such counterintuitive behavior—not withdrawing warmth and empathy in the face of a client crossing appropriate boundaries—is distinctly nonlinear.

Boundary and Role Management II: Multiple Roles

A therapist having a "dual" or "multiple"[3] relationship with a client provides clear challenges to the therapeutic relationship. What is a multiple role? Perhaps the easiest way of setting the context for a discussion of multiple roles is an example.

A man who has developed a very successful business would very much like to have his son and daughter become involved in the business. Even under the best of circumstances, good intentions, and positive familial relationships, it will oftentimes be hard for the participants in such an arrangement to determine when they are relating to each other as *business associates* or when they are relating as *parent and child*. Directions or feedback that may be given by the father as the founder-owner of the company may be interpreted by his children as being harsh, unfair, or rejection by their father. Given this example, what constitutes a *multiple role* in the context of being a therapist?

Lazarus and Zur (2002) defined a multiple relationship as "any association outside the 'boundaries' of the standard client-therapist relationship—for example, lunching, socializing, bartering, errand-running, or mutual business transactions (other than the fee-for-service)" (p. xxvii). But there are other, more complicated variations of engaging in *multiple roles* with a client.

Karl Tomm (2002), a distinguished writer and practitioner of couples and family therapy, importantly differentiates between multiple relationships and exploitation:

Exploitation in relationships is always exploitation, regardless of whether it occurs in a dual relationship, a therapy relationship, a supervisory relationship, or a research relationship. A dual relationship is one in which there are two (or more) distinct kinds of relationships with the same person. For instance, a therapist who has a relationship with someone as a client and who also has another relationship with that person, such as an employer, an employee, a business associate, a friend, or a relative, is involved in a dual relationship. While dual relationships always introduce greater complexity, they are not inherently exploitative. Indeed, the additional human connectedness through a dual relationship is far more likely to be affirming, reassuring, and enhancing, than exploitative. To discourage all dual relationships in the field is to promote an artificial professional cleavage in the natural *patterns that connect* us as human beings. It is a stance that is far more impoverishing than it is provocative. (p. 33)

Just like the brief example of the man involving his children in his business, there are circumstances in which a therapist engaging in two roles with a client would be inappropriate despite noble intentions or the particular therapist involved having the highest ethical standards. Examples of someone engaging in multiple roles include a psychologist providing therapy to a graduate student enrolled in the psychologist's course or a psychologist treating someone who is also a supervisee. The significant vulnerabilities of the student or supervisee render great power imbalances in such complementary relationships. With such imbalances, it becomes relatively easy for the student or supervisee to be subjected to unfavorable transactions. As Peluso (2007) has stated,

When a therapist has more than one relationship with a client (i.e., business relationship, friendship, etc.), the ability to remain neutral, or act in the client's best interest[,] is compromised (or at least can be called into question). Thus, the prohibition against therapists having more than one relationship (that is, the professional, therapeutic relationship) is a boundary designed to protect both the clinician and the client(s) from manipulation, collusion, boundary confusion, and exploitation (p. 313)

See Clinical Exercises 7.1 and 7.2 for examples of therapists acting in multiple relationships.

Clinical Exercise 7.1: A Conflict of Interest?

An experienced and compassionate female therapist worked in a clinic that provided services to indigent clients. One of her clients was an unemployed car mechanic who was in debt and could not find work. The therapist contracted with the mechanic to do some work on her car and agreed to pay him for his services. When confronted with the impropriety of such a multiple role, the therapist's reply was that she was being helpful to someone who needed work.

1. Is this transaction appropriate? After all, wouldn't the man's earning money as a mechanic help him to pay some bills, improve his self-esteem, increase his motivation, and so on?
2. If this multiple role is inappropriate, what is it that is inappropriate?

Being a therapist is challenging whether at Level I or beyond. Clinical Exercise 7.2 is meant to challenge the Level I therapist and follow up on the case above by rendering a semifictitious case with circumstances still more complicated than those previously noted.

Clinical Exercise 7.2: The Only Game in Town

The Department of Veterans Affairs made it possible for disaffected veterans who are mistrustful of bureaucratic organizations and regimentation as a result of their military experiences in Vietnam to obtain more convenient psychological treatment for their emotional problems in "Vet Centers" located in the local community and not attached to any large VA hospital. Many Vet Centers are located in rural areas, far removed from larger urban areas, and with significant populations of veterans.

For this exercise, assume that you are a therapist in a Vet Center located in a relatively small community several hundred miles from the nearest larger size urban area. As one of your clients, you are seeing a man who maintains the only car and truck repair service in the town. You have discovered that your car is in need of repairs. The only other repair shop is several hours' distance.

1. Would you take your car to your client's shop for repairs?
2. If so, why so? If not, why not?
3. What do you see as the ultimate determining factor(s) in making this decision?
4. What would be your rationale for either decision?

Flexibility of Boundaries

Clearly, the cases noted above can quickly become quite complex. Thus, there are some experts who have held the line and stringently maintained that *no* multiple roles are appropriate (Lazarus & Zur, 2002; Pope & Vasquez, 1998). In keeping with such a stringent position, they suggested that practitioners who engage in *any kind* of a multiple role should be subjected to professional review and have professional association memberships suspended and licenses revoked. But, there are less complicated circumstances with more benign outcomes, as Peluso (2007) has illustrated:

> In the "real world" of most people's lives, there are individuals that have operated on more than one level at any given time. According to Coale (1998), these occasional dual roles can be "invigorating, healthy, and conductive to healing, as along as they are not secretive or skewed toward therapist interest at the expense of the client" (p. 103). For example, if a therapist is stranded due to car problems and a client drives by and offers to help (change a tire, give the therapist a ride)[,] should the therapist refuse based on the fear of violating the dual role boundary? Probably not, in fact the therapist would be silly to continue to be stranded. In fact, these occurrences can be empowering to the client, or humanize the therapist for the client. (p. 314)

The central construct regarding multiple relationships is a therapist's "conflict of interests." As a human being, the therapist has "interests" in his own well-being (i.e., getting his car conveniently repaired without having to travel a great distance). But, a therapist incurs a responsibility to put the interests of his client *ahead of self-interest*.

As mentioned in the discussion of the need to maintain appropriate boundaries, the most egregious violation of a therapist forgoing his fiduciary obligation to a client is sexual involvement. Again, it does not matter that a client acts seductively toward a therapist. Such relationships are forbidden by ethical codes of conduct because of the blatant nature of exploitation inherent in the situation. The therapist is obtaining gratification at the expense of his client. That means that the therapist has clearly put *his interests* ahead of the client's interests. The trust implied in the fiduciary relationship between client and therapist has been broken. Rationalizations about having sexual relations with a client "for the good of the client" cannot stand the test of truthfulness.

The issue of multiple roles can quickly become murky in today's complex clinical practice. Baird (2006) illustrated this fact with the observation that anyone with considerable experience in clinical practice will have faced the dilemma of being requested to engage in couples therapy with a client being seen in individual therapy. Although there are many flattering arguments (e.g., faith in the therapist's ability, the client[s] would not have to start therapy from the beginning, and a trusting relationship has already been established) that can be offered in favor of proceeding with such a new therapeutic arrangement, there are many ethical principles that must be attended to as well (e.g., beneficence and nonmaleficence, fidelity and responsibility, and conflict of interest). In fact, one can make a case that referring a client to someone else increases the costs to a client, because of necessity she must start her marital therapy from "scratch." Perhaps the best caution is twofold: (a) A therapist must be alert for the conflicts that can arise when engaging a client in more than one role; and (b) when in doubt, obtain consultation with a trusted colleague, mentor, or supervisor.

Boundary and Role Management III: Therapist Self-Disclosure

The value and propriety of self-disclosure (i.e., the *deliberate* revealing of thoughts, feelings, or personal information by a therapist to a client in treatment for therapeutic purposes) have been debated in the literature for decades. Such disclosure contrasts with the concept of the "anonymous therapist" (i.e., someone about whom a client knows nothing personal, such as marital status, age, and religious preference) long held by psychoanalytic proponents. Given the constraints and caveats noted in the discussions above on boundaries and multiple roles, we will discuss the merits and limits of self-disclosure.

As briefly discussed earlier, therapy and counseling in their essence are *human encounters. Appropriate self-disclosure* can present the therapist as an authentic human being. Thus, there are many instances where well-timed self-disclosure is appropriate, and may actually strengthen the therapeutic alliance. Likewise, there are instances and types of self-disclosure that may be inappropriate. Therapy, as a human encounter, is subject to professional considerations, power imbalances, client vulnerability, misinterpretations, potential exploitation, and inappropriate therapist behaviors, all of which *can* detract from the therapeutic relationship. Thus, even now, self-disclosure is still the subject of discussion. For example, the Psychopathology Committee of the Group for the Advancement of Psychiatry (2001) suggested the following regarding this interesting therapeutic phenomenon:

> In mental health practice, a commonly held view is that therapist self-disclosure should be discouraged and its dangers closely monitored. Changes in medicine, mental health care, and society demand reexamination of these beliefs. In some clinical situations, considerable benefit may stem from therapist self-disclosure. Although the dangers of boundary violations are genuine, self-disclosure may be underused or misused because it lacks a framework. It is useful to consider the benefits of self-disclosure in the context of treatment type, treatment setting, and patient characteristics. Self-disclosure can contribute to the effectiveness of peer models. Self-disclosure is often used in cognitive-behavioral therapy and social skills training and might be useful in psychopharmacologic and supportive treatments. The unavoidable self-disclosure that occurs in non-office-based settings provides opportunities for therapeutic deliberate self-disclosure. Children and individuals who have a diminished capacity for abstract thought may benefit from more direct answers to questions related to self-disclosure. The role of self-disclosure in mental health care should be reexamined. (p. 1489)

Obviously, self-disclosure must be considered carefully because of numerous factors that clients *and* therapists bring to the therapy relationship. Whether or not a therapist engages in self-disclosure is ultimately *a context-dependent decision* to make. Some contextual factors that a Level I practitioner might take into account about self-disclosure are as follows:

- For whose benefit is the particular information being disclosed?
- What is the rationale for the disclosure?

- Does the disclosure strengthen the therapeutic alliance (e.g., is the disclosure straightforward, commonsense, encouraging, and/or facilitating hope?), or does it inappropriately meet an unconscious psychological need of the therapist?
- Is *this* disclosure appropriate for *this* particular client at *this* particular time?

These are complex questions deserving of considerable thought. The Psychopathology Committee of the Group for the Advancement of Psychiatry (2001) has suggested that disclosure may make more sense in certain clinical settings such as clinician-facilitated self-help groups. Most often, clinician-facilitated self-help groups (e.g., for parenting, couples' communication skills, bereavement, or divorce support) are very focused, and self-disclosure is part of the "sharing." A therapist may disclose past experiences as part of the ethic of sharing. As suggested above, such disclosure can help reduce a client's sense of shame and embarrassment, and provide positive modeling and normalization, particularly with regard to transference or countertransference material. Again, the key factor is the impact of the disclosure on the therapeutic alliance. What is the disclosure's potential for strengthening the alliance and leading to better outcomes, and what is its potential for creating a rupture in the therapeutic alliance, perhaps leading to premature termination?

Harm From Disclosure

At first glance, a linear-thinking approach to self-disclosure might suggest, "What's the harm?" To this, we respond with an anonymous description of one former therapy client's interpretation of self-disclosures by her therapist:

> During my therapy with Dr. "X", he shared many of **his own personal problems and conflicts**, including information about his own therapy issues. I used to love it when he would talk about himself because it made me feel even closer and more special to him when he would share his problems and concerns with me. We also had a friendship away from therapy ["dual relationship"] and this enabled me to know even more about him and his life. His own disclosures in our therapy sessions and away from sessions led me to believe that I was truly the *"special friend"* he said I was in his life. Little did I know at the time that this was part of therapy exploitation—that *he was benefiting* from me listening to his problems and feelings and I was helping to meet his needs by expressing my care and concern for him. As the jury concluded, *"it was like she was his therapist."* (Kay C., 2000)

Obviously, the above example is extreme. Nevertheless, it emphasizes that unreflective self-disclosure can lead to inappropriate boundaries and disastrous therapeutic results. Alternately, Mosak and Dreikurs (1975) stated that when a therapist reveals himself as a person, he is acting "authentically": "Self-revelation can only occur when the therapist feels secure himself, at home with his own feelings, at home with others, unafraid to be human and fallible and thus unafraid of this patient's evaluations, criticism, or hostility" (pp. 68–69). Nevertheless, self-disclosure must be approached thoughtfully because of the varied characteristics that individually unique clients *and* therapists bring to a therapy relationship.

Clinical Exercise 7.3: Self-Disclosure

1. Discuss particular formal diagnostic categories that might give you cause for concern about making self-disclosures.
2. Discuss information that you would consider easy to self-disclose if asked by a client. Why?
3. Discuss information that you would consider difficult to self-disclose to a client. Why?
4. Discuss information that you would consider inappropriate to disclose to a client. Why?
5. What is the rationale used for disclosure or nondisclosure in each instance above?

Transference

Transference and countertransference were initially psychoanalytic terms developed by Sigmund Freud. The term *transference* referred to the affective material arising out of the client's unresolved conflicts that were projected onto the analyst by the client, which was analyzed and interpreted for the client. It was the psychoanalyst's job to detect such transference feelings, analyze them, and interpret them to the client. For present purposes, we define transference as thoughts, feelings, and behaviors that (a) a client brings to the therapy, (b) a client attributes to a therapist, (c) may have little to do with actual therapist behavior or intentions, and (d) may need to become the focus of attention for the therapeutic relationship.

With the ultimate decline of psychoanalytic preeminence and relevance (see Hobson & Leonard, 2001), and the development of briefer methods of therapy (e.g., cognitive and behavioral psychology), the idea of transference as a therapeutically useful construct was diminished or forgotten altogether (Gelso & Hayes, 2002). Today, however, an interest in some elements of transference (e.g., relational factors) impacting therapeutic outcome has been resurrected (Christoph & Gibbons, 2002).

For example, if a client begins to feel and discloses romantic (or parental) feelings toward a therapist, it is the therapist's job to reinterpret those feelings as not *really* directed to the therapist (because the therapist cannot return such feelings) but as feelings that contain important information for the therapy itself. In order to tactfully (i.e., without disrupting the therapeutic alliance) deal with this situation, the therapist may ask, "What is it about our relationship—that we have created together—that you find fulfilling?" If that discussion is productive, a variety of follow-up questions can be added, including, "Do you still really need to have that done for you, in your life, etc.?" Further follow-up could proceed along the lines of "If you, indeed, still need that in your life, how might you go about appropriately eliciting that from someone in your life?" or "What is it about our relationship—that we've created together—that you find nurturing that you can ask from someone else, if not yourself?" This allows for the therapy to move forward constructively, compared to a *linear* approach that many novice therapists might take with this situation (e.g., "Um, it is not appropriate for you to feel these things for me. The ethics code tells me to tell you that we cannot have sex"). A linear approach, although technically correct, in the long run can be the least effective means of sustaining the therapeutic alliance, particularly if it causes the client to withdraw from any future therapeutic endeavor.

Clinical Exercise 7.4: Transference

Brainstorm the following client scenarios arising in therapy. Does the issue at hand revolve around a transference theme? If so, why? If not, why not?

- Client expresses attraction for you.
- Client suggests getting together with each other's spouses or partners for dinner and a movie.
- Client offers to hire your child to babysit her children.
- Client begins to yell at you, "All you do is just sit there; you don't *help* me!"
- *Add your own scenario.*

1. How would the interaction between client and therapist be scripted?
2. How would you respond in a way that preserves the therapeutic alliance?

Additional suggestion: In a group setting, share your responses, imagine that you are giving each other peer supervision, and get feedback on how you might handle these situations.

Countertransference

Countertransference refers to affective material arising out of a therapist's unresolved conflicts and personal sensitivities that may be projected onto a client. Countertransference was seen as a significant threat to the psychoanalytic process. It even earned the scorn of Freud (1910, as cited in Gelso & Hayes, 2002), who proclaimed that any analyst who experienced countertransference and failed to "produce results in a self-analysis of this kind may at once give up any idea of being able to treat patients by analysis" (p. 267). As a result, countertransference as a therapeutic issue was grossly minimized by the analytic community for decades out of fear that the therapist would be judged inadequate. In subsequent years, therapists from nonanalytic traditions began to utilize their emotional reactions to a client as an important source of therapeutic information about the client. As a result, countertransference (like transference) found a resurgence (Gelso & Hayes).

A therapist's feelings generated by interaction with a client need to be processed as part of the therapy, *if appropriate*. The important caveat is "if appropriate." By this, we mean that if a therapist's feelings, generated by a client's behavior, stem from unresolved childhood conflicts (e.g., "You tick me off the same way that my sister does, and I haven't spoken to her in 6 years!"), then it is not appropriate for a therapist to relate this to a client. Instead, such issues need to be discussed in supervision, in the therapist's own therapy, or perhaps both. If the therapist does not pay attention to such feelings, conflicts, and the like, then he runs the risk of acting inappropriately with a client. If it does not come from the therapist's unresolved childhood conflicts (i.e., the therapist uses his or her emotions as a "barometer"—as mentioned in Chapter 2), then there could be valuable (if not critical) information that needs to become the focus of the therapeutic relationship.

As a brief example of what is meant by a therapist appropriately using feelings generated by a client's behavior as an important source of therapeutic information, see Clinical Case Example 7.2.

Clinical Case Example 7.2: Therapist Frustration

A successful businessman in his early 50s sought therapy in order to better understand how to respond to his angry wife. He was very open to suggestions made by the therapist and discussed how he could easily improvise and improve on them. At the same time, he seemed to derive few original ideas of how to proceed in relating better to his wife. *The therapist felt frustrated and that he was working harder at the therapy than the client.* When this was disclosed to the client in a friendly and collaborative way with the question "What do you think and feel about that?" it opened an entirely new area of discussion. The client's first reaction to the therapist's observation was "As a child, I was told that children are to be seen and not heard. I gave my opinion only when I was asked for it—otherwise, I kept my mouth shut or paid the consequences!" At the conclusion of the session, the client spontaneously offered the observation that he would have never thought that the discussion would have gone in the direction that it did. He had prepared some things that he wanted to discuss but instead found an entirely new understanding of his characteristic way of relating not only to the therapist but also to his wife. In fact, he indicated that one of his wife's constant comments to him was "You don't talk to me!"

Managing countertransference, according to VanWagoner, Gelso, Hayes, and Diemer (1991), consists of five related factors: self-insight, self-integration, empathy, anxiety management, and conceptualizing ability (see Table 7.1). Taken together, these factors create a matrix wherein countertransference material can be sifted, understood, and utilized. Again, the key is that the therapist must be aware of his or her own feelings and conflicts, and has a handle on his or her propensity for acting upon them in an unconscious way. Hayes et al. (1998) put it best: "The more resolved an intrapsychic conflict is for the therapist, the greater the likelihood that the therapist will be able to use his or her countertransference therapeutically (… to deepen one's understanding of the client)" (p. 478).

TABLE 7.1 Five countertransference management factors

FACTOR	DEFINITION
Therapist self-insight	Therapists' awareness of their feelings, as well as their underlying basis
Therapist self-integration	The integrity of therapists' character structure, ability to maintain boundaries, and ability to differentiate themselves from others
Anxiety management	Therapists' ability to experience anxiety—their own and other people's—without being overwhelmed
Empathy	Therapists' ability to identify with the feelings of others
Conceptualizing ability	Therapists' ability to draw on theory to understand the client's dynamics relative to the therapeutic alliance

Source: Adapted from VanWagoner, Gelso, Hayes, and Diemer (1991); and Gelso and Hayes (2002).

For example, if a therapist finds himself feeling irritated by a client's subtle intellectual bullying in the same way that he used to feel when his big brother would tease him, but the therapist had dealt with these issues long ago, he could utilize them in session to say, "Hmm, it seems like you need to wrestle with me in order to feel connected to this process. Could it be that you really believe, in your heart of hearts, that you are right, and you are trying hard to convince me of that? In addition, could it be that the more that I fail to (or *refuse* to) agree with you, the angrier you get and the more passion you feel for this subject?" Again, the therapist' feelings (e.g., "Why is this person being such a jerk?") are formulated in a therapeutically appropriate way (e.g., "Hmm, it feels like this man is attempting to bully me because he is threatened about losing his prestige") and allow for more of a constructive (and nonlinear) strengthening of the therapeutic alliance.

Direct personalizing of countertransference feelings may be damaging to the therapeutic alliance. In such instances, the countertransference interpretation can still be used, but as indirect, third-person statements. In the example above, feedback might be "Sometimes, it can feel overwhelming to come to therapy and not know what you may hear. It's only natural that you may be on guard so that you won't be surprised. If this is your concern, I'll look out for it as well, and we can discuss it. Therapy can be a somewhat unpredictable process, but it doesn't do any good to be uncomfortable the entire time. Should you start to feel that way, or I sense that you might be feeling that way, we can pause what we are discussing and look at those feelings. What do you think?"

With the responses suggested above, the client is arousing defensive and hostile emotions in the therapist because he is threatened by and unsure of the therapeutic process. The therapist utilizes all five of the factors for managing the countertransference feelings: self-insight (i.e., "I am feeling angry! Why?"), self-integration (i.e., "This isn't about me"), anxiety management (i.e., "I don't have to feel threatened by this"), empathy (i.e., "What is the person feeling?"), and conceptualizing ability (i.e., "What is it that this person's feelings of anger and fear are telling me?").

Clearly, transference and countertransference are potent therapeutic factors that can potentially erode a therapeutic alliance. Managing this material effectively can not only protect but also strengthen the alliance and lead to more successful outcomes (Gelso & Hayes, 2002).

Clinical Exercise 7.5: Countertransference

Brainstorm the following client scenarios. Discuss whether or not a countertransference theme is present. If so, why? If not, why not?

- You feel attraction for the client.
- You feel bored by what the client is discussing.

- You feel frightened by the client.
- You feel frustrated by the client.
- *Add your own scenario.*

1. How would the interaction between client and therapist be scripted?
2. How would you respond in a way that preserves the therapeutic alliance? Are there some scenarios in which it would be better to address it personally? From a "third-person" perspective? Are there situations for which you should seek supervision before addressing it with the client? Are there situations in which you would need to refer the client and deal with the issue personally?
3. Describe how you would utilize the five countertransference management factors in Table 7.1 to help manage the interaction.

Additional suggestion: In a small-group format, imagine that you are giving each other peer supervision. Share your responses on how you might handle these situations, and get feedback.

Ruptures to the Therapeutic Alliance

Sometimes, despite the best efforts by a therapist to positively manage the therapy relationship, threats, "breaks," or *ruptures* to the therapeutic alliance can occur. According to Safran, Muran, Samstag, and Stevens (2002), a rupture in the therapeutic alliance is defined as "a tension or breakdown in the collaborative relationship between patient and therapist" (p. 236). Such breaks can be precipitated by any number of factors, as previously noted: failing to engage and connect with the client (Chapters 2 and 3), failure to consider the client's stage of change, or incompletely assessing client needs and goals for treatment (Chapters 4 and 5). All such missteps lead to a failure to establish rapport (i.e., "resonating together"), as well as a failure in forging and maintaining the therapeutic alliance. Safran et al. conceptualized three major sources of ruptures: differences between therapist and client about the tasks of therapy, differences between them about the goals of treatment, and "strains" in their connection.

The theoretical foundation for their thinking stems from Bordin's (1979, 1994) pioneering transtheoretical understanding about ruptures in the alliance. Bordin suggested that "negotiations" were constantly being conducted between client and therapist about the three major areas (i.e., tasks, goals, and bond) in two dimensions: a conscious level (i.e., surface meaning) and unconscious level (i.e., underlying meaning). Disagreements may be expressed explicitly and sometimes implicitly. However, when ruptures occur, the process of negotiation must be moved front and center in therapy.

Therapeutic Ruptures and Nonlinear Thinking

When ruptures occur, given the prime importance of the therapeutic alliance, it is *essential* that efforts are directed at repair. Much like the discussion above regarding transference and countertransference, repairs can be addressed in a variety of ways that actually strengthen the alliance. In keeping with a major emphasis of the present text, Safran et al. (2002) suggested that there are "direct" and "indirect" means of dealing with disagreements. For example, more direct means might be exploring the possible meaning of a client's refusal to do a homework assignment, clearing up misunderstandings, or reiterating tasks and goals in different words to assure greater clarity. "Indirect means" bear strong resemblance to the present authors' nonlinear thinking. For example, a therapist can ally herself with a client's resistant behavior or can begin to define uncooperative behavior as a useful indicator of a new way of experiencing the therapeutic relationship, which we will discuss in more detail in Chapters 12 and 13. In addition, the depth of the rupture is important to consider. Some ruptures are manifested at a *surface* level (e.g., disagreements about topics being discussed or procedures being followed) or on the *underlying meaning* level (e.g., relationship issues such as transference and countertransference, or boundary issues).

Identifying Ruptures to the Therapeutic Alliance

Regardless of the underlying issues, once a rupture in the alliance has occurred, it is the responsibility of the therapist to attempt immediate repair. In order to do this, the therapist must first recognize that a rupture has occurred. The two types of behaviors that seem to indicate that a rupture has occurred are *withdrawal* behaviors and *confrontation* behaviors (Safran & Muran, 2000). Withdrawal behaviors are any actions that seem to limit the client's participation in therapy and signal his *disengagement*. Confrontational behaviors are expressions of anger, frustration, or resentment toward the therapist or the therapeutic process. Each of these types of behaviors is designed to *stop* the therapeutic process, and force the therapist to react. The therapist's reaction will generally determine whether the rupture will become a breach in the alliance (and effectively end the therapy) or will be repaired in an attempt to salvage (and possibly strengthen) the alliance.

Repairing Ruptures to the Therapeutic Alliance

Following a decade of research, Safran and his colleagues (Safran et al., 2002) developed a conceptually useful four-stage framework for repairing alliance ruptures that is effective in maintaining the therapeutic alliance. Briefly, these stages are (a) attending to the rupture behavior (i.e., withdrawal or confrontation), (b) exploring the rupture experience, (c) exploring the client's avoidance, and (d) the emergence of a wish or need (see Table 7.2).

There are several topics that Safran and his colleagues (Safran et al., 2002) suggested exploring in the repair process, namely, core relational themes (e.g., a client's experience of the therapist, and strains in the relationship): clarifying misunderstandings, reframing the meaning of tasks or goals, and allying with the resistance.[4] In particular, some research findings related to therapeutic ruptures suggest that clients frequently have negative feelings about the therapist or therapy but do not give voice to them. In fact, it is generally not until the end of the therapeutic endeavor, when a client terminates therapy, that most will express any negative emotions or experiences to the therapist. In general, research has revealed that the reasons for clients not expressing negative feelings concern fears regarding the therapist's reactions. As a result, a therapist must be sensitive to this general situation (not wanting to voice negative comments) and be the *first* to talk about it in order to "set the stage" for clients to talk about these feelings when they (inevitably) arise (Safran & Muran, 2000; Safran et al.).

TABLE 7.2   Stage process model of repairing therapeutic rupture

	STAGE	DEFINITION
1	Attending to the rupture behavior	Therapist recognizes behavior that signals the therapeutic rupture (either client withdrawal or increased confrontation toward the therapist and therapeutic process).
2	Exploring the rupture experience	Allowing a client to discuss feelings of dissatisfaction or hurt and resentment regarding the therapist's action, while the therapist facilitates the experience in a nonthreatening way and offers his or her perspective.
3	Exploring the client's avoidance	Exploration of any actions or feelings of client withdrawal or avoidance, defensiveness, and inability to discuss these openly with the therapist.
4	Emergence of wish or need	Client expressing the desire to express negative feeling, or having the power to alter the course of therapy.

Source: Adapted from Safran, Muran, Samstag, and Stevens (2002); and Safran and Muran (2000).

Clinical Exercise 7.6: Repairing Alliance Ruptures

Examine the following scenarios of ruptures in progress, and create a rupture repair rationale (including the possible reasons for the rupture) utilizing the four-stage model outlined above.

1. A depressed client has been in treatment for six sessions. He has begun to make progress when suddenly he skips his last session, calling at the last minute to say that he couldn't make it.
2. A client who is a single parent has initiated therapy to develop better methods of parenting her two preteen children. You have seen her three times, and in the last session you pointed out that she was making some progress. In the next session, she complains bitterly that her children still won't listen to her and states, "This is just a waste of my time; we aren't getting *anywhere*!"
3. A client has been in therapy for approximately 1 year. During one session, you notice that his attention has started to wander and that he tends to give one-word or very brief answers.

Additional suggestion: Share responses in small groups, imagining that you are giving each other peer supervision. Get feedback on how you might handle these situations as well as why you might handle them in that way.

What essentials can a Level I practitioner take from this discussion about the practice of therapy? As noted previously, client feedback to a therapist about the therapy is important in facilitating a positive treatment outcome. That feedback should also include *negative feelings* as well as *any different perspective* that the client may have. Though this might seem counterintuitive (or nonlinear), the process of discussing a client's expression of negative feelings and thoughts can be a source of growth while simultaneously helping to resolve a possible therapeutic rupture. Therapists also need to be mindful of the possibility that perceived "attacks" by a client can prompt retaliation using expressions of veiled hostility or defensiveness. Such interactions can ultimately result in further deterioration of the alliance and a premature termination.

Safran et al. (2002) ended their discussion with sobering advice to clinicians derived from relevant research: It can be difficult to train therapists to constructively deal with a client's negative expressions toward the therapist that, in turn, can precipitate hostile, negative, and/or defensive reactions in the therapist. For the Level I practitioner, we add the following two other points regarding client expressions of negative feelings: (a) The use of a linear, friendly, and cooperative discussion of the client's disagreement with the therapist is legitimate; and (b) nonlinear thinking about a client's disagreement, as mentioned above, can promote growth and a strengthening of the therapeutic alliance.

SUMMARY OF CLINICAL UNDERSTANDING REGARDING THE THERAPEUTIC RELATIONSHIP AND ALLIANCE

All of us have engaged in human "relationships" since infancy—it is an inescapable fact that fundamentally we are social beings. Thus, by its very nature, a therapeutic alliance shares certain common characteristics that all human relationships have, while maintaining distinctive, professional qualities that make it different from everyday relationships. Given the plethora of consistent findings about the therapeutic relationship and alliance, we offer the following summary:

1. Unfortunately, an understanding of diagnosis and labeling or of identifying psychopathology does not have very much to do with positive outcomes in psychotherapy.
2. Likewise, the belief that psychotherapeutic "technique" (i.e., "tactics") or type of therapy represents the essential ingredient in successful therapeutic outcomes is largely unfounded, as consistently revealed by studies of outcome.
3. The most powerful predictor of successful therapeutic outcomes is the strength of the therapeutic relationship and therapeutic alliance.
4. The quality of the relationship and alliance is essential, as are helpful comments, insights, and a sense of therapeutic optimism from the therapist.
5. There are numerous components that contribute to a therapeutic alliance, such as establishing rapport, trust, caring, congruence, and warmth, and maintaining appropriate boundaries.
6. Therapists are well advised to be alert for ruptures to the alliance and must be prepared to deal nondefensively and constructively with such ruptures.

CONCLUSION

This chapter concludes our discussion of Level I domains. Beginning therapists who have learned to master connecting with and engaging a client, assessing (i.e., client readiness for change, themes, needs, resources, and goals), as well as building and maintaining therapeutic alliances are aware that these tasks are essential for creating conditions under which change can occur. But, they are ultimately *insufficient* by themselves for producing successful therapeutic outcomes. However, with such an understanding, Level I practitioners are prepared to help move clients forward by "working through" issues. In closing, we note Safran et al. (2002) and their sage counsel:

> The initial stage of treatment is a period when patients become mobilized and hopeful. They then experience a phase of ambivalence when they may begin to question what therapy can provide. If this phase is successfully negotiated, the alliance is strengthened and termination can be worked through. (p. 245)

In other words, the next level in counselor development and the therapeutic endeavor is to delve further into clients' issues and address their fundamental ambivalence for change in all of its manifestations.

ENDNOTES

1. Recall from Chapter 2 that a *rabbit hole* is a reference to Lewis Carroll's *Alice in Wonderland*, in which Alice followed the rabbit down into a "wonderland" of the bizarre.
2. We do not mean to imply that the Level I therapist is wrong to be concerned about ethical violations, especially when a boundary crossing would be an egregious violation.
3. Traditionally, the term *dual role* has been used to describe any set of conditions in which a therapist encounters a conflict of interest with a client. Recently, the term *multiple roles* has been favored in order to illustrate the multifaceted nature of the therapeutic endeavor and the potential for good and bad that these multiple roles place on the therapist (see Peluso, 2007).
4. Part 4 of this text is devoted to the processes of nonlinear thinking in psychotherapy, which include such things as allying with the resistance and reframing.

PART THREE

The Level II Practitioner: Supervisory and Developmental Considerations

Introduction to Part 3

The Level II Practitioner

CONTENTS

Level II is perhaps the most difficult of the stages of development to describe and experience. It is a phase of therapist development that is "awkward."

The "awkwardness" we refer to is expected and natural. The developing therapist has certainly become much more comfortable in being with clients. The Level II practitioner is also more at home in clinical settings, is more at ease with clients, and genuinely understands (and has experienced) the value of establishing rapport, developing therapeutic relationships, and even creating positive and enduring therapeutic alliances. The Level II's *listening skills, both linear and nonlinear,* and ability to more effectively "read between the lines" of what a client is saying have also improved markedly. Level II practitioners listen not just mechanically but also with the enthusiastic understanding that such listening serves the therapeutic relationship.

At the same time, this stage of development, with its palpably increased feelings of confidence and comfort, is somewhat illusory. The Level II practitioner may not have yet fully understood, appreciated, and integrated into everyday practice very significant subtleties, nuances, and intricacies of becoming a professional counselor. In fact, the Level II practitioner's ability to think nonlinearly is still limited despite feelings of growing confidence and comfort. Such limitations are reflected when clients with more complex and obscure problems appear to be closed and locked doors that Level II practitioners struggle to "force" open. When a very positive relationship and working alliance do not seem to move the treatment along, Level II practitioners may try one clinical "technique" or "trick" from the repertoire they have confidently developed, but they will not encounter the success they expect. Under such circumstances, they are likely to try "more of the same" things but with more effort, only to encounter more of the same disappointing results. They learn quite sharply that "techniques" as a linear inventory of things to try in a semirandom manner hold little particular value when it comes to influencing treatment outcomes.

Considering these advancements and limitations, the present depiction of the Level II practitioner is meant to further "normalize" the process of professional growth and development. As such, our intention is to provide a description of commonly encountered professional and personal concerns and considerations that arise at this level of professional maturity and offer a measure of reassurance that such apprehensions and reflections are normative.

At any rate, the Level II practitioner has reached a point where more obviously naïve considerations about clients have been dissolved. Those more unsophisticated understandings are replaced by much more sophisticated considerations, questions, and challenges. As such, it is somewhat unfortunate that Level II is also, in certain ways, analogous to a later stage of professional adolescence or early professional maturity—the Level II practitioner is capable of performing many "adult" tasks at an effective adult level but perhaps is inconsistent in doing so, is sometimes stymied by client chaos and complexity, at times feels like he or she is at a dead end, and does not always follow through. At Level I, invidious comparison and feelings of inferiority, those age-old phenomena with historical roots as far back as Cain and Abel, prompt practitioners to compare themselves with their peers. Scott Miller (see Walt, 2005) wondered early in his career why it was that everyone else seemed to be having much more "success" with their clients than he was.

Similarly, the Level II practitioner has begun to conclude that not everyone progresses at the same pace in the development of comfort with their professional role, the understanding of complex phenomena, and skills. Part of the awkwardness of emergence into Level II is due to the fact that some Level II practitioners coalesce their understandings rapidly, and some much more slowly. Unfortunately, therapist development is far from a uniform process. Thus, as everyone at Level II reading this text has discovered,

- No two individuals grow and develop physically at the same pace.
- No two individuals mature psychologically at exactly the same pace.
- No two individuals establish a relationship in the same way.
- Some individuals have a greater natural capacity to listen more empathically than others.
- No two individual clinicians develop in precisely the same way at the same pace.

So, clinicians at Level II have begun to *substantially* integrate the idea that clinicians are as different and as varied as the clients they see in treatment.

Alas, the real challenge of professional development is much more a function of having things come together and work well together rather than having them come together in a slipshod manner and just get by. At Level II, the question of just how "expert" others may seem in comparison with one's own effectiveness begins to wilt. Faded are the agonizing comparisons of oneself with other therapists, the illusions that ask the question "Am I the best at this?" The metric that begins to form at Level II is some variation of "How can I improve to be the most effective clinician that I can be? How can I best serve the needs of the troubled others who seek my guidance? Am I *enjoying* the practice of my profession?"

Some of the more difficult understandings that this practitioner must yet fully integrate are simple in nature yet profound in implication. For example, not every practitioner can help every client that he or she encounters—not even the most profoundly gifted of the masters. This is a fact of life, and one that should be learned early. Another general consideration that Level II practitioners still have to fully learn is that clients make small and incremental changes in thinking and behavior in response to therapeutic interventions. Furthermore, every practitioner works better and more effectively with some clients than with others. The simple truth is that for maximum benefit, some clients need to be referred to other practitioners or other hospitals, clinics, or programs. Finally, it is our understanding that confidence and hubris can sometimes be indistinguishable—especially to oneself. As such, on the one hand, hubris may inform the Level II practitioner of a lesser need for supervision. Its reciprocal, humility, advises the need for modesty and the continuing need for supervision. Supervision at Level II is critical in facilitating the emergence of a more complete clinician. Even the most advanced practitioners consult with colleagues, an indication of a desire to learn, be open to blind spots, and serve the needs of one's clients and not one's ego.

FOCUS OF ATTENTION

As in Stoltenberg's (1993) model of supervision, perhaps the biggest change that occurs as practitioners evolve from Level I to Level II is a shift in the focus of attention. At Level II, the practitioner has learned to *focus attention on a client's specific cognitions, emotional states, complaints, and motivations*. Such a shift in orientation can take place only when a practitioner has an increased sense of calm, comfort, confidence, interest, and fundamental understanding of the nature of the work of therapy. Such a shift occurring with an increased sense of comfort and understanding greatly facilitates an increased ability to *concentrate on a client and his or her concerns, purpose for seeking treatment, and goals.*

Intuitively, increased feelings of confidence would appear to be inversely related to subdued levels of anxiety. As noted in Level I practitioners, such anxiety stems from feelings of inadequacy. At Level II, the practitioner's focus of attention remains notably inconsistent as cases emerge of increased difficulty (e.g., a personality disorder), complexity (e.g., a dual-diagnosis patient), threat (e.g., a client mentioning thoughts of suicide), and/or novelty (e.g., a request for assisted suicide). Nevertheless, Level II practitioners are much more comfortable with the requirements of engaging in the formal professional-level practice of therapy. They have ready internal understanding of and access to the network resources of the agency (e.g., a hospital, clinic, counseling center, or community affiliate) in which they operate. They also have a greater fluid and intuitive understanding of and access to performing more formal diagnostic procedures as an aid in addressing more complex clients. Such increases in the professional level of functioning are seen to be directly correlated to a Level II clinician's greater sense of an emerging professional identity.

According to Stoltenberg, just as focus can fluctuate according to the case at hand, motivation can also fluctuate: When therapeutic "success" is high, motivation will be correspondingly high—and when therapeutic "failure" looms, motivation will likely diminish. The consistency–inconsistency continuum needs constant attention at Level II.

At Level II, consultations with a supervisor, consultant, or mentor are less threatening than they were at Level I and can serve as a partial antidote to inconsistencies arising from waxing and waning therapeutic outcomes. Stoltenberg (1993) and Haley (1996) have wisely observed that at times, trainee *reactance* is prominently observed in the context of supervision. Such reactance (i.e., resisting threats to autonomy) can come when therapeutic successes and corresponding feelings of independence run high only to be replaced by increased feelings of dependence when therapeutic failures loom. Through supervision, the growth of the Level II practitioner can be greatly enhanced as tolerance for greater ambiguity and case complexity grows. Encountering cases of clinical complexity beyond the Level II practitioner's competence (e.g., discussing end-of-life issues with a patient in a medical setting when the practitioner has little or no knowledge of biomedical ethical issues) can have discouraging results for the client as well as the therapist. Also, cases with severe emotional volatility can be daunting for the Level II and damage the sense of therapist confidence.

DECREASED LEVEL OF ANXIETY

Under conditions of greater confidence and diminished anxiety, a Level II practitioner has become more facile with the development of clinical understanding. At this level, there is a richer, more intricate, and more sensitive conceptualization of clients' symptoms, circumstances, and personal formulation of their own difficulties. Concomitantly, a Level II practitioner has become more adept at fostering, nurturing, and maintaining the therapeutic alliance. The overarching goal for a Level II is an increased sense of autonomy and responsibility for treatment. Concomitant with a greater sense of autonomy and responsibility for treatment, Level II practitioners demonstrate significant improvement in the sense of clinical judgment as their confidence expands and experience base grows. Also notable at Level II is the managing of one's anxieties and countertransference issues and a generally more effective and appropriate regulation of self-disclosure.

To foster greater autonomy and sense of responsibility, the concept of *supervision* to guide therapist development might better yield to the concept of *mentor*. Mentoring acknowledges more of a peer status and a sharing of thoughts regarding clinical issues rather than the above-below status implied by the supervisor–supervisee relationship.

With the development of an enhanced sense of autonomy and responsibility for treatment issues, the Level II becomes prepared for entrance into the journeyman status of the Level III practitioner.

It may very well be a hallmark of therapist development at Level II to see a client's behavior as separate from (and not a reflection of) one's own performance or abilities. Level II clinicians are able to operate with sufficient competence in the three domains of Level I domains (see Chapters 2 to 7) to begin to work with a client and also calm any of their own fears or anxieties about themselves.

Staying calm allows for focus on more *dynamic elements of the therapeutic process*. In effect, a Level II practitioner gets to test his or her mettle regarding the "sexier" part of being a therapist. One of the major factors interfering with practitioners fully enjoying the work of therapy is a desire to see major therapeutic progress in a short period of time. Although a few clients can and do make such progress, the vast majority of clients require work that is quite plodding and time-consuming. The expression "Patience is a virtue" comes to fruition in being a therapist. Master practitioners understand that feelings of self-esteem cannot hinge on whether or not a client makes major improvements. On the other hand, establishing rapport, a therapeutic relationship, and a therapeutic alliance can occur quite rapidly. That sets the stage for the oftentimes more plodding and painstaking work of treatment.

All too often, a Level II practitioner may desire a client to change more intently than a client desires to change. A master understands that making changes in one's life is in the client's hands. A therapist provides the opportunity and circumstances in which changes can be made.

ASPIRATIONS OF A LEVEL II PRACTITIONER

Perhaps as a result of having experienced a modicum of success, a Level II clinician begins to view videotapes of master practitioners interviewing clients. After witnessing such expertise, a Level II practitioner is subject to experiencing the "WOW" factor. That is, he or she is overwhelmed at the seeming ease, elegance, and effectiveness of the master. As a result of the study of masters at work, a Level II will consciously or unconsciously desire to imitate a particular master. Although such desires are considered to be quite natural and well intentioned, they are considered very misguided and reflective of the fact that the learning curve for a Level II is still quite steep.

At Level II, practitioners are frequently interested in having a very specific definition of a master practitioner—so they can "nail it down" and replicate everything in the definition. Unfortunately, that would represent *linear thinking*. Master practitioners are not concerned with being master practitioners— they are much too busy being themselves, being available to clients, listening with incredible intensity, responding in a genuine manner, making mistakes and learning from them, learning from clients at least as much as they teach clients, and growing all the time.

Expertise as demonstrated by a master practitioner is not to be emulated, as though anyone could imitate another practitioner. Master practitioners intervene in therapy in a particular manner with certain therapeutic principles, understandings, orientations, and thinking processes according to the dictates of their own unique personality. When witnessing the *what* and the *how* of a master, perhaps the best that anyone can hope to do is *incorporate* what it is that they believe is of value that the master does according to the particular dictates of their own personality. "The master does things *that* way;

because of who I am and how I operate, I would need to modify things and do it *this* way, which would suit my personality."

THE DEVELOPMENT OF UNDERSTANDING AND NONLINEAR THINKING

There are a number of "understandings" that begin taking shape for the Level II practitioner. The first of these understandings is the difference between *insight* and *understanding*. Insight is being aware of something but not necessarily in a way that has an impact. To understand something is to know it and appreciate it in an intimate and consequential way. In today's parlance, *understanding* is the equivalent of "Now I get it!" It is such understandings that define this level and elevate the manner in which a practitioner functions. The understandings are no longer cursory but well considered, reasoned, more thoroughly engrained, and more natural.

Beyond understanding the primacy of the therapeutic relationship, perhaps no other characteristic quite typifies the development of Level II practitioners more than the maturity they begin to demonstrate in their understanding of the therapeutic process and the nature, role, and value of *nonlinear thinking*. Such understanding and thinking represent a quantum leap from the Level I of the novice. At the same time, such understandings underscore that mastery will require more experience, supervision, study, and reflection. In effect, a Level II sadly learns that there are no shortcuts. Nevertheless, the application of *nonlinear thinking* reveals that such an awakening paradoxically can be quite liberating. That is, Level II practitioners can begin to relinquish their struggle to *make something happen* in treatment and instead *let it happen*—in other words, they become facilitators of things therapeutic. Master practitioners *guide* the process of therapeutic discovery, change, and the relief of suffering rather than being pushed to come up with "the answer" to a client's difficulties.

Understanding the distinctions and differences between "making" and "letting" becomes the gateway to the world of the Level III practitioner and the feelings of mastery. As such, the gateway is an entrance into the world of how master practitioners *think differently* about people, problems, and making changes. It is in many respects the world of *nonlinear thinking*.

Another insight to emerge from Level II has to do with choosing a particular theoretical orientation or frame of reference. Such a frame of reference may consist of a theory of therapy (e.g., cognitive-behavioral), a school of thought (e.g., systems), or a theory or personality (e.g., Jungian). Staunchly eclectic practitioners may decry the necessity for making such choices. In fact, this text proposes that *regardless of theoretical orientation*, there are universal principles of therapy to which master practitioners pay attention, albeit from their own theoretical frame of reference. The advantage of choosing a particular frame of reference is that it provides a particular metaphorical underpinning and understanding to the process of therapy and "the way things work." The Level II practitioner begins to understand that there is value in knowing that research has developed universal principles of effective therapy *and* in having a specific theoretical orientation that reflects particularly interesting nuances and appealing constructs. In a sense, such an understanding allows for a practitioner to have his or her cake and eat it too—the best of both worlds!

The integral relationship between clinical concepts comes to be understood by the Level II practitioner. Foremost among such awakenings within Level II clinicians is the view that "things" are not necessarily what they seem. That is, "cognition" may appear quite *distinct* from "emotion," but functionally they are not necessarily *separate* from one another. To elaborate, cognitions are easily definable as thoughts based on a "schema." Obviously, clients are routinely troubled by thoughts that they harbor, and many times they are reluctant to reveal them to their therapists. It is equally obvious that clients express feelings and emotions and vividly describe them in poetic terms such as *overwhelming*, *dismal*, and *terrifying*. How can two such human functional activities, thinking and feeling, not be separate?

We propose very simply that the Level II practitioner begins to understand that human experience is truly integrated—a person is a functional unit, not a conglomeration of disparate parts or systems. This is not mere speculation but rather is demonstrated in the experience of everyday living and in the delicate and painstaking research of neuroscience. Hence, an informed understanding of cognition and emotion emerges as being part and parcel of the process of integrating human experience. What sort of integration are we proposing? In a truncated manner, we propose that the Level II therapist *begins* to understand the following elegant and complex relationship between cognition and emotion supported by clinical and neuroscience research:

- Schemas are assumptions, understandings, and representations about major aspects of the world. Individuals have schemas about the self, life, the world, people, and so on.
- Everyone has schemas.
- Schemas are organized into holistic themes that provide unique qualities to an individual that are reflected in his or her thoughts, feelings, and actions; that holistic theme is called the *personality*. Schemas are difficult to change.
- Schemas can be detected by the specific cognitions (i.e., beliefs) that an individual espouses.
- The neural architecture of the brain contains the capacity for human beings to scan and appraise the environment for perceived threats to the person or personality and perceived enhancements to the person or personality.
- The scanning process has been debated in the literature for decades and is known as *appraisal*.
- Perceived threats to schemas are stressful. Typically, the more rigidly held they are or the more outlandish schemas are, the greater the reaction to a perceived threat. Perceived enhancements to schemas are often pursued in one manner or other.
- Reactions to perceived demands or threats from the environment (e.g., interactions with others, or circumstances) to schemas that are held dear to the personality will generate strong feelings and emotional reactions.
- Transient demands or threats from the environment (e.g., others, life circumstances, or both) are perceived as stressful; more permanent such threats are experienced as intolerable and produce symptoms of anxiety, stress, depression, somatic complaints, insomnia, and the like.
- When demands upon or threats to core schemas do not recede and core schemas are maintained without modification, their interaction creates and is experienced as *ambivalence*.
- Ambivalence is a core dynamism commonly operative in clients who want to maintain their core schemas that are, however, incompatible with the perceived demand or threat from life that does not recede.
- The resolution of such ambivalence becomes *the* major challenge and focus of therapy (see Chapters 12 and 13).

A discussion of cognitions, emotions, and their relationship to one another is a major focus of attention in this section of our text. It is such "understandings" that begin to emerge and come to fruition at Level II.

Clearly, the Level II practitioner's understanding of client cognitions and emotions is at a much more sophisticated plane than it was at Level I. There is another order of understanding of cognitions and emotions that begins to develop, however, which is equally important. Regarding the former, the dictum "Know thyself" takes shape. The Level II begins to understand the value of understanding oneself, what kind of clients one works best with, and what clients one does not work well with—and why that is the case. Regarding emotions, the Level II has become more clinically enlightened. Although Level I therapists allow their feelings to distract and disrupt them from the task at hand, Level II therapists have the dawning nonlinear awareness of their feelings as an important source of *information*. That is, if sexual feelings are being aroused, is the client being sexually provocative or is the therapist allowing prurient self-interests to distract from the task and responsibility at hand? If angry feelings are stimulated in a Level II therapist, reflection is intended to reveal more precisely what it is about a client's behavior that is provocative. Is the client's behavior stimulating a sensitivity within the therapist? Or, is the client acting in a typically provocative manner unconsciously designed to elicit like behavior or rejection? And so on.

For some Level II therapists, the nonlinear dawning value of feelings aroused within will be easier to understand than for others; such is simply the nature of diversity among therapists in the same way that diversity exists among the clients they see in treatment. Although no one in particular cares to look at the phenomenon very carefully, the truth of the matter is that therapists do vary in their degree of "emotional intelligence," or emotional competence as it is also called. Unfortunately, the ability to fulfill the requirements for an academic degree does not necessarily translate to the emotional self-awareness that master practitioners demonstrate. Nor does such an academic qualification help individuals to know how to use such awareness to inform their responses to their clients. At Level II, some therapists begin to realize that they develop feelings about clients; for example, whether they like a client or not, or are attracted to a client (or not). For some, such awareness is anxiety provoking. For others, it is an awakening. For those who take heed from an awareness of their feelings, it is an easier growth spurt to learn that feeling reactions to what a client is saying and doing comprise an important source of *information* that can be enormously helpful in the therapeutic process.

Finally, it is characteristic of a Level II practitioner that many fantasies and illusions regarding being a therapist begin to fade. There is a measure of sadness and a void created at the evaporation of professional innocence and the dashing of unrealistic goals and aspirations. Nevertheless, successful emergence into Level II and eventual entry into Level III and beyond can yield satisfactions and wonderment that one has participated in facilitating the personal growth of other human beings as well as helped in the relief of their suffering. The Level II understands that being a therapist can yield such rewards, and that in itself can more than compensate for the void created by the loss of professional innocence and the crumbling of unrealistic goals and expectations.

The Domain of Understanding Clients' Cognitive Schemas

8

Part 1: Foundations

CONTENTS

INTRODUCTION

In the novel *Clan of the Cave Bear*, J. M. Auel (1980) described the cognitive life of the Neanderthal hominids living within their restricted world:

> The clan had changed so little in nearly 100,000 thousand years they were now incapable of change, and the ways that had once been adaptations for convenience had become genetically fixed … when the brain

was developed ... and their memory made them extraordinary ... they could recall the past with the depth and grandeur that exalted the soul, but ... a limitation ... they could not see ahead.... The clan could not think of a future any different from the past, could not devise innovative alternatives for tomorrow ... all this knowledge, everything they did, was a repetition of something they had done before ... the result of past experience ... the more memories they built up ... changes became harder ... there was no room for new ideas ... the clan lived by unchanging tradition ... every facet of their lives was circumscribed by the past ... it was an attempt at survival, unconscious and unplanned ... doomed to failure ... they could not stop change, and resistance to it was self-defeating, anti survival. ... A race with no room for learning, no room for growth, was no longer equipped for an inherently changing environment ... they would be left. (pp. 24–30)

The heroine of Auel's *Clan*, Alya, was a Cro-Magnon, and her prefrontal neocortex development made her capable of problem solving, planning, and conscious decision making, which enabled her to face future challenges of the environment. Her entrance into the clan, however, stimulates tension and generates anxiety between the comfort of understanding and doing things the old familiar way versus life's demands for adaptation, flexible thinking, and new behaviors. The clan owes its loyalty to the old way, but life's incessant demands for new ways won't go away!

WHAT ARE SCHEMAS?

Our clients, and indeed all of us, can be somewhat inflexible in our thinking. Changing the way we think and behave is difficult for most human beings. Defined beliefs (conscious and unconscious) and set ways of thinking make up our *worldview*. But it is nothing more than a "map," a *construct*, or a systematic theory for how the world works (Kelly, 1955; Shepris & Shepris, 2002). Each individual constructs a worldview based on his or her own perception of self, others, and the world. The worldview isn't the way the world *really is* but rather an interpretation of the world *constructed by each individual*. Thus, everyone functions according to a set of rules or *expectations* about the way the world operates and how we *believe* it *should* operate. This is referred to as a person's *schemas*. We follow our schemas (i.e., our interpretation of the world) with intense loyalty and change little, which provides us with a sense of continuity, stability, functionality, and predictability in life.

Schemas represent a "template" or reference manual that each individual has on how to deal with life. The reference manual helps us to appraise and interpret experience while mediating and guiding emotional responses, attitudes, action tendencies, and behaviors in general and problem solving in particular. As with all reference manuals, however, schemas are very functional but simultaneously limited. Obviously, they have proven useful in accomplishing whatever we have accomplished but limiting because they cannot constructively address all circumstances that life generates. Goldfried (1989) suggested a clinically useful description of a schema:

[A] schema refers to a cognitive representation of one's past experiences with situations or people, which eventually serves to assist individuals in constructing their perception of events within that domain. Although there are varying definitions of a schema, most reflect three basic assumptions: a schema is said to involve an organization of conceptually related elements, representing a prototypical abstraction of a complex concept. From a clinical vantage point, these complex concepts are likely to consist of types of situations (e.g. being criticized) and/or types of persons (e.g. authority figures). Specific examples are said to be stored in a schema as well as the relationship among these exemplars. Second, a schema is induced from the "bottom up," based on repeated past experiences involving many examples of the complex concept it represents. Finally, a schema is seen as guiding the organization of new information, much like a template or computer format allows for attending to or processing some information but not others. (p. x)

Personal schemas contain patterns of important information that are useful and essential. When individuals adhere to schema content, they can go through life with a sense of stability without being overwhelmed. Schemas guide the organization and interpretation of information from the world, as well as an individual's reactions to what is being evaluated. Individuals thus become more efficient, and life is made more predictable, more manageable, and, to a certain extent, safer. Schemas also provide a guiding sense of what it is that each human being seeks and strives for. In more primitive humans, the guiding and striving function of schemas increased chances of survival—obviously a good thing. In contemporary humans, schemas enhance not just physical survival but also a sense of personal worth (i.e., self-esteem), social significance, and avoidance of failure.

SCHEMAS HELP GUIDE OUR RESPONSES TO NEW EXPERIENCES

Without schemas, life would be a constant series of challenges or threats to which an individual would not know how to respond. It would be very similar to patients with head traumas who suffer with antero-grade amnesia (i.e., they can't form new memories). If a new person or new situation comes into their lives, they have no way of remembering anything about them (or the situation). When that new person (or situation) arises, the amnesic patient acts as if he is meeting the person (or doing an activity) for the first time, even though he may have encountered them dozens of times.[1] Schemas also help us to recognize patterns of encounters in life so we don't have to treat everything as new and unfamiliar, which would be time-consuming and energy wasting; and they protect us from entering harmful situations or becoming involved with people who may take advantage of us.

Although schemas are efficient, they often contain information that does not address life circumstances appropriately. In such instances, understanding the information that schemas contain becomes very important. If an individual begins to understand her schemas, she can hopefully do something constructive about them. Like the example of Alya and the *Clan*, she can become more open to new experiences, and flexible enough in her thinking to grow and change. When a person does not, she runs the risk of encountering the same problem over and over again.

OVERVIEW OF CLINICAL USE OF SCHEMAS

When therapists can identify underlying themes, rules, beliefs, or values that govern a client's personality, they can make better sense of their attitudes and behavior (no matter how apparently lacking in sense or bizarre they may seem). In the domain of understanding client schemas, master clinicians demonstrate their skills in utilizing *nonlinear thinking* to be helpful to some of the most difficult clients (e.g., those with Axis II personality disorders). Without understanding the context or "big picture" (i.e., schemas) regarding a problem or complaint, a *linear-thinking* therapist may feel lost in trying to understand a client's often contradictory or confusing behaviors. A *nonlinear-thinking* master practitioner, on the other hand, understands that everything derives its meaning from its context and starts his investigation there. Such a practitioner understands that knowledge of a client's context or worldview is what makes it possible to "make sense" of a client's behavior and attitudes, and be effective in treatment. Such knowledge can also be the starting point for Level II practitioners to make real and lasting interventions (i.e., *second-order changes*)[2] that impact a client's worldviews and alter her behavior. When a therapist understands a client's *schemas* (i.e., how a client operates as a result of how she views herself, other people, and the world around her), he knows *what makes a client tick*. This chapter presents an overview of

- the domain of understanding clients' schemas (i.e., the content and organization of particular beliefs and values into patterns of thinking and reasoning); and
- some of the skills that are useful in understanding and assessing *the content and pattern(s)* in a client's thinking.

Skill in this domain is a further extension and refinement of a clinician's ability to listen, respond, and think in both *linear* and *nonlinear* ways. Awareness and recognition of how *a client thinks* build upon the clinical work accomplished in the Level I domains. Information Box 8.1 discusses the history of schemas.

Information Box 8.1: Background and History of Schemas

The role played by thinking in poor adaptive functioning (and in healthy functioning as well) has been recognized going back to the early 20th century (see Ellis, 1989). As far as we can determine, Alfred Adler (1927, 1929, 1956)[3] was the very earliest clinician-theorist to recognize the role that distorted thinking plays in the ills of individuals seeking psychological help. He used the term *private intelligence* to denote the unique way of seeing things (e.g., beliefs, or *scheme of apperception*) a client holds:

> For the neurotic [the equivalent of today's term *personality disorder*[4]], coming to understand his own picture of the world—a picture which he built up early in childhood and which has served as his "private map," so to speak, for making his way through life—is an essential part of the process of cure. When one is attempting to redirect his life to a more nearly normal way of living, he will need to understand how he has been seeing the world. He will have to re-see the world and alter his old private view in order to bring it more into harmony with a "common view" of the world—remembering that by common view we mean a view in which others can share. (Adler, 1956, p. 254)

Adler's references to the neurotic's "picture of the world" and "private map" were his poetic metaphors for the neurotic's distorted thinking processes and the need for the therapist to understand and help reconfigure them so they are more in harmony with a "common" way of thinking about things—not a skewed, radical, or extreme way. He used the term *schema of apperception* to denote the private understanding of self, others, life, relationships, and the world that each individual develops early in life.

In the same era, Bartlett (1932) experimentally demonstrated how individuals will distort new information (e.g., stories taken from non-Western folk tales) to fit within familiar ways of understanding (many times, either by rewriting the events they heard or by deleting the unfamiliar elements), giving some additional validation to the power of a priori schemas. In 1955, however, George Kelly produced a seminal work on "personal constructs" that advanced the idea that schemas exert a powerful influence on how people view the world:

> Man looks at his world through transparent templates which he creates and then attempts to fit over the realities of which the world is composed. (pp. 8–9)
> Constructs are used for predictions of things to come, and the world keeps on rolling on and revealing these predictions to be either correct or misleading. This fact provides the basis for the revision of constructs and, eventually, of whole construct systems. (p. 14)

The concepts and language used between Adler and Kelly to describe *thinking* are strikingly similar. Both acknowledged the self-creation of belief systems, described the building of a "map" (i.e., a "picture" or "template") of the world and the way in which the individual imposes his or her beliefs or map upon reality, and implied a need for the revision of beliefs and constructs in keeping with what is, in effect, reality. Much of the literature regarding "cognition" in therapy has come to be known under another name: schema.[5]

In fact, in the early development of cognitive therapy, Beck (1967) identified client schemas as an important

> structure for screening, coding, and evaluating the stimuli that impinge on the organism.... On the basis of the matrix of schemas, the individual is able to orient himself in relation to time and space and to categorize and interpret experiences in a meaningful way. (p. 283)

Two decades later, Goleman (1986), a cognitive psychologist, independently noted and advanced a conceptualization clinically very congruent with those of Adler, Kelly, and others:

> A schema is like a theory, an assumption about experience and how it works ... in the words of David Rummelhart (1978) a 'kin of informal, private, unarticulated theory about the nature of events, objects, or situations which we face. The total set of schemas we have available for interpreting our world in a sense constitutes our *private theory* of the nature of reality.... Just as theories can be about the grand and the small, so schemas can represent [anything from] knowledge about what constitutes an appropriate sentence in our language to knowledge about the meaning of a particular word to knowledge about what patterns of (sound) are associated with what letters of the alphabet.' (Rummelhart, p. 13). (pp. 76–77; emphasis added)

Mozdzierz, Murphy, and Greenblatt (1986) suggested that authors of widely different theoretical orientations have actually described, condensed, and summarized many similar observations regarding the thinking and reasoning processes of troubled individuals. Arkowitz and Hannah (1989) voiced similar observations. Innumerable authors, regardless of their theoretical orientation (e.g. cognitive therapy, cognitive-behavioral therapy, control mastery therapy, psychodynamic therapy, rational emotive therapy, Adlerian psychotherapy, attachment theory, neurolinguistic programming, or dialectical behavioral therapy), basically have recognized that a client's dysfunctional belief system and distorted thinking play a major role in their misery and emotional dysregulation.

PERSONALITY DEVELOPMENT AND CORE SCHEMA DYNAMICS

Considering how important schemas are, where do they come from, and what do they contain? The simple answer is that schemas are built from a person's experiences, especially those in childhood. In turn, childhood experiences typically shape the three core elements of a person's schema dynamics: the *view of self*, the *view of others*, and the *view of the world and life*.

No matter what family or culture they grow up in, children gather experience with life, other people, and the world. When children learn about the world, however, they do not have the maturity to understand very complex topics such as self-concept, the world, life, other people, virtue, success, failure, and so forth. As a result of the innate creative capacity of human beings to make meaning, children interpret their experiences and draw conclusions that may not be (and frequently are not) accurate (e.g., a child believes that his father drinks because the child gets into trouble in school, or that the world is unfair because a sibling was born, taking his parent's attention away). Thus, although children are makers of meaning, the meanings that they make (schemas) might not necessarily be valid. Instead, they have characteristics of private (i.e., *nonlinear*, or not commonsense) meanings. Although an individual's private meanings (i.e., schemas) make them more *efficient* in functioning (because they act as a roadmap, a guide through life, etc.), they are often skewed and do not necessarily render them more *effective* at getting along with others or meeting life's diverse challenges.

Obviously, parents play a big role in shaping and guiding the development of the meanings children give to their experiences. How parents respond to children, their attitudes toward children, and their behavior in general are all reinforcers that help shape their children's schemas (see Gottman & DeClaire, 1997, for a practical description of the different ways in which parental responses to and interactions with children affect child development, self-image, emotional competence, etc.). Likewise, sibling relationships and other experiences in the family are powerful influences in the creation of an individual's *view of self*, *view of others*, and *view of the world and life*. These will be discussed further in this chapter.

Culture also plays an important role as the context in which a person forms her or his schemas. The particular culture in which a child is raised frames and guides the development of the meanings children give to many important issues. Particular meanings and values held for countless generations change only slowly (e.g., the value of male over female children, religious beliefs, and the concept of "arranged marriages" held by some cultures). In addition, emotionally charged situations that are repeated can become the basis for children drawing erroneous conclusions that become part of the client's schema dynamics. For example, how a child interprets (i.e., appraises) what siblings and others attribute to him can and does contribute to a child's view of self, view of others, and view of life and the world.

One's view of self, view of others, and view of life and the world represent core schemas or a "map of the world." The most typical problems for which individuals seek treatment relate in some way to these core schemas. The master practitioner understands and pays attention to the fact that this particular person with this "complaint" or "problem" sees himself as _____, sees others as ____, and sees life and the world as _____. The problems that a client experiences are derived, in part, from the way in which the client sees him or herself and others, or how he or she sees the world. Thus, any effective therapist must work on the schema level, and help clients see where their flawed thinking gets them into trouble. Clients in trouble are often unaware of the skewed nature of schemas that are relevant to their problems.

VIEW OF SELF

A core element of a client's schema is the view that a person has of him or herself. This takes the form of definitional statements about the self, and answers the question "I am ...?": for example, "I am stupid," "I am smart," or "I am clumsy." More than anything, a view of self[6] contains a *subjective evaluation* that may or may not bear any resemblance to factual information. As such, it contains subtle nuances and implications that are difficult to verbalize and can be either realistic or unrealistic.

Seligman (1990) has described this view of self in terms of how an individual thinks about the causes of the unfortunate and misfortunate events, whether big or little, that befall everyone. He called this view of self an "explanatory style":

> Some people, the ones who give up easily, habitually say of their misfortunes: "It's me, it's going to last forever, it's going to undermine everything I do." Others, those who resist giving in to misfortune, say: "It was just circumstances, it's going away quickly anyway, and, besides, there's much more in life." Your habitual way of explaining bad events, your explanatory style, is more than just the words you mouth when you fail. It is a habit of thought, learned in childhood and adolescence. Your explanatory style stems directly from your view of your place in the world—whether you think you are valuable and deserving, or worthless and hopeless. It is the hallmark of whether you are an optimist or a pessimist. (pp. 43–44)

Clinically, consider the example of someone who is intellectually gifted as measured by standardized IQ and achievement tests in school. If a person is repeatedly exposed to negative parental reinforcement regarding how "stupid" she or he is, the self-view that can easily emerge via underdeveloped abilities to reason effectively can be one of "I must be stupid because my father says I'm stupid. … I am stupid." Furthermore, such an individual will scan the environment for "evidence" confirming his or her negative self-evaluation and ignore those instances (e.g., good grades in school, or encouragement by the teacher) that do not fit such a negative self-evaluation.

An example of a realistic view of self might be a person who enjoys playing the piano for recreation, but doesn't have the musical refinement to play at a professional level. She still enjoys it, but does not delude herself into thinking that she will play at Carnegie Hall. Such a person is able to put her ability (and lack of ability) into a realistic context in harmony with other aspects of her life. People with a realistic view of self are able to take a more balanced look at themselves and be able to see their good qualities and shortcomings (i.e., "I know I tend to procrastinate and wait until the last minute"). They are also less likely to be dependent on others' opinions to determine self-worth. Individuals with *unrealistic* views of self may tend to discount their own perceptions (i.e., they can't trust in themselves) and "buy in" to others' opinions more easily—the client who appears to be appropriately dressed and groomed claims that she is "a mess" because her mother says so (or see the example of the "stupid" person, above).

View of Self and Optimism

A view of self can also be globally positive or negative, as well as realistic or unrealistic. Individuals with a positive view of self are generally more optimistic about their own abilities and talents. Schnieder (2001) suggested that cognitive and motivational processes such as realistic optimism contribute to a sense of well-being in life:

> Within our reality, we may often be able to discover a positive perspective on our situation—not a distortion or illusion, but a legitimate evaluation, within reasonable limits of what we do and do not know about our reality—that helps us to achieve peace of mind, appreciation for our experiences, and mobilization for future endeavors. This perspective invites emotions such as hope, pride, curiosity, and enthusiasm, which are likely to be powerful contributors to the essence of meaning, as well as powerful motivators. … The illusion of the good life is likely to break down for those who lull themselves into complacency with self-deceptive beliefs, but the illusion is likely to become reality for those who are optimistic within the fuzzy boundaries established by active engagement in life. (p. 261)

Individuals with a more positive and optimistic view of self tend to believe in their ability to accomplish tasks. Correspondingly, individuals with a negative view of self will tend to be more pessimistic and downgrade their strengths, accomplishments, or capability to do things. When combined with whether a person is realistic or unrealistic, the schematized view of self exerts powerful influences over a person's action tendencies, attitudes, engagement with life, and behavior.

If a person is realistic and positive, he may be appropriately self-critical, but generally optimistic nevertheless. He has the capacity to set and obtain goals, and is not generally self-destructive. Individuals with a negative and realistic view will tend to self-denigrate, or downplay others' expectations of them. Such individuals may indeed be successful and capable, but generally refuse to see these qualities in themselves, preferring to see any accomplishment as a matter of luck rather than skill or hard work. Individuals with a positive, though unrealistic view of self may seem overly optimistic and inflated in self-appraisal of their ability. They may feel that they can do anything, and cannot see the remote possibility of failure. Extreme forms of this could be seen in mania. Some individuals may feel a high sense of entitlement, or that they should get what they want.

Conversely, individuals with negative and unrealistic views of self can be pessimistic to the point of self-loathing. They often cannot see anything positive about themselves, despite overwhelming information to the contrary. This contrasts with individuals who have a negative and realistic view of themselves, who can at least be persuaded by the results of their work that they have talent. Negative and unrealistic individuals may seem to lack motivation to do things (i.e., "give up" on themselves) and may even exhibit signs of severe depression. Clinical Exercise 8.1 gives some examples of these.

Clinical Exercise 8.1: View of Self

Directions: Read each statement. Decide if the individual's view of self is realistic or unrealistic, and whether it is positive or negative. (*Answers at the end of chapter.*)

1. A client comes to therapy to address her fear of public speaking. She is interested in pursuing a career as an executive, and knows that this is an important part of attaining her career goals. She also understands that this will entail some skills training on her part that might make her uncomfortable.
2. A woman comes to a therapy session complaining of depression following a recent layoff from her job as an accountant. She states, "I am good at what I do, but I knew when I heard the rumors about layoffs, it would happen to me. All my life, stuff like that seems to happen to me."
3. A man comes for counseling because his family is concerned that he was becoming depressed. He is a highly intelligent, though aloof computer programmer who was working as a convenience store clerk because he was "waiting for the right job." The client was asked what he has done to find it, and replied, "I've e-mailed my résumé, but no one has called me. I figured I wasn't good enough."
4. A client tells his therapist that his wife sent him to counseling in order to deal with his anger problem. He states that he resented his wife for thinking that he has a problem: "It's not me. I know that I always give people a fair chance. Ask anyone who knows me, and they will tell you that I only get angry when the idiots around me do stupid things!"

Variation: Once the elements of the view of self (positive or negative, and realistic or unrealistic) are determined, discuss how this might impact or influence the therapeutic process. Form small groups, or discuss as a larger group.

View of Self and the Family of Origin

Each of these elements of the view of self (i.e., positive or negative, and realistic or unrealistic) is shaped by an individual's early experiences, especially in the *family of origin*. Most people would agree that an individual's family of origin is an important influence on his or her perception. The family, however it is defined (from a traditional two-parent household to a *kibbutz*, orphanage, stepparents, etc.), serves as an individual's first exposure to life, the world, and others. As a result, a person chooses[7] to take a realistic or unrealistic, and positive or negative, view of self, in part based on what was modeled to him or her.

Seligman (1990) suggested there are three crucial dimensions to an individual's "explanatory style": permanence, pervasiveness, and personalization. He described the permanence dimension as being characteristic of individuals who believe that causes of bad events and circumstances that occur are permanent (i.e., bad events are unrelenting and will continue to linger), causing them to give up easily. Pessimistic, easily discouraged individuals also believe that negative events are more pervasive and universal than they are episodic, specific, and transient. Finally, Seligman indicated that pessimistic individuals personalize:

When bad things happen, we can blame ourselves (internalize) or we can blame other people or circumstances (externalize). People who blame themselves when they fail have low self-esteem as a consequence. They think they are worthless, talentless, and unlovable. People who blame external events do not lose self-esteem when bad events strike. On the whole, they like themselves better than people who blame themselves do. (p. 49)

Children's values and explanatory styles (i.e., what is important, not important, to be strived for, and to be avoided) are influenced by the modeling of parents and culture. Those values strongly influence children's unconscious choices about how they see themselves, how easily they give up or persist, what they will strive for, and what they will avoid. We revisit a case from Chapter 5 ("Theme of Hopelessness: 'I Have a Chronic Problem'") to illustrate this in Clinical Case Example 8.1.

Clinical Case Example 8.1: A Chronic Problem

Recall from Chapter 5 the widow in her 60s with a long history of treatment. She presented as neat and well groomed, though dressed in somewhat plain, out-of-style clothing and mildly overweight. She was articulate and logical, and demonstrated an impish, "off-the-wall" sense of humor. Her presenting concern was a chronic depression she has struggled with her entire adult life. She furthermore described herself as "supersensitive," angry, chronically annoyed, and wanting to stay in bed, although she forces herself to go to work. She denied she was suicidal.

In reviewing her history, her childhood was laden with criticism by her parents with high expectations but little demonstrable love, affection, and positive reinforcement (especially when compared to her siblings). She describes failure to thrive over the years (i.e., her depression and symptoms) as being due to the many years of deprivations and hardships in her family of origin.

It is easy to see that she has a negative and unrealistic view of self. Growing up in her family, she was presented with a set of standards that she believed was too high for her to reach. In addition, the little physical affection, warmth, or other demonstrations of love she received were too sparse for her to encourage efforts to even attempt to excel at anything, which added to a negative view of self (i.e., someone not worthy of being loved). The essence of these experiences was "I am ordinary," "I am not (able to be) successful," or "My only claim to fame is to be critical, irascible, outspoken—that's who I am." This view of self is unrealistic because it is so pervasive and renders her unable to see positive attributes or accomplishments (e.g., she had a successful marriage, maintained steady employment, helped others less fortunate than herself, and engaged in volunteer community activities) as sufficient to warrant a self-view of "I'm OK—not perfect, but OK." She did have numerous other positive traits, including a sense of humor and anger (which can be a positive trait and will be discussed in the next chapter) that allowed her to form a positive therapeutic alliance where these strengths were revealed.

Before leaving this section, we wish to address how clinicians can reflect back to a client his view of self. Although the classification of positive or negative and realistic or unrealistic is useful for a clinician to organize her thinking, it may not prove very useful for a client to hear such feedback presented in that way. We suggest that a clinician needs to translate this conceptualization into an easily understandable format that is more personally relevant to her client. This would be in the form of "Perhaps you believe, 'I am ...'" "You seem to see yourself as ..." or "Could it be that you see yourself as ...?" thus representing a summary statement of a client's view of self that is easy to understand and perhaps reflected in daily life. A statement can be in the form of a theme or a metaphor,[8] drawn from a client's own statements, or it can be derived from the therapist's imagination based on discussions in therapy. It also highlights individually unique qualities while placing them within a more standard format. In Clinical Exercise 8.2, we revisit Clinical Exercise 8.1 to practice translating view-of-self categories into "I am ..." statements.

Clinical Exercise 8.2: View of Self

Reread the statements in Clinical Exercise 8.1, take the view-of-self categories, and translate them into "I am ..." or "You seem to see yourself as ..." statements.

Example: A client comes to therapy to address a fear of public speaking. She is interested in pursuing a career as an executive, and knows that this is an important part of attaining her career goals. She also understands that this will entail some skills training on her part that might make her uncomfortable.

Suggested answer: "I am a cautious person, but I like stepping out on a limb if it will help me grow."

Variation: Form small groups, and compare "I am ..." or "You seem to see yourself as ..." statements.

VIEW OF OTHERS

An individual's schema regarding *view of others* conforms to many of the same structures as one's view of self. Again, more than anything, a view of others contains a *subjective evaluation* that may or may not bear resemblance to "factual" information. Whether one's view of fellow human beings is realistic or unrealistic, and positive or negative, it is uniquely influenced by an individual's early life experiences, particularly in the family of origin, culture, and society. For example, closely knit cultures, tribal and insular in nature, will tend to convey meanings regarding "others" transmitted from one generation to another—likewise for such cultural phenomena as racial and ethnic prejudice.

Fundamentally, the view of others guides individuals through life by answering the statement "People (or others) are ..." As examples, we cite, "Others are out to get you," "Other people genuinely want to help you," "You can never trust a ..." "Other people are supposed to make things easy for me," and "*Those* people are no damn good." One's view of others can be reflected when negatively describing someone's character, "name calling," or suspecting his or her motives. This negative view of others might take the form of "They are *always*_____" (dishonest, incompetent, bad, weak, mean, etc., or a derogatory term). Such a negative view of others is also unrealistic as it globally describes the person's character or motives, rather than describing a specific event, encounter, or situation. In turn, a negative view of others tends to shape an individual's action tendencies. Of course, as with other elements of a client's schema, subjective evaluations of other people contain deficiencies and omit essential information. A key component to this is whether this view of others is realistic or unrealistic.

A more realistic view of others may contain beliefs such as "Although you can't be too trusting of strangers, friends who demonstrate that they are trustworthy can be relied upon to be loyal," or "Family members are more likely to stick by you; look out for them, and they will look out for you." More unrealistic views of others might be reflected in such qualities as excessive gullibility (e.g., "Everyone likes me," "No one would want to hurt me," and "Everyone has some good in them")[9] or excessive suspiciousness (e.g., "You just can't trust anyone," "Do unto others before they do unto you," "Other people wait to take advantage of you," and "Others do it to me, so I'm going to do it to them").

People with realistic views of others encounter trouble when others violate these personal rules (e.g., a friend runs off with your spouse, your brother steals your TV to feed his drug habit, or your best friend doesn't show up for your birthday party and doesn't call to explain). However, these individuals are able to put such unfortunate events in proper perspective (e.g. "It was one person, and he was sick," or "He was just a bad apple, but most other people are honest"), and "bounce back" after a period of disequilibrium. On the other hand, people with an unrealistic view of others can create problems all their own (e.g., regularly getting taken advantage of, or adopting a paranoid stance and having difficulty relating to others).

View of Others: Positive or Negative

Another aspect of the "view of others" is whether it is generally positive or negative. Individuals with positive views of others often adopt a belief that people are generally good and that the motives for their behavior are benign. This allows individuals to generally relate well to others and establish positive working relationships. If the individual also has a realistic view of others, then relationships with others will usually be mutually satisfying, and based on trust. An individual with a positive view of others, however, may demonstrate a "Pollyannaish" or innocent disposition—believing people are incapable of malevolent motives, especially about oneself. This can lead to being taken advantage of, or (at worst) victimized. Such a view can also be adaptive, however, because sometimes it inoculates individuals from being too disappointed by the actions of one person, thus giving credence to the idea that "ignorance is bliss." Such "bliss" can be protective. Conversely, a negative view of others most often translates to a generally defensive posture toward others. If realistic in orientation, a person may be "slow to warm up" to people but can and will eventually form and establish relationships. If an individual maintains an unrealistic as well as negative view of others, however, she is more likely to be both reticent and unwilling to engage, or possibly adopt an aggressive stance toward others. For example, a person may say, "People are dangerous; if you let your guard down, they'll take advantage of you." Likewise, such a person may be more likely to act in ways that would "turn people off" (e.g., being aloof or cold toward others), thus missing out on opportunities to make lasting friendships. Ample research has long shown that a lack of satisfying close affiliation and support from others can have a detrimental effect on both physical and mental health (Cohen, 1988; Myers & Diener, 1995; Reis, 1984). Clinical Exercise 8.3 offers some examples of these different views of others.

Clinical Exercise 8.3: View of Others

Directions: Consider that each brief statement is from an initial assessment of a client regarding social support (family, friend, etc.). Read each statement, and decide if the individual's view of others is realistic or unrealistic, and positive or negative.

1. "I don't have much use for friends. Anyone that I have gotten close to winds up hurting me, screwing me over, or leaving me in the end. I figure, 'Why bother?' I leave them alone, and they leave me alone."
2. "I have some very good friends that I can rely on. I have always been fortunate in making friends. Sometimes, I have had people who weren't good to me or for me, but I usually end those relationships quickly."
3. "I have a ton of friends! People are always helpful and so nice to me. I love helping back, too. I can't think of anyone that I have had a problem with. I am sure that I must have, but I can't remember it."
4. "It is tough for me to get to know people. I have a really busy schedule, and I don't have many friends, outside of a couple of guys I've known since childhood. At work, I generally get along, but I don't like to get too personal."

Answers: (1) Unrealistic/negative; (2) realistic/positive; (3) unrealistic/positive; and (4) realistic/negative.

Variation: Once you have determined the elements within the schema called *view of others* (positive or negative, and realistic or unrealistic), discuss how this might impact or influence the therapeutic process. Form small groups, or discuss as a larger group.

View of Others and the Family of Origin

As with the "view of self," each person has unique factors that make his "view of others" truly his own. These primarily arise out of early-childhood and family-of-origin experience. For example, if a family is wealthy or poor, abuses drugs, has social status or not, or is from a minority group, all can contribute to not only one's view of self but one's view of others as well. Attitudes about the role of men and women in society are created and passed along within a family and cultural context.[10] As mentioned earlier, culture also greatly influences one's "view of others." It is a transporter of value and meaning, whether good or bad. Together, family of origin and culture provide the context for the development of lifelong feelings and attitudes of racial, religious, and ethnic biases and prejudices. Such biases can be (and oftentimes are), unfortunately, the foundation for the development of racial prejudice, overt hatred, and violence toward people from other groups. Culture is a transporter of value and meaning. Even promulgating the value of boy versus girl babies is a means of promoting gender bias and the pseudo-inferiority of women.

As mentioned earlier, relationships with parents and siblings, culture, social position, as well as birth order can all play roles in the development of any particular individual's view of others. It is a client's perspective, interpretation of, and attitude toward such factors, however, that matter the most. Although some clients will unquestioningly accept family or cultural influences on their view of others, others may reject them and adopt an opposite view. Each of these instances are clinically valuable for therapists to explore.

Again, as with the view of self, the conceptualization of the view of others (positive or negative, and realistic or unrealistic) is helpful for a clinician. In order to personalize the view of others that a client holds, clinicians may use statements such as "Others are …" or "You seem to see others as …" Clinical Exercise 8.4 illustrates this point.

Clinical Exercise 8.4: View of Others

Return to the statements created in Clinical Exercise 8.3 on the view of others, and translate each of them into "Others are …" or "You seem to see others as …" statements. When you have finished, form small groups and share your responses. Then discuss with the class.

VIEW OF THE WORLD AND VIEW OF LIFE

An individual's view of the world in many respects is very similar to her view of others—but it has a somewhat broader scope. The *view of the world* refers more to an individual's perspective on living life itself. A view of the world and/or life addresses the following questions: "What is it like to live life on this earth?" and "What kind of a place is this earth?"[11] A Level II practitioner *must* suspend his or her own beliefs about such issues and assume the challenge of learning about someone else's view of life and the world. Does a client belief that life is a struggle, painful, dangerous, a piece of cake, sucks, my oyster, a jungle, hell, survival of the fittest, a race, exciting, uncertain, or something else? Developing an understanding of a client's view of life has multiple implications. Whatever the "theme" of an individual client's narrative, the view of life and the world addresses the "stage" and setting in which that person believes he must live out his particular drama and pursue his goals. If he believes that life is a jungle, then it follows from his nonlinear logic that the "survival of the fittest" (e.g., only the strong survive) may very well apply. On the other hand, an individual who believes life is a jungle may also believe that he is not the strongest creature in the jungle and that the only way to survive is to carry a low profile and go largely unnoticed by the predators in the jungle. A person's behaviors must be understood from his particular point of view.

Again, like the other components of a person's schema, it can be realistic or unrealistic, and positive or negative. In the instance of a client with a view of life and the world as a "jungle," it might be more accurate (i.e., realistic) to say that there are many things in life that are competitive, but not accurate (i.e., unrealistic) to say that there is no place for those who are not particularly competitive. Unique experiences from an individual's early upbringing help to shape a person's view of life and the world. Individuals with a realistic view of the world see life, society, and so on in a balanced, realistic way. Such a view allows individuals to be able to see the world as it is (i.e., realistically, both good and bad), rather than in a particularly skewed way or how they would want it to be. An individual with a view of the world may have views that depart significantly from reality. Individuals holding unrealistic views can easily distort reality to conform to their view in ways that cause many problems. As such, to the ordinary (commonsense) person, individuals with unrealistic views of the world may hold seemingly idiosyncratic beliefs, perverted values, extreme biases, and so on.

An individual's view of the world can also be either positive or negative. Those who have a positive view of the world are fairly optimistic and believe that the world is a *relatively* safe place. Individuals who have a negative view of the world tend to see the world somewhat as a dangerous place that requires an individual to be vigilant. On the surface, it may seem that individuals with a negative view of the world might be misanthropic and chronically troubled. It is possible, however, for a person to have generally positive views of self and others that are realistic, but to also have a negative view of the world. For example, if someone believes life requires "survival of the fittest," he may also feel confident about his ability to survive as well as have meaningful relationships with others. Clinical Exercise 8.5 provides examples of different views of life and the world

---

Clinical Exercise 8.5: View of Life and the World

Directions: Read over each statement. Decide if the individual's view of life and the world is realistic or unrealistic, and whether it is positive or negative.

1. Client focuses on terrorism, security, killer storms, disease, and "threats," and states, "If you aren't careful, you could be injured by a comet or global warming."
2. Client comes to session and states, "Life is a struggle. People should get ahead by hard work. However, many times *who* you know wins out over what you can do. You have to seize opportunities when they come to you."
3. Client states, "Life is good. If you just take it easy, things will work out. There is no need to get so worked up about things."
4. Client comes to session and states, "There is a balance in life, but no guarantees. Hard work and good faith attempts will usually turn out well, but that is not always certain. However, cheating isn't a good option, because that never works in the end."

Answers: (1) Unrealistic/negative; (2) realistic/negative; (3) unrealistic/positive; and (4) realistic/positive.

Variation: Once the elements of the view of life and the world (positive or negative, and realistic or unrealistic) are determined, discuss how this might impact or influence the therapeutic process. Form small groups, or discuss as a larger group.

View of Life and the World, and Family of Origin

A person's view of life and the world is also shaped in large measure by perceptions a child makes while living in her family of origin. If parents were overprotective and instilled a great deal of fear, then their children are likely to develop a tentative, negative, and unrealistic view of the world. They are prone to be anxious about perceived threats, and fear that they will not be able to cope with them. As a result, such individuals often adopt a self-protective, cautious stance. Many times, this can manifest itself as generalized anxiety, or even a sense of entitlement. In either case, such individuals feel that the world is dangerous. This development can be seen early in life with very young children, even in preschool.

Consider the case of a child accustomed to getting his way at home by throwing temper tantrums, a display of helplessness, withdrawal, and so on. Such a child is likely to believe that other adults and children should give him what he wants (e.g. toys, or his way) when he wants it. Some children will be successful in fulfilling this schematized view by bossing others around, whereas other children may not be successful (because other children resist, or a teacher intervenes). Such children may then adopt a view of the world that "Life is unfair," "No one understands me," or "Grab what you can at all costs, because you aren't guaranteed anything!" If a person has had consistent and balanced role models, however, her view of the world is likely to be more realistic (e.g., "Life is balanced, though not always fair. No one gets what they want and wins all the time").

Again, as with the view of self and view of others, a more personal translation of the view of life and the world for clients is characterized by statements such as "You seem to see life (or the world) fundamentally as …" Again, this is informed by the classification of the view of life and the world as well as the unique elements of the client. We present Clinical Exercise 8.6 for you to practice understanding the view of life and the world.

Clinical Exercise 8.6: View of the World and Family-of-Origin

Return to the statements created in Clinical Exercise 8.5 on the view of life and the world, and translate each of them into "The world is …" or "You seem to see life as a …" statements. When finished, form small groups and share your responses. Then discuss with the larger class.

A realistic view of life allows an individual to contend with the ups and downs that are inherent in *everyone's* life. We revisit a case from Chapter 4 to illustrate this in detail.

Clinical Case Example 8.2: A Woman Tired of Being Anxious

Recall from Chapter 4 (Clinical Case Example 4.2) the case of a pregnant woman with a diagnosis of a generalized anxiety disorder that included hospitalization and suicidal ideation. She eventually found relief and resumed a normal life. She presented herself for treatment because of several major life changes that triggered her anxiety (e.g., not working following a period of success in her career, incurring debts, having problems with her marriage, and being several months pregnant). She moved out of her family's home at age 18 and put herself through undergraduate school and graduate school as well. Several weeks before calling to make an appointment with her therapist, she "caught" herself "spiraling down" (i.e., became aware of the fact that she was "depressed") due to her not sleeping well, not eating well, being fearful as well as "paranoid" (i.e., easily feeling attacked or criticized and very insecure due to losing an attractive figure while pregnant), and battling with what she called "panic attacks."

She summarized her current position by stating, "There are so many things I'm afraid of. ... I realized that I couldn't take any medication like in the past because of the baby. ... I was in that mode of everything falling apart and that triggered, 'It's (i.e., being anxious) a state of mind, like I learned about in therapy.' One day I got so mad! I was sick of this being anxious, being afraid, sick of the negativity, and I refused to feed it. I just woke up and said, 'That's it!' I was *catching myself*, being more proactive versus allowing this stuff to take over and snowball. I *decided* to call you and set up an appointment. I think it's taken a lot of effort to confront it. It's like a creeping vine that's starting to grow. It's something that's said or that I see, and if I don't chop it off it takes over!"

EXERCISE

1. What might be this woman's view of life and the world?
2. How have such a life view and worldview manifested themselves?
3. Hypothesize about other elements she may hold within her schema of life and the world.
4. How might her previous experience in therapy help her to understand her present situation?
5. How might her schema dynamics be employed to help her?

Another area of special interest for discovering a person's view of the world is the assessment of loss early in a client's life, primarily regarding divorce or the death of a parent. By no means do such events automatically create a negative or unrealistic worldview. On the other hand, a child's early experience of the totality and irrevocability of death, or the perceived reality of parental loss through divorce, can leave lasting impressions that the world is cruel, is unsafe, and does not conform to one's wishes or desires. Such realizations might then be incorporated (into one's schema) and manifested in a person's approach to the world.

Contextually Cultural in a Box 8.1: The World's "Hot Spots" and the Development of Posttraumatic Stress

It is not only the loss of a parent that can profoundly affect one's view of life and the world. *The Economist* ("The Invisible Scars," 2006) described one of the world's crises, the dispute between Indian- and Pakistani-held Kashmir, and the devastating impact such a crisis has upon the populace. Médecins Sans Frontières (MSF: also known as Doctors Without Borders)[12] conducted an interview survey of 510 people in the region:

The results are frightening. Of the 510 people interviewed, one in ten had lost immediate family members in the violence, and one in three had lost members of their extended families. One is six had been forcibly displaced and 13% had witnessed rape. Virtually all had endured one or more raids on their houses. Not surprisingly, fewer than half felt safe more that occasionally. Arshad Hussein, a local psychiatrist, talks of the "midnight-knock syndrome." People feel so unsafe that they prefer staying in the hospital to going home ... of the female patients, 50% were suffering from depression and PTSD, according to Dr. Hussein, often because they had suddenly become the head of a household. ... Dr. Margoob[13] worries about the mental health of the young. "An entire generation is growing up," he says, "that does not live one day without fear." And this will trouble Kashmiri society for generations to come, even if peace should prevail tomorrow. ("The Invisible Scars," p. 42)

Such astounding data prompt one to pause as one takes an inventory of the world's "hot spots." International conflicts are precipitating posttraumatic stress now as well as in the future on ordinary citizens in unimaginable numbers. What sort of view of the world will they develop?

Krauss (2006) has described the powerful impact that culture has on the development of human schema (or view of life and the world) and behavior:

That is, people, though at root animals, excel the others in cognitive competency. Once humans have ideas they try to actualize them, to live within them and by them. The most significant of humankind's cognitive creations is the concept of the negative or "not" of an action, thing, or idea. Because of this humans can, think "I shalt not." Being able to do this, Burke believes, makes choice and "morality" possible. And, in Burke's system, choice and morality are essential to character and character is essential to the human personality. Their cognitive aptitude and their need and ability to actualize their cognitive schemata necessarily estrange humans from Nature. Nature alone does not determine human actions nor fully circumscribe human behavior; culture is their managing director. Even the expression of necessary biological processes such as eating and elimination, defending and copulating, [is] channeled, modified, and regulated by culture, hence anorexia and martyrdom. Once an idea has been conceived or a culture has been produced, humans are driven to perfect it. (p. 4)

HOW SCHEMA DYNAMICS RELATE TO PSYCHOLOGICAL DISORDERS

Once a therapist understands the components of a person's schema (view of self, view of others, and view of life and the world) and the numerous sources of influence in their formation, there are two important questions to address. The first is, can an individual modify his schemas? Arkowitz and Hannah (1989) made two important hopeful points: Individuals can change, and it makes no difference what particular theoretical point of view that one takes in order to help such changes come about:

Persons may learn that they are more capable than they previously believed or that they do not need to succeed in everything in order to be loved. Whether these new conclusions about oneself are couched in the relatively nonmentalistic language of behavior therapy, the rational language of cognitive therapy, or the historical and conflict-based language of psychodynamic therapy, each provides some way of reconceptualizing oneself and the world. (p. 164)

The second question is, how do schemas contribute to people's problem(s)? In Chapter 4, we introduced the two broad classifications of client issues, psychological disorders (coded on Axis I) and personality disorders (coded on Axis II). Each of these two broad classifications of client disorders is influenced by clients' schemas. We will present a discussion of these next.

SCHEMA DYNAMICS AND COGNITIVE DISTORTIONS

Spearheaded by pioneers such as Albert Ellis and Aaron Beck, practitioners in the 1960s and 1970s began recognizing and identifying certain definable automatic and unconscious (i.e., the client is unaware of) patterns of client thinking. By uncovering these "automatic" negative thoughts (ANTs) and pointing out their negative effects on clients, therapists were able to emphasize and establish *client control* over distorted and automatic thinking. Guiding behavior, such thoughts and thinking are so rapid and powerful that they prompt clients to believe they are beyond the threshold of control. By describing and highlighting such thinking, therapists are able to persuade and guide clients in refuting or arguing against such thoughts in order to stimulate acting differently (i.e., in a more positive way) or not succumb to these automatic thoughts. Using clients' schema dynamics, therapists can help clients gain an understanding into these cognitive distortions and begin to change how they react to such automatic thoughts. Common methods that clients use in distorting cognitions are listed in Information Box 8.2.

Information Box 8.2: Common Methods of Distorting Cognitions

Arbitrary inference: Making a conclusion that has no supporting evidence or contradicts existing evidence. Examples of this include "catastrophizing," or thinking the worst of any situation.

Selective abstraction: Drawing conclusions about events by taking information out of context or ignoring other information.

Overgeneralization: The process of making a general rule on the basis of one or more isolated incidents and then applying it to unrelated situations.

Magnification and minimization: Involves viewing something out of proportion, as either less or more significant than it really is.

Personalization: Occurs when individuals attribute external events to themselves even when there is no evidence of a causal connection.

Labeling and mislabeling: Defining one's identity based on imperfections and mistakes made in the past.

Dichotomous thinking: Conceptualizing an experience in either-or terms (e.g., seeing a situation as all good or all bad).

Exercise: Take each of the cognitive distortions above, and describe what schema dynamics (positive or negative, and realistic or unrealistic, view of self, view of others, and view of life and the world) would contribute to its development.

Source: From Beck and Weishaar (2005), Corey (2005), and Nystul (2006).

SCHEMA DYNAMICS AND AXIS I DISORDERS

It is important for a nonlinear-thinking therapist to remember that it is not schemas themselves that become problematic, but how a client applies them to life's challenges. Problems arise when a client applies schema dynamics to a given set of life circumstances that are not appropriate. People do this because of schemas' perceived effectiveness in the past. We re-present a case study from Chapter 3 to elaborate.

Clinical Case Example 8.3: A Drinker With "Bumps" in His Childhood

Recall (in the section on nonlinear responding of Chapter 3) the example of a man with an admitted drinking problem who came to therapy. In the second session of treatment, during the process of describing his early family life, he indicated that there were "bumps" while growing up in a "good" family atmosphere. When the therapist followed up on this statement by asking, "I'm not sure what having some 'bumps' means to you. Can you tell me what you mean?" The client responded that his mother had become paralyzed when he was only a toddler and that he had to live with his grandparents many miles from his family home for a number of years. Obviously, the "bumps" he described were of a significant nature and indeed much different from the "bumps" that occur in most people's lives.

Exercise

1. What elements of the client's schemas (view of self, others, and the world) can be gleaned from this brief description of his situation?
2. What type of nonlinear listening and responding is utilized to discover schema elements?
3. Which cognitive distortions presented in the first part of the chapter does the client employ in describing his "bumps"?
4. Might this client's schemas be helpful in managing life? Might they get him into trouble?
5. How can you personalize the client's schema dynamics (using the "I am …", "Others are …", and "The world is …" statements)?

In Clinical Case Example 8.3, based on his experience with his mother's paralysis and his subsequent drinking problem, we hypothesize that his view of the world is generally negative (e.g., "Life is full of big problems, and most people have bigger problems then me; I'd better not complain"). In addition, he may also have a negative and unrealistic view of self (e.g., "My problems are never important enough to trouble anyone with").[14] His expressed view represents a pattern of cognitive distortion that arranges his life experiences to fit with his schema: minimization. By minimizing his own needs (e.g., for attention and affection). he manages life by not creating demands on an already very stressed situation in his family. Such a schema was useful at the time. Such behavior, however, led him to suppress his needs, or distort reality to the point where his needs became virtually nonexistent. This might have helped him to get through the trauma of his childhood, but we cannot distort or suppress our needs as a permanent way of living. There is a cost for such distortion and suppression of needs. Cognitive distortions became hurtful—use of alcohol helped him to minimize his needs but only compounded his problems over time. In treating this person, a nonlinear-thinking therapist would begin by discussing the dual nature of his schema (i.e., how and where it is helpful, and where it is hurtful) and its particular distortions while exploring more adaptive approaches to one's needs and their expression.[15]

Beck and Weishaar (1989) asserted that certain diagnoses have certain "systematic biases" (i.e., have similar schema dynamics) that impact the client's way of thinking (viz., cognitively distorting). Table 8.1 incorporates Axis I disorders and corresponding systematic biases (according to Beck & Weishaar, 1989) or schema dynamics about view of self, world, and others.

TABLE 8.1   The cognitive profiles of Axis I Psychological Disorders

DISORDER	SYSTEMATIC BIAS
Depression	Negative view of self, experience, and future
Hypomanic	Positive view of self, experience, and future
Anxiety disorder	Physical or psychological threat—negative view of others, life, and the world
Panic disorder	Catastrophic misinterpretation of bodily or mental experiences—negative view of self
Phobia	Threat in specific, avoidable situations—negative view of life and the world
Paranoid state	Attribution of negative bias to others—negative view of others, life, and the world
Hysteria	Belief in motor or sensory abnormality—negative view of self
Obsession	Repetitive warning or doubting about safety—negative view of life and the world
Compulsion	Rituals to ward off doubts or threat—negative view of self, life, and the world
Suicidal behavior	Hopelessness—negative view of self
Anorexia nervosa	Fear of appearing fat (to self or others)—negative view of self or others
Hypochondriasis	Belief in serious medical disorder—negative view of life and the world

Source: Adapted from Beck and Weishaar (1989).

HOW SCHEMA DYNAMICS RELATE TO PERSONALITY DISORDERS

According to Benjamin and Karpiak (2002), half of all clients coming for treatment have an Axis II personality disorder. However, a majority of manualized treatment protocols have focused on treating only the Axis I disorders and ignoring the personality disorder despite the fact that researchers have shown that there is a close association between the two. Why do many therapists appear to ignore or dismiss personality disorders? The reasons for this are varied. Some do it for theoretical reasons, believing either that DSM diagnoses are culturally insensitive or that diagnoses stigmatize clients (Coale, 1998). Other therapists may underreport Axis II disorders for financial reasons because such diagnoses are often not reimbursed by third-party payers (Koocher, 1998). Unfortunately, many other therapists underdiagnose personality disorders because they are often intimidating, therapists don't have the skills to treat such individuals, and they are so draining that the work seems unrewarding. Linear-thinking therapists generally attempt to treat clients by ignoring the personality disorder and focusing on the co-presenting Axis I disorder symptoms. They quickly find that therapeutic approaches that are effective for many Axis I disorders are simply not efficacious with personality disorders (Benjamin & Karpiak; Young, Zangwill, & Behary, 2002). Perhaps this accounts for many of the treatment failures that beginning therapists encounter, as well as problems that some manualized treatment protocols have in replicating laboratory validations of their approaches.

Consider the definition of a *personality disorder*. According to the DSM-IV-TR (American Psychiatric Association, 2000), all personality disorders (coded on Axis II) share the following characteristics: an enduring pattern of inner experience and behavior that deviates markedly from the expectations of the individual's culture (on the cognitive, affective, and interpersonal levels) and that is inflexible and pervasive across a broad range of personal and social situations. In addition, these patterns of behavior lead to clinically significant distress or impairment in important areas of functioning (e.g., social or occupational). In other words, personality disorders are simply disorders that arise from one's schemas.

One critical schema dynamic that all personality disorders have in common is that they are all unrealistic in nature, in the client's view of self, others, or the world. Horney (1945, 1950)[16] suggested that individuals with personality disorders demonstrate dysfunctional schemas that are in some manner *irrational, insatiable, impossible, inappropriate, intolerant, wanting things without effort, egocentric, vindictive,* or *compulsive* (she referred to "overdriven attitudes," now known as schemas). The rigid inflexibility of the particular schema dynamics makes it difficult for *linear*-thinking therapists to treat personality disorders; master practitioners, utilizing *nonlinear* thinking, encounter less resistance. Utilizing *nonlinear* thinking, they direct their attention toward the central organizing patterns of a client's problem (the schema, or view of self, others, and the world). The makeup of these elements gives the nonlinear-thinking therapist the ability to engage a client on a more meaningful level, as well as providing a better conceptualization of the peculiarities of the client's behavior.[17] Clinical Case Exercise 8.1 illustrates these points further.

Clinical Case Exercise 8.1: Anxious and Dependent

A well-educated, pleasant, happily married woman with a young child sought therapy because of overwhelming anxiety and an inability to comfortably leave her baby in the custody of others except for her husband and parents. She recognized this as aberrant but felt helpless to bring it under control. She reported her "ton of anxiety" as resulting from her baby's medical problems with numerous legitimate trips to hospital emergency rooms and a felt need for more than typical parental vigilance and new mother nervousness. Although medical authorities assured her that her baby would grow out of his condition, such reassurances had little ameliorating impact on a daily basis. She relied frequently and heavily on her parents in the event of *any* troublesome circumstances that she believed she simply could not deal with on her own—"I don't know what I would do without them!"

During the first session, she reported that she had "done a lot of thinking" and concluded that "as far back as high school," she could remember herself being consistently "excessively worried about something." In the process of collecting early-childhood and family-of-origin material, it was discovered that she had a very positive and endorsing family that was physically affectionate and supportive. At the same time, careful nonlinear listening to the woman's description of the family atmosphere revealed very subtle expressions of a nervous quality underlying the positive and loving picture. As the "baby" of her family, much older siblings could overwhelm and "beat up" on her as they would play roughhouse. Such encounters, although oftentimes fun, would also scare her and require her to call for help in need of "rescuing" by her parents or oldest sibling. Her mother and father's method of discipline included being "strict" with her, and "yelling" to gain "control" over rambunctious and energetic children. She also described her mother as somewhat nervous in nature, a person who did not easily relax. Then. too, there were tornadoes to be frightened of and scary monsters she imagined that would prompt her to run for the cover of her parents' bedroom at night. In describing what her life was like in school, she casually related that teachers and authority figures in general were "intimidating." The net result of all of these nuanced descriptions revealed a pattern of thinking. There was a "nervous edge" to her experience of growing up as a child.

Nevertheless, she did well in school, had friends, and was well liked and successful in a beginning career before marriage. At the time of entering therapy, she was living in a healthy and successful marriage with a husband who was very "supportive and caring." Despite these positive factors, she still experienced the "ton of anxiety" over her child. She stated her goals for therapy as follows: "I'm looking for ways to think about things differently!"

In the case noted above, address the following questions:

1. What is the client's view of self? Realistic or unrealistic? Positive or negative?
2. What is the client's view of life and the world? Realistic or unrealistic? Positive or negative?
3. What is the client's view of others? Realistic or unrealistic? Positive or negative?

4. What unique experiences in this person's life impacted her schema?
5. What messages did she pick up from her family of origin that may have impacted her schema?
6. How might her birth order or sibling relationships impact her schema?
7. How have these "schema" dynamics played a significant role in this woman's personality?
8. What Axis II personality disorder might this client have?
9. Does understanding this woman's schema dynamics make her chief complaint more understandable?
10. Can you translate the client's schema dynamics into a more useable, personal statement or statements—for example, "I am …", "Others are …", and "The world is …"

A *nonlinear*-thinking therapist realizes that schemas—even very problematic ones—have been reinforced and evolved over a lifetime (aided by self-fulfilling prophecies, family of origin, personal experiences, etc.) as a way of helping an individual navigate through life. They represent a client's attempt to solve the problem of "How am I going to manage my life without getting hurt or being immobilized by a fear of getting hurt, making a mistake, failing, losing, etc.?" This is how schemas become a roadmap providing guidance to an individual throughout life. It helps the individual to filter information and make sense of the world, organize an immense amount of information in need of processing, guide interactions with other people, and generally define who he or she is as a person. As mentioned earlier, attitudes or behavioral responses adopted in schemas are adaptive, but when they are highly skewed or misapplied, this can lead to trouble. They can be difficult to alter. But, understanding, classifying, and interpreting schema dynamics in collaboration with a client in a consistent fashion can effectively help the client to address his or her concerns.

CONCLUSION

We have defined the core elements of a crucial domain that all effective clinicians utilize—client schemas. An understanding of the dynamic meanings underlying a client's schema can give a clinician vital clues that unlock central themes that contribute to the client's concerns. In the next chapter, we discuss ways to both assess and use the information about a client's schema dynamics.

ENDNOTES

1. This has been used as a plot device in movies, such as *50 First Dates* (Segal, 2004) or *Memento* (Nolan, 2000).
2. We will briefly discuss first-order and second-order change later in this chapter and in more detail in Chapter 10.
3. Adler's work, although cited as published in 1956, is a text of his collective writing edited by H. Ansbacher and R. Ansbacher. In turn, they cited Adler's original works going back to the early 20th century.
4. The term *neurotic*, as used by Adler, fell out of fashion but can be considered roughly the equivalent of today's *personality disorder*.

5. Although Carl Jaspers' work in the 1912–1913 era used the term "schema," various authors have noted the similarity of his work with that of Adler (see Adler, 1956, p. 14).

6. For the purposes of this text, we do not differentiate between *view of self*, *self-image*, or *self-concept*.

7. The word *chooses* may seem odd regarding a child "choosing" to take a positive or negative view of self. The word *choose* represents a constructivist viewpoint—it is the child who concludes whatever it is that she concludes about self. Thus, in effect, a child "chooses." But, because a child has an unconsciously determined and limited understanding of complicated things, she cannot be held fully accountable for the view of self that she develops. Despite such limited culpability, whatever is concluded about oneself in the view of self, it *is* the individual who concluded it and correspondingly must take ownership of it. The discouraging aspect of this incongruous conundrum is that we are all held responsible for conclusions about the self made as children. It is encouraging that by taking responsibility for childhood conclusions, we can influence and change them.

8. The subject of metaphors will be discussed later in the chapter.

9. Although everyone *may* have some good in them, it is perhaps more difficult for such good to demonstrate itself in the generally sociopathic and predatory individuals in society. And even "good" people, as the saying goes, may have larceny in their hearts. Additionally, different cultures may differ widely in what constitutes the "good."

10. As examples, consider that fetal ultrasound in India has been abused—if a female fetus was detected in utero, women have been more disposed to have an abortion than if pregnant with a male fetus. In China, with a "one child per family" policy, there is a huge preference for males over females, and government efforts to "regulate" population growth have resulted in unwanted female babies being given up for adoption in vast numbers compared to male adoptions. In turn, China is becoming a society with males for whom there are not enough women to marry.

11. The view of life and view of the world can be separated into two separate views for reasons specific to a particular client.

12. Doctors Without Borders is "an independent international medical humanitarian organization that that delivers emergency aid to people affected by armed conflict, epidemics, natural or man-made disasters, or exclusion from health care in more than 70 countries"; see http://www.doctorswithoutborders.org/aboutus/index.cfm (Doctors Without Borders, n.d.).

13. Dr. Margoob is identified as the head of the Psychiatric Disease Hospital in Srinagar, India.

14. There really is not enough information to speculate about the client's view of others, though the reader is free to do so.

15. This is done through the appraisal process, which will be discussed in detail in the next chapter.

16. She referred to "over driven attitudes," which is a precursor name for what today are called *schemas*.

17. Along the same vein, Millon (1996) has suggested that various personality disorders identified by the Millon Clinical Multiaxial Inventory harbor certain "functional processes" and have certain "structural attributes." A prominent feature of each personality disorder is a common way of thinking and feeling.

Answers to Clinical Exercise 8.1: (1) Realistic/positive; (2) realistic/negative; (3) unrealistic/negative; and (4) unrealistic/positive.

The Domain of Understanding Clients' Cognitive Schemas

9

Part 2: Assessment and Clinical Conceptualization

CONTENTS

NARRATIVE UNDERSTANDING OF CLIENT CORE SCHEMA: WHAT MAKES A CLIENT TICK?

As mentioned in Chapter 8, although "view of self, others, and the world and life" are strategically useful in understanding clients and in helping clients to understand themselves, core *schemas* are best communicated back to clients in a holistic theme that one might call a client's "story." It is as though a client is saying, "Because I see myself as _____, and other people are _____ and the world is _____, therefore I'm having difficulty with this issue (e.g., a relationship, set of circumstances, unexpected event(s), need to change, or life demand)." We expand on this to provide practical strategies for using information about schemas.

One way of understanding a client's "story" is to listen for its "plot." Listening for a plot is greatly facilitated by both *linear* and *nonlinear listening*. A master practitioner listens for a client's narrative theme automatically—much like being intimately involved in absorbing and understanding the plot in a movie or a novel. In movies or stories, characters operate by clearly defined rules (i.e., their roles). Traditionally, there are two main characters: a protagonist, a hero or heroine usually motivated by honor or duty; and an antagonist, a villain usually maneuvering by malevolent motives—for example, greed, jealousy, or revenge. In most stories, these distinctions are obvious. The audience has a clear understanding of the characters and their motives, and can interpret behaviors easily.

Everyone operates like a character in a story with defined beliefs (i.e., schemas) and set ways of thinking. Beliefs help us to put events into a context (just like watching characters in a movie), and help us to assign meaning to what we experience (e.g., "This is important to me because …"). Again, the ability to make meaning out of the events and circumstances of life is a universal human quality that transcends cultures. In turn, understanding the traditional values of a client's family and culture can be very helpful in understanding what makes a client tick.

Master practitioners have trained themselves to understand a client's "story" by automatically listening for its "plot" in both *linear and nonlinear ways*—much like being intimately involved in absorbing and understanding the plot in a movie or a novel. Narrative themes may stand out boldly or may be much more muted. Skilled listening and observing are required to identify themes hidden among comments, reflections, and descriptions that clients make about their purpose in seeking therapy.

Master practitioners derive understanding of client schemas from any number of sources. In the next section, we describe how master practitioners utilize a variety of methods to weave core themes in the client's story (i.e., the schema dynamics of view of self, others, and life and the world) into a coherent narrative to understand *what makes the client tick*! Some of the methods used to accomplish this are *linear* and *nonlinear* listening and responding, assessment, relationship building, understanding family-of-origin dynamics, and early childhood memories.

LINEAR THINKING, LISTENING, AND RESPONDING TO CORE CLIENT SCHEMAS

Recall that linear listening has two components: *listening for content and information* and *listen for feeling*. But, schemas filter information and generate feelings. Thus, clients do not relate "pure" information or fact, but rather unconsciously screened, altered information—a map of reality. A prudent *linear-thinking* therapist is sensitive to listening for subtle clues about a client's schemas (i.e., view of self, others, and the world and life embedded in the "facts" of their story). When *listening for content or information*, therapists need to be mindful of specific questions to discover key elements of a client's schemas. *What* is the client saying about him or herself, others, or the world? Are these statements generally positive or negative? Does the client seem rigid or inflexible about these statements? For example, clients often make statements such as "I can't ever seem to do anything right," "You can't be too careful around people," "*Every* time that I …" "I just can't ever seem to relax," and "It's a dog-eat-dog world." Each of these relatively straightforward statements suggests a negative view of self ("I can't …"), a negative view of others ("You can't be too careful around people"), or a negative view of the world ("It's a dog-eat-dog world").

O'Hanlon (2003) suggested that another way of understanding the linear aspects of a client's story is to look for "injunctions": "One way to think of the presenting problem in therapy is that it reflects an injunction … Inhibiting Injunctions such as can't/shouldn't/don't. Intrusive/Compelling Injunctions such as have to/should/must" (p .33). As such, injunctions are commands, rules, absolutes, and the like imposed on a client that can come from parents or other authority figures and are assimilated and incorporated as part of schemas in the personality. It is as though a client is following certain "orders" accepted in childhood as valid and obligatory. They can be detected in early childhood recollections[1] and spontaneous comments about childhood (e.g., "My mother always told me to 'turn the other cheek!'"). O'Hanlon suggested that such injunctions are oftentimes best dealt with through the use of interventions he called "counter-injunctions" (e.g., "Permission statements mirror injunctions nicely"; p. 33) that are based on *nonlinear* thinking. This is an example, however, of the use of linear listening for content that can reveal nonlinear schema dynamics.

Listening for feeling is another important linear source for identifying portions of a person's schema. As mentioned in Chapter 2, listening for feeling provides "shading" or nuanced information. Listening for feelings helps a therapist to refine an understanding of the elements of a client's schema. For example, if a client makes the statement "I just can't win!" but he or she gives a wry smile and a giggle (both tending to contradict what has been said), it may signify a more positive view of self (i.e., "I tried to get away with something, and got caught with my hand in the cookie jar!"). On the other hand, a client looking sad and forlorn, with tears in her eyes, sighing deeply and saying, "I just can't win!" may be indicating a more negative view of self and life—someone who feels that "life" is unfair and perceives that she "always" gets the "short end of the stick." The verbal statements are identical ("I just can't win!") but qualified differently (i.e., one is more playful, and the other more painful). Clinical Exercise 9.1 presents a linear-listening activity designed to help define elements of a person's core schema.

Clinical Exercise 9.1: Linear Listening for Schema

Directions: Read each of the statements below, and decide which of the elements of a person's schema (view of self, others, or the world or life) it reveals, and whether it is positive or negative.

1. "I don't know why I am so gullible, but I guess I never see the bad in people until it is too late!"
2. "Ugh! Men are such pigs! I mean it. They just are. I hate 'em!"
3. "I think that the problem is that people get too worked up about things. If people would just chill out more, things would work out for them."
4. "I try to keep a level head about most things, and I think that I do a good job of it; but sometimes I guess I lose my temper. Not often, but sometimes I just blow off steam."
5. "You know, we could all die tomorrow. A killer asteroid could hit, or they could drop the bomb, and it would all be over."
6. "I'm such a loser."

Variation: Create examples of statements that would translate the various elements of a person's schema (positive or negative view of self, others, or the world or life) into something more personally relevant to the client. Form pairs or small groups, and identify schema elements underlying each of the above statements.

Counselors can use linear listening and responding to help figure out what can be useful in establishing reasonable hypotheses as to what a client's schema dynamics (view of self, others, and life and the world) are. For example, when a client's "view of self" is connected to the presenting problem or complaint, a therapist can present that hypothesis in a respectful way for consideration. For example, "It sounds to me like you see yourself as _____ (e.g., helpless, or an innocent bystander)" or "Could it be that you see yourself basically as _____ (e.g., helpless, or an innocent bystander)?" This is an extension of the "translation" mentioned in each of the view of self, others, and the world and life sections in Clinical Exercise 9.1. Consider the 60-year-old widow cited in Clinical Case Examples 5.3 and 8.1. To respond to her effectively, it was necessary for the therapist to understand and appreciate her underlying self-schema. *All* of her complaints (e.g., wanting to stay in bed; being chronically annoyed, irritated, and critical; not wanting to visit relatives; being "fed up"; and chronically feeling unappreciated) needed to be taken into account to understand how they reinforced her negative view of self (i.e., "I feel less worthy than other people"). In turn, her irritability toward others allows her to act in ways that turn other people off. Such behavior garners negative feedback and leaves her feeling unappreciated, unsuccessful, and "less than" others. In addition, her decision not to visit relatives reinforces others' views of her as irascible. Sensing the "plot" of the client's story, the therapist communicated his ideas about her view of self via an image of the "family ugly duckling." This characterization allowed for a better working alliance (i.e., "This therapist really understands how bad I feel about how I see myself!") and other effective interventions as well.[2] This is a good example of how basic skills (linear and nonlinear listening and responding) can be combined with advanced (Level II) skills (understanding a client's schema dynamics) to effectively work with a difficult client. We will discuss how to use these in more detail next.

NONLINEAR THINKING, LISTENING, AND RESPONDING TO CORE CLIENT SCHEMAS

We have emphasized that linear and nonlinear methods must be used together in order to be most effective with the client. This is especially true with understanding the influence of schema dynamics on a client's behavior. Sometimes, hypotheses that a therapist creates using linear listing (listening for content or feeling) can be confirmed or rejected by nonlinear listening. Straightforward client statements must be consistent and supported by other (often subtle) information. Nonlinear listening for subtle comments can expose faulty logic flowing from schemas, which provides information that supports hypotheses (or fails to). When this is fleshed out, a therapist can make more effective suggestions and interventions. In addition, nonlinear listening can often help a clinician to find the right image or "theme" for a client's "story." We present some of the more common types of client statements that reveal their "logic" and the nonlinear listening that is utilized to understand them: "What if ..." "If such and such is the case, then ..." and "absolutes, polarities, extremes, and exclusionary thinking."

Linear and Nonlinear Listening for "What If ..."

A client posing the question "What if ..." can reveal important information regarding a client's schema dynamic. According to Gula (2002), such a question is a personal "domino theory" that can literally induce immobilization of self-efficacy. It is a veiled attempt to predict and control the future (an impossibility) as a way of keeping oneself safe. Safety and danger are the central dynamic issues behind this schema (i.e., a negative view of the world or life) expressed in many different ways by anxiety. Although revealed in a client's verbalizations about the present, such a schema is typically developed in early childhood and reflects a pervasive dynamic. Clinical Case Example 9.1 illustrates this.

Clinical Case Example 9.1: *Anxious*

A college senior with a history of psychiatric treatment for depression (including liberal use of antidepressive medications) dating back to grammar school came to therapy again depressed, anxious, and discouraged. He had few friends, lived with his parents, worked part-time, did not date, commuted to and from school, and was not having very much fun in life. Problems in concentrating, shyness, phobias, and so on all were part of his narrative. A significant theme noted during the first session was the young man's complaint about "anxiety." He noted that when he would challenge himself to become more involved with others, he would quickly respond to such a self-suggestion with the counterargument, "*What if* others reject me like when I was younger?" He also had mentioned that in driving to the therapist's office and while driving places on a daily basis, he would pose anxiety-inducing questions to himself such as "*What if* that car decides to come into my lane?" or "*What if* that car coming the other way decides to come into my lane and hit me head-on?"

QUESTIONS
1. How would you formulate this client's schema dynamics?
2. What linear information (content, feeling) is revealed?
3. What nonlinear information is revealed by the client's statements? What methods of nonlinear listening would you use?
4. How can you put this client's schema dynamics into a more personally useful statement to feed back to the client?

Relevant to Clinical Case Example 9.1, Beck and Weishaar (1989) noted that human beings are information processors who use several learned "related coding systems" that form the basis for useful information (i.e., schemas), such as "Strangers may be dangerous." They described it thus: "[I]n anxiety, the relevant coding system consists of the following parts[:] (1) attention—hypervigilance for data relevant to danger; (2) selection of data relevant to danger; (3) overinterpretation of danger; and (4) increased access to danger themes in memory" (1989, pp. 22–23).

Clients expressing schemas reflecting "danger" typically have a negative and *unrealistic* view of the world. They are quick to come up with reasons not to take risks, voiced as "What if ..." statements. A *nonlinear*-thinking therapist in this case uses listening for *inference* (i.e., a client is catastrophizing and scaring himself into immobilization in an attempt to prevent something remote from happening).

Returning to Clinical Case Example 9.1, the therapist noted to the young man that perhaps he was "scaring" himself. Furthermore, he pointed out that the client was very good at it but also added the comment that his being good was not the essential thing. The therapist suggested that *scaring oneself* indicated an underlying ability *to influence oneself.* Following this line of reasoning, the therapist suggested that if the client could influence himself in a negative way, perhaps he could also choose to influence himself in a positive way. The client smiled and said that he had never thought of that. He was intrigued by such a suggestion, and his physical demeanor and facial expressions perked up. The therapist then suggested that perhaps as a "homework assignment" (he was, after all, a college student), the client could work at "catching" himself in the act of scaring himself, and tell or suggest to himself that he could influence that behavior now that he was aware of it. The client left the therapy session in quite good spirits, eager to implement a bit of new learning.[3] The therapist succeeded in bypassing potential client resistance by not engaging in a discussion about the "What ifs," and redirecting the discussion to the suggestion that the client himself could be a source of insuring his safety.

Linear and Nonlinear Listening for "If Such and Such Is the Case, Then ..."

Also according to Beck and Weishaar (1989), schemas can be revealed by "conditional assumptions" (p. 24). An individual operating on the basis of such a schema might reason as follows about different topics:

- "*If* I don't get something the first time, (*then*) I don't want to do it because it is beyond me."
- "*If* something appears too hard to learn, (*then*) I don't want anything to do with it because it is too much work."
- "*If* everyone doesn't like me, (*then*) it must signify that I'm not worthwhile."
- "*If* I'm not good all the time, (*then*) it must mean that I'm really bad."
- "*If* I don't get attention and recognition for being 'special' and helpful, (*then*) it means I'm not worthwhile."

Gula (2002) urged caution when individuals use the word *if* because it can be used in deadly inaccurate reasoning that its proponent is hardly aware of.

Master practitioners look for "logic" that flows from a client's schemas. If a client didn't hold the fundamental schemas that she does, she would reason differently and perhaps have other problems.

How rigidly a client holds to a set of beliefs reflects unrealistic schema dynamics and creates greater dysfunction (i.e., personality disorders). A *nonlinear*-thinking therapist listens for a combination of *congruence*, *presence*, and *resistance* when a client uses "conditional assumptions." Listening for congruence (or *incongruence*) provides information about the strength of a belief or conviction. For example, a client states, "I would *never* stay married if my husband cheated!" But, when an infidelity is revealed, she does not file for a divorce. Such *incongruence* could indicate that there are additional competing schemas involved (e.g., "Divorce is a sign of failure, and I must *never* fail").

Likewise, listening for *presence* (e.g., nonverbal behaviors, and tone of voice) adds to a therapist's understanding of how *intensely* someone feels about his beliefs, and how *deeply conflicted* someone is about how he thinks things should be and how they are. Consider the following: An individual believes himself to be indispensable to his office and has a positive but unrealistic view of self. When "downsized," he cannot fathom being replaced. He may have difficulty finding a new job and place many (unreasonable) conditions on taking a new job, such as "I will apply for a job with them *only* if I don't have to travel." Declarations made in anger or frustration with corresponding body language give clues that the client is having trouble with his new reality. *Resistant* clients frequently avoid making a commitment to change by using *conditional statements* (e.g., "Yes, but ..." or "I'll try. ..." statements). This is also generally indicative of conflicts between clients' core schemas and the realities they have to face.

Linear and Nonlinear Listening for Absolutes, Dichotomies, Extremes, Polarities, and Exclusionary Thinking

Statements that include absolutes (always or never), dichotomies (this *or* that), extremes (the best *or* the worst), polarities (right *versus* wrong), and exclusionary thinking ("There is *no way* I could ...") reveal rigidly held beliefs that typically flow from unrealistic schema dynamics. Perhaps the most common of these is the use of "absolute" words—such as *every, everyone, everything, all, always, never, no one, none,* and *nothing.* Clients use these terms to describe many experiences, describe the breadth and depth of their problems, and/or rationalize their behavior, despite the fact that they are rarely justified (Gula, 2002).

Yet, for a nonlinear-thinking therapist, such statements yield valuable clues about the client's schema dynamics. As described earlier, Seligman's (1990) concept of "explanatory style"[4] (i.e., view of self) is useful in this regard. Pessimistic individuals who give up easily see negative things as permanent and are prone to the use of terms such as *never* and *nothing* (e.g., "I can never get a break," or "Nothing ever goes my way"). They are also prone to seeing negative events as "pervasive" in their lives. Rather than perceiving unfortunate events (e.g., the breakup of a relationship) as indicative of specific circumstances (e.g., "Pete is a jerk!"), they tend to perceive such events in terms of universals (e.g., "All men are jerks!" or "I'll never find someone to marry").

Optimists tend to use qualifying words such as *sometimes* (e.g., "Sometimes, I get so discouraged that I just want to quit," or "Sometimes, there are days being a parent that make me want to say I never heard of motherhood"). Optimists also tend to explain events to themselves in terms of permanent causes such as one's traits, one's abilities, and the use of the unrestricted qualifier *always* (e.g., "Lady Luck always smiles at me!"). Again, careful listening (linear and nonlinear) is critical for picking up on these important verbal clues about a client's schema dynamics.

Nonlinear listening is helpful in unraveling seemingly *incongruous* behaviors. Consider, for example, a client who comes to therapy complaining of being depressed and yet espouses an extreme philosophy of going for the "gusto" and "Eat, drink, and be merry." Her philosophy appears to be an expression of optimism and an enjoyment of life, but her complaint is one of being depressed and unhappy. Thus, such an individual may very well harbor an underlying philosophy that reflects the *second half* of the optimistic expression, "Eat, drink, etc.—for tomorrow we die!" Such a philosophy may very well be related to a pessimistic *view of life* that the client attempts to assuage by getting all the pleasure that she can because she knows it won't last.

Listening for *congruence* and for *absence* are powerful tools for the *nonlinear*-thinking therapist in understanding the schema dynamics behind statements a client makes. Clients can rarely justify statements such as "Nothing ever goes my way" when a therapist calls attention to them. A therapist can supportively ask, "Are you saying that *every* time you _____, there has never been a *single* instance in your life that has gone your way?" In addition, a therapist listening for *absence* searches for what it is the client is *not* saying or talking about.

Mature individuals hold more realistic views of themselves, others, and life and the world. They understand and accept that rigid dichotomies, absolutes, exclusionary thinking, and so on are simply not very functional in this less-than-perfect world. Nevertheless, human beings readily indulge in thinking such as "Either I get an 'A,' or I'm no good," "You're either for me or against me," and on and on. Client use of either-or thinking is simply not very functional in a world that is filled with shades of gray.

ELEMENTS OF FORMAL ASSESSMENT IN UNDERSTANDING A CLIENT'S SCHEMA DYNAMICS

Readiness for Change

As previously discussed, a client's readiness for and willingness to change (i.e., stages of change) are important components of any evaluation. Highly skewed, unrealistic, and rigidly held schemas are difficult to influence and directly affect a client's preparedness for change. These clients may get stuck in the precontemplation, contemplation, or preparing for action stage. Client motivation to change, however, is uniquely influenced by schema dynamics, and moving them from one stage to the next is heavily dependent on a therapist's understanding of the client's *view of self*, *view of others*, and *view of life and world*.

Client Resources

A therapist must tailor specific interventions in accord with a client's schema and resources. Effective therapy goes "with the grain" of a client's schemas, not "against the grain." Clients' unrealistic and dysfunctional schemas place them at odds with others, their own ultimate best interests, or life circumstances. The contrariness of highly skewed schemas typically results in emotional discomfort as well as being dysfunctional in important areas of life. When clients encounter life circumstances that need to be addressed and will not recede (e.g., recall Clinical Case Example 4.4, in which the client says that he's been arrested three times for DUI offenses), but that contradict schematized views of self, others, or the world (e.g., "I am not an alcoholic," "I do not have a problem," and "I am responsible"), then individuals can become immobilized. This can lead to a therapeutic impasse because *dysfunctional* elements of the client's schema (that are not useful in the current circumstances, and are actually harmful) do not change. Rather than forcing the impasse and encountering resistance via a power struggle with a client, a *nonlinear-thinking* therapist searches for unused or overlooked resources and untapped empowerment to help a client reconcile such impasses. Such therapeutic focus can help identify the *positive* or *useful* elements of a client's schema (e.g., the man with three DUI arrests is dedicated to his job and family; or a young man with a lung transplant, who feels worn out and tired and doesn't want to do anything, is viewed as tough and resilient to have survived all that he has).

Themes

For the seven themes that are described in Chapter 5, there are corresponding schema dynamics that each theme suggests (see Table 9.1). Consider the client with a DUI. The theme is one of defensiveness. As a result, a clinician can assume that his schema dynamics include a positive and unrealistic view of self, and a negative view of others or view of the world and life. In fact, when therapists discover these themes, they also are uncovering the "plots" to the client's story (mentioned in "Narrative Understanding of Client Core Schema," above). As another example, if a client has a theme of hopelessness ("a chronic problem"), then she probably has a negative view of self, others, and life and the world. Thus, the nonlinear-thinking therapist can (again) simultaneously combine beginning (Level I) and advanced (Level II) skills in order to help a client effectively.

TABLE 9.1 Relationship Between the Theme in a Client's Story and Schema Dynamics

UNDERLYING THEME OF CLIENT STORY	SCHEMA DYNAMICS (SUGGESTED)[11]
1. Desperation	Positive or negative view of self; negative view of life and the world
2. Helplessness	Negative view of self
3. Hopelessness	Negative view of self, others, and life and the world
4. Defensiveness	Positive view of self; negative view of life and the world
5. Exhaustion	Negative view of self and life and the world
6. Despair	Negative view of others and/or life and the world
7. Double bind	Positive view of self; negative view of life and the world

Client Goals

Last, the role of goals in understanding schemas cannot be underestimated. Some individuals come to therapy with minor difficulties when compared to others who enter therapy with major long-standing personality difficulties. A client's goals for therapy (both stated and unstated), if originated by the therapist, must *initially* be congruent with the client's schema. In the example from Clinical Case Example 4.4 (of the DUI client), if the therapist's goal is to coerce the client into accepting that he has a problem, there will most likely be a premature termination. If, however, the therapist understands the client's view of self as "I don't have a problem," "I take care of my family," and "I am responsible," then the initial goal will be to help the client to not have a problem and to take care of his family. How to best accomplish this goal is a focus of exploration for the client and therapist. For this DUI client, this might take the form of presenting a challenge for the therapeutic relationship: "What do you think we might focus on to help you deal with this current dilemma and keep you taking care of your family?" The ultimate goal of moving the client toward greater readiness for change and better adaptive functioning, however, will have been preserved. Also, the therapeutic alliance is preserved and perhaps strengthened in the process.

USING THE THERAPEUTIC RELATIONSHIP TO BETTER UNDERSTAND A CLIENT'S SCHEMA DYNAMICS

Therapeutic Alliance

Understanding a client's schema (i.e., *what and how* a client thinks and feels—confirmed by the client) makes it easier to identify, empathize with, and address important client issues and particular dilemmas. When this occurs, a client understands that the therapist sees, hears, and feels his point of view: "My therapist 'gets' me, understands me and the spot I'm in. She's not critical or rejecting of me. She's not trying to get me to relinquish what it is that I believe and feel, nor is she demanding that I do something I'm ill prepared to deal with or change." Such perceptions strengthen the working alliance and help a client to unravel the particular mystery of the problems for which he seeks relief.

Therapeutic Ruptures and Client Schemas

A client's schemas and skewed thinking can (and do) affect the therapeutic alliance, including how quickly it is established and its depth. In fact, client schemas are a potential basis for transference issues that have the potential to destabilize and rupture the therapeutic alliance. Recall from Chapter 7 the successful businessman in his early 50s who sought therapy to better understand how to respond to his angry wife. In treatment, the therapist grew increasingly more frustrated with the client, feeling that he was working harder than the client. Exemplifying how schemas can influence the therapeutic alliance (including transference and countertransference issues), the client's response to the therapist raising this issue was "As a child, I was told that children are to be seen and not heard. I gave my opinion only when I was asked for it—otherwise, I kept my mouth shut or paid the consequences!" Following this exchange, the client began taking a more active role in discussing issues that he needed to work on without being prompted by the therapist. Once a therapist understands a client's particular schema dynamics (negative view of self), and his actions are placed in a proper context, individual instances of *behavior* (e.g., seeming not to participate fully in therapy, and not answering questions) are more understandable.

To this point, we have shown how a *nonlinear*-thinking therapist utilizes skills in the Level I domains to gain an understanding of client schema dynamics. The following discussion is devoted to facilitating an understanding of how to identify and work with client schemas that can be revealed from a variety of sources. In particular, we will introduce three nonlinear methods that master practitioners often use to assess client schema dynamics: the family of origin, sibling position, and early childhood recollections.

Using Family-of-Origin Dynamics to Understand Client Schema Dynamics

The influence of an individual's family of origin (however it is comprised) on the development of a client's schema cannot be underestimated. The family, as an individual's first exposure to life, the world, and others, has a pervasive influence on the development of schemas. For the most part, positive family experiences *increase the likelihood* that an individual will derive a somewhat positive outlook, and likewise, negative family experiences increase the likelihood of a somewhat negative outlook, although they don't guarantee it. Alas, positivity and negativity do not reveal the entire story. Children learn about values (i.e., what is important, not important, to be strived for, and to be avoided) from their parents (or surrogates), who convey (and reinforce) those values overtly and unconsciously. Thus, getting information about a client's family of origin is critical in understanding schema dynamics.

Sibling Position and the Development of Schemas

Understanding a client's birth order[5] is an important source of valuable information for master practitioners learning about client schemas. Different sibling positions predispose individuals to adopt certain roles, behavioral paths, attitudes, and so on rather than others. As an example, firstborn children from different families are more likely to share common personality characteristics than a firstborn and second-born from the same family. The adoption of different roles is guided by schemas that in significant ways are shaped by one's sibling position.

Kluger (2006) has described a recent burgeoning popular and scientific interest in understanding sibling position and birth order:

> Within the scientific community, siblings have not been wholly ignored, but research has been limited mostly to discussions of birth order. Older sibs were said to be strivers; younger ones rebels; middle kids

the lost souls. The stereotypes were broad, if not entirely untrue, and there the discussion mostly ended. But all that's changing. At research centers … investigators are launching a wealth of new studies into the sibling dynamic, looking at ways brothers and sisters steer one another into—or away from—risky behavior; how they form a protective buffer against family upheaval; how they educate one another about the opposite sex; how all siblings compete for family recognition and come to terms—or blows—over such impossibly charged issues as parental favoritism. (p. 1)

Clinical Exercise 9.2: Sibling Position

Form small groups determined according to birth order—born first, second, youngest, or an only child. Participants are to list and discuss the advantages and disadvantages of being in a particular sibling position. The groups are then to report back to the larger group and discuss how sibling position influenced the development of one's "role" *in life* and what such a role signifies about one's schemas.

QUESTIONS

1. What advantages (of any sort) did you encounter as a result of your particular sibling position?
2. What disadvantages (of any sort) were encountered from your particular sibling position?
3. How do you think your particular schema dynamics (i.e., view of self, others, or life or the world) were affected as a result of being in a particular sibling position?
4. Did your gender and the gender of sibling competitors affect the development of schemas? If so, in what ways?
5. Did the difference (in number of years) between siblings' ages possibly affect the development of certain schemas? In what way(s)?
6. Did your family lose (e.g., by the death of an infant, or by a miscarriage) a sibling? How does that affect or not affect the development of schemas?

Clinical Case Example 9.2 demonstrates the influence of siblings on personality and schemas.

Clinical Case Example 9.2: An Unhappy Couple in Crisis

A woman and her significant other had moved in together with plans to marry. In their late 30s, each was intelligent, educated, verbal, and eager to have their relationship work because each had been previously unhappily married and divorced. Soon after purchasing a house together, the woman found herself increasingly unhappy but complaining little. After months of such unhappiness, Susan felt depressed and then erupted in emotional tirades against her suitor. Sensitive and responsive, Bob made efforts to amend his behavior to take her complaints into account. The complaints centered on his two young children, who were barely school age. After brief individual therapy, Susan sought couples' counseling.

Bob's children split their time between living with their mother and living with their father. Susan readily admitted that Bob's children were likable, respectful, caring, well mannered, and well behaved, and in that regard she had no complaints. In fact, she genuinely liked the children and felt that they liked her. If this was the case, what was the "problem"?

Susan had a difficult time in explaining what her complaint was other than saying that she did not "feel as though we are a family unit." She explained, "Bob doesn't take me into consideration in different ways and in different scenarios. When I explain what I mean, he doesn't get it, and we argue." In turn, Bob felt overwhelmed (i.e., "flooded") with the extent of Susan's anger and troubled by her apparent unresponsiveness to his efforts to address her concerns. Susan simply felt that Bob and his children didn't take her into account, didn't need her, and seemed to do things without consulting her. Even when consulted, she felt it was only temporary and that things would revert to "the old ways."

After the first few sessions of couples' therapy, Bob reported that they had reached a "crisis" and that they were at a serious point in their relationship. During that crisis session, each revealed understandings from childhood that shed light on their current dilemma. In Susan's family of origin, her father was a severe substance abuser who was absent from the home much of the time. Although overt conflict seemed to be lacking, she perceived her parents as uninvolved with each other and basically unhappy. With numerous siblings, such conditions led to Susan's mother relying heavily upon her to get things done. She provided babysitting for her younger siblings, cooked, did the family laundry, and "had to make everything 'OK' for them." Susan described herself as playing a "central role" in maintaining the family despite her father's alcoholism. She felt *important* (i.e., valued) in that role! Susan felt that she, her mother, and her siblings were "very *connected and close* and looked out for each other."

In listening to the depiction of her position in her family of origin, the therapist suggested that she seemed to have not only a significant role (i.e., a social place of value) but also a substantive, important, and *central role*. In contrast, her present circumstances led her to feel as though she not only did not have a substantive, central, and well-defined role but also had no role at all because of the highly functional way in which Bob and his children seemed to work together without conflict. Susan beamed at this explanation as being precisely what it was that she had been trying to convey to Bob without success. She didn't feel as though she had any "central" role in their system, and in fact she felt excluded at times. Her unconscious view-of-self schema informed her as if to say, "The way things *should be* is that others rely on me, I am *central* and *essential* to the family, we are all close, we have fun together, and I have a well-defined role and am needed. That's how I derive my sense of feeling worthwhile. My present circumstances don't seem to give me that feeling. Bob and his children seem to do very well without significant input from me! I don't have a defined role of what (my schema unconsciously informs me) I'm supposed to be doing."

In Bob's depiction of *his* childhood, it was clear that although he was well behaved and obedient, he also felt as though his alcoholic mother singled him out for special unjustified scrutiny, suspicion, and verbal abuse. Similarly, he felt under "attack" by Susan, who acted just like his mother, who was regularly and frequently inebriated, out of control, verbally abusive, and unpredictable, and often mean-spirited. When the therapist noted that Bob seemed to be saying that he felt Susan was unjustly scrutinizing and verbally abusing him just like he felt his mother had done, Bob's face flushed, and he acknowledged complete agreement. It was *his* view-of-others schema that informed him that he was being unjustly accused, verbally abused, and unfairly scrutinized. That was intolerable and unacceptable. Bob and Susan subsequently went their separate ways.

Master practitioners listen intensively for spontaneous client comments revealing information about the family of origin, its beliefs, the roles played, the values reinforced, feelings, and so on. Such client disclosures strongly suggest that schemas are operative in a client's current dilemma. Exploring such possibilities is encouraged—especially how a client viewed the particular family dynamics in question and how such dynamics relate to her current dilemma.

EARLY CHILDHOOD RECOLLECTIONS

Early childhood recollections (ECRs) can be an especially rich source of clinical understanding about client schemas and thinking. But before discussing what can be learned from ECRs, it would be prudent to establish working definitions, describe subtle distinctions, and highlight new understandings about memory.

Cognitions in general are best described and understood as the *process of thinking* (i.e., a psychological activity) rather than by understanding them as "things" (i.e., concrete objects). Kandel, Schwartz, and Jessell (2000) addressed "memory" by subtly describing it as the process involved in acquiring, codifying, storing, and retrieving knowledge. The implication of this for clinicians is that memory and memories are not cast in stone. As Gonsalves and Paller (2000) and Shacter (1996) have indicated, memories do not provide a perfect rendering of what has transpired in a person's life. Rather, at retrieval, *memories are constructed* according to the particular methods that are used to retrieve them. Furthermore, Garry and Polaschek (2000) noted,

> The "autobiographical memories" that tell the story of our lives are always undergoing revision precisely because our sense of self is too. We are continually extracting new information from old experiences and filling in gaps in ways that serve some current demand. Consciously or not, we use imagination to reinvent our past, and with it, our present and future. (p. 6)

Because they are constructed, it is prudent to consider childhood memories as *recollections*—a *re*gathering of the past rather than a tape recording of events. Hence, these recollections are subject to some "editing" by the client, and the conclusions drawn from them (schema dynamics) are modifiable as well.[6] Although research is limited, it suggests that ECRs have both *linear* and *nonlinear* dimensions that must be considered to maximize their usefulness and validity. Josselson (2000) noted,

> If early memories [EMs[7]] are indicative of an individual's present worldview or attitude toward life and offer insight into an individual's current ego organization, they should change in parallel to developmental change in the individual. If, however, they represent "core" aspects of personality, they should remain stable over time. (pp. 464–465)

What research findings reveal is equally *linear* and *nonlinear*. Watkins (1992) reviewed 30 studies of early memories and concluded,

> EMs are consistent with current interpersonal behavior ... the EMs of psychiatric patients, when compared to normal controls, tend to be more negative in emotional tone, show more fear/anxiety themes, and reflect greater passivity or an external locus of control ... the EMs of psychiatric patients show changes over the course of treatment, with EM content becoming more positive in nature as favorable life changes occur ... the EMs of male delinquents and criminals, when compared with memories of control subjects, reflect more negative emotionality, injury or illness, rule breaking, victimization, and being alone in an unpleasant situation. (p. 259)

In other words, early recollections contain significant clues about a client's schema dynamics. Indeed, in a long-term study of stability and change in early memories, Josselson (2000) concluded,

> Early memories seem to represent both stability and change within the individual in a form similar to musical development of theme and variation. As many writers have suggested, early memories mark unsolved issues that may be expressed, resolved, resurrected, or reexperienced in new guises at different periods of life.... Early memories operate like markers of individual destiny, offering expressive metaphors of core themes in personality that may not be as apparent in the welter of detail that a life story comprises. (pp. 477–478)

Clinical Case Example 9.3: ECRs That Go Bump in the Night!

An example may prove helpful in demonstrating the clinical usefulness of ECRs. The client in Clinical Case Example 8.1 ("Anxious and Dependent") reported the following ECR:

Client: I was really scared in the middle of the night. I was seeing ghosts outside my room. I'd see shadows like dinosaurs. Then, when they went away, I would run into my parent's bedroom and crawl into bed with them.
Therapist: What part of the memory is most vivid to you?
Client: Laying in my bed not knowing what to do—frozen.
Therapist: How are you feeling about the memory?
Client: Scared! I remember thinking they—it—was going to get me.

   The interpretation of the memory is straightforward: The client scares herself with frightening monsters of her own misperception and creation—she makes more of reality than is really there. There are other subtle implications from the memory, as the astute practitioner would discover. The client runs into her parents' bedroom to avail herself of the safety they provide. The possible meaning of this is that she relies on others for safety and reassurance in a life filled with scary things. This implies dependency on others to deal with some of life's scarier difficulties. The adroit practitioner will detect a particularly positive and important, albeit subtle, part of the memory as well: This is a very creative person. That is, in the context of her ECR, she uses her creativity to scare herself. Her *creativity* can also be called upon as *a treatment resource* to help her develop new ways to deal with anxiety-provoking life situations.

   Given the research support that ECRs both are stable *and* change, the interpretation of memories in many respects is certainly as much *nonlinear* as it is *linear.* Several authors (Bruhn, 1990; Clark, 2002; Mosak & DiPietro, 2006) have provided guidance regarding the interpretation of ECRs from different theoretical frames of reference. ECR interpretation is certainly not formulaic and can be approached as part of a collaborative process between client and therapist. We offer the following suggestions regarding ECRs.

   Rather than the factual basis of ECRs (i.e., something did or did not occur), it is the feelings about what is remembered that are critically important. In the final analysis, it is the feelings and emotions divulged by a client about what they remember that reflect what is important—the values. We have feelings and emotions about things that are important to us. Thus, it is the values *behind* the feelings that are important in determining the client's schema dynamics. The important consideration is the answer to the question "What was it about that memory that prompted you to feel that way?" Answers such as "It wasn't fair" betray schema dynamics in which fairness is prominent, and ones like "It wasn't right" point to schema dynamics in which rightness and wrongness are prominent personality values. "I was afraid that …" indicates a preoccupation with fearfulness, uncertainty, doubt, and vagueness—a need for guarantees and certainty in an uncertain world (on a schema level). In most instances, clients are unaware of the existence of such beliefs and the thinking that follows from them, let alone that they were formed during childhood with a child's limited capacity to understand events or put them into a greater context. Nevertheless, such unawareness does not prevent others from operating as full adults according to beliefs and thinking formulated and reinforced in childhood.

   There are caveats that therapists must take into consideration when working with ECRs. This is especially true when working with trauma, abuse, and particularly the phenomenon of "recovered memories." This is discussed as part of working with traumatic emotions in Chapters 10 and 11.

Clinical Exercise 9.3: Working With ECRs to Determine Scheme Dynamics

Instructions: Consider the following two ECRs from the same client.

MEMORY NUMBER 1: CLIENT, AGE 2 OR 3

Client: I remember my mother taking me to day care for infants. She had to go to work. It was the first day she took me to day care. I didn't want to go, and she left. I was there the whole day.

Therapist: What part of the memory stands out to you most clearly?

Client: I remember the room with white walls. I was lying in a bed sitting on a stand.

Therapist: How are you feeling in the memory?

Client: I felt awkward—my mother went away and had to go to work. I didn't appreciate that.

Therapist: What about that prompted you to feel that way?

Client: I was scared that she left me. I didn't realize what was going to happen.

MEMORY NUMBER 2: CLIENT, AGE 6

Client: In America, I remember one time my father was arguing with my mother, and he lost his temper. He picked up a drinking glass and threw it at my mother. He packed his things, and he left for a couple of days. He would provoke fights and make it seem like it's not his fault, like it was mother's fault.

Therapist: What part of the memory stands out to you most clearly?

Client: Everyone was yelling, screaming at one another. Mother was crying. He broke the glass on her back. They weren't talking when he came back.

Therapist: How are you feeling in the memory?

Client: I was very mad at him; I was small, but I wanted to call the police.

Therapist: What about that prompted you to feel that way?

Client: The fact that I was playing with my toys, and he threw the glass and it could have caused a lot worse damage—could have shattered in her eyes. It could have been a lot worse.

QUESTIONS

1. Briefly summarize the major schema theme in each memory.
2. What similarities, if any, can you detect in the two memories?
3. Can you differentiate between the specific contents of the memories and similar underlying commonalities?
4. What could be said about this client's view of self, life, and others?
5. Translate questions 1–4 into personally useful statements for the client.
6. What can you point to that supports your interpretation of the memories?
7. What complaints, preoccupations, concerns, and so on might be predicted about this client as a result of clinical clues derived from these memories?
8. What are likely diagnostic categories for this individual?
9. What leads you to this conclusion?

PUTTING THE PIECES OF THE CLIENT'S STORY TOGETHER: THE "FORMULATION"

One of the signature characteristics of a master practitioner is the ability to assemble disparate pieces of a clinical puzzle (i.e., a client's complaint, behaviors, history, circumstances, ECRs, information about family of origin, etc.) into a cohesive understanding—a "formulation." The formulation attempts to create a useful coherent narrative—a model—of why this person is here at this time and what kind of relief he seeks. Suggesting to a client what it is that he appears to be saying, how he appears to be thinking, and what he appears to be feeling in his narrative is a way of helping a client to make sense of his unique circumstances and the chaos that he often experiences.

Persons (1989) suggested that formulations serve the purpose of sorting through a myriad of biopsychosocial assessment data and formulating a sense of the interconnectedness of relevant data. Such interconnectedness leads to developing a comprehensive treatment plan, often involving multidisciplinary practitioners—either on the treatment team or by other providers in the community.

A formulation serves the necessary purpose of acting as a bridge between assessment data and a comprehensive treatment plan. At the same time, however, the master practitioner is also resolutely mindful that a client's story has more to do with *how a client interprets the "facts"* of her story than the facts themselves. We present Clinical Exercise 9.4 to help readers understand this process.

Clinical Exercise 9.4: Useful Models in Developing an Understanding of a Client's "Story"

Implicitly, a master practitioner poses questions such as those posed below in order to develop an understanding of a client's narrative. What other questions might you suggest that would be useful?

QUESTIONS TO ASK A CLIENT AND ONESELF

- Where is the main character (i.e., the client) coming from (i.e., background, context, history, etc.)?
- What would it be like to come from such a background?
- How has the client dealt with his or her origins to this point? Successfully? Unsuccessfully?
- What (or who) is he or she complaining of?
- What are the "facts," and are they different from what the client is complaining of?
- How is the client interpreting the "facts"?
- How long has the main character been complaining about this?
- What does the client need to explain for the therapist to truly understand his or her story?
- Who are the other main characters in this narrative?
- What roles do they play in the evolution of the client's narrative?
- What "inciting" event(s) transpired in the client's life to bring about a need for therapy?
- What changed in the client's life to bring about the "crisis" to precipitate a need for therapy?
- What are the emotions that the client expresses about the change or crisis?

- No matter how obvious it may seem, what is the value that produces this emotion(s) in the client?
- What are the client's needs at *this particular time*? Comfort, reassurance, someone on his or her side, or the like?
- Where does the client want to go? Is it realistic?
- What resolution would the client consider a "successful" ending to his or her episode of therapy?

WHAT IS OR ARE ...

- A client's explanatory model for behaving the way he or she does (i.e., the reasoning and "private logic" of his or her symptoms)?
- A repetitious pattern(s) in a client's verbal expressions, thinking, and feeling reactions to events he or she is describing that represents indications of underlying schemas?
- Missing elements in a client's story (*absence, inference*) or those that do not fit (*congruence, resistance*)?
- Nonverbal behavior(s) conveying meaning, importance, or context to the narrative (*presence*)?
- Beliefs and reasoning regarding specific problem-solving situations, and how such thinking and reasoning are linked to the development and maintenance of problems and symptoms?
- A client's understanding of the impact of family-of-origin dynamics on present functioning?

For purposes of the present text, the formulation is a brief, concise statement of understanding to a client regarding the source of self-generated suffering revealed in the complaint that led him to therapy. A client leaving therapy with a new and better perspective is very useful, calming, and reassuring. It can suggest, for example, that given the type of circumstances the client has described, his history, and his makeup, anyone in similar circumstances would feel or behave similarly. Such a depiction of a client's dilemma is "normalizing." For longer therapy, a formulation becomes the vehicle for the working-through process. *Linear*-thinking therapists may present the formulation in a very straightforward manner, whereas *nonlinear*-thinking therapists usually employ more creative ways to present case formulations that increase the likelihood of a client engaging in therapy and successfully altering his schema. The final section of this chapter focuses on the process of changing schemas via assimilation and accommodation.

WORKING WITH A CLIENT'S CORE SCHEMA

Accommodation and Assimilation

What are the underlying psychological processes for facilitating change? One of the earliest pioneers of schema theory was Swiss developmental psychologist Jean Piaget, who believed that children constructed schemas to help organize, classify, and understand the world (Myers, 2007).

According to Piaget, in order to be able to react to new life experiences, a person's schema naturally had to be flexible enough to change. Some changes merely take a new phenomenon and incorporate it within the structure of the existing schema (e.g., "I've never seen a soccer ball before, so I didn't know what it was; but I know it fits the 'rules' for a ball, so I will include it in my 'ball' schema"). *Assimilation* is the psychological process whereby new experiences are interpreted in terms of a current framework or schema (Myers, 2007).

Sometimes, however, an existing schema does not fully account for a phenomenon. These "rogue" phenomena require a person to either change her beliefs about how things should be (e.g., "Maybe all round things aren't balls?") or dismiss the event (e.g., "The orange object that smells like citrus is a 'ball,'" and "That oblong thing with laces that flies in the air just isn't a 'ball'! That's the way it has always been, and that's the way it will stay!"). Perhaps Sherlock Holmes, the greatest fictional detective ever, said it best when cautioning about clinging too hard to theories (schemas): "Insensibly one begins to twist facts to suit theories, instead of theories to suit facts" (Doyle, 1892/1986, p. 13). Instead, schemas that are no longer fully accurate must be adjusted to some degree to fit new experience. *Accommodation* is the psychological process of adjusting schemas (Myers, 2007).

There are times when a client needs to assimilate new information or experiences into his schematized perceptions of the world. At other times, a client's schemas are not sufficient to cope with the world as it is, and behaviors that "logically" flow from it are responsible for developing impasses with changing life circumstances. As a result, accommodation or alteration of a client's existing schema dynamics is necessary in order to resolve disparities between what is and what exists in schemas. Recall the case presented earlier of Bob and Susan. In order to be able to live together peacefully, each would have had to assimilate new information (i.e., Bob: "My partner is not persecuting me") *and* accommodate their schemas (i.e., Susan: "I am not being rejected if I am not in the center of things; I am important and belong, although, at times, I play a peripheral role in the family"). Oftentimes, when individuals, couples, or families have to both assimilate and accommodate schema dynamics, therapeutic success can be elusive (hence, Susan and Bob's breakup in the end).

Linear Methods of Intervening With Client Schema

Interventions that focus solely on the client's problem or deficit are indicative of *linear thinking*. There are times when the "problem" has to do with accepting a new reality, or assimilating new information into the client's existing schema, and hence linear approaches are reasonable. These usually take the form of specific skills training (e.g., assertiveness training, social skills training, time management, relaxation training, and self-hypnosis for stress management) that helps a client in developing a situational specific competence. If a client's stated purpose for counseling is to obtain "assertiveness training," honoring such a request and providing such training represent a linear response to a linear request. But a therapist must also listen in a *nonlinear* manner to determine if there are more dynamic issues operating.

Cognitive therapists assist clients in identifying maladaptive thinking processes (i.e., a negative/unrealistic view of self, others, and life and the world) and help them to develop more positive ways of thinking. They assess the pros and cons of the thoughts and beliefs that advance or hinder a client in relation to her goals, and assist clients in challenging the believability of maladaptive thoughts (e.g., "Where is the evidence for this conclusion?" "Could there be another explanation of this observation?" and "If a friend told you this, what advice might you give them?"). Whether done in a conversational way or a more dramatic way, such therapeutic challenges are *never* presumptive and are always respectful of a client and the relationship.

Further linear methods of responding to a client's negative/unrealistic view of self include directly "challenging" his negative self-attributions. Therapist encouragement of the use of "challenging" would be represented by the rational-emotive therapy (RET) of Ellis (1962) and Ellis and Dryden (1987), who advocated catching oneself in the act of negativistic self-attributions and providing a "rational" argument to counter the expressed negative view of self. Consider Clinical Case Example 9.4.

Clinical Case Example 9.4: Overly Sensitive

A successfully married career woman with an advanced degree came to therapy on a monthly basis, mostly for support after the death of her parents. In her family of origin, she was the caretaker for handicapped younger siblings who adored her. Indeed, parental feedback was extremely positive and emphasized how truly gifted and special she was. It did not take long to understand that her core positive view of self related to feeling, "I am special." Because of parental attitudes and behavior toward her, a parenthetical embellishment of her view of self seemed to be "I am a caretaker and special, and I expect others to see and treat me that way." Such a view of self, of course, would prompt her to feel very positively about herself.

She maintained a long-term "complaint" revolving around perceived slights at work coupled with a "sensitivity" to how others treated her. For example, if she wasn't invited to a party, it became cause for extremely hurt feelings. If someone made a comment that pertained to her work, she tended to interpret such a comment as attacking her competence. She would defend her competence and add that the individual proffering the comment had no right to say such things.

During one of her monthly therapy sessions, she reported going to a wake for a distant relative who died quite tragically. At the wake, all the extended relatives seemed to be huddled around and preoccupied with a few members of the extended family who were extremely successful financially and who "everyone idolizes, and I wasn't one of them. *Everything in my family is about achievement for everyone. That's my family; that's it!* I walked out feeling sad and empty."

She then reported talking to a friend about her experience at a social gathering at the mansion of a prominent person in their community. Her friend reported similar feelings— "everyone" seems to cluster around the wealthy and beautiful people, who are the most influential and have the most status, and everyone else is like "chopped liver." She then made two especially important observations. The first was a rhetorical question: "Why is there a little person in me who is kicking and screaming that 'I'm important' (i.e., special)?" The second was her remark that "I'm getting over it."

Regarding her first question, it is quite obvious that her view of self is "I am important (or special, or worthwhile)," whereas her view of others suggests private thinking: "I want (i.e., expect) others to view me as important. When I'm not viewed in that way, there is 'a little person in me who is kicking and screaming' who *feels* 'I'm important.'"

About her latter comment, the therapist posed a question: "How did you manage to get over it?" She replied, "Time. It's a day-by-day thing in which you make small progress and don't let little things bother you. Putting things in perspective is another way of getting over it—I know that I'm important; it's just that at times, I don't particularly feel like it. I get over it by 'calming' myself down."

The woman's comments in Clinical Case Example 9.4 are especially powerful in several respects. They are very descriptive of *how* conscious change comes about—it is generally a gradual process of catching oneself, accomplished in small increments through attention and effort. In addition, in formulating her schema dynamics, she has fairly realistic views of herself, others, and the world.

The value of skills training, like all approaches, lies in being able to apply the skills appropriately with clients in an appropriate context. Skills training generally does not address (or alter) the larger schema dynamics, it helps clients cope with life situations, and it helps them assimilate new information (skills) into existing schemas. But many times, clients interested in linear solutions report that they have "tried that" and have found such methods unsuccessful. *Nonlinear listening* reveals comments such as

"I tried that, and it didn't work" as clinical clues that something more dynamic is operational. At such a juncture, interventions that address larger schema dynamics are appropriate.

Nonlinear Use of Metaphor

In the TV show *House, M.D.*, the lead character, Dr. Gregory House, is a misanthropic (but gifted) character who handles the most complex and mysterious medical cases. He and his team of doctors are often stymied by a patient's symptoms, whereby he utilizes metaphors to describe the "behaviors" of a patient's illness. This is meant to help him and his colleagues conceptualize and predict the course of the illness and arrive at a diagnosis. In one episode, a patient's systemic illness that attacks one organ system after another is metaphorically compared to a "freight train" speeding down the track from one station (or organ system, lungs, kidneys, etc.) to another. House and his colleagues struggle to stop it before it reaches the next "destination" and destroys another organ system, or before it reaches the "terminal" (i.e., death).

Metaphors are useful ways to describe and relate complicated client issues in a simple way. They often entail the use of concise, descriptive events or phrases to draw parallels between the present (and complex) situation and the simple (and often commonly understood) phrase or story.[8] Instead, metaphors can help the therapist to describe the "plot" of the client's story or schema dynamics (see Brink, 1982; Kopp, 1995; Matthews & Langdell, 1989). A clinician might try to say to a client, "Hmmm, it appears that you have a negative and unrealistic view of the world that keeps getting you into trouble when you encounter new situations." Although accurate, such an appraisal might fail to impact a client in a personally meaningful way. A clinician could also employ a simple image[9] as a metaphor that would make the same point. For example, "You seem to consistently *see the glass as either half empty or with a hole in it*. Either way, *it never seems to hold enough water*, and you seem to feel as though you are going to get cheated or that *anything good is just going to leak out the bottom of the glass*." Such a metaphor has the potential to be more effective because, if accurate, it appeals to how the brain processes information—both cognitive and emotional aspects of a core schema.

The use of metaphor requires linear and nonlinear thinking, as well as accurate understanding of the salient components of a client's schema (view of self, others, and the world and life). It also requires therapists to be creative in devising a coherent and comprehensive image reflecting a client's schematized worldview—her "template." Sometimes, a client will be the one to provide a metaphor—"I feel like an emotional ping-pong ball!"—whereas at other times, it is the therapist who must. In that case, using linear and nonlinear listening (*congruence, absence, inference, presence*, and *resistance*) can provide essential information.

Strategically, it is important to find a metaphor that encapsulates as many key aspects of a client's problem, worldview, sentiments, and the like as possible. Master practitioners are open-minded and receptive. Such a disposition is exceptionally useful in becoming sensitive to and absorbing themes from classical and contemporary literature, history, movies, books, media, music, TV, mythology, aspects of nature, and even elements of daily living.[10] In turn, such themes are useful in encapsulating key aspects of a client's problem, worldview, and so on. Clinical Exercise 9.5 provides an opportunity to practice the use of metaphor.

Clinical Exercise 9.5: Imagination and Metaphor

Directions: In order to bring into conscious awareness each individual's personal storehouse of imagery, stories, and creativity, we present the following exercise. Read each question below, and answer as fully as possible.

1. Think of five movie characters. Derive a brief metaphor or image of them.

2. Think of five fairy tale stories or ancient myths. Derive a brief metaphor or image of them.
3. Think of the most peaceful place that you can. Derive a brief metaphor or image.
4. Think of the most disturbing place that you can. Derive a brief metaphor or image.

Next, form small groups and discuss the following:

A. The answer to each question.
B. What suggestions can group members make for improving the image or metaphor?
C. How quickly were you able to come up with the answers to each? Was it easy or difficult?
D. Discuss how some of the metaphors or images could be useful in helping to describe a client's schema dynamics. Discuss with the entire class.

This exercise will hopefully stimulate the art of creating metaphors and images to describe to clients.

In addition, paying close attention to a client's background, culture, family history, and employment can help. Matching a metaphor with characteristics from a client's background tends to enhance its effectiveness. We present a brief example in Clinical Case Example 9.5 to illustrate.

Clinical Case Example 9.5: A Noble Health Care Worker

A very competent nurse came for treatment in order to understand a relationship that had gone wrong so that she would not make the same mistakes again. Her idealistic commitment to patient advocacy, her noble but impossible hospital-political issues, her friends, and her relationship gone asunder comprised a consistent thread weaved throughout her life. The therapist suggested that she resembled "Joan of St. Luke's" (a reference to the name of the hospital where she worked). From that point on in therapy, when she discovered herself acting in an idealistic but unrealistic manner, she referred to herself as Joan of St. Luke's, an obvious reference to Joan of Arc. Joan of Arc was idealistic (some of her critics at the time maintained that she was possessed), but ultimately her idealism led to her being burned at the stake (i.e., victimized).

The most reliable indicator of how effective a metaphor is is how well it *resonates* with a client (like a tuning fork; see Chapter 6). A good metaphor captures the client's imagination both *visually* and *verbally*. Metaphors that paint a vivid *visual* picture to illustrate a client's schema and verbal metaphors resonate like an *auditory* "catchphrase" that provides a client with a powerful way of remembering key concepts (such as the woman in Chapter 18, Clinical Case 8.1 who found the phrase "Life makes me nervous" very helpful). Kinesthetic and tactile images are also possible. When these connections are made, the therapeutic alliance is strengthened as well. Another example, given in Clinical Case Example 9.6, might be helpful.

Clinical Case Example 9.6: A Visual and Visceral Metaphor

If a client frequently feels taken advantage of by family members and coworkers who don't seem to care about her needs, a therapist might intervene by saying, "You seem to take so much abuse from your family that you feel like an *emotional pin cushion*. You take their jabs, which hurt, and don't ever say anything back." In this example, the pin cushion metaphor is visually evocative of a passive red bag that has dozens of metal pins sticking out of it. The catchphrase *emotional pin cushion* has visual, visceral, and tactile components that help to cement the image for the client.

An important step in presenting a metaphor to the client is to *verify* that it is accurate and useful. This is typically accomplished when a client signifies this either *verbally* (e.g., by stating, "WOW! That is *so* right!") or *viscerally* (e.g., through "recognition reflexes"; see Chapter 2). Successful metaphors must make sense to clients and should provide additional insight about their schema. This introduces and invites clients to look at themselves from a different perspective. The metaphor of an *emotional pin cushion* allows the therapist to give feedback on the client's view of self (negative and unrealistic) and view of others (negative and unrealistic) that guide her passive behavior in dealing with her family and coworkers. A metaphor also invites and facilitates a client reconsidering whether or not she wants to be a pin cushion any longer, which could help move the client from one stage of change to another (see Chapter 4). We present Clinical Case Example 9.7 to illustrate this further.

Clinical Case Example 9.7: High-Powered Saleswoman

A successful single mother sought family counseling for her 12-year-old son, who was attending an exclusive private school and making B grades, which was unacceptable to the client. Her main complaint was "I am paying a fortune in tuition; I don't expect to get B minuses!" The client was herself an attractive, high-powered woman who was a successful advertising saleswoman for a major media outlet. She was highly self-motivated and concerned with being successful. This was clearly part of her motivation for therapy with her son and was part of her overall schema dynamics. She stated repeatedly that she did not want her son to become like his father (who she thought of as a "loser" because, though he was successful in his own right, he was not as driven as she was). In therapy, she was intense, often trying to dominate the conversation, and would become very defensive if the therapist might not agree with her. The therapist became aware of some countertransference feelings of irritation with the client.

In her childhood, the client strongly identified with her father, who was highly competitive, demanded perfection from his children, was frequently absent from her life, but was very successful. Her parents were divorced when she was 10.

The client was married in her early 20s after a brief courtship. Each of the spouses was successful by any objective measure, but when compared with her husband, she was slightly more successful. As this happened, she began to see her husband as "weak" and "lazy." This was augmented by the fact that he bought old homes, rehabilitated them, and then sold them at a profit. As a result, he did not have a "9-to-5" job, and often worked out of the family home. Tensions over such issues led to an eventual divorce when their only child, a son, was 5 years old. Although she took primary custody of her son, her ex-husband maintained a presence in her son's life. Following the divorce, the client had a series of relationships with men that did not last. She felt that the men she dated always seemed to "disappoint" her and couldn't meet her needs. For the most part, her son agreed but stated that there were some "cool" guys, adding, "Just like always, she would run them off." The client seemed embarrassed by this characterization and rebutted, "A lot of times, men find me too aggressive and I frighten them off, when all I am trying to do is help them *improve* themselves."

QUESTIONS TO CONSIDER BEFORE READING FURTHER

1. How should the therapist deal with the countertransference feelings of irritation?
2. What are this client's basic schema dynamics (view of self, view of the world, and view of others)? How could these be translated into more personally useful statements (e.g., "I am ..." "Others are ..." and "The world is ...")?
3. Are there any metaphors that come to mind that might be useful to describe to the client her particular schema dynamics, how they might be helpful to her, and how they might be contributing to her problems in her life?

The therapist was aware of feelings of irritation that arose out of a sense of feeling dismissed by the client when he was working to help her. Such awareness proved to be useful in assessing the client's dynamics: She did not like having to ask for help (i.e., therapy), and she was reacting to feeling "one down" compared to the therapist. The therapist next drew connections between his experience of the client in the therapy (i.e., irritating and aggressive), the client's history (i.e., competitive and successful), and the current problem with her son (i.e., being too demanding and unrealistic). Given these factors, he surmised that she felt like she had to compete with the therapist. The common element between these relationships was her schema. In response, the therapist formulated the following: Her view of self is positive and unrealistic (based on her unbounded confidence in herself), and her view of others is negative and unrealistic (based on her history of relationships, and how she was viewing her son's predicament and reacting to the therapist).

But, what is the best way to present this to the client without risking a therapeutic rupture and premature termination? Relating to particularly difficult clients through the use of a metaphor can be very useful. In this case, the client provided an excellent metaphor for describing her schematic worldview. Although it was her ex-husband who did it for a living, the client boasted that she had also been investing in real estate on the side. Borrowing from the metaphor, the therapist told her that she seemed to treat people in her life like her real estate investments—find people who were in need of "rehabbing," invest a lot of her time and effort in them, and then "sell" them off better than they were (i.e., get rid of them before they could outdo her). The therapist explained that this is a profitable business strategy, and a noble way to approach life, but there were three major flaws: (a) Her son was becoming a project, with his actions a reflection of his fear (and perhaps hers) that if he is successful, she would have to "sell" him off like everyone else; (b) she was so good at "fixing" people (via giving advice, telling people how they could improve, etc.) that it actually turned them off, which explained her sense of loneliness and lack of close friends; and (c) she was so good at being the "fixer" that she didn't know how to be the one needing care. This frequently led to neglecting her own needs and demanding that others meet them for her (i.e., her boyfriends and son). When these people were incapable of doing so, she would "cut her losses" and decide to either "gut" them completely (by tearing them down emotionally) or get rid of them fast.

In Chapter 4, we introduced the concept of two tuning forks—a metaphor—to describe how a client and therapist needed to be "in synch" (i.e., have a strong therapeutic alliance) in order for the therapy to be effective. A successful metaphor that describes a client's schema dynamics accomplishes this (e.g., "Gee, you really get what it is that I'm saying!"). In the example above, the dominant metaphor came from the client's life and activity (i.e., buying and renovating houses). It also served to express what she does in her relationships with other people, including her son. The boy may be fearful that if he is "too good," Mom might "sell him off"; but if he continues to be in need of "fixing up" (i.e., getting B grades), she might be forced to keep him around, even though she is unhappy with him. The metaphor allows a discussion of these issues in a nonthreatening way for either client, as well as a discussion with the therapist about how to address it (by either assimilation or accommodation). Lastly, metaphors provide client and therapist with a quick reference point for checking in on a client's progress (e.g., "Well I have met someone that I am dating, and I am not trying to do any refurbishing to him!").

SUMMING THE CRITICAL SIGNIFICANCE OF UNDERSTANDING SCHEMAS

Recall the example of Alya from the story *The Clan of the Cave Bear* (Auel, 1980) presented in Chapter 8. The clan, with its inability to grow or change, represents clients who have skewed, unrealistic, and rigid schema dynamics. But therapists can direct their efforts with intractable clients toward helping them assimilate new information into their existing schemas. Alya, however, represents clients who are capable of accommodating new information and can alter their schema dynamics. It is no wonder, then, that more cognitively flexible creatures endured, whereas those who were not flexible became extinct. It is very similar with clients: Those who are able to accommodate and assimilate find relief, whereas those who are not flexible continue to struggle. Information Box 9.1 discusses findings on the use of schemas.

Information Box 9.1: Research Findings on Schemas

Tomorrow's practitioner must engage in treatment methodologies that are informed by research. The cognitive-behavioral therapy (CBT; i.e., using a variety of methods to help clients challenge their beliefs, assumptions, and schemas) movement has generated a substantial amount of empirical research demonstrating that therapy is effective in treating depression and anxiety. It has also been demonstrated to be as effective (in some cases) as psychopharmacology in the treatment of some forms of depression (Young, Beck, & Weinberger, 1993). At the same time, however, several authors have noted that cognitive-behavioral therapy has its limitations (e.g., Corey, 2001; Halford, Bernoth-Doolan, & Eadie, 2002; Young, 1990). Furthermore, several studies have reported attrition rates (clients who drop out of treatment) for CBT of 20–40% for depression and 0–50% for anxiety disorders (as cited in Halford et al., 2002). In addition, for those clients who make gains in treatment, nearly half have a recurrence of depressive symptoms within 2 years (Gortner, Gollan, Dobson, & Jacobson, 1998). Curious about these findings, Young, an associate of Beck's, postulated that something deeper had to account for these treatment-resistant clients. He observed that these individuals frequently had "much more rigid cognitive structures; more chronic, often lifelong psychological problems; and more deeply entrenched, dysfunctional belief systems" (Kellogg & Young, 2006, p. 446). He began to explore the idea that schemas may hold the key for addressing these more difficult clients.

In point of fact, the emphasis on schemas in the psychotherapeutic literature has continued to grow since the 1980s. Many new approaches, particularly in the work of Johnson and Greenberg's (1985) emotion-focused therapy, Snyder's pluralistic approach (Snyder & Schneider, 2002), and Young's (1999) schema-focused therapy, ground themselves directly in concentrating on client schemas, or indirectly by utilizing tenets of attachment theory. All of these authors and others as well have attested to the importance of understanding that what clients are thinking and recognizing patterns within their thinking are just as important as recognizing and understanding client behavior patterns.

CONCLUSION

A client's schemas give rise to affect—the emotions—that a client expresses. It is as if a client is saying, "I hold these beliefs, convictions, values, view of myself, the world, etc., and what I am now encountering in life threatens them. That provokes and fuels me to feel these emotions (i.e., anger, embarrassment, jealousy, depression, anxiety, etc.)—and that's what prompts me to come to therapy!" Encountering transient demands, threats, and challenges from the environment (i.e., others, life circumstances, or both) is part and parcel of what it is to be human; nevertheless, such life encounters are experienced as threatening, stressful, and irritating. Perceived demands and threats from the environment to rigidly held schema (e.g., confrontational interactions with others, overwhelming life circumstances, and extreme impasses) generate strong feelings, correspondingly strong emotional reactions, and impulses to action. More permanent such threats are experienced as intolerable and produce symptoms of anxiety, stress, depression, somatic complaints, insomnia, and so on. There is an inexorable relatedness and intimacy between cognitions and schemas and the emotions they generate. Hence, it is important to understand a client's schemas and her emotions as reciprocal partners. What are *emotions*? How do they specifically relate to schemas? How does a master practitioner deal with them in treatment? These and other questions are the subject to which we now turn our attention.

Brain in a Box 9.1: The Neurobiological Basis of Early Childhood Recollections

Early childhood recollections (ECRs) are a rich source of dynamic understanding about the clients who consult us, whether those recollections are systematically collected or arise spontaneously. Obviously, the brain is the specific body organ that stores memories and unconsciously retrieves and uses them in the service of the goals of the personality. The mystery of how ECRs become such a revealing part of personality is slowly being unraveled by cognitive neuroscience. Paradoxically, in order to understand ECRs, one must first understand fear.

LeDoux (1996) has advocated that the brain's "fear system" is a particularly good anchoring point for understanding the organization of other emotions in the brain. He gives three reasons for selecting fear in this way: (a) It is pervasive throughout humankind and the vertebrate kingdom, and yet paradoxically William James noted that humans are distinguished from other animals because of their ability to reduce conditions of fear under which they live; (b) whether it is anxiety, panic, phobias, posttraumatic stress disorder, or obsessive-compulsive disorder, fear plays an extensive role in psychopathology; and (c) fear is similarly expressed in humans and other animals.

To LeDoux's (1998) list of human fears, we would add an observation made by Adler (1956): the fear of "failure" that comes in an infinite variety of forms. Master practitioners are sensitive to the human fear of failure dynamic apparent in their clients, albeit disguised. Although apparently endemic to the human condition and sharing similar properties between individuals, fear of failure in its subtleties and nuances is unique to each individual.

The amygdala plays an essential role in fear mediation. LeDoux (1998) has called it the "hub in the wheel of fear" (p. 170). In turn, "fear" as a universal (i.e., all human beings are fearful of something, including failure) and a uniquely defined experience (i.e., each individual has different things, experiences, etc., that he or she is fearful of, including different sorts of failure) is an emotional and physical survival emotion. Without it, we would not know to be afraid of things in life that can destroy us physically and hurt us emotionally. We *learn* to be fearful of specific things. LeDoux has suggested that through a process of classical conditioning that takes place in the brain of a child, human beings learn to associate certain experiences with certain fears or other emotions such as embarrassment. But, there are "multiple memory systems" (p. 239).

It is the hippocampus of the limbic system and related cortical areas that are responsible for storing *specific* conscious memories, whereas "unconscious memories established by fear conditioning mechanisms" (p. 239) operate through an amygdala-based system. LeDoux (1998) concluded that:

when stimuli that were present during the initial trauma are later encountered, each system can potentially retrieve its memories. In the case of the amygdala system, retrieval results in expression of bodily responses that prepare for danger, and in the case of the hippocampal system, conscious remembrances occur. (p. 239).

In their summaries of relevant research, Cappas, Andres-Hyman, and Davidson (2005) and Eichenbaum (2001) pointed out that once something is learned, the hippocampus begins to process that information, with consolidation of learning occurring over a period of years. The implication of this for clinicians to understand is that early childhood experiences (e.g., repeated physical abuse, neglect, pampering, anxiety-laden experiences, embarrassments, and being victimized by bullies) are processed by the hippocampus until consolidated as "old knowledge at which point it is organized in the neocortex" (Cappas et al., p. 376). We suggest that (a) a child creatively organizes such understandings into thinking templates (i.e., schemas); (b) a child automatically, unconsciously, and creatively concludes that her thinking template represents "truths" or operating principles through which she appraises experience and by which she acts; and (c) those core operating principles become the unique, defining, thinking principles of an individual personality.

A related issue pertains to the validity of a human memory and whether or not a recollected event did or did not factually occur. Experimental neuroscience data are growing that "false memories" can indeed be generated. With their particular experimental procedures using event-related potentials (ERPs), Gonsalves and Paller (2000) concluded that people

occasionally misattribute their memory of an imagined object to a memory of actually viewing a picture of that object.... We were thus able to use brain potentials to study neural processes related to the occurrence of false memories, both at encoding and at retrieval. (p. 1318)

It is not, however, whether something did or did not occur that is clinically relevant, as some theories question. Therapeutically, the important issue is the client's *belief* that something did occur. Although some clients may be preoccupied with the validity of a memory, for other clients Edelstein and Steele (1997) suggested that it really isn't whether recollected events took place that is presently harming a client but rather that "beliefs about them are harming you because you are following them now" (p. 209).

Given this analysis, spontaneous early childhood recollections divulged by a client in treatment can be particularly revealing and helpful. If correctly deciphered with the collaborative help of a client, such memories can reveal *unconscious* meanings, both cognitive and emotional, that clients have given to certain types of childhood situations when they occurred. The *paradigm* or blueprint laid down in the amygdala without specifics is sensitized to recognize similar threats in the adult environment so that the personality can take appropriate safeguarding actions. The hippocampus and related cortical structures make available a *specific* memory that a client recalls when he states, "There was this one time.... I was about 4 years old. I remember ..." The neocortex represents the template that an individual follows with as much loyalty as a personal religion, but it can be influenced by corrective experiences.

ENDNOTES

1. Early childhood recollections are discussed later in this chapter.
2. Upon feedback from a client, a therapist can ask how her client sees such a self-image affecting his behavior. As a follow-up, an inquiry can be made about how he might like his self-image to be.
3. The client returned the following week, and after exchanging pleasantries, the therapist asked him how his week was and how the homework assignment went. He responded that for a short time, he began catching himself and was encouraged by the homework almost completely stopping his "What if ..." behavior. He then noted that he asked himself, "*What if* it (i.e., catching himself) doesn't work?" At that moment, the therapist asked the young man to repeat what he had just said. He did so without recognizing what it was that he had said. The therapist asked him to repeat himself once again, and he did. The second time around, he "got it." His face reddened, and he laughed heartily and shook his head in awe of how automatic and unconscious his "What if ..." orientation really was.
4. One's explanatory style is highly reflective of an underlying core schema.
5. *Sibling position* rather than *birth order* is a better term because absolute birth order is not as clinically revealing as the term *sibling position*. Birth order simply refers to an ordinal ranking—who was born first, second, third, and so on, devoid of other meaningful information. Absolute birth "order," however, does not reveal the entire story. As a simple example, it is one thing to be born into one's family as the "youngest of four" same-sex siblings who are far apart in age, and it is entirely another thing to be born as the fourth sibling and only boy—especially when the children are close in age and the parents desperately wanted a son. Because such an individual's arrival on this earth is a prized event and he is greatly loved and admired by all family members, it is quite likely to affect *his* personality development (*and* that of his siblings), perhaps by being spoiled by his mother and older sisters (cf. Bank & Kahn, 1982, for more details).
6. Many therapists observe the experience that over the course of successful therapy, a client's ECRs change. At times, recollected events become less threatening and more temporized. At other times, a client becomes more competent, with a greater sense of social connectedness in the re-recollected memory.
7. EM is the term Watkins (1992) used to refer to early childhood memories.
8. *Metaphor* is in actuality an umbrella term that incorporates the use of "multiple levels of communication" and includes such communications as the use of analogy, puns, jokes, and folk language (see Erickson & Rossi, 1976).
9. We hypothesize that "images" are powerful nonlinear, right-brained media that represent how the brain processes a good deal of emotional information. See Pinker (1999).
10. Note that this proposed list of potential sources for metaphors is not considered exhaustive but rather suggestive! Furthermore, the most powerful source of metaphor is the creative capacity of the therapist.
11. These suggestions should always be checked with the client's actual circumstances and disposition.

The Domain of Addressing and Managing Clients' Emotional States

10

Part 1: Basic Understandings

CONTENTS

INTRODUCTION: *GOOD WILL HUNTING* AND EMOTIONS

Good Will Hunting (Van Sant, 1997) is an Academy Award–winning film about a brilliant young man (Will Hunting, portrayed by Matt Damon) who is unable to handle his emotions, despite his intellectual gifts. Unbelievably talented in mathematics and bestowed with a photographic memory, Will experienced horrible childhood physical abuse at the hands of his father and other foster parents. As a result, under the surface of an easygoing manner (and despite his intellect), he has a seething rage that explodes several times in the film, and leads him into trouble with the law. In addition, he is unable to form close, meaningful relationships with people other than his small group of friends (including Ben Affleck) who seem to be going nowhere in life. Will works as a janitor at MIT and lives a somewhat aimless, beer-soaked, working-class life in South Boston, seemingly wasting his immense gift for complex, theoretical math.

While mopping the corridor outside of a major lecture hall at MIT, Will anonymously solves a math problem placed on the hallway chalkboard by a famous math professor as a challenge to the students in his class. When no one takes credit for having solved the problem, the professor places yet another more challenging problem on the board that Will again solves with unbelievable ease—this time he is caught solving the problem but escapes. After yet another encounter with the criminal justice system, Will finds himself in jail. By this time, the professor has tracked him down and spoken to the judge about Will's giftedness. The judge agrees to release Will under two conditions: He is to be subject to the professor's supervision, and he is to undergo psychotherapy. The two conditions are posed because the professor recognizes that a person with Will's talents comes along so rarely in life.

The first two attempts to find a therapist for Will by the professor (who is also working out some "issues" relative to his fame as a mathematician) are abortive disasters. In fact, Will has fun using his intellect in mocking the entire therapeutic process. Of course, this is also a defense against having to deal with his complex, confusing, and painful emotions. His third encounter is with Dr. Sean McGuire, a psychologist played by Robin Williams. His performance is a powerful portrayal of a therapist's encounter and relationship with an aggressive and apparently angry young man who does not want to be in therapy. But, not even he is immune to being pushed by Will's crushing sarcastic intellect—Sean nearly chokes Will during a powerful exchange.[1] This emotional explosion forces Sean to recognize that Will's intellectual talents, his provocation of others, and his explosive temper are all linked. They are attempts to keep others at arm's length to avoid getting close to other people, and avoid potentially being hurt by them. When Sean confronts Will about this, they slowly move forward and negotiate a powerful therapeutic alliance based on acceptance, trust, and mutual respect.

At the same time, Will's charming nonconformity is a magnet to Skylar, an upstanding, orphaned medical student portrayed by Minnie Driver, who provides Will with another challenge—managing his affection for her. He is powerfully attracted to her and, at the same time, is afraid of their closeness. As they become closer, she attempts to learn more about his past. When she notices his many scars and cigarette burns, he lashes out verbally at her and attempts to push her away. He is successful only to find, however, that when she is gone, he truly wants to be with her. Through his relationship with Sean, he begins to understand his own reactions and the emotions that make him tick. Ultimately, he decides to take a risk and follow after the woman he loves to California, leaving the comfort of his familiar Boston home, friends, and going-nowhere life, though he has no guarantee that she will take him back and forgive him (the ultimate in being vulnerable to someone else).

There is a theme inherent in the story of *Good Will Hunting* that is common in classical fiction. That theme concerns the protagonist, a successful and powerfully intellectual character who also has a beastly "dark side" of emotional turmoil. *Dr. Jekyll and Mr. Hyde* and *The Incredible Hulk* are but two popular examples of a character such as Will, a rare mathematical genius capable of an unbridled expression of emotions that can be overwhelming and uncomfortable. Are emotions and "intellect" incompatible, as stories of Will, Jekyll and Hyde, and the like suggest? We suggest that there are two common universal lingering misperceptions regarding emotions.

LINGERING MISPERCEPTIONS OF EMOTIONS

Emotions Are Weak, Feminine, and to Be Feared

Emotions are often contrasted with intellect. Whereas intellect is stereotypically seen as calm, rational, and civilized, emotions are seen as wild, irrational, and uncontrollable. Paradoxically, at the same time, emotionality has been seen traditionally as something "weak," childlike, and feminine (e.g., the 19th-century diagnosis of "hysteria"). Intellect is chauvinistically seen as the domain of rational, strong-minded men, whereas emotionality is seen as the domain of weepy, indecisive women in need of "rescue." Thus, the emotions, and their expression, are often seen (by both men and women) as something to be feared or avoided—a form of weakness. The reality is that human emotions *are* often puzzling and demanding. But, experiencing, understanding, and using the full range of emotions (both good and bad) are crucial to our survival as a species. They are essential to our ability to form relationships with others, and necessary in order to lead a fulfilling life. According to Greenberg and Paivio (1997),

> Emotions provide a rich source of information about our reactions to situations. Emotions, or more accurately those constituents of emotions that may have been out of awareness, can be brought into awareness to enhance the way in which we evaluate our needs, desires, goals, and concerns. What is required, particularly in therapy, is an understanding of what emotions indicate to us about the way in which we are conducting our lives. (p. 4)

Emotions Are to Be Avoided, Contained, and Neutralized in Treatment

A second common misperception regarding emotions concerns how they are addressed in treatment. Greenberg and Paivio (1997) and others (e.g., Nathanson, 1996; Plutchik, 2000; Schwartz & Johnson, 2000) noted that psychotherapists overwhelmingly tend to shy away from understanding both emotions and the information that they contain. They act as if emotions either do not exist or are something that must be dominated and controlled by reason. Many psychotherapists are taught "cutting-edge" theories with very effective methods of dealing with the cognitive aspects of a client's concerns (viz., "automatic negative thoughts," or ANTs, discussed in Chapter 8; see Kirsch & Lynn, 1999). Unfortunately, these methods tend to diminish the impact and role of emotions. Therapists taught such approaches are often awkward and even inept with client discussions of feelings and expressions of powerful emotions. According to Plutchick, therapy conducted without a fundamental and thorough understanding of emotions is limited and often ineffective. Consistent with the theme expressed throughout this text, dominating and controlling emotions, or outright ignoring them as something unpleasant or disruptive to treatment, reflect extremely *linear* thinking.

In fact, there are sad examples of various once-fashionable approaches (and theorists) that attempted to work in a *linear* way on either cognitions *or* emotions while ignoring the other. Psychotherapy researchers such as Norcross, Koocher, and Garofalo (2006) have cautioned *all* clinicians against working on merely the affective domain because such one-sided efforts (e.g., abuses of "primal scream" therapy, and the "EST" movement) are to the detriment of the client's welfare. Some of the damage inflicted on clients was due to poorly trained therapists using "gimmicks" or "techniques" that fail to consider emotions, emotional expression, and their true functions within the context of a broader understanding of human functioning and problem solving. Other damage to clients stems from the misguided notion that feeling strong emotions (that were often stifled or "repressed") by a client is sufficient to produce change.[2]

Catharsis of Emotion as Sufficient for Change

The idea of ridding one's system of emotions stems (in part) from the idea of *catharsis*, a Greek term meaning "to purge" or purify. It was used by Aristotle to describe a release from emotions such as fear and pity that might be evoked when watching a tragic play.[3] In early psychoanalysis (and subsequent systems of psychotherapy), it referred to the release and sense of relief that clients felt as a result of the expression of strong emotion previously repressed or suppressed. Although in some cases this might be true, when taken to its *linear* extreme (e.g., "Well, if some catharsis is good, a lot of catharsis will be really good!"), catharsis for its own sake can be misguided. Such misapplication of this principle led to dangerous abuses, particularly when therapists did not know how to place the emotional expressions into *context*. That is, therapists did not know how to help clients see how emotional states and expressions either fit with schema dynamics or offered a way or impetus to change their schematized views of self, others, and life and the world. Without such therapeutic guidance (via the therapeutic alliance), however, the connection between emotional expression and one's schematized worldview, clients are likely to feel tremendously vulnerable, or (re)victimized by the experience. According to Yalom (1995), catharsis without insight is not helpful, and insight without catharsis is equally unhelpful: "We must experience something strongly, but we must also, through the faculty of reason, understand the implications of that emotional experience" (p. 28).

Skovholt and Jennings (2004) found that master therapists distinguish themselves in this domain by demonstrating an ability to attend to and effectively work with clients' emotions and emotional states, while simultaneously paying attention to their own emotional states. As the work of Jackson, Brunet, Meltzoff, and Decety (2006) have demonstrated, there are similar brain processes operating when we are in pain *and* when we are empathizing with others' pain. But although these neural processes overlap, they are not identical. That allows therapists to not only be empathic but also remain objective and maintain appropriate professional boundaries. When their own inappropriate emotional issues enter the therapeutic alliance (viz., inappropriate countertransference), many Level I practitioners become somewhat befuddled, making it impossible for them to manage clients' emotions effectively. At the same time, clients *are* sensitive to their counselors or therapists failing to react (i.e., acknowledging, joining with, and responding to clients' emotions) or reacting poorly to their emotional expressions because of countertransference or anxiety issues associated with their role as counselor. Piercy, Lipchik, and Kiser (2000) and Schwartz and Johnson (2000) noted that a client's sensitivity to such inabilities leads to feelings that her therapist is not in synch with her. This creates potential for a therapeutic rupture and the beginning of disengagement from the therapy process, which can likely result in premature termination (as discussed in Chapter 7).

Thus, the purpose of working with a client's emotions is to help him understand a given reaction (i.e., emotional expression) that is either: (a) out of the ordinary for a client, (b) not understood, or (c) out of a client's control. To do this effectively, a *nonlinear-thinking* therapist is obliged to reflect about and understand (a) a client's schema dynamics; and (b) the function of and relationship between a client's emotional states, internal feeling, and experiencing of those emotional states and their expression. We discuss these in detail, beginning with basic definitions.

UNDERSTANDING AND DIFFERENTIATING: EXPRESSIONS OF AFFECT, INTERNAL FEELINGS, EMOTIONAL STATES AND MOODS, PRIMARY EMOTIONS, SECONDARY EMOTIONS, AND BACKGROUND EMOTIONS

Expressions of affect, internal feelings, and emotional states (i.e., moods) can be as difficult to distinguish, describe, and make use of as they are to work with. Each is a distinct term, however, and each has a part to play in understanding a client's overall emotional experience of her life. In this section, we define each of these elements (i.e., expressions of affect, internal feelings, and emotional states or mood). We also discuss moderating and mediating influences on each (i.e., the appraisal process, and schematized views), and conclude with a discussion of the difficulty in communication and translation of all these elements for clients, and how this becomes an important clinical issue deserving of attention. We begin by working backward—discussing emotional expressions that are observable by others.

Expressions of Affect

A person's *affect* is composed of a variety of internal (e.g., thoughts, memories, and reflections) and external (e.g., posture, facial expressions, body movements, and voice) *expressions* making up a person's emotional response. According to Othmer and Othmer (1989),

> Affect is the *visible* and *audible* manifestation of the patient's emotional response to *outside* and *inside* events, i.e., thoughts, ideas, evoked memories, reflections, and performance. It is expressed in posture, facial and body movements, and in tone of voice, vocalizations, and word selection. (p. 124; emphasis added; see also Othmer & Othmer, 1994)

In other words, *expressions of affect* are the more readily observable indicators of *internal feeling states* being described by a client. Thus, affect can be considered the *end product* of a person's experience of having an emotion. It represents the particular configuration in which an emotion in a particular person makes itself known at a particular time.

Expressions of affect are readily observable and detectable through *linear* and *nonlinear* listening and observing for congruence, absence, and inference via facial expressions, voice qualities (e.g., tone and pitch), and content of conversation. Such outward expressions signify that someone is *experiencing*—that is, something is going on "inside" an individual *that he is not necessarily expressing in a linear manner*. Subtle or blatantly overt expressions of affect are the equivalent of clues that reveal a client's *internal feeling* states, but they must be examined, not assumed.

Internal Feelings

In their essence, *feelings* are mild elemental experiences based upon what human senses (i.e., visual, auditory, tactile, gustatory, and olfactory are the five basic sensations) perceive that can be described as either pleasant or unpleasant in nature. In a landmark work still referenced today, Arnold (1960) described feelings in the language of everyday life as revealed by such expressions as "I *feel* cold." Such expressions represent elemental *sensory experiences* of something either pleasant or unpleasant. Everyday language also reveals expressions such as "I *feel* that I'm right!" To paraphrase Arnold, such expressions suggest that the speaker has reached a conclusion or decision that is correct, although she may not necessarily be able to "prove" it or describe the elements that led to that conclusion. Other expressions such as "I feel angry" are descriptions and statements of direct *emotional* experiences. Arnold succinctly summarized the complex topic of feelings as follows:

> If feeling is used to indicate awareness of some bodily or psychological state which I experience directly, that state itself can be felt as either pleasant or unpleasant. If it is neither, it will be reported as indifferent. In every case pleasantness and unpleasantness refer to the way in which this state is felt: how it feels to have a sensation or an emotion, to make a deliberate effort, or to engage in psychological or physical activity. (pp. 20–21)

In other words, when we experience an emotion whether we recognize it or not, we *feel* it. Through our consciousness, feelings are the vehicle by which emotions are experienced.[4] Clinically, listening acutely to the verbal expressions that clients use to describe what it is that they are feeling is critical to understanding what they are trying to tell us—it is *information*. Consider the following few client expressions of *sensations* they are experiencing to describe various emotions:

"It's a heavy, heavy sensation in my chest that won't go away" to describe feeling the emotion of sadness

"I get a warm feeling—sort of a glow—throughout my body every time I'm with him" to describe feeling the emotion of infatuation

"My blood runs cold whenever I have to deal with that man" to describe feeling the emotion of intense fear

"I felt ill—sweaty, clammy, headachy—it's like I tried to scream and I couldn't. I gasped, like not enough air in my lungs" to describe feeling the emotion of intense anxiety

To review, in the chain of human emotional experiences being described, expressions of affect (i.e., emotion) are the *external manifestations* of what is going on *inside*, and feelings are the elemental, sensory-based means by which we consciously experience emotions. If this brief discussion of affect and feelings appears multifaceted, intricate, and revealing, the discussion of emotion that follows is equally so.

Emotional States

The consensus amongst many theorists is that emotions explicitly serve two biological or evolutionary functions (Damasio, 1999; Greenberg and Paivio, 1997; Plutchik, 2000). The primary biological function that the emotions serve is to produce biochemical and neural responses for a particular reaction to an event that stimulated the emotion. For example, emotions *produce the appropriate physiological changes and reactions[5] necessary* to flee, fight aggressively, make passionate love, withdraw, and so on. The second biological function that the emotions serve is to *regulate specific internal physiological states* so that an individual can be prepared for the specific reaction required. Damasio (1999) has put it this way:

> [T]he biological "purpose" of the emotions is clear, and emotions are not a dispensable luxury. Emotions are … part and parcel of the machinery with which organisms regulate survival … a fairly high-level component of the mechanisms of life regulation … sandwiched between the basic survival kit (e.g. regulation of metabolism; simple reflexes; motivations; biology of pain and pleasure) and the devices of high reason, but still very much a part of the hierarchy of life-regulation devices. … And as a result of powerful learning mechanisms such as conditioning, emotions of all shades eventually help connect homeostatic regulation and survival "values" to numerous events and objects in our autobiographical experience. Emotions are inseparable from the idea of reward or punishment, of pleasure or pain, of approach or withdrawal, of personal advantage and disadvantage. Inevitably, emotions are inseparable from the idea of good and evil. (pp. 54–55)

Damasio was essentially describing the interface between the realms of cognitive schemas and emotions. Fundamentally, emotions serve human beings as "survival" mechanisms. The primitive "survival" mechanisms that Damasio referred to can be seen as those emotions of our Neanderthal ancestors that signaled whether objects they perceived in their environment were something to be eaten or something that wished to eat them. The contemporary counterpart of "survival" mechanisms can be seen in the emotions brought about by the complexities of modern social living. As a result, there are several levels of emotional states that have been identified: primary emotions, secondary emotions, and background emotions or mood.

Primary Emotions

The work of Paul Ekman, (Ekman, Levenson, & Friesen, 1983; and see Ekman, 1992), represents landmark research on an understanding of human emotions. Whether a given individual is from a primitive culture or a modern culture, it has been determined that there are commonly recognized, "primary," universal, cross-culturally validated emotions: happiness, sadness, fear, anger, surprise, and disgust. By studying *facial muscles*, Ekman et al. (1983) found emotion-specific autonomic nervous system activity that not only differentiated positive emotions from negative emotions but also differentiated among the negative emotions. Cross-cultural universality suggests that there is a common neural architecture mediating emotional responses that are shared by all human beings.

Secondary Emotions

Damasio (1999) has been particularly eloquent in expanding our understanding of the relationship between having emotions and the experience of consciousness of those emotions. He proposed the term *secondary emotions* to describe embarrassment, jealousy, guilt, and pride. Obviously, such emotions have somewhat of a "social" quality to them in that being embarrassed suggests discomfort in front of others, jealousy suggests covetousness toward others, and so on (see Contextually Cultural Box 10.1). Today's "survival" mechanisms can be seen as those secondary emotions stimulated by perceived threats to self-esteem, the need to save face or maintain a sense of superiority, feelings of belonging, and so on. Precisely what each individual interprets as a challenge or threat today is brought about by "values," that is, what someone deems worthwhile as "good" or "bad." According to Pinker (1999),

> Goals and values are one of the vocabularies in which we mentally couch our experiences. They cannot be built out of simpler concepts from our physical knowledge the way "momentum" can be built out of mass and velocity or "power" can be built out of energy. *They are primitive or irreducible, and high-level concepts are defined in terms of them.* (p. 315; emphasis added)

As discussed in Chapters 8 and 9, values arise from schemas, are "unconsciously" (i.e., unknowingly, or "primitively") held by an individual, and spontaneously give rise automatically and intuitively to emotions. As addressed in Brain in a Box 9.1 in Chapter 9, whereas the amygdala is the sentinel that contains information about what is threatening to an individual (i.e., his values, and things held to be important), the emotions are its messengers, calling forth the perceived appropriate response for maintaining the "survival" of the modern-day personality. As such, among their other properties, *emotions are informative in nature* (Greenberg, 2004). If attended to, sorted out, and interpreted well, they inform us of important values, beliefs, positions, and so on that we harbor, some of which may be nonnegotiable in nature. *We emphasize that human beings have emotional reactions to those things in life that have meaning (i.e., "value" to us).*

Contextually Cultural Box 10.1: Cultural Sensitivity, Diversity, and the Secondary Emotions

The secondary emotions having a "social" quality suggests the necessity for clinicians to take into account a client's cultural background in order to understand her emotional reactions. As Krauss (2006) has stated, "Culture is a transporter of value and meaning whether good or bad" (p. 2).

In turn, cultures differ widely in values and meanings. Thus, what might produce embarrassment in one culture might not be embarrassing in another, even though there may be an overlapping of circumstances that prompt embarrassment. Certain values in one culture (e.g., arranged marriage, in which parents of the bride and groom select mates for their children) may produce extreme emotional reactions to the point of suicide in one of the betrothed, whereas in another culture an arranged marriage is not even remotely taken into consideration when thinking about or planning to get married.

Such considerations essentially require clinicians to be "culturally sensitive." What precisely is "cultural sensitivity"? In the broadest sense, we propose that cultural sensitivity has at least three meanings. The first meaning refers to a clinician's specific knowledge base of the particular culture from which a client comes. Such knowledge disposes a clinician to be particularly responsive to issues for one client that might not be as relevant or might even be irrelevant for another client.

The second meaning of culturally sensitivity refers to differences between macro and micro issues. Macro sensitivities are differences in culture highlighted between the client's and clinician's backgrounds. A therapist must acknowledge such differences so that they are minimally influential in therapist decision making about interventions. Would this intervention be personally offensive in some manner and not interpreted according to the *therapist's* cultural norms? Such macro issues are large, are obvious, and speak for themselves. For example, a therapist trained at the doctoral level living a fairly affluent lifestyle cannot interpret psychological behaviors according to his cultural environment when working with impoverished immigrant clients living in a homeless shelter suffering from posttraumatic stress encountered in their war-torn country of origin. The micro issues are much more subtle, as suggested, for example, by a clinician with a Midwestern cultural background and values versus someone from the deep south or perhaps the west coast. A clinician sharing a similar micro background with a client still might have different values as expressed in one being a first-generation American and another being a fourth-generation American. Likewise, whereas individuals from the same country of origin may share many values, they may differ considerably regarding religious beliefs, issues of sin and guilt, and so on. Therapists' alertness to every client's unique background is a form of cultural sensitivity.

The third meaning of cultural sensitivity proposed is that reflected by master clinicians who are constantly alert to those influences from a particular client's background that possibly may affect why it is that a client believes and correspondingly feels the way he does about an issue. Such cultural sensitivity is seen as a subset of a clinician's general capacity to *listen in a nonlinear* manner for the possible meanings that clients attribute to circumstances and the feelings and emotions that are generated by those meanings.

As an example, we cite a case whose derivation is unknown. A well-educated, successful professional woman consulted a therapist reporting that she felt someone had placed a "curse" upon her. Originally from Haiti, she had not lived on the island for years. Nevertheless, the extent of her emotional reaction to the belief that a curse or spell had been placed upon her was profound—she was convinced that she would die if the curse was not removed! *Linear thinking* might prompt a clinician to regard the woman as paranoid, perhaps decompensating, and requiring psychotropic medications and psychotherapy. *Nonlinear thinking* suggests otherwise. Evaluating the woman's profound belief in the curse and the emotions it produced, the therapist helped the woman to locate a shaman from Haiti who lived in a part of the city with a large component of Haitian refugees. An appropriate spell to neutralize the curse she believed had been inflicted upon her by nefarious others promptly produced full and total symptom remission for the woman.

As Krauss (2006) has indicated, "Nature alone does not determine human actions nor fully circumscribe human behavior; culture is their managing director" (p. 1).

Background Emotions, or Mood

Damasio (1999) also added a third category of emotions that he referred to as "background emotions" (p. 51), which for practical purposes can be considered a person's *mood*. Although not ordinarily considered in a discussion of emotions, the concept and label *background emotions*, or mood, are of particular relevance to clinicians at all levels and require them to develop and refine the acute skills of linear and nonlinear observing and attending that we have described in Chapter 2. Othmer and Othmer (1989) defined *mood* as a "long term feeling state through which we filter all experiences" (p. 128).

Nonlinear listening to, observing, and attending to what a client is divulging about her emotional state serve as extremely valuable sources of information for clinicians. Damasio (1999) described background emotions as follows:

> When we sense that a person is "tense" or "edgy," "discouraged" or "enthusiastic," "down" or "cheerful," without a single word having been spoken to translate any of those possible states, we are detecting background emotions. We detect background emotions by subtle details of body posture, speed and contour of movements, minimal changes in the amount and speed of eye movement, and in the degree of contraction of facial muscles. (p. 52)

Othmer and Othmer (1989) suggested that mood has five dimensions: *quality, stability, reactivity, intensity*, and *duration*. They suggested that perhaps the best way of understanding the *quality* of a mood is by relating it to a "theme" that permeates an individual's functioning. The seven themes outlined in Chapter 5 were built around a client's particular *mood* (e.g., themes of desperation, hopelessness, or sadness). The nonlinear-thinking clinician understands how such themes and their emotional accompaniments impact a client's internal feelings and affective expressions. As we will discuss below, *themes* and their emotions and feelings relate to a client's schema dynamics. *Stability* refers to how lingering and steady a client's feelings are or, conversely, how *unstable* she may feel (e.g., "up" one minute and "down" the next). *Reactivity* refers to whether or not an individual's feelings respond to appropriate changes in her social environment. That is, does a client's mood perk up when she is shown attention, or does her mood remain "down" no matter whom it is that may be attempting to interact with her? *Intensity* of affect refers to the degree to which someone is experiencing her particular feelings—in panic disorders, feelings experienced are described as intense, and likewise for someone who is "high" (i.e., manic). In contrast, schizophrenic clients are typically described as having a flat or shallow mood. The final quality of a mood that Othmer and Othmer (1989) described is *duration*—whether it is of short or long duration: "Dysphoria lasting hours or days is seen in personality disorders, sociopathy, alcoholism, and drug abuse, while depressive mood of affective disorder last two weeks or longer. The same is true for elated mood" (pp. 131–132).

The role of "background emotions" in our lives and especially in the lives of clients who consult us is important to understand. As suggested immediately above, understanding such background emotions and moods helps clinicians to discern differences between those emotionally acute crisis situations for which individuals consult therapists and those lingering and longer term emotional states with which some people live chronically almost as a way of life. Thus, a client might seek consultation for contextual issues (e.g., working long hours of necessity, the stress of raising children, feeling overwhelmed by medical problems, or fatigue) that generate strong emotions, both of which might be addressed via clinical interventions such as teaching a client self-hypnosis, meditation, or other relaxation techniques. Just as primary or secondary emotions are most often signals to a clinician that schema dynamics are at work, likewise background emotions of long duration can also reveal that schema dynamics are at work.

Indeed, background emotions seem especially to operate closely with a client's overall schema dynamics (positive or negative), which will be discussed later in this chapter. Generally, a client's emotional states represent three essential elements in a person's life: the universal survival mechanisms of all human beings (primary emotions); information about the complex societal rules and values that either clarify or regulate the client's internal feelings and affective expressions (secondary emotions); and, last, information that is unique to the individual's views of self, others, and the world (background emotions). It should be clear by now that therapists who ignore or downplay a client's emotions (expressions, feelings, and states) are missing valuable clinical information.

Clinical Case Example 10.1: Chronic "Low-Grade" Depression

We reprint the case from Chapters 5 and 8 (Clinical Case Examples 5.3 and 8.1) of a widow in her 60s with a long history of intermittent treatment. Recall that her presenting concern was that she has struggled with chronic depression her entire adult life. She furthermore described herself as "supersensitive," angry, chronically annoyed, and wanting to stay in bed although she forces herself to go to work. In reviewing her history, she felt criticized by her parents, who had high expectations but showed little demonstrable love, affection, and positive reinforcement (especially when compared to what she believed her siblings received). She also described her failure to thrive over the years (i.e., her depressive symptoms, chronic job dissatisfaction, few friends, etc.) as being due to the many years of deprivations and hardships in her family of origin.

Growing up in her family, she was presented with a set of standards that she believed was too high for her to reach. In addition, the little physical affection, warmth, or other demonstrations of love and affection she received from her family were too sparse to encourage efforts for her to even attempt to excel at anything, which added to a negative view of self (i.e., as someone not worthy of being loved). The essence of these experiences was "I am ordinary," "I am not (able to be) successful," or "My only claim to fame is to be critical, irascible, outspoken—that's who I am." In terms of her schema dynamics, she had a negative and unrealistic view of self. It was unrealistic because it was pervasive and she was not able to see any of her positive attributes or accomplishments (e.g., she had a successful marriage, maintained steady albeit constantly changing employment, helped others less fortunate than herself, and engaged in volunteer community activities) as sufficient to warrant a self-view of "I'm OK—not perfect, but OK."

QUESTIONS

1. Describe the client's expressions of affect.
2. What internal feelings does the client appear to be struggling with?
3. How would you describe the client's emotional state?
4. What kind of emotions are present? Primary, secondary, or background?

Emotions, Mood, and Affect

As a helpful clinical suggestion, Othmer and Othmer (1989) distinguished clients' expressions of affect and their emotional states and mood according to four criteria:

1. The first criterion is that *affect is more fleeting and shifting than mood*, which can last for months and even years.
2. The second criterion is that emotions are *reactive*. That is, they are produced in response to internal stimuli (e.g., what someone is thinking about can produce a certain emotion) or external stimuli (e.g., a reaction to what someone encounters), whereas a mood state can change spontaneously.
3. The third criterion they proposed is that *affect maintains the "foreground" of experience*, whereas *mood is the emotional "background"* (p. 125).

4. Finally, Othmer and Othmer (1989) suggested that it is a *practitioner* who observes signs of affect, whereas a disturbed mood is typically reported by a *client*.

The point to listening (both linearly and nonlinearly) in order to recognize and understand what emotions a client is feeling is to *convey that understanding to the client*. As described in Chapters 2 and 3, by summarizing, paraphrasing, and reflecting back to a client an understanding of his or her feeling experience, a practitioner establishes and begins to solidify a fundamental requirement (i.e., the therapeutic relationship and alliance) for further therapeutic work.

Expressions of affect are the only part of the system that is "visible" to others. As noted earlier, as the amygdala generates a fundamental emotional state or states, it biochemically generates or stimulates appropriate *feelings* that, in turn, generate (direct or indirect) expressions of affect. It is important to note that this system can become disrupted because of the powerful, extremely fast, and automatic nature of emotions and the way the brain is "wired" to generate emotions. That is, clients can and do "act out" without being able to recognize their internal feelings (e.g., "I just snapped"), let alone the emotions generating those feelings. Clients can also have feelings without having an understanding of their emotional states or the reasons for feeling the way they do (e.g., having an upset stomach but not relating it to being anxious about something). It is an important therapeutic task to "reconnect" these elements of a client's emotional system. A client can then develop some awareness of how the components of the emotional system work and fit together to influence a behavior. Three other elements impact the emotional system, namely, the primary appraisal process, schema dynamics, and the secondary appraisal process. We will discuss each of these elements below.

It is very important for clinicians to understand and help a client in interpreting expressions of affect, internal feelings, and emotional states. It is also important to help a client recognize and clarify whether the emotional states are primary, secondary, or background. If a client isn't aware of (or minimizes) internal feelings, then the affective expressions are likely to be incongruent with her emotional states. In addition, if a client is not fully aware of (or can't interpret) her feelings, she may not be able to describe her particular emotional states. In turn, if clients cannot interpret their emotional states, they may be unable to fully explain or understand why they are acting in certain ways. Thus, when a therapist asks, "What seemed to prompt your feeling _____?" a client may answer, "I don't know." It is a therapist's role to help a client find ways to become aware of her affective expressions, internal feelings, and emotional states *and what they mean*. Nonlinear listening is essential in helping a client who is "detached" in some way from her emotional system. Although we will discuss specific methods of helping a client understand her emotional processes later in this chapter, we first will discuss one other crucial element in understanding emotions: the appraisal process.

THE APPRAISAL PROCESS

Appraisal is a key component to understanding individual differences and emotions. Richard Lazarus (an early champion of appraisal) noted that emotions "involve appraisals of the environment and the individual's relationships with others and his or her attempts at coping with them" (quoted in Plutchick, 2000, p. 56). Just as with an appraisal of a house or a diamond ring that establishes its monetary value or worth, appraisals of people, the environment, and events in the environment are judgments involving personal value or worth. It is essential to reiterate that although we typically associate the term *environment* with our social surroundings, it may also pertain to our *internal* workings as well. For example, if a person receives "bad news" about his health and becomes frightened, and "scans" how he is feeling, he is basically appraising his internal "environment." Thus, our emotional appraisals and "scanning" not only search our external environment but also alert us to our internal environment for signs of threat. In general, emotional appraisal is the automatic process by which a person assesses whether other person(s), an event, or the environment (a) poses a threat (physical, social, psychological, etc.), or (b) will help an individual meet her needs or achieve her goals. Again, Arnold (1960) has put it well:

> As soon as we appraise something as worth having in an immediate and intuitive way, we feel an attraction toward it. As soon as we intuitively judge that something is threatening, we feel repelled from it, we feel urged to avoid it. The intuitive appraisal of the situation initiates an *action tendency that is felt as emotion*, expressed in various bodily changes, and that eventually may lead to overt action. (p. 177)

In the last sentence above, Arnold is spelling out the relationship between the appraisal process, schema dynamics, affective expressions, feelings, and emotions! Correspondingly, appraisal has two components, primary and secondary.

Primary Appraisals and Assessment of Threats and Benefits

Primary appraisals evaluate the environment or the events in the environment that individuals deal with in terms of whether these represent immediate or potential threats, or if there is *a benefit* to be gained (Plutchik, 2000; and see Arnold, 1960). Primary appraisals are intuitive and automatic, and take place very quickly, without the individual being aware of it. In essence, the appraisal system mediated by the brain's limbic system (and especially the amygdala) is the basis for Gladwell's (2005) *Blink* or "thinking without thinking." Such rapid appraisals are possible because of the design of our central nervous system. The neural architecture of the brain (i.e., how the brain is constructed) contains a capacity for human beings to scan the environment for perceived threats quickly using sensory organs (sight, hearing, touch, etc.). If there is no appraisal of harm or benefit, no emotion is aroused (Arnold; Plutchik).

In evolutionary psychology terms, the automatic nature of primary appraisals is considered to be adaptive for the species, because it was not a good idea for our ancestors to be deliberating whether a hungry tiger was a threat! Threats to modern humans can be physically real (as in bodily harm), psychologically real (as in being verbally abused), or merely perceived (as in imagined menaces to a schema). As an example, an individual may be in physical danger if about to be struck by a car, whereas a psychological threat might be attending a staff meeting where an individual fears being unfairly and publicly criticized by a tyrannical boss. Each one will generally produce a change in one's emotional state, as well as a strong (negative) internal feeling. Examples of *perceived* threats might be conjuring up images of potentially getting into a car accident, or images of being in the meeting. In each case, the brain evaluates threat primarily through the limbic system with the amygdala, a limbic structure playing an exceptionally critical role in that process (see Damasio, 1994, 1999; Ekman, 1992, 1995; Ekman et al., 1983; Goleman, 1995, 2006; LeDoux, 1998; Myers, 2007; Tolson, 2006).[6] If the primary appraisal produces some emotional change, then a secondary appraisal—involving structures of the brain responsible for judgment and personality (i.e., schema)—generally takes place (unless there is reason to act immediately, as when a person puts her hand on a hot stove or is facing down a tiger).

Secondary Appraisals and Responses to Threats

Secondary appraisals of the environment or events in the environment are those in which an individual decides *how to best deal with what has been judged either a threat or a benefit*. Central to this is the idea of coping, which is the individual's response to manage and respond to the threat or benefit (Plutchik, 2000). Secondary appraisals involve judgments, but not necessarily conscious ones. This has led Damasio (1959) to comment that "the brain knows more than the conscious mind reveals" (p. 42). Such *action tendencies*, however, tend to operate in line with a person's schema dynamics, and are more readily apparent (i.e., they result in observable behavior and expressions of affect).

Relative to how best to deal with what has been appraised, according to Lazarus and Lazarus (1994), the two categories of coping are *problem-focused* coping and *emotion-focused* coping. Problem-focused coping is a way of dealing with problems or issues through action that changes or alters the event or environment (e.g., agreeing to do something if a good opportunity presents itself). Hence, problem-focused coping works primarily on the link between a person's internal feelings and his expressions of affect to motivate action. Emotion-focused coping, by contrast, is a style that primarily avoids the problem situation and instead attempts to change the emotion that is perceived (either by seeking out comfort and soothing, or by distracting and denial) (Myers, 2007). As a result, this style of coping works by altering an individual's emotional state, or by dampening his internal feelings. Returning to the brief examples of the approaching car and the painful meeting, a problem-focused coping style might result in the individual stepping on the brake or confronting the criticizing individual. An emotion-focused coping style would lead an individual to reduce the fear of being hit by a car and getting support or feedback from a trusted coworker about how to handle the criticism encountered.

Clinical Exercise 10.1: Identifying Client Emotions

Directions: Recall this exercise from Chapter 8. This time, read over each brief statement and answer the questions below.

1. A client enters therapy to address her fear of public speaking. She is interested in pursuing a career as an executive, and knows that public speaking is an important part of attaining career goals. She also understands that this will entail receiving certain specific skills training that might make her uncomfortable.
2. A woman comes for a therapy session complaining of depression following a recent layoff from her job as an accountant. She states, "I'm good at what I do, but when I heard the rumors about layoffs, I knew it would happen to me. All my life, stuff like that seems to happen to me."
3. A man sought counseling because his family is concerned that he was becoming depressed. He is a highly intelligent, though aloof computer programmer who was working as a convenience store clerk because he was "waiting for the right job." The therapist asked the client what he has done to find "the right job," and he replied, "I've e-mailed my résumé, but no one has called me. I figured I wasn't good enough."
4. A client tells his therapist that his wife sent him to counseling in order to deal with his anger problem. He resents that his wife thinks he has a problem: "It's not me. I know that I always give people a fair chance. Ask anyone who knows me, and they will tell you that I only get angry when the idiots around me do stupid things!"

QUESTIONS

1. What emotion does each client seem to be feeling?
2. For each client, is it a primary, secondary, or background emotion?
3. What do the clients' expressions of affect tell you about their emotions?
4. What might their primary appraisal be if confronted with a threat?
5. What coping style would they likely use: problem focused or emotion focused? What actions would they take?

Variation: Process together in a small group or with the whole class.

Knowing how the appraisal process works in individuals is an important part of understanding how emotions work. It is also one of the first areas that a therapist can help a client work on. First, a practitioner must understand how expressions of affect, internal feelings, and emotional states are linked, as well as understand how they can break down. Then a clinician must assess where a particular problem is taking place. After that, a therapist can utilize the appraisal process to direct a client's attention to what she is experiencing without distortion or alteration. This is part of what is commonly referred to as *awareness*. Simply put, awareness is the process of helping clients to understand how to connect with their own internal feelings, becoming alert to their expression of affect, and making connections to their emotional states. (We will discuss specific therapeutic methods for doing this later in the chapter.) There is one more very important moderating structure in the emotional system that exerts a strong influence on both the appraisal process and emotions: schema dynamics.

The Relationship Between Schemas, Appraisal, Emotions, and Behavior

We have described how the appraisal process can evoke or extinguish a person's emotional reaction, based on whether there is a perceived threat or benefit that warrants action (or coping). Precisely what each individual interprets as a challenge, a threat, or something desirable is determined by "values"—*what* someone deems as "good" or "bad." As discussed in Chapter 8, values are embedded in schema and guide choices but are "unconsciously" (i.e., unknowingly) held by an individual. As "unconscious" entities, schemas give rise automatically and intuitively to emotions. We have emotions (i.e., emotional reactions) toward those things in life that have meaning (i.e., "value" to us). An early definition of emotions again came from Arnold's (1960) classic work:

> [T]he felt tendency toward anything intuitively appraised as good (beneficial), or away from anything intu- itively appraised as bad (harmful). This attraction or aversion is accompanied by a pattern of physiological changes organized toward approach or withdrawal. The patterns differ for different emotions. (p. 182)

The link between emotions and schema dynamics is *nonlinear* in nature. Many theorists and clini- cians treat the two—(a) schemas and the beliefs that result from them, and (b) emotional states and the internal feelings or expressions of affect that result from schemas and beliefs—as discrete and separate entities. For the purposes of this text, we prefer to see them as two distinct domains with each having unique qualities that are integrally and systemically related. It is a clinician's challenge and responsibility to manage them together. To capture the essence of what we wish to convey, consider an ordinary electri- cal cord. The cord is a single entity, but it has two distinct wires, one black and one white. Although each has a particular function, they work seamlessly together to bring electrical current to an appliance. So it is with schemas and emotions.

Just as it was impossible in the Level I domain to connect with and engage a client without simulta- neously working on the therapeutic relationship, so too it is impossible to separate work on the cognitive or schema level from work on the emotional level. If a person has a generally positive schematized view of self, others, and life and the world (see Chapter 8), she will be more likely to operate from a generally positive or optimistic emotional framework (i.e., background emotions) and less likely to have prolonged "bouts" of negative emotional experiences. When she does have any such "bouts," they will generally be short. When the situation passes, she will return to what is "normal" or baseline. In the same way, individuals who have generally negative schematized views of self, others, or the world are more likely to operate from a more negative emotional framework, and are likely to achieve brief experiences of posi- tive emotions before returning to a more negative (or, at best, neutral) baseline. It also becomes quickly obvious that these schema dynamics (positive or negative) affect the appraisal process and the emotional action tendencies they generate. According to Greenberg and Paivio (1997):

Emotions regulate mental functioning, organizing both thought and action. First they establish goal priorities and organize us for particular actions. ... Second, emotions set the goals towards which cognitions and actions strive, making affect a crucial determiner of human conduct. ... Someone who is sad and in need of comfort will find his or her perceptions and actions influenced in a number of ways. For example, one person will begin to move toward comfort; another will begin to think more and more sadness-enhancing thoughts such as "I'm all alone, no one cares" or will begin to retrieve sad memories and yearn for contact, comfort, and companionship. The first person who has enjoyed good attachments with significant others and so learned that comfort is possible, will eventually reach out and make contact with others. For those like the second person, above, who have learned that needs are not met, resignation, which is the poison of action, sets in. They quickly feel, "Its no use, I never get what I need" and give up. Here thought and action are unable to be mobilized in the service of goal attainment. Thus emotion sets the desired *end goal*; cognition and learning provides the *means* whereby the goal is met or not met. Emotions therefore are the guiding structures of our lives especially in our relations with others. Cognition thus sets out to solve the problem of how to reach the emotion-set goal of connecting, of getting comfort, or of separating. (p. 14)

Zaltman (2003) has described that values (i.e., held in schemas) are oftentimes vaguely understood (if at all) and are difficult to articulate. However, when an individual appraises that there is a challenge or threat to a major schema dynamic, an emotional response is evoked (sometimes appropriately, and sometimes not). These emotions give rise to corresponding attitudes, actions tendencies, or behavioral dispositions. Thus, if a given event or set of circumstances fits with a client's schematized worldview, he will be in a pleasant or good emotional state, or at least feel soothed (and not need to act or react).

As Greenberg and Paivio (1997) noted above, emotions guide clients toward actions in ways congruent with their schema dynamics. Even if a client has a generally negative view of self, others, or life and the world, she will at least feel "neutral" about the events (if appraisal is consistent with her schema). But, if an appraisal of a given set of circumstances or events runs counter to a client's expectations (based on schema), she is likely to feel threatened, develop negative emotional states, have negative internal feelings, and display negative affect. In addition, clients with more unrealistic schematized worldviews are more likely to have emotional expressions that are in line with their schema dynamics (i.e., positive or negative) than the opposite. Typically, the more rigidly held they are (e.g., "I must ..." "It should ..." "I can *never* ..." "You *always* ..." or "Only if I can ...") or the more outlandish (i.e., far removed from common sense) schemas are, the greater the potential for the mobilization of a strong *emotional reaction* to a perceived threat.

Because personality disorders are related to unrealistic schema dynamics, their emotional states can also be more difficult to treat (see Chapter 8). In fact, the extreme expressions of affect seen in personality disorders are one of their distinguishing characteristics. For example, desirable things (e.g., a love object) are embedded as values within schemas, and are often pursued despite the fact that they may not be ultimately in one's interests (e.g., when romantic advances are strongly rebuffed in no uncertain terms and considered "stalking").

Clinical Case Example 10.2 may help to demonstrate the intimate connectedness between schema and emotion.

Clinical Case Example 10.2: Feelings, Emotions, and Schema

A middle-aged man appeared for his first therapy appointment that was arranged by his wife (with his consent). When the man appeared for his appointment, it was clear that he was significantly depressed. He reported that he had lost weight (7 to 8 pounds within a 2-month period even though he was not overweight to begin with), could not sleep at night even with the aid of prescribed medications, and had been harboring suicidal thoughts. Although he was not psychotic and his reality testing was unimpaired, he reported that his thinking was very "negative."

As he put it, "I'm a generally happy person—all my life. I've always been an optimistic and positive person. Now, I'm seeing everything negative. I ran into an incredibly difficult situation, and I'm not a happy person at all. I've reached lows that I didn't know were possible. My wife said, 'You're clearly depressed!' When she said it, I knew it was obviously true. She is my number one supporter."

The clinician asked the client what he meant when he said that he "reached lows that [he] didn't know were possible." That's when the client revealed the symptoms noted above. The client's suicidal ideation was the next issue clarified. He revealed that his wife and children were precious to him and he realized that suicide would be a total abandonment of them. Once safety measures regarding the client's comments about suicide were in place, the next issue clarified concerned what it was that had changed in his life to bring about such a profound reaction. The client readily responded that the issue was an impending business failure.

Within the past year, he reported having engaged in a business transaction with several individuals, one of whom he now suspected of being "extremely dishonest." He acknowledged that he should have been more cautious regarding "due diligence." He further described how the impending business failure was making him more and more dysfunctional. Although he believed himself to be very competent, he wasn't able to perform well and manage his business. That led to a continued downward spiral with decreased feelings of confidence, more negativistic thinking and self-recrimination, and so on.

The clinician responded that such sad sets of circumstances were never pleasant and always harsh experiences, but not to suicidal proportions. In fact, he suggested that in this particular case, it appeared that something in the client's "cognitive template"[7] may have something to do with his extremely negativistic view of his circumstances and was prompting him to become more and more immobilized.

In response to this proposal, the man's posture changed significantly. His facial features brightened noticeably, and he responded with the following comment: "My 'template' gave me a purpose, and it was broken in this business. As a result, my goals and purpose didn't make a lot of sense. My mother and father divorced when I was 4 or 5 years old, and father left mother with a lot of money issues. Mother had a nervous breakdown with depression. My most vivid memory is of my mother crying on the stairs, asking how she is going to pay her bills."

He elaborated, "I've gone to the finest schools with the most competitive people you could possibly imagine. All during school, they would say that I'm the hardest working person that they know. Everything in my life has been driven by (a need for and pursuit of) economic security."

In Clinical Case Example 10.2, the client's failure to live up to his schematized values provoked strong emotional states (i.e., sadness and fear) and intense internal feelings (i.e., restlessness, hopelessness, and lack of energy), which were manifested in expressions of affect (i.e., crying, irritability, and a prolonged "down" mood). That understanding, along with the schema the client developed in early childhood, played a prominent role in his present circumstances, and guided the therapist's intervention. Although oversimplified, the client harbors a conclusion (i.e., schema) that economic failure "must" be avoided at all costs because of the dire consequences noted with his mother under such circumstances. Correspondingly, he unconsciously arranged much of his life so as to make certain that he would not fall prey to the fate that befell his mother. Education, hard work, a scientific background, honesty, a good reputation, and so on all entered the mix of entities to pursue in life to insulate himself from the possibility of economic failure that so devastated his mother. In light of his present circumstances, his personality could not deal with the impending collapse and financial failure of his business. At the same time, the feelings of impending failure seemingly would not subside no matter how hard he worked. His defining view of self as a hard worker was being destroyed—he hadn't worked hard enough to avoid a business failure. The appraisal of threat to that schema produced profound fear, signaling that the personality was in danger. Those emotional reactions manifested themselves with his profound feelings of depression.

CLIENT EMOTIONAL PRESENTATIONS AS EXPRESSIONS OF SCHEMA

Clients present themselves for treatment in countless ways. Some come for help without any overt expression of affect, some simply can't stop crying, some report feeling chronically anxious, others express feeling "numb," and so on. The point to looking at, listening to, and understanding the deeper meaning (i.e., schema dynamics) of a client's emotions is to reflect and ultimately *convey that understanding to a client*.

Clinical Case Example 10.3 may help demonstrate the profound and sometimes confusing nature of the relationship between schema, behavior, and emotions.

Clinical Case Example 10.3: Schema, Emotions, and Symptoms

A woman in her 40s returned to therapy after a hiatus of several years. She and her husband had consulted the same therapist several years previously regarding a thoroughly unsatisfying marriage. At that time, the husband complained of never having loved his wife. The wife complained of her husband's 20-year history of marital infidelity, chronic lying, and deceit. Several years before, she had rescinded filing for divorce, and they resumed their unhappy and unsatisfying marriage. The current issue for which she was seeking consultation was the same as it had been before: Her husband was still philandering with a narcissistic air of entitlement and lying about it in a thoroughly unconvincing manner. But this time, his paramour was married with children, in the process of a divorce, and pregnant with his child. The wife once again filed for divorce, and they assumed separate residences. In the meantime, her husband provided no support money for her and their children during their separation.

By every metric of contemporary society, the client was an attractive woman—tall, slender, statuesque, athletic, and stylishly dressed with tasteful use of cosmetics. She revealed that in her social encounters with other men, it was clear that they found her attractive and would "come on" to her. She was equally clear and very firm in setting appropriate moral and psychological limits with other men, discouraged their advances, and engaged in no extramarital relationships—period. Her childhood history revealed that she was never given feedback for being a pretty girl but rather for being athletic. Hence, she acknowledged that she has never allowed herself to see herself as attractive.

Also during the course of their discussion, the woman disclosed that her husband appeared to be on the cusp of securing an important job for which he was well qualified. In keeping with his other imperfections, he had been consistently financially irresponsible and had filed for bankruptcy a number of years ago although making an above-average living.

A Level II practitioner cannot help but ask, "Why would a woman want to stay in such an abusive relationship? What would motivate her?" Is it "masochism"? Dependency? Fear of being alone? The "answer" in this particular instance was not found in any of the above.

In pursuing an understanding of what it was that motivated her to remain in such a dysfunctional marriage for so long, she revealed a specific early childhood memory. In the essence of the memory, she recalled that as a child, she was in a race with cousins to see who could get to the door first. Although she "won" the race and was first to get to the door, she was pushed from behind and wound up breaking the glass in the door with her hand, for which she had to go to a hospital emergency room for stitches. Despite bleeding heavily, she reported being curious but unafraid at that time. Her reaction to this memory was "I was glad to get there first. I wasn't afraid to get stitches. I was happy I won. I wanted to be first."

The therapist suggested that perhaps an operative basic schema ("template") was that she wanted to "win"—that is, be a winner. Getting divorced would make her a "loser," and she had been willing to put up with all manner of pain, embarrassment, and humiliation vis-à-vis her husband's infidelity in order to maintain being married. No matter how many women her husband might have in his life, she would be the wife and hence "first." The painful reality was that her husband would not fulfill her expectations—he always seemed to put his wants, impulses, and so on first. To her, staying married was the psychological equivalent of "winning." In response to this, the woman began crying profusely. This emotional reaction was the equivalent of an important schema dynamic being revealed with all of its primitive and painful emotional accompaniments.

CONCLUSION

To be certain, the model proposed between schema, behavior, problems, and emotions is neither whimsical nor slanted toward a particularly poetic psychological theory. Rather, it is rooted in neuroscience research that struggles to discover the relationship between emotions, reason, and the human brain and how human beings perceive, think, and react. Damasio (1994) has expressed this particularly well:

> The picture I am drawing for humans is that of an organism that comes to life designed with automatic survival mechanisms [i.e., human emotions[8]], and to which education and acculturation add a set of socially permissible and desirable decision-making strategies that, in turn enhance survival, remarkably improve the quality of that survival, and serve as the basis for constructing a *person* [i.e., an individual]. At birth, the human brain comes to development endowed with drives and instincts that include not just a physiological kit to regulate metabolism but, in addition, basic devices to cope with social cognition and behavior [i.e., limbic system]. It emerges from child development with additional layers of survival strategy [i.e., schemas]. The neurophysiological base of those added strategies is interwoven with that of the instinctual repertoire, and not only modifies its use but extends its reach. The neural mechanisms supporting the suprainstinctual repertoire may be similar in their overall formal design to those governing biological drives, and may be constrained by them. Yet they require the intervention of society to become whatever they become, and thus are related as much to a given culture as to general neurobiology [i.e., emotional system]. Moreover, out of the dual constraint, suprainstinctual survival strategies generate something probably unique to humans: a moral point of view[9] that, on occasion, can transcend the interests of the immediate group and even the species (p. 126)

We next discuss some of the most common emotions encountered in therapy and major issues in working with those emotions, followed by a discussion of *linear* and *nonlinear* therapeutic methods of working with client emotions.

ENDNOTES

1. The ethical issues regarding such behavior will be discussed later in the chapter.

2. This is why we *strongly* argue that therapists avoid becoming too enamored with gimmicks or techniques, but should rather develop their ability to understand *how therapists think*, especially regarding all of the domains of effective psychotherapy. Gimmicks or techniques are too easily adopted out of context.

3. http://www.english.hawaii.edu/criticalink/aristotle/terms/catharsis.html.

4. Over a very long time, amongst specialists in the modern era (e.g., Arnold, 1960; Damasio, 1999; Goleman, 1995; Greenberg, 2004; LeDoux, 1998), there are many different orientations and philosophical issues that a complete grasp of feelings (and emotions) entails. Contemporary society and neuroscience research (see "I Think, Therefore I Am, I Think," 2007; Tolson, 2006) have developed a passionate and intriguing search for the relationship between mind and body, looking for an answer to the question of what ultimately determines "consciousness." Central to this issue is an understanding of what it is that makes us aware of feelings, emotions, and a sense of self. Damasio (1994, 1999) appeared to strike the philosophical and neurobiological core of the issue of feelings and emotions with his analysis of the relationship between body, emotion, and consciousness. In essence, one of the conclusions he reached is that "the brain knows more than the conscious mind reveals" (Damasio, 1999, p. 42).

5. For example, to flee a situation in fear, it is necessary for the body to secrete adrenalin, increase heart rate and blood pressure, dilate the arteries to accommodate an increase in the flow of blood, and so on. A corresponding set of physiological reactions must occur for a variety of different emotional reactions, and those reactions must and do occur automatically. Upon alert from the amygdala, the thalamus and hypothalamus trigger the appropriate biochemical releases that a particular emotion calls for.

6. It should be noted that there are some neuroscientists who debate the centrality of the amygdala in this process, but most agree that as part of the limbic system, it is a key component in relaying sensory information to specific regions of the brain that are responsible for initiating the particular biochemical triggers appropriate for a particular emotion to be enacted.

7. The cognitive template was briefly described to the client as a series of beliefs, convictions, values, and so on concluded early in childhood (i.e., a *schema*) that, when challenged by life circumstances, can produce seemingly insoluble and overwhelming dilemmas.

8. The "automatic survival mechanisms" to which Damasio referred are human emotions.

9. The "moral point of view" to which Damasio referred are human values, which are contained in schemas.

The Domain of Addressing and Managing Clients' Emotional States

11

Part 2: Managing Common Negative Emotions in Therapy

CONTENTS

INTRODUCTION TO COMMON NEGATIVE EMOTIONS IN THERAPY AND COUNSELING

It is impossible to address the subject of emotions in one chapter. Discussing a general conceptual framework for emotions, their relationship to cognitions, methods of working with emotions in treatment, and providing a comprehensive overview of specific emotions are daunting. In Chapter 10, we described Ekman's six primary emotions. There are, however, literally thousands of gradations and combinations of emotions that human beings experience. As a result, we will not attempt to categorize or catalogue the entire range of human emotions.[1] There are specific emotions, however, that clients commonly present that require clinical attention, which we will address before discussing therapeutic methods for working with emotions. They are *fear/anxiety* and *sadness/depression*. We will discuss the structural elements of each emotion (expressions of affect, internal feelings, and emotional states), as well as briefly discuss the relationship to schema dynamics and the impact on the appraisal process.

Fear/Anxiety

Even if you have never seen the film, almost everyone knows the theme from the movie *Jaws*. The first few strains of the low-pitched theme music followed by an ominous silence only to recur clearly convey the impression that *something deadly and unseen* lurks. The music and cinematography make the heart race and goose bumps percolate in a sympathetic terror with the actors on the screen. The reality is that fear is perhaps the most powerful emotion that human beings possess. According to Greenberg and Paivio (1997), its purpose is encoded in the survival of our species, as it helps to warn people that something potentially dangerous lurks. Fear helps to motivate a person to take flight from whatever the danger is, or to confront and change the fearful stimulus. Clients' expressions of affect may reveal a worried look, an easily triggered startle response, "skittishness," and an unwillingness to take suggestions related to what is prompting the fear.[2]

Closely related to fear is the experience of *anxiety*. Anxiety is anticipatory, that is, the dread of something to occur in the future. It keeps people "on edge" and at a state of alert. Individuals experiencing anxiety often operate with a belief that something bad may occur, and that they have to be prepared for it. Clients may describe their bodily sensations of fear or anxiety as "cold," or that they feel distracted or "antsy." Some people may manifest physical symptoms when they are feeling anxious or fearful (i.e., feeling sick to their stomach, or having a headache). Such experiences of fear and anxiety put an individual in an emotional state in which they are "on guard." If clients have unrealistic schema dynamics, however, they may be unable to distinguish what is a real threat from what amounts to scaring themselves for nefarious interpersonal purposes. We re-present a case from Chapter 8 (Clinical Case Example 8.1) to illustrate (see Clinical Case Example 11.1).

Clinical Case Example 11.1: Chronic Worry and Anxiety

A well-educated, pleasant, happily married woman with a young child sought therapy because of overwhelming anxiety and an inability to comfortably leave her baby in the custody of others except for her husband and parents. She recognized this as aberrant but felt helpless to bring it under control. She reported her "ton of anxiety" as resulting from her baby's medical problems with numerous legitimate trips to hospital emergency rooms and a felt need for more than typical parental vigilance and new mother nervousness. Although medical authorities assured her that her baby would grow out of his condition, such reassurances had little ameliorating impact on a daily basis. She relied frequently and heavily on her parents in the event of *any* troublesome circumstances that she believed she simply could not deal with on her own—"I don't know what I would do without them!"

During the first session, she reported that she had "done a lot of thinking" and concluded that "as far back as high school," she could remember herself being consistently "excessively worried about something." In the process of collecting early-childhood and family-of-origin material, it was discovered that she had a very positive and endorsing family that was physically affectionate and supportive. At the same time, careful nonlinear listening to the woman's description of the family atmosphere revealed very subtle expressions of a nervous quality underlying the positive and loving picture. As the "baby" of her family, much older siblings could overwhelm and "beat up" on her as they would play roughhouse. Such encounters, although oftentimes fun, would also scare her and require her to call for help in need of "rescuing" by her parents or oldest sibling. Her mother and father's method of discipline included being "strict" with her, and "yelling" to gain "control" over rambunctious and energetic children. She also described her mother as somewhat nervous in nature, a person who did not easily relax. Then. too, there were tornadoes to be frightened of and scary monsters she imagined that would prompt her to run for the cover of her parents' bedroom at night. In describing what her life was like in school, she casually related that teachers and authority figures in general were "intimidating." The net result of all of these nuanced descriptions revealed a pattern of thinking. There was a "nervous edge" to her experience of growing up as a child.

Nevertheless, she did well in school, had friends, and was well liked and successful in a beginning career before marriage. At the time of entering therapy, she was living in a healthy and successful marriage with a husband who was very "supportive and caring." Despite these positive factors, she still experienced the "ton of anxiety" over her child. She stated her goals for therapy as follows: "I'm looking for ways to think about things differently!"

QUESTIONS

1. What are the structural elements of this client's experience of anxiety (expressions of affect, internal feelings, and emotional state)?
2. How do her schema dynamics relate to her emotional experience of anxiety?
3. Speculate how this might impact her appraisal process (particularly related to her child), and what coping style she might choose.

The schema dynamics reflective of fear/anxiety consistently communicate to a person, "Watch out: I am in danger! Either I can't trust myself, others are a danger to me, or the world poses a threat to me (physically, emotionally, etc.)! Life just makes me nervous!" Another message that a state of anxiety communicates is "If I am not careful or on alert, then bad things will happen." The client in Clinical Case Example 11.1 anticipates that something troublesome and dangerous lurks and that it may get out of control, especially with her child. If a client is unrealistic in her view of self, others, or the world or life, then even if everything is going well, she will nevertheless continue to scan her environment for potential problems on the horizon—in effect, one can never rest assured. As a result, the primary appraisal of events is likely to amplify such a client's fear or anxiety, whereas the secondary appraisal will trigger a coping-style response that is not necessarily congruent with the circumstance. Regarding clinical interventions, linear confrontations (e.g., "So, there is never a time when it is good to trust someone you don't know well?") are typically ineffective. Often, clients experiencing anxiety disorders will have ready rationalizations for continuing to maintain their vigilance: anecdotal evidence to support their claims of a need for wariness, instances when they or others let their guard down and were taken advantage of, or others they have heard about who have encountered "bad" things. Hence, a *nonlinear* approach is necessary (see below).

Sadness/Depression

Sadness is the result of experiencing a form of loss or disappointment in life.[3] This can range from the mundane (e.g., missing a train, or not getting the last jelly doughnut) to the life altering (e.g., losing a job, or getting a divorce) to the tragic (e.g., the death of a child). Much like the link between fear and anxiety, sadness and depression are linked, but distinct.[4] Sadness is triggered by an event (in the present or past) in which something did not turn out the way it was hoped. Depression can be related to prolonged episodes of melancholy, to the point that future events are predicted to be as disappointing as past or present events and circumstances, and in which the sadness experienced overwhelms most other feelings of emotion (i.e., an inability to feel pleasure in anything, which is called *anhedonia*). Such episodes can be mild, moderate, or severe, and reactions can last from hours to decades.

Sadness and depression have very similar, and limited, expressions of affect. Clients typically may cry when they feel sad, or will have a very blunted (stoic) affect. They may seem downcast, and are remarkable for what is *absent* (smiling, laughing, etc.). Some clients may mask depression with anger or other destructive behaviors (e.g., suicidal ideations or ruminations, or addiction), and must be thoroughly evaluated (see Chapters 10 and 11). In terms of internal feeling states, clients experiencing sadness or depression have a wider range of feelings than their expressions of affect. Specifically, they may describe feelings as "blue," "down," and unhappy, and report a lack of energy or enthusiasm to do anything. Sometimes, depressed individuals will describe their internal feelings as "dull," blank, and dark, or that there is no feeling at all. In these circumstances, a client's emotional state will be characterized as hopeless, defeated, and generally negative (Greenberg & Paivio, 1997). Clinical Case Example 11.2 revisits Clinical Case Example 9.3

Clinical Case Example 11.2: Disappointment and Sadness

A successfully married woman with an advanced degree came to therapy on a monthly basis, mostly for support. In her family of origin, she was the caretaker for handicapped younger siblings who were appreciative and even adoring of her. Indeed, parental feedback was extremely positive and emphasized how truly gifted and special she was. She maintained a long-term "complaint" that revolved around her "sensitivity" to how others treated her (e.g., perceived slights by coworkers or social snubs). For example, if she wasn't invited to a party, it became cause for extremely hurt feelings. If someone made a comment that pertained to her work, she tended to interpret such a comment as an attack on her competence. She elaborated that she was very competent and the individual proffering the comment had no right to say such things.

During one of her monthly therapy sessions, she reported going to a wake for a somewhat distant relative who died quite tragically. She said that at the wake, all the extended relatives seemed to be huddled around and preoccupied with a few members of the extended family who were extremely successful financially. She noted, "Everyone idolizes (them), and I wasn't one of them. *Everything in my family is about achievement for everyone.* That's my family; that's it! I walked out feeling sad and empty."

Questions

1. What might be the structural elements of this client's experience of sadness or depression (expressions of affect, internal feelings, and emotional state)?
2. How do schema dynamics relate to her emotional experience of sadness or depression?
3. Speculate how this might impact her appraisal processes, and what coping style she might choose.

Some individuals (e.g., with biochemical imbalances in the brain or lifelong bouts with depression) may have encoded (or accommodated) negative schemas (e.g., "I am unlovable," "I am worthless (or useless)," "Other people will only disappoint me, and I don't trust them," and "The world only wants to grind you into dust"). As a result, most of their secondary appraisals are likely to be emotion focused and motivate their assuming more defensive positions. They are more likely to withdraw from others for fear of further rejection, disappointment, loss, or alienation. Rasmussen and Dover (2006) have described the dynamics and "adaptive" aspect of depression:

> In the face of recurrent or chronic battle, one option that is nearly always available is retreat. One can give up the challenge. However, it is important to note that no one happily retreats from a desired activity or goal (*i.e., schema dynamics*). The more critical the victory is to the individual's sense of worth, dignity, and integrity (i.e., superiority), the greater the hesitancy to abandon the battle and the greater the pain associated with the retreat. When a person becomes hopeless and does not want to alter his or her goals but does not posses the skills necessary or does not want to do what is necessary to achieve those goals, then depression becomes adaptive. More explicitly, it may be more useful to do nothing when one perceives nothing useful to do, when the costs outweigh the benefits or a major roadblock has been encountered en route to a life goal (Nesse, 1998). As Gilbert (2002) suggested, depression is the emotion that removes a person from a battle that he or she is not going to win. (pp. 378–379; emphasis added)

Effective therapeutic interventions for such clients target the appraisal process, and help the client to use more problem-focused coping strategies. These are described below.

We have attempted to briefly discuss how the emotional system (appraisal, expressions of affect, internal feelings, and emotional states) applies to two of the most common emotions presented in therapy. We now present an exercise in the application of the same analysis to other emotions.

Clinical Exercise 11.1: De-Constructing Emotions

Instructions: Choose one of the emotions in the list below.

- Anger
- Pain/hurt
- Shame/guilt
- Happiness

Record what you believe to be the following:

1. Structural characteristics (i.e., expressions of affect, feelings, and emotional state or mood)
2. Schema dynamics (i.e., view of self, others, and life and the world)
3. How the emotion relates to the appraisal process (primary and secondary)
4. How each coping style (problem focused or emotion focused) is likely to be utilized by an individual experiencing the emotion

Variation: Form groups according to the emotion that was chosen. Share your answers with one another, and create a group answer to the questions above. Then discuss as a class.

At this point, we turn our attention to the therapeutic aspects of dealing with a client's emotions, particularly the *nonlinear* aspects that master therapists utilize. First, we discuss elements of listening and responding.

SPECIFIC CONSIDERATIONS IN DEALING WITH CLIENTS' EMOTIONS

Listening and Responding

Nonlinear listening for expressions of affect: A particularly important therapeutic task is *nonlinear listening* (as well as *observing*) for expressions of affect (emotion), no matter how subtle they may be. A less experienced Level I practitioner may be hesitant to ask a client about the tears welling up in his eyes for fear of prompting further client discomfort. However, it might just be the case that drawing the client's attention to his expressions of affect may be the most important experience for him *to express and understand*. Recognizing that such moments contain the most potential opportunities for client growth is the mark of a master practitioner. We will discuss some of these below.

Linear and nonlinear listening for and responding to incongruence: Clients are typically conflicted about what is at the core of their "problem." Typically at the heart of a client's conflict are feelings of ambivalence (a topic of focus in Chapters 12 and 13). Because of this ambivalence, a client may demonstrate a certain incongruity or perhaps a disconnect between *what* she is saying and *how* she is saying it. Observing such disconnects and incongruities is important to the therapeutic process in that it affords an opportunity to explore and understand the ambivalence clients feel, and begin to focus the client's attention on her emotional system. To accomplish such exploration, a therapist can make statements to a client such as "I notice that your heart doesn't seem to be in what you are saying," "You seem to be saying one thing and your body seems to be saying something else," "I notice that you appear to be hesitant in talking about ..." and "That was an awful big sigh that went along with what you were thinking at the moment." Such statements reveal a therapist's sensitivity to and awareness of his client's *feelings of ambivalence* about her situation.

Linear and nonlinear listening for absence of feelings: Frequently, a master practitioner will observe that a client does not appear to express feelings when it would be quite normal to do so, given the situation being described. Observing such behavior, therapists may ask themselves, "What are the feelings that are *not* being expressed? Why are they not being expressed? Are they too painful, too embarrassing, or too overwhelming?" In turn, such questions can be transformed into inquiries to the client: "I notice that you don't seem to express much feeling much about ..." "That sounded awful to me but I notice that ..." or "How do you keep going without being upset when ...?" Such questions are meant to give clients a safe environment and an opportunity to delve into what they are feeling but not expressing—a necessary step on the road to self-understanding and freedom from the tyranny of symptomatic behavior by reconnecting the elements of the client's emotional system.

Linear and nonlinear listening for inference: The feelings that a client expresses are connected to the *values and value system* to which he adheres. Put another way, a client's expressions of affect, internal feelings, and emotional states are connected to his schema dynamics. When what a person believes and values is stimulated (i.e., positively or negatively through threat or what he is attracted to), emotions are automatically triggered with corresponding feelings. Thus, helping clients recognize what they are feeling becomes a gateway to what they believe in their schemas. If a client didn't believe what it is that he believes, he wouldn't feel the way he does. Feelings would not be aroused as a vigilant alarm that an individual is perceiving threat of some sort. Thus, *linear thinking* subtly suggests that emotions are an entity unto themselves—a human mystery. On the other hand, using *nonlinear thinking*, master practitioners can extrapolate and infer from a client's feelings that there are beliefs and convictions underlying those feelings.

Linear and nonlinear listening for presence: In essence, this entire chapter is about listening for the expression of client feelings. The most obvious, outward sign of these is the client's expression of affect. Overwhelming client feelings can and do begin to subside. When they do, it is often helpful to ask clients how that came about—is the client doing something differently that led to an attenuation or resolution of what she had been feeling (e.g., "I could be wrong, but it appears to me that you had tears in your eyes just a moment ago when you were describing …")? An accompanying question is to inquire how she was able to accomplish such an attenuation or resolution of such strong feelings. The latter question is important because it highlights to the client how *her own* resources, resolve, actions, decisions, and so on were instrumental in her feelings subsiding—the client brings about the change with the therapist as the "coach." It is naïve *linear thinking* that suggests that a therapist can take credit for therapeutic movement; it is *nonlinear thinking* that returns credit for bringing about change to the client.

The Therapeutic Relationship and Emotions

Master practitioners' *listening* for presence, absence, congruence, inference, and resistance plays a prominent role in dealing with client emotions. *Responding* to client expressions of emotion plays an equally prominent role. As Marci, Ham, Moran, and Orr (2007) have recently demonstrated, exactly *how* a therapist responds to client emotions is a significant variable in determining client perceptions of therapist empathy. A contemporary understanding of emotions informs us that they do not simply exist within a *client*; the therapist can *conjointly* experience what a client is experiencing—in fact, that is the *essence of empathy* (see Chapter 4).

As described in the Level II Introduction, therapists at this stage of development have developed a much greater proficiency at attenuating any personal feelings of anxiety about their professional role. Obviously, achieving a greater sense of comfort in a therapy setting allows therapists to be less encumbered by internal processes that can easily detract from listening ever more acutely for feelings that a client is expressing directly or indirectly, or not expressing. When a therapist is relaxed, engaged, interested, hopeful, and empathic, a client can experience it.

THE RELATIONSHIP BETWEEN EMOTIONS AND SCHEMA DYNAMICS: THE USE OF NONLINEAR THINKING

Earlier in this chapter, we described how schema dynamics introduced in Chapters 8 and 9 (i.e., view of self, view of others, and view of the world and life) played a role in the appraisal process. In addition, we described how it can be problematic for individuals who are not aware of the influences that their schema dynamics wield. We now revisit some of these ideas in order to show how therapists' use of *nonlinear thinking* can help clients connect the elements of their emotional system, and help clients connect their emotional system to their schema dynamics, in order to reappraise their problematic circumstances. For example, to simply admonish a client in linear ways with comments such as "Stop feeling that way" or "Don't feel that way" is obviously ill advised, ill fated, and somewhat foolish. After all, if someone were able to do so, he would most likely not require a therapist in the first place. On the other hand, a comment such as "Your strong emotional reaction to what happened is very interesting. Let's look into that some more" is somewhat more encouraging of a process that can help a client to connect the elements of his emotional system's reactions with his schema dynamics—what was it about a particular set of circumstances that prompted the client to feel that way?

It is important to remember that the emotional system of the brain is an inherent part of what we are born with—the architecture of the limbic system. It is built to appraise! But, what is it supposed to appraise? The appraisals automatically made by the emotional system evaluate threats (physical, social, and psychological) and goals and desires to be pursued. But, each individual appraises threats or things desirable differently and to different degrees. Thus, we have an appraisal system (i.e., the limbic system structure and amygdala in particular) that determines threats and goals (i.e., values), whereas *what* to appraise as threats or desires comes from the beliefs, values, desires, and so on (i.e., schemas) that we have concluded early in life. The difficulty for a client comes from the fact that she oftentimes does not necessarily make connections between her problematic circumstances, the feelings and emotions generated by those circumstances, and what her schemas dictate. To a certain extent, this is understandable because the emotional system has the capacity to overwhelm with its qualities of speed, intensity, unreflectiveness, and spontaneity. Indeed, according to Greenberg (2004),

> Thus, people need both capacities [i.e., emotions and conscious capacities/schema dynamics as well as what they have learned culturally[5]].... They need emotions to tell them, without thought, that something important to their well-being is occurring, and they need their thinking capacities to work on the problems that emotions point out and that reason must solve. (pp. 29–30)

Greenberg was asserting several things. First, he noted that one's emotions inform the client and the counselor that something, which is important or of *perceived* value, is transpiring. A simple illustration of Greenberg's last point is if someone smells smoke in the kitchen or hears a smoke alarm. As Dobbs (2006) has put it, "A direct path from the thalamus to the amygdala makes you jump ... a second, slower path, through the sensory cortex[,] assesses if you should run from the flames or pop up the burning toast" (p. 49). This "normal" behavior (checking to see if it is just toast burning in the toaster) is a good example of the role that schema dynamics play in the appraisal process, and the subsequent decisions that are made in light of strong emotions. In this example, the "rational" behavior assumes that a person has an overall realistic view of the world (i.e., not all "alerts" are emergencies that the world is going to end), which allows the person to make the reasonable determination to just pop up the toast. By contrast, an irrational behavior would be to immediately run into the street in a bathrobe, screaming that the house is on fire.[6]

As several neuroscientists (Damasio, 1994, 1999; LeDoux, 1998) have maintained, *emotions are cognitive in nature.* This is entirely in keeping with a clinician's need to develop *nonlinear thinking.* Unfortunately, all too often, cognition and emotion are considered separate and distinct entities. Although they may be distinct, they are not separate. Emotions provide emotional *understandings* and *information* rather than rational understandings of such things as psychological threats. Making the most use of information that the emotions provide requires *rational cognitive processes.* Kiser, Piercy, and Lipchik (1993) described it thus: "Emotions are intuitive appraisals that initiate action tendencies ... while corresponding cognitive processes determine whether or not impulses will be acted upon" (p. 235).

Nonlinear thinking is required to consider *both* the emotions as providing valued information *and* rational cognitive processing to evoke an understanding of what to do about it. *In other words, each needs the other in a seamless relationship.* In fact, according to Greenberg (2004) and others, in order to be maximally effective with clients, a practitioner must be able to work on both the cognitive and schema levels. This is where the "reconnecting" process becomes essential.

When the System "Goes Down": Being Overwhelmed by the Circumstances and Emotion

Some clients come for treatment with a sense of their emotions being "out of control" (see Chapters 4 and 5). This is most typically expressed by some variation of one of the following phrases: "I feel so overwhelmed," "I can't help feeling ..." "I feel so confused," "I feel so torn," or "I'm so very tired." Furthermore, clients also express little understanding of why they feel the way they do and are seemingly unable to get beyond the expression of emotion. They feel "stuck." This indicates that a client's emotional system (i.e., expression of affect, internal feelings, and emotional state) is dominating his functioning; it also indicates that the client is unaware of the connections between his emotional system and schema dynamics. As an example, often medical or surgical clients feel totally overwhelmed by their encounter with devastating illnesses. In some instances, their encounter has been life threatening; at other times, it has not been life threatening but extremely debilitating. Such encounters gnaw at one's ability to function in daily life and are totally draining of energy. Clinical Case Example 11.3 may help the reader to understand the feelings and emotions that such encounters bring.

Clinical Case Example 11.3: Expressions of Emotions

A well-educated professional man in his late 40s with no prior history of psychological problems appeared for treatment self-referred. He was on medical leave from a very responsible corporate job and sought therapy because of a lingering illness of 5 months' duration. He had been hospitalized every month for 5 months for an acutely painful episode and complications of diverticulitis, an inflammation of a diverticulum, which is a small sac that has formed within the bowel. Although it can often be treated medically and with changes in diet, diverticulitis can also become a serious medical condition requiring surgery, as it did in the case of this man. The particular surgical correction for his condition required the removal (i.e., "resection") of a certain part of diseased bowel. If complications were encountered during the gastric resection, as part of the informed consent process, the surgeon had warned him of the possibility that he would have to perform an ileostomy. That procedure involves not only removing the diseased part of the bowel but also attaching the small intestine (called the *ileum*) to a surgically created opening in the abdominal wall with an external "bag" to capture fecal matter.

Exercising conservative judgment, the surgeon decided that he would not only have to resect part of the bowel but also have to perform the ileostomy. After surgery, the man was left with the management of the ileostomy bag. If all went well, however, within a few months of the original procedure, the bowel could be reattached and the ileostomy bag removed.

As he described his present circumstances and feelings, he said, "I'm not a crier, but I'm having a hard time with this. I'm not sitting around. I'm doing things, but I'm crying a lot. I know it's only temporary until I have the ileostomy reversed. There I go (crying). What's my problem?" he asked rhetorically.

The therapist, an experienced clinician, asked him, "Is there anything in particular that you feel you need to talk about?"

After a considerable pause without a response, the clinician said, "That very long pause suggests to me that you are going through a rolodex in your mind of different things that you really could talk about, and perhaps you really don't know which of them you would want to start with."

In a very excited voice, the man exclaimed, "That's it exactly!"

In many ways, this case example is typical of the verbalizations that clients use to express emotional feelings regarding their particular circumstances. As a brief clinical exercise, address the following questions:

1. What particular expressions and behaviors used by this man suggest strong emotional content?
2. What contradictions do you note, if any, in this client's descriptions of his particular circumstances?
3. What questions would you want to ask this man?
4. What rationale do you use for proposing those particular questions?

5 The Level II clinician has begun to assume more of a natural disposition for nonlinear listening and responding. What do you note about how the therapist responded to this man?

6. What is this man's view of self?

7. What confusion does the man express?

8. What is the relationship between his confusion and his complaint?

9. What is the prognosis for this man?

10. What is the basis for making that prognosis?

Therapeutically Working With Emotions: "Coaching" the Therapist's Approach to Working Successfully With Emotions

Working with clients' emotions can be very difficult for many therapists. As we mentioned at the beginning of this chapter, some therapists avoid actively engaging with client emotions because of their own issues, or their own lack of competence in this domain. In one form or another, many of the master practitioners in this domain—such as Greenberg (2004), Yapko (1997), and Seligman (1990)—all make use of the idea of the therapist as an emotional "coach." This is a fitting metaphor regarding "emotional coaching" when considering what a good "coach"[7] does. Coaches are important because they (a) collaborate with a client in strategizing to achieve specified goals, (b) confer responsibility for success upon the "player" (i.e., client), and (c) are supportive at moments that require calming, focusing, energizing, and so on.

Coaching is also an extremely useful metaphor for counselors to conceptualize what they can provide a client regarding emotional regulation. Within the context of the domain of establishing and maintaining a therapeutic relationship and the therapeutic alliance (see Chapter 7), appropriate coaching provides clients with greater potential opportunity for growth and better functioning. Coaches maintain clarity regarding the boundaries of the relationship, and recognize that responsibility for success belongs to the "player" (i.e., the client), not the other way around.

Greenberg (2004) has defined two specific phases in the emotional-coaching process:

- "Arriving" (i.e., the process of helping a client come to a more informed awareness and acceptance of her feelings)
- "Leaving" (i.e., the process of deciding whether the particular "place" her feelings reveal is good for her or not good for her)

"Arriving" entails four steps: (a) identification of what a client is feeling; (b) "welcoming" and accepting of what one is feeling, as "it is what it is"; (c) "labeling" or putting into words and developing a vocabulary to describe what one is feeling; and (d) exploring a client's emotional experiences and determining what the core or "primary" feelings are (e.g., if a client expresses anger regarding someone, the therapeutic task is to determine if the anger betrays a feeling of being belittled, marginalized, etc.).

"Leaving" also entails four steps: (a) the process of assisting a client to assess if a "primary feeling" (or the core feeling being experienced) is healthy or unhealthy, and if it is the latter, it requires processing; (b) the process of identifying maladaptive destructive schema(s) (e.g. "I am worthless," or "Life sucks") connected to particular maladaptive emotion(s); (c) the process of gaining entrée to "alternate adaptive emotions and needs" (e.g.. helping clients key in on what their "needs, goals and concerns" are); and (d) the process of facilitating a client in transforming maladaptive emotions and beliefs that are destructive.

Therapeutically Working With Emotions: Coaching and Level II Clinicians

Clearly, a Level II clinician (in an emotional-coaching role) encourages a client to reflect on distressing feeling states and "work through" them via thoughtful, rational, and reflective processes in order to develop (a) a greater sense of understanding about the purpose of the emotion (i.e., what important information the emotion reveals about what a client values), and (b) a greater sense of mastery of the emotions (e.g., reconnecting the elements of the client's emotional system and developing a sense of understanding about the emotion[s]). Such understandings promote a client feeling less victimized and overwhelmed by his emotions as well as more in control of himself. Facilitating such emotional reflection for clients through "coaching," however, is not the entire object lesson regarding the process of examining feelings.

As discussed in the Introduction to Part 2, a Level II clinician is as interested in her own emotional arousal to a client as she is in a client's emotions. Nonlinear understandings of emotions aroused within a therapist are viewed as a valued source of knowledge that provides information regarding potentially important issues (see Chapters 6 and 7). For example, the astute Level II clinician asks, "Are the feelings I'm experiencing being stimulated by 'issues' that I have? If so, do they represent 'unresolved' concerns that I have about certain sensitive areas of my life? Or are these feelings being aroused within me because of some sort of provocative behavior in the client?" This is especially true if the "coach" has been in the game at some point (i.e., countertransference; see Chapter 7). The answers to such questions help guide treatment efforts in more productive directions.

Recall that the goal of any effective therapist in working with clients' emotions is to help clients reconnect the three elements of their emotional system (expressions of affect, internal feelings, and emotional states), as well as connect with their schema dynamics in order to reappraise their situation and make different behavioral choices. Thus, it is easy to see that the metaphor of "coaching" is appropriate for counselors when dealing with emotions. Like all other coaches, "emotional coaches" have a variety of means at their disposal (i.e., recognizing, emotional differentiating, focusing, soothing, and "fighting fire with fire") to help clients work through their emotional states. We turn our attention to some of those methods.

Therapeutically Working With Emotions: Attending

Recognition of one's emotions is, in a nonlinear way, a *cognitive process*—an *awareness* of the fact that one is experiencing an emotion. Gottman (1997) described this as "emotional competence," whereas Goleman (1995) and Mayer and Solovey (1997) referred to it as "emotional intelligence." As they described it, emotional competence or intelligence involves a number of identifiable processes, including recognizing what one is feeling, being able to put a label on it, and expressing it in an appropriate (i.e., rational) way. Although this may seem elemental and self-evident, many people are not aware of what they are feeling, let alone able to label and articulate it. This is due, in part, to the fact that the limbic system is faster than the frontal lobes in processing information. Hence, many emotional reactions occur quite rapidly and spontaneously without a person's full awareness that he is having them, let alone why.

Goleman (1995) expanded on several well-defined "styles" for attending to and dealing with emotions that were identified by Mayer and Stevens (1993). They are the *self-aware*, *engulfed*, and *accepting* styles. The "self-aware" style of attending to emotions demonstrates a significant "sophistication" in recognizing emotions. Associated with awareness of their emotional states, those possessing this style tend to be autonomous, have an acute sense of their boundaries, and in general enjoy good psychological health. Bad emotional moods don't occupy them for long because they tend to let them pass without ruminating or obsessing about them. This is very similar to what Skovholt and Jennings (2004) found in their research on master therapists (see Chapter 1). This level of sophistication in recognizing and sorting out emotional information is crucial for effective therapists.

Mayer and Stevens (1993) identified another manner of attending to and dealing with emotions called the "engulfed" style. Such individuals are perhaps best characterized by their feeling overwhelmed or "swamped" by their emotions and somewhat "helpless to escape them, as though their moods have taken charge" (Mayer & Stevens, p. 48). Correspondingly, such individuals are not very aware of their feeling states, do not feel much of a sense of being able to identify their feelings, and have a very meager sense of being able to influence or control their emotions. It is as though they are chronically stressed by a feeling of being overwhelmed and emotionally out of control but without being aware of it. Indeed, many clients come to therapy with this style.

The third way of attending to and dealing with emotions identified by Mayer and Stevens (1993) is the "accepting" style. Such individuals are in synch with their emotional feelings and are accepting of what they are feeling. But the "accepting" style has two variations: the positive and the negative. The positively inclined are typically in good moods, with little incentive to do anything about such an upbeat state of emotional affairs. The negatively inclined, however, are those who are clear about what they are feeling, but it is mostly downbeat. Nevertheless, they accept their typical emotionally distressed pattern of living and do little to change it. Both variations have clinical significance, and the ramifications of this will be highlighted in Chapters 12 through 17.

Therapeutically Working With Emotions: Recognition and Emotional Differentiation

The primary purpose of emotional differentiation is to help a client determine if the powerful emotions that she recognizes and is experiencing are adaptive or not. This focuses the client's attention on her emotional states (primary emotions, secondary emotions, and background mood) as a way to help reconnect her to her internal feelings, as well as to her schema dynamics. Obviously, if emotions are adaptive, they are endorsed and supported as authentic. If they are not adaptive, intense negative emotions must be subjected to a process of scrutiny. The first step in such scrutiny is to facilitate a sense of calm.

Overall, although it is desirable to decrease the overreactivity of the arousal mechanism, facilitating a sense of calm can be challenging due to the nature of the perceived threat, the schema, and the emotional arousal mechanism (we will discuss the regulation and soothing aspects of these below). Nevertheless, clients can be assigned "homework" to practice examining less intense and disruptive negative emotions on a daily basis to encourage *the processes* of recognition and differentiation. As Goleman (1995) has indicated,

> [T]he emotional brain engages those response routines that were learned earliest in life during repeated moments of anger and hurt, and so become dominant. Memory and response being emotion-specific, in such moments reactions associated with calmer times are less easy to remember and act on. If a more productive emotional response is unfamiliar or not well-practiced, it is extremely difficult to try it while upset. But if a response is practiced so that it has become automatic, it has a better chance of finding expression during emotional crisis. (p. 147)

It is from calmness that rational processes are much more dominant in the workings of a personality (i.e., schema dynamics). As mentioned earlier, maladaptive intense emotional states can overwhelm a person with their speed, intensity, and spontaneity, so one must practice "catching" oneself reacting. Thus, within microseconds of a perceived emotionally (or physically) threatening event or encounter, an individual can become flooded with uncomfortable basic emotions. Because such encounters bypass the slower functioning of the neocortex that is associated with thoughts from higher rational processes, the discomfort mediated by the amygdala and other limbic system nuclei occurs almost instantaneously (Cozolino, 2002). It is here that helping a client to develop an awareness and appreciation of the process of *reappraisal* is critical.

Strong negative emotional states always touch upon essential needs of human beings—belonging, being loved, feeling abandoned, being rejected, feeling unappreciated, being emotionally denied, and on and on.

In studying emotion in treating instances of childhood maltreatment and affective disorders, Greenberg and Paivio (1997) discovered that core maladaptive feelings mainly tended to be connected to shame and fear/anxiety. With such powerful early emotional responses as shame and fear triggered in response to contemporary events, it is easy to understand that "catching" oneself is not easy and requires *patience* and *practice*—both of which must be pointed out to a client. As Goleman (1995) pointed out, all strong emotions carry with them action tendencies that must be kept in check. Simply put, that means restraining oneself from *acting* on the basis of strong negative emotions. Again, the overall goal of this process is to help a client thoughtfully and rationally reconnect the elements of his emotional system (i.e., expressions of affect, internal feelings, and emotional states), as well as his schema dynamics, in order to allow for a reappraisal to occur, and the client to make different behavioral choices (viz., "catching oneself"). The reappraisal also involves a thoughtful and rational examination of schemas that are based on unrealistic considerations, overgeneralizations, distortions, exclusions, deletions of important information, and so on (see Chapters 8 and 9). All beliefs based on such skewed and biased information can and do interfere with rational problem solving.

Therapeutically Working With Emotions: Revelation, Reflecting, and Focusing

Revelation or reflection refers to an individual not only being aware of her feelings but also reflecting upon them. Greenberg (2004) has astutely observed that there are two types of awareness. One type of awareness is based in the "here and now" and reveals that an individual is aware of what she is feeling but otherwise lacks an informed understanding of what she is feeling. The second type of awareness that Greenberg referred to is a more thoughtful sort of awareness. In such a state, an individual is not only fully aware of what she is feeling but also able to assess whether or not she *wants* to feel that way. Once this information is reflected on by the client, she can then decide what it is that she wants to do about this particular feeling state. These awareness assessment processes are *reflective and revealing* in nature. Once again, Greenberg was helpful in summarizing this process:

> This state of being aware of one's conscious feeling of emotion allows one ultimately also to be aware of the lived past and the anticipated future and to make decisions about one's emotions in the present. One recognizes what one is feeling and considers whether one accepts one's response as appropriate. Developing and applying this capacity is an important aspect of emotional intelligence. (p. 30)

In practical terms, how does one go about encouraging a client to "reflect" on his feelings? Once again, the process is counterintuitive and nonlinear. As previously discussed, clients typically infer "not wanting" to feel in some particular way—they want to be rid of particular feelings, thus eliminating the discomfort attendant to such a feeling(s). The Level II practitioner may encourage a client to begin accepting the feeling, in effect as though the feeling was attempting to inform the client that something important is stirring. The next relatively simple step is to assess if it is drawing the client *toward* something or *away from* something—is it a friend or foe? Is the feeling healthy and adaptive, something a client should nurture and use its energy to move toward one's wants, or is it an unhealthy and maladaptive feeling, an obstacle to one's sense of well-being and goals and needing to be replaced (Greenberg, 2004)? One may also consider in this "reflection" phase suggestions from Gendlin (1978):

> What is the worst of this feeling?… What really is so bad about this?… What does it need?… What should happen?… Don't answer: wait for the feeling to stir and give you an answer.… What would it feel like if it was all O.K.? (p. 178)

Such reflection is cognitive in nature, though it refers to a process of regulating one's emotions (to be discussed below).

Therapeutically Working With Emotions: Focusing to Foster Recognition and Reflection of Emotions

As noted above, the process of differentiating positive and negative feelings and "catching" oneself in the process of having strong negative emotional moods can be daunting because of the very nature of the emotional process. The daunting aspect of dealing with feelings can result in a client feeling "stuck" and thus "disconnect" from her emotional states and her internal feelings. Gendlin (1978) developed a therapeutic process called "focusing" that was designed to help clients cope with this vague sense of being "stuck," being uncomfortable, and not being able to move on (or what we would call *being disconnected from internal feelings*). His research demonstrated a crucial difference in successful versus unsuccessful therapy outcomes:

> We found that it is not the therapist's technique—differences in methods of therapy seem to mean surprisingly little. Nor does difference lie in what the patients talk about. *The difference is in how they talk ... what the successful patients do inside themselves.* (pp. 4–6)

Gendlin further demonstrated that this difference consisted of attending to a "felt sense" of sensations, feelings, and cognitions located in a client's body and that this was a teachable skill. This is very similar to Bitter's (2008) exercise (see Information Box 11.1), identified as "the Inner Act." The first step is to recognize and get in touch with this vague feeling of being "stuck" and its affective expression (even if the expression is to do nothing). Then, it is important to begin to connect that expression with the internal feeling sensation of being "stuck." Pursuing this allows the client to begin the process of reconnecting his internal feelings with his emotional states and affective expressions.

Information Box 11.1: Assisting Clients to Recognize and Reflect on Emotional Processes

Throughout the history of psychotherapy, several prominent practitioners focused considerable attention on the emotions and emotional processing. Three such practitioners were noted family therapist Virginia Satir (1964), and Erving and Miriam Polster (1974) from the Gestalt therapy school pioneered by Fritz Perls. Bitter (2008), a master practitioner who has studied with and was influenced by both Satir and the Polsters, effectively integrated their approaches. In understanding emotions, both Satir and the Gestalt schools emphasized present experience and directing a client's attention to experiencing the physical sensations (both the affective expressions and internal feelings) as a means of helping a client to connect to the emotional state and schema dynamics that underlie (and drive) affective expressions (behaviors). Bitter directly tied in the client's schema dynamics as well by utilizing a variation of the early childhood recollection (ECR) techniques described in Chapter 9. We briefly describe the process below:

- A client describes in detail the issue that she wants to work on.
- The therapist asks the client to describe any feelings that she is aware of regarding the issue.
- Then the therapist asks about the client's internal feelings. Specifically, the therapist asks the client to create as many *sensory connections* as possible to the feeling in order to strengthen her recognition of the feeling, and also asks the following:
  - Where is the feeling located on the client's body?
  - Does the feeling have a particular shape?

- Does the feeling have a particular texture? Is it smooth, coarse, rough, sharp, or the like?
- Does the feeling have a particular temperature to it (hot, cold, etc.)?
- Once the client has a clear visual and verbal picture of the feeling, the therapist asks the client to recall the earliest memory she has of feeling this way. Clients generally associate the present concern to the early childhood memory as well as the emotional processing surrounding it and to a particular schema dynamic.
- The therapist will then help the client to recognize the impact of her emotions, and invite her to reflect on the connections to help with the original presenting concern.

As described in the discussion of early childhood recollections (ECRs; Chapter 9), there is an important relationship between what someone is feeling in a recalled childhood memory and *what about the circumstances that she described prompted her to feel that way*. As Bitter (2008) pointed out in Information Box 11.1, what prompts someone to feel a particular way betrays an important emotional schema that contains a value for a client. Otherwise, what value would there be in feeling that way? For example, if a client expresses uncertainty, vulnerability, anxiety, and fear in an ECR, obviously, the important value (i.e., schema) being expressed is safety. Correspondingly, she is not expressing a sense of invincibility, bravado, and so on. Moreover, by extension, she is indicating that the perceived vulnerability expressed in the memory (e.g., "I was so small, and it was so scary!") requires the personality to be vigilant to perceived threats to safety. Of course, some things perceived as threats in adulthood will be unfounded or exaggerated, and the price paid for such misperception may be that of living in a state of chronic alertness and anxiety.

If the feeling being expressed in an ECR is "outrage" over something that was perceived at the time of the memory to be "unfair," fairness (or the perceived lack of it) is perhaps a value being expressed in the schema behind the memory. And so on. But the emotional reactions generated may not necessarily come with an awareness of the connections to underlying schema dynamics. It is such emotional reactions that need to be regulated, and regulation begins with understanding.

It is also important to remember that in the basic list of universal emotions, the unpleasant emotions (i.e., anger, sadness, fear, and disgust) identified by Ekman and Friesen (1975) outnumbered the pleasant emotions (i.e., joy and surprise) by a ratio of 2:1. In fact, Shaver, Schwartz, Kirson, and O'Connor (1987) determined that individuals have three times as many terms to describe nuances in unpleasant emotions as they do to describe nuances in pleasant ones. These salient facts suggest that the basic brain architecture of human beings, in addition to its "programming" (i.e., early learning), is clearly inclined toward being sensitive to and aroused by threats to "survival" (i.e., both physical and psychological). As a result, many clients may not have the vocabulary to appropriately label their experiences (see the discussion of Greenberg's [2004] "arriving" and "leaving," above). Recall from Chapter 3 Clinical Exercise 3.1, "Increasing Your Feeling Vocabulary." In the exercise, you were asked to create synonyms for high-, medium-, and low-intensity words for each of the primary emotions. This exercise can also be helpful for clients to be able to begin to help them identify their internal feelings and connect them to their expressions of affect and emotional states.

Therapeutically Working With Emotions: Regulation

The purpose of helping a client to recognize, identify, and reflect upon her emotions is to establish the beginnings of a *rational* process—a more conscious and reflective *reappraisal*—of circumstances, if alternative interpretations of those circumstances are plausible, if alternative reactions are possible, and so on. It is, in effect, a *working through* and *integration* of the elements in the emotional system (i.e., affective expression, internal feelings, and emotional state) with the schema dynamics. We caution the reader *not* to mistake the term *rational process* with the idea that cognitive processes (thoughts, cognitions, beliefs, or "logic") are superior to emotions and can be used to "control" emotions. This has been a bias in the counseling and helping professions that has led to the view of emotions as "second-class citizens" (i.e., weak and "feminine," or something to be feared). Moreover, helping a client to develop such rational processes facilitates an increased sense of competence in dealing with emotions in the present and on an ongoing basis. Establishing such rational processes ultimately facilitates clients' understanding of the particular schema dynamics that may be responsible for generating the particular emotion(s) they are experiencing by reconnecting the emotional system. Such processes at times produce an "I never thought of that" reaction, along with strong affective expressions (e.g., powerful abreactive crying or a wry smile).

Rational processes can and do lead to regulation of emotions—that is, understanding and dealing more appropriately and effectively with emotions and emotional reactions. In fact, using one's cognitive powers of attention, recognition, and thoughtful reflection begins the process not only of regulating emotions but also of actually *using* them for one's benefit (i.e., to see emotions as informative in nature) rather than seeing them as powerful autonomous entities that overwhelm and victimize. Examples of such recognition include comments such as "I was really embarrassed because ..." "Confrontation doesn't bring out a very good side of me," "I know I'm awkward at that because my sister was so good at it," "I'm uncomfortable with being late—it reflects poorly on me to others," and "This situation makes me somewhat anxious because ..." Greenberg (2004) has summarized this very well:

> They (i.e., clients) need emotions to tell them, without thought, that something important to their well-being is occurring, and they need their thinking capacities to work on the problems that emotions point out and that reason must resolve. (pp. 29–30)

Thus, everyone needs their emotional capacities and processes to enlighten them about issues of importance, as well as their rational cognitive processes to make sense out of the emotional information provided.

Therapeutically Working With Emotions: Soothing

Another way to effectively help clients regulate their emotions is to teach them the natural and universal process of *soothing*. The process of learning self-soothing begins in childhood and is clearly facilitated by good parenting. If self-soothing has not been learned in childhood (and incorporated into one's emotional system and schema dynamics), it becomes challenging to learn as an adult. Indeed, Frija (1986), Goleman (1995), Gross (1999), and Greenberg (2004) have all advocated soothing, or "emotional regulation," as being essential to emotional competence. In a linear way, soothing can be seen to stem from the nurturing and intimate nature of the relationship between mother and child. With an ideal set of conditions, an infant who is upset and in distress because of the pain of hunger, being startled, and so on is highly amenable to the soothing nature of his mother's (or mother surrogate's) sight, voice tone, and touch. Likewise, an older child learns that her mother (or father) can provide the necessary soothing to assure her safety. It is axiomatic that a felt sense of safety in a child is essential for feeling comfortable in venturing out in the world.

In adult life, human beings learn that a spouse, significant other, relatives, friends, or even trusted coworkers are important sources of emotional support and soothing under a myriad of difficult circumstances that life can conjure. Although all of these are necessary and wonderful sources of comfort in a world and life that can be harsh, emotional competence demands more. It also requires self-soothing. However, the processes of allowing others to sooth and self-soothing require appropriate reappraisals and being aware of one's schema dynamics.

The objective of self-soothing is for an individual to provide feelings of emotional comfort to himself as an antidote to a wide spectrum of negative thoughts, urges, and feeling. This is accomplished through a variety of methods such as promoting a dialogue with himself, treating himself well, and engaging in a healthy feeling experience. When an individual focuses on engaging in pleasant, nonharmful experiences (e.g., a warm bath, listening to one's favorite relaxing music, or engaging nature through a walk), this allows for a *disengagement* from emotions that for the moment are sensed as overwhelming. Such disengagement allows an individual a respite from the intensity of negative emotions and simultaneously demonstrates to a client in a *nonlinear* way that he has *the capacity* to exercise control over his emotional life.

Clinical Exercise 11.2: Therapeutic Methods for Self-Soothing

Directions: Think about and write down five self-soothing behaviors, activities, or rituals. Then think of five additional ways that you could recommend to a client.
Variation: Form groups, and create a list of self-soothing behaviors, activities, or rituals to share with the class or group.

Another method for facilitating self-soothing also involves internal dialogue—a client learns to say things to the abused or hurt child of her early life that the child needs to hear to promote healing. Again, this is a schema-level intervention that connects to the client's emotional state and her expressions of affect. As a brief example, a woman in her mid-60s sought help for long-standing issues stemming from childhood that were emerging in her current adult life. After many years of being substance free through active participation in a 12-step program, she still harbored significant emotional instances in which she felt overwhelmed by feelings of shame identical to those she experienced in childhood. The therapist asked the mature woman, who was very successful in overcoming her substance abuse, what it was that she might say to the little girl in her life who felt so shamed. She replied to the therapist, "I'd say to her, 'You did nothing wrong, and you need to know that. I'm here to protect you and make sure nothing happens to you like it did then!'" She reported that she revisited such dialogue many times with significantly reduced feelings of "angst."

As described in Chapters 8 and 9 on schemas, a negative view of self that is repeatedly reinforced is the antithesis of self-soothing. In this regard, a person with a borderline personality disorder who has so much difficulty in managing strong emotions aroused with incredible speed and intensity has much to benefit from self-soothing; he or she will also find that learning how to implement such self-soothing is daunting but doable.

A key to learning self-soothing in the face of persistent negative emotions is nonlinear thinking. Equally ironic, it involves, as a first step, embracing whatever it is one is feeling. Clearly, this is counterintuitive because most individuals just want to be rid of negative emotions (e.g., "I don't want to feel this way!"). Nevertheless, a client must learn at first to tolerate and own what emotions he is feeling, and embrace them before he can learn from them, neutralize them, or bring about their metamorphosis.

Finally, the therapeutic alliance can be seen as a primary source of soothing. With a therapist in the client's "corner" and providing a "safe place," it becomes possible for the process of healing to begin. Although few may see it as a source of soothing, the therapeutic alliance should be that place in life in which a client *feels* it is safe to be exposed, vulnerable, honest with oneself, and accepted just as she is—unconditionally. Such unconditional acceptance, as described by Rogers (1957) many years ago, is nothing short of soothing.

Therapeutically Working With Emotions: Putting It All Together

Regulation and soothing are rational-cognitive processes. In Chapters 4 and 5, we discussed listening for the particular verbalizations that people use to describe their goals for treatment. In Clinical Case Example 11.3, note that the client stated, "I'm not a crier, *but* I'm having a hard time with this." In this case, his life circumstances are making it difficult for him to soothe himself. One therapeutic goal is to help soothe the client's immediate concerns. However, the second is to teach the client how to soothe himself and thus regulate his emotions (via reconnecting the emotional system with his schema dynamics so that he can reappraise the situation). Yet, before one can do that, it is important to note what listening for *absence* reveals. He does not state what his self-image schema *is* but rather what it *isn't*. In developing a more refined "formulation" for this particular client, the Level II clinician might ask, "What schemas (i.e., about his view of self) have precipitated this man's crying and feeling emotionally despondent in the set of circumstance that he has described?" One can easily extrapolate with *nonlinear thinking* that it has something to do with exactly the *opposite* of being "a crier." In fact, he subsequently described himself as someone who has a great deal of *chutzpah*.[8] How is this contradiction to be reconciled?

Clinical Case Example 11.4: A Planner Who Couldn't Plan!

As previously highlighted, very typically unconscious schemas are unknowingly and automatically followed much like a personal religion. Thus, when they come into direct conflict with life circumstances that won't go away, the result can be a spontaneous, automatic, instantaneous, and intense experience of emotional anguish. Return to Clinical Case Example 11.3. Treatment helped this man to develop an awareness of what schema(s) lay behind his crying and having a hard time. That understanding was helpful in his developing more of a sense of being in control of his emotions and what they mean rather than being a victim of them.

To further elaborate on this particular case and the identification of his view-of-self schema that might be responsible for his symptoms with no previous history of dysfunction, note the following. During the course of the first interview, the man revealed an adult history of repeated serious medical problems, surgeries to correct them, difficult and painful recoveries, and lingering chronic conditions subsequent to recovery that left him functional but with both physical and mental scars. Nevertheless, although describing himself as "an optimistic person by nature,"[9] he expressed confusion about his emotionally labile reaction, tearfulness, sadness, and so on. But, he did not report any biological signs of depression such as a loss of appetite or sleep disturbance.

With this having been his first encounter with therapy, toward the end of the initial interview, the therapist asked him if he had experienced anything that was different in the session from what he had perhaps expected. He replied that the discussion had allowed him to see (i.e., rationally understand) at least part of the basis for his intermittent crying and tearfulness:

> I learned that I'm *afraid* that this ileostomy is going to be more chronic than any of the other stuff (i.e., medical problems) that I've had in the past.[10] With the other stuff, I'd have a procedure and it was over; I was left with problems but they were not unmanageable and I could deal with those, get better over time and put them away … get them behind me. Now I have other diverticuloses. With this ileostomy, I'm afraid that there'll be more diverticulites, more surgeries and the bag will become permanent. Will they be there destroying the rhythm of my life? When it (i.e., diverticulosis) comes, it's quick and intense. *I'm afraid, and I'm not a generally fearful person.*

In the discussion that followed the above comment, the man spontaneously and unconsciously revealed another major aspect of his self-image schema to go along with his "not being a crier" and having "chutzpah": "I'm a planner. Methodical. That's how I go about things. No matter what the problem is, I lay out my strategy, *and I usually succeed.* I'm a terrific strategic planner and problem solver in my job."

Question: Link the three elements of the client's emotional system with the client's schema dynamics. Write a brief description.

In Clinical Case Example 11.4, what possible connection can there be between his being a methodical planner, a strategizer, and successful in his career and indeed throughout his life and the anticipated circumstances (i.e., possible further surgeries) that he foresees? One may hypothesize the following: His schema(s) dictates that literally *all problems* are to be approached by carefully laying out the facts, methodically planning, and devising a strategy on how to approach a particular problem given a set of facts. They also reveal that he is courageous. By acting in accordance with his view of self, he has been successful in life as a professional person, spouse, and father, and as someone with legitimate chronic ailments. The therapist related his thoughts that *perhaps*[11] this understanding of himself represented a major "template" (i.e., schema dynamic) for him. He further elaborated and described the "template" in his description of the ileostomy bag—that it was a smelly, messy, dirty, unsanitary, and unpredictable thing that leaked and made him chronically feel dirty and sexually unappealing. He then suggested that a major "organizing principle" in his personality (i.e., schema dynamics) was searching for a way to deal with his present medical circumstances as well as potential future circumstances (i.e., a planned methodology), but he could not find a way. His medical condition had too many perceived uncertainties for him to be able to make plans according to the traditional way (i.e., schema dynamics) to which he was accustomed. He continued to apply his "life strategy" (i.e., schema dynamics), and it yielded no solution to anticipated life circumstances. The man responded with tears of recognition, thus tacitly acknowledging the accuracy (and empathy) of the therapist's comment.

Note the richer and fuller understanding of the client's view-of-self schema that ongoing *linear* and *nonlinear listening* revealed: not a crier, has chutzpah, and is organized, methodical, a strategizer, and successful. And yet, when these major schema dynamics in this particular man's personality encountered life circumstances that would not bend to his will, his symptoms (e.g., crying and tearfulness) spontaneously emerged (expression of affect) and became the *emotional* representation of the perceived insolubility of his situation. He did not know or understand that this long-established, successful, and powerful but now ineffective (or at least perceived to be ineffective) personality schema would not change and that the unpredictability of his medical circumstances would not go away. Understanding this particular schema and the perceived unsolvable problem it generated under his medical circumstances was highly relevant. In fact, it was integral to dealing with his circumstances and present psychological symptoms (e.g., crying, sadness, and feelings of impending doom) and was essential to his treatment.

The "regulation" of this man's crying, realistic unrealistic fears, and so on involved his cognitively and rationally *gaining an understanding* that a major schema (i.e., using the "template" as a metaphor for the schema) was involved and that he experienced it to be ineffective. Consciously and unconsciously following the dictates of that schema had been a major source of life success for him.

Nonlinear listening and thinking revealed that he spontaneously disclosed major characteristics of his schemas. Quite paradoxically, those same schemas (i.e., his view of self is that he is successful and goes about methodically planning, strategizing, implementing, and continually being successful in problem solving) could be applied to his present unpredictable circumstances! The therapist could pose the question "How would *you* go about planning, strategizing, and implementing a solution to a problematic situation in which the future was uncertain, unpredictable, difficult to plan for, and possibly very discouraging?" In this way, a major schema of his personality could once again be employed to his advantage, thus again providing him with a sense of control and efficacy in his life.

Clinical Exercise 11.3: Questions of Assessment and Formulation

Discuss the following questions regarding Clinical Case Example 11.4:

1. What assets or strengths, if any, do you perceive this man to have?
2. How would you characterize such assets, if any, as being helpful in strategically working with this man?

3. What nonlinear thinking might you apply to treating this man?
4. What linear thinking might you apply?
5. What is your opinion of the use of nonlinear thinking in helping this man?

In fact, that is exactly what the therapist did. As a result of focusing and reflecting on his feelings, reconnecting the elements of his emotional system, and then finally linking it with his core schema dynamics, he was able to reappraise his situation (with the help of the therapist's comments). The client's response to such a conundrum was instantaneous: "I need to apply my principle of 'reduce your expectations by an appropriate magnitude.'" In the discussion of that principle, the therapist described his understanding of this principle as involving the "shrinking of one's frame of reference." That would involve taking not only one thing at a time but also one day at a time. Furthermore, it involves reducing one's time frame of reference to dealing more with the here and now every moment of every day. Such a frame of reference puts one more in control of one's life because we can always do something right now. In addition, the past cannot be changed, and the future has not arrived—indeed, it may never arrive for us. But the true value of such a therapeutic intervention is its nonlinear quality: It elicits use of *the client's* major schema—carefully plan, devise a strategy, implement, and so on—and applies it to his dilemma, which he was construing as unpredictable, uncertain, and the like. Prior to treatment, he had been unable to do that because of the emotions that he was experiencing.

Information Box 11.2: Soothing by Getting Emotional Distance,
the Breakout Principle, and the Relaxation Response

Many Eastern "mindfulness" approaches (as well as the "relaxation response") help clients attain a level of emotional soothing by teaching some basic relaxation (and mindfulness) techniques. There are three essential elements in this process: (a) being in a relaxed state by focusing on one's breathing, (b) practicing "choiceless awareness"[12] as distractions occur to the client (which they inevitably will), and (c) gently returning to the breathing and breath focus. This is the posture that a therapist takes toward her own feelings and that she models for the client to the client. Much like Greenberg's (2004) "arriving" phase in emotional coaching, mindfulness is the posture a therapist adopts in "being with" a client, and it is also the posture that a therapist encourages clients to adopt toward their own feelings (Benson, 1975, 1985, 2000; Benson & Proctor, 2003). This is the embodiment of being "in tune," discussed in Chapter 6. Sometimes, client feelings can be so overwhelming, however, that it is difficult for a client to nonjudgmentally accept them without reacting to them. In such cases, a therapist can help a client to create some distance from his feelings by "clearing a space" for them: "You don't go into the problems.... [S]tand back just a little way.... [S]tand back a few feet from your problems.... [Y]ou can walk up and touch them if you like.... [Y]ou can pull back whenever they begin to get too threatening" (Gendlin, 1978, pp. 71–72).

One can also search for a "felt sense" (Bitter, 2005; Gendlin, 1978) of where in the body this sensation is located; its intensity, color, and shape; and a name it resonates with—all of which help to create distance and a greater sense of control.

Therapeutically Working With Emotions: "Fighting Fire With Fire"

There are times, however, when attempts to soothe a client are not effective. In such instances, the old adage "fighting fire with fire" may reflect a *nonlinear* approach to helping clients to develop a greater sense of emotional competence. Remember that the goal is to help clients connect the three elements of their emotional system along with their schema dynamics in order to reappraise their circumstances. In reality, setting "controlled fires" is a way in which firefighters attempt to prevent the possibility of a spontaneous fire that may be much more difficult to contain. In the present context, "fighting fire with fire" refers to conjuring other emotions to deal with troubling negative emotions. As unusual as it may seem, a common cultural example of this can be found in attending the wake of a good person. Ironically, bereaved relatives and friends will not infrequently remember good times, humorous anecdotes, and funny stories about their experiences with the deceased as a way of transforming the emotions of loss and sadness by enjoying memories of the deceased. Greenberg (2004) has clinically described this approach to dealing with troublesome negative emotions as "changing emotion with emotion" (p. 62): "shifting attention, accessing needs and goals, positive imagery, expressive enactment of the emotion, remembering another emotion, talking about an emotion, expressing an emotion on the client's behalf and other methods of expressing emotion" (p. 194).

In this approach, therapeutic focus is on changing the uncomfortable emotions as an immediate priority of treatment and attending to cognitions and schemas later, if necessary, after a measure of relief has been gained. If negative emotions can be troubling to deal with, they can also be powerful resources put to good use. "Changing emotion with emotion" uses the power of another emotion to neutralize or transform a maladaptive emotion. As an example, a somewhat overweight woman, tearfully sensitive to the fact that her waist and thighs were large and contributed to her being overweight, commented to her therapist that she had had a colonoscopy. When asked what the results of the test conveyed, she commented that her doctor told her that she had a very "slim" colon—a relevant fact for her medical condition. She spontaneously commented, "I may have fat thighs and a big waist, but I've got a really sexy-looking colon!" Her comment revealed the use of humor to transform sensitive and doleful emotions emanating from her general medical condition into something much more adaptive.

Greenberg (2004) suggested that "maladaptive anger can be undone by adaptive sadness, and maladaptive shame can be replaced by accessing both anger at violation and self-comforting feelings and by accessing pride and self-worth" (p. 63).

The methodology of "fighting fire with fire" is active and promotes self-efficacy—through reconnecting the emotional system and allowing for a reappraisal of the client's situation. It moves preoccupation with the negative emotion that is "center stage" to a different part of the "theatre" that is human consciousness. Essentially, this replaces the destructive emotional cycle with healthier and equally powerful emotions.

Clinical Exercise 11.4: An Analysis of *Good Will Hunting*

Review the movie *Good Will Hunting* (Van Sant, 1997). Address the following issues:

1. Write a clinical assessment of Will Hunting's behavior.
2. Can you identify a major theme in your assessment?
3. How would you describe the relationship between Will and Sean?
4. Did Will and Sean have a therapeutic alliance? If so, why? If not, why not?

5. What is the turning point in their relationship?

6. Describe the problems encountered in establishing a relationship with a client like Will.

7. What major schema dynamics (view of self, others, and life and the world) do you see operative in Will's personality?

8. How do those schema dynamics demonstrate themselves in *all* of Will's relationships (i.e., his friends, Skylar, the math professor, and Sean)?

9. Describe the elements of Will's emotional system. Where do(es) the emotional "disconnect(s)" occur?

10. Describe the connection between a fundamental "schema" (i.e., "value") that Will harbors and the affect he demonstrates.

11. How would you characterize the dilemma confronting Will regarding his schema and the demands of his life circumstances?

12. What major schema dynamics (view of self, others, and life and the world) do you see operative in Sean's personality?

13. What affect is generated by Sean's schema dynamics?

14. Describe the boundary issues, if any, that you detect in the relationship between Will and Sean.

15. Which of the issues concerning boundaries would you have difficulty with, if any?

16. What is the basis of those boundary issues?

17. How does Sean connect emotionally with Will in order to influence his reappraisal of his circumstances?

18. How close to "real life" do you believe the therapeutic encounter and dialogue between Will and Sean really are?

19. What subtle lessons, if any, might be learned from the film about "technique" in therapy?

SUMMARY

In having a richer appreciation of emotions and their manifestations, meanings, functions, and ability to convey useful information, a Level II practitioner can begin to understand more about what Sroufe and Waters (1977) meant by stating that there are "no more important communications between one human being and another than those expressed emotionally" (p. 197). It is the emotional communication between client and therapist that transforms a professional relationship from one that is somewhat distant, mechanical, officious, and artificial into the vibrant human partnership described in Chapters 5, 6, and 7 as the *therapeutic alliance*. This does not mean that appropriate boundaries and professional behaviors are not maintained. Quite the contrary, a therapist emotionally in tune with a client—one human being relating to another in as fundamental a manner as can be—can simultaneously convey the rapport, empathy, and support required for solid therapeutic work to be accomplished *and* maintain appropriate objectivity and boundaries. Such an understanding of emotions greatly facilitates the transition of therapeutic work from being conducted at Level I to being conducted at Level II. As previously described, at Level I, anxiety and the struggle to do things "right" often dominate; at Level II, clinicians are more relaxed, more authentically themselves, and emotionally in tune with clients.

CONCLUSION

In this chapter, we have presented the complex issue of human emotions, including a model for understanding the different behaviors that clinicians see in a counseling session. In addition, we have discussed the link between the emotional system, the appraisal process, and a client's schema dynamics. In all, the domain of understanding and working with a client's emotional system has both linear and nonlinear aspects. Finally, we presented both linear and nonlinear therapeutic interventions to help clients recognize, reflect, and regulate their emotional reactions. The focus of this chapter has also been on those instances in which there is only one emotion that is dominant for a client at a particular time. Human emotional experience is not constrained by simplicity. We next turn to instances in which there can be numerous emotions present. Such complexities create feelings of ambivalence—an emotional reaction that can immobilize a client and the therapeutic process if not attended to skillfully.

Information Box: 11.3: The Brain and Chronic Anxiety and Posttraumatic Stress Disorder (PTSD)

Although there are few absolutes in life other than "death and taxes," it is an absolute that many of the problems human beings encounter are because of difficulty they have in regulating their emotions. In some individuals (e.g., those with PTSD and generalized anxiety disorder [GAD]), emotions not only are difficult to regulate but also appear to have a life of their own. Research to unravel the mystery of emotions such as anxiety and fear has been based on both learning theory and brain functioning. For example, in reviewing contemporary learning theory perspectives on the etiology of anxiety, Mineka and Zinbarg (2006) have emphasized that "perceptions of uncontrollability and unpredictability play a role in the development and course of PTSD" (p. 19). Furthermore, the same authors contended that

> people who have a history of uncontrollable and unpredictable life stress may be especially prone to developing GAD. Worry about possible bad outcomes or dangerous events, the central characteristic of GAD, seems to serve as a cognitive avoidance response that is reinforced because it suppresses emotional and physiological responding. Because attempts to suppress or control worry may lead to more negative intrusive thoughts, perceptions of uncontrollability over worry may develop, which is in turn associated with greater anxiety, leading to a vicious cycle. (p. 20)

On the other hand, Joseph LeDoux (1998), the eminent neuroscientist, declared, "While fear is a part of everyone's life, too much or inappropriate fear accounts for many common psychiatric problems. ... Fear is a core emotion in psychopathology" (p. 130). We would add that due to humans' incessant striving from a felt minus to a felt plus, noted many years ago by Adler (1956), fear of failure (in its innumerable forms) and fear of not belonging loom large in the human psyche.

But what role does the brain play in mediating fear responses and in the regulation of fear? LeDoux (1998) has called the amygdala a "hub in the wheel of fear" (p. 170). The amygdala is part of the midbrain and the limbic system. Although even very low levels of cortical sensory input can activate the amygdala, *the hippocampus provides the emotional context*. Goleman (1998) has described the contributions of these two organs very aptly:

While the hippocampus remembers the dry facts, the amygdala retains the emotional flavor that goes with those facts. If we try to pass a car on a two-lane highway and narrowly miss having a head-on collision, the hippocampus retains the specifics of the incident, like what stretch of road we were on, who was with us, what the other car looked like. But it is the amygdala that ever after will send a surge of anxiety through us whenever we try to pass a car in similar circumstances. As Le Doux put it to me, "The hippocampus is crucial in recognizing a face as that of your cousin. But it is the amygdala that adds you don't really like her." (p. 20)

It appears, then, that the amygdala can be overactive in some individuals, who become so upset with emotional overload that they are unable to think very effectively and use rational cognitive processes to inform, advise, and calm themselves. There is no mistaking it: Anxiety or fear generated by the sentinel function of the amygdala affects performance. Collins, Schroeder, and Nye (1989) studied the state and trait anxiety scores of 1,790 students training to be air traffic controllers, a profession with extensive stress. Among the findings of the study were that anxious students are more likely to fail and successful candidates demonstrate a higher amount of tolerance for circumstances that might produce stress in others. Likewise for a wide variety of academic performance. Seipp (1991) conducted a meta-analysis of 126 different studies on academic performance that included over 36,000 subjects in total. In short, the study concluded that the more disposed a student was to worrying, the poorer was his or her academic performance no matter what measure of performance was used, be it test grades, GPA, or achievements (as cited by Goleman, 1995, pp. 83–84).

Other parts of the brain function as regulators for the emotions. Although the emotions can overwhelm, they can also play a crucial part in making decisions as when the mind and clear thinking appear to be saying one thing and the "gut" (i.e., amygdala) appears to be saying something else. It is from the compromises affected by head and gut that wise decisions and clear thinking arise (Goleman, 1998, p. 27). Gladwell (2005), in his widely popular book *Blink*, has referred to decision making that apparently is done without conscious rational thought as "thinking without thinking," a reference to the role that centers in the brain for emotions play in daily life.

According to LeDoux (1998), fear responses are "programmed" into our genetic makeup for very good reasons—survival is at stake:

[C]onsiderable evidence shows that there is a genetic component to fear behavior ... identical twins (even those reared in separate homes) are far more similar in fearfulness than fraternal twins. This ... applies across many kinds of measurements, including tests of shyness, worry, fear of strangers, social introversion/extroversion, and others. Similarly, anxiety, phobic and obsessive compulsive disorders tend to run in families and to be more likely to occur in both identical than in both fraternal twins. (p. 136)

The good news is that even severe instances of trauma and the anxiety it can precipitate as a chronic condition (as represented by PTSD) can be better understood today with hope for its future cure. A study conducted by Rachel Yehuda, a psychologist and neurochemist at Yale University School of Medicine specializing in PTSD, reported on by Goleman (1992) was the first research to report "distinct biological changes" in Holocaust survivors with PTSD. That is, they demonstrated elevated norepinephrine, a well-known stress hormone. Likewise, similar elevated levels of norepinephrine have been discovered in Vietnam veterans plagued by PTSD. It is believed that many of the symptoms common to PTSD such as nightmares, flashbacks, insomnia, hypervigilance, and so on are due to a sympathetic nervous system that is too easily aroused. Nevertheless, Yehuda's research revealed that about a quarter of Holocaust survivors are free of PTSD symptoms. Addressing and correcting the condition of an overactive nervous system provide hope that such debilitating conditions as PTSD can be overcome.

ENDNOTES

1. There are numerous texts available (for the layperson and the professional) that look at the entire spectrum of emotions, or specific emotions. See Plutchick (2000) for a thorough review and classification system for emotions.
2. Again, we wish to convey to the reader that this is not an exhaustive list of the experience of fear or anxiety.
3. Again, the topic of depression is vast and well beyond the scope of this text. Any practitioner is well advised to study this in greater detail.
4. There is a movement within contemporary psychiatry not to consider sad reactions to the normal unhappy events and losses of everyday living as "depression."
5. Comment in brackets has been summarized from Greenberg.
6. Note that if the house *is* on fire, then the reverse is true and running from the house *is* the rational thing to do. The point is that there must be a realistic appraisal of the situation to do this.
7. In addition to the metaphor, there is the subclinical field of executive (or life) coaching that has become very popular
8. A slang of Yiddish origin suggesting audacity and boldness.
9. As an operating hypothesis, this self-description is perhaps also a reflection of her self-concept schema.
10. This is perhaps an oblique reference by the client to a basic schema (i.e., a self-perceived and self-described lifelong optimist) colliding with the automatically mediated fear of pessimistic circumstances (i.e., chronically gnawing postsurgical circumstances that are not manageable) that won't abate (i.e., he can't get out of his body).
11. Such "interpretations" are always respectfully, tactfully, and tentatively proposed to clients as hypotheses and not statements of fact. It is only a client that can address the degree of accuracy of any such hypotheses.
12. That is, nonjudgmentally accepting and welcoming all thoughts, feelings, sensations, urges, and cravings that enter the person's awareness; perhaps naming or labeling them; and even perhaps noting them with an attitude of "Welcome sad thought" or "Here comes afraid."

The Domain of Addressing and Resolving Ambivalence

12

Part 1: Understanding and Identifying Client Ambivalence

CONTENTS

INTRODUCTION: ODYSSEUS'S DILEMMA

Metaphors that relate to epic works of fiction are some of the most widely known and commonly used that psychotherapists (see Horowitz, 1983) have drawn upon to describe a variety of therapy-related topics. One such epic tale of struggle that parallels the plight of so many clients is Homer's *Odyssey*. In it, Odysseus, a Greek hero of many battles in the Trojan War, must face a number of trials set forth by the jealous gods before he can return to his home.[1] One of the most poignant trials that Odysseus had to face was that of sailing past the mystical Sirens.

Enchanting creatures, the Sirens were part woman and part bird, but with voices that were literally and potently hypnotic. Their singing would call sailors to seek them out and sail in their direction, only to steer their boats onto the rocks where they would languish until they died. Odysseus was a powerful hero in the war, and wanted to be *the only human being* to hear the Sirens singing without being destroyed in the process. At the same time, he and his crew had fought long and hard in the Trojan War and wanted to go home. Circe, a sorceress and lover of Odysseus, outlined the dimensions of Odysseus' challenge, telling him,

> First you will come to the Sirens, who bewitch every one who comes near them. If any man draws near in his innocence and listens to their voice, he never sees home again, never again will wife and little children run to greet him with joy. (12: 40–44, trans. W. H. D. Rouse)

The problem is now clear: If he does what he wants and listens to the Sirens' singing, he will be drawn to them like all of the other voyagers and be destroyed; yet if he sails straight on through to safety, he will not have heard their song. This is his *dilemma*, and although the subject of Odysseus' dilemma is obviously unlike dilemmas faced by clients today, his dilemma is *very much* like those of so many other troubled human beings: He wants "to have his cake and eat it too." That is, by being the *only* human being to hear the Sirens singing without being destroyed—a prestigious accomplishment—Odysseus would become quite unique in the annals of history. His ego is clearly at stake! In essence, his *desires* to be *the only human being* to accomplish the feat of hearing the Sirens sing *and* sail safely past them carry with them a very powerful positive emotional valence. It is as though he is reflecting a view of self that says, "I want to be known as someone very special because I believe that I am special." But to accomplish that, he has to encounter danger and his probable demise. On the other hand, if he preserves his safety and returns home—a very appealing alternative, considering that he has been away for a long time and fought a war along the way—he will not have heard them singing.[2] In this classical, millennia-old tale, Homer conveys the fact that he understood the connection between values, beliefs, and desires, as well as the feelings they generate. Odysseus could choose safety and return home (i.e., an obvious positive value), or he could choose a course of action that would be unique in the annals of history (i.e., an extremely appealing alternative for a Greek hero). In fact, he wants both! In essence, that represents the ambivalence of a double bind: *wanting to have our cake and eating it too.*

To further drive home the point, Homer again addressed a similar dynamic clothed in new circumstances. Odysseus confronts another perilous dilemma while homeward bound: He wants something that is virtually impossible to attain without peril. Circe advised that in another task, after passing the island of the Sirens, Odysseus must sail through a passage between two overhanging rocks. She says, "When you have got clear of them (i.e., the Sirens), there is a choice of two courses, and I will not lay down for you which to take; use your own judgment. I will just say what they are" (12: 68–72, trans. W. H. D. Rouse).

Each of the two courses that Circe highlights is ominous: No one has ever safely passed through one of the routes,[3] and the other course she outlined for Odysseus is equally forbidding and has *two* ominous and deadly cliffs. Circe informs him that one of the cliffs is inhabited by the evil monster Scylla, who has six heads: "No seamen can boast that they have escaped scot-free from her: she grabs a poor wretch with each head out of the ship as it sails along" (12: 120–124, trans. W. H. D. Rouse). Upon the other cliff dwells Charybdis, a monster in the form of a mighty whirlpool that sucks down any ship that goes past: "Three times a day she spouts it out, three times a day she swallows it down: she is a terror—don't you be there when she swallows! No one could save you from destruction[,] not Earthshaker [Poseidon, the sea god] himself" (12: 129–135, trans. W. H. D. Rouse). Although he wants to avoid peril, he must choose a path even though each has a very heavy price associated with it![4] Hence, it is the source of the modern-day expression that someone is "stuck between a rock and a hard place."

Under personal circumstances with similarly perceived ominous consequences, clients clearly experience feelings of emotional discomfort and immobilization by trying to engage *only one side* of the polarities that they experience. They become focused only on what they want and not necessarily on what the circumstances of their life situations demand. Like Odysseus, they want to avoid both the rock *and* the hard place. This is simply not realistic, however. The realities of life continue to impose themselves, and a client is faced with the necessity to make a decision "this way or that way" and go forward with her life. This precipitates feeling pulled in two directions at the same time, and feeling immobilized, "stuck," and unable to make a commitment. Clinically, practitioners label this phenomenon as *ambivalence*.

Ambivalence is an inherent factor universally found in human problem solving, and problems both big and small can stimulate it. To advance their level of sophistication and ability to help and influence clients who consult them, therapists must (a) learn first about the nature of ambivalence; then (b) understand how to recognize it in all its subtleties; and, finally, (c) learn how to therapeutically respond to it. Master practitioners are skilled at all three of these tasks. As previously discussed, Level I and Level II practitioners, prone to linear thinking, often see a client's feelings of ambivalence as an obstacle to treatment (or "resistance"). Such practitioners are also prone to experiencing client ambivalence as a judgment of or a poor reflection on their ability to be an effective therapist, thereby undermining professional confidence.

Nonlinear thinking reveals that clients' expressions of ambivalence are a natural part of the change process. A client's expressions of ambivalence are also likely to be reflected in feelings about therapy and the therapeutic process because (a) these are potentially threatening to the client's customary ways of thinking and operating, and (b) the client can feel coerced (i.e., psychological *reactance*) by the therapeutic situation into choosing one or the other of two distasteful options. A nonlinear-thinking therapist also understands that most clients, to some degree, *want to have their cake and eat it too, feel pulled in two directions at the same time* (between the process of change and the fear of change), and ultimately *find themselves stuck between a rock and a hard place*. In actuality, these three commonplace expressions represent the essence of the domain that will be explored in this chapter. But how is it that human beings develop ambivalence?

UNDERSTANDING CLINICAL AMBIVALENCE

Definition

The term *ambivalence* was originally coined in 1911 by Eugen Bleuler, who is perhaps best known for suggesting the term *schizophrenia* as a substitute for what had been called dementia praecox. A contemporary of Freud, he used the term *ambivalence* to describe one of the symptoms of schizophrenia. Although Bleuler (1950) described ambivalence as being of different types (i.e., emotional, intellectual, and volitional), today it appears to be used more as a general term reflecting coexisting but antithetical emotions, attitudes, beliefs, or desires toward a given set of circumstances or a given "object" (e.g., a person; see Hinsie & Campbell, 1970). The prefix *ambi* is Latin, meaning "both" or "in two ways." The word *valence* comes from the Latin and means having strength or a powerful attraction, or the degree of attractiveness of a goal (Merriam-Webster's, 2006).

For present *clinical* purposes, we refer to ambivalence as a client's experience of being stuck *between a rock and a hard place* because *he wants to have his cake and eat it too*. This poetic definition comes both from clinical experiences with clients as well as from the etymological origins of the word. Thus, in a clinical context, ambivalence refers to a person being *pulled in two directions*, alternately attracted to or repulsed by *both* sides (i.e., valences) of alternative choices inherent in a given set of life circumstances that ultimately become described as a "problem." Intrinsic in a client's experience of ambivalence is a desire to maintain the status quo (typically reflective of schema dynamics—view of self, view of others, and view of the world and life) versus the need to adapt to demanding life circumstances that are typically perceived as threatening because they call for some sort of change. This is especially true when a client has to make a decision or solve a problem. Ultimately, it is a client's schemas that interfere with making decisions and constructively solving problems.

Erickson and Rossi (1980) described it thusly: "Psychological problems develop when people do not permit the naturally changing circumstances of life to interrupt their old and no longer useful patterns of association and experience [i.e., schema] so that new solutions and attitudes may emerge" (p. 71).

Mozdzierz, Greenblatt, and Thatcher (1985) have described the role of schemas and the reasoning that flows from this role as follows:

> When the demands of life require a solution different from one's long-held ways of thinking (private logic), the individual is caught in a double bind: the solution does not fit the puzzle. Yet the individual cannot discard the solution since it is sensed as a part of oneself and would represent, in effect, a disavowal, repudiation, and rejection of self. (p. 456)

Decision making has become the focus of a great deal of attention in the research literature. The role of schema dynamics has become quite prominent among the many salient variables that have been identified to help explain how human beings come to decisions. Ajzen (1996) has described the role of schemas in this way:

> Perhaps their greatest contribution to our understanding of decision–making processes … can be found in theory and research that link social judgments on the one hand to carrying out a behavioral decision on the other. Even if biased, the various cognitive and motivational processes [i.e., schemas] that have been identified lead to the formation of beliefs about the alternative courses of action, about their advantages and disadvantages, about the resources they require, about the expectations of other people, and so forth. Although subjective and not necessarily accurate, these beliefs guide the decisions people make, and *it is by examining the beliefs people hold that we can gain an understanding of decision making in real-life situations*. (p. 316; emphasis added)

Thus, ambivalence results when a client is faced with life circumstances requiring a choice in which either or both of the perceived options run counter to her schematized view of self, others, or life or the world. On the one hand, clients' dilemmas represent their beliefs and experience of what they want (or don't want). On the other hand, they are confronted with what their life situation demands, which is incompatible with what they want (or don't want).

The therapist's job is to use the therapeutic alliance, described in Chapter 5, to support clients (via the therapeutic alliance) as they "work through" the issues at hand, help clients explore the pluses and minuses of their alternatives in a safe and trusted environment, and help clients develop the courage to face their "trial." Part of the "working-through" process involves guiding clients to become aware of and understand the powerful influences that *unconscious values*, *beliefs*, and *attitudes* have on them and the *anxiety* that is generated when those beliefs are threatened. In the light of such threats, clients can demonstrate great resistance to any demand that they need to select an alternative and change the status quo, even when they accept that it is necessary. For example, a client may come to counseling to "control his temper" because his bursts of anger have caused him difficulties with his wife or boss. He does not particularly want to come for treatment, but does so to avoid negative consequence (losing his job or spouse). The reality may be that he does not feel that it is a problem that requires "help," because his "temper" usually allows him to "get his way." As a result, he is most likely to be in the precontemplation or contemplation stage of change. After all, human beings have great loyalty to their unconscious values, beliefs, and attitudes and attribute many successes (and avoidance of failures) to them. In essence, clients are threatened with giving up a "winning formula."

Clients may describe this phenomenon in a number of ways, such as "an internal conflict," "wanting to" versus "not wanting to," fear of doing something in their lives, "my head says one thing and my gut says something else," "wanting my cake and eating it too," and being "caught between a rock and a hard place." Briefly stated, a client has at least two distinct alternatives (valences poles, or sides of the dilemma) from which she must choose. Each available alternative has advantages and disadvantages for the client that are based on her beliefs and desires about the issues in question. Choosing may be very anxiety producing. Once a therapist understands the meaning a client attributes to her various perceived options (*from the client's point of view*), it becomes clearer why it is that a client feels stuck. This is important because clients' understanding of the reasons for their powerful feelings of ambivalence is most often vague, and leads to impasses in therapy. Such vague understanding is thoroughly in keeping with the unconscious (i.e., "I want to have my cake and eat it too") dimensions of ambivalence.

Clinical Exercise 12.1: Dilemmas

Practical examples of personal dilemmas abound: to get married or not; needing to choose one man or another; needing to choose one woman or another; going to college but not wanting to work hard at one's studies, and/or facing failure; completing a degree or not; applying for a promotion and risk not being chosen; wanting more money in a job, but not wanting to take on more responsibility; the decision to start a family or forgo children in marriage; having an abortion or giving birth; keeping a child born out of wedlock or giving it up for adoption; and so on.

DIRECTIONS

1. After reading the personal dilemmas above, generate five additional dilemmas that people commonly face in life and record them.
2. Share them with the class to create a list.
3. Discuss what it is that causes life choices and circumstances to develop into these dilemmas.
4. Flesh out how these circumstances represent a person feeling *pulled in two directions at the same time* and *wanting to have her cake and eat it too*, while *being stuck between a rock and a hard place*.
5. Do you notice any *patterns* (i.e., repetitions) that are *commonly* repeated among the various circumstances listed?
6. How might you describe the patterns, if any, that you have identified?

Types of Ambivalence

Kurt Lewin (1935, 1938) is credited with having drawn scientific attention to the need to resolve conflicts generated from competing "forces" of attraction and repulsion when human beings need to make complex decisions.[5] An individual experiences "forces" that render him unable to make a decision as a "conflict." Individuals become therapy clients when the competing forces of attraction and repulsion become immobilizing and life circumstances are demanding a decision. (See Information Box 12.1 for examples.)

Lewin's concept of "conflict" is classical and can be useful to clinicians in *recognizing* double binds and their associated ambivalences (a client "theme" originally described in Chapter 5). He identified four types of conflict: *approach–approach*, *avoidance–avoidance*, *approach–avoidance*, and *double approach–avoidance*. An *approach–approach* conflict represents a choice between two alternatives that both have positive valences or poles that are attractive, and the person must find a way to choose the *best option*. Typically, a person fears making a choice and regretting the choice she made because it did not include *all* of the positive elements that she desired. This is often called *buyer's remorse*. In an *avoidance–avoidance* conflict, the choice is between two options that have negative valences (i.e., are not attractive). A simple example of this might be having to choose between getting an immunization shot in the arm or a shot in the leg—both are going to be painful. Many times, clients will delay taking action because taking no action is seemingly less painful than taking action (though it might not be for their long-term benefit). The third conflict identified by Lewin was *approach–avoidance*, in which both options that a person must choose from have both positive and negative valences. Individuals feel compelled to make a choice between options that simultaneously attract them (which brings a fear of regret) and repulse them (which leads to a desire not to act), or to do nothing and stay the same. Finally, there is *double approach–avoidance*, in which both options that a person must choose from have both positive and negative valences. This is a "double whammy" because individuals must make a choice between two options that simultaneously attract them and repulse them. An example of this is often faced by cheating spouses, who must choose whether to stay with their spouse (who is familiar and safe, but feels hurt by the betrayal from the infidelity) and the lover (who is exciting, but who is also a reminder of the unfaithfulness and guilt over leaving the spouse). These individuals seem to vacillate the longest.

Individuals become immobilized and often enter therapy when the competing forces of attraction and repulsion are experienced as intolerable in the face of life circumstances that demand a decision.

Information Box 12.1: Examples of Each Type of Conflict

APPROACH–APPROACH CONFLICT

A client enters therapy and states that she has a choice of two jobs. Each pays approximately the same, and both are attractive to her. She worries about making the wrong choice.

AVOIDANCE–AVOIDANCE CONFLICT

A client in counseling complains of having a difficult decision to make: whether or not to put his elderly mother, who is suffering from Alzheimer's disease, in a nursing home, or have her move in with him and he becomes her primary caretaker.

APPROACH–AVOIDANCE CONFLICT

A client states that it is her life's ambition to attend medical school and fulfill her dream of becoming a doctor. At the same time, she expresses fears of what she will do if she fails to gain entrance to medical school. Correspondingly, she continues to postpone taking the Medical College Admission Test (MCAT).

DOUBLE APPROACH–AVOIDANCE CONFLICT

John was married to Michelle and best friends with Danny. They all worked together as partners in a small but successful company. As a result of some late nights working closely to each other, Michelle and Danny began a flirtation, which soon became a mutual interest in each other. Danny feels great conflict between the options of pursuing Michelle and not pursuing Michelle.

EXERCISE

On a separate sheet of paper, define the "poles" in each of the conflicts above.

- What is the attraction (approach pole)?
- What is the repulsion (avoidance pole), if applicable?
- Speculate about what kind of behaviors the client may use to signal his or her conflict or ambivalence.

Variation: Develop examples for each of the four types of conflicts given above. Share with classmates in dyads or small groups, and challenge them to define each of the poles of the dilemma.

In the 1950s, Miller and Dollard (Dollard & Miller, 1950) took Lewin's ideas and empirically tested them with rats. The reader might wonder, what does 6-decade-old rat research have to do with the practice of psychotherapy today? The answer is that their work does shed light on what people do when confronting many of these difficult decisions. They placed rats in long boxes that could have food at either end (positive valence) or deliver a foot shock to the rat at either end (negative valence). They found that in the *approach–approach* situation (i.e., food at both ends and no shocks), rats placed in the box would vacillate; but as soon as they got closer to one end (i.e., randomly, by coincidence, or by convenience), they started moving toward that end and never "looked back." In the *avoidance–avoidance* situation, rats had shocks at both ends (but no food). Under those circumstances, the rats tended to just vacillate between the two ends without committing to one side or the other. In the *approach–avoidance* situation, the food and shocks were on the same side; the rats would move toward the goal (food) until they received the shock. Then they would back off and vacillate. Lastly, in the *double approach–avoidance*, the rats would vacillate (like in avoidance–avoidance), until they would get exhausted and try to escape somehow from the (closed) box (see Dollard & Miller).

What happens if an individual faced with a decision like Dollard and Miller's (1950) rats cannot comfortably come to make a choice? Ajzen (1996) has described it as follows:

Consistent with the cognitive miser view, people are assumed to maintain the status quo and avoid the stress associated with decisional conflict unless circumstances demand a change of behavior. Little conflict is generated if an acceptable alternative is readily available, but if it is not, the resulting stress can produce *defensive avoidance*: procrastinating, shifting responsibility for the decision to others, exaggerating the desirability of the status quo. … Alternatively, the person may be stricken with panic, a state called *hypervigilance*, with a paralyzing effect on action. (p. 310)

In many ways, these observations help to explain many of the behaviors of ambivalent clients. Their behavior may look like they are *immobilized, endlessly vacillating*, or *trying to escape or avoid*; or if they do make a decision, it may be due to *random chance*. That is the time an individual may seek help.

Clinical Case Example 12.1: Ambivalence and "Life or Death"

A married woman in her mid-50s with grown children was referred for psychological evaluation and possible therapy because of her adjustment to a severely damaged heart muscle. She had developed dilated cardiomyopathy (i.e., an "enlarged heart"), a condition in which the heart muscle's pumping efficiency has decreased severely. This means that it gradually becomes more and more ineffectual at perfusing other vital body organs with oxygenated blood. At that time, because those other vital organs (i.e., the liver, kidney, lungs, and brain) begin to fail, the patient develops what is called *multi-organ system failure*. After thorough medical evaluation, her cardiologists determined that the only treatment available to save this woman's life was cardiac transplant.

Medically, the woman was a good candidate for transplant. A discussion of her possible need for transplant had arisen with her doctors several years before, so the idea was not new to her. As her health deteriorated in keeping with the gradual decline in her cardiac functioning, she did not seem to want to discuss being listed[6] for transplant with her doctors. According to the referring cardiologist, for this woman, "time was running out."

During a discussion with the psychologist performing the evaluation, the question came up as to what her thoughts and feelings about transplant were. She replied, "It's not that I'm against transplant. It's just that I've heard things about it such as there can be complications and problems after surgery—it can be dangerous." She was neither refusing to obtain transplant nor consenting to seek such treatment. The treatment team and her physicians did not know how to proceed given the woman's ambivalence, but they knew that without transplant she would die soon. This dire prediction is about as certain as any that modern medicine can make.

The woman's dilemma is rather straightforward but fraught with life-and-death alternatives and consequences. On the one hand, she clearly needs transplant, or she will die prematurely. On the other hand, the information she has gathered about transplant and her interpretation of it have led her to conclude that it is equally dangerous. Although her present health is poor, she is alive and functioning, albeit with great limitations on her physical activity. Such functioning and denial of the urgency of her circumstances may be blinding her to the true risks of opting to forgo transplant versus taking her chances with a new heart.[7]

The woman in Clinical Case Example 12.1 appears to be in a double approach–avoidance scenario. On the one hand (or "pole"), if she chooses to be listed for transplant, she could face "complications" (e.g., not surviving surgery, organ rejection, or a posttransplant life of unending multiple medical complications). On the other hand, if she chooses not to be listed, she would maintain her current life status (i.e., alive and not rejecting a new organ), but her medical condition (i.e., enlarged heart) and quality of life (i.e., severe physical limitations) will continue to deteriorate until she dies. Too often, clients in such circumstances are characterized as being in a state of denial.[8] Of course, when clients decide not to make a decision regarding the choices that they have, they are actually "deciding." But, as such, they relinquish control of their life and are "deciding" to leave outcomes to chance, letting "fate" work things out (i.e., *random chance*). In Clinical Case Example 12.1, as a result of the woman's constant equivocation, her behavior appeared to transplant team members as constant stalling (*immobilization*) and deliberating (*vacillating*) about change or making a decision, *denial* about how seriously ill she really was, or some form of distancing or dissociation from the reality of the problem situation (*escape*). Although the choice may seem simple and straightforward, until they are actually in such circumstances, no one knows the immobilization that can result from life-or-death decisions. For practical purposes, this woman *was being pulled in two directions* (i.e., having the transplant but being exposed to the risks of surgery and those of transplant as well, or remaining in poor and declining health most likely leading to death), *feeling stuck between a rock and a hard place* (i.e., each choice is fraught with risk), and *wanting to have her cake and eat it too* (i.e., being in poor health but alive without subjecting herself to the dangers of transplant surgery). Neither alternative is perceived as pleasant or appealing. The treatment team faced the pressure of time to make a decision and "list" the woman for transplant in time to provide an opportunity to save her life or use palliative measures until she dies. But, whenever the subject would arise, she would waver with ambivalence. It is important to note that not all clients have such life-threatening dire circumstances, but their dilemmas are usually just as debilitating for them.

LINEAR AND NONLINEAR VIEWS OF AMBIVALENCE

With linear thinking, ambivalence can be misinterpreted as a lack of commitment to the change process, dissembling (i.e., changing one's story), uncooperativeness, and the like. Indeed, some Level I or even Level II therapists may misinterpret ambivalent behaviors as "resistance" and attempt to pathologize the client (e.g., as "oppositional-defiant"). Even more misguided, ambivalences can be misinterpreted as behaviors that must be overpowered by such interpretations such as "You don't seem to be interested in treatment," "You don't seem to want to change," or "You don't seem to want to get better." Such therapeutic comments are counterproductive, corrosive to the therapeutic alliance, and born of frustration (see Chapter 7).

A *nonlinear* view of ambivalence is to understand that it is *part* of what can be expected in the change process and not an aberration (or sabotaging) of the treatment process. Miller and Rollnick (2002) put it succinctly thus:

> It is easy to misinterpret such ambivalent conflict as pathological—to conclude that there is something wrong with the person's motivation, judgment, knowledge base, or mental state. A sensible conclusion from this line of reasoning is that the person needs to be educated about and persuaded to take the proper course of action [*linear* thinking] … we regard ambivalence to be a natural phase in the process of change. It is when people get stuck in ambivalence that problems can persist and intensify. Ambivalence is a reasonable place to visit, but you wouldn't want to live there. [*nonlinear* thinking]. (p. 14)

Although there is an advantage to the discomfort that a client feels when he is stuck in his ambivalence (e.g., not having to let go of either of two attractive alternatives, or not having to choose between two equally unpleasant alternatives), "working through" the ambivalence can come at a cost as well. Among other things, it can mean such things as

- giving up something enjoyable (e.g., alcohol, fatty foods, cocaine, or promiscuous sex);
- facing circumstances that are personally demanding (e.g., having to exercise, watching what one eats, doing the "right thing," finishing a degree, or applying to graduate school);
- facing circumstances that are uncertain and, in extreme situations, even life threatening;
- accepting responsibilities that one would rather avoid;
- facing possible failure, loss of prestige, harsh realities, or the like;
- modifying deeply held beliefs that are core to one's personality; and
- being viewed by others in a negative light.

Clinical Exercise 12.2: Personal Ambivalence

Prepare your *personal* responses to the following:

1. Identify circumstances in your life (or the life of someone you know very well) such as those listed above that have prompted ambivalence and strong reluctance to change, make a decision, or the like.
2. Identify those elements of ambivalence that made choosing an alternative especially difficult.
3. How long did it take for you (or the person you are referring to) to make a decision?

4. What rationale can you provide as to why it took as long as it did to resolve the ambivalence? Or, if you (or the person you are referring to) have not resolved it as of yet, what prevents you (or that person) from resolving it?
5. What was it like to go through the process of resolving ambivalence? Or, if a decision has not been reached, what will it take for you (or the person you are referring to) to resolve it?
6. Could anything have accelerated the process? If yes, what? Does that represent some action on *your* part? Does it represent *wishing* that life circumstances would change so they would be easier?
7. How did you resolve the situation?
8. What were you feeling (i.e., what emotions did you have) during the process?
9. How did you feel once you resolved the situation?
10. What are your thoughts as to what clients go through after having reviewed the life circumstances you faced and the ambivalence it generated?

Yes, "working through" a client's ambivalence can be arduous, painful, time-consuming, and demanding on the client. A Level II therapist (particularly a nonlinear-thinking one) has the maturity to focus his efforts more fully on clients' concerns and is more comfortable in realistically being able to differentiate client behavior from his own performance or abilities. Skillful Level II clinicians utilize the knowledge of all three Level I domains (see Chapters 2–7), and the other two Level II domains (Chapters 8–11) to be able to help the client to resolve ambivalence. We now point our attention to describing how master practitioners recognize and work with client ambivalence.

LISTENING FOR AND RECOGNIZING AMBIVALENCE

In Chapter 2, we presented *linear* and *nonlinear* approaches to listening as major elements in the domain of communicating and engaging with clients. The same *nonlinear listening* can be used to detect client ambivalence, and is often the first step in successfully resolving it.

Expressions of Language

Nonlinear listening for expressions of ambivalence is particularly important because clients are often unlikely to state that they are ambivalent. This is in keeping with Pinker's (2007) observations that people don't necessarily say what they mean. Instead, a therapist must listen for clues in a client's verbalizations that suggest that she is ambivalent about change or therapy itself. Listening for *congruence, absence, inference, presence,* and *resistance* are all important in this process. For example, a client making statements that are incongruous with accompanying behaviors (e.g., voice intonation and facial expression) or incongruous with how she expresses themselves emotionally can be signs of ambivalence. We discuss nonlinear-listening skills and linguistic patterns as a means of detecting client ambivalence.

Listening for Congruence

A client can reveal ambivalences through direct expression of *equivocation*, a statement that is not literally false but that cleverly avoids an unpleasant truth (*American Heritage Dictionary of the English Language,*

2004). Equivocation reveals that one side and then the another side of the ambivalent polarities have their pitfalls and unpleasant truths; it can also reveal that a client wants the perceived advantages of one option but does not want to relinquish the perceived advantages of another incompatible option. Listening for congruence or, more specifically, *incongruence* in a client's story can help to reveal the equivocation. This can alert a clinician that a client is feeling ambivalent about the situation or issue at hand.

Listening for Absence

Many times, a client's ambivalence manifests itself as behavior that effectively detours around a given problem. *Detouring* refers to diverting attention to less significant concerns along with devoting extraordinary amounts of time, energy, and resources to them (e.g., see "land mines," "rabbit holes," and "red herrings" from Chapter 2). For example, a client may enter therapy because of experiencing recurring intrusive thoughts, but instead of discussing those thoughts, when they occur, under what circumstances, and so on, he engages in stories about him and his wife's sexual escapades. Such diversions may have the effect of temporarily minimizing one of the poles, which either allows a client to escape the dilemma or lets fate decide what choice should be made. Listening for absence allows a therapist to pick up on the minimized pole and helps bring the full picture into focus for the client (this will be discussed further below).

Listening for Inference

Formally, the word *if* is a part of speech called a *conjunction*, meaning that it brings two things together. In terms of ambivalence, the client is bringing together the two poles of her dilemma. When clients express a linguistic pattern that states, "If only …" (something would occur, stop, go away, or the like), "then" this entire "problem" would go away. For example, a client may use feelings of depression as a way to slow down (or hesitate) any change from occurring. She may say, "Oh, if only I didn't get so depressed, I would have the energy to make the changes you suggest, and I could be a better wife (mother, worker, etc.)." Typically, it is other people, the world, or life that a client is "demanding" to be altered (e.g., things shouldn't be so hard to accomplish) and not her central values (e.g., wanting ambition fulfilled but not wanting to learn what is necessary to fulfill it). The inference, or "wish," that is contained in the "If … then" statement reveals a client's schema or core beliefs: "If only others would change or the world would go away, then I could be happy—then I wouldn't be in this bind that I feel." The conjunction implicitly brings together both poles of a dilemma: Clients more infrequently express themselves as wanting to stay the same while is life demanding a change—hence, they *want to have their cake and eat it too.*

Vague client expressions of "stress" also reveal ambivalences. Recall from Chapters 10 and 11 that stress is caused by "stressors," those elements in the environment that an individual perceives (via the appraisal process) as threatening and for which they have not devised an effective means of coping. Stressful situations can easily reveal double binds and their inherent ambivalences by carefully analyzing a person's particular environmental circumstances (e.g., changes and/or demands in relationships, work, or commitments). As a brief example, a client might come to therapy asking for help with time management skills, particularly because he always seems to wait until the last minute to get things done. Such behavior disrupts his life, "stresses" him, and eventually upsets his family or others in his social environment. After accumulating basic information, if a therapist begins to make some tentative suggestions regarding being more organized (e.g., setting reasonable goals, and getting a day timer), and almost immediately the client begins to protest that he never seems able to do those things, the *inferred* message that the client is sending is that he would like to be more organized without having to make any real changes to his life (e.g., without having to exert any effort or assume responsibility). Listening for the inferred meaning of *stress* and what the client would like to do with it can help to uncover the underlying ambivalence.

Listening for Presence

Clients who are ambivalent often demonstrate their feelings through their nonverbal behaviors. A client's emotional arousal and emotional reactions to discussing a particular topic will often reveal ambivalence. Although they may say one thing, their body language tells a different story. When clinicians listen for presence, they listen for the conflicts and dilemmas that are paralyzing the client. These can be brought to the client's attention by *developing discrepancies*, *externalizing the problem*, or *looking for exceptions* (these will all be discussed in Chapter 13).

Listening for Resistance

In Chapter 2, we described "Yes, but ..." as a common indicator of resistance (and now ambivalence). Just like the term *if*, linguistically the word *but* is a conjunction and connects the two poles of the dilemma. The word *but*, however, usually means that the second choice negates the first, even if they are both in the same sentence. Such masked *equivocation* is clearly an expression of ambivalence and a reluctance to be held to one alternative or another. Either alternative (or pole) may be perceived as impinging on a core client value or belief (i.e., schema dynamic), regardless of the life circumstances. As a brief example, consider a client entering therapy who states that he wishes to lose weight. When, however, the therapist suggests a plan that includes an exercise routine, the client responds initially by agreeing and then immediately talking about his lack of time, his discomfort with going to gyms, his aesthetic displeasure in sweating, the distance to travel to a gym, and so on, effectively negating the suggestion. Many client behaviors that hinder the pursuit of important (or obvious) therapeutic goals because the clients do not complete homework tasks or instead make meager commitments to challenges (e.g., "I'll try. ..." from Chapter 2) are manifestations of ambivalence. A therapist must listen for resistance, understand the poles of the dilemma that are essential to the experience of ambivalence, grasp the underlying schema dynamics, and intervene to keep a client focused on the therapeutic task at hand.

In addition to these nonlinear-listening skills, the assessment skills described in Chapters 8 and 9 are vital in helping to detect ambivalences that a client is living with but can't necessarily articulate very well. It is essential to remember that, for a variety of reasons (e.g., anxiety about coming for treatment, confusion, emotional turbulence, and uncertainty about what the therapist's reaction to their "problem" will be), clients frequently "don't know where to begin" and don't necessarily provide a coherent history and logical narrative of their problem(s) and efforts to solve them. Clients often are somewhat oblique in how they go about telling their "story" and reason for seeking help. Both *linear-* and *nonlinear-listening skills* are vitally important in this regard because it is not necessarily very often that a client will directly articulate a dilemma as a double bind. That is why master practitioners find it useful in asking such questions as "What is it that prompted you to seek counseling at this particular time? Why not 6 weeks ago or 6 months ago? What is it in your life that has changed?" This line of inquiry is important; it helps a therapist to identify particular events that have tipped the balance of equanimity and are part of the creation of the client's double-bind equation. In addition, understanding the *theme* of the client's story (also from Chapter 5) can also provide a therapist with some important clues about the role that ambivalence will play in the therapeutic process (e.g., themes of desperation, hopelessness, and helplessness).

Emotions and Emotional Reactions

If understood, a client's expression of emotions can frequently reveal ambivalences of sufficient magnitude to warrant attention. What a clinician is listening for is the emotional impact that a client's alternatives have. It is a client's emotional arousal, emotions, and emotional reactions to the discussion of a particular topic that will often reveal immobilizing ambivalence and the prompting of symptom development. As mentioned above, an individual is placed in a "double bind" when life in its infinite variety presents circumstances that must be addressed but require behavior in conflict with "core" values. It is exactly those things that people value that they have feelings about. Emotions (e.g., anger, resentment, and frustration) are aroused because the client appraises the situation to be threatening to his beliefs or schema dynamics. Symptoms are experienced (e.g., depression, anxiety, insomnia, and bulimia) as a result of ineffective and maladaptive coping strategies to these situations that cause feelings of ambivalence.

Clinical Case Example 12.2: Ambivalence Expressed via Symptoms

A bright, college-aged client was in treatment on an episodic basis due to school commitments during the academic year and work commitments during the summer hiatus. Nevertheless, she worked steadily at her initial presenting problem—bulimia. Over a 2-year period, she came for a total of 18 therapy visits. As she seemed to decrease the frequency of her episodes of bulimia, the therapist reinforced the idea that her symptom was an expression of her attempts to problem-solve. To complicate matters, as her bulimia would occasionally wane, she found herself inexplicably taking a razor blade and making very small surface cuts in the skin on her arm. With concern about their very serious and potentially lethal consequences, the therapist followed up on what those symptoms might be about. The young woman indicated that she had no intention of harming herself and had no thoughts of suicide either before or after engaging in such behavior. She was certain that it was another manifestation of an attempt to "problem-solve," as had been discussed in therapy previously. Appropriate safeguards for potential suicide were taken to both the client and the therapist's satisfaction. In addition, her bulimia had never progressed to a point of substantial weight loss.

In "working through" her problem, it was clear that she perceived herself as a "good girl" (i.e., a core schema reflecting view of self) who found it difficult to express negative feelings or dissatisfactions for fear of offending others, thus threatening her sense of identity as a "good girl." This was especially the case with family members. Mother in particular was someone whom she described as controlling and difficult for her to talk to at times. This appeared to be a characteristic manner in which her mother related to the world—having things the way she wanted, including her children. But, as the young woman improved and progressed in confidence, the focus of therapy was more and more directed toward her recognizing feelings and constructively telling Mother and others how she felt.

During the 18th visit, the therapist asked about how she was doing with her symptoms. She indicated that it was now over 6 months since she had vomited or cut herself. She explained, "I've kicked all the bad habits. ... If I'm not 'throwing it up'[9] and not throwing it away, I have to 'sit on it.'...[10] Mother would be coming at me in an accusing way with a rude tone, and I used to throw it back at her[11] ... (as if to say) who can hurt the other person more." The difference now seemed to be that she had begun to identify what she was feeling and was expressing it more and more appropriately, withdrawing from hostile confrontations from her mother until she was more approachable, and listening to what her mother had to say, all of which were compatible with goals of therapy—finding other ways of dealing with her feelings besides bulimia and cutting herself while still considering herself to be a "good girl."

QUESTIONS

1. What are the significant values (i.e., view of self, others, and life and the world) to which this woman adheres?
2. How do her symptoms (i.e., bulimia and cutting) allow her to have her cake and eat it too?
3. As briefly as possible, describe the double bind she faced.

4. How do feelings reveal the existence of ambivalence in this particular case?
5. What environmental impact could her symptoms be seen to have?

Stages of Change and Ambivalence

In Chapter 4, we introduced the stages of change (SOC) model as part of the domain of assessing clients' needs and accessing resources and goals for treatment. The SOC model suggests that not all clients come for treatment with the same preparedness or motivation to change. Likewise, *nonlinear thinking* suggests that clients also have differing levels of ambivalence. For example, precontemplators (i.e., resistant, rebellious, resigned, and reluctant) are likely to demonstrate ambivalence with certain characteristics. Behaviorally, their ambivalence may resemble Chamberlain, Patterson, Reid, Kavanaugh, and Forgatch's (1984; as cited in Miller & Rollnick, 2002) four categories of disruptive client behavior (i.e., arguing, interrupting, negating, or ignoring—see below). Usually, this is a reflection of the fact that precontemplators are caught between the two poles of "having" to come to therapy (e.g., being forced by the court, one's family, or an employer), and not wanting to come to therapy at all. The ambivalence comes as a result of their trying to avoid the unpleasant consequence of not coming or not making some attempt (halfheartedly) at changing. Consider the following example.

A client enters individual therapy after staying out all night drinking with his buddies—the fifth time in the past year that he has done this. His fiancée believes that this is a problem and threatens to break off their engagement if he does not seek help. He doesn't want to lose her and feels badly about his behavior, but he also enjoys his drinking activities with his buddies. He reluctantly comes to therapy. He really doesn't believe that he has a problem, however, and refuses to engage in the therapeutic process. Clearly, he is ambivalent: He comes for treatment, although he doesn't want to and won't make any changes, just to avoid a worse consequence. Such clients have some motivation (e.g., they feel that they are demonstrating motivation by keeping their appointment)!

Those clients in a contemplation mode of treatment are more likely to be acutely ambivalent. They recognize their dilemma (e.g., that what they are doing is bad for them), and yet they perceive something of value in maintaining the status quo. The typical methods of coping with ambivalence in this stage of change are reminiscent of Lewin's (1941; 1938) and Dollard and Miller's (1950) descriptions of behavior when facing a dilemma: *letting random chance decide, vacillation, paralysis,* and *escape.* Obviously, such coping strategies impede the change process.

Even clients in the "preparing for action" stage express ambivalence. The trap of endlessly preparing to make some change and believing that action is actually taking place is an example of the underlying struggle of *wanting to have one's cake and eat it too.* To the *nonlinear*-thinking therapist, endless preparation for change reveals a client's vacillation as ambivalence. We discuss specific strategies and methods for working through ambivalence later in this chapter.

Behavioral Manifestations of Ambivalence

Ambivalence is a human behavior that has been documented throughout human civilization. Earlier in the chapter, we utilized the literature of ancient Greece to capture the heart of ambivalence (*feeling pulled in two different directions at once, being stuck between a rock and a hard place,* and *wanting to have one's cake and eat it too*). In the first-century CE writings of St. Paul, he poetically outlined the experience of struggling with ambivalence:

I don't understand myself at all. I really want to do what is right, but I can't. I do what I don't want to do— what I hate. I know perfectly well that what I am doing is wrong, and my bad conscience proves that I agree with these laws that I am breaking. ... No matter which way I turn, I can't make myself do right. I want to, but I can't. When I want to do good, I don't; and when I try not to do wrong, I do it anyway ... there is something else deep within me, in my lower nature, that is at war with my mind, and wins the fight, and makes me a slave. ... Oh, what a terrible predicament I am in! Who will free me from my slavery to this deadly lower nature? (*The Living Gospel*, Romans 7:15–24)

St. Paul's words could have come from the lips of many clients coming to any contemporary practitioner's office. Clients don't understand themselves and their behavior. They oftentimes know what they are doing is ill fated and bad for them but can't "make" themselves change. Those feelings and the words that typify them (i.e., "What a terrible predicament I am in. ...") describe people as feeling helpless to become calmer, feel less depressed, eat according to their diet, maintain sobriety, stop yelling at the kids, get along with their spouse, fall asleep naturally, and so on. St. Paul describes all of those things that he doesn't want to do. Without too much extrapolation, when St. Paul states that "something else deep within me, in my lower nature ... *is at war with my* [conscious] *mind, and wins the fight*" (emphasis added), he sounds like all troubled human beings who feel trapped by such apparent polarities (e.g., what someone wants to do, knows they should do or doesn't want to do and knows they shouldn't do it) and yet powerless to change. Immobilization, fretting, anxiety, depression, confusion, and the like (i.e., the development of symptoms) become the expression of the fact that an individual is being squeezed between these polarities. The contemporary client is as confused as St. Paul is by the fact that he cannot "make" himself do what he "knows" is the "right" thing. Modern psychotherapy research and literature have identified a number of psychological means by which practitioners can recognize client manifestations of ambivalence. They include the flight into illness or flight into health, secondary gain, resistance, and reactance. When viewed *nonlinearly*, the reality is that these behaviors actually begin to make sense! We detail these below.

FLIGHT INTO ILLNESS AND FLIGHT INTO HEALTH

As discussed in Chapter 4, a prudent clinician must exercise caution when assessing psychological symptoms. Such symptoms can overlap with signs of a physical illness. Thus, the possibility of a client having an organic illness must always be balanced with people's propensity to use illnesses as excuses. This is especially true if they feel that such complaints are likely to gain sympathy and concern from significant others in their life circumstances or provide some other advantage. This is analogous to the child who has not done his homework and does not want to go to school to "face the music." He might complain to an overanxious mother of a having a "stomachache," who then lets him stay at home "sick." Although he is *excused* from facing the consequences in school, he does pay a price by being confined to a bed and not being able to play outside.

Of course, the symptoms most frequently encountered by clinicians are some variation of anxiety and depression. *But it cannot be emphasized sufficiently that symptoms can also be generated by somatic conditions* (e.g., a heart condition)! In turn, a rule of thumb for the prudent practitioner is that somatic complaints by a client must always be taken as possibly having a true physiological origin. *As such, they must be evaluated by a physician until a client and his or her physician believe that there is no physiological basis for the person's somatic complaint(s).* In effect, one of the consequences that ambivalence can have is to prompt behavior known as a *flight into illness* or a *flight into disease*. A psychoanalytic term in origin, it represents the following: "flight away from a threatening reality by means of the conversion symptoms describes the paranosic or primary gain of the illness" (Hinsie & Campbell, 1970, p. 304). Under the influence of strongly felt and unrelenting ambivalence, a *flight into illness* can represent a client's maladaptive attempt to "solve" his dilemma—as illustrated with the client above, who solves his dilemma caused by not having done his homework by pretending to be sick. The "illness" or "disease" and its accompanying symptoms essentially *excuse* or *absolve* an individual from having to address those life circumstances that demand attention and will not relent. Simultaneously, the self-esteem of the individual is preserved. It is as though a client is addressing the significant individuals and life circumstances that he believes to hold him accountable and says, "I would have attended to this but for my illness!" After all, who can find fault with someone who is "sick"? In fact, Adler (1920/1959, 1956; Mosak & Shulman, 1967), taking a different view from that of Freud about the nature of symptomatic behavior, came to understand symptoms as having a purpose, namely, to preserve self-esteem and/or to excuse. Clinical Case Example 12.3 may prove useful in illustrating this.

Clinical Case Example 12.3: Flight Into Illness

Upon the advice of his family doctor, a middle-aged man with excellent job performance and more than 15 years at the same company sought treatment for a virulent depression. He reported a number of significant losses in the past 2 years (i.e., a very sad if not quarrelsome divorce, the loss of both parents, and the permanent disability of a sibling). His major complaint at the outset of treatment, however, concerned his depression over an unrelenting work environment with a boss who seemed to care nothing for people but rather only about getting the job done regardless of safety issues for his employees. That was a view with which the client disagreed. He had felt abused by this boss much as he had been physically and verbally abused by his stepfather. But in addition, he complained of a variety of other vague physical symptoms (e.g., headaches and episodes of confusion).

Upon the advice of the psychiatrist prescribing his medications, the client went on extended but paid sick leave. As his time on sick leave lengthened, he complained of periodic unrelenting headaches, lightheadedness, blurred vision, and bouts of confusion (e.g., on a trip with his girlfriend to see relatives, he woke up in a hotel room and was unclear about where he was and how he got there). In addition, he had sleep apnea, and was obese and diabetic. Under such circumstances, his physician rightly ordered specific tests for his apnea (i.e., to determine the precise pressure levels that would be necessary for his bi-pap machine, which he needed to help him breathe), blood work, and an electroencephalogram (EEG) and computerized tomography (CT) scan of the man's head to rule out such things as a possible space-occupying lesion and seizure disorders. In addition, a spinal tap was being contemplated to rule out still other possible organic causes for the man's varied physical complaints. Human beings don't necessarily come to see counselors, therapists, and others in the helping professions in pristine physical condition, and their complaints may be organic in nature.

Vague complaints of fatigue, chest pains, headaches, numbness and tingling in one's extremities, and so forth may very well have a physiological basis. Although they may also be psychological effects of wanting one's cake and eating it too, the prudent clinician does not make such an assumption. But upon receiving his disability compensation, the client was able to maintain his financial responsibilities to his family and was able to preserve his self-esteem as a responsible person. He applied for temporary disability and then permanent disability.

QUESTIONS

1. What are the "poles" of the ambivalence in this case?
2. What is or are the benefit(s) to the client of the vague physical complaints for which no organic explanation could be found?
3. What is or are the detrimental negative valence(s) of the client being "ill"?
4. What kind of nonlinear listening might be helpful in uncovering the client's ambivalence?

Unfortunately, the "success" of the symptoms at excusing oneself and escaping a more direct resolution of one's ambivalence extorts a heavy price. In Clinical Case Example 12.3 (the obese, diabetic, depressed man with varied other complaints), the client must now present himself as someone who is disabled. Use of nonlinear listening is a critical method for recognizing ambivalence when it manifests itself through a "flight into illness." In particular, listening for congruence, absence, presence, and resistance can help unravel the constructed illness and the poles of the client's ambivalence.

A *flight into health* (the reverse of a *flight into illness*) is another potential consequence of ambivalence. It is defined as "a relinquishing of symptoms that occurs not because the patient has resolved his neurosis, but rather as a defense against further probing by the analyst into painful, unconscious material" (Hinsie & Campbell, 1970, p. 304). As defined, the flight into health can be an expression of a client's *additional ambivalence* about (a) being in therapy, or (b) having to address the issues underlying his problems as a result of therapy. Such ambivalence can appear precipitously, with a symptom or problem temporarily getting better without a client really making any changes. This behavior is similar to that demonstrated by precontemplators. A *flight into health* alleviates further need for therapy, and a client is allowed to keep doing the things that were harmful in the first place, avoid the pain of addressing the problem, or both. Clinical Case Example 12.4 may prove helpful.

Clinical Case Example 12.4: Obsessive Thoughts

During an initial interview, a client reported that he has obsessive, intrusive thoughts while driving. Those thoughts suggest to him that he has hit someone. Even though he knows that is not the case, he feels compelled to stop every few blocks, get out of his car in order to check for evidence of a collision, and convince himself that he has not hit anyone. Asking somewhat routine questions, the therapist asks about the client's past, to which he gives vague answers. At the end of the session, the therapist suggests that given the current information about the problem as stated, it might be prudent to explore more information about his family of origin.

Before the next scheduled session, the client calls to tell the therapist that he has not experienced the thoughts and that he no longer needs therapy. Although it is impossible to say definitively whether he was "cured," the chances are that the client was feeling ambivalent about addressing issues related to his family of origin. Instead, the client developed a solution that allows him to avoid discussing such issues: He took a "flight into health." The "flight into health" allows the client to avoid the threat (whatever it might be) of discussing his family of origin.

QUESTIONS

1. What are the "poles" of the ambivalence in this case?
2. What are the benefits to the client of being "healthy"?
3. What are the liabilities to the client of being "healthy"?
4. What kind of nonlinear listening might be helpful in uncovering the client's ambivalence?

The behavior of the client in Clinical Case Example 12.4 is a form of maladaptive "problem solving." It is maladaptive because such "solutions" resolve the *immediate* problem (i.e., the client "escaped" potentially having to discuss or confront something that he viewed as threatening), but the client's "solution" leaves him with his original problem (albeit temporarily in abeyance). The more likely reality is that in such instances, the respite is temporary, the "problem" doesn't change, and the person continues to suffer. What is abundantly clear is that the client is not prepared to engage therapy with the "resolute perception" (see Hanna, 2001) needed for a successful outcome.

The flight into illness and the flight into health are both good examples of *client nonlinear thinking*. That is, the "flights" are behaviors motivated by *privately logical thinking* and not common sense. "Flights" are *privately logical* because they are based on skewed schemas and not based on common sense. Such reasoning motivates and allows a client to escape a threatening situation while her underlying issues remain unaddressed.

Commonsense problem solving is direct and addresses an issue in a straightforward way. In Clinical Case Example 12.4 (i.e., the individual who does not return to therapy), common sense suggests that when the therapist brings up the issue of family of origin, the client would likely say that talking about his family of origin is something that makes him feel anxious and is something that he doesn't want to talk about. That would be important information for the therapist. The master practitioner hearing such important information would endorse the client's courage in acknowledging the difficulty in discussing his family of origin, pay careful attention to that topic, and afford the client an opportunity to revisit it when the timing was appropriate (e.g., when the client is more comfortable in therapy and makes an oblique reference to family).

SECONDARY GAIN

On the surface, both a flight into health and a flight into illness are *useful* to a client. They have a *primary gain*. That is, the client derives a *direct* and *immediate* benefit from the effects of her behavior: The client is able to escape a threat because of "health" or "illness." In addition to a client deriving a direct and immediate benefit from a "flight," she can also derive a more subtle gain that is called a *secondary gain*. Secondary gains represent interpersonal or social advantages or actual financial compensations that are derived *indirectly* from symptomatic behavior. This is one reason why it is essential for nonlinear-thinking therapists to pay attention to the issue of ambivalence and the way it might be expressed in therapy: Client behaviors have potential hidden benefits (i.e., *secondary gains*) associated with behaviors that are difficult to relinquish (Rogers & Reinhardt, 1998).

Although not always evident, secondary gains are frequently very powerful reinforcers and motivators for behavior. An example can be found in the obese, insulin-dependent, diabetic client mentioned in Clinical Case Example 12.3. As a result of his "condition," he continues to collect most of his salary, even though his depression and vague physical complaints have no physiological basis. Another more brutal example would be that of a man physically abusing his wife. Such behavior gives the perpetrator a sense of power and control over his spouse by intimidation and coercion. When such an individual is asked to change (and even when he too espouses wanting to change), his resulting ambivalence is understandable. This is one reason why it is essential for nonlinear-thinking therapists to pay attention to the issue of ambivalence and the way it might be expressed in therapy: Client behaviors have potential hidden benefits (i.e., *secondary gains*) associated with behaviors that are difficult to relinquish (Rogers & Reinhardt, 1998). Although clients can never be "accused" of simply wanting to achieve *secondary gains* (e.g., compensation in the form of a settlement from a lawsuit, being excused from having to work, or being excused from responsibilities because of "illness"), the possibilities of such gains must be taken into account in one's "formulation of the problem" (see Chapter 9).

The concept of *secondary gain* has been discussed by both psychodynamic as well as behavioral schools of therapy, and has become a commonly accepted concept in understanding some client behavior. For psychodynamically oriented theorists, secondary gain is motivated by the protection from trauma that it affords the psyche. According to Rogers and Reinhardt (1998), "Incapacitation largely exempts an individual from social expectations and subsequent failures. Adoption of a sick role provides a socially acceptable escape from threatening circumstances and personal inadequacies" (p. 58).

On the other hand, behaviorally oriented theorists ascribe the motivation behind secondary gains to be the avoidance of negative or painful stimuli. That is, when individuals are placed in circumstances that produce pain or fear and discover behavior (e.g., becoming sick, or being docile and meek) that reduces the pain or fear, it becomes reinforced. Such reinforced behavior is adopted and becomes *learned* behavior. For example, recall the discussion of nonlinear thinking from Chapter 1 about the client who kept obsessing about his wife. The linear and primary "gain" for this behavior was that the client was hurt and upset over the breakup, and not able to "get over it" (*self-protecting*). The more threatening fear, however, was the need to "start dating again" and possibly being rejected and hurt. In order to reduce this fear, he found that obsessing about his ex-wife spared him from the potential pain of those circumstances, and thus obsessive behavior became *self-reinforcing* and represents a secondary gain (Rogers & Reinhardt, 1998). This is a classic example of ambivalence: A client feels like *he is being pulled in both directions* (i.e., "I should give her up, but I don't want to") while *wanting to have his cake and eat it too* (i.e., "I can still have her in my thoughts, even though I don't have her in reality"), and ultimately *finding himself stuck between a rock and a hard place* (i.e., "This really hurts because it reminds me that I really don't have her, but it's just as bad as having to start all over and be rejected with nothing").

Regardless of the proposed explanation[12] for a secondary gain (psychodynamic or behavioral), *nonlinear*-thinking processes are at the heart of understanding a client's development of the behavior. That is, the ostensible reason for a problem may not bear correspondence to the *underlying* reason. Rather, there are hidden (i.e., privately logical, *nonlinear*) motivations for behaviors that *make sense* or *serve a purpose* for a particular individual that may not be readily apparent.

Nonlinear listening (especially congruence, absence, and inference) can be very useful in discovering underlying ambivalence. This is especially so when there are schema-driven reasons for the secondary gain (e.g., unconsciously harboring thoughts such as "Everyone is in it for themselves," "I am lovable when I am vulnerable," or "I'm *entitled* to this insurance settlement money even though I'm not that disabled"). Three types of behaviors can be generated by the ambivalence underlying under such circumstances—"resistance," "reactance," or "safeguarding"—but they are all expressions of being *pulled in both directions*, while *wanting to have one's cake and eat it too*, but ultimately finding oneself stuck *between a rock and a hard place*. We will discuss in this chapter how each of these reveals the *nonlinear* nature of client thinking.

Resistance

Client demonstrations of ambivalence have been well-known since the beginnings of psychotherapy. From Charcot and Janet to Freud, the earliest clients of psychotherapy displayed ambivalence (e.g., hysterical paralysis), and making sense of this behavior was often difficult. In his early work, Freud interpreted ambivalent behavior demonstrated by his clients as being a sign of noncompliance. Thus, when they would not comply with his therapeutic interventions, he called it "resistance." In traditional psychoanalytic theory, resistance is a "defense mechanism" employed by the client in an effort to "repress intra-psychic impulses that conflicted with social expectations and self-perceptions" (Beutler, Moleiro, & Talebi, 2002, p. 130). As an unconscious process, resistance allows a client to avoid certain thoughts and feelings that may cause anxiety or embarrassment. Resistance is thus used in the service of protecting the ego (or "self") and is associated with a fear of change (Beutler et al., 2002; Bugental & Bugental, 1984; Hanna, 2001).

Whether or not resistance is considered a sign of psychopathology (as in the analytic sense), it is certain that it can be disruptive. As Beutler et al. (2002) have put it, resistance "is likely to be disruptive to relationships and social activities" (p. 130). Correspondingly, resistance has generally been viewed as disruptive to the treatment process. According to Chamberlain et al. (1984; as cited in Miller & Rollnick, 2002), resistance is often seen as some form of arguing, interrupting, negating, or ignoring behavior. They interpret all such behaviors as being designed to interrupt or halt therapeutic progress (see Information Box 12.2).

Information Box 12.2: Four Process Categories of Resistant Client Behavior

1. Arguing
   A. Challenging: challenging the accuracy of what the counselor says
   B. Discounting: questioning the counselor's personal authority
   C. Hostility: expressing direct hostility at the counselor
2. Interrupting
   A. Talking over
   B. Cutting off
3. Negating
   A. Blaming: Other people are at fault for the behavior.
   B. Disagreeing: "Yes, but …"
   C. Excusing.
   D. Claiming impunity: Client claims not to be in danger.
   E. Minimizing.
   F. Pessimism.
   G. Reluctance: expresses reservation.
   H. Unwilling to change: lack of desire to change.
4. Ignoring
   A. Inattention
   B. Nonanswer
   C. No response
   D. Sidetracking

Source: Taken from Chamberlain, Patterson, Reid, Kavanaugh, and Forgatch (1984), as cited in Miller and Rollnick (2002, p. 48).

All of the resistance categories outlined by Chamberlain et al. (1984) can be seen as attempts at gaining power over the therapy process or the therapist. Thus, historically, resistance was considered something that has to be overcome in order to move therapy forward so that a client could bring into conscious awareness material (e.g., unwanted thoughts, behaviors, and feelings) that is being repressed. Beutler et al. (2002), however, suggested that there is a sizeable body of literature implying that *the process of therapy is not necessarily enhanced by directly confronting or arousing resistant behavior* in the client: "Effective psychotherapy may well have the aim to induce as little resistance as possible while still moving the patient toward his or her goals" (p. 132). Merely avoiding client resistance, however, could be considered a demonstration of *linear* thinking (i.e., *linear thinking* implies that if a therapist avoids client resistance, the therapy will turn out well). More to the point, however, therapists must understand a client's behavior and tailor their therapeutic interventions to *meet a client's needs in light of resistant behavior*.

In discussing the stages of change model in Chapter 4, a client who may be attempting to avoid the therapeutic process by "forgetting" to do a "homework" assignment does not need to be managed in the same way as a client who is openly hostile toward her therapist. Both are manifestations of behavior with underlying ambivalence, but each requires a different therapeutic approach that (a) takes into account a client's ambivalence and stage of change, and (b) preserves or repairs the therapeutic alliance. As with the other manifestations of ambivalence, using nonlinear listening is crucial in helping a client to get beyond the resistant behaviors to the underlying ambivalence. In addition, understanding a client's schema dynamics (i.e., view of self, others, and life and the world) is important in defining the poles of the ambivalence. Often, by understanding a client's schema dynamics and her emotional states, a *nonlinear*-thinking clinician can determine how to best help his client work through ambivalence. In other words, one size does not fit all. Client factors (e.g., a client's readiness for change, schema dynamics, and emotional factors) need to be taken into account when determining how to best to best help one's client work through ambivalence. This requires *nonlinear* thinking.

Reactance

Thus far, our discussion of client manifestations of ambivalence suggests a paradoxical phenomenon: Those clients who voluntarily come for counseling or psychotherapy will demonstrate resistant behavior(s). Linear thinking suggests that this contradiction is confusing: If clients want the help of a therapist, why would they be resistant to such help?

Many nonpsychoanalytic or psychodynamic therapists find it difficult to adopt constructs from a dynamic perspective. The assumptions and implications of these constructs simply do not match up with their view of the therapeutic process. In the process of encountering client ambivalence, however, many nondynamic therapists have needed a way to understand it and address it. One construct that has been adopted from social psychology by cognitively or behaviorally oriented clinicians was the construct of *reactance*. Reactance in a person occurs

> whenever he or she believe[s] that free behaviors are being threatened with elimination. Thus, even normal reactance tendencies are both differentially responsive to an individual's disposition to perceive threat and motivational in that they direct the individual toward restoring the threatened behaviors. Once activated, reactance is observed in oppositional behavior, noncompliance, and rigidity. (Beutler et al., 2002, p. 130)

In other words, reactance occurs as *a typical response* that human beings demonstrate to threat or coercion, not a response that arises from more unconscious processes that prevent thoughts or feelings from being expressed. This explanation has allowed for nonanalytic therapists to devise methods for working with this manifestation of ambivalence. We propose that clients who demonstrate reactance manifest ambivalence by trying to escape (i.e., oppositional behavior), vacillating (i.e., noncompliance), becoming immobilized (i.e., rigidity), or letting fate decide, just as Dollard and Miller's (1950) experiments suggested.

In therapy, reactance can be thought of as a naturally occurring process. As described above, at some level a client intuitively senses that a therapist will try to persuade him to change his usual pattern of behaviors—and that may be perceived as a threat to the client's freedom (Beutler et al., 2002; Brehm, 1966; Brehm & Brehm, 1981). According to Hanna (2001), clients who are actively engaged in therapy may feel the ambivalence of giving up control of their lives: "People who actively fight beneficial change do so because their beliefs and general outlook are so delicately in balance that change appears as a threat" (p. 21).

We conclude this brief discussion of *reactance* by noting that clients are ambivalent about issues that are troubling them *and* ironically they are ambivalent about getting the help that they need to resolve the problem for which they have sought treatment! As a result, clients express their hesitancy to therapy itself in the form of noncompliance with the therapist, *because therapy itself is a process that naturally arouses varying degrees of reactance*! Hence, therapy produces the feeling of being *pulled in two directions* (i.e., "I want to change, but I don't want to be forced to change") while *wanting to have one's cake and eat it too* (i.e., "I know that I need outside help to change, but I don't want to give up control"), and ultimately finding oneself stuck *between a rock and a hard place* (i.e., "I can't stay the same, but I'm not sure I want to change"). Understanding such ironies is part of the challenge and excitement of becoming a therapist. Recognizing such challenges and knowing how to comfortably react to them comprise a mark of a *nonlinear*-thinking master practitioner.

CONCLUSION

A *nonlinear*-thinking master practitioner is more likely to sense a client's feelings of ambivalence, and he or she (a) expects it as a natural part of the therapeutic process, and (b) understands that a client's behavior might be a method of protection from threat (e.g., the therapist, or change itself). If therapists are able to discern these nonlinear thought processes and utilize their alliance and rupture skills (i.e., "vibrating" with a client's feelings like a tuning fork; see Chapter 6), they may be able to see past a client's flights, gains, resistance, or reactance, and understand its true meaning: an expression of client ambivalence. Seen as such, it is easier to engage a client than by seeing her behavior as uncooperativeness or a power struggle. Understanding the manifestations of ambivalence and their impact on clients on and the change and therapeutic processes are only half the battle. We now turn our attention to the practitioner's role in helping clients to resolve their ambivalence.

ENDNOTES

1. The "journey home" was a metaphor that Homer used to convey man's search for freedom from suffering.
2. In case you were interested to know what happened to Odysseus: Circe helps him to resolve the double bind he is in by instructing Odysseus to have his crew tie him to the mast while they row through to safety with their ears plugged with wax. He listened to Circe and did just this. Odysseus was able to hear the Sirens' song and sail safely toward home—although the story doesn't end there.
3. Except for Jason, but he wasn't able to do it without the intervention of one of the gods.
4. Odysseus chose to avoid Charybdis, but doing so was at the expense of losing six sailors to Scylla's multiple maws (i.e., mouths with voracious appetites).
5. A great deal of support for Lewin's (1941) model of conflict comes from animal research based on the behavior theories of Clark Hull and Neal Miller (1971).
6. Being "listed" refers to a list of candidates according to priority as determined by criteria developed by the United Network for Organ Sharing (UNOS).
7. The treatment team faced the pressure of time to make a decision and "list" the woman for transplant in time to provide an opportunity to save her life or treat her palliatively. But, whenever the subject would arise, she would clearly waver with ambivalence between alternatives, as described above. The woman eventually acquiesced to the pleading of her husband and children, consented to transplant, was eventually transplanted, and is still alive as of this writing.
8. There are many different manifestations of denial.
9. A clearly symbolic reference to her "throwing up" (i.e., vomiting), which the therapist asked her to repeat. Upon repeating what it was that she said and hearing her own words, she began to smile and laugh at having "caught" herself in a moment of true understanding.
10. A reference to what it was that she was feeling.
11. Perhaps another oblique and unconscious reference to her vomiting.
12. Rogers and Reinhardt (1998) have a third explanatory approach for secondary gain: the forensic approach. This looks for the potential legal or monetary reward as the motivation (or secondary gain) for problem behavior (particularly in the absence of physical evidence of a problem). This is frequently seen in cases of bogus workman's compensation claims, fraudulent disability clams, issues of competency to stand trial, and other legal or quasi-legal proceedings.

The Domain of Addressing and Resolving Ambivalence

13

Part 2: Working With and Resolving Client Ambivalence

CONTENTS

MANAGING AND RESOLVING AMBIVALENCE: THE PRACTITIONER'S ROLE

Level I therapists who tend to focus more on their *own* anxieties are less able to see beyond surface behaviors, and less able to appreciate the true nature of ambivalence. By contrast, a Level II therapist is clearly more focused on client behavior than his own. As such, he is in a better position to be able to discern and understand his client's behavior in terms of its underlying ambivalence (i.e., a type of conflict or dilemma). Aided by *nonlinear thinking*, such focus is more likely to result in moving the therapeutic process forward to a successful conclusion. Given the dynamic importance of ambivalence in the change process and its integral connection to emotions generated by threats to schemas, *nonlinear thinking* is required to manage a client's ambivalence and help the person to resolve it.

MOTIVATIONAL INTERVIEWING AND WORKING WITH AMBIVALENCE

In Chapter 4, we presented research on moving clients from one stage of change to the next. In concert with helping clients to move along the change process, Miller and Rollnick (2002) developed a clinical model called *motivational interviewing* (MI) or *motivational enhancement therapy* (MET), whose central tenet involves addressing clients' ambivalence and helping them to resolve it.

Empirical support for the efficacy of MI also comes from recent empirical research. For example, Miller, Benefield, and Tonigan (1993) and Burke, Arkowitz, and Menchola (2003) have suggested that MI-based interventions are indeed clinically effective and potent in addressing problem drinking, behavior that is difficult to change. As Tashiro and Mortensen (2006) pointed out,

> Meta-analyses have found motivational interviewing for substance abuse to be as efficacious as other treatment modalities but that a lower dose of treatment is required (three fewer sessions) than with typical treatments (Burke, Arkowitz, & Menchola, 2003). This raises the obvious question about why fewer sessions of motivational interviewing produce the same effects as other interventions. (p. 962)

Although the stages of change model (see Chapter 4) identifies where along the continuum of change a particular client may be, MI, in essence, provides a *nonlinear way of thinking* about ambivalence. It *facilitates* psychological movement regarding ambivalence from any one stage of change to the next stage by working *with* a client's natural propensities for growth, competence, changing, and protectively staying the same. Central to MI is the nonlinear understanding that clients paradoxically express a desire to change and simultaneously resist change and seek to maintain the status quo. This is because change (potentially) disrupts a client's schematized view of self, others, or life or the world, which can precipitate feelings of failure, shame, embarrassment, loss of prestige, and the like.

Miller and Rollnick (2002) outlined several strategies for addressing and resolving ambivalence, loosely classified as "reflective responses" and "beyond reflective responses" (see Information Box 13.1, "Strategies for Resolving Ambivalence"). Reflective responses are similar to the *linear*-listening and -responding approaches outlined in Chapters 2 and 3 in which a therapist simply paraphrases and reflects back a client's feeling, sentiments, attitudes, and so on. In this way, a therapist is able to help a client thoroughly explore each side of her ambivalence. It is a method that requires patience and subtlety rather than mimicry. One of the reflective responses, called *amplified reflection*, may include some interpretation or logical extension of a client's argument (at times rendered to the point of hyperbole). For example, a client complaining of having an overwhelming, chronic back pain that precludes returning to work refuses to adhere to his physician's recommendation for treatment. By use of "logical extension" of the dilemma, a therapist can explore all of the ways that a client's life will be impacted when he is no longer able to get out of bed due to the pain (e.g., "So, your back condition *may* take a turn for the worse if you aggravate it, and then there would *really* be a price to pay—you might have to have back surgery, and that can really be treacherous!")

Another of the reflective responses is called *double-sided reflection*, in which a therapist simultaneously affirms both sides of a client's ambivalence (e.g., "I can see how it would be fulfilling to pursue your dreams of acting; after all, how many times do we get to go through life? I can also see how having a steady job and a regular paycheck would calm your fears of having to rely on your parents to support you"). At times, a client may simply be fatigued by the endless back-and-forth and resolve her ambivalence by making a decision (which ends the processing). These are powerful methods for helping to move a client from an earlier stage of change (i.e., precontemplation or contemplation) to a more advanced stage of change in a way that preserves the therapeutic alliance.

Information Box 13.1: Strategies for Resolving Ambivalence

Reflective responses (*linear*)

- Simple reflection
- Amplified reflection
- Double-sided reflection

Other responses beyond reflection (*nonlinear*)

- Shifting focus
- Reframing
- Agreeing with a twist
- Emphasizing personal choice and control
- Coming alongside

Source: Adapted from Miller and Rollnick (2002); parentheses added.

Another response to client ambivalence, called *beyond reflection*, appears to have many elements in common with principles of *nonlinear* thinking, as well as similarities to the *nonlinear* responding outlined in Chapter 3 and elsewhere in this text. These include shifting focus, reframing, agreeing with a twist, emphasizing personal choice and control, and coming alongside (therapeutic paradox).[1] *Shifting focus* refers to parrying or evading a troublesome subject posed by a client, usually to arouse resistance and defensiveness, and derail the therapeutic process (i.e., safeguarding). For example, a teenage client may say, "You're just going to judge me by my appearance and say that I need to listen to my parents, and do what they say." If a therapist tries to deal with this subject confrontationally, he will either get into a power struggle (e.g., "Your parents want what is best for you") or try too hard to ally with the client. Shifting focus sidesteps the ambivalence in the hope of engaging the client in therapy (e.g., "Well, maybe they are right, and maybe you are right, but I know that I don't know nearly enough about your situation to make that determination!"). At this point, the client can decide to explore each side of the conflict (e.g., "I want to do it my way, which will hurt my parents," versus "If I listen to them, I sacrifice my individuality"). The nonlinear methods of listening and responding (e.g., for congruence, absence, inference, presence, and resistance) are useful here as well.

Agreeing with a twist is accomplished when a therapist reflects back what the client says with agreement, but also adds a new frame of reference to it. Consider, for example, that a client is seeing a therapist for depression, but doesn't feel much hope for a recovery from her symptoms: "I've been down this road before, Doc. I may feel better for a while, but it always comes back." Agreeing with a twist, a therapist may respond by saying, "Recurrence is a common feature in people who suffer from your condition, and while one episode may feel like one too many, there are also long periods when your mood seems to be very stable and you can be productive." In other words, the therapist validates that although the client has a right to be concerned, she would be squandering a good opportunity if she didn't make use of her time when she was not sick.

Emphasizing personal choice and control is a way to deflect client criticism and reactance by asserting the belief that it is the client who ultimately has the "say-so" in determining the course of therapy—and his or her life. For example, a client may feel that she is being pressured by her therapist to make a decision and lash out, "I have five kids that I have to look out for. If I leave my husband, who is going to feed them, and clothe them? I'd need to get a job and then pay for day care." The agreement with a twist may sound like "Having a large family is a great financial strain, and going out on your own is an enormous personal strain. Perhaps staying in an unsatisfactory and abusive relationship may be the best option open to you right now." Again, many of the nonlinear-listening and -responding methods discussed above and in Chapters 2 and 3 are helpful in these situations to move the client along the stages of change.[2]

Clinical Exercise 13.1: Nonlinear Listening and MI Interventions to Help Resolve Ambivalence

Instructions: Read each of the following case vignettes, and develop *reflective* (i.e., linear) or *beyond reflective* (i.e., *nonlinear*) responses that best describe the client's behavior.

1. A client comes to therapy following an argument with his wife that became physical. As a result, the police became involved, and the client was required to come to therapy. Although you invite the client to talk about the incident, he devotes much of the time in therapy to talking about how unfair the criminal justice system is, and how "all that the cops and judges want is my money."
2. A client enters therapy and describes how she had been to several therapists but hasn't found the right one yet. She tells you that she has heard great things about you and that in just the brief time that you have been together, she really feels that you will be the one to help her solve her problems.
3. A client comes to therapy and states that he no longer feels any joy from life. When asked about his background, he states that it was "normal," but later proceeds to describe how his mother had to be hospitalized following the accidental drowning of his younger brother when he was 6 years old. Following your empathetic expression of the magnitude of the loss for the family, the client's only remark was to say, "Yeah, mom took it kind of bad."
4. A couple comes into therapy because the wife is diagnosed with major depression, and has been hospitalized twice for it. The husband made the appointment with the therapist and begins the session by saying, "My wife's condition makes it hard to do anything. I have to do a lot around the house, especially when the depression gets bad, but I don't mind as long as she gets well." As the wife begins to tell her story, the husband either attempts to "correct" her or shakes his head to indicate "no" when she makes statements about her illness.

5. A client comes for his second therapy session following what you believed to be a successful first session. The client's presenting concern was anxiety, especially around his supervisor at an accounting firm. At the end of the initial session, you and the client agreed to some specific homework tasks that included speaking up at a staff meeting, setting up an appointment to speak with the supervisor, and inquiring if a female coworker who he has been interested in is dating anyone. When he returns, he says that he didn't accomplish any of the tasks because "the meeting went too long, the secretary was never at her desk to make the appointment, and I just didn't get around to it" (i.e., asking about the coworker).

6. A client comes to session for help in dealing with her 6-year-old son, whom she describes as "uncontrollable." The client discusses how she punishes the child and physically disciplines him by spanking, but it doesn't work. You suggest using logical consequences with the child, and time-out procedures instead of spanking. In response, the client says, "Oh, I don't think that will work," but agrees to try it. At the next session, the client reports that she tried using a time-out, but that the child didn't behave, and that she "had" to use physical discipline.

QUESTIONS

1. Describe the poles of the dilemmas that each client is facing.
2. What kinds of nonlinear listening would be used to best understand the client's ambivalence?
3. Choose one of the MI methods of responding to the ambivalence presented above that would help the client best work through the ambivalence (*amplified reflection, double-sided reflection, shifting focus, reframing,* or *agreeing with a twist*).
4. How do you think that the client in question 3 will react to the intervention that you chose?

VARIATION

Form small groups, and discuss your answers to the questions. Which approaches were chosen? Was there agreement on which approaches might work better than others? Then discuss with the entire group.

USE OF THE THERAPEUTIC ALLIANCE: KEEPING A CLIENT PROBLEM FOCUSED IN THE FACE OF AMBIVALENCE

Even if clients come to therapy and insist that they are ready to make changes, when it comes time to "face the music," they may not feel or be prepared to do so and hence feel very vulnerable. They may engage in many types of behaviors (described above) that can have negating effects on the therapeutic process. It is incumbent on a therapist to see such behaviors as normative to the therapeutic process, and then bring those feelings (and the values, beliefs, and attitudes responsible for them) as clearly as possible into clients' awareness at a pace they can tolerate without being overwhelmed, and help them to resolve those feelings. Erickson (1977) stated,

> The patient does not come to you just because you are a therapist. The patient comes to be protected or helped in some regard. But the personality is very vital to the person, and he doesn't want you to do too much, he does not want you to do it too suddenly. You've got to do it slowly ... gradually ... in the order in which he can assimilate it ... you approach everything as slowly and as rapidly as the patient can endure

the material. … The patient doesn't consciously know what the problems are, no matter how good a story he tells you, because that's a conscious story. (pp. 20–21)

Erickson is cautioning therapists to understand that clients are "stuck between a rock and a hard place"— that they want to change, and simultaneously want things to stay the same and want to be protected. Therein lies the challenge to becoming a master practitioner: *helping to identify and understand a client's ambivalence, bringing it into her awareness*, and *keeping it in the focus of the therapy while at the same time not overwhelming the client, who is in therapy because she is not necessarily prepared to address the life circumstances that are immobilizing to her.*

When a client is faced with the choice of whether or not to move forward in therapy and feels *pulled in two directions at the same time*, a therapist must reassuringly guide him through sometimes paralyzing feelings. In Chapters 6 and 7, we presented research that overwhelmingly supports the importance of the therapeutic alliance as the foundation from which change can occur. As discussed in Chapter 12, clients who are not willing to tolerate their anxiety are more likely to "fly into health" (or "illness"), or they are liable to vacillate and become paralyzed for fear of making a wrong decision. They may resemble precontemplators or contemplators who seemingly don't want to change. But, such clients may be attempting to *protect* themselves from feeling *overwhelmed* about the potential consequences of making changes. As always, the efficacy of all therapeutic transactions, including managing a client's ambivalence, is contingent upon maintaining the therapeutic alliance.

For a therapist, according to Miller and Rollnick (2002), ambivalence, resistant behaviors, and the therapeutic alliance are integrally related: "Counsel in a directive [i.e., linear], confrontational manner, and client resistance goes up. Counsel in a reflective, supportive manner, and resistance goes down while change talk increases" (p. 9).

USE OF THE THERAPEUTIC ALLIANCE: KEEPING CLIENTS FOCUSED ON THEIR PROBLEM IN THE FACE OF AMBIVALENCE

There is a subtle but important distinction between *what* a therapist does and *how* she goes about therapeutic activities. Relative to conducting therapy in general and addressing client ambivalence in particular, we have advocated that it is essential to avoid ruptures to the therapeutic alliance and manage potentially disruptive client behaviors (e.g., resistance and reactance). *How* a therapist goes about addressing client ambivalence, avoiding alliance ruptures, managing disruptive client behaviors, and conducting treatment in general requires certain therapist attitudes, and a certain mind-set and disposition. We will discuss four *general principles or qualities* considered to be central to help guide practitioners in this regard: *professionalism, collaboration, evocation*, and *autonomy* (Miller & Rollnick, 2002).

GENERAL THERAPIST PRINCIPLES AND QUALITIES FOR DEALING WITH CLIENT AMBIVALENCE

Professionalism

As discussed in Chapters 6 and 7, the term *professionalism* refers to a therapist being ever mindful of the need to conduct himself according to the requirements of professional rules of conduct (i.e., ethical principles) and the *fiduciary relationship* between himself and his clients. No matter what the *personal qualities* of a client may be (e.g., appealing or unappealing), fiduciary obligations require that a client's interests are served by the therapeutic relationship and come before a practitioner's interests. Thus, a client must never be taken advantage of by a therapist for the latter's own gratification, and a practitioner is obligated to follow the rules of professional conduct as determined by his profession.

Collaboration

Given today's understanding of the processes of therapy, there are few if any theoreticians, researchers, or practitioners who would deny that therapy is a *collaborative process.* The theoretical orientation of a practitioner is irrelevant in this regard and has been advocated as far back as Adler's (1956) admonition that therapists must "renounce superior authority" and Goldberg's (1977) call for a "therapeutic partnership." *Collaboration* refers to the sense of a partnership between client and therapist whereby a client is treated like and correspondingly feels like and participates in the therapy as an equal partner. As a result, she experiences the therapist as honoring her struggles and perspective.

Evocation

Evocation refers to a therapist's belief that clients have all of the resources and motivation needed for change, but are not necessarily accessing them or utilizing them effectively. In effect, a therapist's job is to evoke a client's intrinsic (i.e., internal) motivation and resources in the service of therapeutic goals. This is accomplished by drawing on the client's perceptions and values as well as untapped resources.

Autonomy

Autonomy is a moral value. As Beauchamp and Childress (1989) noted, however, it is actually *respect for autonomy* that is the value. It thus refers to a therapist's reverence for a client's right to self-determination, particularly in therapy, as well as his right to make informed choices. But such autonomy is not absolute.[3] By addressing a client's ambivalence in a collaborative and evocative manner, a therapist demonstrates respect for client autonomy and allows a client to make an informed choice to change or not (Miller & Moyers, 2004; Miller & Rollnick, 2002). These therapist qualities are all compatible with a *nonlinear* approach to therapy. Clinical Case Example 13.1 might be helpful.

Clinical Case Example 13.1: The Right Pace of Therapeutic Movement

A late-middle-aged, multitalented man was engaged in the process of making changes in life-long behavior patterns. Among decisions he had implemented were severing ties with family members who by every measure appeared to have had very toxic effects on him. Gender confusion, cross-dressing, and poor relationships with women were among the issues through which he was making his way. Especially important to him were gains he was making with his burgeoning feelings of true masculinity. On an almost daily basis, he recognized that he was a man, had the feelings of a "man," felt good about dressing like a man, and was looking forward to growing those feelings. The therapist remarked that how he would relate to women (i.e., a therapeutic goal the client and therapist had established) might be the "next" goal. The man remarked, "We're at different understandings. I'm just beginning to feel good about wearing my Jockey shorts and T-shirt, and you're talking about me putting on a tuxedo and cufflinks!"

EXERCISE

1. What are the poles of the dilemma that the client is experiencing?
2. What did the client's remark signal to the therapist?
3. How would you evaluate the client's remarks? Would you consider them positive? If so, why? Would you consider them negative? If so, why so?
4. How might you respond to this client?
5. Which of Miller and Rollnick's (2002) "qualities" listed in the text would you use, and how?
6. How would you now suggest moving the client forward without rupturing the therapeutic alliance?

This is a good example of how the therapist can sometimes be both "wrong" and "right" at the same time, and how a well-established, positive therapeutic alliance can help work through difficulties (particularly with ambivalence). In the discussion that followed, the man indicated that the prospect of engaging in more "normal" relationships with women was immobilizing to him. Although he was making progress, he still felt quite ambivalent. He wasn't fully comfortable with the change in his behavior—yet. With a strong therapeutic alliance, client and therapist were able to reconcile the therapist apparently guiding the client further and faster than he felt ready for. Indeed, without the foundation of a positive therapeutic relationship, the client would not be willing to tolerate the anxiety of facing troubling issues, and would likely try to "escape" (by prematurely terminating the therapy). In this case, the client felt secure enough with the therapist to voice his concern about moving too quickly. Client feedback, as discussed in Chapter 5, proved essential in maintaining the "right" pace of change.

In addition to the *general principles* described above, therapists have a variety of more specific approaches to ambivalence that they can utilize to help clients resolve their ambivalence and move toward desired changes. We discuss some of these below.

MANAGING CLIENT AMBIVALENCE: SPECIFIC LEVEL II STRATEGIES AND INTERVENTIONS

The Level I and Level II domains work in tandem to facilitate change. It is the Level I domains that are important for setting the basic framework for counseling and establishing the therapeutic alliance. The alliance is essential for creating the context and environment for resolving client ambivalence. In turn, it is the Level II domains pertaining to schemas and emotional reactions that are at the very heart of understanding, addressing, and resolving ambivalence and making lasting change in the client. Most conflicts that clients experience are the result of incongruity between their schema dynamics (i.e., view of self, others, or the world or life) and the reality of the circumstances that they face.

Resolving Ambivalence: "Holding a Mirror Up to a Client"

No matter what approach (linear or nonlinear), the underlying goal in this domain—and the most important task that a counselor must perform—is to help clients resolve their ambivalence. *Confronting is a process of directing someone's attention to something* that she *potentially* avoids looking at (either deliberately or unconsciously). The qualifier *potentially* is used because therapists of necessity have *limited certainty* about being accurate in their formulation of exactly what it is that a client may be avoiding due to her ambivalences. Confronting is often thought of as "holding up a mirror" to a client and *asking* her to look at or "bring to light" something that she appears to be avoiding. According to Hanna (2001),

> Confronting is the function of actively observing and closely scrutinizing a problem, issue, thought, behavior, emotion, person, situation, or relationship. The person uses his or her attention and powers of viewing to look into, through and even beyond a problem or issue … In terms of the actual change process, confronting involves an intentional, sustained, and deliberate directing of attention or awareness toward anything that is painful, intimidating, or stultifying. It involves continuing to examine or investigate— "digging in one's heels"—in spite of fear, confusion, or the tendency toward avoiding or acting out. Almost anything at all can be confronted: mental images, memories, emotional pain, behaviors of all varieties, thoughts, thought patterns, beliefs, persons, places, objects, and relationships. (p. 71)

At Level I and at times Level II, perhaps the biggest concern about the use of *confronting* is practitioners' misunderstanding of its true therapeutic meaning and intent. To begin with, *confronting* is mistaken for *confrontation*. Synonyms for *confrontation* are words such as *quarrel*, *argument*, *war of words*, and *conflict*. Unfortunately, all of these synonyms suggest pejorative and aggressive images of being "in your face"! Any therapist behavior that implies being *confrontational* (i.e., deliberately or unintentionally hostile in nature) is decidedly counterproductive, ill advised, and likely born of ill-conceived therapist motivations (e.g., frustration or anger) or misguided intentions. The purpose of being *confrontational* is most likely to prevail over a client (e.g., insisting to be "right") regarding an issue under discussion. This is counterproductive for any therapeutic endeavor (Horvath & Bedi, 2002). Such therapist behavior places a client in a "one-down" position—a place from which it is difficult to move forward. Thus, *extreme caution* is urged regarding practitioners' understanding and use of *confronting*.

The reasoning behind such caution is nonlinear in nature. Rather than being immune from having problematic encounters with life and living, practitioners are human beings. This subject is unfortunately avoided in the psychotherapy literature except in discussion of "therapist burnout" (e.g., see Cherniss, 1995; Kottler, 1993). Correspondingly, therapists are subject to the same frustrations, ups and downs of everyday living, and emotional reactions to situations, circumstances, and people as the clients they serve. The all-too-evident truth is that practitioners at any level are not automatons. As such, from time to time, even journeymen practitioners can find themselves frustrated, feeling ineffectual and even exasperated in response to clients apparently not making any movement toward resolution of ambivalences. Such responses can be perceived by therapists' personalities as threats to *their* view of self (e.g., "I'm not as good at my profession as I should be" or "I'm really not as good a therapist as I think I am"). Should that develop, a therapist's use of *confrontation* (i.e., a learned therapeutic intervention) unfortunately becomes subject to being tainted with defensiveness no matter how slight or subtle. Most clients are already exquisitely sensitive to such "messages" of rejection. Should that occur, it can become highly corrosive to the therapeutic alliance.

Clients must feel that their therapist is aligned with them before they will engage in a dialogue about change. This means that a therapist must walk a delicate tightrope between understanding a client's perspective and supporting the status quo of destructive behaviors. This understanding leads to acceptance of the client (at whatever his stage of change) and a sense of "safety" for the client, which, in turn, facilitates an exploration of ambivalence. Even when a therapist must confront or redirect a client's attention back to the therapeutic tasks at hand, the strength of the therapeutic alliance, empathy, and support expressed will often balance discomfort that a client may be feeling due to his ambivalence. It is the therapist who must guide her client through the sometimes immobilizing ambivalence. But, clients must be prepared to work through their ambivalence, and in order to do so they must be able *to trust the therapeutic relationship.* Thus, it is reiterated that the most fruitful way to understand *confronting* is by keeping the focus of therapeutic attention on clients' problems, their symptoms that result from their dealing with their problems, and the ambivalence(s) that clients have concerning the problems.

To illustrate the care that must be taken regarding the difference between *confronting* and being confrontational, Miller et al. (1993) found that:

specific and observed therapist behaviors commonly associated with the term *confrontational* were found to predict poorer outcomes for problem drinkers. These findings are consistent with earlier reports that a directive–confrontational style evokes client resistance (Patterson & Forgatch, 1985) and is associated with unfavorable outcomes in treating alcohol problems (Miller et al., 1980; Valle, 1981). Indeed, the level of client resistance evoked during a treatment session appeared to be negatively related to long-term treatment success. (p. 460)

In their study of the influence of different therapist styles on client drinking, Miller et al. (1993) also noted, "Therapist styles did not differ in overall impact on drinking, but a single therapist behavior was predictive ($r = .65$) of 1-year outcome such that the more the therapist confronted, the more the client drank" (p. 455). Seemingly contradictory of these findings, Hanna (2001) noted that almost all modalities of psychotherapy confront clients in some way. Orlinsky, Grave, and Parks (1994) found that focusing directly on the problem in therapy was related to positive outcomes in 64% of the findings they investigated. Are these finding contradictory? The answer is "No." Miller et al. appeared to have the most cogent rationale for understanding this subtle but exceptionally important issue:

Confrontation and empathy are not, we believe, inherently incompatible. In its etymology, confrontation literally means "to bring face to face," which does not necessarily mean going head to head. To confront is to help another person face the facts. In this sense, confrontation is a *goal* rather than a therapeutic procedure (Miller and Rollnick, 1991). What constitutes the most effective means for accomplishing this goal remains an open question. (p. 460)

The "key" to understanding how to keep a client focused on her ambivalences regarding the choices she faces without alienating her is *empathy* and understanding that confrontation is a "goal" rather than a method or "technique." We present Clinical Case Example 13.2 to illustrate.

Clinical Case Example 13.2: Facing ("Confronting") Ambivalence

A female client in her late 20s entered therapy because she had been having panic attacks and was beginning to have difficulty leaving her home (agoraphobia). During her initial visits, it is learned that she is living with her boyfriend of 4 years; she loves him very much and doesn't want to jeopardize their relationship. They met at a club, and much of their dating life has revolved around the "club scene" (i.e., music, drinking, dancing, and late nights). About a year ago, the client began to feel tired of the same old "scene." She mentioned to her boyfriend that she wanted to do other things besides the "clubs." She reported to her therapist that her boyfriend said, "I couldn't be with someone who isn't into this scene. That is one of the things that I love most about you. Besides, you know that I don't want to be tied down."

About 6 months later, she had her first panic attack in a club while there with her boyfriend. Subsequently, she has had three other panic attacks. Each time she experienced such an episode, she reported that her boyfriend was supportive—but she expresses fears that he is beginning to think that her panic attacks are becoming "old."

EXERCISE

1. What kind of dilemma (i.e., conflict—e.g., approach–approach) would you describe this as?
2. How would you describe the "poles" of the dilemma?
3. How did the client's ambivalence manifest itself? As far as can be determined, what are the client's schema dynamics?
4. How would a therapist directly "confront" her about this?

5. Recalling the exercise described in Exercise 2.3, "Beginning the Use of Nonlinear Thinking," devise five different ways in which a therapist might bring this client "face-to-face" with her behavior. Remember that tone of voice, inflection, emphasis, body posture, empathy, and the like, as well as judgment, rejection, and so on, all can convey a sense of "confrontation."
6. Speculate on what you think a client's response might be to the various methods of "confrontation" itemized in Question 5.
7. Which of these methods intuitively appeals to you as having the most potential for being effective? On what do you base that judgment?

In the case above, the client's dilemma appears to be that, on the one hand, she no longer wants to participate in the "club scene;" but on the other hand, if she quits the club scene, she risks losing her boyfriend, who has made it clear where he stands on the issue. The panic attacks have a *secondary gain* for the client: They allow her to *have her cake* (i.e., she doesn't have to risk losing her boyfriend over the issue of not wanting to go to the club) *and eat it too* (i.e., she doesn't have to go to the club because her ostensibly involuntary panic attacks *excuse* her from responsibility for going). At the same time, however, she knows that this is not going to be helpful for her relationship in the long run, which becomes a motivating factor for her to address it in therapy. Her fear of losing her boyfriend can trigger feelings of ambivalence, which in this case are manifested by panic attacks. The therapist must be persistent in keeping a client's focus on the issue at hand and not becoming sidetracked.[4] In other words, in order to overcome ambivalence, a client must develop resolute (i.e., determined) focus. Such determined focus must take place within the bounds of a safe therapeutic relationship that can effectively "hold" or contain a client's emotional processes while confronting the painful aspects of her life despite the pain. According to Prochaska (1999), it is important for therapists to move clients from precontemplation to at least the preparation for action stage within the first three sessions, or else they are more likely to prematurely terminate from therapy. Although this may or may not be reasonable in all cases, it is worth considering. Thus, a client needs to be made aware of her problem and—connected to that—understand the necessity of facing it and working through her ambivalence. That increases her chances of being successful in therapy.

Awareness, Ambivalence, and Effective Treatment

Clients who are willing to experience this anxiety (or ambivalence) are ready to face the emotional turmoil and pain that accompanies decision making. They either recognize the long-term benefit of experiencing discomfort, fears, and so on, or see the futility of endlessly utilizing behaviors that avoid difficulties in their life. In fact, Orlinsky et al. (1994) found that being open to experiencing anxiety is highly predictive of successful outcome. Individuals willing to experience anxiety are generally more honest with themselves about the severity of their problem (i.e., "own the problem"), likely to be in the preparation for action or action stage of change, and hold a belief that some sacrifice (e.g., experiencing anxiety or ambivalence) is required in order to be successful, especially with change (Hanna, 2001).

Clinical Case Example 13.3: A Client Willing to Experience Anxiety

Recall from Chapter 5 the case of the pregnant woman (Clinical Case Example 5.2) who is afraid of needles (in the section entitled "Theme of Helplessness: The Symptom Is Out of Control"). When asked what she would like to realistically accomplish through treatment, she indicated that she would like to get through her labor, have a healthy child, and not hurt her baby. She also specifically stated, "It's not to have hypnosis give me a quick fix! My goal is not just to get blood samples or vaccinations!" Rather, she revealed that she would like to "go through the delivery like an adult!" As a result, she is ready to face the unpleasantness of her particular anxiety so that she can achieve her goals—growing up and acting as an adult. This is an individual who understands that she is going to experience the pain of childbirth, but she mitigates it by reminding herself of the reason that she is in therapy. As the philosopher Friedrich Nietzsche (1968) wrote, "He who has a *why*, can endure any *how*."

As in Clinical Case Example 13.3, the mother-to-be must be aware of what her underlying fears are in order to face the unpleasantness of her situation and the anxiety it produces. In other words, clients have to (a) be *aware* of their problem (not deny it, run away from it, etc.), (b) understand what kind of problem they have, and (c) have a meta-awareness about the fact that they are ambivalent about changing their behavior so that they confront themselves eventually. In Clinical Case Example 13.3, the woman recognizes that she has a problem, and by coming to therapy, she faces her fear and anxiety. In addition, she recognizes that a "quick fix" (i.e., hypnosis) is available, but not the solution. Hanna (2001) described this process:

> Awareness has to do with a client's recognition of or clarity of perception about a problem. It is the function that brings a mental, emotional, or environmental issue in from the edge of consciousness and into focused detail. In general, awareness is the identification or pinpointing of issues or relationships that are in need of addressing as part of the therapeutic process and its tasks. (p. 62)

In other words, a client's awareness allows therapy to continue and progress even when the client begins to display ambivalence. Awareness includes knowledge of schema dynamics and how they are related to the ambivalence. Such awareness allows a therapist to point out how client behavior relates to his ambivalence in a way that will bring his focus back on the issue at hand—or his reason for therapy in general. The use of metaphors described in Chapter 9 can be especially useful in keeping a client's focus on the issue at hand, especially when he is trying to escape, becomes paralyzed, vacillates, or lets fate decide.

Conversely, clients who are not aware resemble the precontemplators (i.e., reluctant, rebellious, resigned, or rationalizing) or contemplators described in Chapter 4, and they behave like the ambivalent clients described above (e.g., vacillating, attempting to escape, and utilizing safeguards). They may be characterized by being vague, noncommittal, "back and forth," and even oblivious to their surroundings or condition (often saying, "I don't know …" or "I guess …"). They may be meek and kind, but "clueless"; or they may be bellicose and blame others outside of themselves for their problems (e.g., "It is all my parent's fault") or act passive and feel helpless ("There's nothing I can do"). Such clients can be very frustrating and even tempt therapists to give up on them. This is, however, merely a symptom (i.e., reactance, or safeguarding) of underlying ambivalence about making a change and a way for them to demonstrate to the therapist how much they *want to have their cake and eat it too, feel pulled in two directions at the same time*, and are ultimately *stuck between a rock and a hard place.*

Pacing, Confronting, and Nonlinear Thinking

The confronting that "maintains and sustains attention in spite of the impulse to avoid, give into confusion, or act out" advocated by Hanna (2001, p. 74) must be balanced by Erickson's admonition, "The patient comes to be protected or helped in some regard" (1977, p. 20). Indeed, Hanna (2001) also urged caution regarding clients who are not prepared to encounter the level of self-examination required in a therapist's confronting. He indicated that such clients are generally in an earlier stage of change, highly ambivalent about therapy, and probably engaging in safeguarding behaviors. For them, Hanna (2001) advised therapists to exercise caution:

Forcing a person to confront too much, too soon, is traumatic by definition. Bringing a client to contact painful phenomena must be done with care and attention to the person's level of tolerance. Overwhelming a client with mental, emotional, or environmental material that is too much to confront will not only bring about early termination, it will cause harm. Thus, exposure to sensitive memories, feelings, or beliefs should be done gradually so the client will be successful and not view therapy as a source of failure and pain. (p. 241)

There are two important factors that must be honored simultaneously: (a) pursuing the objectives of the therapy, even though it can be uncomfortable, frightening, or even painful; and (b) doing so at a pace that a client can tolerate. If only one is done and not the other, the result will be therapy that is either too aggressive, overwhelming, and/or hostile, or too timid. Hence, confronting cannot be done unless the therapist is also operating with a friendly tone within all of the domains previously discussed (i.e., engagement, assessment, and maintaining the therapeutic alliance). The linear-thinking practitioner will find this more troublesome, both conceptually and clinically, than the nonlinear-thinking practitioner. When it is done with relationship considerations in mind, however, a client is more likely to be receptive to what a therapist has to present (even though it may be uncomfortable) rather than reject it outright because it is too threatening. We present several additional, nonlinear methods for managing ambivalence below that take these two principles into consideration.

Rolling With the Resistance

Motivational interviewing has its origins in the treatment of substance abuse. For many substance abuse counselors, confronting an addict (i.e., confrontation as "in your face") has been an important traditional step toward "breaking through" clients' denial. In addition, such confrontation has been viewed as an indispensable prerequisite to fully engaging clients in treatment and recovery. Thus, when Miller and Rollnick (2002) originally proposed that the best way to deal with resistance was *not* to fight it, but to "roll" with it, a considerable controversy was born. However, they made a convincing argument for their unconventional approach:

> Reluctance and ambivalence are not opposed but are acknowledged to be natural and understandable. The counselor does not impose new views or goals; rather, the person is invited to consider new information and is offered new perspectives. "Take what you like and leave the rest" is the permissive kind of advice that pervades this approach. It is an approach that is hard to fight against. (Miller & Rollnick, p. 40)

They described resistance and ambivalence about change as two sides of the same coin (a decidedly *nonlinear* approach). When a client is discussing the need for change, why something is the right thing for her to do, or the like, she is embracing "change talk" (i.e., dialogue that leads to change and is one side of the resistance coin). On the other hand, clients will also advocate for *not changing* or engage in "resistance and counterchange" talk, which essentially preserves the status quo. The clinician's primary task is to decrease a client's level of resistance and keep resistance low. In doing so, a therapist can develop "discrepancies" more clearly, and clients can engage in more change talk and ultimately resolve their ambivalence about the problem. Clinical Case Example 13.4, which revisits one of the cases give in Clinical Exercise 13.1, may be helpful.

Clinical Case Example 13.4: Noncompliance With "Homework"

A man comes for his second therapy session following what you believed to be a productive first session. His presenting concern was anxiety, especially around his supervisor at an accounting firm. At the end of the initial session, you and the client agreed to some specific homework tasks that included speaking up at a staff meeting, setting up an appointment to speak with the supervisor and inquiring if a female coworker who he has been interested in is dating anyone. When he returns, he says that he didn't accomplish any of the tasks because "the meeting went too long, the secretary was never at her desk to make the appointment, and I just didn't get around to it" (i.e., asking about the coworker).

QUESTIONS

1. What are the poles of the dilemma that the client is facing?
2. Speculate on what the client's schema dynamics (particularly view of self and view of others) might be, and how they are contributing to the client's ambivalence.
3. How might a *linear*-thinking therapist handle the client's behavior?
4. How might a *nonlinear*-thinking therapist "roll with the resistance" in this example?
5. What signs of effort (if any) did the client show?

Motivational-interviewing theorists see resistance as developing frequently as a result of a client perceiving an infringement on his personal freedom (i.e., reactance) by a therapist engaging in confrontational interventions rather than in a collaborative process. Rather than viewing it as a static trait that belongs to a client, MI views resistance as a dynamic process that can ebb and flow between client and therapist. Change occurs at lower levels of resistance; thus, therapists must keep resistance low. Resistance is *not* something a client has or doesn't have; it is more useful to view it as a continuum that is always moving back and forth between resolution and doubt—just like the dilemmas (e.g., approach–avoidance) outlined in Chapter 12. Nonlinear-thinking clinicians who roll with the resistance recognize that anyone who continues to be stuck in this state of flux feels awful. As a result, a client may search for someone (e.g. a spouse, friend, coworker, or therapist) to take one side of his ambivalence for him (and *from* him) so he can argue for the other side, and seemingly make a decision. Of course, the side that a client usually takes is the side that says, "Keep doing what you are doing; don't change." Thus, "rolling with the resistance" (a nonlinear paradoxical way of thinking) frustrates that strategy by avoiding the trap of taking a side and instead moving a client to keep vacillating in his ambivalence until he is ready to act. Oftentimes, it calls for a therapist to utilize different approaches (or to employ knowledge of different domains) that are tailored to a client's specific needs. In fact, according to Miller and Rollnick (2002), resistance is often the first signal for a therapist to take a different approach with a client. Such is the point in time that a clinician may find it useful to "develop discrepancies."

Developing Discrepancies

As previously noted, some clients present themselves for treatment on an involuntary or mandated referral basis. Other clients enter treatment when their circumstances have become intolerable. Many times, such clients will attempt to distort realities and reflect little or no desire to see things as they actually are (e.g., "This whole DUI thing has been blown way out of proportion. I mean, sure drinking and driving is bad, but I didn't have *that* much to drink. It was bad timing that I got stopped"). Many times, they would also prefer to express feelings about the way they would like things to be (e.g., "I wish this whole thing would just go away instead of me having to deal with lawyers, the court, and alcoholism counseling. This is costing me a lot of time and money over something that has all been a big mistake"). The blurring and/or denial are manifestations of ambivalence being expressed in order to justify the status quo.

As described above, in light of such client protestations, a nonlinear-thinking therapist's first approach is to "roll with the resistance." That is, allow the client to have her say, and do not contradict her. The next, more active step is to develop discrepancies. *Developing discrepancies* refers to expanding upon inconsistencies between circumstances as they are, and the way a client proclaims that she would like them to be. The "Columbo Approach" (see Chapter 4) can be very useful in developing discrepancies in a non-threatening way.

According to Miller and Rollnick (2002), a client who is "blurring" or distorting reality and not seeing any difficulty with his behavior should be a clinical opportunity for the therapist to give voice to the arguments for change, not just against it. For example, a therapist might respond to the fictional DUI client's protestations against being arrested for a DUI by saying, "You seem really upset by this mess of having to deal with a lawyer, a court date, maybe losing your driver's license, going for alcoholism counseling, spending a bundle of cash for all of this, and so forth. I don't know if you have a drinking problem or not, but if you did have a drinking problem, how might that affect your life? What do you think it would mean to you?" From a *nonlinear* perspective, therapists are required to point out the fact that the present state of affairs is very different from how a client wants them to be. At the same time, a therapist must not appear to be an advocate for any particular position. By utilizing her communication skills (both *linear* and *nonlinear* listening and responding), a therapist can draw very clear distinctions between the two poles of a client's conflict and reduce the "comfort" that a client may derive from "blurring." This is akin to "holding the client's feet to the fire." Unlike confronting, merely having a therapist *not advocating for one side of a client's ambivalence or the other* puts a client in a less threatening position.

Sometimes, simply bringing a discrepancy to the surface is enough to motivate a client to begin embracing the desire to change. The likelihood of this occurring is greatly enhanced when a client perceives his behavior to be incongruous with important personal values or goals. As a brief example, a client who had deeply disappointed his family by his errant ways commented in therapy that his epiphany occurred when he saw the depth of the "pain and hurt" his wife and children were experiencing as a result of his behavior. Having come from a dysfunctional family of origin, he had vowed as a young man never to inflict upon his own family what his family of origin and especially his father had inflicted upon him. Yet here he was, having hurt the ones he loved the most.

At other times, discrepancies result when the cost of clients' behavior is brought into stark relief and they must acknowledge that the personal and psychological expense of the problem behavior is not worth the cost. Two MI exercises commonly useful in developing discrepancies to facilitate client discussion of their ambivalence are *values clarification* and *weighing the cost of behavior*. Such an exercise allows a therapist to develop discrepancies more sharply in the hope that it "overrides the inertia of the *status quo*" (Miller & Rollnick, 2002, p. 39). For example, in Clinical Case Example 10.3, in which a wife was wrestling with her feelings of rage at her husband's infidelity, the therapist might point out that, on the one hand, the client valued her commitment to marriage; whereas on the other, she valued integrity. She acutely feels the dimensions of the dilemma she is in: If she continues to be hurt, angry, and upset and decides upon divorce, she will be a "loser"; on the other hand, if she stays with her husband, she is constantly reminded that he chose to be intimate with someone else over her, which also defines her as a "loser" (i.e., a second choice). By clarifying and labeling the client's values, as well as the cost of continuing versus the cost of not continuing the behavior, the therapist provides a framework for the client to make a decision (about the ambivalence).

It takes a master practitioner to uncover such dynamics and present them without stimulating additional anxiety or imposing a sense of coercion on a client that is likely to prompt reactance or safeguarding behaviors. Consider Clinical Case Example 13.5.

Clinical Case Example 13.5: In a Quandary

Jane is in a quandary. Cumulatively, she has many stressors in her life, particularly with work. Despite the fact that there were several coworkers who were senior to her, she was promoted to project director over her area. On some level, she was proud of the title and the authority to manage. On the other hand, she did not like having to confront her coworkers, nor did she like dealing with some of the day-to-day operations (along with the occasional crises) that drained her of time and energy. Nevertheless, Jane has felt a strong sense of duty since she committed to the position. But, she has felt that it has taken her away from other parts of her job that give her greater satisfaction. After a year of doing this and making some progress, Jane started to feel tired and unappreciated at work. Her sense of duty and commitment drove her to continue in her position, but she began to resent it more and more.

Finally, a senior coworker, someone who Jane trusted and confided in, confronted her about her performance. She cautioned Jane that she was in danger of "burning out" and it was starting to show. She was greatly embarrassed by the feedback and reluctant to admit it, although she felt her colleague's comments were accurate. At the same time, the colleague offered to take on Jane's duties for her. Despite her trust in and relationship with the colleague, Jane suspected her motives (i.e., the job entailed better pay, more flexibly in work assignment, etc.), though the colleague denied it.

QUESTIONS

1. What are the poles of the dilemma that the client is facing?
2. Speculate on what the client's schema dynamics (particularly view of self and view of others) might be and how they are contributing to the client's ambivalence.
3. In what sort of dilemma does the client find herself (e.g., approach–approach)?
4. How might a *linear*-thinking therapist handle the client's behavior?
5. How might a *nonlinear*-thinking therapist "develop discrepancies" in this example?

Jane's dilemma is clear: On one hand, she would like to enjoy the "perks" of her job, but she dislikes the hassles it poses for her. On the other hand, she finds the idea of "freedom" from the burden of this job very appealing. At the same time, the thought of shirking her duty was very unappealing to her—it wouldn't leave her feeling very good about herself. Thus emerges her feeling ambivalent about what choice to make: She felt that she was *being pulled in two directions* (i.e., give up the job, or remain in the uncomfortable position), *feeling stuck between a rock and a hard place* (i.e., there is no good alternative), and *wanting to have her cake and eat it too* (i.e., have the perks of the title and the power to make decisions, but also be free of hassles). As a result, her behavior may look like endless stalling and deliberating (i.e., vacillating) about change or some form of distancing or dissociation from the reality of the problem situation (i.e., escape).

Developing discrepancies serves the purpose of providing motivation for a client to make a decision by making certain that a client's ambivalence remains the focus of therapeutic attention. This is done by extrapolating the consequences of the client's action or lack of action. In the example with Jane, if she does not have the courage to make a choice about her situation, she would either do nothing and eventually be removed from the position, which would be embarrassing, but at least she wouldn't have been the one to make the decision. The therapist would respectfully draw this distinction, and remind the client that the choice is ultimately hers. Too often, when clients decide not to face the conflict that they are in, they give up control of their life, and leave things to chance and let "fate" work it out for them (e.g., develop a physical, stress-based illness). Put simply, they are merely reacting to being *pulled in both directions* while *wanting to have their cake and eat it too*, and so on.

Clinical Exercise 13.2: Developing Discrepancies

Return to a previous Clinical Case Example in chapter 12 (Clinical Case Examples 12.1 to 12.4) and this chapter (Clinical Case Examples 13.1 to 13.4), and think about how a therapist could begin to develop discrepancies with that client. Share your ideas with a small group or with the entire class.

LOOKING FOR EXCEPTIONS TO HELP RESOLVE AMBIVALENCE

Many times, clients will demonstrate their ambivalence by discussing the chronic nature of their problem or the failure of attempts that they have made to "fix" it (see "Theme of Desperation: 'I Have a Problem That I Need to Work On!'" or "Theme of Hopelessness: 'I Have a Chronic Problem'" from Chapter 5). Nonlinear listening for *absence* would detect that most often, there is little mention of anything positive in the client's story, whereas nonlinear listening for *resistance* would detect the "Yes, but ..." nature of any attempts at "intervention" on the counselor's part (e.g., "Have you tried ...?" and "Oh yes, I tried that already, but it didn't work"). Such impasses can often leave linear-thinking therapists feeling frustrated by a client's lack of cooperation. A way to have the client actively engage in trying to resolve his ambivalence was developed by de Shazer (1985; de Shazer, Dolan, & Korman, 2007) and expanded by Berg (1994; Berg & Szabo, 2005). It evolved as a direct response to the problem-obsessed and problem-focused nature of psychotherapy—as if understanding the problem alone will somehow yield its solution. As its name implies, solution-focused therapy centers its attention on solutions rather than problems. Toward that end, solution-focused therapists rely on the power of a client's subjective perspective, and operate with the assumption that clients are merely stuck (i.e., struggling with their ambivalence) rather than sick and that they have the capacity to orient toward wellness by choosing better solutions than they have done so in the past (Hoyt, 2002).

In solution-focused therapy, "problems" are approached in a *nonlinear* way. That is, a client's problem or concern is seen as a client's attempt at a *solution* that once worked, but is not working any longer. In terms of working through the ambivalence, the therapist focuses the client's attention on times when she has been successful, and *not* when she was ambivalent. As an example, see Clinical Case Example 13.6.

Clinical Case Example 13.6: Call for Attention

A young man who discovered and acknowledged his homosexual identity during high school found himself in therapy shortly after graduating from high school in order to deal with overwhelming feelings of depression and suicidal thoughts. As an adolescent, after convincingly discovering and owning his sexual orientation, he suffered unimaginable taunting, derision, and threats of violence at the hands of thoughtless other male high school students. Nevertheless, he felt "liberated" from being in the "closet," and as a point of fact, he seemed to revel in the attention that he garnered, albeit negative in nature.

Feeling ignored by his father, he lived in the shadow of an older sibling who followed and fulfilled parental expectations and appeared to be the apple of the father's eye. Again, it was the father's attention that the client seemed to crave. With his older sibling excelling in school, the client found poor school performance to be an effective way of garnering family attention, but again it was negative in nature. In his interpersonal style, the client craved excitement and used outrageous, histrionic, mischievous, and somewhat flamboyant behaviors to garner the attention and excitement that he craved. Without a college career, and with few marketable skills and his adolescence behind him, he found himself going through a succession of jobs, drinking, smoking, and keeping late hours with friends, but without any real direction in life. Jobs that seemed to have potential lasted a few weeks.

His antidepressant medications seemed to have little effect on his mood, and subsequently he was hospitalized on three occasions for suicidal ideation after episodes of drinking. His suicidal thoughts were described in outlandish terms and received legitimate expressions of concern from his friends. He discovered in therapy that his view of self ("I only feel worthwhile if life is exciting and I am the center of attention") was leading him to garner attention but only in self-destructive and nonproductive ways. The therapeutic task was to determine how it was that he would be able to get attention and excitement in his life in new ways—other than those that have been so destructive. Although seeking excitement and acting flamboyant, histrionic, and overreacting to life's everyday circumstances had once been effective in garnering attention, such behaviors were now only resulting in largely negative consequences.

From a solution-focused perspective:

1. If you were to choose a solution-focused approach to intervening with this client, what questions would you present to him?
2. What is the basis for your choosing those particular questions?
3. How would you go about differentiating this client expressing suicidal thought that are motivated by a need for excitement and attention and those that may result in his acting on such thoughts?
4. What is the client's dilemma (approach–approach, avoidant–avoidant, etc.)?
5. What are the poles of the dilemma?
6. What are the relevant schema dynamics in this client example (view of self, etc.)?

Solution-focused therapy is an exploration of how a behavior ("solution") used to be functional for a client and what could now be done either to make the solution functional again or to substitute a new solution that will be less problematic. This is accomplished by discovering *exceptions* to the problem (e.g., "Tell me when the problem is *not* a problem"). *Exceptions to the problem* refer to those times when a client's goal is already happening at least a little, or when the problem is not happening as much. In other words, the therapist asks the client to find a time when he was able to resolve her ambivalence, or when it did not exist. In these *exceptions* to the problem, the focus is why and how these exceptions were able to take place. The line of inquiry that a therapist pursues concerns what was different about what a client was doing, thinking, saying, feeling, or relating. When a client is imagining a future of what life would be like without the problem and when he is looking at what was different during these *exceptions* to the problem, a therapist is engaging his client in "solution talk" rather than problem talk—hence, the dialogue is *solution focused* and not *problem focused*. This focus can be utilized to help resolve a client's ambivalence by gently challenging his rigid, unrealistic schematized views (i.e., "I always ..." or "I never ..."). When exceptions are generated, a therapist can probe for what his client did differently. This allows for one of two things to happen: (a) A client can explore specific instances in which an outcome was different, which is a potential "roadmap" out of his current dilemma; or (b) a client may begin seeing himself in a new light (i.e., accommodating his schemas). We illustrate this in Clinical Case Example 13.7.

Clinical Case Example 13.7: Looking for Exceptions

Return to the case of Jane (in Clinical Case Example 13.5), who was in a quandary about her work responsibilities and coworkers. Speculate regarding what kind of family she may have come from and what her school experiences were like. Brainstorm ideas for *exceptions* from her past that might help her present dilemma. Finally, conjecture as to what her particular schema dynamics might be, and develop "exception" scenarios that involve either or all of the following:

1. Family experience (feel free to make up her siblings and family members)
2. An experience in school
3. A related work experience

VARIATION

Form groups or work with the entire class, and brainstorm how you would utilize these exceptions to create a "roadmap" for helping her resolve her feelings of ambivalence in the present dilemma.

If a client cannot identify *exceptions* to the problem, the solution-focused therapy also asks a *miracle question* in which a client imagines what life would be like if a miracle happened during the night and the client awoke to find that his problem no longer existed. This approach is very useful when the ambivalence is manifested as a flight into illness or flight into health, or if there is a "secondary gain" involved. The task or plan is to then ask a client what small part of this he might begin implementing, acting "as if" the miracle occurred; and if these exceptions are effective, a client is encouraged to do more of them (Walter & Pellar, 1992). A variation of this is to ask, "Suppose a miracle occurred overnight and the problem would be gone. How would you know? What would be different in your life?" Again, as with exceptions to the problem, the "miracle question" is related to a client's schema; it can be helpful in resolving ambivalence by exploring similar "roadmaps" or by expanding a person's views (schema accommodation).

Many times, follow-up questions are used to clarify exactly how the "old solution" negatively impacts a client and how to begin to create new solutions (de Shazer, 1991; Hoyt, 2002). One such follow-up inquiry is a scaling question (e.g., "On a scale of 1 to 10 …") to measure the relative strength of the problem to the client. As a method for resolving ambivalence, scaling each of the poles of the dilemma gives a numeric weight to each of the sides, and can help "tip" the balance one way or another.

Clinical Exercise 13.3: Revisiting Solutions

Return to a previous Clinical Case Example in Chapter 12 (Clinical Case Examples 12.1 to 12.4) and this chapter (Clinical Case Examples 13.1 to 13.6), and look for ways that a therapist could begin to use a solution-focused approach (e.g., looking for exceptions, asking the miracle question, or asking a scaling question) with that client. Share your ideas with a small group or with the entire class.

EXTERNALIZING THE PROBLEM

Too often, a client's expression of ambivalence is an internal one. The client goes back and forth in her own mind, until she feels trapped. Language becomes the method by which this ambivalent (distorted) thinking becomes entrenched or enshrined (e.g., "I am bipolar"), with individuals becoming bound up by their (problem-focused) language. Likewise, *relanguaging* a problem (or *restorying*) is one of the chief methods for helping clients resolve their problems and their ambivalence. Therapists using narrative therapy[5] adopt a "not-knowing" stance, which places them in an equal (or even inferior) position to a client and allows a therapist the privilege of listening over questioning. Clearly, this is a *nonlinear* approach to therapy as well as addressing ambivalence.

One of the more unique and revolutionary elements of narrative therapy is *externalizing the problem*. When narrative therapists place the problem outside of a client (or couple, family, etc.), an individual becomes free to stop fighting against himself or, in the case of a couple, fighting against each other, which can prolong ambivalence. Such fighting creates a useless cycle of shame, blame, and denial. Instead, a client (i.e., an individual, couple, or family) can join together to fight against the problem. A couple can gain a greater sense of control by labeling what the problem is (an extension of externalizing) or can begin to exert a measure of influence over it by setting some boundaries on the problem's influence. For example, instead of a person being diagnosed with "depression" and having his identity bound up in the illness, "depression" is conceived of as an entity outside of the individual. The entity is then something for the individual and others (e.g., spouse, partner, friends, and/or family) to combat. This frees the individual to look for unseen, unused, or untapped resources (see Chapter 4), rather than being victimized by the illness. In turn, a client can rewrite, or "restory," his narrative from one of weakness to one of strength. As discussed in Chapter 8, this story or narrative reflects a client's schematized views, but externalizing the problem allows him to make either first-order (i.e., surface) changes (assimilation) to his schemas or more substantial second-order changes (i.e., accommodation). In essence, a client creates a new story in which he is more important than the problem (Carr, 1998; Freedman & Combs, 2002; Sperry, Carlson, & Peluso, 2006; White & Epston, 1990). This, in turn, helps to resolve ambivalence by taking the problem from inside the client to outside the client. Clinical Case Example 13.7 may prove helpful.

Clinical Case Example 13.7: A Marital Couple

A young, highly successful, accomplished, and attractive couple sought marital counseling due to emotional distance that had grown between them for a variety of reasons. Both earned six-figure salaries, both had graduate degrees, and both had exceptionally bright future career prospects. They had made progress in understanding the basis for their "emotional" distance from one another and sufficiently working through certain crises.

During their fifth session of therapy, which had been spread over the course of approximately 2 months, the discussion turned to how their work schedules, career paths, and future choices concerning careers affect their marriage. The woman bemoaned the fact that she was tired of seeing others taking credit for projects she had designed and seen to completion and being promoted as a result of her efforts. Very tearfully, she lamented the fact that she was very nearly within grasp of being given a promotion that would clearly mean recognition, success, and her future career path. As the oldest child in her family of origin, she felt she had been achievement, career, and success oriented since early childhood, thus reflecting strong family values of what constitutes self-worth.

At the same that she articulated the above central orienting values in her personality, she began to sob that she knew that her children desperately needed her at home at this critical preschool time in their lives. Although she could change her employment status with her current company to part-time, she knew that it would be the death knell for a strong upward career move and the promotion, recognition, and status she covets. She also recognized that if she devoted more time and attention to her children, who need her at home, she could return to full-time employment in the future and resume her achievement orientation. But, she also believes that by then she would be an "also-ran" in the company thicket of high achievers.

QUESTIONS TO CONSIDER

1. What are the client's schema dynamics?
2. What are the poles of the client's dilemma? What kind of dilemma is presented here (e.g., approach avoidance)?

3. How does the client's language construct and maintain the problem?
4. How could she "relanguage" or "restory" the problem to be externalized?
5. How would externalizing the problem help relieve the ambivalence?
6. What could the counselor do to help externalize this problem?

What is the wife in Clinical Case Example 13.7 to do? Should she forgo what she believes that she has been groomed and trained for all of her life in order to care for her children, who need her? Or, should she sacrifice the needs of her children and continue with a career path that she truly enjoys? The pendulum of her schema dynamics sways her in one direction, whereas the circumstances of her life sway her in another. Therein lays the ambivalence that torments her. She would like to be able to *both have her cake and eat it too.* That is, she would like to continue with her career path *and* care for young children who she knows need her, but she perceives these two alternatives as being largely incompatible. She feels that she cannot have it both ways and must make a choice, and it is a painful choice to make, with no one able to give her the "right" answer. Her husband is supportive but knows he must leave the decision to her. The therapist urged careful balancing and consideration of the two alternatives that confronted her. Because of other subtle comments the woman made, the therapist suggested that some of her tears *appeared* to be the result of "letting go" of at least some of her career aspirations—not only a sign that she was "mourning" their loss but also a healthy sign that she was beginning to get on with her life (i.e., listening and responding to presence). As the oldest child in her immigrant family of origin, she values success, achievement, and all its accoutrements (e.g., status, money, and overcoming the disadvantages of being an immigrant). When she developed those values, however, she had not been married or had any children. Having children became a value that ultimately came into conflict with career success as a value. But, that does not mean that career success and all that it signifies to her as a longheld value will simply evaporate in the cognitive schema she has held dear and worked very hard to fulfill for many years. By externalizing the client's issue or symptom (in this case, her career ambitions), however, the therapist can help the client work through the ambivalence and make a choice, or be able to "restory" the ambivalence and incorporate it into her life choices.

In order to be able to utilize these narrative practices, a therapist is required to prize listening and understanding first and questioning second (i.e., *nonlinear* listening). Questions should be used only to help couples to see that the narratives of their lives and relationship are actively constructed rather than passively recounted and given. Therapists who begin to use a narrative approach are

> interested in collaborating with people to change their lives through enriching the narratives they and others tell concerning their lives.… It seems that through these alternative stories, people can live out new identities, new possibilities for relationships, and new futures. (Freedman & Combs, 2002, p. 308)

In other words, they are invested in maintaining a robust therapeutic alliance with a client and realize that it is a primary method for helping to resolve ambivalence and begin a conversation that elicits "change talk."

Listening for and Eliciting "Change Talk"

One way that therapists begin to make progress in helping clients to resolve ambivalence is through the development of "change talk" (see Miller & Rollnick, 2002; Watzlawick, 1978). According to Miller and Rollnick, change talk reflects movement of the person toward change, whereas resistance represents and predicts movement away from change. Although the initial stages of therapy focus on building motivation for change utilizing principles outlined above, the "working-through" phase of therapy focuses on instituting and stimulating change. This can be seen as the movement of a client from a precontemplation or contemplation stage toward a preparation for action and even an action stage of change. From our perspective, in order to elicit such change talk, therapists must be able to listen and respond nonlinearly (i.e., congruence, absence, inference, presence, and resistance, as outlined in Chapter 3). Likewise, *non-linear* listening and responding can also help a clinician to reflect back to a client when she is beginning to use change talk, make positive decisions, or work through her ambivalence. For example, if a client has habitually come to therapy talking about how difficult it is to manage her daughter, and instead comes to therapy and discusses her daughter's positive traits, *listening for absence* can help the therapist to identify her positive movement via the change talk. Change talk is also similar to *solution-focused speech* (in solution-focused therapy) and *externalizing* (in narrative therapy). Ultimately, change talk indicates that the client is in the processes of considering second-order change, or change in the schema level of her awareness. Thus, it is important for clinicians to listen for and be aware of a client's change talk, which falls into one of four general categories:

1. *Disadvantages of the status quo*: Dialogue that highlights the disadvantages of the status quo signals that a client has begun to realize that the way things are is presently no longer acceptable or desirable (i.e., moving from precontemplation to contemplation). For example, a client with a history of substance abuse who has consistently perceived his drug usage as "partying" or "recreational" begins to have real consequences for his behavior (loss of job, family, etc.). A client realizes, "This is more of an issue in my life than I thought. ... I never realized how much this affected my family." At times, therapists can elicit disadvantages by asking questions such as "What worries you about your situation?" and "How has this prevented you from doing what you want?" Listening for *congruence, inference*, as well as *resistance* is important for identifying this type of change talk. Looking for exceptions and developing discrepancies are useful additional strategies for eliciting "disadvantages" as well.

2. *Advantages of change*: Dialogue that highlights the advantages of change signals that a client has begun to consider how life might look different (better) if a change took place (i.e., moving from the precontemplation to contemplation stage). For example, a wife in a marriage with incidents of repeated domestic violence may begin to "dream" (visualize) what it would be like to live a life without fear. A client realizes, "Hmmm, without (the particular problem) I'd be able to ..." or simply "I would feel so much more relaxed, and I'd be able to do so much more." In addition, sometimes therapists can elicit this by asking questions such as "How would you like things to be different ..." (i.e., the "miracle question"). Listening for *congruence, absence*, and *presence* can also be important for identifying this type of change talk.

3. *Optimism for change*: Dialogue that highlights a client's sense of optimism signals that a client has begun to accept that change is possible for him (i.e., moving from the contemplation to preparation for action stage). For example, the substance-abusing client above, after some initial work on his motivation for change, may begin to feel a measure of confidence in his ability to bring about change (self-efficacy). The client states, "I did (make a positive change) before. ... I think I could again if I put my mind to it." In addition, therapists can support such optimism by asking questions such as "Who could offer you support (to make this change)?" "When in the past have you made a change like this?" and "What was helpful to you?" Listening for *congruence, absence*, and *presence* can also be important for identifying "optimism for change" talk.

4. *Intention to change*: Clients' expressions of their intention to change are signals that they have made a decision to implement change and no longer see advantages to their previous behavior (i.e., moving from the contemplation to preparation for action stage). An expression of intention to change is a sign that significant ambivalence *may* have been resolved.[6] For example, a client in a violent relationship may recognize that her husband is not going to stop his behavior and decides that she must leave in order to protect herself and her children. Such a client may realize, "I think it is time. ... I don't want this for my family anymore. ... I have to do something." In addition, therapists can stimulate intentions and resolve by asking questions such as "What

do you intend to do?" or "Let's not be concerned about how you might accomplish this for now and instead focus on how you want things to be!" Listening for *congruence*, *absence*, *presence*, and *inference* are also important for recognizing this type of change talk. Again, looking for exceptions and developing discrepancies are useful strategies for eliciting this type of change talk.

Clinical Exercise 13.4: Change Talk

Instructions: Read each of the statements, and answer the questions below.

1. A client comes to therapy and complains that he no longer feels any pleasure from his life. As a result of therapy, he comes to understand that his career is "draining" him, despite the fact that he is successful at it. He has spent a great deal of time going "back and forth" on making a career change, weighing the positives and negatives of each. Finally, during one session he excitedly talks about the possibilities that a new career would bring, and how energized he was feeling about what was in store.

2. A client has been in therapy to address panic attacks. His attacks frequently disrupt his family and work life, requiring the people around him to drop everything and care for him. Although he has made progress in therapy, it has been strongly recommended that anti-anxiety medication would be most effective for his type of anxiety. The client has actively resisted this, stating, "I don't want to have to be dependent on medication to feel normal." But, after a particularly debilitating panic attack, the client began asking about medication, saying, "I just can't do this to my family and friends anymore."

3. A client with a history of substance abuse comes to therapy as a condition of probation. Although she knows that it can be helpful to her and that her abuse is problematic, she also finds it difficult to give up her habit. The therapist gives her a homework assignment of tallying up the cost (in both time and money) of her abuse. The client came back, stating, "I seriously underestimated how much of my life this was consuming. It is really taking over, isn't it?"

4. A client has been dealing with issues of guilt surrounding the death of her mother over a year ago. She was her mother's primary caregiver and has found her death difficult to come to terms with—despite her mother's long-known terminal illness. As a result, she has frozen her life (including her home) to keep things as they were the day her mother died. Her husband has found this difficult and strongly suggested that she "get some help." After several sessions of therapy, where the client began to grieve her mother's loss, the client came in and began to talk about what she could do with her life now that she had extra time on her hands.

QUESTIONS

1. What is the dilemma that is presented in each of the scenarios?
2. What kind of nonlinear listening would you use in each?
3. Which of the strategies presented above for handling ambivalence might be useful in these situations?
4. What kind of change talk is the client in each scenario using?

SUCCESSFUL RESOLUTION OF AMBIVALENCE

Clients come to therapy feeling ambivalent. Miller and Rollnick (2002) suggested signs that a client has successfully resolved her ambivalence and is ready to begin implementing changes:

1. Decreased resistance
2. Decreased discussion about the problem
3. Resolve
4. Change talk
5. Questions about change
6. Envisioning
7. Experimenting with new behavior

They cautioned, however, "It is quite tempting to assume that once the client is showing signs of readiness for change … the decision has been made and it is all downhill from there on" (pp. 128–129).

What is known about the change process is that the most lasting change comes about slowly and that even when a person has made a choice, feelings of ambivalence may still linger. If therapists are successful in helping a client to resolve his ambivalence, the client can begin on a path to change. Yet, these first steps are tentative, and a client may not be fully committed to them. It is like starting a fire in a fireplace—although a spark may ignite a flame, it is the therapist who can contribute to the fire by adding a warm glow—or let it die out. Although it is a client's responsibility to continue the change, the therapist must encourage client efforts toward change. At the end of it all, there is no one best approach to resolving ambivalence; such thinking would be decidedly linear. There is a wide variety of choices within this domain that, when artfully employed, represent the best in nonlinear thinking regarding facilitating a client to resolve his ambivalence and advancing the therapy toward a successful outcome.

CONCLUSION

Clients may come to therapy feeling ambivalent, or swaying between and being *pulled in two directions*, while *wanting to have their cake and eat it too*, and ultimately finding themselves stuck *between a rock and a hard place*. There is one further intervention recommended by Miller and Rollnick (2002) in managing client ambivalence. Although they referred to it as "reframing," this intervention deserves much more thorough discussion because of its pervasive, transtheoretical, and universal use in the therapy literature. In fact, "reframing" reflects the epitome of nonlinear thinking. As such, our discussion of this topic is quite comprehensive, and section 4 of this text is devoted to that task.

Information Box 13.2: Brain in a Box

As Goldberg (2001) has said, it is the "executive brain" in the form of the frontal lobes and *prefrontal cortex* that

> plays a central role in forming goals and objectives and then in devising plans of action required to attain these goals. It selects the cognitive skills required to implement the plans, coordinates these skills, and applies them in a correct order. … Human cognition is forward looking …

driven by goals, plans, aspirations, ambitions, and dreams, all of which pertain to the future and not to the past. These cognitive powers depend on the frontal lobes and evolve with them. In a broad sense, the frontal lobes are the organism's mechanism of liberating itself from the past and projecting into the future. The frontal lobes endow the organism with the ability to create neural models of things as a prerequisite for making things happen, models of something that does not yet exist but which you want to bring into existence. (p. 24)

It is clear that the frontal lobe takes us where we want to go in life. It is the "executive" that carries out our "plans." And yet, clients report feeling helpless, feeling powerless to change, being "out of control" and being "unable to help myself." They *experience* not being able to execute goals, plans, ambitions, and so on. What accounts for this?

A reasonable hypothesis is that we are complex *psychological* creatures and equally complex *neuropsychological creatures* with a robust emotional life as well. Our emotional life, vis-à-vis the limbic system of the midbrain, sends us cautionary messages about danger signals with which human contemporary life is fraught. Especially vibrant among those cautionary signals in humankind's life is the fear of failure with its seemingly limitless variations.

A considerable measure of symptomatic behavior appears to be the result of individuals wanting to attain their goals but being "ambivalent" about exactly what it is that would be involved. The ambivalence clients express is disguised as "I want to have my cake and eat it too" in statements such as "I want to get married but maintain two girlfriends because I 'can't' seem to choose which would be the better choice," "I want to be slim but don't want to change my eating habits or exercise," "I want a divorce because of what my husband did but I don't want to be recognized as a divorcée," "I want a new car but I don't want to part with the money," and "I want to divorce my husband but if I do I'll be a loser in the eyes of society—someone who couldn't hold her husband's interests."

In our estimation, such ambivalences represent a variation of "moral dilemmas" in which an individual must make a decision posing tension (i.e., the "moral dilemma") between two equally deleterious and reprehensible alternatives. Such tensions are personally agonizing and loudly proclaim, "I want to have my cake and eat it too, but I can't do it. What am I to do?"

In faced with making such decisions and choices that portend a felt sense of *failure or diminution*, the "executive function" in human beings in effect becomes immobilized and instead focuses on the symptoms (e.g., anxiety, depression, and obsessing) they have developed in struggling to resolve such dilemmas rather than solutions that require courage under conditions of uncertainty.

Recent research by Greene, Nystrom, Engell, Darley, and Cohen (2004) has provided data that such moral dilemmas are likely mediated by different brain structures. Executive functions mediated by the dorsolateral prefrontal cortex (DLPFC) provide the "rational" answers as to what the "right thing to do" is (from a utilitarian perspective of the most good for the most people), whereas the "emotional" thing to do (i.e., something we want or want to avoid) appears to be mediated by the limbic system. The anterior cingulate cortex appears to be a limbic system–associated area of the brain that elicits prefrontal cortex activity in resolving such conflicts.

Therapy is meant to "connect and engage" a client in a "safe" relationship. What can such a "safe" (e.g., due to the therapeutic alliance, providing support, calming and reassuring the client, and extending hope) relationship accomplish? House, Landis, and Umberson (1988) have demonstrated that another person's mere presence can decrease anxiety and distress (mediated in the limbic system) in individuals in intensive care units, as determined by physiological measures (i.e., decreased heart rate, lowered blood pressure, and lowering secretion of fatty acids found responsible for depositing plaque on artery walls). In turn, Marci, Ham, Moran, and Orr (2007) discovered a significant relationship between patient and therapist "physiological concordance" (i.e., measures of skin conductance collected during psychotherapy sessions). The higher a patient perceived his or her therapist's empathy, the higher the congruence between the physiological responses of patient and therapist. Extrapolating from such research, the therapeutic relationship is meant to help attenuate the anxieties and stresses that stem from the eruptions of the emotional cauldron of the limbic system in the face of perceived threats to modern survival—in other words, "failure," however it is construed (e.g., as embarrassment, disappointment, or rejection) by a client. Through a collaborative effort of their relationship and perceived human empathy, a therapist assists her client in calming down, thus reengaging the decision-making, planning, and goal-oriented functions of the client's frontal lobes. This can sometimes be accomplished quickly, and sometimes more slowly, but it can be accomplished. Of course, this depiction is an oversimplified *model* of the way in which the brain functions, but it is reasonable in light of what research is revealing about the brain and how it operates. As a result, the nonlinear-thinking therapist must be able to work with both conscious and unconscious processes. Ajzen (1996) has put it this way:

> Most theories of decision making, as well as social psychological models that link beliefs to attitudes, and attitudes to intentions and behavior, have dealt primarily with conscious, deliberate, volitional processes. People's beliefs and attitudes are said to follow reasonably from the available information, and their decisions and actions are taken in a deliberative manner to be consistent with their beliefs and values. Work on dual-mode processing of information, however, suggests that the deliberate mode of operation may have to be supplemented by a spontaneous mode in which cognitive and motivational processes operate at an unconscious level and influence decision and actions automatically without extensive cognitive mediation. (p. 316)

Ajzen (1996) reflected an understanding revealed by psychological and cognitive neuroscience research in recent years that conscious-mode processing is mediated by the executive function of the prefrontal cortex and unconscious-level processing of perceived threat is mediated by the limbic system and especially the amygdala.

ENDNOTES

1. Reframing and therapeutic paradox will be discussed in greater detail beginning in Chapter 14.
2. Note: *Coming alongside* is a type of intervention called a "paradox" that will be discussed in much more detail in Part 4 (the Level III section) of the text.
3. A psychotically depressed client in danger of committing suicide or someone who announces in therapy his intent and plan to harm an identified person cannot claim autonomy and confidentiality.
4. Hanna (2001; Hanna & Puhakka, 1991) defined this process as "resolute perception." Resolute perception is a process whereby a client, with the help of her therapist, makes a decision to become single-minded in facing whatever mistaken beliefs, poor choices, or maladaptive behavior sequences that are allowing problem behavior to continue.
5. *Narrative therapy* was first described by Michael White and David Epston (1990, 1992). It draws on the philosophy and writing of Michel Foucault and his critical analysis of the interplay of language, knowledge, and power on society's marginalized individuals (e.g., "the others," sick, insane, or criminal).
6. However, this does not necessarily mean that the change is certain. Recall from Chapter 4 that many clients can be stuck in the preparation for action stage with the false belief that they are making changes. It is significant in terms of client adherence to treatment.

PART FOUR

The Level III
Practitioner Profile

Introduction to Part 4

The Level III Practitioner Profile

CONTENTS

GENERAL CONSIDERATIONS

Mastery is a thing of beauty, whether it is in a trade, profession, or creative endeavor. Master practitioners make the things they do look effortless. The irony is that once someone achieves true mastery of her province, she seems to care less about being a master and more about bringing out the best in herself. Paradoxically, master practitioners understand that although earlier aspirations (i.e., those at Levels I and II) may have been driven by a desire to *be* a master, they now have little concern or preoccupation with such matters. They are more concerned with being themselves, relating in an authentic way, and being fully available to clients. They are continually involved in the process of *becoming* a master practitioner rather than an end point of *being* one. The reader will note that, throughout this introduction, there is an implied relationship between practicing at Level III and becoming a master practitioner. The reasoning for this interchangeability is that *practicing one's profession at Level III is the gateway to becoming a master practitioner.*

At Levels I and II, there is a measure of *angst* regarding being in professional settings. In contrast, Level III is familiar with and comfortable in such surroundings, whether it is a hospital, an outpatient clinic, private practice, or a counseling center. Likewise, Level III practitioners are equally comfortable in their professional role. Clearly, Level III practitioners experience a palpable sense of comfort with their ability while remaining simultaneously aware of their limitations.

Level III practitioners understand that their chosen life's work continually evolves as a product of personal maturation and professional growth. It takes years of practice and study to aspire to becoming a sorcerer. Becoming a master practitioner is also fraught with disquiet, frustration, query, setbacks, and the like, as demonstrated in the feeling of sometimes taking two steps forward and one step back in one's professional development. This has been well expressed by Scott Miller:

> I, on the other hand was plagued by doubt. Even later, as a fully *bona fide* treatment professional, seated opposite a particular client, I often felt like I had missed the one crucial day in graduate school—that one day when they taught you the secret handshake, the secret ingredient in the "Big Ma" of therapy. (Quoted in Walt, 2005, p. 1)

Being sensitive to and humbled by many varieties of human suffering but not overwhelmed by them, the Level III practitioner is intuitively empathic with the anguish that his clients experience. Despite their intuitive empathic concern, Level III practitioners are ever mindful of a need to also maintain professional boundaries and responsibilities. In that regard, the practitioner at this level is able to provide warmth, comfort, reassurance, and validation to troubled clients without violating appropriate boundaries. Master practitioners also maintain a muted sense of understanding that if clients were not intransigent, irascible, and disquieting, they would have little need for being in a therapist's office. Under challenging conditions prompted by such client behavior, the masters understand that maintaining a hopeful outlook and a positive therapeutic alliance are paramount.

Through clinical experience with a wide variety of clients, thoughtful supervision, personal reflection, and the development and integration of basic skills, the Level III counselor demonstrates a keen awareness of the cognitive, emotional, and relational aspects of the interaction between a client and herself. Therapists at this level can listen reflectively with the "third ear," calculate the impact of particular interventions on a client, sense the direction of client movement, and see the client completely within his or her context without losing objectivity or losing sight of the empathic therapeutic alliance that is necessary if the therapy is to be effective. They also realize that they must deal with each client as unique.

They have a well-calibrated sense of the impact of their interventions and accept client feedback regarding the fruitfulness of the treatment process or lack of such progress. Correspondingly, Level III practitioners are able to critique their interventions and use client feedback as a self-correcting mechanism that guides. They incorporate client feedback into their work as an important source of information for making certain that the client's goals and their own therapeutic goals are in alignment. Miscues are taken in stride without a sense of guilt, immobilizing self-denigration, or feeling of failure. In keeping with the characteristics of "resilient" individuals (see Seibert, 2005), Level III practitioners do not define themselves according to therapeutic frustrations, reversals, adversities, or misfortunes. Rather, with the help of professional values, they ground themselves with a devotion to learning from such setbacks because they understand that they are building another dimension of clinical experience.

Level III practitioners are also able to balance perspectives between the micro and macro issues of therapy. Correspondingly, they can move between the use of micro skills and techniques, on one hand, and the macro issues of the big picture and what is transpiring in treatment, on the other. Movement back and forth between micro and macro issues is fluid, and the relationship between them understood.

Just as all human development is not "linear" (i.e., it does not proceed smoothly from one level of functioning to another across all areas of activity but rather in an irregular pattern), the road to Level III functioning and beyond is not linear either. Although they demonstrate professional autonomy, at times, Level III practitioners may sense their particular clinical efforts with a client reaching a plateau and consult with others. But, their "consultation" reflects more of a quality of sharing than a dependence upon others. In addition, instead of perceiving a plateau with a specific client or in general professionally as an end point and acquiescing to it, they have become familiar with its being a time of unconscious consolidation of what has been learned. They are confident of emerging from plateaus with new understanding.

Level III practitioners do not proceed in a linear, lockstep, and systematic manner when they consider such things as empirical research and an evaluation of its efficacy—nor do they blindly incorporate what such research has to offer in their work with clients. They *do* evaluate their understanding of relevant research findings in the nonlinear light of a particular client in a unique context and the best course of treatment. This is especially the case regarding evidence-based practice (EBP). The Level III therapist makes a careful assessment (see Chapters 4 and 5) of a client and his complaint and circumstances, including a client's stage of change, level of distress, and so on, in determining the propriety of applying any intervention, especially "EBPPs." As Norcross and Hill (2003) have put it, there is a need for "tailoring" the therapy according to certain "patient behaviors or qualities" (see Norcross, Hogan, & Koocher, 2008a; 2008b).

At the threshold of becoming a master practitioner, a Level III therapist understands that no two clinicians are identical in the way in which they conduct treatment. Therapists differ in their personalities, style, theoretical orientation, and so on. As such, not only are interventions "tailored" to a particular client, but they are also by definition tailored according to the individual characteristics of the practitioner.

CRITICAL THINKING AND CLINICAL JUDGMENT

At a Level III stage of professional functioning, therapists and counselors demonstrate qualitatively different therapeutic behaviors, internal states of being, and ways of thinking about their clients, life, and problems encountered in living. Although the concept is not well articulated in the psychological literature, the development of clinical judgment is perhaps the sine qua non characteristic of the master practitioner. According to Facione and Facione (1996), across the entire spectrum of professional endeavors, clinical judgment shares a great deal in common with what has been called *critical thinking*. Clinical judgment is demonstrated in knowing what to do regarding such knotty issues as

- when to refer to another practitioner;
- when to recommend hospitalization, and how to do so;
- what sort of treatment approach to utilize in dealing with a particular client's concerns;
- when and how to confront;
- how to contend with termination-of-treatment issues;
- what to avoid focusing upon as a red herring;
- when and how to suggest a medication evaluation;
- discussing end-of-life decision making; and
- addressing questions pertaining to ideation of self-injury and harming others.

As the reader can readily fathom, the list is literally endless regarding how issues of clinical judgment arise. As a concrete and specific example, we offer the following. A demonstration of sound clinical judgment concerns what sort of treatment approach to utilize in dealing with a particular client's concerns. For example, the Level III respectfully recognizes the value and necessity of formal diagnosis while simultaneously understanding that strict categorization alone does not necessarily determine the most appropriate or effective treatment. As such, he is able to evaluate and gauge EBPs and adapt them to a specific client at a particular time according to the client's unique context. According to Gill (2005),

> What Evidence-Based Practice in Psychology (EBPP) does in the health care systems ... is to develop guidelines for best possible practice. It provides a comprehensive approach to the conceptualization of those guidelines. It relies heavily on the availability of adequate scientific and clinical evidence concerning the intervention being applied and the diagnostic condition being treated. (p. 5)

The adoption of EBPP has been defined as one of the most important issues adopted by the American Psychological Association (Gill, 2005). It has also been considered an important step in clinical decision making. According to John Norcross, "Clinical decisions should be made ... with consideration for the probable costs, benefits and available resources and options" (as quoted in Gill, p. 5). It is clinical judgment that determines when and how to apply EBPs. Level III practitioners also know what type of research has been used in producing a particular EBP and how much credence to place in the validity of any such research as it pertains to a particular client under consideration. The Level III practitioner addresses these issues with confidence, not in the correctness of her assertions but in the appropriateness of the need to address the issue at a particular time. Obviously, such confidence requires critical-thinking skills.

The sense of *clinical judgment* is not an easy capacity to define. Although the "ideal" critical thinker does not exist, according to Facione and Facione (1996) this person demonstrates a certain "profile":

> The dispositional profile of the ideal critical thinker is described by the Delphi [see Facione, 1990] experts as follows: The ideal critical thinker is habitually inquisitive, well-informed, trustful of reason, open-minded, flexible, fair-minded in evaluation, honest in facing personal biases, prudent in making judgments, willing to reconsider, clear about issues, orderly in complex matters, diligent in seeking relevant information, reasonable in the selection of criteria, focused in inquiry, and persistent in seeking results which are as precise as the subject and the circumstances of inquiry permit. (p. 134)

These attributes are surely impossible to attain in any one individual but are worthy of being an aspirational ideal. The embodiment of these qualities would indeed serve to form the ideal critical thinker as perhaps exemplified in the Level III therapist or the master practitioner in any profession. Specifically as applies to therapists and counselors in general, however, critical thinking is necessary but not sufficient to bring about effective outcomes, which are the product of a strong therapeutic alliance. Critical thinking also concerns being able to say, "I don't know," as opposed to being inauthentic, "faking" a response, or having an answer for everything. Clients understand "not knowing" even coming from an "expert" because they too have been in a position in which they did not know something. Clinical judgment is borne in a crucible of challenges that come from diverse clinical experiences, clinical supervision, common sense, and the facets of critical thinking described by Facione and Facione (1996) above.

From a general perspective, Level III practitioners do not see rigid distinctions between assessment and treatment, but rather are comfortable with the fluid borders between the two processes and how they complement each other. On an ongoing basis, they assess and evaluate client perceptions and progress, and adjust and refine their interventions accordingly. In that ongoing assessment process, Level III practitioners have trained themselves and honed *nonlinear-listening skills* to be exceptionally sensitive to key dynamic components (e.g., client "complaints," symptoms, life circumstances, and new dynamisms) operating within clients as well as changes in the status of those components. Furthermore, they are responsive to changes in dynamic components. Listening more effectively and strategically, the Level III practitioner recognizes, assesses, and addresses sudden changes that can and do impact current functioning and the goals of treatment.

Rather than having a fixed agenda of what the practitioner wants the client to address or believes the client needs to address, the Level III practitioner is flexible in addressing client concerns that have emerged between sessions and can recognize when such concerns represent the authentic versus the avoidant. Although a practitioner's ongoing assessment is crucial as the alliance and course of treatment evolve, the Level III understands that *the client's* appraisal of the progress of the treatment is essential (Miller, Mee-Lee, Plum, & Hubble, 2005).

Likewise, the master is keenly mindful of developmental tasks that a particular client might need to address that are new, looming, or settled unsatisfactorily. Aging, unexpected or forced retirement, the loss of a loved one, the breakup of a long-term relationship, the running of a woman's "biological clock," and so forth are all "developmental" tasks and may play a part not only in the formulation of a client's current problem but also in the formulation of potential solutions.

Furthermore, the Level III practitioner is mindful of that part of a client's narrative that suggests that the personality's old, trusted, reliable, and formerly successful methods of coping and problem solving are not adequate to the current set of circumstances. Or, correspondingly, a client has been applying inappropriate methods of coping to a particular set of circumstances, such as attempting to "get his way" in circumstances that make it virtually impossible to do so.

In their ongoing assessment of client functioning, Level III practitioners are sensitive to human nature's propensity for construing the choices resulting from life's challenging and problematic circumstances in terms of lose-lose alternatives: "I get to choose whether I want to be boiled in oil or burned at the stake." When closely examined, human beings are extraordinarily vulnerable to the development of such double binds. Although oversimplified, the individual's "life plan" (i.e., personality organization, values, beliefs, and sentiments) comprises relatively unchallenged "givens." As such, it is like a "personal religion" that demands all of one's loyalties. However, life's impartiality knows no such allegiances—it just is. Life has inherent demands and tasks that must be addressed; if not addressed, there are perceived consequences. How the personality of a client typically approaches such life demands may not be adequate to the task. In such instances, life and its inherent demands will not go away, and the individual finds it difficult or even unimaginable to modify the personality characteristics that are perceived as previously successful and "hardwired."

EMOTIONAL CHARACTERISTICS

Master practitioners have a sense of equanimity, especially about what they know and what their professional abilities are. With passion, they pursue knowledge and understanding of what the work of counseling and psychotherapy is all about, and they are never satisfied with what they know—they are constantly seeking to expand their knowledge base. In effect, they are not arrogant about their ability as therapists. Correspondingly, they are quite aware of their limitations.

In the *emotional domain*, Jennings and Skovholt (1999) described several categories that master therapists access and use: (a) They appear to have emotional receptivity, defined as being self-aware, reflective, nondefensive, and open to feedback; (b) they seem to be mentally healthy and mature individuals who attend to their own emotional well-being; and (c) they are aware of how their emotional health affects the quality of their work. Hence, Level III therapists are nonreactive in the face of a client's strong emotional reactions, can appropriately use their emotional impulses to illuminate the therapeutic discourse, and have sufficient capacity to soothe themselves in the moment when their emotions are stirred up.

Furthermore, Level III therapists are able to separate the "business" components (i.e., time costs money) and the caring components (i.e., the care and concern for clients are free). They also understand that it is a privilege to participate in the partnership of a healing relationship and the intimacy that clients share with them. They value foremost the trust displayed by clients.

It is ironic that the Level III practitioner is at the cusp of becoming a master practitioner but, after the work and passion devoted to her craft, is not particularly interested in such status or prestige. At this level of functioning, it is most likely that such practitioners do not even care about recognizing themselves as such. Such appellation would suggest self-aggrandizement, and master practitioners are by and large modest and humble about their abilities. They fully recognize that they are forever striving in pursuit of improvement but have long ago abandoned the fiction of achieving perfection in their work, if they ever pursued it at all. Thus, without the slightest expectation of ever arriving at perfection, they are in constant pursuit of improvement and excellence—to be the best that they can be.

Another hallmark of a Level III practitioner is that he has long ago relinquished any idea of "changing" a client through his interventions. If a clinician has "relinquished" such ideas, what sort of ideation is it that he *adheres* to? What is it that the practitioner *does*? Through the therapeutic relationship, Level III practitioners understand that they provide *the circumstances* within which change becomes possible. It is the client who must reorganize his or her thinking and behavior; it is the practitioner who provides the input that can make that possible. Furthermore, the Level III has achieved a level of comfort with not feeling obligated to change people. The Level III practitioner has learned to trust the processes of change—establishing and maintaining the therapeutic relationship, commitment to intense listening, access to nonlinear thinking, flexibility to changing client circumstances, creativity, and so on all are signal indicators of the processes of change.

SUMMARY

More than anything else, Level III practitioners are aware of how differently they now *think* from when they first began. We maintain that the hallmark of Level III practitioners is that they have learned to *think in nonlinear ways*. Nonlinear listening and becoming sensitive to the information it provides set the stage for nonlinear interventions—those universal, transtheoretical, paradoxical responses to clients that have the capacity to transform. It is to a further consideration of *how master practitioners think and intervene in nonlinear paradoxical ways* that we now devote our attention.

The Domain of Paradoxical Interventions

14

Part 1: Definition and Neutralizers

CONTENTS

INTRODUCTION: *PATCH ADAMS*

In 1998, Robin Williams played the lead character in the movie *Patch Adams* (Shadyac, 1998). The film is based upon the true story of a young man who eventually became what we would identify as a nonlinear-thinking physician. He challenged the staid medical establishment of the 1960s to embrace different points of view regarding the practice of medicine. In the course of a unique journey to find himself, Patch encountered an eccentric man in a mental hospital who claimed to have "nine fingers" on one hand. When questioned by his doctors about how many fingers *they* had when they held up one hand, he also told them that they had "nine fingers." In every other way, the gentleman seemed "sane," and even became Williams' mentor in terms of character issues. But, because of his preoccupation with having "nine fingers," Patch determines that the man is not well. In an important moment in the movie, late one night Patch is reading a book under low light. Fatigued and suffering from eye strain, he took off his eyeglasses, rubbed his eyes, and looked at his hand. As he attempted to refocus his eyes, he noticed that when he stared at a point just beyond his hand, he saw his fingers split into two! *Voila!* In a serendipitous moment, he discovered that, from *this* point of view, he indeed had "nine fingers." After informing the old man that he, too, now has "nine fingers," the man smiles knowingly at him and says, "*Sometimes you just have to approach things from a different vantage point.*"

In many respects, clients get "stuck" and develop perceptual ruts much like the scenario depicted in *Patch Adams*. As described in Chapters 12 and 13, impasses (or dilemmas) develop when there is conflict between schemas and life circumstances. These dilemmas seem unsolvable and produce feelings of ambivalence. When individuals experience feelings of ambivalence, they attempt to resolve them by vacillating endlessly, becoming immobilized, trying to escape, or letting fate decide. Most often, such ill-fated attempts to resolve seemingly irresolvable ambivalence result in the development of symptoms that clients complain of (e.g., depression or anxiety) in counseling. Symptoms then become excuses for not being able to solve life's challenges as well as preoccupations from which there is no escape—"How can I be expected to do anything about *that* when I'm so miserable and overwhelmed with *these symptoms*? I can barely function!" As a result, clients then focus on what have become disturbingly evident problematic symptoms (e.g., preoccupation, worrying, anger, stress, insomnia, depression, and nervousness) and cannot see the root cause of their dilemmas. Oftentimes, because of their focus on troubling symptoms, clients are unable to see circumstances in their lives differently (i.e., "9 fingers"). And yet, it is seeing something differently that creates the potential for clients to become more adaptive and functional. The question for counselors and therapists becomes, what can be done to facilitate and stimulate clients' "reappraisal"[1] of their circumstances (i.e., seeing things differently, more positively, and with more hope), diminish ambivalence, and help them cope in more constructive directions? To answer this question, we propose the following.

The concept of nonlinear thinking has been highlighted throughout the domains of Levels I and II in order to illustrate how master practitioners *think* about the practice of counseling and psychotherapy in order to be effective. As demonstrated, the domains are *evidence-based practices*. That is, the research literature supports the practices delineated in all the domains. We have also delineated how *nonlinear thinking* is exhibited within each of the common domains that underlie all effective therapy[2] to maximize successful client outcomes. There is one more level of counselor development, in which all of the Level I and II domains merge together: paradoxical interventions. Paradoxical interventions represent perhaps the most universal, sophisticated, and elegant of the *nonlinear thought processes* demonstrated by master practitioners (*regardless of their theoretical orientation*). As such, explicit use of paradoxical interventions is a hallmark characteristic of Level III practitioner development and deserving of consideration as another unique domain. Through the use of *nonlinear thinking* as expressed in *paradoxical interventions*, therapists are able to intervene with clients in a way that seamlessly integrates all Level I and II domains using both *linear* and *nonlinear* thinking. But, what is a paradox, and what are paradoxical interventions?

DEFINITION OF PARADOX AND PARADOXICAL INTERVENTIONS

For our particular purposes, there are actually several different ways of defining or looking at what a paradox is. The *Random House American College Dictionary* (2006) defines *paradox* as follows: "A statement or proposition seemingly self-contradictory or absurd, and yet explicable as expressing a truth" (p. 878). For example, the old saying "Sometimes you have to go slow in order to go fast" expresses a truth about people who are in a rush. This is because more often than not, such people are rushed, get sloppy, make mistakes, and have to do something over again (thus taking *more* time). It is contradictory (and even absurd) because on the surface, it doesn't seem true—slowing down does not appear to be an intuitively logical (or linear) way of getting something done quickly! On the other hand, human experience reveals an element of truth entailed in having to redo something because of carelessness in working too fast.

A second understanding of paradox related to the description above is that it can also be viewed as a statement or situation that contains two true elements that cannot simultaneously coexist, although most often they do coexist, which defies logic, or is counterintuitive. That is, although each statement is true, when put together they don't seem to make logical (i.e., *linear*) sense. In fact, the word *paradox* actually comes from Greek and means "beyond belief." As a brief example of this view of a paradox, we cite a classical paradox in Figure 14.1.

If "Everything in this box is a lie," then the statement must be the truth; but if the statement is the truth, it says that everything in the box is a lie! Both statements can't exist simultaneously, although each statement can be considered "true."

Paradox: Counselor's Perspective

In order to understand paradoxical interventions in treatment, each of the above perspectives on the definition of a paradox is relevant. *The first definition of a paradox presented above is pertinent to a counselor's perspective.* That is, an explicit paradoxical intervention consists of seemingly self-contradictory and sometimes even absurd therapeutic comments about a client's circumstances. Although they are seemingly self-contradictory, or even absurd, effective paradoxical comments *contain an element of truth*. In many of the previous chapters, when we have illustrated a *nonlinear* response to a client's concern, we have utilized a paradoxical intervention. For example, in Chapter 10, the therapist told his client (Clinical Case Example 10.3) that she was emotionally stuck in a bad marriage because she wanted to be a winner

Everything in this box is a lie.

FIGURE 14.1   View of a paradox.

(she was still the wife) and getting a divorce would make her a loser (she would have "lost" to another woman). Thus. it can be seen that staying in a bad marriage made her a winner *from her point of view* and thus contains an element of truth. Hence, some paradoxical interventions help the client find *new meaning* (i.e., something positive) in a client's symptom or complaint, whereas others "prescribe" the symptom (i.e., advocating that a client reproduce or engage in a symptom or complaint for constructive purposes). More specifically, practitioners use paradoxical interventions to:

1. neutralize the negative impact of critical, negativistic, inflammatory, or disparaging remarks directed at the therapy or the therapist;
2. tranquilize and help to calm clients upset and overwhelmed with emotion;
3. positively energize and mobilize client resources in more useful rather than useless directions; and
4. challenge client behaviors that are disruptive to client functioning and/or well-being.

Although paradoxical statements and perspectives—by nature of their contradictory or absurd elements—challenge clients' views of their circumstances, they do so by *joining* rather than opposing symptoms, complaints, problem behaviors, resistance, and reactance.[3] At the same time, paradoxical therapeutic interventions *always* contain positive qualities such as empathy, encouragement, and at times humor.[4]

Paradox: Client's Perspective

When clients experience dilemmas (i.e., approach–approach, avoidance–avoidance, approach–avoidance, and double approach–avoidance; see Chapter 12), they typically feel highly ambivalent, which places them in a double bind. The double bind (or dilemma) contains two true elements that cannot exist simultaneously: "If I choose to address this issue in a direct way, it will go against my schematized worldview (e.g., 'I am afraid that I might fail, or lose something that I value fundamentally"). At the same time, if I don't face this issue, it won't go away, and I am failing to meet what I perceive that life is demanding of me." The person is stuck in his ambivalence because both poles contain an element of truth that cannot coexist. The symptom (e.g., vacillating endlessly, becoming immobilized, trying to escape, or letting fate decide), however, allows for these to coexist, though at a price (a person's health, anxiety, functioning, etc.). This price creates a "tension" that requires some sort of "resolution." When clients try to "resolve" the dilemma on their own, however, without understanding the underlying ambivalence and the paradoxical nature of their wanting their cake and eating it too, the results are typically highly dissatisfying and only add to their apprehension and confusion.

Paradoxical interventions are therapeutically effective because they mirror the tension of a client's ambivalence or dilemma. In fact, the second definition of paradox is *the same* as the one for a double bind described above (a statement that contains two true elements that cannot coexist simultaneously, yet *do* coexist). This pertains to the *client's perspective* on her circumstances and how she experiences paradoxical interventions. The resolution of the ambivalences stemming from a dilemma doesn't come from the client's struggle with her problematic symptom such as vacillating endlessly, becoming paralyzed, trying to escape, or letting fate decide. As Watzlawick, Weakland, and Fisch (1974) indicated, such efforts are all members of the same "class" or "logical type" of effort. Instead, resolution comes from a different "class" or "logical type" of effort—the practitioner's new (e.g., absurd or illogical) reinterpretation of the client's dilemma and circumstances. The practitioner's reinterpretation of the client's dilemma and circumstances results from a *nonlinear* understanding (i.e., a different "logical type") of the client's schematized worldview, understanding how the present circumstance creates ambivalence, and so on. Such understanding unbalances the "tension" and presents new possibilities that accommodate client schemas, reappraises the current problematic circumstances, and resolves ambivalence. Just like *Patch Adams*, the client sees things from a different point of view that allows both seemingly inconsistent statements (i.e., a man says he has nine fingers, but people have only five fingers on one hand) to be true.

As an example, a young man says, "I want to be with Jane, the love of my life, but she wants to get married. I would marry her; *but* I am afraid to lose my freedom. Jane expects a commitment, and I don't want to lose *her*. As a result, I've become very, very anxious and depressed and I'm barely functional. But, getting married would compromise my freedom!" This young lover cannot have it both ways and may seek a counselor or therapist to help him regarding what he should do. He *truly* loves Jane, and he *truly* loves his freedom (to come, go, and do as he pleases), but from *his* vantage point he can't have both conditions be true at the same time—one has to go because of life circumstances. Jane is telling him that it is time for him to make up his mind about what he wants! She either wants to "take things to the next level" or move on with her life without him. This set of circumstances (i.e., the demands of the situation and the client wanting both Jane and his freedom) creates ambivalence for the client, and he becomes *stuck between a rock and a hard place*, while *being pulled in two different directions at once*. Anxiety, nervousness, and depression develop, and ultimately provide an excuse from the prospect of having to choose between Jane and his freedom. Continued preoccupation with nervousness, anxiety, and so on prompts him to seek treatment for his symptoms as a compromise to his dilemma. Thus, he has found a way to *have his cake and eat it too* but at the price of experiencing and suffering with his symptoms. In the process, his self-esteem is preserved because he has a "reason" for not addressing the life circumstances that demand attention. Therefore, from the client's perspective, it is not *him* but the involuntary symptomatic behavior that "prevents" a more direct and commonsense attempt at a solution of the problem.

Linear approaches to helping a client resolve her ambivalence and dilemma usually fall far short of desired outcomes because of the complex nature of client concerns. On the other hand, *nonlinear* paradoxical interventions can be most helpful in that regard. A client perceives a paradoxical intervention as two statements of fact (or truth) that seemingly cannot coexist, but do. That prompts a client to constructively react (emotionally) against her therapist's interpretation or directive and her own symptom or complaint. A paradoxical intervention prompts an emotional response that either broadens a client's perspective in order to see her problem in a different way; or advocates for the status quo (or maintaining the problem), which shows the client that the problem is within her control. To make sense of such interventions, clients are required to shift their perspective or reappraise the problem or symptom in a way that allows therapy to move constructively forward.

Returning to the example above, if the young man's therapist gave him a benign but firm directive *not* to make a decision with his current symptoms of anxiety, depression, and nervousness (i.e., "strong emotional conditions") because it might be the wrong decision, he would essentially be intervening in a paradoxical way. The therapist is advising that the client do what he is already doing—do not make a decision—*but for benign reasons*. Such a directive contains an absurdity because the client is already not making a decision. It is also absurd because the therapist is agreeing with the client (after the client has defined his not making a decision as a problem)! But, the therapist may add that it is generally not a good idea and not in the client's interests to make a decision under such strong emotional conditions (an element of truth). This promotes an affective expression that highlights the client's flawed thinking and behaving. We present Clinical Case Example 14.1 to illustrate.

Clinical Case Example 14.1: Redefining a Complaining Wife

A man whose wife discovered him in an adulterous affair came to therapy struggling to maintain his marriage and learn how to deal with his desire to "crawl under a rock" due to how he had betrayed his wife and children. At the same time, he indicated that he had great difficulty in reconciling certain patterns he had observed in his marriage even *before* his brief affair. Although he was "mortified" over his own behavior, he maintained that his marriage was far from perfect prior to his affair. Communications with his wife were characterized by seemingly incessant questioning by her that ended up with her "never being wrong." Their children had made the same observation of their mother: that she "always had to be right." Everyone likes to be right, but an extreme need to be "right" (or never "wrong") can clearly be aggravating to others. In the present instance, this pattern of relating left the husband feeling like he was "groveling" and constantly apologizing without ever feeling as though he was being forgiven for anything, let alone for having had his affair.

Obviously, this distraught man was *interpreting* what his wife's behavior was all about, and he didn't like what he was looking at or feeling. Seeing that the man had made some very keen observations about his marriage both pre- and post affair, the therapist first gave the dispirited man a note of encouragement by complimenting him on his recognition of this pattern in his marriage. Note that the man is dispirited, is guilty, and wants desperately to reclaim an honorable life. The encouragement is directed at his having an ability to make observations. Knowing that this man was a highly paid executive in a very responsible position, the therapist asked the man if he was a "data-driven" manager. He enthusiastically responded, "Yes!" The therapist then offered the following "prosocial" paradoxical explanations by stating that his wife was not very much different from many women who, by questioning their husbands, were looking for *information*. For someone who has a privately vested interest in being "right" (i.e., "perfect"), however, there can never be enough information. Being "right" and having the information to be "right" are what make her "tick."

The man responded by enthusiastically noting, "That spins it so differently! I take it (i.e., *privately logical*) as questions—like how I was brought up with my mother and father constantly demeaning me. That's intriguing if that's the case. I never think to answer the questions because I'm pissed off! That might be the most enlightening thing I've ever heard about my relationship with my wife. That rings true! I was verbally abused by my mother and father for 20 years. When I hear those questions from my wife, it's like I'm being verbally abused. It might be me overreacting to circumstances of verbal abuse in my childhood!"

Consider how Clinical Case Example 14.1 fits the definitions of a paradoxical intervention. First, the paradoxical intervention was seemingly absurd because it didn't fit the picture that the client had painted about his wife (complete with "independent corroboration" from his kids) as a nagging and controlling woman who alienated everyone. The client developing such a picture of his wife is stimulated by his long-held schema dynamics (i.e., the verbal abuse he experienced as a kid). However, when he looks at his wife's behavior from another vantage point previously unavailable to him, then the more benign (i.e., positive, prosocial) interpretation of his wife's behavior (*seeking information*) becomes more acceptable to him. Thus, from the client's point of view, the idea that she may have a more benign purpose for her questioning behavior mollifies and accommodates his predefined (schematized) idea about her.[5] This helps him to *reappraise* his beliefs and emotional reactions toward her, as well as embrace another perspective. Her questioning is not of the same "logical type" of verbally abusive behavior as that of his parents; it is of a different "type" of behavior. The new interpretation of his wife's behavior allows him an avenue of opportunity to continue to stay in the marriage, which is something that he wants to do. Otherwise, he is stuck with his double bind: "I want to stay in the marriage, but to do so is to continue to take abuse (which my schemas won't allow me to do)!"

Thus far, we have attempted to define and discuss paradox and paradoxical interventions within the larger context of *nonlinear* thinking, as well as discuss the use of paradoxical interventions from client and counselor perspectives. Next, we examine some of the *basic elements* of paradoxical interventions. In this regard, we will define reframing and its central place in the use of paradoxical interventions. Then, we will examine the *nonlinear thinking* behind paradoxical interventions, or how paradoxical interventions work to help the client resolve his dilemmas. Next, we demonstrate how *nonlinear* listening helps a therapist decide what paradoxical intervention a client needs from therapy, as well as how to construct the paradoxical intervention.

FUNDAMENTAL ELEMENTS OF PARADOXICAL INTERVENTIONS

The Strategy and Use of Paradoxical Interventions: The "How-To" of Nonlinear Process

Utilizing paradoxical interventions effectively (e.g., how to find a positive dimension to a client's symptom or complaint) can appear daunting, but there are a number of basic nonlinear principles that can assist the process. We begin with the basic elements of reframing, and then discuss the use of *nonlinear* listening and responding as the building blocks of paradoxical intervention. The key elements of the contradictory or absurd messages with an element of truth that need to be contained in the paradoxical intervention are revealed by the skill of nonlinear listening. Understanding this along with the client's schema dynamics guides a client's interventions.

Reframing

Reframing, or *redefining* as it is sometimes called, is a *nonlinear* paradoxical intervention that provides new meaning for a problematic concern. Generally, reframing offers a *positive* implication or significance to what a client has been appraising as negative or problematic. Thus, it is most typically *unexpected* (i.e., "anti-expectation") and requires a client to *reappraise* her concern (e.g., symptom, complaint, circumstances, behavior, or beliefs), most often in a different and more positive way. Upon hearing and understanding what the therapist has paradoxically reframed, the process of *reappraising* something that has had negative meaning can produce emotions and their concomitant feelings that are calming, liberating, relieving, and change stimulating. All of the paradoxical interventions that we describe in some way involve the process of reframing: redefining and conveying new meaning, which stimulates reappraisal within a client. The use of such reframing is universal in the therapy literature (e.g., see Mozdzierz, Lisiecki, & Macchitelli, 1989).

In Clinical Case Example 14.1, the *redefinition* of the wife's behavior as *seeking information* was a more benign (i.e., positive, prosocial) interpretation of his wife's behavior than understanding it as reminiscent of the early childhood verbal abuse he encountered that was now unacceptable to him. The specific goal and intended effects of this redefinition were to *tranquilize* and *calm* the man as a result of a new understanding. The different and more benign definition of his wife's behavior provided such calming. He was cognitively "stuck" in a repetitive *personally nonlinear* mind-set about his wife, which continued to agitate him and cause him to respond negatively toward his wife. The reader will note the numerous ways in which this nonlinear paradoxical reframing of the wife's behavior affected the man: He recognized the strong emotional connection to the chronic feelings of being in a defensive and angry mode stimulated by his wife's nagging. After hearing the paradoxical reframing, he *reappraised* the difference between his wife's "seeking information" and his parents' abuse, and, literally, new associative learning in the client's emotional system had taken place. Although not all redefining results in such new understanding, very often perceiving new meanings to problematic life circumstances can provide significant emotional relief (e.g., tranquilizing or calming) to clients.

Reframing and Looking for Opposites, Positives, and Opportune Moments

A major orienting principle in understanding how to formulate and apply paradoxical interventions concerns making use of dialectics. Dialectics is the process of contrasting a thing with its opposite in order to create a new meaning. In terms of *reframing*, the dialectic process involves looking for the *opposite* of what a client is describing as "the problem." For example, in Clinical Case Example 14.1, the client's perception of his wife's incessant questioning was posed as her seeking information. What would be the opposite of "questioning" (with all its pejorative connotations for this particular man)? Although questioning can be a "Spanish Inquisition" type of torture (perhaps not unlike what the client was experiencing), it can also be simpler, more benign "information seeking" from someone who was not an easy conversationalist. This reinterpretation of his wife's behavior not only resonated in a different, more positive way with his understanding of *her* but also resonated with his understanding of himself (i.e., schemas) and why he was chronically in an irritated and angry frame of mind, especially with his wife's manner of relating. His responses and demeanor toward his wife's questioning dramatically changed for the positive. As a result of the dialectic process (considering the opposite), the therapist's paradoxical intervention allowed the client to create a new meaning (i.e., a "reappraisal") and resolve his ambivalence toward his wife.

Reframing and Looking for the Positive in the Negative

In advocating for a symptom in order to effectively use paradoxical interventions, a practitioner can ask herself, "What is something *positive* that a client's symptom, complaint, etc., accomplishes? Does it help a client to avoid, excuse, postpone, achieve a private sense of triumph (albeit at a price), etc.? Does it provide a possible solution to the client's struggle with ambivalence? What positive *new meaning* can be derived from the symptom?" When something positive can be gleaned from what it is that the symptom, behavior, complaint, or the like accomplishes, positive effects are conveyed to the client in an encouraging and thoughtful manner. For example, if a client is avoiding something, new meaning is found in reframing it as *preventing something bad from happening.* If he is postponing something, new meaning can be found in reframing such postponement as an indication that the client is not yet prepared for something and it is better to be prepared before committing himself. Can anything good happen from being unprepared for something?

Nonlinear Listening: Determining What a Client Needs

In formulating and using effective paradoxical interventions, a therapist must clearly understand a client's schema dynamics, her emotional responses, and the nature of her ambivalence (i.e., what kind of dilemma she is in—approach–approach, etc.). This begins with assessment that comes from nonlinear listening. As outlined in Chapter 2, and discussed in other chapters, *nonlinear* listening provides therapists a valuable window into a client's schema dynamics, emotional system, and underlying ambivalence about change. Listening for congruence (or the lack of correspondence between what is said and what is meant), listening for absence (or what is *not* being said), listening for inference (or the purpose behind "I don't want …" statements), listening for presence (or the nonverbal behaviors that add meaning), and listening for resistance (or the desire *not* to change) all provide the starting point for a therapist's use of paradoxical interventions. They provide the contextual information about the client (schema dynamics, etc.) that makes the paradoxical intervention unique and specific to the client, which, in turn, makes it more effective.

Nonlinear Responding: Advocating (Benignly) for the Status Quo

When a therapist *advocates (benignly) for the status quo*, she suggests or instructs a client *to continue* with certain symptoms or behaviors but for benevolent purposes. Remember that a client's symptoms represent attempts to resolve dilemmas created due to ambivalences felt when a client's schema dynamics are found incompatible with life's demands or the circumstances that clients are facing. Advocating for the status quo must be done in a *benign* manner to provide an opportunity for a client to maintain schemas until such time as he feels safe enough to modify them and address life's demands more constructively or the circumstances change. Thus, *he can have his cake and eat it too*; at the same time, continuing the behavior produces feelings of discomfort at the lack of change. This is paradoxically absurd because it sends a message to clients to keep engaging in a problematic behavior that they want to change. It is paradoxical because the intervention is working to change the behaviors by telling the client *not* to change the behavior.

When *advocating (benignly) for the status quo*, it is important to remember that a client has typically been "fighting" (i.e., with herself, her symptom, despairing, etc., or with other people, e.g., being resistant, rejecting, or forming impasses). As a result, when using a paradoxical intervention that *advocates (benignly) for the status quo*, a therapist "joins" with the symptom or complaint in a way that is accepting, embracing, and endorsing, while empathically acknowledging a client's right to feel the way she does and be the way she is. Acceptance and joining are important considerations, for they encompass the contextual and prosocial aspects of paradoxical interventions. Such interventions authenticate a client's experience. That allows a therapist to assume a position of symptom advocate while reinforcing the therapeutic alliance. Such behavior gives a client nothing, or at least less, to be resistant to or "against." The therapeutic "leverage" and energy a client has invested in her symptom are advantageously and ironically utilized to help her.

In some interventions, a therapist *paradoxically advocates (benignly) for the status quo* by encouraging a client to teach or demonstrate the behavior, or by directing the client *not* to change. For example, in the movie *Don Juan DeMarco*, which we first discussed in Chapter 6, Marlon Brando's psychiatrist character recognizes that Johnny Depp's character is not ready to shed his "Don Juan" persona (which offers him protection from a broken heart and a disappointing life), and advocates that he maintain it by "playing along" with him. In *advocating (benignly) for the status quo* or prescribing the symptom, a therapist provides the *unexpected opportunity* for an unconscious client *reappraisal of* his symptom, circumstances, behavior, beliefs, and so on in a way that is different and more positive from what he has perceived or has not previously considered. Clinical Case Example 14.2 may prove helpful.

Clinical Case Example 14.2: A Woman Complaining of Dizziness

A 50-something single woman with multiple chronic medical problems (i.e., COPD, diabetes, heart condition, hypotension, etc.) who was semiretired from her work in the health care industry found herself unexplainably depressed after two brief successful outpatient surgical procedures. Her depression led to a brief stay in a psychiatric hospital and referral for outpatient medication and therapy follow-up.

Upon beginning outpatient therapy, she described her chronic medical conditions and had numerous complaints, which began with her still being depressed. She legitimately described being depressed because she had no interest in doing anything, nothing gave her satisfaction, and she had "no life." This latter comment meant that she had *no* relatives and *no* friends other than at her place of part-time employment, to which she couldn't return until she obtained medical authorization. She was bored at home with "nothing to do but watch TV" and complained of insomnia and chronic anxiety that she had never experienced before. Her psychiatrist explained that he had prescribed three benzodiazepine drugs from which the woman reported no relief—something the psychiatrist had never encountered before. Her antidepressant medications also seemed to provide no relief.

Toward the end of the first session, she bitterly complained that she had always been productive, busy, and a generally neat and thorough housekeeper all of her life but that her home was now looking shabby with laundry undone, dishes piling up, and no desire to address any of it. She could not address any household tasks because of one of her medical problems. That is, she suffered from *hypotension*: "Any time that I get up to do anything for more than 10 minutes, I have to go back and lay down because I get dizzy." Her "solution" was to return to bed, which she found intolerable. Her physicians had not put restrictions on her doing the activities of daily living, including light housekeeping, but to little avail.

After listening to the woman's description of her inactivity and hypotension in the context of her quite extensive list of medical problems, the therapist suggested that it seemed important for her to be busy, but it was also necessary for her to be cautious—namely, she did not want to provoke an episode of passing out, which could have serious complications. The therapist then suggested that *if* she was going to do anything around the house, it was important for her to limit her activities to no more than 10 minutes. She was then to return to bed and lay down.

At the very beginning of the next therapy session, the woman somewhat smugly reported that for some reason within a day of her last session, she cleaned the entire house, vacuumed, did all her dishes, and finished numerous loads of laundry as well with no ill effects. Although she continued to complain of her depression and unrelenting anxiety, from that point on she continued to be more active. Although she still complained of a variety of things, she joined a support group, went shopping for groceries, began searching for a new church affiliation, and so on, also with no ill effects.

In Clinical Case Example 14.2, there were many "complaints" that the client was making. The immediate assessment concerned her complaint about being bored and having much to do but being unable to do it for more than 10 minutes. One "solution" that this woman seemed to apply to her dilemma and circumstances involved trying to do things but becoming discouraged, frightened, bored, or perhaps a combination of those reactions. When benignly encouraged to maintain the status quo (i.e., *limit her activities to no more than 10 minutes*) and then return to bed, the woman responded with a somewhat prolific burst of activity that seemed to continue. Her movement *toward* housework was abortive; the therapist suggested moving *away* from her housework by engaging in only a few minutes of such activity and then returning to bed *for safety reasons* (i.e., benign purposes). Also important in Clinical Case Example 14.2, the woman demonstrated disdain toward several of her physicians and, by extrapolation, other authority figures (e.g., supervisors). *Nonlinear listening for congruence* revealed the discrepancy between the physician's treatment and the client's lack of progress, suggesting that there may be a hidden agenda and considerable ambivalence. Detecting and understanding such a personal characteristic helped guide the therapist's intervention by posing a suggestion that would have one of the following outcomes: Either the woman was likely to disregard it, or it would help keep her functioning within the safe boundaries of "10 minutes" of physical activity. As a result, the therapist was able to construct a paradoxical intervention that is absurd ("Do no more than 10 minutes and return to bed"—something that she was already doing). From the client's perspective, she receives two true messages that cannot coexist (for her): "You shouldn't try so hard" and "Listen to me; I know what is best for you." The first message was a comfort (in a way) because it didn't challenge her to do anything other than what she already had been doing. But the second message made the comfort in the first statement intolerable because her view of herself was that she was *always* capable of doing things and her view of others was that they didn't know what was best (especially doctors).

If this sounds much like the martial art of jujitsu (judo), you wouldn't be far off. In many ways, the art of judo and clinical practice deal with similar "structural issues." (For a greater discussion of martial arts and the process of therapy, see Crommpton, 1998; Gleser & Brown, 1988; Mandel, Weizmann, Millan, Greenhow, & Speirs, 1975; Koizumi, 1960; Saposnek, 1980; Sneed, Balestri, & Belfri, 2003; Westbrook & Ratti, 1974.) Clients want change and yet strangely resist change. To deal with this contradiction, there are acceptance strategies and change strategies such as that identified in Clinical Case Example 14.2. Likewise, judo is composed of two concepts: *Ju* is the practice of *yielding* to an opponent's strength, whereas *Do* refers to the way or the teaching. Within the small confines of the practice mats or a clinician's office, a client wanting change is pushing and pulling to resist that change. To meet force with force (i.e., power struggles) is counterproductive. Instead, when a client pushes (e.g., advocates for a change), a clinician yields, and when a client pulls (e.g., resists change strategies and suggestions via linear thinking), a clinician goes with the pull. In the pushing and pulling, the clinician "joins" the client's "force," whichever way it is moving. The purpose of the clinician yielding or joining the client's force is to unbalance the client, to create uncertainty for the throw, or for a different point of view, a view of the other side of the ambivalence polarity or dialectic so that something new can emerge. Also, in judo the defender often tries to throw an opponent without creating any unbalance. In therapy also, a clinician may attempt to persuade or argue with a client without creating any unbalance in his point of view. In paradoxical thinking and dialectics, the unbalance is created by the nonlinear dialectical thinking, which allows a client to engage the other side of his dialectic ambivalence. As Sneed et al. (2003) have suggested, a clinician's task is to engage a client in his dialectical struggle in order to reach a synthesis of the polarities by unbalancing the client and playing out the dichotomous ambivalence that exists in the patient's mind. It has also been suggested that clients want to change (for reasons of social approval or health) and, at the same time, do not want to change (for reasons of a sense of inadequacy or loss of pleasure and safety). As we discuss specific paradoxical interventions, we will illustrate how many of them work to paradoxically *advocate* (benignly) *for the status quo.*

Nonlinear Assessment: Searching for Previous Solutions

Another *nonlinear* principle useful in planning paradoxical interventions is to identify not only what the complaint is but also what the client has tried to do about it (as well as tracking what typically happens as a result). What a client has done represents her *solution* to her symptom or complaint. As a client discovers her solution to be ineffectual, she typically engages in doing *more of the same* (as with the woman in Clinical Case Example 14.2). For example, a typical complaint is "I can't sleep!" A client will then report all the ways she has tried to *make herself go to sleep.* This is a contradiction, however. No one can make herself fall asleep; we have to allow ourselves to fall asleep. Or, for example, when a client's spouse is unresponsive to subtle messages, the same messages are repeated but louder and oftentimes with increasing amounts of acrimony, and so on.

It is helpful to understand that clients' solutions are variations on a *theme.* In Chapter 5, we introduced the idea that there is typically a central theme of what a client does in order to contend with his problem or complaint. In Chapters 8 and 9, we discussed how these themes are related to an individual's schema dynamics. In Chapter 13, we discussed how solution-focused approaches look at what clients have tried before (themes); these solutions can also be starting points for paradoxical interventions. In many respects, the theme is like listening to a familiar song such as "Happy Birthday," but it is played in a different musical key, in a different tempo (e.g., rock, reggae, or jazz), or by a different instrument. The different key or the different instrument may make it temporarily appear like a different song, but *the relationship* of the notes to one another will disclose that the song is the same. It is likewise listening to *what theme* a client expresses as a *solution* to his problem. Understanding the theme underlying a client's solution to his problem provides an insight into where not to go while simultaneously expressing a direction to explore in perhaps redefining a situation.

MAINTAINING THE THERAPEUTIC ALLIANCE: CONVEYING PARADOXICAL INTERVENTIONS

There are several important considerations involved in a therapist actually conveying paradoxical interventions in a way that maintains the therapeutic alliance. The first is the therapist's conviction that, indeed, there is a positive element of truth to what she is conveying to her client; the therapist must be able to see, feel, hear, and understand the element of truth in the paradoxical intervention. It is also important to understand that the "truthfulness" of the intervention is relative and not absolute.

Furthermore, it is essential that a clinician understands and believes that *this is* the best way to facilitate client change.

Furthermore, if counselors understand that behaviors, symptoms, and complaints do not have just one meaning, and that a different view of the situation is necessary for lasting (i.e., "second-order") change, then it becomes possible to understand that *reframing* provides another meaning—a more constructive and benign meaning—that the client hasn't come upon. Thus, if a client continues with a symptom or complaint, he is cooperating with the therapist and moving in a more constructive direction; and if the symptom is abandoned, the client is also served. A therapist's belief in what she is paradoxically suggesting is important in helping a client believe in it.

Another important component of conveying a paradoxical intervention is to remember that such interpretations *are not forced* upon a client. They are simply offered for his consideration. *A therapist must never fight with a client.* Despite what is demonstrated in movies and TV dramas in which a "therapist" *definitively* tells a client what he has done right or wrong, fighting with a client, according to many researchers, is not very productive (Beutler, Moleiro, & Talebi, 2002; Norcross, 2002; Salovey & Fraser, 2007). Instead, a therapist must always approach the client in a spirit of seeking a deeper understanding of the client as well as more detailed information from him. One approach to this, outlined in Chapter 3, can be seen in a clinician adopting a stance of "not knowing" (often thought of as the "Colombo"[6] approach). This presents a therapist as less threatening and potentially allows a client to disclose more information (e.g. "I know what I mean when I say that I am anxious, but I am not sure what you mean when you say you were anxious in that argument with your father"). In addition, the nonlinear-thinking therapist utilizes her impressions to deliver a paradoxical intervention in the form of statements such as "I noticed that ..." or some variation of "It occurred to me ..." or "Could it be that ...?" This allows clients to absorb paradoxical directives without becoming defensive while increasing their impact.

Clinical Case Example 14.3 may prove helpful in bringing together many of the characteristics of paradoxical interventions described above.

Clinical Case Example 14.3: Unacceptable Sexual Behavior

A hard-working, well-educated, and multitalented man in his mid-40s diagnosed with bipolar disorder had worked diligently to manage "highs" and "lows." He took his medications regularly and came for therapy approximately once a month after more regular weekly sessions no longer appeared necessary. Because of his own poor childhood experiences of being victimized by bullies, he sought to treat others according to the "Golden Rule." That is, as an operating philosophy he treated others with a respect and thoughtfulness that he would like to have from others. As such, he presented himself as genuinely friendly, likable, outgoing, and considerate. It was a successful formula that worked well for him, and more often than not he was rewarded in kind. He was scrupulous about adhering to it and was equally scrupulous about other aspects of his life as well.

Having been divorced several years earlier, he dated consistently only to realize as time went on that several of his serious relationships had fallen short of what it was that he was looking for in a life partner. At such times, he would take time to heal, but he would acknowledge in therapy that he would rent pornographic videos and masturbate. He complained that he felt terribly guilty (i.e., had strong emotional cognitions stemming from high moral standards) and believed such behavior to be immature, regressive, and even "sinful." Nevertheless, sexual gratification is a legitimate human need, and at certain times he would indulge but feel guilty.

QUESTIONS

1. What are the "poles" of the client's dilemma?
2. What schema dynamics (view of the self, others, and life and the world) can you detect?
3. How might you construct a paradoxical intervention (using the two definitions above)?

In Clinical Case Example 14.3, the client's *ambivalence* about his behavior is clear: His view of self dictated that he is a "good" person in more ways than one. That is, not only does he want to treat others well and be treated that way in return, but he also wants to conduct himself morally well. When he masturbates, he believes that he is not conducting himself morally well (i.e., not living up to his perceived view of self). But, the evidence is overwhelming that physical-sexual gratification is a highly desirable human pursuit. Like all human beings caught in this kind of dilemma, he wants to have his cake and eat it too. That is, he wants to be perceived as being a good person (i.e., the expression of having his "cake"), but he engages in a sexual activity (i.e., "eating it too") that he considers morally bad (and something a "good" person wouldn't do). In his mind, he can't be a good person and indulge in masturbatory behavior at the same time, even though each is something desirable. The question is, how does a therapist respond in an encouraging way to someone who is "confessing" such behavior and expressing such guilt? The answer to the client's paradoxical dilemma is a *nonlinear paradoxical intervention*.

In this particular instance, the therapist suggested that the masturbatory behavior was perhaps an "expression" or "communication" from his inner mind suggesting that he was lonely and in need of some sort of comfort that masturbation seemed to provide. Indeed, the few times he "confessed" such behavior seemed to occur when he had just ended a relationship that had not gone well. Perhaps the view of self (i.e., "I'm a good person") can accommodate the added dimension that he is a "lonely" good person who temporarily needs comfort in this particular way. The therapist also added that perhaps his client could look at how high he had set the bar for acceptable behavior and that he might want to examine if it indeed was so excessive that no one might be able to live up to it. The man's response was "I think you may have something there!"

From the client's perspective, he experiences two truths that cannot coexist simultaneously: "I'm a bad person because I'm doing something that I consider morally 'wrong' and immature, but my view of self is that I am a good person!" From the therapist's perspective, the client is a good person who is lonely; masturbation is not so much something that is wrong but rather a communication that he is lonely and needs comfort. A set of circumstances in which the client believes he is engaged in bad behavior but is a good person represents two contradictory statements that can nevertheless be rationalized as expressing a truth.

In Clinical Case Example 14.3, the therapist's paradoxical comments *reframed* the client's masturbatory behavior in a *prosocial manner*. Those comments enabled the client to have a different emotional reaction that allowed him to reappraise the situation, accommodate his schema dynamics, and reconcile both his unacceptable behavior (i.e., masturbation) *and* a positive view of self (i.e., still being a good person, albeit a lonely one)—effectively resolving his ambivalence toward it. The interventions were paradoxical in nature because the same *problematic* masturbatory behavior was presented in a *more positive and acceptable way* (i.e., two truths can't exist simultaneously). The comments presented an interpretation of the client's situation that was *unexpected and beyond* what he had previously considered (i.e., outside of his perceptual rut and *at odds with his expectations*). And yet, each comment was presented in a context, manner, and framework that made his current situation more understandable, acceptable, and hopeful.

When deconstructing the therapist's intervention, the following is revealed. The therapist first considered the nature of the complaint. *Nonlinear listening for inference* suggested that the client's complaint was that masturbation is something "bad" and, for him, "sinful." Although it may seem unreasonable to view masturbation as sinful, it is clearly reasonable that it represented *the client's reality*. The *opposite* of being sinful concerns removing masturbation from the realm of "sin." Thus, although his "symptom" was disconcerting because it was not compatible with his being a "good" person, it also served numerous useful psychological purposes. For example, it allowed him to avoid seeking connection that he wanted with others but was temporarily too afraid or hurt to seek, and it provided *comfort and relief*, both physical *and* psychological.

Thus, the reinterpretations (or *reframing* of his symptom or complaint) were effective because they (a) gave the client an opportunity to consciously and unconsciously *reappraise* his behavior in a manner he hadn't considered—his view of self limited the ability to consider other possible meanings for his masturbation; (b) fit with the man's self-schema as a "good" person; (c) provided a positive and truthful component to his previously perceived negative behavior; (d) took full advantage of the client's readiness for change (i.e., his stage of change); and (e) provided an opportunity for the client to see and feel that the therapist was on his side and did not morally admonish him or think less of him, which, in turn, strengthened the therapeutic alliance. Also, the therapist understood the client's perspective and position (i.e., his schema demanding a "good" self-concept) regarding his circumstances, particularly in light of the other convergence factors.

CATEGORIES OF PARADOXICAL INTERVENTION

Having defined paradoxical interventions and their basic elements, we next discuss how such interventions can *neutralize* certain behaviors disruptive to the therapeutic endeavor, and how they can be utilized to *tranquilize* client distress.

Neutralizers: The Primary Paradox

Neutralizers represent a class of interventions that are closest to having a generalized nonlinear paradoxical mind-set. In most instances, the neutralizing influence and effects of a "primary paradox" consist of a simple, unexpected, ironic therapist response to certain types of client verbalizations or behaviors:

- Negativistic, inflammatory, or disparaging remarks directed at the therapy or the therapist
- Aggrandizing, elevating comments that put a therapist on a pedestal from which she can be toppled and the treatment sabotaged
- Land mines, rabbit holes, and red herrings (first discussed in Chapter 2)
- The recalcitrance of precontemplators and mandated clients
- The corrosive effects of power struggles

By responding with neutralizing paradoxical interventions, the therapist does not confirm, deny, dispute, or otherwise react or overreact to a client's accusations or statements (as outlandish as they might be), but rather attempts to "neutralize" them. Such neutralizing interventions are an especially important consideration in addressing the need to nurture, preserve, and maintain the therapeutic relationship.

Assumptions Underlying the Use of Neutralizers

There are several nonlinear assumptions underlying the need for the use of *neutralizers*. The first assumption concerns clients' potential use of negativistic, disparaging, and so on comments. The nonlinear-thinking practitioner understands that for any number of reasons, clients may not be in the therapist's office of their own willing accord (see Chapters 2–7 and 12–13). Likewise, some individuals may have difficulty in forming cooperative relationships or relationships in which there is a disparity in authority (e.g., doctor–patient, or supervisor–supervisee), and thus may subtly attempt to disrupt such a relationship as not helpful. There is a considerable disparity in the felt sense of power and authority between client and practitioner. Being in a counselor's office is at some level a tacit indication of one's life being unmanageable. On the other hand, counselors implicitly carry an aura of knowledge, authority, and skill that renders them in a "one-up" position relative to that of their clients.

For some clients, disparaging comments may be intended to provoke what the client believes to be an inappropriate counselor response, thereby providing the client with an excuse for leaving treatment prematurely. But, under such conditions, the client is able to leave therapy without feeling responsible for doing so. Returning to the film *Good Will Hunting* (discussed in Chapter 10; Van Sant, 1997), Matt Damon's character (Will Hunting), as part of his probationary plea bargain to work with a math professor at MIT, must go to therapy (against his will). Arrangements are made for him to see a therapist, whom he mocks, followed by another therapist, with whom he repeats his mockery before being seen by Robin Williams' character, Sean. In each scene with the other therapists, the mocking behavior that Will displays is designed to disrupt the therapeutic process. In each case, he is successful. When he finally starts to see Sean, he attempts to sabotage the therapy, just as he had done before. Will begins to jokingly critique a painting that Sean had done, and begins to probe his personal life. When Will hits upon the subject of Sean's deceased wife, Sean became enraged and grabs Will by the throat.[7] When they meet again, Sean takes him for a walk to the Charles River. He explains his behavior, and then he describes why Will does what he does. He explains that he uses his intellect to push people away, but in doing so he never really experiences life. He says, "I could ask you about love, and you would probably quote me a sonnet." Will is at a loss for words, reacts with silence and stonewalling in therapy, but eventually begins to engage in treatment and open up to Sean. In other words, Sean effectively neutralizes Will's negative behavior.

Therapists who do not respond appropriately to disparaging client comments may be reflective of a failure to engage clients, which contributes to the high "dropout" rate in therapy (see introduction). Neutralizers are therapeutic responses that are meant to defuse the potential of such comments to undermine the work of the therapist and/or therapy. Master practitioners are skilled in recognizing and benignly responding to overt and subtly disparaging comments to nurture the therapeutic relationship and heal ruptures to well-established alliances.

A second nonlinear assumption concerns clients' potential use of aggrandizing, idealistic comments that flatter a therapist but may subsequently be used to hold the therapist responsible for the failure of the therapy! A client is ultimately responsible for making progress from treatment. She gets the credit for gains made, and she is responsible for making changes. The therapist is a facilitator of change and bears responsibility for making certain that all possible salient domains of therapy are appropriately brought to bear. Therapists create the conditions that are necessary for a client to move through the stages of change and cope more effectively and constructively.

Table 14.1 describes brief examples of client remarks that can be disruptive to treatment. Disruptions to treatment can occur from disparaging the therapist and/or the therapy, and could corrode a therapeutic relationship. Before proceeding to the exercise, please cover up the right-hand columns. Think about and record what a therapist might say in response to such a client comment so that you might subsequently review your rationale. Then examine and discuss each suggested response that has been provided, one at a time.

How Neutralizers Work

A metaphor that may be helpful in describing the meaning and impact of neutralizers on clients' behaviors is that of an antacid—relatively simple compounds whose purpose is to neutralize the destructive, corrosive activity of acid in the digestive tract. For example, imagine someone consuming a large meal

TABLE 14.1   Possible aggrandizing, disparaging, inflammatory, and negativistic client comments, and possible practitioner responses

CLIENT COMMENT	TYPE OF CLIENT COMMENT	POSSIBLE NEUTRALIZING THERAPIST RESPONSE
"You don't seem interested in me!"	Disparaging of the therapist	"That's interesting. Let's explore that."
"Last session, you gave me several examples of clients to illustrate valid points. I didn't like that. I've listened to other people all my life, and this is my time for someone to listen to me!"	Expression of negativism by the client	"Thank you so very much for showing me the sort of trust that allowed you to express that to me."
"You don't seem to like me!"	Inflammatory	"Hmmm. Tell me more about that."
"WOW! Your fee is really high!"	Negativistic and inflammatory	"I disagree—it's outrageous. At the same time, I don't know anything that isn't expensive."
"I don't want to be here!"	Negativistic	"I don't blame you. You didn't ask for this."
"You're confusing me!"	Disparaging and possibly inflammatory	"I sometimes say things, and they don't come out right."
"You're my last hope."	Aggrandizing and perhaps setting up the therapist or therapy for failure	"I like to believe that there are numerous practitioners who are able to help you. Let's see what we can accomplish."
"You come very, very highly recommended."	Aggrandizing and perhaps setting up the therapist or therapy for failure	(With humor) "I deny everything unless I have a chance to talk to my lawyer."
"Dr. Smith says you are absolutely the best and will solve my problem."	Aggrandizing and perhaps setting up the therapist or therapy for failure	(Said with humor and mild exaggeration) "I don't know about that Dr. Smith and how he tends to exaggerate everything."
"This discussion is very difficult."	Possibly negativistic	"I'd like to caution you that most likely tonight, you are going to be thoroughly exhausted. Many clients have reported such exhaustion following the sort of session that we're having."

EXERCISE PART 1	EXERCISE PART 2	EXERCISE PART 3
1. Describe what sort of comment (i.e., aggrandizing, disparaging, inflammatory, or negativistic) each of the following client statements might be. 2. Is the client's comment directed toward the problem or toward the therapy or therapist? What is the difference? 3. What might be a client's purpose in making such a comment?	1. Defend each of the interpretations made above.	1. What was *your* reaction to each of the possible counselor comments above? 2. Did you expect the sort of response that is indicated? 3. How does each comment address the possible purpose a client may have had in making the comment? 4. After this exercise, what other sort of *neutralizing* responses might you make to such client comments?

TABLE 14.1   Possible aggrandizing, disparaging, inflammatory, and negativistic client comments, and possible practitioner responses (Continued)

CLIENT COMMENT	TYPE OF CLIENT COMMENT	POSSIBLE NEUTRALIZING THERAPIST RESPONSE
"I don't know if I'm getting anything out of this."		(How would you respond?)
"Judging from what I've seen and heard from you, I don't seem to be getting any relief, and I don't know if you can help me."		(How would you respond?)
"I'm thinking of finding a new therapist."		(How would you respond?)
"You never talk to me."		(How would you respond?)
"You absolutely saved my life!"		(How would you respond?)
"I couldn't have done this without you."		(How would you respond?)
"Have any of your clients ever committed suicide?"		(How would you respond?)

of spicy food. The stomach secretes hydrochloric acid in significant quantities in order to digest the spicy food into nutritious energy for the body—an obviously useful and beneficial function. In some instances, however, as a result of a particular menu choice, the once-helpful acid continues to pour out, eating away at the lining of the stomach. In addition, the acid can back up into the esophagus, a part of the digestive tract that has little protection against stomach acid, and causes a painful, burning sensation (commonly referred to as heartburn!).[8] All of this results in a disruption of pleasurable activities and causes significant discomfort. Within a few minutes after chewing two antacid pills, however, the antacid *neutralizes* the stomach acids and stops the pain of heartburn, providing significant relief.

In the same way, for any number of reasons, some client behaviors are disruptive to the therapy, acting very much like an acid. Such attitudes or behaviors can have corrosive effects that can prevent the development of or eat away at a therapeutic relationship or alliance. By paradoxically counteracting clients' negativistic or disruptive comments (e.g., by making an absurd statement that contains two true elements that seemingly cannot coexist) and rendering them harmless (or at least noncorrosive), neutralizers act like an antacid that soothes a client's acidic comments. Clearly, it is the master practitioner who has developed a general nondefensive and paradoxical mind-set—not as a "technique" but as a nonlinear way of thinking about such corrosive client comments, the treatment process, and even life itself.

Nonlinear Thinking and Neutralizers

A therapist's neutralizing responses evolve from a nonlinear mind-set. This means sometimes using irony to respond to a client's negativistic comment about the therapy or therapist, and perhaps agreeing with it wholeheartedly; hyperextending a client's point further than the client intended; using humor; "looking at the flip side"; or adopting a neutral stance. Natural differences in clinicians' personalities have much to do with what sort of response (i.e., humorous, ironic, "straight," etc.) they can comfortably deliver in replying to caustic client comments (see Mozdzierz et al., 1989).

A therapist must never deliver neutralizing comments with contempt, sarcasm, or any other form of defensiveness or hostility—the purpose of a "primary paradox" is to simply *neutralize* clients' depreciating, aggrandizing, and so on comments in order to allow therapy to continue. Maintaining such a *nonlinear* mind-set is what master practitioners do to understand the purpose of a client's comments and then effectively neutralize any acidity or aggrandizement of the therapist. This is in keeping with the initial goals of early treatment, namely, to always keep sight of establishing and maintaining rapport, nurturing and preserving the healing potential of the therapeutic relationship or alliance, and *not provoking* further client negativism or premature termination. Clinical Case Example 14.4 is an illustration.

Clinical Case Example 14.4: Neutralizing the Rebellious Behavior of a Reluctant Nun

A nun was referred—actually, "ordered"—by her mother superior to go for treatment. She was overtly unhappy about being forced into treatment with reduced professional responsibilities, but because she had taken a vow of "obedience," she reluctantly and unhappily complied with the referral. She made it abundantly clear that she felt betrayed at being sent for therapy. Assessing her grave reluctance to be in therapy, the therapist gingerly broached the subject, and she agreed that she did not want to be in treatment.

Although she was very devoted to religious life, she felt unappreciated and that colleagues perceived her very negatively. This clearly colored her perceptions and interactions with others, which she made clear to the therapist from the beginning. Neutralizing the toxicity of her position, the therapist said, "I really don't want to see people who don't want to be here. It's counterproductive. People benefit the most from counseling if they are willing participants." With that, she seemed to perk up. It seemed to the therapist as though she perhaps wasn't feeling quite so "forced" to be in treatment. He then asked if he might make a "suggestion," which she agreed to listen to.

He then proceeded to ask, "How would it be with you if we were to agree to three more sessions spaced out every other week? (Jokingly) Almost anyone can tolerate me for three sessions. During that time, you can tell me your story of what led to your being sent here and how you are feeling about it. At the end of that time, if you don't find anything of value in our discussions, I will be happy to write a letter to your mother superior informing her that we have concluded our business." She smiled and readily agreed to the proposition. She ended up staying in treatment for six months, finding herself more and more committed to understanding things about herself that she had long neglected.

QUESTIONS

1. What were the poles of the client's dilemma?
2. What was the "neutralizer" paradoxical intervention used?
3. What was "neutralizing" about the therapist's response to this woman?
4. Identify principles about the use of neutralizers that would be helpful in determining what the therapist said.
5. Discuss the paradoxical nature of the reframe for the client (i.e., two true elements that were mutually incompatible, yet true) and the counselor (an absurd or contradictory statement that contains truth).
6. What, if any, was the impact of neutralizing the nun's negativistic attitude about treatment on the therapeutic alliance?
7. Given this client's personality characteristics and circumstances, speculate on what might have happened had the therapist chosen to "interpret" the client's "resistance" about being "forced" into therapy.

By and large, as mentioned earlier, neutralizers are a means of making certain that a therapist does not provide a client with an excuse for leaving treatment prematurely. That was the therapist's primary intention in Clinical Case Example 14.4. What *was* paradoxical about the intervention was the two true statements that the therapist made: (a) implying that staying in therapy was counterproductive unless it was voluntary, and (b) acknowledging that the client had been forced into therapy and was expected to stay. As a result, if the client was going to benefit from treatment, her perception of the therapy would need to change from something forced upon her to something that she chose to do. The therapist aligned himself with the client by providing her with what she wanted (i.e., early termination of treatment, which was in keeping with her feeling of being forced into treatment). But, he also suggested that they could perhaps renegotiate their arrangement after three sessions. Again, this allowed the client to make a *choice* about being in treatment.

Neutralizers and Ambivalence

It is necessary to deconstruct these events to understand the subtleties of this intervention. The client's ambivalence concerns having taken a vow of obedience (i.e., a promise to follow the orders of her mother superior) and being in a situation that she did not want to be in. The intervention essentially addressed both aspects of her ambivalence: She *was staying* in treatment for three more sessions and 6 more weeks, which allowed her to feel good about keeping her vow of obedience. Being provided an option to terminate treatment early allowed her to keep faith with *herself and her desires* to not be in or need therapy.

The intervention neutralized the acidic effects of her negative reaction to being "ordered" to go to therapy, which she demonstrated toward the therapist. In addition, when the therapist communicated that he understood her predicament (of being "forced"), he communicated respect for the client, supported her position, and in fact agreed that therapy is most effective and beneficial with people who want to be there—similar to "agreeing with a twist," which was described in the last chapter. This allowed both client and therapist to work on creating a therapeutic alliance. Lastly, the therapist augmented the impact of certain truths: Therapy *does* work best with people who want to participate in it; they could conclude their work, albeit very limited, early; and he was willing to write a letter in support of their work being concluded after 6 weeks of "brief" therapy. Using that frame of reference, however, if he could stimulate the client to agree to a course of three sessions, they would have a good chance of fostering a strong enough relationship to make a better determination about what the client needed regarding counseling. All of this could not have been accomplished without the neutralizing paradoxical intervention.

THE STRATEGIC USE OF NEUTRALIZERS

Neutralizing Power Struggles

As discussed in Chapters 12 and 13, clients who come to therapy are often in a state of ambivalence about giving up their problem behaviors. Even if they verbally express a desire to rid themselves of a bad habit or immobilizing behavior, they may struggle when a therapist attempts to intervene. Clients often misrepresent themselves to their therapists, pleading that they need help in making a change (i.e., the theme of despair in Chapter 5). If the therapist succumbs to such pleading (i.e., the side of making changes), it allows clients to argue strongly for staying the same (i.e., something they appraise as and feel "safer" with because its effects are a known quantity). Linear-thinking therapists who fall into this trap are vulnerable to finding themselves in "power struggles" with clients. The reality is that entering into verbal harangues with a client, mobilizing defensive responses, and arguing are quite counterproductive (i.e., acidic); only accentuate feelings of ambivalence within a client; and all too frequently lead to premature termination (Beutler et al., 2002; Horvath & Bedi, 2002). *Neutralizing* power struggles is the most effective way to handle these traps. Consistent with Miller and Rollnick's

(2002) work with motivational interviewing, we have found that offering no direct obstacles to a client's resistance, uncooperativeness, or symptomatic behavior is the most "antacid-like" and productive approach. According to Beutler et al., a therapy setting that is devoid of an overt struggle for power and has a spirit of mutual respect is more effective. This is the effect of a neutralizing paradoxical intervention. It allows for the therapist to avoid power struggles with clients, while at the same time fostering a therapeutic alliance.

Dealing With Precontemplators and Mandated Clients

Clinical Case Example 14.4 (i.e., the reluctant nun) is reminiscent of the precontemplators discussed in Chapter 4. Recall that precontemplation is the first stage of Prochaska and DiClemente's (1984) stages of change model, and it is incorporated as part of the domain of assessing client readiness for change, needs, strengths, and goals. In Chapter 4, we detailed how clients in the early stages of change model are often unwilling or not ready to commit to change. We also discussed the research of Prochaska and DiClemente (2005), which determined that failure to move a client from a stage of precontemplation to the preparing for action stage in the early phase of therapy typically resulted in premature termination (as seemed likely with the nun in Clinical Case Example 14.4). Each type of precontemplator (rebellious, reluctant, resigned, and rationalizing) can embroil a therapist in a power struggle, and the most efficient and effective way of managing their behaviors, while maintaining the therapeutic relationship, is to neutralize a client's acerbic comments and attitudes.

SUMMARY

In summary, neutralizing is an important way of defusing and detoxifying comments and situations that are potentially hazardous to the development of a positive and fruitful therapeutic relationship. We emphatically reiterate that neutralizing represents more of a nonlinear (i.e., paradoxical) mind-set than it does a "technique." The use of neutralizer paradoxical interventions helps to address essential therapeutic tasks such as helping to engage clients when they may be reluctant to do so, defusing potentially toxic situations, moving a client along the stages of change, and developing and preserving the therapeutic alliance. The use of neutralizing agents is but one aspect, however, of how to think and respond in a nonlinear manner utilizing paradoxical interventions. We venture forth into still other aspects of nonlinear thinking as we discuss the tranquilizers.

ENDNOTES

1. Our use of the term *reappraisal* is quite deliberate. It relates to a client specifically *reevaluating* circumstances in a way *different* from the evaluation provided by schema dynamics.
2. That is, connecting to and engaging with clients; assessing client readiness for change, needs, resources, and goals for treatment; establishing and maintaining the therapeutic alliance; understanding clients' cognitive schemas; addressing and managing clients' emotional states; and addressing and resolving clients' ambivalence.
3. Similar to the principles of motivational interviewing (see Chapter 13).
4. See Mozdzierz, Macchitelli, and Lisiecki (1976) and their definition of paradoxical interventions as "encouragenic dialectics."

5. In one way, the wife's behavior may have been nagging, which left him feeling as though he was "groveling"; but an element of truth is that she *was* seeking information. He had been preoccupied with, resentful of, and resistant to her incessant questioning and felt victimized, angry, and hurt when he was working so hard to amend his behavior and save his marriage.

6. As reported in Chapter 4, Colombo is a fictional detective from a TV series of the same name staring Peter Falk. Colombo typically presented himself as somewhat bumbling, not understanding, quizzical, and the like.

7. Clearly, this is an instance of countertransference that is inappropriate. In real life, such therapist behavior could be subjected to charges of assault and a malpractice legal action.

8. The reader is advised that not all stomach conditions simply reflect eating spicy foods. Gastric esophageal reflux disease (GERD), stomach ulcers, and other serious conditions can also cause stomach upsets.

The Domain of Paradoxical Interventions

Part 2: Tranquilizers

15

CONTENTS

DEFINITION

The "tranquilizers" represent a group of paradoxical interventions that help to calm people who report that they are "upset" (e.g., anxious, nervous, or overwhelmed) about themselves or life circumstances. They usually feel that their lives are "out of control" and that they can't seem to calm themselves. Outside of precontemplators and mandated clients, many clients who come for treatment find themselves in such feeling states—critical incidents may have occurred, traumatic events taken place, the need for changes they are unable to accommodate become an intolerable crisis, and so forth. For all practical purposes, these clients feel immobilized. From this basic formulation, it stands to reason that treatment calls for such clients to be calmed, soothed, reassured, relieved, empathized with, and so on (because they are presenting themselves as "upset"). Indeed, many clients respond that they feel much better after a therapy session because of the soothing influence of the therapist, the therapeutic relationship, and the therapy context, namely, it is a "safe place." But calming a client in and of itself is not an end point. Therapeutic movement cannot take place when clients feel immobilized. Indeed, if

335

clients are calmer, they can begin the process of being receptive to thinking differently and behaving more confidently.

The therapeutic task is to determine a way (or ways) to "tranquilize" such clients' fears, anxiety levels, and so on without scaring them out of therapy. In Chapters 10 and 11, we discussed some practical strategies for doing this. However, adding to those, the therapist must remember that the energy that a client uses to embroil family members, coworkers, and eventually the therapist into her issues is a manifestation of ambivalence. It is the same type of dysfunctional or immobilizing effort that keeps her from more constructively dealing with her circumstances. Tranquilizing comments, interpretations, or suggestions are designed to calm, relieve pressure, deliver psychological reassurance, emotionally sedate clients with humanistic concern, and potentially restore a measure of emotional equilibrium to them. Without such calming, they are otherwise prevented from fuller participation in therapy and the achievement of more specific therapeutic goals. The problem is that the client's "activity" is *not* helping but rather hurting her. If it continues, it will jeopardize the therapy. Therefore, the behavior must be tranquilized to move forward.

NONLINEAR LISTENING AND TRANQUILIZERS

As with other elements in this text, *nonlinear listening* is important in determining what a client needs. In general, *linear listening* reveals that clients who need tranquilizing complain that they are "upset." They use a wide variety of linear descriptors to convey their upset such as *anxious, nervous, stressed, confused, down, overwhelmed, pressured, depressed,* and so forth. Those words are accompanied by phrases such as "I can't take it anymore," "I'm coming apart at the seams," "I've got to *do* something," "I can't stand the pressure any longer," "I don't know what to do," "I want to end it all," and "I'm doing all this stuff (i.e., 'spinning my wheels') but not getting anywhere" (endlessly vacillating)." Such clients may come for treatment in a "crisis" (e.g., "in emotional turmoil," or "emotionally upset") because they are literally exhausting themselves (and others) and unable to calm themselves. Their particular situation may reflect a long protracted period of being unable to resolve a situation that seems to get worse with everything they do, or it may be a more recent and immediate traumatic crisis with which they can't cope. In couples and family therapy, a client may complain that a spouse or family member is not as concerned as he is, not putting in the same effort as he is, or not (re)acting the same way that he is.

In most such instances, clinicians must listen not only in a linear manner but also for *congruence* (does the client really want the help she is seeking for herself as the identified client?), *absence* (is what the client *says* is the problem really the problem?), *inference* (what is the client telling me that she *doesn't* want?), *presence* (what is her agitated behavior saying that she is not telling verbally?), and *resistance* (how does a client respond to a concrete linear suggestion—does she "Yes, but ..."?). Assessing for themes, determining a client's schema dynamics, understanding the client's emotional system, and determining the source of her ambivalence also are important for the therapist to know. Each of these elements provides the *nonlinear*-thinking clinician with information about what a client needs from therapy, as well as provides the building blocks for paradoxical interventions.

TYPES OF TRANQUILIZERS

We have identified four types (or "P's") of paradoxical "tranquilizer" interventions: permission, postponement, prohibition, or persuasion. Each of them seeks to paradoxically interrupt dysfunctional behaviors, symptoms, complaints, and so on by proposing the absurd idea that a client continues doing the (negative) thing he is doing or avoiding the (positive) thing that he doesn't want to do. The Level III therapist understands that a client's symptoms and manifestations of ambivalence have been generated to serve a function and a purpose, namely, to excuse him from some possible threat or failure or to protect self-esteem (hence, ambivalence). The therapist recognizes that these clients are stuck between their schema dynamics (views of self, others, or the world) and circumstances that they face (or don't *want* to face). When a therapist intervenes by using one of the "tranquilizers," however, a symptom or complaint is transformed so that it no longer accomplishes what it was originally created to do. For example, if a client has used procrastination as a way to avoid failure but comes to therapy to "cure" her procrastination, a therapist might recommend that the client "postpone" tackling this issue until she is *really* ready. At this point, the client is confronted with the idea that her procrastination is out of control, which is a sign of failure (and contrary to her schematized view of herself). She might then decide to "prove" that she can accomplish tasks, and no longer procrastinate. Her procrastinating behaviors are successfully "tranquilized," and the therapist can begin to explore the deeper issues of what the perceived failure or threat might be.

As a client engages with his ambivalence (e.g., procrastination behaviors), the therapist also engages in the client's dialectical struggle (e.g., advocating for change while also recommending caution regarding what change will mean). That is the *nonlinear thinking* at the heart of Miller and Rollnick's (2002) "Rolling with the Resistance," "Developing Discrepancies," "Agreeing with a Twist," and (of course) paradoxical interventions (see Chapter 13). Paradoxical tranquilizer interventions have the added benefit of addressing the client's schema dynamics and emotional system as well as his ambivalence. When that happens, clients feel relieved, calmed, or "tranquilized." At the same time, feeling calm and relieved, the client can begin to think more clearly and may be more receptive to therapeutic movement. When calmer, clients have an opportunity to take stock of their ability to cope with issues, engage in planning, set attainable goals, and make more reasonable decisions. We next discuss applications of each of the types of the tranquilizer paradoxical interventions.

Permission

Permission is the verbal "tranquilizer" by which a therapist gives her client the authority to continue with present behavior or have his symptoms or complaint, albeit cast in a slightly different light. This directive is seemingly absurd, but has an element of truth embedded in it. Our experience supports the idea that it is not only the symptom or complaint alone that discourages individuals. Rather, it is clients' *feeling of struggling* (unsuccessfully) with their problem that adds to their suffering along with the redundant, useless, circular, and no-win solutions they have attempted. Of course, such struggling only makes their situation worse by prompting feelings of frustration, helplessness, and loss of control. A therapist giving a client permission to have his symptom makes such an intervention paradoxical because it absurdly proposes a constructive purpose for continuing with the present problematic behavior. Several general examples of permission that reflect paradoxical thinking will hopefully illustrate this principle:

- A client who is highly paranoid is advised that it is fortunate that she is suspicious. Because she has been hurt by others in the past, her present vigilance is perhaps the best way of possibly preventing other such hurts. Whatever discomfort being suspicious yields, it is better than the hurt that ensues from trustful expectations followed by betrayal.
- A compulsive client is advised that it is wise to be careful in the way in which he approaches life and the world, both of which can be gnarled and chaotic.
- A client who reports being frustrated by not being able to make decisions because she is easily "confused" is advised that her confusion may be protecting her from making a *hasty decision* on matters that she may not even be aware of presently. Confusion can be a means of slowing things in life so that we can make more sense of them.

Clinical Exercise 15.1

Instructions: Read each of the three client descriptions described in the text.

1. Discuss how each intervention described is paradoxical (via the definition of paradoxical interventions from the client and counselor perspectives).
2. Describe how each is a redefinition of the client's dilemma.
3. How does each give a client permission to have his or her symptoms (albeit from a different perspective)?
4. How might the proposed redefinitions be related to the client's schemas?
5. How might you describe the ambivalences generated within each of these clients?

The reader will note how important it is in each of these case vignettes for a therapist to have successfully engaged and established rapport with his client. If the relationship isn't well developed, then the preceding comments could be misinterpreted by the clients as cynical or mocking, which would only arouse their resistance while continuing with their problem behaviors. As a result, for basic *reframing* to work, the therapist has to see the positive in the negative behavior. Furthermore, as previously discussed, therapist conviction is also important regarding the "element of truth" contained within each example of giving permission. A specific example of giving permission in Clinical Case Example 15.1 comes from group therapy with a member who has been largely silent through many sessions.

Clinical Case Example 15.1: Shyness in a Group Setting

Despite having a good rapport with the group leader, a group member could not seem to make the leap and speak up in group. When asked about this, the client agreed that he should speak up in group but then "freezes," and feels anxious and guilty. In fact, this "shyness" has been problematic for him all of his life, preventing him from being successful at work and so on.

In this scenario, it is the client's silence (paradoxically!) that needs to be tranquilized. He is told that perhaps he should continue to remain silent for a while longer, as his reticence to talk could be protection against revealing more about himself than he is prepared to reveal at the present time. Again, this is a variation of "rolling with the resistance" in order to counteract the client's ambivalence. The client is not bullied or cajoled into speaking up. In fact, he is to be commended for the courage it took to even mention his dilemma!

Should the group leader have wanted to pursue this even further, he could have suggested that he is confused (i.e., developing a discrepancy). That is, on the one hand the client has *an admitted problem with shyness*, but on the other hand *he speaks up* and is able to announce that he has a problem with shyness, which is a contradiction!

Hence, permission (and tranquilizers in general) calms and frees a client from the pressure of being "backed into a corner" relative to her ambivalence. When individuals perceive that they are in a psychological corner (whether they put themselves there or not), they usually feel that they have only one choice. That "one choice" typically is sensed as a need for defensiveness as reflected in "black or white" thinking. Such thinking leads to constriction in their actions (i.e., doing what is "safe" by not acting at all), even if this continues to bring them trouble. This is one of the reasons why direct-assault, or linear, thinking by a therapist typically results in resistance from a client. If a client feels that her back is to the wall, and that she lacks trust in her therapist, she is highly unlikely to hear (let alone heed) the interpretations or suggestions of the person giving her counsel. Permission gives a client the "psychological space" and authorization to step out of the corner that she is backed into (i.e., her dilemma) and begin to consider other alternatives. It is quite paradoxical in nature because clients *expect* a therapist to tell them to stop doing whatever it is that they are doing—possibly in an authoritarian or disapproving manner—just like others in their social environment have most likely done. When a therapist "rolls with the resistance" and gives a client "permission" to continue with her behavior while rendering a "plausible explanation" for doing so, the client is given room to question the "plausible explanation" underlying a behavior that she knows to be problematic. As we will show, this is what was at stake for Clinical Case Example 15.2, which illustrates how paradoxically giving permission made an impact.

Clinical Case Example 15.2: One More Child to Raise

Another example that shows how nonlinear paradoxical permission can act like a tranquilizer for a client's symptomatic behavior comes from a female client who was in her late 40s. Referred to therapy for depression by her psychiatrist, the client complained of restlessness, lethargy, increased irritability, and feelings of hopelessness. To add to her woes, she had also recently been diagnosed with borderline hypertension (although not high enough to require medication). Although she had recently been placed on medication for depression, her psychiatrist felt that individual therapy was what she truly needed.

Reluctant at first, she openly expressed her doubts about therapy. The client reported that she was happily married for over 25 years, and had three children, the youngest of whom was about to graduate from high school and move out. She was looking forward to being an "empty nester," and having more time with her husband as well as for herself, and to start developing "adult relationships" with her children. Less than a year before, however, the client's younger sister was hospitalized for drug abuse—one of many such hospitalizations. In addition, the sister's 6-year-old daughter came to "temporarily" stay with her. At that time, she was the only person who could assume care for her niece because the child's father was, likewise, a substance abuser. Other family members, including the child's paternal grandmother, agreed to help during school breaks, summer vacations, as well as other times during the year whenever the client needed a break. When she actually asked for help, however, no one ventured forth. In fact, when she complained, she was chided by her brother, who asked her, "You think you're the only one with problems?"

At this point, she felt trapped: On the one hand, she really loved her niece and felt badly for her. By all accounts, the niece was a well-behaved little girl. On the other hand, she did not like the idea of sacrificing herself and the rest of her adult life to raising another child, telling her therapist, "I've raised my own, already."

QUESTIONS

1. What is the client's dilemma?
2. What *ambivalence*, if any, can you describe?
3. What kind of *nonlinear* listening helps you discover this?
4. Can you suggest an intervention or paradoxical "permission" for this client? How would the particular suggestion you are suggesting give the client "psychological space"?
5. Identify various aspects of paradoxical interventions in what you have suggested.
6. Discuss the paradoxical nature of the reframe for the client (i.e., two true elements that were mutually incompatible, yet true) and the counselor (an absurd or contradictory statement that contains truth).

Variation: Form small groups or work as an entire class, and compare responses. Discuss which might be the most effective approach as a tranquilizer.

Regarding the client in Clinical Case Example 15.2, when the counselor hypothetically mentioned to the client that she could turn her niece over to someone else in the family, or even to the child service worker who would place her in a group home, she adamantly refused to consider it, saying, "I couldn't do that!" Upon being given *permission* to do what she was complaining of, she raised objections. She was a firstborn who took on the role of family caretaker after their mother died a few years prior: "Her mantle had passed on to me." It is clear that her schema dynamics dictated loyalty to the role of "caretaker." It was equally clear that a commonsense linear suggestion would not be effective in bringing this woman relief from her torment. The therapist's assessment determined that the woman needed relief and calming. As a result, he suggested, "It seems to me that you are very interested in being her (the child's) aunt, and doing all the things that an aunt would do; but you are not interested in being her mother." The client immediately seized on the idea and agreed. The therapist continued, "It doesn't seem fair that you are forced to be her mother because no one else will be." Again, the client agreed. In the same vein, the therapist continued, "The thought of you just 'giving her up' would relieve you of the problem; but, the issue is just that giving up on her is not very palatable to you." This assessment clearly reflected the *ambivalence* that the client felt. She became quiet and nodded in agreement as the therapist added, "But what would happen to her if something happened to *you*?" This apparently reflects the development of a *discrepancy* in the client's thinking and *private reasoning*.

The client was stumped. The therapist persisted, "I mean, what would happen if you died suddenly in a car accident, or got sick and developed some life-threatening condition that made it impossible for you to take care of the child? Who would do it?" The client admitted that she didn't know, but that "something" would have to happen. The therapist suggested that this might be worse than "giving her up"; it would be abandonment! The therapist further suggested that she already had a condition that was beginning to make it difficult for her to stay healthy—borderline hypertension. The client was told about the interplay between hypertension, heart disease, depression, and cancer, and that if she continued to ignore her health, her body would force a solution to her problem that she might not like! This was the essence of the paradoxical intervention for the client. From the counselor's perspective, the absurd or contradictory statement that contained an element of truth was the idea that this woman, who was the only person in the family to take this child in, might actually *abandon* her!

From the client's perspective, the two concepts that were true but couldn't coexist were that she *did* want to be relieved of the responsibility of raising this child *and* that she felt that she was "ordained" to be the child's parent figure (a schematized view of self, revealed in the phrase that her mother's "mantle had passed on to me"). At this point, the client agreed that if things continued the way they had been going, something would have to happen. The therapist invited her to think about developing a "contingency plan" with other family members and the child's welfare worker about what might happen. It was further suggested that she might want to brainstorm with these interested parties to take steps now, and give herself a break before it was too late.

In this example, the client was in a classic *double approach–avoidance* dilemma. When the client was given permission to actively think about giving up the child, as well as recasting her role from its present status of being mother and sole nurturer, to her desired status of being aunt and a support to the child, she was able to feel less stuck. The therapist's comments provided an opportunity for her to reappraise her situation, resulting in a more schema-friendly emotional response and corresponding positive feelings. Once she was given permission to be freed from the self-imposed tyranny of "I must take care of her (be her mother), because no one else will," "No one will help me," and "It's so unfair," she was able to reach out to other family members and ask for help.

As a result of the paradoxical intervention, the woman was able to write family members a letter explaining her situation, her concerns, and her disappointment. Because of this process, she decided that she really didn't want to give up the child, but rather wanted some relief. In addition, she also reported feeling less depressed, more energized, and able to enjoy life more. As an added note, the child also benefited because she now *did* have a contingency plan for her care!

Postponement

When using postponement, a clinician is encouraging a client to delay or prolong a decision, required action, or felt need to act into the undefined future. A crisis situation usually requires the client to make a decision that can arouse considerable anxiety and uncertainty. Fear of failure (embedded as part of a client's schematized view of self) is often the underlying issue that inhibits clients from making a decision they need to make. Although this can often be a "successful"[1] strategy, the impending need for a decision can precipitate a crisis for the client. The pressure to make a decision can trigger feelings of ambivalence, especially if it entails doing something that the client does not want to do (or making a commitment to a particular course of action *at this point in time*). Oftentimes, such individuals will have vacillated, become immobilized, or tried to escape, but the circumstances have forced a crisis necessitating a decision (see Chapters 12 and 13 for details). The last option (besides making a decision) in resolving their dilemma is to let fate decide, which may result in a negative outcome for the client and produce the failure that the client fears. Encouraging a client to paradoxically postpone a decision provides significant relief to a client (i.e., *tranquilizes*), enabling a reestablishment of a sense of control, tranquilizing, and providing an enormous sense of relief that is desperately needed at times of significant apprehension. It is often much better to deal with the consequences of postponement than it is to deal with the consequences of a decision that one feels ill prepared to face. Under conditions of *relief*, a client increases his chances of making a more well-reasoned decision in the future. Clinical Case Example 15.3 provides an example.

Clinical Case Example 15.3: Wife or Girlfriend?

An example of the use of postponement can be seen in a group therapy client who came to one session with a "serious" dilemma. He explained that he was becoming more and more dysfunctional because of his inability to make up his mind about whether to stay with his wife or divorce her and elope with his girlfriend, who was now several months pregnant. His health was starting to deteriorate as a result of the strain of the situation he was faced with. When he asked for and received feedback from fellow group members, he essentially engaged in "Yes, but ..." behavior (see Chapter 2). That is, when group members argued for him to stay with his wife, he would argue "but" she had not been able to conceive a child for him and therefore he had never become a father, which was extremely important to him. He had fathered a child illegitimately, and as far as he was concerned others might take such an event lightly but he could not do so. It was thus impossible for him to give up his girlfriend and his child.

Then, when several group members argued for him to stay with his girlfriend, the client would say that was a good idea, "but" his wife had treated him well throughout 13 years of marriage. She had been loyal to him during extended times when he needed hospitalization on numerous occasions, and so on. He explained that he loved her for her devotion, support, and loyalty and that leaving her was impossible.

The client complained of exasperation and physical exhaustion that had resulted from not being able to choose between the two women in his life as well as from running back and forth to each of them, attempting to satisfy both, which was in itself physically and emotionally draining him.

QUESTIONS

1. What are the poles of the client's dilemma? What kind of dilemma is it?
2. How does the client's behavior demonstrate his ambivalence?
3. What schema dynamics can you decipher, if any, from the information given?
4. What are the elements of the client's emotional system (i.e., emotional state, internal feelings, and affective expressions)?
5. What is the behavior, symptom, or complaint that needs to be tranquilized? How is that creating problems for the client and getting in the way of therapeutic progress?
6. What types of nonlinear listening would you use to understand the client's situation?
7. How would you use the therapeutic paradoxical intervention of postponement with this client?
8. Discuss the paradoxical nature of the reframe for the client (i.e., two true elements that were mutually incompatible) and the counselor (an absurd or contradictory statement that contains truth).

Variation: Form small groups and share answers with the class, or discuss answers to the questions above as a class.

In Clinical Case Example 15.3, the therapist suggested that perhaps neither the group nor the client could make a decision because of several reasons: To make a decision might be premature at this time; no one really knew enough information about the client, the women, the situation, and circumstances to make a decision; and besides, the baby was not due for months. The therapist essentially suggested postponing a decision, which is what the client was doing anyway. But, the therapist then *shifted the focus* of the group discussion from the client's obviously irresolvable problem to a more immediate and legitimate concern. That is, the client's "physical and emotional well-being" was being jeopardized by the physically, sexually, and emotionally demanding schedule he was keeping by going back and forth between the two women in his life to whom he felt loyalty. This nonlinear approach defocused (i.e., *disengaged*) the client's ill-fated struggling with his "decision dilemma" for which there was presently no acceptable solution. It simultaneously focused his attention on a problem about which he could do something: his health. He could make certain that he got sufficient sleep, used vitamins, ate a proper diet, said "no" to either or both women if need be, and so on. *Postponing* what he was already postponing allowed the client to defocus and disengage from the problem (i.e., struggling with the need to make a decision). This particular intervention was effective in helping the client because he was known to have a poor health history and was especially concerned about health issues.

There is an issue of importance to reemphasize in the above example for all therapists. That is, paradoxical interventions are not mechanical "techniques" from which to expect magical results. It can be beneficial to follow such interventions with other suggestions or a shift in the therapeutic focus. In Clinical Case Example 15.3, with the need for a decision postponed, the client was directed to focus on his health *until* he could be in a better position (e.g., by getting more rest, being less anxious, and being able to think more clearly) to make the best decision possible about his relationships. Such a shift in focus interfaces with other domains (i.e., understanding schema dynamics, emotional components, and underlying ambivalence, and having a solid therapeutic alliance). Clinical Case Example 15.4 is another illustration.

Clinical Case Example 15.4: Malingering or Not?

A man came into therapy following a serious injury on the job. He worked in a prison system and had been severely beaten by a disturbed inmate approximately 2 months earlier. Even though he was due to return to work within the month, he did not feel ready to do so. Although he had recovered from most of his physical injuries, he still complained of "headaches." A neurologist had ruled out a physical cause for the headaches, but he continued to report that they still occurred several times a week. Malingering was ruled out, because this man strongly identified with his role as a corrections officer and had received several meritorious commendations from the state for his work. In addition, he had made some attempts to return to duty earlier but was nonetheless plagued by headaches. Later in treatment, he acknowledged being fearful of returning to work, a hypothesis that the therapist had formulated earlier in treatment. As a result, he began to restrict his activities outside his home for fear of triggering a headache that would leave him vulnerable. It was clear that he was on the way to developing a full-blown panic disorder or agoraphobia.

QUESTIONS

1. How would you describe the client's dilemma?
2. What are the schema dynamics that you can decipher from the information given?
3. What are the elements of the client's emotional system (emotional state, internal feelings, and affective expressions)?
4. What behavior, symptom, or complaint might need to be tranquilized? How is it creating problems for the client and getting in the way of therapeutic progress?
5. What types of nonlinear listening would you use to understand the client's situation?
6. How might you intervene using paradoxical postponement with this man?
7. Discuss the paradoxical nature of the tranquilizing approach you are suggesting for the client (i.e., two true elements that are mutually incompatible, yet true) and the counselor (an absurd or contradictory statement that contains truth).

Variation: Form groups to discuss, or share as a class the answers to the questions above.

In Clinical Case Example 15.4, the therapist suggested that the client specifically *not* think about going back to work for at least the next week. The therapist made a reasonable assumption that the client's headaches might be an unconscious means of avoiding going back to work. In effect, the headaches were an expression of his inability to make up his mind about what he wanted to do with his life. He was given *permission* to *postpone* not going back to work—something that he was already postponing. Perhaps he could think about it after that, but until then his sole focus was to think about getting "well." The client was also instructed that if he felt that he wanted to go somewhere out of the house that he should, but only in the company of someone else in the event that he might get a headache.

The next week, the client reported having only one or two headaches that were "mild" and that he had been able to go out to shop with a relative. He complained that it was limiting to have to ask for someone to come and wait for him because he had never been accustomed to being "helpless." It was suggested that for the next week, he should still not think about going to work, but that if he wanted to go somewhere outside the house he could go by himself as long as he felt it was "safe." Again, the following week, the client reported only mild headaches and that he had been successful in going out by himself. Gradually, the issue of returning to work began to be discussed, beginning with the client putting on his uniform at home, but not leaving home while wearing it; then driving to work, but not going in; and eventually returning to work. At the same time, the therapist began to discuss with the client the possibility that part of his symptoms might be "an invitation" (i.e., a positive redefinition of something that was very negative) to explore other career options. Prior to the accident at work, this man might have rejected such an idea. Now, he admitted that he was beginning to think of other things that he could do with his life. This opened up a new avenue of discussion that eventually led to the client enrolling in college courses to change careers.

In each of these examples, the clients involved could see only one choice available to them: a bad one (e.g., "I will hurt myself if I choose the wrong woman," or "I will hurt myself if I go back to work"). Therefore, to spare themselves the perceived tragedy that failure represented, they delayed and ran out the clock in order to let "fate" decide.

In these examples, the therapist used nonlinear thinking and embraced the client's resistance by agreeing that now is not the time to make an important decision. This gives the person the "psychological space" to back away from his entrenched position. Having the space he needs provides a measure of relief and psychological tranquilization.

Prohibition

Prohibition is a tranquilizing paradoxical intervention that is closely related to permission and postponing; however, in this intervention, the therapist in a friendly way benignly "can't support" a client doing what he has already not been doing. The rationale for prohibiting what a client has already not been doing is that doing something could prove injurious in some way. Like the other tranquilizers, it defies *the client's* idea of "common sense." Clients enter counseling or therapy *expecting to be changed or influenced* in some way. Thus, their expectations dictate that a "therapist" would try to reverse "bad" behavior or encourage "good" behavior. This represents clients' *linear thinking*, and doesn't allow for the influence of their ambivalence, emotional factors, or schema dynamics.

Prohibition entails quintessential characteristics of paradoxical interventions because it essentially says that in order to change, you have to *not* change. Such an injunction either provokes a reaction to go against the therapist's directive (and go toward a positive result), or stops a client's agonizing and vacillation. This produces an emotional reaction that allows a reappraisal of the situation and a reconnection of the emotional system and schema dynamics that provides an opportunity for a more lasting solution to emerge. *Nonlinear listening* is helpful, but *listening for inference* (i.e., what the client *doesn't* want) can provide the therapist with the essential clues about what needs to be "prohibited." We provide examples of prohibition, beginning with Clinical Case Example 15.5.

Clinical Case Example 15.5: A Talented Young Musician

A talented young professional concert musician, who previously had been playing successfully in a symphony orchestra, had been unemployed for the last several years. Because of his early learned family role and many other chronic emotional problems, he felt a great deal of discouragement and despaired of ever working again as a professional musician. His work was the highlight of his life. Taking note of an advertisement, he felt compelled to audition for another symphony position while at the same time being terrified at the prospect of either obtaining (not feeling he would be able to "handle it") or being denied the job (hence, another failure and still further discouragement). He felt absolutely certain that he had the technical ability to pass the audition because he was in top form, had continued to practice, was taking a master class, and had a history of successfully auditioning on numerous other occasions. He was no stranger to such a challenge. But, he was nevertheless terrified of the prospects of auditioning and being turned down.

QUESTIONS

1. Discuss how the client "wins" if he isn't offered a position and if he is offered a position.
2. Carefully spell out the ambivalence the young man faced.
3. How would you interpret the client's willingness to actually go for the audition?
4. In what way was prohibiting his taking a position tranquilizing to this man?

It had been suggested to the client that he was in no position to make a professional decision at this time and should consider not going back to work for the immediate future. On the other hand, he *was encouraged* to perhaps follow his prosocial inclinations and audition for the symphony position *with the idea that he had no intention of accepting the position at this time should it be offered.* He was to think of the audition as merely "practice" for a future time when he would be in a better psychological position to be able to make a professional decision and commitment.

The suggestion took into account both aspects of the client's felt ambivalence, namely, wanting to be successful and simultaneously fearing he would fail while delaying a decision and prolonging a crisis with which he was not prepared to deal at *the present time.*

Interestingly, this talented young man embraced the therapist's suggestion. In fact, he auditioned so successfully that he was offered a position with the symphony immediately after his audition. He reported in his next therapy session with thorough glee that he accepted the position on the spot!

In Clinical Case Example 15.5, using nonlinear *listening for inference*, the therapist understood what it was that this man didn't want: facing the possibility of failure because he was so discouraged. By introducing the elements of prohibition and choice, the client became much more relaxed (i.e., tranquilized). He believed that he was not in any danger of failing because he was directed to have *no intention of accepting a position.* There could be no failure! The audition was only to be "practice." As Mozdzierz, Macchitelli, and Lisiecki (1976) stated,

Viewed within this context, a paradoxical strategy employed by a therapist is a means of transforming the patient's symptomatic asocial uncooperative behavior into a cooperative venture between the patient and the therapist. ... If the patient rebels against the therapist, he abandons the symptomatic behavior that was unconsciously designed to preclude cooperation, and he cooperatively participates in society. If the patient persists in the symptomatic behavior he does so while cooperating with the therapist. *The patient wins* (cooperative participation) *either way.* (p. 173)

We present Clinical Case Example 15.6 as another illustration of prohibition.

Clinical Case Example 15.6: Postponing Graduation

A young professional woman with many accomplishments took time from her life to pursue a doctorate in her field. She completed the course requirements, passed her comprehensive exams, submitted her dissertation proposal, diligently collected data for her research, discovered very strong positive findings supporting the hypotheses in her research, and was almost finished writing up the dissertation results. However, she simply could not bring herself to write the final two chapters that would describe her results and discuss them. She sought therapy to help her to work her way through her immobility.

The therapist collected historical information and a full description of her efforts to "solve" her problem. Her efforts to finish the dissertation mostly revolved around "forcing" herself to sit down and write the last two chapters. But, she would discover that no matter how intense her determination to finish "the damn thing," she would inevitably find excuses and other things to do. All of this left her frustrated, angry, and depressed.

In the discussion about this issue, the therapist learned that the woman was apprehensive about what might be expected of her once she finished her doctorate. Despite the obvious evidence of past successes, she feared failure (i.e., not living up to very high personal expectations) in the role of a "doctor." In response to all of this, the therapist suggested that it might be helpful if the woman would consider doing an assignment that might help her with her problem. She readily agreed.

She was instructed to take only 20 minutes per week to work on her dissertation. If it took 20 minutes for her to simply turn on her computer, open her data files, read material, and the like, and she wrote nothing, she was to put away all of the materials until the next week and repeat the procedure. Obviously, with such an assignment the woman's ambivalences could be addressed. On the one hand, she could avoid finishing the dissertation and avoid any possible threat and potential failure because it can take a very long time to finish a dissertation (even only two chapters) working on it only 20 minutes per week. On the other hand, she could satisfy her desire to feel that she was doing something about accomplishing a lifelong goal.

Within several weeks of initiating the assignment and discussing the exaggerated expectations she held about being a "doctor," the woman began violating the 20-minute assignment. The first report of her violation was that she had lost track of time and had written some material over a 2-hour period. The therapist suggested that she return to the 20-minute assignment as soon as possible, but she continued to report violating not only the length of time she worked on the dissertation but also the frequency. Needless to say, within several months the woman had finished writing her dissertation, submitted it to her dissertation committee, and successfully defended it.

The woman in Clinical Case Example 15.6 genuinely wanted to complete her dissertation and enjoy the fruits of her labor. But that represented only one half of her goals and one half of her ambivalence: She also wished to avoid failing. In fact, she had never failed at anything, but she did not know what might be expected of her professionally with a doctorate. It was unknown territory for her. Completing most of her doctoral work allowed her to satisfy one part of her goal, which was satisfying the needs of a self-schema of achievement; demonstrating an inability to finish her dissertation allowed her to satisfy another component of her self-schema—don't fail at anything! Moreover, the therapist's assignment advocated (benignly) for the status quo and allowed her to satisfy both components of her view of self until such time as the achievement needs, coupled with therapist support and being able to talk about her fears and ambivalences, gave her sufficient courage to follow through and finish her work.

A frequent setting for the use of prohibition comes from couples' sex therapy. Performance anxiety is a frequent component in sexual dysfunction. That is, an individual experiences increased anxiety about how "good" he or she is as a lover (i.e., "performance"). As a person worries more about his or her sexual performance, ability to perform suffers more and more. As ability to perform suffers, anxiety increases further and starts a downward cascading spiral of frustration and fear. As a result, a couple will begin to grow distant from one another and argue in order to avoid the painful subject of sexual intimacy. This distance begins to strain the relationship, which can eventually lead to the couple seeking therapy. Many times, even performance-enhancing medications (e.g., Viagra and Cialis) cannot help a couple achieve the intimacy that they desire because of psychological factors.

A standard practice of therapists working with couples experiencing some measure of sexual dysfunction is to teach Masters and Johnson's (1966) technique of "sensate focus," in which each person takes a turn giving and receiving pleasurable stimulation. The receiving partner controls the amount of stimulation being given by telling the partner to start or stop. In the beginning, the couple is required to give only nonerotic pleasurable stimulation. More explicit sexual stimulation is gradually (with each successful episode) introduced. The couple is usually given a directive from the beginning "prohibiting" them from engaging in sexual intercourse. Such "prohibition" is intended to remove the sense of pressure accruing to the couple from "performance anxiety" and the sense of urgency to perform sexually. Instead, they are encouraged to concentrate on the other forms of pleasurable stimulation. Such instruction *disengages* the couple from their struggle with symptomatic behavior and provides them a measure of tranquilizing relief. As a couple experiences a measure of success, they often are unable to comply with the prohibition and come to therapy sheepishly (or proudly) announcing that they "disobeyed" the prohibition against sexual intercourse and had a successful and fulfilling night of lovemaking. In this instance, prohibiting intercourse allows a couple—relieved from the pressure to perform—to relax. They have received a needed psychological "tranquilizer." Thus, they can "disobey" the prohibition and be *successful* at the same time (thus breaking the cycle of performance anxiety or inability to perform). In either event, they win.

Persuasion

Another of the P's of the paradox is persuasion, namely, urging and advocating for symptomatic behavior. It is perhaps one of the last things (i.e., opposite of expectations) that a client *expects* to hear from his therapist. When using paradoxical persuasion, a therapist champions the cause of symptom retention and produces a positive, plausible rationale for such advocacy. Like prohibition and other tranquilizers, persuasion is paradoxical in nature—it is absurd for a therapist to advocate that a client do the very thing he is complaining about or seeking to avoid, but at the same time there is an element of truthfulness in doing so. The rationale pleads that the patient is not yet ready to attempt new behaviors and/or responsibilities from which his symptomatic stress has insulated him. In point of fact, there are many things that clients are thoroughly unprepared for. An argument can also be made to the client that he hasn't fully considered the implications of making a hasty retreat from symptomatic behavior—getting better too fast can be ill advised. The therapist can further insist—seriously, albeit benignly—that the symptom should be retained due to its considerable benefits to the patient that he may not be able to see at this time. This provides a measure of tranquilizing for the patient regarding his problem, symptom, or behavior and allows the client an opportunity to begin disengaging from his struggle with it.

Arguing for the symptom and *joining the resistance* are well-known therapeutic terms that have described this intervention. Recalling the stages of change from Chapter 4, when clients are not ready to make changes, they often engage in a variety of different coping strategies from actively denying that there is a problem (the precontemplation stage) to admitting that there is a problem but they are not yet willing to take the necessary steps for change (the contemplation stage). Persuasion can help a client to make movements from one stage of change to another. It can be especially useful when a patient is advocating a need to change, but there is no concrete information to suggest that positive movement has taken place (i.e., the preparing for action stage). The therapist *argues*, *advocates*, and *persuades* for the benefits of the symptom (traits, behaviors, perceptions, etc.) to be retained because it has certain clear protective advantages. The therapist then might explore how the patient might use the symptom, etc. to her advantage to improve her present and/or future life. Clinical Case Example 15.7 illustrates this.

Clinical Case Example 15.7: A Case of Perfectionism and a Case of Paranoid Disposition

As a relatively simple example, an extremely suspicious and paranoid client might be persuaded that the suspiciousness and lack of trust that he complains about are practical necessities for survival in a modern urban society and a terrorist-infiltrated world. After construing mistrust and suspiciousness in such a light, the therapist might further insist that they be refined and honed to a "keener edge." Because of the patient's "sharp eye," skepticism, and wary way of looking at things, the therapist might inquire if the client ever considered security work.

Another general example of the use of persuasion is that of the truly perfectionist obsessive-compulsive person preoccupied with orderliness and not making mistakes. Such a person might be asked if she has ever considered seeking a career in quality control, accounting, or the like, because those fields represent career paths requiring precisely her natural skills.

In persuading a client, the therapist does not insist that the client practice his trait, symptom, behavior, complaint, or the like—only that he considers its advantages and long-term benefits. In therapy, persuasive rationales might be initiated by the therapist asking herself, "Why *should* this particular client *not* be depressed, or why should he stop drinking, trust people, become more active, express feelings more openly, etc.?" Generally, our experience has shown that this *nonlinear* approach results in a client beginning to not only argue for change but also actually initiate concrete behaviors. Or, instead of a client arguing for change, he may simply begin to *relinquish his struggle* with the need to be rid of the behavior; Clinical Case Example 15.8 illustrates this.

Clinical Case Example 15.8: Paranoid at Home

A poignant example of persuasion concerns a paranoid patient reported on previously:

[A] patient with a litigious paranoid personality was bitterly complaining about and arguing with his young teen-aged daughter, whose boyfriends and girl friends constantly invaded the privacy and sanctity of his home—raiding the refrigerator, dancing "crazily," etc. He expressed the wish that he would be rid of them so he wouldn't have to fight with them and his wife over the issue all the time. The therapist asked the patient to reconsider (i.e.[,] *the therapist "argued for"*) his attitude since having the children at his house so often provided him with an opportunity to "watch" his daughter and her friends very carefully so that no "hanky panky" would go on as it might if they were at someone else's house, at the forest preserve, etc. The patient readily agreed and seemed relieved, resulting in decreased antagonism toward his daughter and her friends. This created a better relationship between the patient and his daughter and his wife and himself so that even with the children at home the patient was more at ease. (Mozdzierz et al., 1976, p. 181, emphasis added)

QUESTIONS

Consider the vignette above taken from Mozdzierz et al. (1976), and answer the following:

1. What are the poles of the client's dilemma? What kind of dilemma is it?
2. What are the schema dynamics that you can decipher from the information given?
3. What are the elements of the client's emotional system (emotional state, internal feelings, and affective expressions)?
4. How would you describe the client's ambivalence, if any?

5. What is the behavior that needs to be tranquilized? How is it creating problems for the client and getting in the way of therapeutic progress?
6. What types of nonlinear listening would you use to understand the client's situation?
7. How did the therapist's *paradoxical use of persuasion* help the client and move the therapy forward?
8. Discuss the paradoxical nature of the reframe for the client (i.e., two elements that were mutually incompatible, yet true) and the counselor (an absurd or contradictory statement that contains truth).

Variation: Form small groups to discuss, or share as a class the answers to the questions above.

Those readers who have encountered staunchly paranoid individuals in their practice know that such clients are challenging, to say the least. They are not persuaded by linear commonsense thinking because their experience (long embedded in schema dynamics) has taught them that they can't trust the world and its inhabitants—that has been their lifelong experience. Extending such a position, why should they trust the therapist? Is it just because you are a therapist or counselor with a good "reputation"? Hardly! Such thinking on the part of a therapist is not consistent with a *nonlinear*-thinking mind-set. Instead, strategies like "rolling with the resistance" and persuasion in favor of a symptom can help to facilitate a therapeutic alliance, as well as facilitate a more rapid disengagement from the problematic behavior.

In Clinical Case Example 15.8, the patient's paranoid view of others and view of the world represented by his sensitivity to being mistreated even included his daughter and her friends drinking his Pepsi and eating his potato chips. As a good example of the "judo" aspect of paradoxical interventions, this appealed to his paranoia by telling him that he could "watch" and "keep an eye on" his daughter so that nothing would go on "behind his back" (the paranoid person's nightmare). This was a powerfully persuasive argument that the patient could easily see because it was compatible with his schema dynamics (hence, using its "force" *against* the client's "complaint" about his daughter's friends). Tranquilizers also allow for discussion of the *real* issue to emerge. In this case, it was the father's ambivalence about his daughter "growing up" and making life choices on her own. Clinical Case Example 15.9 further illustrates persuasion.

Clinical Case Example 15.9: Distraught Woman Whose World Has Collapsed

In another example, an extremely distraught woman from the west coast sought help because her husband had cheated on her. She described a "perfect" family upbringing and what she thought was a "perfect" marriage. The more she delved into her husband's behavior, the more reprehensible things she found, such as his frequenting massage parlors, using Internet porn sites, and so forth. She was devastated, as well as her "perfect" world and "perfect" children, because in her rage she had blatantly divulged his behavior to her children, who found themselves tormented and torn over loyalties to their victimized mother and still wanting to have a connection to their father.

After having "kicked" her husband out of the house and forbidden him from reentering without her permission, whenever they would plan to meet to discuss their predicament and possible options, she found herself verbally assaulting him. As several months passed, the wife found herself calming down and becoming more "rational." She did not appear to want a divorce, perceiving such an alternative as turning her into a "loser." On the other hand, she did not appear enthusiastic about taking her husband back because that would make *him* a "winner" (i.e., he had everything to gain, namely, his wife, his children, and his home) and her a "loser" (i.e., she would be taking a "cheater" back, and her husband was getting the better "deal"). In the process of constantly reevaluating her circumstances and alternatives, she found herself wanting to "punish" him. She also believed that periodically "punishing" him "forever" by rubbing his face in his misdeeds was her way of reminding herself that he was not going to get a "better deal" if she took him back.

QUESTIONS

1. What are the poles of the client's dilemma? What kind of dilemma is it?
2. What are the schema dynamics that you can decipher from the information given?
3. What ambivalence can you detect?
4. What are the elements of the client's emotional system (emotional state, internal feelings, and affective expressions)?
5. What is the behavior that needs to be tranquilized? How is it creating problems for the client and getting in the way of therapeutic progress?
6. What types of nonlinear listening would you use to understand the client's situation?
7. How would you use the therapeutic paradoxical intervention of persuasion to help the client and move the therapy forward?
8. Discuss the paradoxical nature of the reframe for the client (i.e., two true elements that were mutually incompatible, yet true) and the counselor (an absurd or contradictory statement that contains truth).

Variation: Form small groups to discuss, or share as a class the answers to the questions above.

In Clinical Case Example 15.9, the client talked about her strategy and what her options might be, she related that she had better begin finding more positive things to say about him. The therapist persuasively argued that finding positive things about him was not necessarily in her interests! She expressed disbelief. If she was going to take him back, she maintained that her periodic harangues couldn't go on forever. Again, the therapist pleaded his case that it was not in her interests to see good things about her husband because she was at the core interested in who was getting a "better deal." As long as she maintained that posture, it *wasn't* in her interests to find positive things about him. In a core dynamic embedded in her self-schema, she believed that she could only feel good about herself if she was above others and "top dog" by convincing herself that she was getting or had gotten a "better deal" than someone else. That nonlinear, schema-based value had to be addressed in a nonlinear way. Persuading her *not* to abandon her long-held beliefs about her husband's imperfection and unsuitability was an absurd paradoxical statement that nevertheless contained elements of truth *for her*. When the client absorbed the two incompatible concepts (i.e., "He's a loser" and "I'm better than him") while also finding that she still cared for him, she disengaged from her struggle and moved the therapy forward.

In each of these instances, the client's behavior is in a heightened, agitated state. As with the other tranquilizer "P's", the client is expecting a fight. Paradoxical persuasion takes the therapist out of the position of being the "opposite" or "antithesis," and helps avoid a power struggle with the client by advocating for what she is already doing. Instead, the use of persuasion suggests to the client that her complaint isn't so problematic—as a matter of fact, there are advantages to it. The end result is that the client is no longer struggling with attempting to rid herself of the complaint. In the process, the client's ambivalence begins to resolve, and the real issues to be dealt with can emerge.

SUMMARY ON TRANQUILIZERS

There are a number of similarities among the various paradoxical "tranquilizers" that we have described. We would like to clarify at this point that the subtle differential use of these interventions is based upon the distress, excitability, anguish, and so on of a client; the amount of stress he is experiencing to do something about his circumstances; as well as what it is that the therapist is attempting to accomplish on behalf of the client. For instance, prohibition and postponement are meant to tranquilize because the client with whom they are used is in a high degree of emotional excitement and stress. The difference in these two interventions would be the degree of emphasis on the part of the therapist. Postponement generally entails more of a time dimension and allows a client to engage in a variety of activities while delaying any decision as a result of the activities. Prohibition benignly and empathically but formally discourages a particular activity or decision as not being in the client's interests at the present time. Each of these "tranquilizers" is meant to stimulate the resolution of a client's ambivalences regarding his problematic life circumstances. We present one last exercise to stimulate the reader's ability to understand and utilize the tranquilizer paradoxical interventions.

Clinical Exercise 15.2: Summary Vignettes Using Paradoxical Tranquilizers

Directions: Read each case scenario, and answer the questions below.

1. A client who had become depressed due to a recent divorce was having casual sexual relationships with numerous women. His parents (with whom he was living) were putting pressure on him to stop his promiscuity and to settle down with a "decent" woman. The client, however, was in no way prepared to get involved in any kind of intimate and enduring relationship at this point and continued to date three and four women in a single week. But, he strongly felt he should begin to "settle down."

2. A middle-aged man who elected to enroll in a night college course in general psychology. He hoped this would be an opportunity not only to expand his social life but also to enhance his knowledge of other people as he was being promoted to a supervisory position at work. The client was an "action-oriented" man who had poor academic experiences in his youth, even dropping out of school from time to time. About a third of the way into the course, he expressed having the "same old feelings" of once again wanting to quit. This was particularly distressing because it only served to reinforce and remind him of what he considered past failures to improve himself. In fact, he felt these feelings were evidence of an eventual relapse. Although fellow group members encouraged him to "stick it out," the client listened politely but remained discouraged.

3. A young man who acknowledged his gay identity during high school, then came to therapy shortly after graduating from high school in order to deal with overwhelming feelings of depression and suicidal thoughts. Feeling ignored by his father, he lived in the shadow of an older sibling who followed and fulfilled parental expectations and appeared to be the apple of his father's eye. Recently, he found himself going through a succession of jobs, drinking, smoking, and keeping late hours with friends but without any real direction in life. His antidepressant medications seemed to have little effect

on his mood, and subsequently he was hospitalized on three occasions for suicidal ideation after episodes of drinking. Although seeking excitement and responding to life's everyday ups and downs in a flamboyant, histrionic, and overreactive manner had once been effective in garnering attention, such behaviors were now largely resulting in only negative consequences.

QUESTIONS

1. What are the above clients' dilemmas?
2. What kind of *nonlinear* listening helps you discover these?
3. Can you identify ambivalences in these clients?
4. How are their behaviors potentially disruptive to therapy (and thus in need of tranquilizing)?
5. Which of the tranquilizing paradoxical interventions might be appropriate for the client? How would you use it with the client?
6. How is this reflective of *nonlinear* thinking?
7. Discuss the paradoxical nature of reframing for the client (i.e., two elements that are mutually incompatible, yet true) and the counselor (an absurd or contradictory statement containing a truth).

CONCLUSION

This chapter has defined paradoxical interventions and placed them within the larger context of nonlinear thinking as well as the Level I and Level II domains. The types of interventions presented are meant to be heuristic and suggestive—as means of stimulating practitioner nonlinear thinking rather than absolute categories of intervention. From a therapist's perspective, there are numerous *general purposes* for a therapist making paradoxical interventions. Some of the purposes for which a therapist makes a contradictory or absurd statement or directive[2] about a client's symptom, complaint, or the like that contains a truth include the following:

- To overcome the resistance inherent in unrealistic schemas in the service of facilitating a positive resolution of ambivalences
- To establish and facilitate a greater sense of cooperation between the therapist and the client
- To encourage and instill hope
- To enhance self-esteem
- To foster a broader perspective of the client's circumstance
- To create a sense of "beneficial uncertainty" (Beier, 1966), novelty, and unexpectedness

More particularly, we presented two specific classes of paradoxical interventions: the neutralizers, which are meant to detoxify potentially disruptive client intentions; and the tranquilizers, which provide a client with a measure of relief from stressful, circular, unproductive, and ambivalent engagement with his or her symptom or complaint. In the next chapter, we will discuss how further nonlinear paradoxical interventions (more P's of the paradox) can also be used to have the opposite effect on client behavior as we introduce the energizers and the challengers.

ENDNOTES

1. "Successful" from the client's perspective because it allows him or her to avoid making a decision.
2. Directives are instructions given to a client that are paradoxical in nature. They differ slightly from "homework assignments" in that the latter are seen as more linear interventions meant to practice, strengthen, and reinforce certain behaviors.

The Domain of Paradoxical Interventions

Part 3: The Energizers

16

CONTENTS

INTRODUCTION AND DEFINITION

Striving for success and wanting to avoid failure are universal. People are drawn to stories about famous people and their successes and failures. We cite the concrete experience of disappointment and failure that Walter Payton, the great running back of the Chicago Bears football team, went through early in his career many years ago. *Chicago Tribune* sportswriter Cooper Rollow (1977) wrote about the sadness and agony that a young Walter Payton experienced as a result of injuring his ankle on the very last day of the football season. Because he had to leave the game early with his injury, Payton lost his chances to win the National Football League rushing title. Rollow quoted Payton from a speech he gave at a dinner in his honor. We quote Payton here for two reasons: to reflect the powerful influence of the intuitive use of paradoxical nonlinear thinking by people in everyday life, and to highlight the inherent wisdom and influence that such paradoxes possess, to say nothing of the different perspective that they provide. To quote Payton,

> It was, I guess, the low point of my life. So much had been made of the fact that I had a chance to beat O.J. Simpson out for the rushing title. When I found myself lying there on the field and knew I had failed, it was like I didn't want to get back up. … My teammates wanted it so much, they were willing to do anything to get it for me. As a result, I became overly aggressive. And that can be just as bad as not putting out enough.

What it is, I'm a competitor. Being injured, not finishing the game was eating inside of me. I didn't know how to cope. I talked to people about how I felt. To my wife, Connie, and to Ronald Harper. To reporters ... they were doing most of the talking, putting words in my mouth. ... I was just going along with it. But deep down inside of me, I never did really express my inner feelings.

Finally I went home to see my mother in Columbia, Mississippi. I explained to her how I felt. She told me, "Don't worry about it son. It was God's will. It was probably best for you that it worked out as it did. This may be a disappointment right now. But it may help your career in the long run because you have a target to shoot at. Too much success, too young, can be bad." All at once, when her words got through to me, I felt a big sense of relief! (Rollow; *emphasis added*)

Obviously, Mrs. Payton is a wise woman. Of course, what she did was to *paradoxically redefine* her son's experience with failure in such a way as to give him relief from the agony he was experiencing and simultaneously energize him with hope for the future. Who knows what would have happened if he had been successful that early in his career? What we do know is that Mrs. Payton apparently was able to do something for her son intuitively that master practitioners routinely do for their clients. We also know that Payton went on to win many awards, and even a Super Bowl ring. He retired (and recently died) as a much beloved sports hero.

Clients come for treatment with an infinite number of symptoms and problem situations in many ways similar to those described about Walter Payton. In Chapter 14, we introduced paradoxical interventions, and demonstrated how they can be used to neutralize and tranquilize client behavior. However, many times clients demonstrate complacency, negativism, or overt discouragement regarding their circumstances. They find it difficult to make efforts to participate fully in treatment and are resistant. Perhaps the best way of describing such clients is that they are "stuck"—much like Walter Payton was. Frequently, there is a disconnect between (a) their stated needs (i.e., symptom relief), (b) the underlying purpose those symptoms may serve (e.g., protection from failure, or avoidance), and (c) what they are willing to do or feel they can do about their situation. As with many clients, they appear to be reacting to their feelings of ambivalence by endlessly vacillating, being immobilized, trying to escape, or letting fate decide. The result is that they feel powerless and become immobilized.

Well-meaning *linear-thinking* therapists who overtly attempt to encourage such clients to change (e.g., via empathy, or taking one side of the problem) are quickly frustrated in such efforts. If not a chronic problem already at the beginning of treatment, unresolved ambivalences can soon develop characteristics of being chronic and intractable. At times, clinicians will acquiesce to such behavior and accept a client's explanation that his condition is beyond help. We have suggested that the assessment process requires determining what is motivating a client to come into therapy at this particular time. That process helps to determine what direction therapeutic interventions will take. For example, a therapist's interventions need to be directed toward dealing with a client's ambivalence or those behaviors, feelings, symptoms, behaviors, complaints, and so on that interfere with dealing with the ambivalence. There is a class of paradoxical interventions that we have labeled *energizers* to deal with such circumstances.

THE ENERGIZERS

"Energizers" represent a class of nonlinear paradoxical interventions designed to encourage, stimulate, and mobilize clients who, as a result of their experience of ambivalence (i.e., dilemma), have either become immobilized or are endlessly vacillating. Energizers prompt new behaviors that are contrary to the more rigid and maladaptive perceptual and behavioral entrapments of what they have been doing (i.e., "more of the same"). By proposing an energizing paradoxical intervention, a therapist acts as a disturber of a client's defensively closed and lethargic perceptual system. The therapist's intention is to mobilize resources that a client has simply been unable to access either because of faulty appraisal processes (e.g., deletions and distortions) and schema dynamics that prevent action or because of feelings of ambivalence. The results of altering a clients' perceptual system (e.g., like the example of *Patch Adams*; Shadyac, 1998), make it difficult for them to return to the way they previously were seeing things. We cite Clinical Case Example 16.1 as an illustration.

Clinical Case Example 16.1: Chronic Distress Over Bad Thoughts

A young, frail-looking woman in her late 20s sought counseling as a result of her husband being placed in a nursing home 2 weeks earlier. She stated that she felt like a failure for no longer being able to care for him at home. He was in his early 30s and the victim of a fulminating[1] multiple sclerosis, a terrible illness that affects all body motor movements but leaves awareness intact. For 2 years prior to the placement of her husband in the nursing home, she had cared for him at home, even though for much of that time he had been confined to a wheelchair. When his bowel and bladder control failed as well as many other voluntary muscle movements, it became physically impossible for her to care for her husband at home even with professional nursing support on a daily basis. She was truly grief-stricken at the fact that he was "stuck in a nursing home for the rest of his life." Her husband, whom she repeatedly emphasized was such a good person, faced a dim future.

She sobbed movingly about the lack of support from some family members and felt disloyal to her husband when friends and family would tell her to forget about him and get on with her life. The same people advised her to seek another life with someone else because she was still young. She admitted that the future looked bleak for herself and her husband. Although she teetered back and forth with thoughts of suicide, she discounted them because she felt that her husband needed her.

During one session, she asked, "Is it wrong to wish that he would die?" She had been struggling with this question over and over again, and could not stop feeling guilty over entertaining such thoughts. Because of these thoughts, she found herself visiting her husband less frequently because the thoughts were very intrusive, which, in turn, made her feel *more* guilty.

Implicit in her question was a dilemma for the therapist: To tell her it was wrong to wish her husband to die would only make a very courageous young woman feel even guiltier than she already did. On the other hand, to give her permission to wish her husband dead would only make her feel guilty and disloyal. After all, if she did not feel that it was wrong to begin with, she wouldn't have brought the issue up in the first place. Thus, if the therapist told her it was not wrong, she would not have found much comfort. It follows that her schema dynamics did not allow her to comfortably entertain thoughts about wishing him to die. Her schema dynamics also would not permit her to feel good about herself because she felt that she failed her husband by having to place him in a nursing home.

The therapist's response was "For whose benefit do you want such a seriously and hopelessly ill man to linger on? If you wished him to stay alive as long as possible, perhaps it was to help postpone your own loss and grief. To wish a loved one to continue to linger may be for *our* benefit. On the other hand, to wish him dead may in the final analysis be an act of love and courage in that he would no longer have to deal with his suffering, helplessness, and hopelessness."

QUESTIONS

1. What is the woman's dilemma?
2. From the information available, describe more fully some of this woman's schema dynamics.
3. Can you detect what the client's "solution" to her dilemma was prior to the therapist's intervention?
4. How would you describe the therapist's response as "energizing"?

In Clinical Case Example 16.1, the young woman felt and expressed relief on hearing this particular perspective that she had never considered. Although it did not mitigate the grim realities she still faced, she derived a sense of comfort and encouragement from feeling understood and having "an answer." She felt "energized" (i.e., not euphoric but more capable of facing the realities of her life) and more hopeful, and she began visiting her husband with more regularity and no longer complained of being troubled by thoughts of wishing him dead.

Level I and II practitioners frequently encounter difficulty with energizing interventions because they often contravene more "logical" (i.e., *linear*) notions of what it is to be a "helper." As discussed in Chapter 7, for therapists and counselors, the concepts of helping and forging a therapeutic alliance clearly necessitate empathy. Although empathy is a necessary condition for addressing the suffering component of our clients, it is not necessarily sufficient to stimulate the resolution of ambivalence, change, and growth.

Clients who are in need of energizing frequently require an intervention that does the opposite of what they expect. Energizers are designed to stimulate more flexible behavior. They are always implemented within a climate of deep respect for the client. It is important to remember that although energizers present two statements about the client's problem that are contradictory, they still contain an element of truth. When done effectively, such interventions produce what Watzlawick, Weakland, and Fisch (1974) and Fraser and Solovey (2007) discussed as "second-order change." We add a cautionary note to the use of the "P's of the Paradox," as we have called them: Paradoxical interventions do not replace the necessity of "working through" issues that a client brings to therapy. Although at times such interventions represent major aspects of therapeutic success, at other times they facilitate overcoming the corrosive impact of resistance, reactance, and negativism. At all times, it is the client who defines what a successful outcome is. That is why it is so important to solicit feedback from clients about the impact and success of treatment—or lack of it (see Miller & Rollnick, 2002).

NONLINEAR LISTENING AND ENERGIZERS

As with other elements in this text, *nonlinear* listening is important in determining what a client needs. In therapy, clients who need energizing may complain that they are "tired": "I'm doing all that I can just to stay afloat, and have no time or energy to think about doing anything different." The therapist recognizes that these clients are stuck between their schema dynamics (view of self, others, or the world) and circumstances that they face (or don't *want* to face). "Energizers" alter a symptom or complaint so that it no longer has the negative impact on treatment it previously had. In each case, a clinician must listen for

- *congruence* (does the client *act in a manner consistent* with the help that he says he is seeking?);
- *absence* (is a client's inactivity a distraction from working on issues of ambivalence?);
- *inference* (what is the client telling me she *doesn't* want?);
- *presence* (what does a client's behavior tell me that the client is not expressing verbally?);
- *resistance* (when recommendation for change is made, the response is "Yes, but …");
- *listening for beliefs* as a source of information about schema dynamics;
- *listening for feelings* as a valuable source of information about a client's emotional system; and
- *understanding* the client's dilemma and the ambivalence that results from it.

Each of these methods of listening provides the *nonlinear*-thinking clinician with *potential* information about what the client needs from therapy.

TYPES OF ENERGIZERS

We present three types ("P's") of paradoxical "energizer" interventions: prosocial redefinition, practice, and pedagogism. Each of them stimulates *an emotional response* that (hopefully) encourages a client to reappraise his circumstances and move toward new solutions. In turn, this reappraisal simultaneously allows a client to disengage even slightly from problematic behavioral solutions. As a result, a client develops a new sense of possibility. The clinical examples of energizers that follow represent therapeutic efforts designed at invigorating feelings, behaviors, or systems. The possibilities for utilizing energizers are enormous depending on the creativity, sensitivity, and flexibility of the practitioner. Every therapist who uses paradoxical interventions must execute them in accord with the unique characteristics of her particular personality. We reiterate that the categories of paradox are heuristic and suggestive learning devices designed to help practitioners develop a sense of what clients need and what therapists can do to facilitate that (e.g., neutralize, or tranquilize).

PROSOCIAL REDEFINITION

Each client is unique. But although the origins and behavioral manifestations of their diagnoses may not have much in common, there are some elements that most clients seem to share. One common element that clients share was described in Chapter 8 on schema dynamics—the relative inflexibility of their view of self, others, or the world and life. By and large, another common element that they share is that their appraisal processes (described in Chapter 10) are skewed, which creates problems in their coping methods. As a result of skewed schema dynamics and the faulty appraisal processes that follow from them, another common element that these clients share is that their symptoms or behaviors have a tendency to affect other people and their general social environment. Others are often constrained, concerned, pushed aside, or shut out because of the client's behavior. At the same time, clients deny any control over their behaviors and what it is that is troubling them—"I just can't help it!" Even if they want better relationships with others, clients often suffer from poor, failing, or strained human connections. At times, they may have few meaningful relationships at all. Simply said, "neurotic" behavior oftentimes strains (in a variety of subtle ways) or alienates a client's relationships with others.

Consider clients who develop agoraphobia—a most debilitating condition. They fear the outside world *so* much that they confine themselves to the safety of their home. Their schematized appraisal of the world is pessimistic and inflexible (i.e., "There is danger *everywhere*"), and they react emotionally in a volatile way as a result of such appraisals. Now imagine that you are a friend, relative, spouse, or child of this person. The quality of your relationship might be quite strained. Further complicating matters, a phobic individual can wield great power as a means of controlling a relationship(s) while denying that he is doing so—"It is the *phobia* that is controlling, not me! I just can't help it!" Unless someone is willing to conform to the agoraphobic person's "rules" of fear, a relationship is destined for difficulties. All of this can lead to such clients feeling more isolated and alone as individuals affected by their behavior feel unable to be constrained by the agoraphobic's behavior.

Prosocial redefinition is an energizer—a paradoxical intervention that seeks to capture the essence of a client's problematic behavior that pushes others away, and finds a positive aspect to it. Prosocial redefinition reconstructs and "reframes" problematic behavior in a way that reveals it to have a *prosocial* dimension. Recall from Chapter 14 that a major part of using paradoxical interventions is reframing. As a therapeutic activity, Bandler and Grinder (1982) defined *reframing* as follows:

What reframing does is to say[,] "Look, this external thing occurs and it elicits this response in you, so you assume that you know what the meaning is. But if you thought about it this other way, then you would have a different response." Being able to think about things in a variety of ways builds a spectrum of understanding. None of these ways are 'really' true, though. They are simply statements about a person's understanding. (p. 43)

Reframing provides a client with an opportunity to consciously and unconsciously *reappraise the meaning* of her troublesome circumstances in a more beneficial way that she had not previously considered. In this core paradoxical intervention, a therapist must discover a plausible meaning (i.e., one containing an element of truth) for the behavior, and present it as being *prosocial* in nature. Often, this requires looking for a positive or opposite meaning to the behavior (see Chapter 14). Such an interpretation makes it easier for a client to *reappraise* the negative results of inflexible thinking that arises from her schema dynamics when she sees her behavior in a larger context. Again, Bandler and Grinder (1982) described it:

Reframes are not con-jobs. What makes a reframe work is that it adheres to the well-formedness conditions of a particular person's needs. It's not a deceptive device. It's actually accurate. The best reframes are the ones which are as valid a way of looking at the world as the way the person sees things now. Reframes don't necessarily need to be more valid, but they really can't be less valid. (p. 42)

To illustrate prosocial redefinition, we present Clinical Case Example 16.2.

Clinical Case Example 16.2: Total Incompetence

A 50-year-old bachelor with a previous history of long-term employment and other life productivity came to an outpatient clinic for help, complaining of feeling "total incompetence, stupidity, and worthlessness"—it was obvious that he was depressed. Despite having recently finished 3 years of college in a demanding business administration curriculum with very respectable grades, he felt that he was now flunking out of school, and couldn't comprehend what he was reading or do well in his assignments. His conclusion was that he was worthless, stupid, and so forth.

Agreeing to group treatment, he soon disclosed his feelings to the group. As the members of the group attempted to reason with him (i.e., *nonlinear thinking*), he would mightily dismiss any comment that contained the slightest suggestion that there was anything worthwhile about him. For example, comments about having completed 3 years of college were dismissed because he now was in danger of flunking and couldn't concentrate on or comprehend anything he was reading. To the suggestion that he had worked successfully for most of his adult life before quitting to go to college, he retorted that his previously acquired skills were worthless in today's highly competitive job market. To the suggestion that he was relatively handsome and articulate, he replied that he hadn't dated in years, and furthermore, if he had a date he wouldn't have the slightest idea of what to do with her.

And so went the group's discussion for about 15 to 20 minutes. *Nonlinear listening* revealed that there was something very clear: *This man had been able to successfully negate* all encouraging and positive comments directed toward him—he had fended off all of the well-meaning members of the group. *Linear thinking* suggests a dilemma for the group's therapist: If he attempted to encourage the patient as other group members had, it is reasonable to assume that his comments were just as likely to be rejected. If he didn't encourage the client, he would continue with his negativistic thinking and remain discouraged and depressed. *Nonlinear thinking* provided a potential solution: The therapist suggested to the client that he apparently wasn't ready to hear anything positive or encouraging about himself, thus preempting his most likely response to any positive comments made about him. He further suggested that his position was understandable in its own right because people can and do become very "down" on themselves at times. It was then suggested that although he wasn't ready to hear or accept what the therapist was about to say (more preempting), it was "very clear" that the client's ability to think was not only clear but also irrefutable. That is, anyone who could so consistently and successfully negate supportive comments from an entire group obviously had "a fine mind."

Subsequent further assessment and *nonlinear listening* revealed the source of much of the client's feelings of worthlessness: He feels terribly guilty about living with his 89-year-old mother, who, although frail and largely housebound, cooks for him, washes the dishes, does his laundry, makes his bed, cleans the house, and pays their living expenses with her Social Security check. He furthermore states that he is dependent upon her and that it is not right. In fact, he complains that it is painful to watch her work while he does so little. After careful consideration of the *consistency* of the client's complaint, his aforementioned behavior was *reframed in a prosocial manner* beginning with a recitation of the following citation of the "facts":

- His mother is 89 years old, frail, and largely housebound, but in relatively good health.
- She has little, if any, social life.
- All of her friends are deceased.
- They have no other family; thus, the client is her only child.

Nonlinear thinking provided a response: The client was then told in a very compassionate manner that "by staying at home and *allowing your* mother to take care of you, you are giving her a reason, a purpose, for living. Furthermore, by staying home and *allowing* your mother to take care of you, you appear to be *sacrificing* seeking a life of your own *for her welfare*."

Upon the client being told this *prosocial redefinition of his complaint*, he burst into tears, sobbing about how much his mother seemed to enjoy caring for him and that it seemed to be the only thing that kept her alive. Within a few weeks, his depression had lifted significantly, and he had found several job interviews that looked promising.

QUESTIONS

1. What is the client's dilemma in this scenario?
2. From the information given, speculate on the client's schema dynamics.
3. What are the elements of the client's emotional system (i.e., emotional state, internal feelings, and affective expressions)?
4. What "principles" described from Chapter 14 could be helpful in developing the prosocial interpretation of the client's behavior used by the therapist?
5. What is the behavior that needs to be energized?
6. How would you address the urge to respond that the *client* should be doing all of the things that his mother was doing for him?
7. What types of nonlinear listening would you use to understand the client's situation?
8. Discuss the paradoxical *prosocial* nature of the redefinition of the client's behavior (i.e., two elements that were mutually incompatible, yet each is true) and the counselor's behavior (i.e., an absurd or contradictory statement that contains an element of truth).

Variation: Form groups to discuss, or share as a class the answers to the questions above.

Clearly, there are many ways that the client's behavior in Clinical Case Example 16.2 could have been viewed—lazy, highly dependent, avoidant of responsibility, depressed, narcissistic, "enmeshed" and undifferentiated from his mother, and so on. To emphasize and interpret any of these hidden "negative" motivations to the client would have simply put him in a continued deficit position (Hobson & Leonard, 2001). Although these "hidden" dynamics may all have a measure of validity, they emphasize only one way of seeing his circumstances—the negative way. That only feeds the self-defeating, depressed, and hopeless feelings that the client already has, and seldom seems to lead to change.

Assessing in a way that looks for strengths and unused resources (discussed in Chapter 4), however, reveals other possibilities. Furthermore, knowing a client's schema dynamics also allows a therapist to see other possibilities. In Clinical Case Example 16.2, the client was an only child who has always felt the obligation and responsibility of caring for and watching out for his now elderly mother—he was the major focus of her existence. It was of paramount importance to him to hear that his staying at home represented "*sacrificing* seeking a life of your own *for her welfare*" (positive prosocial motivation). It was in keeping with his *view of self* because he had previously supported her until she became elderly and unable to go out because of her frailty (i.e., "I am a good person *because* I have taken good care of my mother"). Also, he was being helpful to his mother, who seemed to have little purpose at this time in her life other than caring for her son—a lifelong view (i.e., view-of-others schema) compatible with his experience of his mother. Such meanings represent other plausible and constructive motives (i.e., they contain an element of truth and are *prosocial*) for his behavior.

His conflict, however, lies in the contradiction of two facts that cannot coexist at this time: At 50-something, he should be pursuing a life of his own (i.e., addressing more of life's embedded developmental tasks such as holding steady employment, having friends, dating, etc.) *and* he should be taking care of his mother (i.e., caring for her as she becomes elderly rather than letting her take care of him). If he continued to stay at home in accord with the prosocial interpretation of his behavior given by the therapist, he was cooperating with the *therapist*! On the other hand, if he chose to be resistant toward the therapist's depiction of his behavior and sought employment, he would be engaged in the prosocial activity of working and resolving the issue for which he came to therapy. The client wins either way.

A dynamic tension exists for him between what he is doing and what he believes he should be doing in life (i.e., a self-ideal), which is reflected in his ambivalence. The prosocial redefinition by the therapist is paradoxical because it is "absurd" according to social rules (i.e., a 50-year-old man allowing his elderly mother to do so much for him), and yet it can be seen to contain an element of truth. For the client, his circumstances represent two true but contradictory realities. The intervention is one that allows for self-esteem as well as a socially useful and acceptable rationale for his life circumstances and behavior.

Looking at the situation in such a manner doesn't change the reality or "facts" of the situation. But it constructs a prosocial and potentially *energizing reappraisal* of his circumstances, which invites the client to find ways to be able to take care of his mother *and* begin to tackle the issues of adulthood. Even if it doesn't lead to immediate change, it is encouraging to the client and strengthens the therapeutic alliance.

Prosocial redefinitions are enormously useful in helping clients make sense of negative emotions as well. For example, anger as an emotion of power and wanting to overwhelm others can be reinterpreted dialectically as representing an expression of helplessness—someone cannot influence or achieve what it is that she wants in transactions with others, so she attempts to overwhelm them with a display of anger. Such reinterpretation can be useful in helping clients to make sense of their internal feeling states as well as future instances in which they feel angry—they can look for other means of influencing, reappraise the situation, and so on. Without such alternate understandings (i.e., a spectrum of meanings), clients can continue to feel guilty about negative emotions that they experience and express. This often leaves clients feeling "stuck."

For example, a husband and wife were in treatment for their long-standing difficulties in accepting one other. During one session, the wife came to couples' counseling depressed and discouraged about her husband expressing great anger toward her. As the "baby" of her family of origin, she had grown to expect that others would not become upset with her but rather admire her for being "cute." Her husband's anger thus ran contrary to the expectations that she had held for men (i.e., her view-of-others schema) since childhood. During the same session, the husband told the male co-therapist that he was angry with him for something he had said the previous week. After a small discussion, the therapist stated that he was encouraged by the patient's expression of anger toward himself and the client's wife. He explained that the expression of anger in a meaningful relationship was a definitive sign of trust in the person toward whom the angry feelings were expressed. The therapist expressed his thanks to the client for trusting him and his wife with his feelings because he didn't do that very often. The client responded that what the therapist had said was accurate in that he didn't often run the risk of telling others how he felt—especially if he was angry. The wife indicated that although it was difficult to accept the expression of anger because of her convictions about the way she felt she should be treated, she was grateful that her husband was able to trust her with his feelings.

The net results of this particular prosocial redefinition were twofold. The husband found an acceptance of his angry feelings, whereas the wife was able to be more accepting of her husband's anger and was able to begin exploration of her own exaggerated expectations of men. As a result of this paradoxical prosocial redefinition, both spouses could "win" in the series of transactions and could hopefully view the expression of anger in a much less destructive light, thus diminishing tensions and the potential frequency of anger's recurrence. As an "energizer," prosocial redefinition helps mobilize clients who are "stuck" in negative, repetitive behavioral patterns, as shown by Clinical Case Example 16.3.

Clinical Case Example 16.3: The Stereo and the Baby

A couple in their mid-20s was participating in marital therapy for help with their relationship. They had made a number of gains in the course of treatment, including steady employment by the husband, declines in long periods of silence between them, increased dialogue of an affirming nature, the purchase of a home, and the wife conceiving their first baby. Unfortunately, soon after they moved into their home, they were burglarized not once but twice while they were at work. In both instances, the major item "ripped off" was a moderately expensive stereo system.

During the session following the announcement of her pregnancy, the wife expressed her concern that she felt that they didn't seem to have much time together. When they did, about the only topic they would discuss was the stereo system and whether to purchase another one or not. The husband was in favor of purchasing a new stereo, whereas the wife was not. They felt genuinely stymied at their dilemma, with both expressing their need to talk about "things" but apparently only able to get as far as unresolved discussion of the stereo.

After a while, it seemed that the couple was fixated on the "stereo"—to the exclusion of anything else. This was especially challenging considering that although they had expressed a desire to have a child, they had not talked about their doubts, fears, and expectations regarding what parenthood might mean to each of them and their relationship. The therapist suggested looking at "the other side of the stereo coin," and how even though it was frustrating them, it might actually be helpful to them. He posited that perhaps at this time the couple needed to be "stuck" with the issue of the stereo, and that although it might stymie them somewhat, perhaps it was better than dealing with their feelings on the issue of the pregnancy, a topic that they were ambivalent about (i.e., "We want kids, we are competent people, but how good will we be as parents when we can't even buy a stereo without getting screwed?").

QUESTIONS
1. How would you describe the clients' dilemma?
2. What are the schema dynamics that you can decipher from the information given?

3. What are the elements of the clients' emotional system (emotional state, internal feelings, and affective expressions)?
4. How would you describe the clients as being "stuck"?
5. What behavior is it that needs to be energized?
6. How is that behavior creating problems for the clients (i.e., interfering with therapeutic progress)?
7. What types of nonlinear listening would you use to understand the clients' situation?
8. How would you use a paradoxical intervention (i.e., prosocial redefinition) with the clients?
9. Discuss the paradoxical nature of the reframe for the clients (i.e., two elements that are mutually incompatible, yet both true) and the counselor (i.e., an absurd or contradictory statement that contains an element of truth).

Variation: Form small groups to discuss, or share as a class the answers to the questions above.

In Clinical Case Example 16.3, the paradoxical intervention prompted both spouses to respond with some surprise, although both agreed that there were issues that each had not discussed because of feelings of being overwhelmed. For the wife, it was the idea of being a good mother, having to give up her job (i.e., independence was part of her view-of-self schema), being a responsible mother, having a child totally dependent upon her, and so on. For the husband, the coming of the baby meant having to choose between the security of his present job (which had limited potential for advancement) and the insecurity of looking for a new job (i.e., "I must not fail" is part of his view-of-self schema) with better future possibilities. It also meant less time for him to spend pursuing personal interests. Both spouses were able to see the intervention as a legitimate assessment of their current needs. That is, both were overwhelmed (by the financial responsibilities of their new home, the two burglaries, and the pregnancy), and neither could face the other with their trepidations and doubts without fear of upsetting the other. They needed the "stereo problem" as a focus of something that they could work on. At the time, it allowed them to avoid thinking about their fears about the birth of their first child. Their "ambivalence" could now be incorporated into a *prosocial function*—being stuck was a necessary respite, a psychological catching of one's breath, before continuing with what they needed to talk about.

Another group of clients who often need "energizing" are those who become entangled with the criminal justice system. The linear thinking of conventional therapeutic and counseling wisdom is based on the idea that successful treatment outcomes are made when the client admits that what he has done is wrong and demonstrates some remorse. Of course, as mentioned in Chapters 12–13, such thinking often leads to a nonproductive power struggle. This is just as true for people who stringently maintain their innocence as it is for those people who "wallow" aimlessly in their guilt in order to atone for their "sins." Recall from Chapter 2 the nonlinear concept of *listening for absence* (or what the client is *not* saying) and the discussion of rabbit holes and useless "war stories." Some clients think that they are making progress with these. More likely, they are "stuck" in the repetitive cycle of doing penance and never being quite finished with making amends (i.e., the "preparation for action" stage of change; see Chapter 4). What they share in common with other clients is that their behavior prevents them from doing any constructive therapeutic work. Finding a way to disentangle such people from their useless solutions and bring them and their behavior back into the mainstream of human society becomes an essential therapeutic task (i.e., helping to get them *out of the hole they have dug for themselves*). Therapists have a frequent problem around knowing exactly how to do this. On the one hand, to minimize a client's feelings is tantamount to approving of his crime, whereas to agree with the client's unrelenting need to express repentance is to give permission to continue wallowing. Instead, a paradoxical intervention can be quite helpful in freeing the person from the negative useless behavior and toward a more therapeutic resolution. We present Clinical Case Example 16.4 as an example.

Clinical Case Example 16.4: A Stalker

A male college-aged client was convicted of stalking his ex-girlfriend.[2] In treatment, the client described how he met his ex-girlfriend in a bar where she had approached and pursued him and engaged in a night of dancing. From there, the relationship became very intense very fast. He believed that things between them were good and was shocked when she suddenly and unexpectedly broke up with him. As a result of the breakup, he felt empty and confused, and tried to contact her several times to find out about what happened. According to the client, it was his persistent attempts to confront his ex-girlfriend to find out why she left him that led to the stalking complaints and his ultimate conviction. In one specific episode, he admitted that he went over to his ex-girlfriend's house, but found that someone was with her. He decided to hide in the shrubs to see who would come out, but did not intend to be discovered. Unfortunately, she found him, became understandably upset, and pressed charges against him. When he was asked why he went to her home and what he was intending to do, he said, looking lost and sad, "I don't know." It was clear, however, that he felt stupid, guilty, sad, and endlessly remorseful.

QUESTIONS

1. What is the client's dilemma in this scenario?
2. What are the schema dynamics that you can decipher from the information given?
3. What are the elements of the client's emotional system (emotional state, internal feelings, and affective expressions)?
4. What is the "stuck" behavior that needs to be energized? How is it creating problems for the clients and getting in the way of therapeutic progress?
5. What types of nonlinear listening would you use to understand the client's situation?
6. How would you use a paradoxical prosocial redefinition with this client?
7. Discuss the paradoxical nature of the reframe for the client (i.e., two elements that are mutually incompatible, yet true) and the counselor (i.e., an absurd or contradictory statement that contains truth).

Variation: Form small groups to discuss, or share as a class the answers to the questions above.

In Clinical Case Example 16.4, the therapist's assessment of this sad young man was that he was in mourning over the sudden and unexpected loss of the relationship, and that the stalking was a way of expressing his grief, albeit in a nonproductive, socially useless way. In fact, his behavior had many characteristics of mourning: denial regarding the loss, behaving as though she was still a part of his life, and so on . The therapist reflected this to the client and added, "Most people when they grieve have a gravesite or memorial place to go to if they want to mourn over the resting place of their loved one. Maybe that is what you were trying to do when you were stalking your ex-girlfriend; finding the 'resting place' of your relationship so that you could grieve and move forward with your life."

Immediately, the young man agreed with the unexpected interpretation. He began to see *what* he did in light of *why* he did it, and began the mourning process and moving forward. At termination, when asked what the most helpful part of his counseling was, he stated that it was the "cemetery" metaphor—"because it made me seem 'normal' and not the 'monster' that they made me out to be in court." Developing a prosocial explanation that was clearly plausible given the man's personal history and the circumstances of his situation, he could acknowledge that he *had* been wrong but that he was not irredeemable. This paradoxical intervention helped him to reappraise the situation as much more benign than he had been feeling and make a choice to change his behavior. Subsequently, he developed a way of saying farewell to the relationship, and disengaging from the pain he felt. Prosocial redefinition helps clients to break away from the self-imposed exiles and old (mistaken) ways of behaving. This "liberation" gives them the "energizing" they require to reengage in resuming a productive life.

PRACTICE

Anyone who has ever tried to learn to play an instrument or a new sport, or develop any new skill, knows the value of practice. As the old adage goes, "Practice makes perfect!" The problem is that with human nature being what it is, many people don't follow through with practicing even though they know it is what they need. The same understanding is equally true in a clinical setting as well—it is often difficult to stimulate our clients and patients to practice new ways of doing things.

Obviously, rigid thinking and repeating ineffectual solutions do not reflect common sense. But such thinking and solutions do reflect a very particular type of personal and idiosyncratic nonlinear reasoning. Motivating these clients to practice a new way of thinking and dealing with their condition is challenging because they have frequently exhausted themselves with rigid and unproductive thinking and ineffectual solutions. A paradoxical intervention that can sometimes help in dislodging a client from counterproductive activity is the energizer we call *practice*. "Practicing" defines the "problematic" behavior, and encourages a client to "practice" it and become better at it but *for benign purposes*. For many clients, such instruction is clearly counterintuitive (like most other paradoxical interventions) because it is *nonlinear*, unusual, and totally unexpected.[3]

Clients are asked to practice their symptoms or demonstrate them during the therapy session in order to demonstrate the client's command over the behavior. When they hesitate to do so or claim that they cannot, clients' schema dynamics, emotional system, or feelings of ambivalence can be revealed. In order to detect those dynamisms, a therapist must rely on nonlinear listening, especially *listening for congruence*, *listening for absence*, and *listening for resistance*. This can be particularly useful in working with individuals who exhibit two types of personality characteristics: paranoia and perfectionists.

Recall from Chapter 8 that a person with a paranoid disposition toward life has a negative and unrealistic or inflexible view of others and the world; such a person cannot afford to let her guard down. These individuals fear being betrayed or taken advantage of by "the enemy," predators, life circumstances, and so on. As a result of this understanding, a therapist can paradoxically encourage such clients to practice being even more "vigilant," often suggesting restraint from making decisions until collecting *more* information. Such a suggestion is thoroughly congruent with the way paranoid individuals see the world. It must be emphasized that this intervention cannot be done mockingly or with amusement. It is only *truly* paradoxical if it is done within the context of a therapeutic alliance, and with a good understanding of the client's schema dynamics.

Understanding the schema dynamics of the truly paranoid person is important. It is *nonlinear thinking and reasoning* that provide guidance in working therapeutically with such clients. Consider the following *nonlinear reasoning*: For the most part, the paranoid person has had lifelong experiences of feeling disappointed, betrayed, and hurt by others. If a therapist comes along and says, "You can trust me!" the paranoid person's defenses will be elevated because it has simply not been their experience that they can trust anyone. But, if a therapist suggests that the world *is* unpredictable and dangerous, it becomes strangely (i.e., paradoxically) empathic and compatible with how a paranoid person sees the world. Thus, urging that the paranoid person collect more information, go slowly, carry a low profile, and so on becomes a paradoxical directive to be more careful—and paranoid.

The paradoxical element of the intervention also comes from encouraging the client to practice *under the direction of the therapist*, which makes it a cooperative act (e.g., if he does go more slowly, or collect more information) and in harmony with the therapist; if he doesn't, he is relinquishing some of the heightened paranoia as unnecessary. The "absurd" element is that the therapist understands the client's point of view and the context in which the behavior is valid.[4] For many clients, the fact that the therapist understands their point of view and doesn't condemn them for it is "energizing." In this way, the therapist is aligned with the client and can use the alliance to begin exploring and understanding the client's emotional system, appraisal processes, and ambivalence. We present Clinical Case Example Case 16.5 to illustrate.

Clinical Case Example 16.5: A Paranoid Young Woman

A young woman in her mid-20s came to therapy at the insistence of her family because of her increasingly disturbing paranoid behavior. In particular, the client's paranoia fixated around FBI agents. She believed that they were trying to entrap her because they mistakenly believed that she was a "terrorist." She claimed that she knew that they were tapping her phone line and trying to "frame" her. It was only because she was very careful with her personal trash, bank statements, and other identifying information that she had not been caught. She claimed that she has known people who have "disappeared" and have been sent to unknown prisons, never to be heard from again.

The woman was intelligent and lucid, and held down a secretarial job that she was good at (because she was so cautious); however, she refused to date. Recently, she had begun to share her ideas with coworkers, which had caused her to be the object of some ridicule. The client now believed that those coworkers may be in on the conspiracy, and are trying to get rid of her. The client stated that she was in fear of her job because of layoff rumors.

QUESTIONS

1. What is the client's dilemma in this scenario?
2. What are the schema dynamics that you can decipher from the information given?
3. What are the elements of the client's emotional system (emotional state, internal feelings, and affective expressions)?
4. What is the "stuck" behavior that needs to be energized? How is it creating problems for the clients and getting in the way of therapeutic progress?
5. What types of nonlinear listening would you use to understand the client's situation?
6. How would you use the therapeutic paradoxical intervention of practice with the client?
7. Discuss the paradoxical nature of the reframe for the client (i.e., two elements that are mutually incompatible, yet each is true) and the counselor (i.e., an absurd or contradictory statement that contains truth).

Variation: Form small groups or share as a class the answers to the questions above.

In Clinical Case Example 16.5, the therapist understood that there was no way to dislodge this woman's paranoid belief system. Instead, he intervened by paradoxically stating, "You know, I can't say if you are right or wrong on this, but what I do know is that sometimes *you can't be too cautious*. What I think you may want to consider doing is to write down a log of instances in the next week when you suspect that you are under surveillance." The client agreed to the assignment. Once the client agreed to the assignment and "practiced" the troublesome behavior, *she had agreed to be cooperative with the therapist*. But when she returned the next week, she stated there were only two entries in her "log." Upon reading them, it became obvious that the client was responding to situations when she felt afraid or alone.

Once the client accepted the assignment and the therapist's "help," her schema dynamics could be explored as well as her emotional appraisal processes. The therapist decided to go a step further, stating, "It seems that whoever is pursuing you may be backing off. Let's give it another week, but this time *really* try to come up with some evidence." The client was unable to produce anything, and the therapist began to introduce to her that there might be another explanation for what she felt. The energizer paradoxical intervention mobilized her to go beyond the problematic behavior and take a second look at her behavior.

Another person for whom practice is often a good interventional "fit" is the "perfectionist." Such an individual often spends significant time and energy making certain that he does not make a mistake or do something poorly. In the process, perfectionists often exhaust themselves. They find that they don't enjoy life, friends, family, and the like as much as they might were it not for the curse of their perfectionism. A perfectionist may come for treatment with dysthymia and a host of depressive symptoms because he cannot stop focusing on his own actions and the constant need to make certain of his perfectionism. Clinical Case Example 16.6 illustrates.

Clinical Case Example 16.6: An Unhappy Perfectionist

The client was a happily married man in his late 30s who came to counseling for help in dealing with coworkers who he supervised. In particular, he felt like a failure because he couldn't get them to take their jobs (or do them, for that matter) as seriously as he did. He was also afraid that their poor performance would reflect badly on him with his superiors. He felt dejected, defeated, and depressed; had lost interest in things that gave him pleasure; was staying later at work; and was beginning to "snap" at his wife. Through the use of *nonlinear listening* during the course of one session, the therapist gauged that he was dealing with a perfectionist and suggested it to the client. The client immediately saw how the theme of perfectionism fit with his behavior and feelings, although he hadn't considered it before. His pursuit of perfectionism was leading to perceived failures; the perceived failures were leading to more useless pursuits of perfectionism.

When all was said and done, this likable but perplexed young man found himself in a "catch-22." He admitted to staying late at work on a regular basis, redoing his subordinates' paperwork to make sure that it was free of errors and up to his standards. Embarrassed, he also reported it was seldom that he gave feedback to these individuals about what he was doing for fear of looking "weak" to them. As he explored his feelings about this, he admitted that he did not want to act like this anymore but that he didn't know what to do.

QUESTIONS

1. What is the client's dilemma in this scenario?
2. What are the schema dynamics that you can decipher from the information given?
3. What are the elements of the client's emotional system (emotional state, internal feelings, and affective expressions)?
4. What is the "stuck" behavior that needs to be energized? How is it creating problems for the client and getting in the way of therapeutic progress?
5. What types of nonlinear listening would you use to understand the client's situation?
6. How would you use the therapeutic paradoxical intervention of practice with the client?

7. Discuss the paradoxical nature of the reframe for the client (i.e., two elements that are mutually incompatible, yet both true) and the counselor (i.e., an absurd or contradictory statement that contains a truth).

Variation: Form small groups or share as a class the answers to the questions above.

Because the client in Clinical Case Example 16.6 spent so much time trying to catch errors or prevent them, the therapist recommended that every day the young man should "practice" deliberately making an error, do something wrong, or do something incorrectly. The rationale given to him for this suggestion was simple enough: It didn't matter what he chose to "screw up" as long as he agreed to practice this habit and allow the natural consequences to result. In addition, he was told that if he found himself worrying about making a mistake, he would remind himself that he already made his mistake for the day and that he didn't have to worry about making another one. The young man agreed to "practice." Remember the irony of the present instance: someone with perfectionistic qualities wants to "practice" because, as we all know, "Practice makes perfect!"

The next week, the young man returned much more energized and more at ease. He reported being able to carry out the suggestion to practice "screwing up" and that he felt "totally different" about himself and his situation at work. The world wasn't "going to end" for him if he was less than perfect. In addition, he was (for the most part) able to put aside chronic worrying about his performance. As a result, he found himself better able to interact with coworkers without the tension that had been permeating his professional relationships. The paradoxical interaction had the effect of creating a second-order change in the client by offering another perspective on his behavior that allowed him to *get out of the hole that he dug for himself*. In subsequent sessions, he was able to work on some of the underlying issues prompting his perfectionistic tendencies as well as develop assertiveness skills in order to ask others for appropriate help in getting his needs met.

In the preceding example, knowing the client's schema dynamics (unrealistic view of self), the strategic value of "practice" can be used as a paradoxical intervention with a client to help free some of his energy that truly allows him to be a success. By contrast, a different therapeutic route could have been chosen such as a more traditional (i.e., *linear*) cognitive-behavioral approach. In such an approach, the client is instructed and encouraged to track thoughts that go with the perfectionistic tendencies. But, such *linear*-thinking interventions would probably take more time. By requesting him to "practice" being imperfect, he discovered a means of disengagement from the more useless method of dealing with work-related problems (i.e., living in fear of making a mistake). In other words, the paradoxical intervention has effects on the cognitive, relational, and emotional levels all at the same time. His disengagement from concern about making mistakes subsequently allowed him to discover the energy to recognize his own value as well as the value of working with others.

PEDAGOGISM

As the saying goes, "Teaching is learning twice." Pedagogism is a gentle but energizing paradoxical intervention in which a client walks a therapist through the processes and the logic underlying what others have oftentimes defined as problematic. As a case in point, defiant adolescents, precontemplators, and mandated clients find themselves in difficulty because of the impact of their behaviors on others, although they may not see their behavior as particularly problematic. Pedagogism is considered a particularly useful intervention to use with such clients, who seem to "dare" a therapist to make them change. Attempts to *make* a defiant client change appear doomed before they begin. The mental and psychological gymnastics that the therapist must go through in order to do this are often the equivalent of a scene from an *Indiana Jones* film in which he has to swing across an open canyon, swim in shark-infested waters, and then figure out impossible clues as to how to safely enter a temple.

But, by using *nonlinear thinking*, a therapist may request such a defiant client to explain the "secret" of her success, namely, a positive framing of what has been defined as troublesome (for others) behavior. More specifically, a defiant adolescent may be asked in an admiring way how she is able to "keep everything together so well" with her parents, school officials, and so on "harping" on her. Such behavior (i.e., apparently not letting anything bother her) is defined and reported to the client as a valuable skill that the therapist would like to know more about and learn from the client so that he might teach it to others.

The paradoxical energizer of pedagogism takes the "problem" behavior, finds its dialectical opposite, and, in a *nonlinear* fashion, "turns it on its head." Using *nonlinear thinking*, the therapist does not attempt to convince the client that his behavior is wrong or maladaptive, which is what the client expects. Obviously, if the defiant adolescent begins relating how he manages to keep things together and not be bothered, he is cooperating with the therapist—previously defiant behavior has been transformed into a cooperative venture between client and therapist. This has the effect of placing the client in the role of "knowledgeable expert" rather than helpless victim (Mozdzierz, Macchitelli, & Lisiecki, 1976). After a while, maintaining such a defiant posture in treatment becomes difficult for the adolescent, and she begins to engage more in the therapeutic endeavor. In a series of classical articles, Marshall (1972, 1974, 1976) suggested this method of intervention for dealing with a variety of child and adolescent problems. Pedagogism can also be used in other contexts, as Clinical Case Example 16.7 illustrates.

Clinical Case Example 16.7: Design a Plan for the Wife to Follow

The following illustration of this comes from a couples' therapy session. The husband initiated the therapy, complaining, among other things, that his wife never picked up around the house as he expected. The husband made it very clear to his wife that because he earned enough money for her to stay at home, the very least that she could do (in his opinion) was to keep the house clean. Upon further assessment, it was discovered that they had three children under the age of 6 and that the wife did actually keep the house fairly clean. The husband, it seemed, was not reacting to filth, but to the "mess" of toys that would be used by the kids and the occasional dirty diaper left in the garbage pail that his wife had not been able to empty before he came home. The exasperated wife defensively explained how she spent most of her time keeping the house clean for her husband, but that he never seemed to appreciate or notice all that she had done but instead chose to focus on the few things that the children had left out.

The therapist intervened paradoxically. He instructed the husband to write up a plan—a set of instructions for teaching—to keep the house the way he expected and bring it back the next week to discuss with his wife. Having "good" ideas about how things should operate is a skill that obviously can be taught. Such an "assignment" obviously met with the husband's belief that something needed to be done about his wife's difficulty in keeping the house the way he thought it should be. He gladly accepted, and the next week he came in with a five-page document on what he expected from his wife's cleaning efforts, and how to implement them. The therapist then, with a completely straight face, asked the husband if he had "field-tested" his plan. The husband first said that he had, and that these were the rules that he had used all his life. When asked, however, if he had actually performed them under the same conditions that his wife encountered daily, he answered "no." The therapist, knowing that the husband had some training as an engineer, stated that any project or plan must surely be pilot-tested before being implemented. The husband reluctantly agreed, and the therapist then asked the wife to take a day, leave the house and the children, and do whatever she wanted. In the meantime, the husband was to apply his manual for an entire day with the kids, to see how well it worked out. The husband tried to protest, but he agreed to put it to the test, with both spouses to report back. The therapist even said that he would be interested in a copy because he had difficulty keeping his house tidy. This is considered central to a pedagogically paradoxical intervention: The client's insistent investment in his complaint is used as something that can be taught—in this instance, to the therapist!

The next week, the couple reported that they had tried to implement the plan, and when the wife came home, she found that half the things on the husband's list were not accomplished. The husband admitted that he really didn't know how much work his wife did with the children, calling it a "full- and part-time job." At this point, the husband began to admit to having some feelings of jealousy and neglect from his wife that ultimately led to his devaluing her work and leading to his attention-seeking complaint behavior (i.e., the heart of the problem all along). The wife protested that she had told the husband that this was the case, but that he had always denied it. "That is because," the therapist said, "until now he didn't really *know* it. The point is that now that he does, you have to decide what do the two of you want to do about it?" At this point, the couple was ready to begin to work, whereas before the paradoxical intervention, criticism of the wife's ability to clean would have dominated the conversation and sandbagged the therapy. Not only weren't his unrealistic "complaints" and demands unchallenged, but also they were elicited as a source of expertise that could be taught to others; however, in the process he would have to acknowledge and learn some important things about running a household with little children.

Pedagogism also works effectively in energizing clients who have been victims of difficult life circumstances. Whether the victim of crime, illness, defective genes, or a random unfortunate event in life, many clients are overwhelmed, are preoccupied with having been victimized, and find it difficult to focus on other areas of strength or resilience in their lives. In addition, their negative focus (i.e., preoccupied, feeling victimized, etc.) leaves them deenergized and can often continue to make them feel stuck. Part of the sense of feeling stuck stems from the legitimate sense of being overwhelmed by the events that such clients have experienced. Their customary templates for understanding life (i.e., their schematized views) have little frame of reference to cope with such circumstances. As a result, they may understandably overestimate or overappraise threats in their environment, or underestimate their ability (e.g., strengths and resources) to cope with these threats. Pedagogism in this instance is a method to energize such clients by helping them to focus on how their experience as a victim has created significant resilience. Clinical Case Example 16.8 illustrates this point.

Clinical Case Example 16.8: Terrorized by a Rare Cardiac Condition

Recall from Clinical Case Example 5.5 the case of the accomplished physician who contracted a rare and debilitating cardiac condition. She was a woman in the prime of life, with a brilliant career, financially doing well, and dating a man whom she cared for dearly. She was very health conscious, exercised vigorously on a daily basis, ate healthy foods, maintained an ideal body weight, generally led a moderate lifestyle, and so on until she was suddenly struck by an illness whose origin is unknown. The disease she contracted is rare and sometimes fatal, and thus must be monitored closely and treated aggressively for life. Treatment consists of a regimen of steroidal anti-inflammatories, immunosuppressive medication, periodic monitoring of cardiac functioning, and frequent lab analysis of the blood (much like that given to cardiac transplant patients).

After being close to death, the woman recovered sufficiently to return to work. However, despite this second chance for life, she felt emotionally and psychologically weakened. She discussed how she felt defeated, frightened, vulnerable, and metaphorically "constantly looking over my shoulder" to scan and monitor whether or not the illness was going to return unabated in the same stealthy manner that it had first overtaken her. She began to worry that it would affect her relationships and her work, and (although she knew that she would never be free of worry) she wondered if she would ever feel close to "normal" again.

QUESTIONS

1. What is the client's dilemma in this scenario?
2. What are the schema dynamics that you can decipher from the information given?
3. What are the elements of the client's emotional system (emotional state, internal feelings, and affective expressions)?
4. What is the "stuck" behavior that needs to be energized? How is it creating problems for the clients and getting in the way of therapeutic progress?
5. What types of nonlinear listening would you use to understand the client's situation?
6. How would you use the therapeutic paradoxical intervention of pedagogism with the client to demonstrate her resilience?
7. Discuss the paradoxical nature of the reframe for the client (i.e., two elements that are mutually incompatible, yet both are true) and the counselor (i.e., an absurd or contradictory statement that contains truth).

Variation: Form small groups or share as a class the answers to the questions above.

SUMMARY OF THE ENERGIZERS

Energizer paradoxical interventions are best used for clients who are immobilized by their particular circumstances or by their ambivalence. Recalling the stages of change from Chapter 4, these are individuals who may be in the contemplation stage (i.e., aware that they have a problem, but not ready to face it) or in the preparing for action stage (i.e., getting ready to make a change, but not taking action yet). For one reason or another, they seem to be stuck in a hole (their problem behavior) and they cannot get out (not energized). Clinicians can figure out that this is happening by paying attention to their own countertransference feelings (from Chapter 7), and subsequently conclude that the client needs an energizer. For example, the therapist feeling very tired and weary in the session (like she is doing all of the work) or feeling that the client or the therapy is stuck may be indicators that the client feels like he is in a hole that he cannot get out of (because of fear, etc.). Therefore, the client needs to be motivated or energized to see that he has the ability to stop the problem behavior and move forward with therapy. We present a final exercise on the energizers.

Clinical Exercise 16.1: Multiple Cases in Need of Energizers

1. The client is a 29-year-old man who works as an attorney for a prestigious law firm in a major metropolitan city. The client has come to therapy to address his struggle with depression that has plagued him since his adolescent years and all throughout college

and law school. He tells you that he often feels so bad that he cannot get out of bed. He reports, however, that he had never missed a day of work or a court date due to his depression.

2. An 82-year-old man was referred for treatment because of depression following the death of his wife. They had been married for 49 years, 11 months, and 2 weeks when the wife died of a heart attack. The client blamed himself for not finding her on the sidewalk so that he might have been able to revive her. While in group therapy, he talked about how he no longer does anything around the house with the possible exception of preparing some very meager meals for himself. He especially talked about how many projects his wife had left for him, from fixing a curtain rod to washing and waxing floors. He then expressed the wish that "If I could only talk to her and give her a message or get a message from her, I could feel much better."

3. An elderly gentleman in his late 70s was diagnosed as having congestive heart failure. Although there were clearly cardiac medications available that would have decreased the severity of his symptoms and made him both more comfortable and more functional, he adamantly refused to take such medications. His reasoning was that such medications were "chemicals" and "chemicals" are bad for the body. He just couldn't get himself to use a "new way" of treating his heart condition but instead wanted to rely on herbal medicine to treat himself (often a very dangerous practice). But he was competent to make such decisions and knew the risks of not taking his doctor's advice.

In each case, address the following questions:

1. What is the client's dilemma?
2. What kind of *nonlinear* listening helps you discover this?
3. How is his behavior potentially disruptive to therapy (and thus needs energizing)?
4. Which energizing paradoxical intervention might be used with this client? How could it be used?
5. How is this reflective of *nonlinear* thinking?
6. Discuss the paradoxical nature of the reframe for the client (i.e., two elements that are mutually incompatible, yet both are true) and the counselor (i.e., an absurd or contradictory statement that contains truth).

Next, we present one of the more complex classes of paradoxical interventions: the challengers!

ENDNOTES

1. Fulminating multiple sclerosis is a particularly devastating and rapidly progressing neurological disorder in which the covering of the body's nerves are destroyed, resulting in a scarring of the nerves, rendering them inoperative, and thus leading to greater and greater paralysis.

2. Although stalking is clearly an issue that can reveal serious psychopathology and require thorough investigation, in this instance, it should be noted that the young man was not considered to be a danger to his ex-girlfriend. He lived several hundred miles from her and was under a strict court-ordered "order of protection" not to enter the town where the infraction took place or go anywhere near her, which he was abiding by (although many times individuals convicted of similar crimes do not).

3. Because the most common expectation that clients have is to be told to "stop" doing what it is that is problematic.

4. This is not to say that the therapist needs to agree with or condone the client's behavior to use this intervention. The therapist does need to believe in the nature of the nonlinear intervention.

The Domain of Paradoxical Interventions

Part 4: Challengers

CONTENTS

INTRODUCTION

The final classification of paradoxical interventions is probably the most difficult to master. They are reserved for those clinicians who have truly grasped the essence of *nonlinear* thought processes demonstrated by master clinicians, have a firm understanding of the other domains of competence, and also feel comfortable using paradoxical interventions. The challengers are that class of paradoxical interventions that are unsettling to a client's status quo. In much the same way that a grain of sand causes an irritating challenge to an oyster (thus causing the creation of a pearl), so too do the challengers provide a positive unsettling feeling to a client in the name of therapeutic movement. As "disturbing" as they are to the client's (maladaptive) status quo, challengers are meant to provoke positive therapeutic movement or prompt a greater sense of *prosocial equilibrium* to a client in maintaining her symptoms.

Just as with the energizers (discussed in Chapter 16), clients who require challengers feel burdened and stuck. The circumstances of their life generally require them to do more than they feel capable of doing, and their behavior (even though it is problematic) is the "best" that they can do. Unlike clients who require energizers and are immobilized and (for the most part) unable to move forward, clients who require challengers are acting in a way that is at best not in their interest, and at worst dangerous. Put simply, the client truly believes that, given his circumstance, he is doing all that he possibly can and that it is the *right* thing to do. Often, clients' schema dynamics (generally, the view of self) contain unrealistic expectations of what they "ought" to be able to do. Their limited resources or fear of failure, however, forces them to "fall short" of what they should or could do. Or, their schema dynamics may dictate that they do not foresee being able to "get" what it is that they want, so they retreat. As a result, such clients are caught in a dilemma and have intense feelings of ambivalence. They become entrenched in their positions with a discouraging, reactionary, and defensive stance toward others and life, and in addition engage in maladaptive (or even dangerous) behavior patterns. They convince themselves, "No one understands what I am going through," and such internal dialogue helps them justify their actions. Such clients never seem to make it into the textbooks and practice cases, and yet they appear in the practitioner's office every day. In fact, it is precisely because such clients are so typical of those who appear in clinicians' offices that we include them here.

NONLINEAR LISTENING AND CHALLENGERS

As always, *nonlinear listening* is especially important in determining whether challenging paradoxical interventions may be needed to mobilize a client. In therapy, clients who need energizing may complain that they are "tired": "I'm doing all that I can just to stay afloat and have no time or energy to think about doing anything more or different." The therapist recognizes that such clients are stuck between their schema dynamics (view of self, others, or life or the world) and circumstances that they face (or don't *want* to face). When a therapist intervenes by using one of the "challengers," however, a client's symptom is transformed so that it no longer does what it been doing. In order to effectively set the stage for such a transformation, a therapist must listen for *congruence* (i.e., is the client really wanting the help he is seeking?), *absence* (i.e., is all this behavior distracting from the *real* issue?), *inference* (what is the client telling me he *doesn't* want to happen?), *presence* (i.e., what is his behavior saying that the client is not telling me verbally?), and *resistance* (when I recommend that he changes, does he "Yes, but …" me?). Such *nonlinear listening* provides a therapist the guidance that she needs in stimulating a client from his lethargy or retreat by appropriate challenging.

TYPES OF CHALLENGERS

There are four types (or "P's") of "challenger" paradoxical interventions: proportionality, prediction, prescription, and positive provocation. Each of them prompts a client to react and (hopefully) *disengage* even slightly from her problematic behavioral solutions with at least a partial restoration of more adaptive functioning. This is perhaps one of the most difficult of the classes of paradoxical interventions for many clinicians because it entails some level of directness. Caution is recommended, however, about being "direct": If challengers are presented too passively, the intervention can be easily dismissed by a client ("Oh, what do you know? You're not going through what I am going through!"). Likewise, if such interventions are done too aggressively, a client will feel that the counselor is unjustly attacking her. Perhaps the most cogent suggestion that we can make is that challengers should be presented with respect and with confidence in their being appropriate in a matter-of-fact manner. Again, like all paradoxical interventions, therapists must be aware of all the other domains to be able to help a client with a challenger paradoxical intervention. We will now present the "P's" of the challengers, as well as case examples to illustrate the principles underlying these paradoxical interventions.

Proportionality

The concept of proportionality refers to the universal and natural striving for balance found in all of life and the universe. There is an inherent sense of this harmony when one leads a "balanced" life. In family systems theory, this is referred to as *equilibrium*. Unfortunately, for one reason or another (e.g., willfulness, misunderstanding, oversensitivity, faulty genes, brain chemistry gone awry, or misinterpretation), human beings seem to have considerable difficulty in achieving balance.

In daily living, individuals must rely on their constant automatic appraisals of life's events (i.e., the capacity for a "blink"—thinking without thinking—response) to inform them of the possibility of threats and/or the possibility of achieving things desirable. Unfortunately, because such automatic appraisals are so incredibly rapid, they come with inherent biases or distortions. Although it may be oversimplified, the extent of the distortion provided by automatic appraisals is contingent upon how far removed from common sense they are. It is quite common that clients seeking treatment have developed *disproportionate appraisals and responses* to perceived threats, failures, and so on in their lives.

When things are distorted, in many ways it's like looking at an old "funhouse" mirror that distorts a person's reflection. The appraisal acts like the warped mirror, which makes the head and body seem to be either too big or small and doesn't fit with reality. In times of stress, which are regular occurrences in today's often hectic, complex, and many times chaotic life, the images we have of ourselves (or situations in which we find ourselves) may become warped or out of proportion due to our distorted appraisals. During particularly stressful times, most people make efforts to bring things back into their proper proportion (e.g., the time spent on work and family life), just like people try to do with their reflections in the funhouse mirror by moving up or down to get a more realistic image. Some individuals, however, get things terribly out of proportion and out of balance, and don't seem to be able to get them in proper balance. They make the best effort that they can to bring things back into proportion, but cannot do it in constructive ways, so they live with "warped" solutions. Eventually, these individuals become stuck in maladaptive and even absurd "solutions," behaviors, strategies, and so on (i.e., distorted responses to distorted appraisals), and are unable to extract themselves from those solutions. The out-of-balance situation becomes "typical" and automatic, which becomes a "problem." Most often, their maladaptive disproportionate responses to life circumstances become problematic for other people.

Rather than using logic, reasoning, commonsense reality, or consensual validation (i.e., *linear* approaches) to deal with all manner of human absurdities, a therapist, using paradoxical interventions, takes a *nonlinear* approach, *joins* with the client's disproportionate appraisal and response, and extends them even further than the client had (i.e., "hyperextends" them). *Nonlinear* thinking is crucial in this process: The therapist knows that the client's "out-of-balance" behavior appears to make sense to *her*. Proportionality consists of taking a patient's unbalanced (i.e., out-of-proportion) position and exaggerating it, taking it to a greater extent than the patient (much like Miller and Rollnick's [2002] "agreeing with a twist"—see Chapter 13). In effect, when a therapist exaggerates the behavior in such a way, it oftentimes renders the patient's out-of-balance position much less palatable or tenable. Clinical Case Example 17.1 may prove helpful.

Clinical Case Example 17.1: A Sad Mother's Visit With Her Adult Children

A very accomplished professional woman sought brief therapy because her oldest adult sons had chosen careers that took them far from home after graduating from college. She quietly lamented how much she missed them, how emotionally close they had been, and how she relished their confiding in her. On one particular occasion, as tears welled in her eyes, she described how they came home every so often and then would decide to spend most of their time staying over at a friend's apartment in the downtown area, where they could reconnect with their childhood buddies and "party" with women friends. Although there was very clearly a sad and nostalgic truth to her story shared by all parents whose children have grown up and left home, it appeared equally clear that she was not fully appreciative of the fact that her children were doing what they should be doing at that time of life and that she needed to get on with other things as well.

The therapist stood up from his desk chair and said, as though pondering something very difficult to figure out, "Let me see if I have this right. (Gesturing with his right hand as though he were weighing what he was saying.) The boys could spend time with Mom (gesturing with his left hand as though he were weighing and comparing it against what was in his right hand)—or, they could spend time with their friends, drink, party, and enjoy their girlfriends. (Obviously exaggerating, with his hands going up and down as though he were continuing to weigh those options.) They could spend time with Mom, or they could party with their friends. Let's see: Young, energetic men with lots of good friends that they haven't seen in a long time could spend time with Mom (continuing to move his hands up and down, as though he were continuing to weigh something), or they could party with their friends."

The woman instantly broke into a broad, knowing smile and laughed, recognizing that she had "exaggerated" her position (i.e., consensually nonlinear thinking) toward her children. Almost instantaneously, she had put things back into balance. It is common sense that young men and women would want to spend free time with their friends, thus establishing a normal life pattern while not meaning to "reject" their parents. The paradoxical intervention allowed the client to reappraise her situation and decide to change her behavior.

Many therapists consider this intervention as analogous to the judo metaphor of many paradoxical interventions (discussed in Chapter 14). The practitioner uses the client's "power" and position to his own (and ultimately) to the patient's therapeutic advantage. That is, the person's natural inclination toward balance is engaged once the therapist hyperextends and exaggerates the client's behaviors. Timing and sensitivity in the application of the concept of proportionality are extremely important considerations, as is the manner of presentation. Developing skill at executing such timing and sensitivity is a hallmark of the master practitioner. As such, we hope the reader will see that at times a somewhat humorous presentation (as in Clinical Case Example 17.1) is called for, and at times a more serious one is needed. In either event, the therapist extends the client's symptoms or complaints to the point of exaggerating something already out of proportion and carrying it to the point of a *reductio ad absurdum* (reduction to the absurd). See Clinical Case Example 17.2.

Clinical Case Example 17.2: Depression, Money, and a New Son-in-Law

The following example of a stubborn, successful, middle-aged man, hospitalized in a psychiatric ward for what appeared to be a rather severe depression, is a good illustration of this point. With a colossal stubbornness, the client would not speak to anyone at all. As the treatment team mobilized its resources, an urgent meeting was scheduled with the man's wife, who had brought him to the hospital for voluntary admission. Team members expressed their perplexity regarding what precipitated the man's depression. The wife responded that she thought that she understood the precipitating cause: They had one child, a beautiful daughter, who had recently announced her intentions to marry the love of her life. According to the wife, their future son-in-law was a nice man that their daughter had been dating for several years. When the young couple announced their intentions to the patient[1] and his wife, he became silently furious and told his wife that he was adamantly determined to refuse to pay for the wedding. Team members asked if perhaps as parents they could not afford to pay for the wedding, but the woman indicated that her husband was a very successful entrepreneurial professional man and they had done very well financially. They lived frugally, and because they had but one child, they could easily afford to pay for her wedding.

The attending psychiatrist asked, "Well, then, what's the problem? Why is your husband so depressed and refusing to pay for the wedding?"

The wife replied, "He hates the man our daughter intends to marry!"

QUESTIONS

1. What is the client's dilemma in this scenario?
2. What are the schema dynamics that you can decipher from the information given?
3. What are the elements of the client's emotional system (emotional state, internal feelings, and affective expressions)?
4. What is the "stuck" behavior that needs to be challenged? How is it creating problems for the client and getting in the way of therapeutic progress?
5. What types of nonlinear listening would you use to understand the client's situation?
6. How would you use the therapeutic paradoxical intervention of proportionality with the client?
7. Discuss the paradoxical nature of the reframe for the client (i.e., two elements that were mutually incompatible, yet both are true) and the counselor (i.e., an absurd or contradictory statement that contains truth).

Variation: Form small groups to discuss, or share as a class the answers to the questions above.

In Clinical Case Example 17.2, a *nonlinear*-thinking therapist needs to appreciate how *out of proportion* the client's behavior is relative to the problem. *Listening for congruence* (the symptoms don't add up) and *presence* (the stubborn silence communicates anger and frustration) provides valuable clues to a possible way of intervening. Specifically, the client believed that he was powerful and that his wishes should be respected. Instead, his daughter's defiance demonstrated that he was *powerless* in this situation. From his history, it is clear that he has been entrepreneurial and very successful, thus achieving what it was that *he wanted*. By extension, in the present circumstances, he was *not getting his way*. This was intolerable to him, and it resulted in him being caught in a dilemma. The client's behavior was an expression of his ambivalence about his daughter (he loved her and wanted to be a part of her life, but he hated her choice of a husband, which would make it impossible to be a part of her life). Fully armed with this information, the therapist decided to employ a proportionality paradoxical intervention. When the patient sat down, it was clear that even though he was depressed, he was interested in what would be transpiring. When informed about what his wife had said, the man appeared somewhat grudgingly interested. The therapist then said,

> Mr. Jones, your wife has informed us about your dislike of your future son-in-law and your refusal to pay for your daughter's wedding. It is my considered opinion that you appear to be either suffering from delusions of poverty or you are an exceedingly cheap guy. Which is it?

Despite the admittedly outrageous comment, the man soon began talking in group therapy about his dilemma: He didn't like the idea of giving away his only daughter, the apple of his eye, to the man she chose to marry. Soon, he was able to be discharged to outpatient status. The intervention can be considered effective because his choice of continuing to be depressed and powerless became "unbalanced." That is, the therapist's input gave the client a perspective that he had not considered before and that he didn't like: He wanted credit for being successful, and he did not want to be considered "cheap" when it came to his only daughter! His silent, stubborn, and depressive symptomatic behavior had carried him further in a direction than he had ever intended because it had side effects that he didn't like. The outrageous, exaggerated, and equally out-of-balance comment by the therapist had disturbed the patient's precarious equilibrium, caught his attention, and started him talking. That was the purpose of the "outrageous" comment: to *disengage* the man from his unproductive struggle and engage him in something much more common sense in nature, such as talking about the loss of his daughter and his feelings about his future son-in-law. This was an ordinary developmental life task—namely, the marriage of a daughter—but the patient's response was disproportionate to the circumstances. Follow-up revealed that his daughter did marry the love of her life and that the patient not only paid for it but also learned to live with the inevitable.

Regarding this case, we hasten to add that, obviously, for a Level I or II practitioner to offer an apparently irreverent comment to a patient (or client) is fraught with *caveats*. First, the comment must be made with the intention of helping the client to disengage from unproductive behavior (e.g., refusing to talk, withdrawing, and being depressed as a silent protest and an expression of stubbornness). Second, the comment must be made within an atmosphere of respect for the client without malice and certainly without sarcasm (Horvath & Bedi, 2002). To do this effectively, the therapist must understand the client's schema dynamics, and show (through an absurd comment) how his behavior is disproportionate in some way. In this example, the client was invited to see how his behavior was out of balance, struggling with something that was inevitable, and a result of the "shock" of losing his daughter (without being able to do anything about it).[2] The antidote was to "challenge" him (i.e., provide an *unexpected disproportionate response*) by giving him an opportunity to relate with others, acknowledge his displeasure, and ultimately get on with life.

The unexpectedness of the therapeutic response in containing such *dis*proportionality can be utilized with couples as well as individual clients, as demonstrated in Clinical Case Example 17.3.

Clinical Case Example 17.3: Queen for a Day

An example of this involved a young couple that entered a couples' group for marriage counseling 6 months following the birth of their first child. The wife was a very attractive young woman and the "baby princess" (i.e., the youngest and the only daughter) of her family of origin who obviously reveled in her beauty, her femininity, and being the center of attention. The husband was the oldest boy of four sons. As such, he had a strong work ethic and was committed to being hyperresponsible for his family, his job, his obligations to friends, and so on. The wife, as the "beautiful baby" of her family of origin, had been accustomed to getting a great deal of attention from her father. Since being married, she expected the same kind of unrealistic amount of attention from her husband. She was accustomed to the considerable economic security that she had experienced at home and expected her husband to provide similar security for her.

After the birth of their child, things began to change as they do for all new parents, and soon a double-bind contingency with associated ambivalences was precipitated between them. The wife spent many hours alone with their baby, lamenting feeling "fat" and lonely with her husband spending longer and longer hours away from home to earn money for their family. When he did so with a succession of second jobs in addition to his full-time employment, his wife felt depressed, neglected, unattractive, and unable to deal with her new role as mother, and she complained about it. The husband then would be prompted to quit his second job, but within a few weeks she would become upset because there didn't seem to be enough money available or anticipated to ease her anxiety about their financial security. With that, the husband, true to his commitment to being a responsible provider, would acquire another second job. Soon afterward, his wife again would soon feel lonely, fat, and depressed all over again. Neither solution seemed able to break the cycle that had been created.

Questions

1. What is the couple's dilemma in this scenario?
2. What are the schema dynamics of each individual that you can decipher from the information given?
3. What are the elements of the couple's emotional system (i.e., emotional state, internal feelings, and affective expressions)?
4. What is the couple's dilemma or double bind?
5. What is the "stuck" behavior that needs to be challenged? How is it creating problems for the clients and getting in the way of therapeutic progress?
6. What types of nonlinear listening would you use to understand the couple's situation?
7. How would you use the therapeutic paradoxical intervention of proportionality with this couple?
8. Discuss the paradoxical nature of the reframe for the clients (i.e., two elements that were mutually incompatible, yet both are true) and the counselor (i.e., an absurd or contradictory statement that contains an element of truth).

Variation: Form small groups to discuss, or as a class share the answers to the above questions.

Clearly, in Clinical Case Example 17.3, the husband as the oldest son was dutiful and worked hard to please his wife, although he was becoming more and more frustrated. Her father had treated her "like a princess." Now, the wife was only expressing what she had become accustomed to as her father's favorite: She wanted what she was used to and expected the same from her husband. As this situation crystallized in the couples' group therapy, the wife was asked if she would be willing to participate in a group assignment, and she said she would. She was then made "queen of the group." As such, she could demand whatever she wanted in the group, and the group members would do their best to provide it for her. As she expressed her commands and wishes, her fellow group members would scurry about, bringing her whatever she asked for. She demanded a pedestal for her feet, and someone brought it to her. Coffee with cream and sugar, and it was provided. The young husband watched in astonishment, and the more he watched, the angrier he became; the wife soon felt uncomfortable and stated, "This isn't realistic; you can't expect to get everything you want in life."

The husband expressed that when others were scurrying around the room, he got in touch with how foolish he felt as he worked continuously trying to please his wife in an exaggerated and unrealistic manner (i.e., his previous *thinking* that was privately "logical" and not "commonsensical"). The wife got in touch with the fact that many of her demands were unreasonable and out of balance (i.e., her consensually *nonlinear thinking* that was privately "logical"). The husband realized that he did not have the power to please his wife (i.e., *consensual* linear thinking) because her being pleased was not based on something reasonable: He was damned if he got another part-time job, and he was damned if he didn't get another part-time job. He also understood that he believed he had not been following common sense regarding doing what he needed to do. The wife became more reasonable and secure in knowing that her husband would not respond unrealistically to her demands. This example of proportionality in a group setting certainly did not "cure" this couple, but it was instrumental in helping them to use their emotional system to reappraise their situation. From this, they were able to develop a new perspective on the exaggerated and out-of-balance nature of their system. From that point, they not only were able to understand their repetitive exaggerated behaviors but also began exploring alternatives to falling into those same "warped" patterns. Another example might be useful.

At a workshop on the development of paradoxical thinking, participants were encouraged to ask questions and bring up examples. One particularly earnest participant asked about a client that he was working with. The seminar presenters asked a few pertinent questions and subsequently made one or two suggestions, to which the young man replied, "I tried that, and it didn't work!" Another suggestion was made by the other of the seminar presenters, to which the seminar participant replied, "I tried that, too, and it didn't work!" Again, the first seminar presenter suggested still another paradoxical intervention, to which the young man replied, "That didn't work, either!" The second seminar presenter then suggested, "Perhaps you're not working hard enough at trying to get this client to change!" The entire room of participants erupted in laughter, as did the young man. Obviously, the seminar participant had not realized how unrealistically hard (i.e., disproportionately) he was pushing to change his client. It was only through *exaggerating his efforts* that he was able to obtain a new perspective.

In all of the above examples, proportionality was used to make a point by overstating the client's exaggerated and disproportionate (i.e., *nonlinear*) position. Simultaneously, critical flaws in the client's thinking and behaving were exposed (or overexposed). As a result, the client disengaged from a nonproductive disproportionate solution to a set of life circumstances. That disengagement fostered a more "commonsense" approach to that set of circumstances and a more natural inclination toward balance. Sometimes, it is by challenging a client's exaggerated perception and position that one is able to help her leave the "funhouse" of wavy mirrors and strange solutions (i.e., *nonlinear* thinking)!

Prescription

Ironically, though it is being presented and discussed toward the end of this work, prescription (or "prescribing the symptom") is perhaps one of the most common perceptions of what paradoxical interventions are all about. Although prescription, which refers to a therapist encouraging the continuation of disruptive behaviors but under the direction of and *in cooperation* with the therapist, is a powerful tool, it isn't (as we hope the reader is aware by now) *all* of paradoxical thinking. In fact, prescription should be used only when appropriate (i.e., *not* for someone who is actively suicidal because of the risk to the individual). Again, from our perspective, to arbitrarily use prescription in order to "*be* paradoxical" is gimmicky, risky, thoughtless, and not at all reflective of a true understanding of the nature of this challenger. Any intervention that takes on the characteristics of being simply a "technique" that seeks to manipulate a client devoid of context and client understanding will only rupture the therapeutic relationship and is not recommended. We provide an example of paradoxically prescribing the symptom in Clinical Case Example 17.4.

Clinical Case Example 17.4: Divorced, Lonely, and Frightened

A prime example of what we mean by the "prescription of a symptom" or complaint comes from the case of a middle-aged, mildly depressed man who had recently received his final divorce papers just before coming for help. He had been married for a long time, and after his divorce he was lonely, depressed, and leading a rather spectacularly uneventful and reclusive life. He worked long regular hours and occasionally visited his grown children, but otherwise he mostly stayed at home watching TV or repairing his car. He reported that some friends in a neighboring state had invited him for a holiday weekend and offered to arrange a date for him with a widow they knew. The patient told the therapist about this invitation and expressed a desire to accept his friends' invitation because it would probably be good for him, while simultaneously expressing grave doubts about getting "fixed up" with a blind date that "wouldn't work out" and thereby having a bad time.

Sensing the patient's ambivalence, the therapist commented on the man's simultaneous desire to go and his doubts about how disappointed he might be. It was then suggested to the man that he might as well "go with" his desire to accept the invitation to visit with his friends but keep his distance from the blind date and expect *not* to have a very good time. This would allow him to *have his cake and eat it too* by allowing him to accept the invitation *and* honor his legitimate desire not to get hurt. The paradoxical intervention prescribes that the client should do both things: Go on the trip *and* expect to have a bad time, rather than the either-or dichotomy of "I really want to share my life with someone" but "Because I don't want to get hurt again, I lack the courage that it takes to go out" that the client was wrestling with. Basically, then, his complaint had been prescribed for him as the antidote.

At the following session, the patient reported that he went for the weekend visit and "I didn't have a bad time." He also announced that he expected to make a return visit the following month. As a result, he encountered some good-natured humor about "getting lucky" with the blind date from fellow group members, to which he responded with smiles.

One thing that Clinical Case Example 17.4 demonstrates is that sometimes both poles of a dilemma are legitimate and must be honored. At the same time, clients sometimes create more of a problem than really exists. Prescription (like proportionality) has the effect of hyperextending a client's logic to the point that she is challenged and feels uncomfortable with the implications of her activities. This is similar to the motivational-interviewing method of "agreeing with a twist" (described in Chapter 13), whereby a therapist agrees with the client's perspective *too much* and the client begins to back away from her original position. We present Clinical Case Example 17.5 to demonstrate this further.

Clinical Case Example 17.5: Scraps of Paper to Compensate for a Poor Memory

Another example of prescription involves a man in his late 50s who had been to see a succession of physicians for consultation about his chronic postnasal drip and his feeling of a deteriorating memory. Medical findings consistently revealed no evidence for either condition. The patient persisted in his position, and eventually he was referred for psychiatric, neurological, and psychological evaluations. Each of these, in turn, agreed with the conclusions of all previous findings.

The patient was attending therapy sessions and continued to disbelieve the results of the evaluations. He also continued to complain about how bad his memory was and that he was reduced to writing notes, memos, phone numbers, appointments, grocery lists, and so on on scraps of paper, the inside covers of matchbooks, the edges of newspapers, toilet tissue, and the like that he wouldn't throw away. He quite dramatically pulled out a 2-inch-thick wallet that was chaotically stuffed with such scraps of paper to illustrate his point. He further pulled a small disorganized bundle of such scraps of paper from his pockets. All previous reassurances had failed to encourage the patient about the state of his memory, and he had chosen to disbelieve all evaluations of his not having organic memory impairment.

QUESTIONS

1. What is the client's dilemma in this scenario?
2. What are the schema dynamics that you can decipher from the information given?

3. What are the elements of the client's emotional system (emotional state, internal feelings, and affective expressions)?
4. What is the "stuck" behavior that needs to be challenged? How is it creating problems for the client and getting in the way of therapeutic progress?
5. What types of nonlinear listening would you use to understand the client's situation?
6. How would you use the therapeutic paradoxical intervention of prescription with the client?
7. Discuss the paradoxical nature of the reframe for the client (i.e., two elements that were mutually incompatible, yet both are true) and the counselor (i.e., an absurd or contradictory statement that contains an element of truth).

Variation: Get into groups to discuss, or share as a class the answers to the questions above.

In Clinical Case Example 17.5, after listening to the client's story about how his memory was failing and how he was reduced to the level of attempting to keep track of so many facts on scraps of paper, the therapist decided to take a *nonlinear* approach. He suggested that perhaps he could get a spiral notebook to keep better track of all the facts that he had difficulty retaining in his memory. He was further instructed that it should be a large notebook, so that if he forgot where he placed it, it would be conspicuous. The patient stopped and looked at the therapist in total disbelief. He said, "I'm not that bad, am I?" The therapist suggested that perhaps the patient knew best after all and that the testing and evaluation procedures he had gone through had failed to detect the organic dysfunction of which the patient complained. The patient began arguing with the therapist that he would have to be "really bad" to carry around a notebook and that he just couldn't see himself as "that bad." In essence, the therapist had prescribed the client to do exactly what he already had been doing but in a preferably *large notebook*.

The paradoxical intervention *supportively challenged* the client to confront the two central questions of his dilemma that he had been avoiding, namely, "I'm not that bad, am I?" versus "I'm not good enough." The client's schematized view contained the beliefs that "I must be good and on top of things, because when I am not, bad things happen"; and "I cannot rely on others; they get things wrong a lot." The client wanted to be just bad enough to not be perfect all the time, and thus be excused from the unrealistically high expectations that he set for himself when he failed (which was inevitable), but not be so sick that he may have a real condition that would need treatment. By purposely and artfully, albeit unconsciously, making himself imperfect with his nonlinear thinking, he provided himself with a ready-made excuse for when he *really* was imperfect. As a result, therapists and doctors were "set up" to be the counterpoint to which he could argue and keep his dysfunctional behavior. When his therapist refused to do this, the client had to disengage from his symptomatic position, absorb both sides of the argument and see the absurd and distasteful nature of it, and make a decision to change or keep going (albeit without the same "payoff"). In the next 3 weeks, the therapist noticed that the patient no longer complained about his memory, and indeed he indicated that for some unexplained reason, he seemed less troubled by his memory. The patient soon terminated therapy under amicable conditions, stating that he felt better.

Prescription takes the client's solution and gives the client the "authorization" to keep on doing what she is doing. When these ambivalent clients find themselves still in the same place, however, they interpret the therapist's intervention paradoxically because it contains two true statements that should not be able to coexist, but do. Generally, these statements are (a) You don't like what you are doing (or what happens to you when you do it), and you want to stop; and (b) given the chance, you will keep doing it. By explicitly feeding into the second statement (giving permission), the implication of the first statement becomes more pronounced for the client. This is the "absurd" underlying nature of the paradoxical intervention. We present Clinical Case Example 17.6 to illustrate this.

Clinical Case Example 17.6: Mechanically Inclined and No Desire to Study

A bright young man with a natural inclination and talent for mechanical and electrical work was attending a technical school to complement and develop his aptitudes and doing very well at it. He had been in therapy with his wife regarding marital strife arising in part from his attendance at school, the prospect of graduating, his getting a job, and so forth. His wife was getting impatient, and he was becoming more and more anxious that if and when he got a job after finishing school, he would have to "produce." He was frightened because his period of prolonged dependency on his wife would be coming to an end—she had been supporting the two of them. On the other hand, it was frightening his wife to think that after 5 years of married life and supporting her husband, if he wouldn't graduate from technical school, he wouldn't be able to get a job and she would still have to support the two of them. She wanted to start a family.

One day, he came to therapy complaining very desperately that he wanted to be able to study in order to sustain the nearly "straight-A" average that he had worked very hard for. But, he indicated that he recently had found that he could not force himself to do so. He felt that it was essential to "know everything" there was to know; he didn't want to be "just another one of those guys who got 'straight A's' but didn't know anything."

His sibling position in his family of origin had been that of a middle child. As such, he was overshadowed in schoolwork by his older brother and younger sister, who were "straight-A" students, whereas he was a spectacularly average student. Now he wanted to do as well as he could and know all that he could, but at the same time he was academically surpassing his customary scholastic mediocrity. When he went home after school, he felt his books "calling" him, and he felt himself not listening.

QUESTIONS

1. What is the couple's dilemma in this scenario?
2. What are the schema dynamics that you can decipher from the information given?
3. What are the elements of the couple's emotional system (emotional state, internal feelings, and affective expressions)?
4. What is the "stuck" behavior that needs to be challenged? How is it creating problems for the clients and getting in the way of therapeutic progress?
5. What types of nonlinear listening would you use to understand the couple's situation?
6. How would you use the therapeutic paradoxical intervention of prescription with the clients?
7. Discuss the paradoxical nature of the reframe for the clients (i.e., two elements that were mutually incompatible, yet both are true) and the counselor (i.e., an absurd or contradictory statement that contains an element of truth).

Variation: Form small groups to discuss, or share as a class the answers to the questions above.

In Clinical Case Example 17.6, the man was asked if he was up to an assignment, and he readily agreed without hearing what it was. The therapist suggested that the young man set out his books, work manuals, study guides, and everything else that he usually needed to do a good evening's studying. He was then told to open his books and notes to the appropriate pages and then to promptly leave his book, manuals, desk, and so on for the period of time that he ordinarily would spend studying. Furthermore, he was told that he seemed to be *pushing himself much too hard* (i.e., an oblique reference to the exaggerated expectations he had of himself after graduation) and *he was allowing his books and studies to control and dominate him rather than him being in charge of the studying!* When he protested that he must study because otherwise he would fail, he was politely told that he was defeating himself because he couldn't bring himself to study whenever he tried (i.e., he heard his books "calling," but he wasn't listening). The nonlinear logic suggested to him was thus "Because you are defeating yourself and not studying anyway, why not take the time off?" Just as with externalizing the symptom or problem (in Chapter 12), the therapist had thus changed the *context for the client's not studying*. As a result, when the context was changed, the meaning of the behavior changed. His wife was requested to conveniently leave him alone while he could have time to relax and demonstrate that *he* was in charge of his books and was proving it! She was coached that perhaps she could busy herself by enjoying a book or relaxing while he was busy proving to his books that he was in charge.

At the next session, the wife reported that she came home from work to find her husband studying diligently. He was then told that should this development reoccur, he was to make certain that he "defy" his books by opening them but not studying in order to demonstrate his domination of his studies and that he was only to study when he wanted to rather than when he felt compelled to. If he should ever feel compelled to study, it was suggested that such feelings were signs that his studies and books were running his life, and he needed to demonstrate that he was in charge of studying and not his books. Thus, from the client's perspective, the therapist's intervention had two true statements: (a) The client did not want to fail, and (b) the client did not want to be forced to study (especially by his wife). The absurdity of these two "truths" made the element of choice clear for the client, and he was able to construct a better solution. Several months later, this young man graduated—and became gainfully employed!

In each of the cases above, the clients (who were arguably capable enough) were unable to accomplish their goals because they were "hamstrung" by maladaptive schemas or highly skewed appraisal processes, accompanied by self-limiting behaviors. The challengers, and prescription in particular, afforded them an opportunity to disengage from a maladaptive and self-defeating pattern that frustrated their verbalized desires. Only after relinquishing the maladaptive pattern can an individual grasp a new solution.

Prediction

In the paradoxical intervention of prediction, a therapist uses knowledge of a client's schema dynamics, emotional system, and current situation, and any feelings of ambivalence on the client's part, to "prophesy" that certain "events" (e.g., behaviors, ideas, thoughts, and communication patterns) will "probably" occur under certain conditions the client is about to encounter. This is not as "gimmicky" as it may seem. It actually requires that a therapist have a solid theoretical grounding from which to base a prediction. It also requires an equally sound case conceptualization that allows the therapist to identify the client's particular dilemma and characteristic behavior responses to certain circumstances, and then make a prediction. The therapist prophesized the client's behavior: what he would "probably do anyway" in a given situation. The client then can engage in his maladaptive and repetitive behavior, but because it was "predicted," it will not provide the patient with any "payoff" (i.e., secondary gain; see Chapter 12) if the predicted outcome occurs. If the predicted outcome does not occur, then although the therapist was proven "wrong," the client has been helped to move in a more prosocial and constructive direction. Clinical Case Example 17.7 is suggested as an example.

Clinical Case Example 17.7: Expecting to Have a Bad Time

An articulate and intelligent man who was coming to therapy to address his marked obsessive-compulsive character traits informed his therapist that he a problem that he had to work on. Namely, he had to attend a relative's wedding but did not want to do so because he knew he wouldn't have a good time. From previous sessions, knowledge of the patient's character traits, the patient's typical reactions to feeling forced to do something, and his characteristic way of dealing with social situations, the therapist reasonably intuited what the man's experience would be. Thus, he "predicted" that the man would probably have a "bad time" attending the wedding. The "bad time" would begin with difficulty in deciding on what to wear. Once he finally made that decision, he would probably have to leave the house in a hurry because the decision required so much time and he would be in danger of being late for the occasion—an obviously "unpardonable" thing to do. Because he "can't stand" being late, he would probably have to drive fast and "run the risk" of being stopped for exceeding the speed limit. Whether or not he was stopped, he would arrive at the wedding a little harried but exactly on time. Once there, he would probably find the music too loud, the liquor too weak, the food too cold, and the service too slow. Most likely, he would end up being critical for having such a bad experience and leave the wedding, not having enjoyed himself that evening.

Regarding Clinical Case Example 17.7, how is it that the therapist can make these "predictions," and what is the therapeutic benefit of doing so? First, the therapist reasonably knew something about the general behavioral traits of someone with the client's diagnosis. For example, regarding the difficulty of deciding what to wear, it is well-known that many people with obsessive-compulsive character traits have a good deal of difficulty with ordinary everyday personal decisions. Being perfectionistic in nature, they want to be "right" and make the "right" decisions and choices—they hate being wrong, which is a sign of being less than perfect. Having so many options available in deciding what to wear to a wedding would prove to be a formidable task. Again, being perfectionistic, it would prove difficult for a man who wants to avoid being late to drive within the speed limit. And so goes the reasoning. Such people are often critical and cynical as well. They consistently see the glass as half-empty.

Second, the therapist drew on the strength of the solid therapeutic alliance and an understanding of the client's schema dynamics. Because he has been told ("predicted") that this is how he typically operated within such social situations, this man can either prove the therapist correct and have a miserable time or "prove" the therapist wrong by being cognizant of the predictions made about him and have a pleasant time. In effect, this would represent a new experience (on the emotional level) for the client and would be a change in his inflexible response to social situations. Should he have a good time for whatever reason, he will have "risen to the challenge" and relinquished an old maladaptive pattern of behaving. Even if the client remains powerless, gets caught up in the current of his own behavior, and proves the therapist correct, he will see that his behavior is predictable. In addition, he will know that his therapist understands him and his problem, thus enhancing the relationship (another example of the "tuning forks" from Chapter 7). Consider Clinical Case Example 17.8.

Clinical Case Example 17.8: Predicting Husband and Wife Behavior

In another example of predicting, a husband being seen in treatment with his wife asked for an individual session with the full consent of his wife. During the session, the husband spoke of his genuine concern for his wife. He was fearful of her intense bouts of seemingly unexplained anger, "black depression," and uncontrolled spending. Of course, he was the "superior"-role spouse who was being brought to his knees by his wife's "inferior" behavior, namely, spending large amounts of money frivolously (see Mozdzierz & Friedman, 1978). He asked what the prospects were for his wife learning new behaviors and, indeed, expressed some optimism regarding genuine improvements that she had made in recent months. The therapist seized this opportunity to caution the husband that within a short time, he might expect a relapse in his wife's behavior.

In true keeping with the predictive efficacy of systems theory, about 3 weeks later in her individual therapy session, the wife related an incident in which she acted like a "screaming bitch." She further related being "stunned" in amazement at her husband's response. He was reassuring, and did not try to control her behavior or talk her out of it. She stated that this response helped her to "see my way out of my black mood." She then made some compensating gestures toward her aging mother-in-law that were greatly appreciated by her husband but that she previously had a great deal of difficulty doing.

Several months passed, and the woman continued to make progress in various areas of her life. The therapist predicted that because she continued to make progress, the wife should expect to see some regressive behaviors in her husband. This is not uncommon in "overadequate/underadequate" spouses (see Mozdzierz & Friedman, 1978). She, too, expressed amazement at this. Several weeks later in therapy, she reported that her husband's drinking had increased, and he was now coming home on a regular basis quite drunk. He was also responding quite irrationally to some of her behaviors that were decided improvements in an objective sense from what they had been.

In each instance in Clinical Case Example 17.8, the predictions of the therapist were seen to greatly facilitate the treatment process. They demonstrate to the client that the therapist has truly heard and understood them and knows what is transpiring between them. Prediction is one of the most sophisticated skills to master because it requires a deep understanding of the client in light of all the previous domains (his or her schema dynamics, goals, strengths, emotional system, etc.). By predicting a characteristic pattern based on an understanding of the dynamics of that logic and past performance, the client is "challenged" by being exposed to many therapeutic possibilities. Such prognostications tend to dampen the impact of their occurrence—should they occur, that is! In the abstract, predictions can be used to predict an attitude, thought, feeling, behavior, and way of seeing things. In the concrete, it can be used to predict relapses, an unhappy weekend pass from the hospital, a quarrel with a family member between sessions, being late for appointments, and a disappointing vacation, but it can also be used to predict such things as loss of a job, and being suspicious of new surroundings and/or people. It is paradoxical because it is absurd to predict (essentially, "bet on") what a client will do. That is, it can be used to predict any behavior with which a client is symptomatically involved. It becomes the closest thing to magic in therapy, and makes master therapists *look* like master sorcerers!

Positive Provocation

At first glance, it would appear that the term *positive provocation* is an oxymoron. How can something be "positive" and "provocative" at the same time? It is exactly in the *combination* of being *supportive* and simultaneously *confrontational* that the paradoxical nature of both the intervention *and* therapeutic benefit lies (two truths that cannot simultaneously coexist, but do, etc.). As might be suspected, however, intervening in such a manner requires considerable thought about the essential elements of any intervention. Where is the client stuck? What are the complaints? In light of the client's complaint, what behavioral objectives would the therapist like to accomplish to stimulate therapeutic movement? Nonlinear listening is crucial in such instances, as the client will report that there are things that she is not doing that she wants to do or things that she should be doing but can't seem to get done. On the other hand, she may report she is doing things that she doesn't want to do. In addition, such clients often report that they can't control certain symptoms such as anxiety, depression, nervousness, insomnia, and so forth. These are the signature characteristics of ambivalence and the schema dynamics underlying that ambivalence. It sends the message "I want this to stop. I want to get off!" but the client doesn't see how.

Therapists frequently find themselves at a loss as to what to do about such complaints and impasses. At the same time, those complaints and impasses keep coming up. But, if the therapist begins to question how the complaint can be broached and not broached at the same time, certain "answers" typically arise as to how to stimulate therapeutic *movement* (i.e., not "cures") by being provocatively supportive. We hope to elaborate an understanding of this by the following examples. We begin with Clinical Case Example 17.9.

Clinical Case Example 17.9: A Cowboy's Word

A burly man in his early 60s dressed in blue jeans and traditional cowboy clothing (western-style plaid shirt, cowboy boots, cowboy hat, and an elaborate and genuine-looking cowboy belt buckle) was referred to an intake and evaluation group.[3] He was accompanied to the group by his wife because of a drinking problem. The wife expressed a belief that she and professional mental health workers who had previously spoken to her husband were helpless in instructing, threatening, and encouraging this caricature of a displaced cowboy to quit drinking. According to the man's wife, nothing "worked." As the wife explained her predicament, the cowboy appeared bored and restive in the group, and resolutely refused to be hospitalized for his drinking problem, all the while maintaining that he could stop drinking on his own. In the exchange among the group therapists, one politely but strongly insisted that the patient required immediate hospitalization for detoxification because he gave no indication of being able to stop drinking long enough to be medically safe. The other group therapist felt that the gentleman could be treated as an outpatient.

As the two therapists engaged in a professional "quarrel" between themselves in full view of the group and the patient, the disagreement appeared to have all the qualities of being a minor melodrama played out with a "good cop" and a "bad cop." A third staff member, knowing some details of the man's background, interjected that this was obviously a man from the "west" who has worked with horses and as such could be considered a man of his word. This therapist went on to elaborate in rather detailed imagery that it takes a "real man," a specific kind of man, to be able to relate to such dumb, stubborn, and powerful animals as horses in a consistent and reliable way. He added that if this man said he would stop drinking and be an outpatient, then he, as a member of the staff, would be willing to go along with him because he was obviously "a man of his word."

The first therapist continued to argue for hospitalization and detoxification, insisting to the opposing therapist that the cowboy would not be able to abstain from drinking, adding that the mythology about western cowboys was all well and good, but it did not pertain to the present situation. We note that it is extraordinarily magnetic to be talked about by others in a group. As such, it is difficult to be present without paying very rapt attention to what others are saying about you. Thus, the cowboy, whose original demeanor was rife with boredom originally, began to pay more attention. In fact, it appeared that he was attending to the exchanges of dialogue about him with a new and unmistakable alertness and interest. His head swiveled back and forth between the therapists as each stated his case. Then, in very few words and in a rather challenging and defiant way, he stated that he could indeed refrain from drinking until the next meeting. The first therapist remained fixed in his supportive yet provocatively (i.e., challengingly) pessimistic prognosis, adding that he couldn't go along with that because there were significant health risks at stake.

The client returned the following week smiling. He turned to his "tormentor," the first therapist who had given him such a "hard time," and proudly proclaimed a full week's sobriety, which was attested to by his wife. In reply, the therapist turned to him and said, "Well, anyone can stay sober for a week, but it takes, in effect, a 'real man' to stand the *real* test of being sober and abstinent for more than a few weeks." The mini-drama began again, renewed with a different focus: Would the cowboy be able to stay sober 2 weeks in a row?

The cowboy's "allies" portrayed the picture of hopeful optimism that he would not give in to his weakness for drinking. And, even more importantly, the cowboy was a man of his word because he had remained sober for a week just like he said he would! His "antagonist" would not budge; there were significant health risks at stake. Another appointment was scheduled for the following week.

Once again, the patient proved his provocateur "wrong" and came to the group having been sober now for 2 successive weeks, which was again confirmed by his wife. In the months of sobriety that followed, the patient and his wife were transferred to a married couples' group, where they successfully worked on issues that had gone unattended for quite some time in their marriage (and in their lives in general) due to the patient's drinking. The man's need to demonstrate his oppositional orientation, masculinity, and honor as well as his need to thwart his "provocateur" were greater than his need to drink, thereby promoting therapeutic movement in the direction of sobriety.

QUESTIONS

1. What is the client's dilemma in this scenario?
2. What are the schema dynamics that you can decipher from the information given?
3. What are the elements of the client's emotional system (emotional state, internal feelings, and affective expressions)?
4. What is the "stuck" behavior that needs to be challenged? How is it creating problems for the client and getting in the way of therapeutic progress?
5. What types of nonlinear listening would you use to understand the client's situation?
6. How would you use the therapeutic paradoxical intervention of positive provocation with the client?
7. Discuss the paradoxical nature of the reframe for the client (i.e., two elements that are mutually incompatible, yet both are true) and the counselor (i.e., an absurd or contradictory statement that contains an element of truth).

Variation: Form small groups to discuss, or share as a class the answers to the questions above.

We certainly do not recommend Clinical Case Example 17.9 as a standard "treatment" for alcoholism, but it does illustrate how positive but respectful provocation with genuine concern can be used for a patient's benefit. Although the provocative therapist was being challenging, the paradoxical element of truth is that it can be and frequently is medically dangerous for someone who has been drinking for a prolonged period to precipitously stop. Such an abrupt cessation of alcohol consumption can lead to seizures. Such truthful concern for the patient was presented to the patient as being *in his best interests*. Another illustration is presented in Clinical Case Example 17.10.

Clinical Case Example 17.10: Take Your Choice

Another example of positive provocation with a twist of humor can be seen in the case of a moderately well-to-do couple being seen for marital strife. The wife complained that earlier in their marriage, the husband had showered her with small but thoughtful gifts, but that during the last 3 years he had become a "miser." In turn, it appeared that the husband had been harboring a grudge against his wife over her insistence on buying a new home purchased 3 years earlier. His position on thrift appeared to have been born from feeling forced to purchase their new home; other than that, he apparently would have had little difficulty in once again satisfying his wife's doubts about his love for her with small, thoughtful gifts throughout the year. Although the woman was aware of the economic strain prompted by the financial burden of paying for their new home, she still had doubts about his new thriftiness (i.e., being a "miser") and was threatening divorce.

QUESTIONS

1. What is the couple's dilemma in this scenario?
2. What are the schema dynamics that you can decipher from the information given?
3. What are the elements of the couple's emotional system (emotional state, internal feelings, and affective expressions)?
4. What is the "stuck" behavior that needs to be challenged? How is it creating problems for the clients and getting in the way of therapeutic progress?
5. What types of nonlinear listening would you use to understand the couple's situation?
6. How would you use the therapeutic paradoxical intervention of positive provocation with the clients?
7. Discuss the paradoxical nature of the reframe for the clients (i.e., two elements that were mutually incompatible, yet both are true) and the counselor (i.e., an absurd or contradictory statement that contains an element of truth).

Variation: Form small groups to discuss, or share as a class the answers to the questions above.

In Clinical Case Example 17.10, in earlier sessions the husband had expressed sarcastic remarks about the conspicuous consumption of lawyers, who lived well on income derived from the misery of the "common people." To him, it was "obvious" that they "didn't work very hard for their money." Co-therapists suggested that it looked like the husband would have to take his wife out to dinner and a movie occasionally or consider the following: The husband's lawyer would use his hefty retainer to pay for a new Cadillac and a Las Vegas vacation. To add further to the provocation, the therapists added visual imagery of an attractive Las Vegas showgirl at the lawyer's side and the lawyer wearing an expensive suit, also purchased with the client's money! Both the husband and wife were in touch with the tragedy, comedy, absurdity, and potential reality of the intervention. In subsequent weeks, the husband was able to reassure his wife that his grudge was yielding to love for her by meeting some of her requests at face value, requests that were indeed reasonable.

Some readers might be thinking, "Well, that's fine for the kind of people you see in your practice, but I work for an agency where the clients aren't at a very high level of functioning. Such things wouldn't work with my clients!" It is with this reader in mind that we describe our final example of positive provocation in Clinical Case Example 17.11.

Clinical Case Example 17.11: An Unbelievable Stink!

A fast-aging woman recovering from substance abuse and a recent brief depression that required hospitalization in a state facility was complaining of her teenage son. As a single parent, she lived in poverty on public assistance with her other adult children, who demonstrated psychiatric symptoms of one sort or another. She had attained less than a complete grammar school education, had never held a job for more than a few months, but was able to maintain a marginal existence in the community with the help of her day treatment program and appropriate medications. Although she suffered from a variety of psychiatric symptoms, she was determined to be a "good mother." She sought specialized counseling from the day treatment staff for a problem that she was having with her 16-year-old son.

Mostly due to a lack of supervision, no father in his life, and little motivation, the boy had become a school truant who passively defied his mother's halfhearted pleas for him to go to school. He met such pleading from his mother with complaints that he was too "weak and tired" to go to school.

In keeping with the clinical needs of the situation, day treatment staff made an appointment for the boy to meet with the consulting psychologist to determine his level of intellectual ability and his potential for employment. As part of the evaluation, the boy and his mother were interviewed together. As is so often the case, the line between assessment and intervention became blurred during the evaluation, and some of the dynamics of their family system soon became obvious. The mother complained of the boy's lack of activity and openly "shamed" her son in front of the therapist by revealing his "laziness." As an example of his laziness, she cited the fact that he refused to get up in the middle of the night and go to the bathroom. Instead, she explained, he would urinate in a 5-gallon "pee bucket" that she complained smelled "terrible," especially in the summer because they did not have air conditioning. The boy simply shrugged his shoulders and said that he didn't feel good. He expressed being interested in getting a job, to which his mother countered that he should go to school. In some of the dialogue that followed, he insisted that he didn't want to go to school.

QUESTIONS

1. Who is the client? Support your choice.
2. What is the client's dilemma in this scenario?
3. What are the schema dynamics that you can decipher from the information given?
4. What are the elements of the client's emotional system (emotional state, internal feelings, and affective expressions)?
5. What is the "stuck" behavior that needs to be challenged? How is it creating problems for the client and getting in the way of therapeutic progress?
6. What types of nonlinear listening would you use to understand the client's situation?
7. How would you use the therapeutic paradoxical intervention of positive provocation with the client?
8. Discuss the paradoxical nature of the reframe for the client (i.e., two elements that are mutually incompatible, yet both are true) and the counselor (i.e., an absurd or contradictory statement that contains an element of truth).

Variation: Form small groups to discuss, or share as a class the answers to the questions above.

In Clinical Case 17.11, the therapist entered the impasse by insisting, just as the boy had maintained, that he was obviously "too weak and sickly" to be able to sustain any type of work. In point of fact, the boy was a model of youthful physical fitness. As support of his position, the psychologist noted, "Aren't you too weak to be able to go all the way to the bathroom in the middle of the night? Aren't you too weak to be able to empty the pee bucket?" The boy appeared to absorb the provocation and promptly replied, "I am strong enough to get a job." To this, the therapist replied, "That appears to be nonsense. You should be at home taking care of yourself! You are definitely too weak to go to school or get a job!" The mother insisted that he go to school. The boy insisted that there was a job available at the local Burger King that he wanted to investigate.

And so it went. The young man's oppositional spunk appeared to be well mobilized. He and his mother left the interview with him muttering that he was going to "show" the therapist that he wasn't "too weak to get a job." As they parted on friendly terms, the mother insisted that they return the following week in conjunction with her day treatment appointment. When the day of her appointment arrived, the mother told the therapist that her son didn't get the job at the Burger King, but rather he was now employed at the local McDonald's. Apparently, the boy's need to take an oppositional stance against what his mother wanted for him was satisfied in a more constructive way. Although staying at home and being truant from school certainly appeared to accomplish this end, his job at McDonald's also appeared to accomplish that, albeit provoked by the therapist's insistence that he was "too weak" to go to work. The boy was positively provoked and mobilized into therapeutic movement when other motivations offered by his mother apparently carried no weight.

The curious reader may wonder, "What ever happened to the pee bucket?" Well, we might have responded that some things are simply better off left as is! Nevertheless, there was follow-up over a longer period of time with this woman. In fact, over the next 4 years, she would occasionally encounter the psychologist, who would ask about her son. When the young man turned 17 years of age, he enlisted in the military with his mother's permission. While serving his country, he completed his high school education with a GED and subsequently fulfilled his military service with distinction. *We can only assume that he had no further need for the bucket!*

SUMMARY ON CHALLENGERS

Clinical Exercise 17.1: Summary Exercise on Challengers

1. A young client in his mid-20s who had been diagnosed with schizophrenia came to his therapy situation looking very tired and "washed out." When asked if he had been sleeping well, the patient responded that he had spent a "terrible night." He explained that he was having difficulty falling asleep because he had been paying increasing attention to the sound of airplanes on their way to landing at O'Hare Airport. The more preoccupied he became with these thoughts, the more anxious he became. He then became convinced that one of the planes could very well crash into the trailer in which he was living. Soon, he found himself even more unable to sleep, pacing intermittently through the nights and bizarrely turning his house-trailer lights on and off in an effort to "warn" approaching aircraft of his presence. It was usually morning before he was able to fall asleep.

2. Recall from Chapter 13 the Clinical Case Example (13.4) of a man who came to therapy to address his anxiety, especially around his supervisor at an accounting firm. At the end of the initial session, you and the client agreed to some specific homework tasks that included speaking up at a staff meeting, setting up an appointment to speak with the supervisor, and inquiring if a female coworker who he has been interested in is dating anyone. When he returns, he says that he didn't accomplish any of the tasks because "the meeting went too long, the secretary was never at her desk to make the appointment, and I just didn't get around to it" (i.e., asking about the coworker). He states that he intends to do it at the beginning of the next week.

1. What is the client's dilemma in the scenario above?
2. What schema dynamics can you decipher from the information given?
3. What are the elements of the client's emotional system (emotional state, internal feelings, and affective expressions)?
4. What is the "stuck" behavior that needs to be challenged? How is it creating problems for the client and getting in the way of therapeutic progress?
5. What types of nonlinear listening would you use to understand the client's situation?
6. How would you use the therapeutic paradoxical intervention of positive provocation with the client?
7. How is this reflective of *nonlinear* thinking?
8. Discuss the paradoxical nature of the provocation for the client (i.e., two elements that were mutually incompatible, yet both are true) and the counselor (i.e., an absurd or contradictory statement that contains an element of truth).

Variation: Form small groups to discuss, or share as a class the answers to the questions above.

CONCLUSION

The use of challengers is often considered when clients have taken entrenched, extreme, and oppositional positions toward life and others as a means of problem solving. As with all of the challengers, but especially with positive provocation, the client is in effect saying to the therapist, "No one (and you neither, Ms. Therapist) can make me give this up (i.e., a symptomatic behavior) or make me do this!" The "irritation" of provocation in particular and the challengers in general provide patients with strong medicine in the service of a need to help them to "disengage" themselves from maladaptive entrenched behavioral, attitudinal, or emotional "solutions" when they are unable to do so. As stated at the beginning of Chapter 16, in the real world of seemingly impossible clients, therapists create conditions that stimulate change to occur with their clients, they burn out and clients terminate therapy prematurely, or therapy wanders somewhat aimlessly. This is why we believe that nonlinear paradoxical thinking is the essence of thinking like a master therapist and why it is a convergence factor for all successful therapies across schools of psychotherapy.

Contextually Cultural 17.1: Paying Attention to Diversity

Current professional literature (e.g., American Psychological Association, 2003; Ecklund & Johnson, 2008; LaRoche & Maxie, 2003; Mishne, 2002; Swartz et al., 2007) continues to emphasize the necessity to develop cultural competence amongst clinicians in the practice of psychotherapy as well as assessment. Within disadvantaged minority populations and especially women of such groups, dropout rates and "no-shows" for treatment are a continuing problem. Among the many injustices suffered by women in this culture, it is apparent that being female, poor, and from an ethnic or racial minority group creates a kind of "perfect storm" of conditions for therapy failure. Based on core principles of ethnological interviewing and motivational interviewing (see Miller & Rollnick, 2002), Swartz et al. (2007) and Swartz et al. described the "engagement interview," which is designed to increase chances of disadvantaged minorities to stay in treatment.

Ethnological interviewing respects the fact that individual cultures have culture-specific stressors, values, explanations for illnesses and problems, definitions of treatment success and goals, and nontraditional culturally specific coping resources (e.g., spirituality and family) that must be respected to connect with and engage disadvantaged minority clients. Grote et al. (2007) and Swartz et al. (2007) emphasized the need for clinicians to suspend their own personal and usually dominant cultural biases. In addition, they noted how all such clients have a number of barriers to effectively utilizing treatment:

- "practical" (e.g., time, cost, transportation, and child care or other family responsibilities);
- "psychological" (e.g., misinformation, stigmatization, doubts about therapy's effectiveness, hopelessness, or the debilitating effects of the symptoms themselves, whether social anxiety, fear of unfamiliar places, or low energy); and
- "cultural" (perhaps unintended but felt nonempathic responses from a clinician of a dominant culture in the past).

Hence, Swartz et al. (2007) recommended specific suggestions for coping with such clients and their highly sensitive circumstances:

- Concrete problem solving for solutions for practical barriers
- Providing information regarding psychological barriers that will hopefully destigmatize a client's problem and provide hope
- Asking about past treatment experiences
- Making inquiries about a client's feelings concerning a clinician possibly being of a different culture
- Encouraging clients to voice feelings that something a therapist is telling him or her might be culturally dystonic

Although all clients potentially have these barriers to treatment, they are exacerbated by poverty and a client's cultural minority status. In addition to ethnological interviewing, the engagement interview strategy (Swartz et al., 2007) also incorporates the core principles of motivational interviewing (MI)—especially for the resolution of ambivalence regarding treatment engagement.

Swartz et al. (2007) cited the MI principles of empathic reflective listening and MI interventions like "double-sided reflection," "amplified reflection," "reframing," and "emphasizing personal control and choice" (as opposed to argumentation, persuasion, advice, mandates, and warnings of dire consequences) and "client as expert" of his or her own situation—which result from nonlinear thinking. Although the engagement interview (Swartz et al.) is a one-session pretreatment intervention that can be combined with the intake, its philosophy would enhance the practice of cultural competence throughout the course of treatment.

As Swartz et al. (2007) suggested, paradoxical interventions are no less valid with disadvantaged minorities than with any other group, especially reframing and tranquilizing, provided that basic principles of respect, empathy, linear and nonlinear listening, and connecting with and engaging a client are observed.

Information in a Box 17.1: Novelty, Paradox, and the Brain

As described throughout the sections of this book, a "neurotic" problem, once established, continues unabated and resistant despite "common sense," self-exhortations, and even therapeutic efforts. In other words, people continue to do more of the same—they continue to do what they've always done, and they get what they've always gotten regarding their ambivalences and maladaptive problem-solving efforts to life circumstances. Why? There are abundant data from brain research that provide at least a partial explanation.

Although it may be a lack of courage that psychologically prompts us to avoid dealing with problem situations *when they occur* (e.g., fear of failure or social disapproval), thus maintaining lingering ambivalences, it may be brain-derived routineness and impoverishment that keep neurotic and ineffectual problem solving going. Problem-laden clients oftentimes continue to see things and correspondingly feel things in the same way. Relevant to this dilemma, Thornton (2006) reported that the brain supports a neural center that seeks novelty as well as a center that seeks to maintain things as they are. Obviously, such an understanding is neurologically supportive of the dialectic ambivalence dynamic that we have described when clients espouse a desire to change and at the same time resist it.

According to Thornton (2006), neuroscience research has demonstrated that the brains of rats from an "impoverished" environment (described as single rats in solitary confinement with no rat companionship or "toys" for stimulation) were underdeveloped and withered. On the other hand, the brains of rats from an "enriched" environment (defined as a large cage filled with "toys" and a dozen rat companions) had much thicker brain cortexes, neurons of increased size, and many more neuronal connections—all of which are known to contribute to problem-solving ability. Indeed, the brains of rats from a "standard" environment (three rats in a large empty cage) resembled "normal" rat brains.

Learning something new occurs in the *right* side of the brain, whereas keeping it going is on the left side of the brain; left-sided thinking about problems keeps the "same old, same old" going as people continue to do what they've "always done" and are surprised to discover that they are getting what they've always gotten. It is the newness, novelty, and uniqueness of something that prompt the *right side of the brain* to "wake up" and be alerted that something new is present. That is why creative (nonlinear) responses to "neurotic" behaviors, difficult circumstances, and so on are likely to be more effective than "intellectual" (i.e., left side of the brain) clinical interpretations of those same behaviors. That is the role that therapy in general and disengagement and paradox interventions in particular play in the change process. Paradoxical responses in therapy prompt the engagement of the right side of the brain, which becomes active because such responses are novel, different, new, and unique. In turn, those responses *interrupt* the repetitious, same-old-rut, left-brain responses. It is the *therapeutic relationship and the trust it radiates* that allow a client *to be* receptive to new things coming into awareness. Decreased anxiety associated with trust, safety, and a feeling of belonging allow for a greater sense of receptiveness—change takes place at low levels of anxiety (resistance).

Mikulciner and Shaver (2005) have dramatically demonstrated that they could activate circuits dormant in the brain to even stimulate a sense of emotional security. Their research efforts resulted in people becoming more willing to donate blood, do volunteer work, and even feel more compassionately toward ethnic groups different from their own. Although Mikulciner and Shaver's research efforts resulted in greater emotionally secure and empathic behavior through the use of overt or subliminal cues to activate brain circuits, the therapeutic relationship and benign paradoxical interventions can stimulate similar behavioral inclinations.

Likewise, being in a psychological rut can be seen as a short-term perspective on problem solving when it is clear that maintaining the status quo is detrimental for clients' long-term well-being. Research by McClure, Laibson, Loewenstein, and Cohen (2004) has demonstrated that the brain maintains short-term processing and decision making in the limbic system, which demands immediate gratification, whereas longer term decisions are steadfastly a function of the prefrontal cortex. Disengaging clients from their fixed emotion-based functioning to be able to think differently about their circumstances and use emotional input as a source of information is a very desirable outcome for therapeutic endeavors. Nonlinear paradoxical interventions are a particularly effective means of accomplishing such outcomes.

ENDNOTES

1. The designation *patient* is appropriate in the present instance because the man was in a hospital.
2. See Rossi 1973 for a description/definition of "Psychological Shocks" and "Creative Moments" in psychotherapy.
3. Details of this case were previously published in Mozdzierz, Elbaum, and Houda (1974).

Ethically and Effectively Helping the Client to Disengage

How and Why Nonlinear Thinking and Paradoxical Interventions Contribute to the Making of a Master Therapist

18

CONTENTS

INTRODUCTION

The purpose of this textbook has been to present innovative and cutting-edge instruction and learning on counseling and psychotherapy. Our work is unique in its frame of reference derived from a wealth of useful clinical understandings provided by contemporary research—the what, who, how, when, and why of therapy. Our perspective begins with a simple premise: As in any professional endeavor, there are levels of experience and expertise that novices and journeymen must traverse. Novices are best served by learning and understanding fundamentals so that they can use them as building blocks upon which to grow. The domains of Level I (i.e., connecting with and engaging a client; assessing client readiness for change, needs, assets, and goals; and building a relationship and a therapeutic alliance) are the fundamental, transtheoretical, and universal building blocks of understanding and skill for becoming a counselor or therapist: *Why and how* to be attentive, listen, and respond; *why and how* to engage and connect; *why and how* to empathize with human suffering; and *why and how* to assess and intervene all lead to the development of clinical understanding and astuteness as well as professional judgment.

Also as in any endeavor, there are experts—master practitioners—whose work transcends that of the more average therapist and from whom others learn. We have surveyed the vast literature of therapy and determined that there are transtheoretical and universal domains to which master practitioners devote their attention and in which they excel. Across all the domains, we have concluded that master practitioners demonstrate *unconventional* thinking processes that we have described as *nonlinear*. We have also attempted to nuance our understanding of the change process by paying attention to research from neuroscience and to culture and diversity issues of both the client *and* the clinician.

The domains in this text represent what master practitioners pay attention to and what they *do*. Ultimately, we have come to understand the work of therapy or counseling as being a way to guide clients so that they can achieve changes that result in resolving their problem and leading more functional and satisfying lives. Typically, this requires *two reciprocal developments*: (a) Clients must "stop"—or *disengage* from—old, maladaptive patterns of thought and behavior; and (b) they must *engage* in different, more positive behaviors. This is just as true for clients with more chronic lifelong problems as it is for clients who are acutely distressed.

Disengagement is at the heart of the change process, as well as its ultimate goal. It is the means of helping a client to *discontinue struggling* (e.g., remove himself from preoccupation, and stop fighting) with his problem and the inappropriate solutions that he has been using to cope (generally manifested as a form of ambivalence; see Chapter 12). This chapter will demonstrate how the domains and other major concepts of this text serve the purpose of disengagement or change.

There are many avenues that therapists use to help clients disengage, with some more effective than others. Many therapists focus their therapeutic efforts on clients disengaging from their problematic behavior by attempting to *arrest* or stop a particular behavior. This is the defining characteristic of a *linear* approach. In terms of its effectiveness, if a client is ready to change (i.e., in a preparing for action or action stage of change; see Chapter 5), this approach *can* be effective. But, as mentioned above, disengagement is only one part of a *reciprocal process*. If clients are to "stop" or disengage from doing something, they also need to embrace something—engage in thinking or behaving patterns that are more adaptive and constructive than those they are "stopping." This is not done in a structured formulaic manner but rather by

- empathically relating to a client in a strong therapeutic relationship;

- reflecting *to the client* the therapist's understanding of the client's feelings and circumstances, and receiving client concurrence of the therapist's understanding;
- gauging what the client needs (e.g., via her behavior); and
- helping the client more deliberately to work through (i.e., resolve) ambivalences stemming from maladaptive schemas by understanding and altering them, even subtly; or finding a paradoxical means of mobilizing change processes, as described in Chapters 14, 15, 16, and 17.

In this chapter, we elaborate on how nonlinear thinking (and paradoxical interventions, in particular) facilitates the disengagement (or change) process. First, we will examine the ethical dimensions of nonlinear thinking. Next, we present how fostering change at a structural level is the most effective type of change. Then, we will discuss how *nonlinear* approaches and the use of paradoxical interventions are central to helping clients disengage by altering their contextual understanding (i.e., their unconscious appraisal processes), helping them to find new positive and redemptive meaning, defocusing, externalizing, and embracing the novelty of new experience. Last, we will discuss how the process of mastery represents a therapist's disengagement from the struggle of *doing* effective therapy to *being* an effective therapist. We begin with a discussion of the ethical dimensions of nonlinear thinking and paradoxical interventions.

PARADOXICAL INTERVENTIONS AND ETHICAL PRACTICE

Introduction

Do no harm is the primary rule of ethics in medicine, and it can be considered an equally appropriate caution for all of health care, including psychological and counseling services across the spectrum of approaches. All disciplines, regardless of theoretical orientation, share a fundamental starting point regarding the practice of therapy with their clients: All practitioners of psychotherapy and counseling have a *fiduciary* relationship to their clients. There is a *relationship of trust* that exists between the practitioner and the client. The practitioner *must* put the interests of the client above his or her own interests. Any exploitation—such as engaging in a sexual relationship; dual relationships (i.e., boundary issues) involving finances, goods, or services; or interactions that serve to entertain the clinician or punish or invalidate the client—can *never* be justified as being for the benefit of the client (see Chapter 7).

Regarding paradoxical interventions, then, the question is, *are* such nonlinear methods for the benefit of the practitioner or the client? Practitioners can, on the surface, appear blunt, direct, uncaring, or sarcastic if and when they engage in paradoxical interventions. They could also appear as though the interventions were designed more to show how brilliant the therapist is rather than help the client. If that is the case, then paradoxical interventions can be seen to violate the trust in the relationship between practitioner and client, and thus be considered unethical at worst, and completely insensitive at best. We believe such instances, although rare, unfortunately are not unheard of. In fact, we maintain that a paradoxical intervention *cannot* be effective if other elements of therapeutic effectiveness (particularly a good therapeutic alliance) are not present and vibrantly maintained. A good, ethically sensitive relationship cannot be exploitative, by definition, as it is derived out of a sense of maturity, care, and responsibility to the client.

The second reason to consider the ethical dimensions of nonlinear paradoxical interventions is that they can appear "manipulative" of a client and thus also in violation of the trust that a troubled person places in a care provider. The word *manipulative* as commonly used today implies a shrewdly and deviously managed way of controlling a relationship, that is, a nonstraightforward (i.e., unethical) way of dealing with others. But actually, one of the primary meanings of the word *manipulate* is *to move something in a skillful manner*, like a microsurgeon delicately and expertly manipulating a scalpel or laser to operate on a patient. That is precisely the intention of the psychotherapy and counseling processes: to help move and encourage someone in a healthier or more positive direction than they have been pursuing and in the process facilitate the relief of many varieties of human suffering. Indeed, that is the purpose of using non-linear paradoxical interventions: to facilitate disengagement from symptomatic behavior; to aid a client in developing a new understanding or new relationships (vis-à-vis new neural brain connections) to such behavior; and to facilitate more positive (e.g., more "prosocial," cooperative, and other-oriented) movement away from self-absorption, away from an *external* locus of control (where the client feels victimized and powerless), and more toward an *internal* locus of control (where the client has choice and agency). These are the reasons why clients come for help; they are out of synch with how the majority of the world functions and copes. Thus, paradoxical interventions are not aimed at "manipulating" *a person* in order to "control" that person's behavior or to "force" a person to change. They are aimed at influencing the mechanisms underlying how human beings operate (i.e., modes of thinking). They are aimed at influencing, expanding thinking, counterbalancing opposing ambivalences, and shifting inertia, not controlling or manipulating (negatively) a person. They are aimed at helping the client to adopt a new perspective or point of view in order to disengage from "crazy" (e.g., ineffectual, or non-commonsense-based) ways of thinking and acting that are not functional, and when linear (commonsense) approaches are not effective. In fact, given the power and effectiveness of these interventions, we believe that it is unethical *not* to use them in the appropriate context!

Paradoxical Interventions and the Ethical Principles

There are five principles of ethics to which all psychotherapists and counselors aspire to adhere: autonomy, fidelity, nonmaleficence, justice, and beneficence. Although initially elements of biomedical ethics, they have been adopted and expanded by all of the therapeutic helping professions (see Peluso, 2006). We present our discussion of how paradoxical interventions are not in conflict with, but actually *fulfill*, these important principles.

Autonomy: Respect for the Individual

Respect for autonomy is one of the ethical principles that is relevant to the use of paradox in psychotherapy and counseling. The principle of respect for autonomy demands that patients who consult us are esteemed as autonomous rational agents whose consent to treatment must be elicited. Furthermore, their consent to treatment must be freely voluntary, without controlling coercion, as well as based on a full understanding of what the treatment entails.

Competent patients, that is, those individuals who are capable of making informed, intentional medical decisions in their best interests on their own behalf, have a right to refuse *any* treatment, even life-sustaining medical treatments. That right to refuse even a life-sustaining treatment is a guarantee stemming from the "right to privacy" that is protected by the U.S. Constitution. Are the "right to privacy" and "respect for autonomy" violated when a therapist or counselor employs nonlinear thinking and paradoxical interventions? We believe that clients' autonomy is not being contravened because bringing *new information* (i.e., a new meaning, or a different way of seeing things, stimulating the brain to make new associative connections) into awareness enhances autonomy rather than restricts it. It offers additional choices! The client can accept or reject it, but, once presented, she *must* consider it, if even for a brief moment. And *in* that brief moment, she is open to a new possibility, and even a new reality. The key is not forcing the client to accept the information (that would be a violation of the principle of autonomy). Indeed, such additional choices simultaneously enhance the disengagement process.

Fidelity: Respect for the Truth

A fundamental component in the definition of paradox is that it contains an element of truth. Thus, being presented with a paradoxical intervention is being presented with a truth to which the person must respond. Remember that in order for a paradoxical intervention to be effective, the therapist must also believe in the truth of what he is proposing to a client (i.e., "Perhaps your feeling so depressed is a way for you to engage in a strategic withdrawal because you feel so unprepared for …"). If the therapist does not believe that there is another meaning for the depressive symptoms and is trying to utilize a paradoxical intervention, it will likely fail in its effectiveness as a result of violating the ethical principle of fidelity!

Nonmaleficence: "Do Not Harm"

The biomedical ethical principle of nonmaleficence requires that we do not intentionally, needlessly harm or injure someone we are treating by either an act of commission or an act of omission. An act of omission—not doing something we should have done as part of our professional obligation to a patient, which causes harm—can be the basis for a malpractice suit based on negligence. Causing someone harm intentionally (other than the harm, for example, inflicted by the basic nature of a surgical procedure, i.e., cutting someone open) would be a violation of the principle of nonmaleficence. Does the use of paradoxical interventions intentionally inflict harm on someone, and hence become a violation of the principle of nonmaleficence? We think not.

The processes of psychotherapy and counseling are fraught with painful memories, losses, failures, sad realizations, fears, anxieties, and the like. Such experiences are endemic to the process of therapy. In addition, most clients have the expectation that therapy or counseling is going to "hurt" in some way, but in the long run it is going to "help"; it's the paradoxical nature of the therapeutic beast! In this regard, we have consistently presented paradoxical interventions as having an intrinsic *prosocial* nature. By facilitating the patient's disengagement from symptomatic preoccupation, healthier processes become possible, and that is the purpose for which clients come for help. Again, any paradoxical intervention that is used as a "technique" or gimmick, or that is done without a strong working alliance, is negligent and runs the risk of violating the nonmaleficence principle.

Justice: Doing What Is Right

It has been suggested that paradoxical interventions like "prescribing the symptom," though elegant, might not be ethical because they encourage the client to actively engage in a harmful behavior. In such cases, it is crucial for the counselor to employ caution when utilizing these interventions. Proper assessment, and thorough understanding of the client's schema dynamics, his emotional system and the nature of his ambivalence must also be taken into consideration. Therapists are responsible for maintaining the therapeutic alliance and attending to therapeutic ruptures (see Chapter 7). As a result, they must act in ways that are fair as well as beneficial to the client. Coale (1998) commented about the issues of therapeutic relationships and what transpires in them, which is relevant to our consideration of justice:

> Establishing therapeutic relationships based on mutual interconnectedness involves working within therapeutic paradoxes—establishing equality in a hierarchical relationship, mutuality in a nonmutual relationship, empowerment in a power-imbalanced relationship, and respect for *client* meaning and belief within a frame of therapy theories and beliefs. … Setting boundaries in the context of such therapeutic paradoxes is a joint process between therapist and client. It is not just something that the therapist can do *to* the client but rather something that, in interaction, the client and the therapist do together. The client must agree to respect the boundaries that he and the therapist set together. He must be open to what the therapist has to give. (p. 97)

But, what about the argument that prescribing the symptom is an evasion of the patient's informed consent? We maintain that it is logically impossible to fully inform a client about *all* the processes of therapy. For instance, if we know that a strong positive relationship is one of the truly effective ingredients of the therapy and counseling process, should we "inform" the patient, "I'm now in the process of support-ing, endorsing, and affirming you so that you will feel like we have a strong bond in a healing context in which to work"? Not really. Instead, the therapist must work to maintain an atmosphere of respect for the client, and act in ways that do not exploit any position of power and authority.

Beneficence: Doing What Is Good

The ethical principle of beneficence is to do good. If anything is clear about the work of counseling and psychotherapy, it is that their foundations are at best based on theories, highly poetic metaphors, and beliefs about the way things work, which are supported by ongoing research. It is an aspirational field, and the best practitioners are ones who believe that the best is possible for each person. To do this often (paradoxically) means taking clients where they may not want to go in order to explore their ambivalence or dilemma. Beier's (1966) therapeutic concept of "beneficial uncertainty," in addition to being a part of nonlinear thinking, is relevant to the concept of paradoxical interventions and beneficence:

> The patient, within the experience of a permissive atmosphere, has to be challenged to experience and tolerate uncertainty; but as such a challenge does occur within the framework of a permissive atmosphere, the sense of uncertainty experienced by the patient is likely to beneficial—one which leads to an explora-tion rather than defense. (p. 57)

Beier noted, however, that simply creating uncertainty is not sufficient in clinical activity. He emphasized that it must be "beneficial," meaning *it is created nonjudgmentally with a sense of concern for the cli-ent's well-being*:

> The presence of concern and the freedom from having judgment imposed permit the patient to interpret the responses to his messages as beneficial rather than threatening. The messages of the therapist are, in a true sense, persuasion; they are designed to give the patient both hope and courage to dare into the unknown. (p. 9)

This is similar to a physician showing concern regarding the serious nature of a medical condition and the need for surgery. All clients bring problems, concerns, anxieties, and uncertainty to therapy. In practice, "beneficial" uncertainty frequently involves a clinician saying the unthinkable, which brings the client's worst fears into the open (Beier, 1966). Beier cautioned, however, that these interventions can be dangerous and must be delivered free of countertransference, free from being entertained by the client, and free of an urge to retaliate, harm, punish, or reject the client.

Given the universality of nonlinear thinking by master practitioners and its demonstrated efficacy (see Information Boxes 18.1 and 18.2 later in this chapter), the use of paradoxical interventions—when utilized properly—is in keeping with the highest ethical standards of the profession. We now turn to a discussion of *how* it is that nonlinear thinking and paradoxical interventions work to effect such dramatic and lasting change.

NONLINEAR THINKING AND SECOND-ORDER CHANGE: EFFECTIVE MEANS AND EFFECTIVE ENDS

Fraser and Solovey (2007) analyzed the relevant literature on therapy and its effectiveness. They asserted that there is a common element in all effective psychotherapies—a "golden thread that unifies all effec-tive treatments." What is this "golden thread"? Fraser and Solovey identified this as none other than paradoxical or *second-order change*—borrowing from the work of Paul Watzlawick and his colleagues from the Mental Research Institute. In other words, they concluded that both the practices of master practitioners and "empirically supported therapies" (i.e., evidence-based psychological practices, or EBPPs) are effective because their interventions occur at a "second-order" level of change. This is an important theoretical and practical consideration because it contributes to bringing us closer to reconciling the debate between those advocating for EBPPs and those advocating for a strong therapeutic relationship (along with other factors) as the basis for effective treatment.

We have mentioned them only briefly in this text, but first- and second-order change deserve more explanation here. Based on Whitehead and Russell's (1910–1913) "Theory of Logical Types," Watzlawick, Weakland, and Fisch (1974) described first-order change as representing direct attempts to coerce change *on the same level of reality* (i.e., within the same "logical type," or class). Examples would be arguing with a spouse and demanding that he changes his behavior, insisting that a loved one stop drinking, managing anxiety by avoiding potentially threatening situations, wrestling with depressed feelings in an effort to make them go away, and the like. Such change efforts are "first order" because they represent the same level of reality and the same logical type or same class of behaviors. Practically speaking, first-order changes are those things that clients have been *trying* as "solutions" to their problems. They represent *linear thinking*, and are mostly ineffective in bringing about the sort of long-term changes that people desire.

Second-order change takes place on a different level (e.g, schema accommodation, or reappraisal). Watzlawick et al. (1974) summarized the essence of what is involved in second-order change thusly:

a. Second-order change is applied to what in the first-order change perspective appears to be a solution, because in the second order change perspective this "solution" reveals itself as the keystone of the problem whose solution is attempted.
b. While first-order change always appears to be based on common sense (for instance, the "more of the same" recipe), second-order change usually appears weird, unexpected, and uncommonsensical; there is a puzzling, paradoxical element in the process of change. Applying second-order change techniques to the "solution" means that the situation is dealt with in the here and now. These techniques deal with effects and not with their presumed causes, the crucial question is what? and not why?
c. The use of second-order change techniques lifts the situation out of the paradox-engendering trap created by the self-reflexiveness of the attempted solution and places it in a different frame (as is literally done in the solution of the nine-dot problem).[1] (pp. 82–83)

In other words, in order to be effective at the second-order level of change, therapists must (a) understand that *linear* solutions are often just the first step in truly understanding a client's problem; (b) intervene in a fundamentally paradoxical manner (one that is seemingly absurd to the client); (c) realize that it is necessary for an individual to face and resolve the ambivalence that she is feeling *now*, rather than focus on past hurts, distant causes, or future fears; and (d) help create accommodations to an individual's schema by *altering her perspective* (i.e., changing the context and prompting a reappraisal of circumstances) regarding the problem. Recall the example in the Introduction of the man who kept obsessing over his ex-wife. Applying the principles of second-order change outlined above, his "problem" (obsessing over his ex-wife) was actually a *solution* to his real problem (he was not ready to move on with his life). Next, the therapist's suggestion that he might not be ready to stop thinking about his wife is absurd because, if he did, he might have to think about more immediate and pressing things (e.g., his heart disease). Third, the focus is on his readiness to engage in his new life now, rather than on his ex-wife. Last, when the client hears the therapist's paradoxical intervention, he must reappraise his "problem" and put it into the larger context of his ambivalence (between the reality of changed life circumstances and his schematized view of the world). Based on this, we conclude that *how* therapists facilitate genuine client second-order change is through *nonlinear* approaches.

Such interventions can and do facilitate a rapid change in a client's perspective about (and reaction to) his particular problematic circumstances by changing the context in which they occur. It is worth reiterating that Fraser and Solovey's (2007) discussion of second-order change is remarkably similar to our discussion of paradoxical intervention and nonlinear thinking. In addition, moving a client toward

TABLE 18.1   Table of characteristics of first- and second-order change

IF THE CLIENT'S TENDENCY IN ATTEMPTING TO SOLVE A DILEMMA (I.E., "FIRST-ORDER" CHANGE) IS TO ...	THEN THE PARADOXICAL INTERVENTION (I.E., "SECOND-ORDER" CHANGE) IS TO ...
... go away from the problem.	... go toward the problem.
... overpursue the problem.	... stop and reverse the pursuit.
... not attend to the problem.	... acknowledge the problem and take necessary problem-solving action.
... overly complex.	... simplify the problem and narrow problem-solving efforts.
... overintervene in everyday ups and downs.	... tolerate and accept the natural unpleasantries of everyday living.
... read too little difficulties or simplify to the point of trivializing things.	... honor the complexities of the problem or situation.

Source: Adapted from Fraser and Solovey (2007).

flexibility and complexity is a hallmark of nonlinear thinking that impacts the schema level. The reality is that second-order change is dependent on the therapist being able to think nonlinearly.[2]

Table 18.1 summarizes more examples of the nonlinear nature of Fraser and Solovey's (2007) conclusions. For example, if a client's tendency is to move away from the problem (a first-order change that temporarily stops the problem), then the paradoxical intervention (and second-order change) suggests that a client be directed to move toward the problem. This is *nonlinear* in that it does not "logically" flow, and it is paradoxical because it is seemingly absurd to the client, though it contains an element of truth.

Fraser and Solovey (2007) suggested that that EBPPs (as discussed in Chapter 1) are also quite paradoxical. That is, whether a clinician is providing paradoxical interpretations, prescribing symptomatic behavior, or suggesting that a client engage in a structured systematic EBPP exposure to something that she has reported as the problem for which she is seeking help, a client's context is paradoxically altered in substantially positive ways. Fraser and Solovey's suggestion is an important one in several regards. As mentioned above, philosophically, theoretically, and clinically, it bridges a significant disagreement between proponents of EBPPs and those who argue their limitations, and attenuates the sharpness of the disagreement, as Kazdin (2008) has suggested is necessary. This understanding accommodates clinicians who prefer the structured, formal approach in their work that is suggested by EBPPs for some problems, and those who prefer more of a relationship-based approach.

As a review of some of the ingredients required to think like a master practitioner, we present Information Box 18.1, as a summary of nonlinear thinking reflected in all of the domains.

Information Box 18.1: A Review of Nonlinear Thinking Throughout the Domains as Facilitators of Disengagement and Second-Order Change

Nonlinear thinking facilitates disengagement or second-order change because it is the following.

INTRODUCTION AND CHAPTER 1

- Disproportional to its inputs (like an equation), or, to put it in more generic terms, "The sum is greater than the whole of its parts."
- Unlike linear thinking, does not resemble a straightforward, characteristic, one-dimensional, logical approach to human problem solving.

- The sort of thinking that turns things upside down and inside out, and departs from the linear way of thinking about things in the physical universe.

CHAPTERS 2 AND 3

- *Listening* not only with one's ears but also with one's eyes, feelings, and intuitions and a generally open mind.
- *Hearing* things that aren't spoken or are conspicuous by their absence.
- *Understanding* the significance of discrepancies between *what* is said and *how* it is said.
- Developing the capacity for understanding the *potential implied meaning of messages.*
- Seeing *beyond* what is present to what is absent, as a result of therapist curiosity being piqued by what a client *isn't* saying or discussing.

CHAPTERS 4 AND 5

- Understanding that not all clients seek treatment with the same motivation or readiness for change.
- Recognizing and endorsing the value of client strengths and resources, and utilizing creative methods for including them in the therapeutic dialogue.
- Integrating both a client's problem or symptoms *and* the client's strengths or resources into a multidimensional picture of the client and a plan for his or her treatment.

CHAPTERS 6 AND 7

- Facilitating rapport and empathy to develop a therapeutic alliance.
- Mirroring the client's exceptionally idiosyncratic nonlinear thinking as a vehicle for achieving therapeutic progress (like a tuning fork).
- Utilizing countertransference to inform therapy.

CHAPTERS 8 AND 9

- Understanding that the client's worldview or schema is what makes it possible to "make sense" of a client's behavior.
- Directing client attention toward the central organizing patterns of their problem (the schema, or view of self, others, and life and the world).
- Understanding that schemas—even very problematic ones—have evolved over a lifetime of reinforcing experiences (aided by self-fulfilling prophecies) as a way of helping an individual navigate through life—sometimes successfully and sometimes problematically.

CHAPTERS 10 AND 11

- Extrapolating and inferring from a client's affective expressions, internal feelings, and underlying emotional states.
- Utilizing client emotions as an opportunity to *empathize* with a client and help a client to understand that emotions *inform*.
- Demonstrating to a client in a *nonlinear* way that he has *the capacity* to exercise control regarding his emotional life.

CHAPTERS **12** AND **13**

- Understanding that most clients, to some degree, want to have their cake and eat it too, feel pulled in two directions at the same time, and ultimately find themselves stuck between a rock and a hard place.
- Understanding that ambivalence is a method of protection from threat (e.g., the therapist, or change itself), and thus a *part* of what can be expected in the change process and not an aberration of the treatment process.
- Understanding that paradoxically, clients express a desire to change and simultaneously resist change and seek to maintain the status quo because change has the capacity to disrupt the client's schematized view of self, others, or life or the world, which prompts feelings of failure, shame, embarrassment, loss of prestige, and so forth.

CHAPTER **14**

- Nonlinear thinking is reflected in paradoxically *neutralizing* client behaviors, attitudes, emotions, and the like that can disrupt treatment.

CHAPTER **15**

- Nonlinear thinking is also reflected in paradoxically *tranquilizing* clients who are upset.

CHAPTER **16**

- Nonlinear thinking is reflected in paradoxically *energizing* clients who are discouraged.

CHAPTER **17**

- Nonlinear thinking is also reflected in paradoxically *challenging* clients who have become immobilized.

Using *nonlinear* thinking, practitioners can make interventions that both *arrest* the problematic behavior (first-order change) as well as *resolve* the underlying dilemmas and ambivalence (second-order change). As we have demonstrated, this disengagement process can be fostered or accelerated by the use of paradoxical interventions. Paradoxical interventions stimulate a change in the way a client relates to his problem and/or symptomatic behavior, similar to Fraser and Solovey's (2007) description of interventions that act on the second-order level: They are often surprising, humorous, unexpected, novel, and confusing, and serve to stimulate separating the person from the problem, creating distance from it, or depersonalizing the problem. For example, assume that a client is mandated to come for treatment by someone (e.g., a judge, attorney, spouse, or employer) and that he is not happy about it (i.e., he is a precontemplator). The client verbalizes hostile expressions about therapy and the therapist. Such negative behavior represents a client's struggling with his symptom or problem (i.e., he simply doesn't want to be in therapy—period). Attempting to start a "fight" with the therapist can be an "excuse" to leave treatment that the client does not want, is threatened by, or may be unprepared for. When a therapist neutralizes the client's hostile expressions, it gives the client a new perspective from which he can see that there is no reinforcement derived from being negative. In this case, disengagement increases the probability that the client will at least stay in treatment.

If a client's demeanor requires tranquilizing, disengagement occurs by attributing new meaning to the symptomatic behavior that is calming, protective, and reassuring. This is a change on the second-order level of change, as the symptomatic behavior is experienced as positive rather than negative. If a client needs to be energized, disengagement frees up the energy that was once bound up in (and by) the problematic behavior. Again, the client's relationship to the problem (i.e., second-order level) is changed when the therapist not only gives "permission" for the client to continue to have the symptoms but also goes so far as to suggest that it could be "dangerous" to relinquish them if a client is not prepared to do so. Finally, if a client's behavior needs to be challenged, disengagement comes from a therapist exaggerating a client's position to a greater extent than he may (unconsciously) have intended. In turn, this alters the client's view of his behavior and prompts him to reevaluate whether this is what he really wants, which is a second-order level of change.

SECOND-ORDER CHANGE, DISENGAGEMENT, NONLINEAR THINKING, AND MODERN APPROACHES

A major focus of this text—a point of view described in Chapter 1—is that there is a convergence of understanding from different theoretical perspectives as to what it is that brings about change. Mozdzierz, Lisiecki, and Macchitelli (1989) analyzed many of the historical and modern approaches to psychotherapy and, utilizing a mandala (i.e., a symbol of unity), graphically represented how paradoxical interventions were ubiquitous and universal across different theoretical perspectives. Many of the differences that exist between classical "schools" are those attributable to poetic metaphors describing various constructs. All of these original-thinking practitioners have discovered and written about how, through the application of a nonlinear-thinking process, troubled people can and do become *disengaged* from their symptomatic behavior and thus able to embrace other, more constructive life pursuits. As a result of the use of *nonlinear*-thinking processes to formulate paradoxical interventions, these practitioners helped clients become engaged with more natural and healthier psychological coping mechanisms (hence, second-order change). Information Box 18.2 highlights a few of the more contemporary orientations (e.g., meditation, the relaxation response, mindfulness-based cognitive therapy [MBCT], acceptance and commitment therapy [ACT], and the "Four R's," which are *relabel*, *reattribute*, *refocus*, and *revalue*) and how each also works on the second-order level through the processes of *disengagement*.

Information Box 18.2: Modern Theoretical Perspectives on Disengagement

- We believe that the mechanisms involved in the effectiveness of "mindfulness" and meditation are the same as those involved in the use of dialectics and paradox, namely, disengaging from the struggle with the problem (e.g., unwanted thoughts, behaviors, images, feelings, urges and cravings, and sensations) and developing a new relationship with the problem. There are several contemporary "schools" of psychotherapy based on the Buddhist practice of "mindfulness." The fact that Buddhism can be dated to 500 BC, and its concepts are used today in therapy speaks to both its timelessness and universality. Although mindfulness is a Buddhist practice of meditation, many clinicians feel that it is also a useful psychological tool that does not require the adoption of any religious beliefs while it is simultaneously compatible with a person's existing beliefs.
- Outside of the eastern Transcendental Meditation movement, the "relaxation response" (Benson, 1975, 1985, 2000) was perhaps the initial introduction of a mindfulness type of practice to assist people in changing their struggling relationship to problems. Based on principles of meditation, a person centers himself in a quiet place with a comfortable posture and simply focuses on a mantra (e.g., a word or sound with no meaning,

breathing, or the flame of a candle). Whenever he becomes aware of being distracted from his focus, he simply and gently returns to the focus of his attention rather than experience attraction or disgust to the distraction.

- Mindfulness-based cognitive therapy (e.g., Segal, Williams, & Teasdale, 2002) is a blend of mindfulness and cognitive therapy techniques. It has been successfully utilized (Teasdale et al., 2000) in the treatment of major depressive disorder—mindfulness is applied during the remission phase of major depressive disorder, and cognitive therapy techniques are employed during the acute phase. During the remission phase, clients are taught to develop a "mindful mode of processing" or an accepting, nonjudgmental, "decentered, detached, disengaged" awareness of the automatic and habitual depressing patterns of thinking (e.g., negativity, self-devaluation, and hopelessness) activated by normal passing dysphoric thoughts and feelings that can cyclically escalate into a relapse of depression. By learning to treat mood states more as passing "mental events" rather than accurate facts about reality that need to be acted upon, with no attempts to challenge or change (i.e., struggle with) them, a person can disengage from such mood states before they escalate and lead to relapse. The person can then engage in healthier pursuits and coping.

- Acceptance and commitment therapy (ACT; Hayes, Strosahl, & Wilson, 1999; see also Bach & Hayes, 2002) is another mindfulness-based therapy that encourages clients to "just notice thoughts rather than treating them as true or false" and to accept uncomfortable thoughts, images, feelings, and sensations as "unavoidable private events." Hayes et al. (1999) pointed to the fact that *avoidance and suppression strategies*, or strategies that teach clients to challenge or attempt to change uncomfortable "events" (i.e., to struggle with the problem), only lead to increased intensity of symptoms and self-preoccupation. By *accepting* these uncomfortable events without needing to act upon them, a client is able to "focus on valued goals" instead. The ACT approach changes the relationship that the person has with the problem away from one of struggle. It seeks to help clients "defuse sources of distress."

- Schwartz and Bayette (1997) utilized a mindfulness-based therapy with clients with obsessive-compulsive disorder (OCD). He believed that the approach is effective with any disorder or problem that is ego-dystonic to the client. Schwartz proposed a "Four R's" model (relabel, reattribute, refocus, and revalue) that encourages clients to become aware of disturbing mental events and relabel or reattribute them to a genetic biochemical "brain lock" condition in which the brain becomes "stuck" in a disturbing way of thinking. Rather than struggle with the uncomfortable thoughts or urges, a client tells himself, "Its not me—its OCD," and refocuses on "valued activities." Over time, this leads to smoother, unlocked functioning. In our estimation, this is another poetic (i.e., "brain lock") and apt description of what disengagement is about.

Another indicator of the "universality" and effectiveness of *nonlinear* thinking (and paradoxical interventions in particular) is whether it can stand the test of scientific scrutiny. Recall once again from Chapter 1 the issue of evidence-based practices in psychology. Although we maintain (along with others) that there are problems with the extent to which positive findings in a controlled laboratory setting have been generalized (only to have the treatment effect be less than that promised in "real-world" scenarios), clinically relevant research is vital to determine the efficacy and effectiveness of various elements of psychotherapy. Over the course of several decades, there have been numerous accounts in the literature that have described positive therapeutic outcomes associated with the use of paradoxical interventions (Avni &

Lazar, 1998; Fisher, Anderson, & Jones, 1981; Haley, 1963, 1984; Rule, 2000; Seltzer, 1986; Watzlawick et al., 1974). We detail some of these in Information Box 18.3.

Information Box 18.3: Paradoxical Interventions: Research Findings

The efficacy of paradoxical nonlinear thinking is not constricted to dramatic outlier cases. In a study of the impact of paradoxical strategies with couples in a brief couples therapy setting, Davidson and Horvath (1997) demonstrated that the paradoxical interventions called *reframing* and *restraining* are helpful in managing conflict. In fact, following the three sessions of treatment, 39% of the couples improved (well over the 20% improvement rate predicted by the dose effect), suggesting that paradoxical interventions help clinicians increase their potency with clients. Related to this, Presbury, Echterling, and McKee (2002) offered a review of postmodern, deconstructive views in the service of brief counseling. In their view, paradox is seen as a valuable intervention that assists "complex systems" to reorganize themselves, thus facilitating growth.

Hill (1987) has perhaps captured the essence of such research findings in his meta-analysis of paradoxical interventions and concluded,

> Thus, on the average, clients receiving paradoxical interventions were better off than 84% of the clients in untreated groups, and 72% of those in placebo groups. An analysis of those studies containing both paradoxical and nonparadoxical treatments revealed that paradoxical treatments were consistently and significantly more effective. (p. 266)

Likewise, Hampton and Hulgus (1993) conducted a meta-analysis of studies using paradoxical interventions with clients across a broad spectrum of presenting concerns (e.g., generalized anxiety, agoraphobia, and depression) and found that these strategies were as effective as cognitive or behavioral techniques. In addition, they also found that paradoxical interventions had longer lasting treatment effects than either cognitive or behavioral treatments.

Another interesting finding regarding the effectiveness of paradoxical interventions was *whom* these interventions were most successful with. According to several researchers, individuals who evidenced more resistant behaviors (in both clinical and nonclinical populations) made the most significant gains from paradoxical interventions (Beutler, 1983; Horvath & Goheen, 1990; Shoham-Salomon, Avner, & Neeman, 1989). Recalling the stages of change model presented in Chapter 4, it appears that paradoxical interventions would work best with clients who are in the precontemplation or contemplation stages. It seems that paradoxical interventions may be effective with such individuals because "they capitalize on the patient's tendency to respond in consistently oppositional manners" (Beutler, Moleiro, & Talebi, 2002, p. 132). More importantly, when clients were followed post treatment, paradoxical interventions continue to maintain therapeutic gains even after the therapy was concluded (Horvath & Green).

In developing "motivational interviewing," Miller and Rollnick (2002) pointed out that therapeutic paradox can be seen as an integrated approach in treating the ambivalent client. As discussed in Chapters 12 and 13, Miller and Rollnick have empirically demonstrated that MI is an effective tool for dealing with "resistant" clients. This approach further exemplifies the effectiveness of the kind of *nonlinear* thinking that goes into the formulation of paradoxical interventions, as will be discussed in this chapter. At the same time, just as we similarly suggest, Miller and Rollnick cautioned against the use of paradox as some sort of clever device or therapeutic gimmick that doesn't respect the fundamental collaborative nature essential to this dialectic process in treatment.

Although there are numerous explanations about the theoretical basis for the effectiveness of paradoxical interventions, such discussion is beyond the scope of the present text. For further discussion of how numerous authors have attempted to systematize and explain paradox, see Avni and Lazar (1998); Fisher et al. (1981); Johnson and Alevizos (1975); Mozdzierz et al. (1989); Omer (1982); Raskin and Klein (1976); Rohrbaugh, Tennen, Press, and White (1981); Rohrbaugh et al. (1977); Seltzer (1986); Weeks and L'Abate (1982); and Watzlawick et al. (1974).

The empirical findings noted in Information Box 18.3, taken along with Fraser and Solovey's (2007) work, and the scholarship presented in this text all point to the fact that *nonlinear* thinking, and in particular paradoxical interventions, is the approach used by master practitioners in order to foster disengagement, or the kind of lasting change that works on the second-order level of change. In the sections that follow, we discuss *how* paradoxical interventions foster the disengagement process and create second-order change, namely, by altering a client's context of understanding and accommodating the client's schemas.

Alteration of Context and Accommodation of Schemas

In the *Star Wars* movies, Jedi master Obi-Wan Kenobi initially tells a young Luke Skywalker that his father, Anakin Skywalker, was "betrayed and murdered" by the evil villain Darth Vader. As a result, Luke comes to see Vader as a purely evil character who must be stopped in order to free the galaxy of the menacing Empire. When Luke rushes off to duel Vader and free his friends (before his Jedi training is complete), Darth Vader reveals the truth to Luke (and the film audience) that he *is actually* Anakin Skywalker—that is, he is Luke's father! Later, when Luke confronts Obi-Wan about this fact, Obi-Wan tells him, "Your father was seduced by the dark side of the Force. He ceased to be Anakin Skywalker and became Darth Vader. When that happened, the good man who was your father was destroyed. So what I have told you was true ... from a certain point of view." Luke, incredulous at this explanation (because it was the basis for all that he thought was good and bad in the universe), questions him further, to which Obi-Wan simply explains, "Luke, you are going to find that many of the truths that we cling to depend on a certain point of view." The new explanation "forces" Luke to reappraise his assumptions from a new point of view, at which point Vader no longer is an evil villain, but a pitiable person who is in need of redemption.

One of the most powerful ways that paradoxical interventions accomplish this is by broadening the client's perspective and altering her context (*through the appraisal processes in the emotional (limbic) system*; see Chapter 10). Numerous authors (e.g., Fraser & Solovey, 2007; Mozdzierz et al., 1989; Mozdzierz, Macchitelli, & Lisiecki, 1976; Omer, 1981, 1991, 1994) have emphasized contextual considerations as very important in the development and use of paradoxical interventions. As we have sought to demonstrate in the Contextually Cultural boxes throughout this text, context includes not just the objective facts but also the subjective appraisals and emotions that are primarily driven by the client's schema dynamics (view of self, view of others, and view of life and the world). It is from within a given context that ambivalence is created, problematic behaviors emerge, and solutions are discovered. Paradoxical interventions help clients to broaden their perspectives using contradictory (or absurd) statements (often condensed in metaphors) that contain elements of truth. When clients experience two messages that seemingly cannot coexist, but do, they typically react by saying, "I never thought of it that way before!" This relieves tension, facilitates the resolution of dilemmas (i.e., underlying ambivalence), and makes a more lasting (i.e., "second-order") change. Hence, enlarging the perspective and context from what schema dynamics have typically permitted provides a client with an opportunity to disengage (i.e., stop struggling) and allow a new focus to emerge ("from a certain point of view").

Clinical Case Example 18.1 offers a relatively simple illustration of changing the context regarding a client's concerns.

Clinical Case Example 18.1: Need for Female Companionship

A Vietnam veteran who presented originally with severe anxiety and a drinking problem came for treatment. He had made a "mess" of his life after returning from the war and finally found his "bottom." He was hospitalized for detox, managed to work a 12-step program, and maintained sobriety. He was also in his final semester of college and realistically expected to graduate with a bachelor's degree from a large urban university. He actually had done very well academically. Despite these quite remarkable accomplishments, he still maintained a considerable anxiety that manifested itself in "the shakes." That is, his hands shook when he became anxious. A number of therapeutic interventions for that specific difficulty, obviously not the right ones, seemed to go nowhere. He was lonely and longed for the companionship of a woman who he could date. There was no one on the horizon. When asked if he was really ready, his commitment to being truthful to himself and in therapy dictated that he say, "No!" The therapist agreed that an attempt to date would be a disaster. Such a brutally frank assessment was merely a reflection of what the client had been telling the therapist. Alas, his expectations for what dating would represent to him were overwhelming. Medications were not an option for this man given his experiences with substance abuse.

As a paradoxical measure, the therapist suggested that what this man needed was "practice." How could he get practice at talking to women and not encounter the paralyzing anxiety that he was likely to generate if he saw someone who he might want to date? When this was proposed to him, he simply didn't think it was possible. His therapist assured him that it was. The question was, would he be willing to agree to the "assignment"? He eagerly agreed.

The assignment was explained by first asking him if he could tell the married women on campus from the unmarried ones. He indicated that he thought he could because married women "almost always" wore wedding rings, and some of them were pregnant. The therapist agreed and further offered that pregnant women were also a "fair," although not foolproof, indication that a woman was married. He was to approach only the married and/or pregnant women, strike up conversations with them, and *avoid at all costs engaging any single woman* in conversation. Obviously, married women were less of a threat to him; they were automatically excluded from being eligible to date. He eagerly delighted in this proposed assignment and reported in therapy that he soon found himself becoming not only desensitized to the fear of talking to women but also soon talking to even single women!

Questions

1. How would you describe the client's symptom or complaint?
2. What is the client's dilemma?
3. How might his symptom or complaint be related to his schema dynamics?
4. Discuss the paradoxical nature of the assignment (i.e., two elements that were mutually incompatible, yet true).
5. Did the paradoxical intervention broaden the client's perspective or advocate (benignly) for the status quo?
6. Describe what the client's stage of change might be.
7. How does the stage of change relate to the client's reaction to the assignment?

In Clinical Case Example 18.1, the client had developed an intense avoidance response to interacting with women, while at the same time feeling lonely and desiring female companionship but knowing that he was not ready to date! Hence, the approach–avoidance ambivalence is apparent and illustrates the principle of *wanting to have one's cake and eat it too.* The therapist's assignment provided the client an opportunity to engage in his avoidant behavior (i.e., interacting with women) and simultaneously not put himself in danger of encountering a woman who might want to go out with him. Presumably, married and/ or pregnant women can be considered less likely to be eligible to date, less likely to respond defensively to a fellow student just making conversation, and the like. Thus, they were "safe"; the client would not be threatened with the prospect of approaching women ineligible for dating. This represented a fundamental "shift" in his thinking, or an accommodation to his schema from "No woman will accept me the way I am" to "Some women will accept me the way I am." This prompted an emotional response that allowed him to reappraise his circumstance and altered his subjective view of women. This also altered his interpretation of their intention (i.e., context), which led to him being able to approach women ("... from a certain point of view"). The alteration of his context allowed him to both address his loneliness for female companionship and not date (something he admittedly was unprepared for). This fulfills the definition of a paradoxical intervention (i.e., two truths that cannot coexist) presented in Chapters 14, 15, 16, and 17.

Paradoxical interventions that are appropriate and effective can always be seen to "fit" and grasp a client's frame of reference, or context. Recall the metaphor of the vibrating tuning forks from Chapter 6. The "fit" (or "sympathetic vibration") can be seen in two distinct respects. In the example above, the client saw things in black and white and decided that he couldn't do it (i.e., interact with women). The paradoxical intervention altered his context, and opened him to see new possibilities and make new choices (i.e., reappraisal). Understanding things as the client experiences them (i.e., *their* context) reduces the potential for conflict or resistance. As mentioned in Chapter 9, when therapists "borrow" a client's expressions and metaphors, it allows for empathic understanding, which can alter the context and foster an accommodation of the client's schemas. Clinical Case Example 18.2 provides another instance in which the therapist broadens the client's perspective to provide possibilities that she had not considered.

Clinical Case Example 18.2: A Chronically and Acutely Anxious Woman

As a brief example, a woman in her late 50s with chronic obstructive pulmonary disease (COPD) that required a lung transplant was referred by her physician for counseling to deal with her anxiety and difficulty in eating a sufficient amount of food to maintain a stable weight. She willingly sought treatment, escorted by her very loving and supportive husband. During two sessions in which she readily disclosed a lifelong personality disposition of being chronically anxious, the therapist empathically noted, "Life seems to make you nervous with many terrible and frightening things to worry about—especially if you're alone!" To this summarizing comment, she heartily agreed. In fact, as her medical condition deteriorated in the indeterminate wait for a lung transplant, it was becoming more and more difficult for her to breathe—a condition that can induce extreme panic in almost anyone in very short order.

Her natural disposition, chronic medical condition, acute medical condition, and circumstances all made her extremely "nervous." Understandably, most often such clients wish to be removed from the danger, or "crisis" (or crises), that they are in or that they perceive looming. The therapist's assessment of this woman indicated that she perceived threat, failure, being overwhelmed, and even death looming in her life. For example, she spent seemingly long periods of time alone and largely housebound until her husband would return from work. The woman did not want to be alone for good reason—it was scary. She imagined that anything could happen to her that might require immediate medical attention and she would be alone to fend for herself. She felt unable to cope with such an appraisal of her circumstances but forced to do things that she didn't want to do—be alone and eat more when her physical condition made it extremely difficult for her to do so.

The therapist redefined her anxiety about being alone during the day when her husband had to go to work as "a call for contact with people." Both she and her husband readily agreed. In fact, the woman suggested that when the weather permitted, it was reassuring to her to sit in their back yard, feel the sun, and talk to neighbors who might be outside gardening. In a linear way, the therapist further suggested that perhaps as a couple they could work on seeking some "people medicine." This was an obvious metaphor for making certain that they seek out contact with neighbors, solicit fellow parishioners from the church to which they were very close to drop in on her, make certain that family members (as well as her husband) call her, and so on. The woman's disposition turned noticeably brighter at this suggestion. By the next session, they had made arrangements for her to have more contact with others while her husband was at work. She reported feeling considerably less anxious during the past week.

The suggestion that her anxiety, which was something whose onset she couldn't control, was "a call for contact with people" addressed her anxiety and the ambivalences that both the client and her husband faced: *She* couldn't directly require her husband to stay home, even though she clearly felt less anxious when he did so, because he had responsibilities to support the family. Her dilemma was as follows: If she demanded that her husband stay home, she would jeopardize his job; but if he goes to work, she becomes anxious about being alone. The husband's dilemma was no less acute: If he went to work, he felt as though he was abandoning his wife; but if he stayed home, he felt he was jeopardizing his job and livelihood. Upon the therapist's suggestion, soliciting "people medicine" was a means of addressing both of their ambivalences: She would not be alone as much, which greatly appealed to her, and she didn't have to ask her husband to not go to work. At the same time, he could help solicit people to visit his wife, call her, and still keep his commitments to his job.

The client's other major complaint was that the food her husband prepared was delicious and nutritious but simply too much for her to possibly consume.[3] The therapist inquired if they used regular-sized dinner plates, to which they responded, "Yes." In a nonlinear-thinking way, the therapist suggested that they might consider using much smaller salad plates rather than regular dinner plates. Such a suggestion addressed the ambivalences that each of them faced about the client's weight loss: If she didn't eat enough food, she would lose weight and jeopardize her status on the lung transplant waiting list; but if she tried to eat the amount of food her husband prepared, she was simply overwhelmed by the prospect because it was "just too much food." The husband's ambivalence was no less daunting: If he didn't give his wife enough food, he would feel like he had failed to be a good husband, and her transplant status could be jeopardized; yet when he filled his wife's regular-sized plate with food, as he believed a "good husband" should do, his wife was overwhelmed and discouraged, and probably ate less than she might have otherwise.

The suggestion to move to a smaller dinner plate satisfied her husband's need to feed his wife as much as possible so that she would not dangerously lose further weight (he could still "fill" her plate and feel good about being a good husband). It also satisfied her need to feel less overwhelmed by *how much* she felt she was being expected to eat (after all, there *is* less food on a salad plate than there is on a regular-sized dinner plate).

The therapist asked if he could make one further suggestion that concerned *how* she would eat. In response to the woman's complaint about her inability to eat very much (a legitimate complaint with both physiological and psychological components), the therapist suggested that at this time, the only food she had to worry about was that "at the end of her fork." Her spirits brightened even further. Upon her next visit, she spontaneously revealed that her medical caretakers were quite pleased that she had "maintained" her weight.

The woman survived to transplant and is alive and well as of this writing.

QUESTIONS

1. What, if anything, can you see as tranquilizing about the therapist's responses to this client?
2. Describe and discuss the "real" scary things in the client's life from the "psychologically" scary things in her life.
3. Is the wife or the husband the identified client? Defend your selection with regard to question 2.
4. Can you identify a strategic reason(s) why the therapist chose to see the wife and husband together?
5. What can you tell about the underlying client schemas of this couple?
6. In what way, if any, does the therapist's suggestion that the client need only pay attention to the food "at the end of her fork" address possible underlying schema(s)?

Note that the woman in Clinical Case Example 18.2 had been preoccupied with a *full plate of food on a regular-sized dinner place*. Among other things, this woman wanted to be a "good" patient and eat the food presented to her, but the physiology of failing organ systems tends to mitigate against that. By changing the *context* in which food was presented (i.e., a smaller dinner plate and a preoccupation only with what is at the end of her fork) new, more attainable, and more encouraging prospects that the woman could abide by emerged for her.

In Chapters 15, 16, 17, and 18, we presented several case examples to illustrate elements of the four categories of paradoxical interventions (which we called the "P's"). We revisit some of these cases to demonstrate how paradoxical interventions facilitate accommodation of a clients' schema and/or an alteration of their context. Recall from Chapter 15 the case of the prison guard who was badly hurt on the job by an inmate, and had begun to develop serious headaches and avoided going out in public (Clinical Case Example 15.4). This was interfering with the client's desire to return to work, as well as with his significant relationships. The therapist provided a paradoxical intervention for him to *postpone* returning to work or even *thinking* about returning to work. The intervention had the effect of disengaging the client from his focus on the headaches by altering his context and allowing him to not put pressure on himself. In a brief period, the client was open to changing his view of himself (accommodating his schema) as a corrections officer, and engaging in the ambivalence that he was experiencing about his career.

Clinical Exercise 18.1: Paradoxical Intervention and Cognitive Changes

Instructions: Reread the following case examples in Chapters 16 and 17, and determine how the paradoxical interventions helped the clients alter their context and/or accommodate their schema dynamics.

Case Example 16.6: "An Unhappy Perfectionist"
Case Example 17.5: "Scraps of Paper to Compensate for a Poor Memory"
Case Example 17.10: "Take Your Choice"

Variation: Form small groups, and discuss how each of the uses of paradoxical interventions helped the clients in the cases to disengage.

Second-Order Change, Disengagement, Nonlinear Thinking, and Reappraisal

Recall the discussion from previous chapters that human beings develop a particular way of thinking, behaving, and reasoning (determined by schema dynamics). The particular constellation of schemas they harbor and the reasoning that follows from them represent an unconscious "truth" that is perceived as helpful in navigating life's complexities successfully (i.e., "These beliefs and this way of thinking have more often than not been a successful formula for me! They represent my 'map' of the world that helps me navigate"). At the same, when life circumstances change (also a "truth") and unrelentingly challenge core schemas and our way of thinking and reasoning, the conflicts created (i.e., approach–approach, avoidance–avoidance, approach–avoidance, or double approach–avoidance) result in feelings of ambivalence. Ambivalence develops because *both realities* are perceived as "true" (e.g., we want *two* things but can't have both, or we want to avoid *two* things but must face one or the other). A dilemma is the result. As we have advocated, a new paradigm must be adopted to resolve problematic situations, or a person becomes trapped in a double bind: Troubling life circumstances won't go away, and the client doesn't want to change his or her core beliefs (and the thinking and reasoning that follow from those beliefs) because they have been a successful "strategy" in approaching life. As a practical matter of fact, most individuals do not recognize that they have a *set of assumptions about reality*, let alone that they are operating on the basis of those assumptions.

Paradoxical interventions provide an *opportunity for a reappraisal* of—a new way of perceiving—one's symptoms and/or problematic circumstances that accommodates *both* existing schemas and the circumstances that challenge them (or, to quote Obi-Wan Kenobi, "It is true, from a certain point of view"). We present Clinical Case Example 18.3 to help illustrate this.

Clinical Case Example 18.3: To Go or Not to Go to the Reunion; That Is the Question!

A very gentle, well-educated, retired former school administrator developed symptoms of acute anxiety as a result of an invitation to a "girls-only" family reunion. She badly wanted to attend the reunion to see and touch base with cousins, whom she enjoyed but had not seen in a number of years. The "problem" was the client's sister. For approximately the last 10 years, the client had not been getting along with her sister. As she explained it, every time that she and her sister were alone at any function, she felt that her sister began criticizing her for reasons that didn't make sense. It didn't seem to make any difference what the issue was; the client felt her sister to be critical and contemptuous. She didn't know why that was the case, but that's the way she felt. At the same time, she badly wanted to go to the reunion, but the deal breaker was that her sister would be in attendance. The thought of her sister "cornering" her and berating her when no one else was around prompted her to lose sleep and become increasingly anxious, panicky, and fretful about what to do. Because her husband, who was very protective of her, would not be allowed to attend (i.e., the invitation was for "girls only"), she felt even more exposed and vulnerable.

Recognizing the dichotomy involved in the woman's thinking, the therapist asked her, "Do you think it is possible for you to go and not go to the party at the same time?" Without much thought, she replied, "No! I either go or don't go!"

The therapist suggested that perhaps with a little imagination, it might be possible for her to "go and not go" to the party at the same time. He further suggested that she might go to the party but arrive very late. Of course, she would have to explain the reason for her tardiness. When that was suggested, she and her husband indicated that, indeed, the same day of the party they were scheduled to visit their son, who was institutionalized at a considerable distance from where they lived. The limited availability of visiting hours made it imperative that they maintain their loyalty and keep their regularly scheduled visit with him, as they had for a number of years. They thus readily acknowledged that they could arrive late.

The therapist then suggested that because she wasn't attending the party as scheduled like all the rest of the "girls," it would be an acceptable faux pas for her husband to accompany her to the party for a "late visit" and say "hello" to everyone. The client would have little exposure to being all alone with her sister, and as an added measure her husband would be there to "protect" her if the need should arise. In addition, the therapist suggested as a further *extra* added measure of caution that they could extend their apologies for being late and wanting to leave early because of the long day that they had had traveling to visit their son. Of course, all of the cousins knew about the young man being institutionalized and empathized with the client as a mother who suffered with her son's institutionalization. Upon follow-up with the client, it was revealed that the suggestion made to her (i.e., expanding on her frame of reference, and thus changing the context for her arriving late and leaving early) worked "beautifully." The client resolved her dilemma and was able to *have her cake and eat it too*. It took exactly one consultation session.

Regarding Clinical Case Example 18.3, some people might say, "Isn't this just 'coddling' the client, and shouldn't she be able to make a choice and stick with it?" The first and most important consideration is "What does the client need?" In this case, she wants and needs to go to the party for a variety of reasons and at the same time not be antagonized by her sister. This is a perfectly reasonable expectation. Unfortunately for the client, she had appraised the situation to be one where she did not have an alternative: She judged that she could not go without the possibility of antagonism from her sister. Her dilemma is clear: To go to the party under conditions as described means that she would be in jeopardy from her sister, but to not go to the party means she would miss out on the opportunity to see cousins who rarely gather in one place at one time. The creative (i.e., paradoxical) solution that the therapist suggested allowed her to have her cake and eat it too (i.e., go to the party and be relatively free from bother). By going, the client may discover that her fears were unfounded or that she has the strength to deal with her sister, and she may keep engaging the family. Or, she may discover that it is not a good use of her time and energy to participate in these functions and feel more comfortable with her decision to not go. Either way, through this paradoxical intervention she will have reappraised her context, which allows her to resolve her ambivalence and find a way out of her dilemma, thus creating second-order change.

Another case example from Chapter 14 illustrates how paradoxical interventions that allow for an opportunity for reappraisal can be "freeing" to the client who has been bound down in his dilemma. Recall Clinical Case Example 14.3, "Unacceptable Sexual Behavior," in which the client felt guilty for engaging in masturbation—a behavior that he saw as morally unacceptable because it made him "weak" in his eyes. The therapist utilized a paradoxical intervention that suggested to the client that his behavior was a way of him communicating that he wanted companionship and that he might be needing to date and find a partner (following a particularly bad divorce) to combat his loneliness. The intervention allowed the client to reappraise his situation and make a new interpretation that was less denigrating. In a similar way, in Clinical Case Example 16.1, a woman felt tremendous guilt and depression surrounding her thoughts of wishing that her husband (who was in a nursing home afflicted with multiple sclerosis) would die. The client admitted feeling such tremendous guilt that she had even contemplated suicide. The therapist's paradoxical intervention was as follows: "For whose benefit do you want such a seriously and hopelessly ill man to linger on? If you wished him to stay alive as long as possible, perhaps it was to help postpone your own loss and grief. To wish a loved one to continue to linger may be for *our* benefit. On the other hand, to wish him dead may in the final analysis be an act of love and courage in that he would no longer have to deal with his helplessness, hopelessness, and suffering." This allowed the woman to reexamine her reactions and reappraise her thoughts and feelings from being disloyal and heartless to being loyal and loving.

Clinical Exercise 18.2: Reinterpretation and Reappraisal

Instructions: Reread the following Clinical Case Examples in Chapters 14, 15, 16, and 17, and determine how paradoxical interventions helped the clients reinterpret and/or reappraise their situation and create second-order change.

Clinical Case Example 14.1: "Redefining a Complaining Wife"
Clinical Case Example 15.9: "Distraught Woman Whose World Has Collapsed"
Clinical Case Example 16.8: "Terrorized by a Rare Cardiac Condition"
Clinical Case Example 17.1: "A Sad Mother's Visit With Her Adult Children"
Clinical Case Example 17.9: "A Cowboy's Word"

Variation: Form small groups, and discuss how each use of paradoxical interventions helped the clients in the cases to disengage.

Providing a New Meaning for a Client's Symptom or Struggle

One way to foster the disengagement process is to provide a new meaning for the struggle or symptom for the client. In an unsuccessful struggle with symptomatic behavior, people are aware of the sense of failure on two levels: (1) failing to favorably "solve" (i.e., more positively deal with) whatever issues that life has given them and (2) failing to get rid of their symptoms that won't go away. Perhaps one of the most basic and powerful ways of accomplishing disengagement is through providing the symptomatic struggle with *redemptive* meaning. Redemptive meaning suggests that there is indeed something positive, constructive, and prosocial that stems from this negative set of circumstances. The person is not engaging in a meaningless struggle with symptoms and suffering, but rather the struggle signifies something "redeeming" and saving. The individual is going through this experience and receiving something positive from it that she may not have thought of before. We present an extended Clinical Case Example 18.4 below to demonstrate this.

Clinical Case Example 18.4: A Reclusive Paranoiac or a Real Man?

Another case demonstrating more complexity, longer therapy, and the inherent utility of helping a patient find new meaning is that of an aging man who in some respects resembled the chronically anxious, jittery, and skittish character created by the comedian Don Knotts. If it were not for the true fearfulness and suffering that this man was experiencing, his mannerisms could have been considered comical. Chain smoking in a remote corner of the waiting room, darting vigilant eyes, and a literally cautious slithering walk down hospital corridors in an effort to remain invisible to others all gave muted testimony to his constant and chronic anxiety and wariness.

He always dressed in the most unobtrusive workingman's clothing and most likely would have felt physically vulnerable without his workman-style hat, which he wore whether it was winter or torrid summer. His speech was halting and interspersed with stuttered words, telling his story that was not psychotic although at times quite disjointed.

The first few sessions of therapy were obviously a testing of how much trust he might have in the therapist. It was scheduled for 6:45 a.m. weekly to accommodate the patient's expressed need for "getting in and getting out before too many people are around." A cup of coffee for both the client and the therapist became a part of the relationship's early morning ritual. The issue of trust spread even to the use of medications—except for something to help him sleep occasionally. He wanted nothing to do with "drugs." He felt as though medications dulled his alertness but otherwise did little for him. In keeping with a wary paranoid orientation to life and the world, being vigilant was more important for him than being calmer or sleeping well on a regular basis.

As time passed, he described a series of events in his life that paved his ultimate road to despair. Several of these events were of critical importance. The first was a marriage that ended in divorce 10 years before but that had been deteriorating for years prior to its legal dissolution. The man's original dedication to his marriage was unquestioned. He worked long, hard, physical hours as a tradesman; did side jobs; took little money for himself; and was very faithful to his wife and children. Zealous pursuit of his interpretation of the masculine ideal was perhaps ultimately his undoing. His wife did not appear to demonstrate a corresponding devotion to him or his values, perhaps because of his long hours. She spent the family's money on things that she wanted while neglecting to pay utility bills and occasionally the rent. Thus, he complained that she had been financially irresponsible, and lax in caring for her children's needs. Finally, she was unfaithful to him.

Ultimately, the patient's response to his wife's behavior was poorer and poorer communication between them, arguments, greater withdrawal, and a profound sense of discouragement signaled by an increased use of alcohol. He soon learned that drinking, carousing, and not coming home provided for him more of a sense of "being a real man" than his marriage and family life had. As he discovered, however, it was an overcompensated and false sense of security: He found himself constantly escalating the level of "masculine" behaviors, as he interpreted them. There seemed to be no satisfying his need to make up for his sensed failure as a husband and father. He became sexually promiscuous and a drunkard with ever increasing bravado. As his acting out became more and more pronounced, he "figured" he could try having sex with a man. As he described it, through his private logic, such an act would be truly courageous and masculine: It was "daring," and only a "real man" could dare it. He did this on two drunken occasions: The second time proved genuinely disastrous for he became repulsed by his own actions and physically assaulted the man he encountered, although he was never arrested for this.

He began to decompensate more and more. Intense feelings of suspicion developed that his drinking companions knew of his sexual indiscretion. Although his original thinking was that "a man could try anything and get away with it," he now began to feel that people were staring at him. His overriding guilt and paranoia prompted him to conclude that "there must have been" pictures of his homosexual episode, and that people were staring at him. He became incessantly preoccupied and perseverated on the delusion: People knew him to be "queer" and that "there must be pictures."

Shortly after these incidents occurred, the patient lost his job, became seriously depressed, and was hospitalized, but he told no one of his homosexual episode. He did not work for several years until depleting his savings. Reluctantly, he obtained a job in a completely different field, once again working long hours with overtime with no complaints and no trouble. At the time he entered treatment, he led the life of a hermit, going only to work and then home to his apartment, where he would not even keep a light on for fear of being recognized from the street. For 7 years, that was the sum total of his existence until his apartment was threatened because of his landlady's ill health. He passionately feared having to move because he might be recognized.

As his story unfolded in therapy, it became clear that this man was basically describing what be believed to be a desperate fight for his survival. The fight was so desperate that he felt as though he had to be fully prepared at any time to take flight. His preoccupation with "pictures" was immutable, was impervious to logic and conventional therapeutic intervention, and represented a constant struggle for both physical and psychological survival. He even worried about his car getting older because he needed transportation for a possible "fast getaway." In his trunk, he had stored cash, several cartons of cigarettes, a clean change of clothes, and a tire iron to fend off possible accusers. He had *no* friends and *no* contacts with his children. Despite these concerns, the patient came regularly for therapy sessions early in the morning and never missed a session over a period of one year.

Those readers who have encountered extreme paranoia in someone they have treated will perhaps agree that such patients are among the most difficult to treat. As the therapist pondered this man's impoverished, isolated, and interpersonally sterile existence, he questioned how he might help this man to enjoy a somewhat fuller life. Two dialectical thoughts emerged. The first was that the patient was indeed living a precarious, shallow, and stressful existence. Most of the professional community as well as the patient would most likely agree with that assessment. He was going to believe what he obviously believed, and it was fruitless to attempt to try to talk him out of his beliefs.

The second thought was somewhat more encouraging and had the added advantage of being quite consistent with the patient's history and dynamics: In spite of his paranoid thinking and defensive-reclusive existence, he was working, seeking help, living in the community, and relatively healthy. *In spite* of all the obviously precarious circumstances and struggles that he described, he was functioning. In the therapist's nonlinear way of thinking, the patient's behavior was not *avoidant*, but rather it was nothing less than *heroic*. Once that conclusion was reached, it was a short step to viewing the patient's behavior as classically masculine: a man fighting for survival and being successful in a heroic way against insurmountable odds of being "found out." The more impossible he made and described his situation to be, the more of a "real man" he was. How many people could even think about doing what he had already done and was continuing to do for the last 10 years? How many people could survive such impoverished circumstances? More specifically, how many *men* could do so?

When this line of thinking was introduced to the patient, his reaction was "I think you got something there. ... I think you hit it on the head." The patient was now in what can be construed as a positive double bind: If he persisted in his secluded behavior, he was "a real man" engaged in a heroic struggle for survival; and if he could be persuaded to "venture out" into new activities, he could begin moving in a prosocial direction. Indeed, the patient was encouraged and energized enough to begin asking the therapist if he had "done right" by continuing to work and avoid further hospitalization despite his felt precarious daily existence. He also began inquiring if he should laugh at himself and what had happened to him as a way of dealing with his situation. When asked how he was able to maintain himself for so long (an obvious strength), he indicated that he felt somehow he had to keep going because his children or his aged mother or sister might need him at some future time. Although he persisted in his feelings that "they might be out to get me at any time," the intensity diminished, and he could more easily see a need to keep going *for other people*.

Subsequent to the above intervention, the patient took advantage of a suggestion to become involved in group therapy in order to reintroduce other people into his life. From a short period of time in group, he began to volunteer at the hospital where he was being seen in treatment. He soon found himself the object of the attention of several widows who were also volunteers.

The patient described in Clinical Case Example 18.4 suffered with his struggle for survival by battling with his paranoia. However, when his behavior was reframed as "heroic," it allowed him to disengage in his isolating behavior, and develop a somewhat more palatable view of his lot in life. The issue is that his suffering was transformed—it had a more positive meaning. In other words, his schema dynamics (i.e., "I want to live up to the self-ideal that I have in my head of being a real man") were accommodated, and second-order change resulted. The same behavior remains—struggling, fighting to stay alive, ready to defend himself, and so on—but *what the behavior means is of a different order of reality*. That represents a *second-order change*. Note, however, that this could not have been achieved if the therapist had not adopted the *nonlinear* approach and reframed his client's behavior in a prosocial way. Attempting to change his thinking (e.g., first-order change of attempting to convince him that there weren't any pictures of him and people were not looking for him) would only result in more reason to be on guard. As a result, it encouraged him to go on with his life in more constructive ways. Indeed, considering how much he did struggle, what he was able to accomplish *is* nothing short of heroic.

Another example of how paradoxical interventions facilitate the disengagement process by providing new meaning to a client's struggle with her symptoms comes from Chapter 15 in Clinical Case Example 15.2 ("One More Child to Raise"), the case of the woman who is forced to raise her niece after her sister's parental rights are terminated while other family members who had promised to help became uncooperative. The client felt trapped by her circumstances, yet did not want the responsibility of raising another child after she had successfully raised several of her own. At the same time, she felt obligated by both sympathy for her niece's predicament and a sense of duty that she "inherited" from her mother. The stress took a toll on her, and it was only when the therapist paradoxically related that she was in danger of neglecting the child (a duty she felt strongly) by not demanding help in the event that her health should get worse (in which case, the child *would be* abandoned) that she was able to address the issue. As a result, the client had a new meaning for her struggle (with symptoms of depression, and worsening health), and resolved to *do* something to change it (i.e., *engage* in a new way of behaving) by demanding help.

Clinical Exercise 18.3: Adding New Meaning to the Struggle

Instructions: Reread the following Clinical Case Examples in Chapters 16 and 17, and determine how the paradoxical interventions helped to provide these clients with new meaning for their struggles:

Case Example 16.2: "Total Incompetence"
Case Example 16.4: "A Stalker"
Case Example 17.3: "Queen for a Day"
Case Example 17.4: "Divorced, Lonely, and Frightened"

Variation: Form small groups, and discuss how each use of paradoxical interventions helped the clients in the cases to disengage.

Disengagement Through Defocusing or Externalizing the Symptom or Struggle

Disengagement can also be facilitated through paradoxical interventions that focus attention *away* from preoccupation with oneself and onto someone or something constructive outside of oneself. Self-preoccupation appears to be a universal characteristic of maladjustment. Taking an interest in others or in others' interests (i.e., valuing what is important to others) appears to be a much healthier way of spending one's time and dealing with life. Refocusing a client's attention promotes a shift *away* from the self onto others, or from preoccupation with deficits to the perception of strengths. Shifting a client's focus of attention can remove the debilitating sense that she is helpless and "locked into" a problem without any recourse. This changes the way in which the client relates to the symptom or the problematic life circumstance. Clinical Case Example 18.5 provides a simple illustration of how a shift in therapeutic focus of attention can have a significant impact.

Clinical Case Example 18.5: A Woman Finds Her Voice

As an example of what we mean, a hard-working woman in her 50s suffered a stroke. Although the injury occurred on the right side of her brain, it rendered the left side of her body partially paralyzed. She was very depressed, crying (at times incoherently) and lamenting loudly, "Why did God do this to me? I've never hurt anyone; I always tried to help people. What am I going to do now? Who's going to take care of me? How can I live?"

All of her considerations are weighty, and the more that this woman would ponder them, the more depressed and disconcerted she would become. What can you say to someone in such a position as a human being, let alone as a therapist, that would be encouraging? She was from a blue-collar, hard-working, honest, never-hurt-a-fly, help-others heritage so typical of so many people. She was crying, overwhelmed, emotionally labile, and preoccupied with her deficits, disability, and dysfunction. Reality had little else that she could see. The therapist responded by *agreeing* with her: "You've had a terrible misfortune in life, and it will take you a long time to overcome what has happened to you." (This positively suggested, of course, that she could with time reconcile herself to what had happened to her.) While emphasizing that, the therapist proceeded to state almost incidentally, "I couldn't help but notice, even with all your misfortune, how clearly you speak and how well organized your thinking is." Knowing of the woman's bilingual background and also being bilingual, he proceeded to ask her in the second language, "I wonder if you can still understand and speak Polish?" (The therapist knew that she was able to do so from other sources before seeing her.)

The woman suddenly became alert and instantly stopped crying. She listened intently to what the therapist had to say. She responded to him in Polish that she could understand and speak Polish as well as ever. In turn, the therapist countered by noting how "marvelous" it was that she could understand and communicate in *two languages*, an obvious asset for anyone. The conversation then proceeded to similar encouragements she had received from others in her life, including the physical therapist who complimented her on how hard she was working toward rehabilitation and how much progress she had already made.

All well and good, but exactly what sort of *thinking* enters into such an intervention? In Clinical Case Example 18.5, it was clear that the woman's complaint was that she was upset about her plight, that is, having had a stroke. Her "upset" was the behavior that required *tranquilizing* because it threatened to overwhelm all other issues (as well as the therapy). In turn, the question for the therapist became, *how* could he help tranquilize her? Using nonlinear thinking (i.e., looking not at her complaint per se but shifting focus to look at it dialectically), it is a short step to see *how well and how articulately* she was able to express her complaints while she was feeling so dysfunctional! The nonlinear-thinking therapist *at times* readily shifts the focus of attention, looks at opposites, and juxtaposes different meanings in an attempt to derive a point of intervention. As discussed in Chapters 4 and 5 on assessing a client's needs, goals, and strengths, and in Chapters 12 and 13 on ambivalence, finding ways to either shift a client's focus on her strengths or see the problem as an external force acting against the client are useful methods of reframing the client's situation. By *defocusing* from the *content* of her complaints and discerning the *easily overlooked* positive elements in her life, things at which she was still competent, a foundation was created—something she could build upon. In this case, the positive components noted were her being able to speak as well as she could (i.e., the fact that the speech ability of some stroke patients is severely impaired was also noted to her), retaining her bilingual abilities, and displaying the hard work ethic noted by her physical therapist. By this time, the fruitless portion of her behavior could be left behind, and more of the work of rehabilitation undertaken. We hasten to add that *how* one presents such a defocusing is extremely important. The woman was approached with amazement at how well she spoke in *two languages*, and not with rebuke that she should be glad that she could still speak at all.

Closely related to refocusing is the process of "externalizing the problem," presented in Chapter 13. Externalizing the problem facilitates the client developing a new attitude that separates the client from the problem: "It's not me as a person that is the problem; it's (e.g., the drinking, this inherited trait, or my diagnosis)." More concretely, "It's not me—it's the sadness, OCD, depression, shyness, genetics, addiction or an addictive voice, hurt inner child, etc."). With the process of "externalizing," the person is able to disengage from the struggle with the problem by identifying it as not a part of him. Instead, he is able to focus on his relationship to the problem and how to manage it. Clients rarely say, "I'm cancer," or "I'm high blood pressure." Yet clients frequently say, "I'm depressed," "I'm schizophrenic," "I'm OCD," or "I'm Adult ADHD," instead of "I have schizophrenia" or "I have depression."

By *externalizing* the problem, and thus moving it at arm's length away from oneself, clients can have increased objectivity toward it and its management (i.e., a new "relationship" with it). Instead of struggling with *oneself as the problem* and fruitlessly attempting to recoil from oneself or attempting to push the discomfort away, externalizing allows for major themes to be explored (Flemons, 2003; Hanna, 2001; Hanna & Puhakka, 1991; Hanna & Ritchie, 1995) such as the "problem's" effect on the client and his effect upon the problem, when and how he refused to be ruled by the problem, and so on (White & Epston, 1990). An individual no longer must feel victimized or helpless. Adler (1972) described cases in which the symptom was redefined as a "friend" rather than an enemy that needed to be destroyed. As a "friend," it would return whenever needed to prevent the client from rushing into a commitment to gain social approval that he was not yet prepared to do (e.g., entering college, getting married, or needing to change jobs) or for health reasons (e.g., stopping or starting a health-related behavior). The problem is not what the person has been complaining of but the relationship that he has *with* the problem that is causing his suffering (White & Epston).

Disengagement Through the Novelty of the Unexpected

As mentioned above, the most typical reaction that clients verbalize to a paradoxical reframing of their circumstances is "I never thought of it that way!" As a brief example, an accomplished career woman in her early 50s presented herself for treatment because of childhood sexual trauma that she had never addressed. In addition to the trauma, she rendered an early childhood history of herself as the big, quiet, overweight, unintelligent, ugly duckling sibling of her family who always tried to please others. After a thorough assessment and written feedback, the therapist described some of her adult assets as "intelligent" and "attractive." This was based on very simple observations and factual information: She was a college graduate and had held a responsible job in the demanding financial industry for many years, and she *was* attractive, well groomed, and in good health. As she read those two simple descriptors of herself, she broke into tears, sobbing that *no one* (other than her husband, who seldom told her these things) had ever described her in that way going back as far as she could remember. She described it as so "foreign" to her! The therapist's *unexpected* description of her as intelligent and attractive moved her emotionally to begin considering herself in a light she had never considered. Such interpretations are quite paradoxical because her *self*-description (i.e., self-schema) was so dialectically opposite.

In Chapters 14, 15, 16, and 17, we presented numerous examples of paradoxical interventions that utilized novelty (i.e., "absurd" statements) and demonstrated how it fosters the disengagement process. Recall from Chapter 14 (in Clinical Case Example 14.2) the case of a woman with a medical condition complaining of dizziness when she tried to do anything "strenuous," forcing her to return to bed (despite the fact that she had previously enjoyed an active life). The therapist forbade her to do anything for more than 10 minutes, and then she had to return to bed. This intervention was an absurd hyperextension that forced the client to reexamine whether she was as sick as she believed. It took the novelty of the approach to allow her to choose to disengage from her old way of viewing her condition and see that she had strengths that she hadn't accessed before.

Clinical Exercise 18.4: Paradox, Novelty, and Disengagement

Instructions: Reread the following case examples in Chapters 14, 15, 16, and 17, and determine how the paradoxical interventions used novelty and the unexpected to foster the disengagement process:

> Case Example 14.4: "Neutralizing the Rebellious Behavior of a Reluctant Nun"
> Case Example 15.5: "A Talented Young Musician"
> Case Example 16.5: "A Paranoid Young Woman"
> Case Example 17.2: "Depression, Money, and a New Son-in-Law"

Variation: Form small groups, and discuss how each use of paradoxical interventions helped the clients in the cases to disengage.

Most often, the novelty of paradoxical interventions is unexpected. Our contention is that neurotic problems, once established, continue unabated despite common sense, exhortations, painful consequences, and the like. In other words, people continue to do more of the same; they continue to perseverate on ineffectual solutions, doing what they've always done and getting what they've always gotten. Why? There are abundant data from neuroscience research that provide at least a partial explanation.

There are considerable supportive data of this point of view from a number of diverse sources. For example, Rossi (1973) described "psychological shocks and creative moments as possibly 'the essence of psychotherapy'" (p. 9). As mentioned earlier, Fraser and Solovey (2007) described paradoxical interventions as "the golden thread" that unifies effective treatments. From neuroscience research, Segalowitz (1983) and Galen (1974) early on suggested that the right hemisphere is perhaps more related to unconscious processes and emotional states than the left hemisphere. More recently, LeDoux (1998; quoting Gazzaniga, 1972) has referred to this as "one brain—two minds."

Brain in a Box 18.1: Paradoxical Interventions and Brain Changes

Paradoxical interventions can be viewed as involving the way the brain works. They would appear to engage the brain architecture that governs the client inertia seen in maladaptive solutions, that is, *how* our brains work when they get hold of something, even if it is maladaptive and gives us further grief. Pinker (1999) suggested that there are much data to support this contention:

> [T]he mind has to get something out of forming categories, and that something is inference. Obviously we can't know everything about every object. But we can observe some of its properties, assign it to a category, and from the category predict properties that we have not observed. ... Many cognitive scientists believe that the mind is equipped with innate intuitive theories or modules for the major ways of making sense of the world ... Don't take the 'theory' idiom literally. ...

Don't take the 'module' metaphor seriously, either; people can mix and match their ways of knowing. ... *And we often apply modes of thinking to subject matters they were not designed for, such as slapstick humor (person as object), animistic religion (tree or mountain as having a mind), and anthropomorphic animal stories (animals with human minds). ... Saying that the different ways of knowing are innate is different from saying that knowledge is innate. ...Goals and values are one of the vocabularies in which we mentally couch our experiences. They cannot be built out of simpler concepts from our physical knowledge the way "momentum" can be built out of mass and velocity or 'power' can be built out of energy and time. They are primitive or irreducible, and higher-level concepts are defined in terms of them.* (pp. 307–315; emphasis added)

In many respects, Pinker (1999) has described exactly what it is that people who are troubled do: They apply "modes of thinking" (i.e., schemas) to "subject matters" (i.e., life circumstances) and make inferences (i.e., reason). The problem is that all too often, the "modes of thinking" simply weren't designed for solving the life circumstances being presented. Paradoxical interventions may be as effective as they are because they target the mechanisms underlying how the brain works. The individual experiences difficulties with his problems and "solutions," but has little or no knowledge or awareness of the role that the brain's architecture plays in such circumstances. Although we are aware of the fact that we are aware, an awareness of how we operate as creatures is something that remains very much a mystery to us. That is, people are aware of *what* they are thinking but not necessarily *how* they are thinking or the *premises* (i.e., largely obscure, primitive, and unconscious) underlying that thinking. Paradoxical interventions are very much orthogonal (i.e., at right angles to) to maladaptive attitudes, feelings, behaviors, and the like (i.e., more of the same). As such, the architecture of the brain (i.e., its "modes of thinking") is totally unprepared to deal with something such as paradoxical messages that are so at odds with *how the brain is designed to operate and what information it expects* to be forthcoming. Because of its inherent difficulty with paradoxical messages, the mind breaks— disengages—from its symptomatic inertia and allows for the possibility of new understanding (i.e., mode of thinking), new meaning, new behavior, and a new relationship with the symptom or problem to emerge.

When the architecture encounters paradox, it is ill prepared to deal with it because it is *not* "more of the same." As a result of paradoxical interventions, a client cannot continue to make the same "inferences" that she had been making. Discordant information has entered her "mode of thinking," as Pinker ( ) referred to it. That startling, orthogonal effect that paradoxical interventions appear to have on an individual has been called *beneficial uncertainty, anti-expectation, taking the wind out of the sails,* a *violation of expectations,* and a host of other names. The disengagement from how clients had been thinking, feeling, and behaving (i.e., symptomatically) that occurs in response to paradoxical interventions is often dramatic and extremely powerful. As Benson (2003) has pointed out, healthy biochemical processes are triggered when the release and disengagement from symptomatic behavior occur. Nitrate oxide pours into the bloodstream in significant amounts to counter the unhealthy "fight-or-flight" stress response enacted and perpetuated through the application of maladaptive and unhealthy solutions. Paradoxical interventions are intended to be prosocial in nature and thus seen as healthy as well.

The new meanings that people develop are not simply "psychological" but are in fact related to changes in the brain itself. Doidge (2007), Schwartz and Begley (2003), and others presented their case for the brain's plasticity from clinical case studies and animal and human research. Whether it is patients affected by brain damage from strokes or OCD, the brain can and does change. Paradoxical interventions are seen to facilitate such changes.

THE TERMINATION OF THERAPY AND DISENGAGEMENT

In effect, terminating therapy is a form of disengagement—it is a *disengagement* from the therapeutic relationship and the need for therapy. If engaging a client in therapy is a crucial first step in the process of establishing a therapeutic alliance and successful treatment outcome, then termination is an equally important process. We briefly address a number of different issues that master practitioners appear mindful of in the process of ending therapy.

One of the most important considerations in treatment is to never take the therapeutic relationship for granted and assume that a client will keep coming back until all of his issues are resolved. Master practitioners seem to sense when a client has achieved sufficient success regarding what it is that she wanted or needed to accomplish in treatment. Even so, every session can and should be treated as though it might be the last session with a client. As much as possible, every session needs to end on a positive note. That said, there are a number of specific considerations about termination that come up quite frequently that we would like to address.

Traditional Termination

Under ideal circumstances, after a client has made progress in reaching therapeutic goals, it is the therapist's responsibility to explore what the client thinks and feels about ending therapy. If both parties agree, a mutually determined termination date then can be scheduled. At times, however, when there has been a positive working alliance and the topic of termination is brought up, clients quite often are uncomfortable about doing away with a "winning formula" and would like to continue in treatment. In other words, they are *ambivalent* about termination. Under such circumstances, the prudent practitioner can explore the client's ambivalence and hesitancy and suggest a termination based on several sessions spaced out over a mutually agreed-upon time period. Such a strategy is similar to patients consulting a physician after a bout of illness and receiving follow-up appointments to check that they have maintained the gains they have made. It is reassuring to a client to have such follow-up, but not all clients necessarily require them. Making a one-sided decision to terminate therapy is not recommended because it can be interpreted as abandonment.

If the topic of termination is brought up and a client mentions that she would like to continue in treatment, it is the therapist's responsibility to discuss this with the client. If there are other defined issues to work on, mutually agreed-upon treatment goals can be established, and work begun. If the client is simply ambivalent about leaving therapy, however, the therapist can help the client work through her ambivalence to a successful conclusion.

At times, after a brief number of sessions, a therapist may determine that a client needs to be referred to another practitioner. It is the therapist's responsibility to discuss the reasons for such referral with the client.

One-Time Consultation

It is not uncommon for clients to announce that they are seeking a "one-time professional opinion" about a particular set of circumstances such as a decision they need to make. At times, such individuals have already made up their minds as to what it is that they intend to do and would simply like to satisfy themselves that they "have done everything possible"—including consulting a professional person with an objective opinion—before acting on their intentions. At other times, such clients may simply be at a contemplation stage of change—uncertain as to whether or not they have a "problem" or someone else is the problem. Under these circumstances, a master practitioner is best positioned to help such a client by clarifying his situation as much as possible and, if possible, pointing out the pluses and minuses of the discernible ambivalences and his available alternatives, as well as what the client appears to be feeling about each of those alternatives. If such a client is certain and clear about wanting only one session and the therapist believes that he needs treatment, such a conclusion should be couched in terms of "suggestions" rather than mandates.

THE FINAL SECRET: BACK TO THE SORCERER'S APPRENTICE

We started this text with the aim of presenting nonlinear thinking and paradoxical intervention as critical elements of effective psychotherapy practiced by master therapists. Although it was once confined to mystical and mythic realms, and given only brief consideration in the literature, we have aspired to "expose" the secrets of this and, if not explain how to do it, at least provide a roadmap to this crucial convergence factor.

To begin with, we used the story of the sorcerer's apprentice to explain most people's experience of the master therapist in their use of paradoxical interventions to effect change in their clients. The key, we asserted, was that novice therapists, like the sorcerer's apprentice, may know how to *act* like their respective masters but did not know how to *think* like them. As a result, their efforts would be, at best, successful with some effort until they mastered the final convergence factor (i.e., paradoxical interventions and the nonlinear thinking behind them). This brings us full circle back to Mickey Mouse as the sorcerer's apprentice. He, like many beginning counselors, wants to have the power that he sees that masters have, and tries to *seize* it by mimicking the actions of the master.

In today's society, with a resurgence in secret societies or ancient wisdom (just look at the success of the novel *The Da Vinci Code*; Brown, 2003), it is easy to see how master therapists using nonlinear thinking and paradoxical interventions may look as though they possess some mystical knowledge. And in some respects they *do*, for they understand some of the most basic, fundamental elements of human thought and behavior. However, it has also been our contention that this knowledge is not the sole possession of these masters, and that this knowledge can be taught to and understood by a majority of individuals (rather than a select few). We have attempted to break down, as best we could, the processes of paradoxical intervention, as well as the processes underlying these strategies. Furthermore, we have tried to show how these underlying processes mirror clients' private nonlinear thinking and create a working alliance with them, which decrease any inherent resistance.

However, now that you have finished this book, taken this journey, and discovered the mystery behind the thinking of the most effective clinicians, there *is* one final secret of the masters to share with you: You must go back to the beginning! As you will recall from Chapter 1, Skovholt and Jennings (2004) found that master practitioners were distinguished by their desires to keep learning and to continue to pursue knowledge (both in and out of the counseling field). They kept up their sense of curiosity and never felt that they had "attained" mastery. As a result, they pursued every counseling interaction with a sense of newness and wonder. George Leonard (1992), in his book *Mastery*, found that masters find enjoyment in doing the most basic skills of a given discipline, not in the accomplishment or achievement of some goal. He stated that masters enjoy "practice," whereas individuals who merely "dabble" want to be proficient without the practice.[4]

> The people we know as masters don't devote themselves to their particular skill just to get better at it. The truth is, *they love to practice*—and because of it they do get better. And then, to complete the circle, the better they get the more they enjoy performing the basic moves over and over again. (Leonard, p. 75)

In essence, though they were masters themselves, these practitioners become apprentices again. This time, however, they do not learn from great masters, but instead from clients, students, supervisees, and the practice of the therapeutic process itself! It would be as if Mickey Mouse, instead of becoming afraid of the multiplying brooms and flooding waters, approached the chaos with wonder and excitement about what he would find out about the experience. Indeed, *that* is a nonlinear thought!

In the final analysis, however, interventions that master therapists use are not "magical" or whimsical, but rather the careful application of solid principles of counseling and psychotherapy (i.e., domains) combined with a firm understanding of the processes of *nonlinear thinking*. The reality is that the true master adopts a way of thinking about the practice of psychotherapy that is less interested in power, and is more interested in helping clients see through their pain and out of their trapped circumstances, to a better vision of their lives. Striving to bring out the best in others and oneself is perhaps the best description of mastery. So we invite you to take that next step. Wherever you are in your development (Level I, Level II, or Level III), go back to the beginning of this book and reread the chapters. We believe that the information that is contained within will have different meanings to each person if he or she reads it a second or third time. We also believe that as people develop as therapists and come back to this material, they will see and understand things differently that they can apply in their work, and perhaps to their lives. It is a powerful thought, but as we have attempted to show, *thinking* is what the magic and healing of psychotherapy is all about.

ENDNOTES

1. The nine-dot problem involves connecting nine dots (three rows of three dots each) with one continuous line without lifting the pencil from the paper. The dots cannot be connected without the line leaving the "field" (i.e., the boundaries set by the rectangular arrangement of the nine dots). We urge that the reader try solving this puzzle
2. It is not coincidental that the Mental Research Institute housed both Watzlawick (a proponent of second-order change) and Jay Haley (a proponent of paradoxical intervention) during the same era.
3. In heart or lung transplant patients, there is a complex relationship between the major organ (i.e., heart, lung, digestive, etc.) systems so that when one begins to fail, it can easily precipitate failure in another such system.
4. It is interesting to note that in the counseling field, we call the delivery of services *practice*.

References

Acosta, J., & Prager, J. S. (2002). *The worst is over: What to say when every moment counts*. San Diego, CA: Jodere.

Adams, N., & Grieder, D. M. (2005). *Treatment planning for person-centered care: The road to mental health and addiction recovery (practical resources for the mental health professional)*. Burlington, MA: Elsevier.

Adler, A. (1927). *Understanding human nature*. New York: Greenberg.

Adler, A. (1929). *The science of living*. New York: Greenberg.

Adler, A. (1931). *What life should mean to you*. Boston: Little, Brown.

Adler, A. (1935). What is neurosis? *International Journal of Individual Psychology, 1*, 9–17.

Adler, A. (1956). *The individual psychology of Alfred Adler* (H. Ansbacher & R. Ansbacher, Eds.). New York: Basic Books.

Adler, A. (1959). *The practice and theory of individual psychology*. Totowa, NJ: Littlefield, Adams. (Originally published in 1920)

Adler, A. (1964). *Social interest: A challenge to mankind*. New York: Capricorn. (Originally published in 1931)

Adler, K. (1972). Techniques that shorten psychotherapy: Illustrated with five cases. *Journal of Individual Psychotherapy, 28*, 155–168.

Ajzen, I. (1996). The social psychology of decision making. In E. T. Higgins & A. W. Kruglanski (Eds.), *Social psychology: Handbook of basic principles*. New York: Guilford.

Alighieri, D. (1805). *The Divine Comedy of Dante Alighieri* (H. F. Cary, Trans.). Retrieved September 30, 2008, from http://www.divinecomedy.org (Originally written in 1321)

Allport, G. (1960). *Personality and social encounter*. Boston: Beacon.

American Heritage Dictionary of the English Language. (2000). *4th ed*. New York: *Houghton Mifflin*.

American Psychiatric Association. (1994). *Diagnostic criteria from DSM-IV*. Washington, DC: Author.

American Psychiatric Association. (2000). *Diagnostic and statistical manual of mental disorders* (*DSM-IV-TM*; 4th ed., text rev.). Washington, DC: Author.

American Psychological Association. (1998). *Communicating the value of psychology to the public*. Washington, D.C.: American Psychological Association.

American Psychological Association. (2002). *Ethical principles of psychologists and code of conduct*. Washington DC: Author.

American Psychological Association. (2003). Guidelines on multicultural education, training, research, practice, and organizational change for psychologists. *American Psychologist*. 58, 377–402.

American Psychological Association, Division of Psychotherapy. (N.d.). [Home page]. Retrieved September 24, 2008, from http://www.cwru.edu/affil/div29/div29.htm

Anderson, C. M., & Stewart, S. (1983). *Mastering resistance: A practical guide to family therapy*. New York: Guilford.

Ansbacher, H. (1972). Adler's "Striving for Power," in relation to Nietzsche. *Journal of Individual Psychology, 28*, 12–24.

Ansbacher, H. (1992). Adler's concepts of community feeling and social interest and the relevance of community feeling for old age. *Individual Psychology, 48*, 402–412.

Arkowitz, H., & Hannah, M. T. (1989). Cognitive, behavioral and psychodynamic therapies: Converging or diverging pathways to change? In A. Freeman, K. M. Simon. L. E. Beutler, & H. Arkowitz (Eds.), *Comprehensive handbook of cognitive therapy*. New York: Plenum.

Arnold, M. (1960). *Emotions and personality* (Vols. 1 and 2). New York: Columbia University Press.

Asay, T. P., & Lambert, M. J. (1999). The empirical case for the common factors in therapy: Quantitative findings. In M. A. Hubble, B. L. Duncan, & S. D. Miller (Eds.), *The heart and soul of change: What works in therapy* (pp. 23–55). Washington, DC: American Psychological Association.

Ashby, J. S., LoCicero, K. A., & Kenny, M. C. (2003). The relationship of multidimensional perfectionism to psychological birth order. *Journal of Individual Psychology, 59*, 42–51.

As others see us: Dealing with people changes our minds. (2006, December 23). *The Economist*, pp. 9–10.

Auel, J. M. (1980). *Clan of the cave bear*. New York: Crown.

Augustine. (1909–1914). *Confessions* (E. B. Pusey, Trans.). New York: Collier. Retrieved September 30, 2008, from http://ccat.sas.upenn.edu/jod/Englishconfessions.html (Originally written in 397 CE)

Avni, A., & Lazar, R. (1998). Dynamic perspectives of paradoxical interventions. *Israel Journal of Psychiatry and Related Sciences, 35*, 38–47.

Bach, P., & Hayes, S. C. (2002). The use of acceptance and commitment therapy to prevent the rehospitalization of psychotic patients: A randomized controlled trial. *Journal of Consulting and Clinical Psychology, 70*(5), 1129–1139

Bachelor, A. (1988). How clients perceive therapist empathy: A content analysis of "received" empathy. *Psychotherapy: Theory, Research and Practice, 25*, 227–240.

Baekeland, F., & Lundwall, L. (1975). Dropping out of treatment: A critical review. *Psychological Bulletin, 82*, 738–783.

Baird, K. (2006). The ethical dilemmas involved in going from individual therapy to couples therapy (or the other way around) with the same client(s). *Illinois Psychologist: Newsletter of the Illinois Psychological Association, 43*, 11–30.

Bandler, R., & Grinder, J. (1975). *The structure of magic* (Vol. 1). Palo Alto, CA: Science and Behavior Books.

Bandler, R., & Grinder, J. (1976). *The structure of magic* (Vol. 2). Palo Alto, CA: Science and Behavior Books.

Bandler, R., & Grinder, J. (1982). *Reframing: Neurolinguistic programming and the transformation of meaning.* Moab, UT: Real People Press.

Bank, S. P., & Kahn, M. D. (1982). *The sibling bond.* New York: Basic Books.

Barber, J. P., Connolly, M. B., Crits-Christoph, P., Gladis, L., & Siqueland, L. (2000). Alliance predicts patients' outcomes beyond in-treatment change in symptoms. *Journal of Consulting and Clinical Psychology, 68*, 1027–1032.

Baron, R. M., & Kenny, D. A. (1986). The moderator-mediator variable distinction in social psychological research: Conceptual, strategic, and statistical considerations. *Journal of Personality and Social Psychology, 51*, 1173–1182.

Barry, J. (2006, October 9). "No one wanted to hear." *BusinessWeek*, pp. 91–92

Bartlett, F. A. (1932). *Remembering: A study in experimental psychology.* Cambridge: Cambridge University Press.

Beauchamp, T. L., & Childress, J. F. (1989). *Principles of biomedical ethics.* New York: Oxford University Press.

Beck, A. T. (1967). *Depression: Clinical, experimental, and theoretical aspects.* New York: Harper & Row.

Beck, A. T., Rush, A. J., Shaw, B. F., & Emery, G. (1979). *Cognitive therapy of depression.* New York: Guilford.

Beck, A. T., & Weishaar, M. (1989). Cognitive therapy. In A. Freeman, K. M. Simon, L. E. Beutler, & H. Arkowitz (Eds.), *Comprehensive handbook of cognitive therapy.* New York: Plenum.

Beck, A. T., & Weishaar, M. (2005). Cognitive therapy. In R. J. Corsini & D. Wedding (Eds.), *Current psychotherapies* (7th ed., instr. ed., pp. 238–268). Belmont, CA: Thomson Brooks/Cole.

Beier, E. (1966). *The silent language of psychotherapy: Social reinforcement of unconscious processes.* Chicago: Aldine.

Benjamin, L. S., & Karpiak, C. P. (2002). Personality disorders. In J. C. Norcross (Ed.), *Psychotherapy relationships that work: Therapist contributions and responsiveness to patients* (pp. 423–438). New York: Oxford University Press.

Bennis, W. G., & Thomas R. J. (2002, September). Crucibles of leadership. *Harvard Business Review*, pp. 39–45.

Benson, H. (1975). *The relaxation response.* New York: Morrow.

Benson, H. (1985). *Beyond the relaxation response.* New York: Berkley.

Benson, H. (2000). *The relaxation response: Updated and expanded* (25th anniversary ed.). New York: Avon.

Benson, H., & Proctor, W. (2003). *The breakout principle.* New York: Scribner.

Berg, I. K. (1994). *Family based services: A solution-focused approach.* New York: Norton.

Berg, I. K., Dolan, Y., & Trepper, T. (2007). *More than miracles: The state of the art of solution-focused brief therapy.* New York: Haworth.

Berg, I. K., & Szabo, P. (2005). *Brief coaching for lasting solutions.* New York: Norton.

Bergin, A. E. (1997). Neglect of the therapist and the human dimensions of change: A commentary. *Clinical Psychology: Science and Practice, 4*, 83–89.

Berman, E. M., & Lief, H. I. (1975). Marital therapy from a psychiatric perspective: An overview. *American Journal of Psychiatry, 132*, 583–592.

Berne, E. (1964). *Games people play.* New York: Grove.

Berne, E. (1973). *What do you say after you say hello? The psychology of human destiny.* New York: Bantam.

Bernstein, P. L. (1998). *Against the gods: The remarkable story of risk.* New York: John Wiley.

Beutler, L. E. (1983). The effects of value similarity and clients' persuadability on value convergence and psychotherapy improvement. *Journal of Social & Clinical Psychology, 1*(3), 231–245.

Beutler, L. E. (1989). Differential treatment selection: The role of diagnosis in psychotherapy. *Psychotherapy, 26*, 271–281.

Beutler, L. E. (2000). David and Goliath: When empirical and clinical standards of practice meet. *American Psychologist, 55*, 997–1007.

Beutler, L. E., & Arkowitz, H. (Eds.). (1989). *The comprehensive handbook of cognitive therapy.* New York: Plenum.

Beutler, L. E., & Harwood, M. T. (2000). *Prescriptive therapy: A practical guide to systematic treatment selection.* New York: Oxford University Press.

Beutler, L. E., Moleiro, C. M., & Talebi, H. (2002). Resistance. In J. C. Norcross (Ed.), *Psychotherapy relationships that work: Therapist contributions and responsiveness to patient needs.* New York: Oxford University Press.

Bien, T. (2004). Quantum change and psychotherapy. *Journal of Clinical Psychology/In Session, 60*, 493–501.

Bien, T., & Bien, B. (2002). *Mindful recovery*. New York: Wiley.

Binder, J. L. (2004). *Key competencies in brief dynamic psychotherapy: Clinical practice beyond the manual*. New York: Guilford.

Bitter, J. R. (2008). *Theory and practice of family therapy and counseling*. Pacific Grove, CA: Brooks/Cole.

Blatt, S. J., Shahar, G., & Zuroff, D. C. (2002). Anaclitic (sociotropic) and introjective (autonomous) dimensions. In J. C. Norcross (Ed.), *Psychotherapy relationships that work: Therapist contributions and responsiveness to patients* (pp. 315–334). New York: Oxford University Press.

Bleuler, E. (1950). *Dimentia Praecos: Or, The group of schizophrenias*. New York: International Universities Press.

Bohart, A. C., & Tallman, K. (1999). *How clients make therapy work: The process of active self-healing*. Washington, DC: American Psychological Association.

Bonime, W. (1962). *The clinical use of dreams*. New York: Basic Books.

Bordin, E. S. (1979). The generalizability of the psychoanalytic concept of the working alliance. *Psychotherapy: Theory, Research and Practice, 16*, 252–260.

Bordin, E. S. (1994). Theory and research on the therapeutic working alliance: New directions. In A. O. Horvath & L. S. Greenberg (Eds.), *The working alliance: Theory, research and practice*. New York: Wiley.

Bowlby, J. (1982). *Attachment* (2nd ed.). New York: Basic Books.

Brehm, J. W. (1966). *A theory of psychological reactance*. New York: Academic.

Brehm, S. S., & Brehm, J. W. (1981). *Psychological reactance: A theory of freedom and control*. New York: Academic Press.

Brink, N. E. (1982). Metaphor creation for use within family therapy. *American Journal of Clinical Hypnosis, 24*, 258–265.

Brogan, M. M., Prochaska, J. O., & Prochaska, J. M. (1999). Predicting termination and continuation status in psychotherapy using the transtheoretical model. *Psychotherapy: Theory, Research, Practice, Training, 36*, 105–113.

Brown, D. (2003). *The Da Vinci code*. New York: Doubleday.

Brown, J., Dreis, S., & Nace, D. K. (1999). What really makes a difference in psychotherapy outcome? Why does managed care want to know? In M. A. Hubble, B. L. Duncan, & S. D. Miller (Eds.), *The heart and soul of change: What works in therapy* (pp. 389–406). Washington, DC: American Psychological Association.

Bruhn, A. R. (1990). *Earliest childhood memories: Vol. 1. Theory and application to clinical practice*. New York: Praeger.

Bugental, J. F. T., & Bugental, E. K. (1984). A fate worse than death: The fear of changing. *Psychotherapy: Theory, Research, Practice, Training, 21*(4), 543–549.

Burke, B. L., Arkowitz, H., & Menchola, M. (2003). The efficacy of motivational interviewing: A meta-analysis of controlled clinical trials. *Journal of Consulting and Clinical Psychology, 71*, 843–861.

Buss, D. M. (1996). The evolutionary psychology of human social strategies. In E. T. Higgins & A. W. Kruglanski (Eds.), *Social psychology: Handbook of basic principles* (pp. 3–38). New York: Guilford.

Cahill, L., Uncapher, M., Kilpatrick, L., Alkire, M., & Turner, J. (2004). Sex-related hemispheric lateralization of amygdala function in emotionally-influenced memory: An fMRI investigation. *Learning and Memory, 11*, 261–266.

Cameron-Bandler, L. (1978). *They lived happily ever after: Methods for achieving happy endings in coupling*. Cupertino, CA: Meta Publications.

Campbell, R. J. (1970). *Psychiatric dictionary* (4th ed.). New York: Oxford University Press.

Cappas, N. M., Andres-Hyman, R., & Davidson, L. (2005). What psychotherapists can begin to learn from neuroscience: Seven principles of a brain-based psychotherapy. *Psychotherapy: Theory, Research, Practice, Training, 42*(3), 374–383.

Carkhuff, R. R. (2000). *The art of helping in the 21st century*. Amherst, MA: Human Resource Development Press.

Carlson, J., Watts, R. E., & Maniacci, M. (2006). *Adlerian therapy: Theory and practice*. Washington, DC: American Psychological Association.

Carr, A. (1998). Michael White's narrative therapy. *Contemporary Family Therapy: An International Journal, 20*(4), 485–503.

Carr, L., Iacoboni, M., Dubeau, M., Maziotta, J. C., & Lenzi, G. L. (2003). Neural mechanisms of empathy in humans. *Proceedings of the National Academy of Science, USA, 100*, 5497–5502.

Castonguay, L. G., Goldfried, M. R., Wiser, S. L., Raue, P. J., & Hayes, A. M. (1996). Empirically supported treatments: Implications for training. *Journal of Consulting and Clinical Psychology, 64*, 497–504.

Centorrino, F., Hernan, M. A., Drago-Ferrante, G., Rendall, M., Apicella, A., Langar, G., et al. (2001). Factors associated with noncompliance with psychiatric outpatient visits. *Psychiatric Services, 52*(3), 378–380.

Chamberlain, P., Patterson, G. R.; Reid, J. B., Kavanaugh, K., & Forgatch, M. S. (1984). Observation of client resistance. *Behavior Therapy, 15*, 144–155.

Cheek, D. B., & Le Cron, L. M. (1968). *Clinical hypnotherapy*. New York: Grune & Stratton.

Cherniss, C. (1995). *Beyond burnout: Helping teachers, nurses, therapists and lawyers recover from stress and disillusionment.* New York: Routledge.

Clark, A. J. (1999). Safeguarding tendencies: A clarifying perspective. *Journal of Individual Psychology, 55*(1), 72–81.

Clark, A. J. (2002). *Early recollections: Theory & practice in counseling and psychotherapy.* New York: Brunner-Routledge.

Clay, R. (1997). Researchers harness the power of humor. *APA Monitor, 28,* 1–18.

Clinton, W. J. (2004, September/October). The secret keeper. *AARP: The Magazine,* pp. 76–80.

Coale, H. W. (1998). *The vulnerable therapist: Practicing psychotherapy in an age of anxiety.* New York: Haworth.

Cohen, S. (1988). Psychosocial models of the role of social support in the etiology of physical disease. *Health Psychology, 7,* 269–297.

Cohen, S., & Herbert, T. B. (1996). Health psychology: Psychological factors and physical disease from the perspective of human psychoneuroimmunology. *Annual Review of Psychology, 47,* 113–142.

Collins, W. E., Schroeder, D. J., & Nye, L. G. (1989). *Relationships of anxiety scores to academy and field training performance of air traffic control specialists* (FAA Office of Aviation Medicine Reports). Washington, DC: Office of Aviation Medicine.

Corey, G. (2001). *Theory and practice of counseling and psychotherapy* (6th ed.). Pacific Grove, CA: Brooks/Cole.

Corey, G. (2005). *Theory and practice of counseling and psychotherapy* (7th ed.). Pacific Grove, CA: Brooks/Cole.

Cozolino, L. J. (2002). *The neuroscience of psychotherapy: Rebuilding the human brain.* New York: Norton.

Crits-Christoph, P., Baranackie, K., Kurcias, J. S., Beck, A. T., Carroll, K., Perry, K., et al. (1991). Meta-analysis of therapist effects in psychotherapy outcome studies. *Psychotherapy Research, 2,* 81–91.

Crits-Christoph, P., & Gibbons, M. C. (2002). Relational interpretations. In J. C. Norcross, (Ed.) *Psychotherapy relationships that work: Therapist contributions and responsiveness to patients.* (pp. 285–300). New York, NY, US: Oxford University Press.

Crommpton, P. (1998). *T'ai chi for two: The practice of push hands.* Boston: Shambhala.

Cuber, J. F., & Harroff, P. B. (1996). *Sex and the significant Americans.* Baltimore: Penguin.

Cummings, N. (1986). The dismantling of our health system: Strategies for the survival of psychological practice. *American Psychologist, 41,* 426–431.

Damasio, A. (1994). *Descartes' error: Emotion, reason, and the human brain.* New York: Penguin.

Damasio, A. (1999). *The feeling of what happens: Body and emotions in the making of consciousness.* New York: Harvest Book, Harcourt.

Danaghy, K. (2003). Keynote review: Core tasks of psychotherapy: What "expert" therapists do. *Milton Erickson Foundation Newsletter, 23,* 14–15.

Davidson, G. N. S., & Horvath, A. O. (1997). Three sessions of brief couples therapy: A clinical trial. *Journal of Family Psychology, 11*(4), 422–435.

Davidson, R. J. (2001). Toward a biology of personality and emotion. *Annals of the New York Academy of Sciences, 935,* 191–207.

Davidson, R. J., Kabat-Zinn, J., Schumacher, J., Rosenkranz, J., Muller, D., Santorelli, S., et al. (2003). Alterations in brain and immune function produced by mindfulness meditation. *Psychosomatic Medicine, 65,* 564–570

Davis, N. J. (1999). *Resilience: Status of the research-based programs.* Working Paper. Rockville, MD: Center for Mental Health Services

Deane, F. (1991). Attendance and drop-out from outpatient psychotherapy in New Zealand. *Community Mental Health in New Zealand, 6,* 34–51.

de Bono, E. (1994). *De Bono's thinking course.* New York: Facts on File.

Delphin, M. E., & Rowe, M. (2008). Continuing education in cultural competence for community mental health practitioners. *Professional Psychology: Research and Practice, 39,* 182–191.

Dennis, M., Godley, S., Diamond, G., Tims, F., Babor, T., Donaldson, J., et al. (2004). The cannabis youth treatment (CYT) study: Main findings from two randomized trials. *Journal of Substance Abuse Treatment, 27,* 97– 213.

De Shazer, S. (1985a). *Clues: Investigating solutions in brief therapy.* New York: Norton.

De Shazer, S. (1985b). *Keys to solutions in brief therapy.* New York: Norton.

De Shazer, S. (1991). *Putting differences to work.* New York: Norton.

De Shazer, S., Dolan, Y. M., & Korman, H. (2007). *More than miracles: The state of the art of solution-focused brief therapy.* New York: Haworth.

DiAngelis, T. (2008). When do meds make the difference? *Monitor on Psychology, 39,* 48–51.

DiClemente, C. C. (2005). Conceptual models and applied research: The ongoing contribution of the transtheoretical model. *Journal of Addictions Nursing, 16,* 5–12.

DiClemente, C. C., & Hughes, S. O. (1990). Stages of change profiles in outpatient alcoholism treatment. *Journal of Substance Abuse, 2,* 217–235.

DiClemente, C. C., & Velasquez, M. M. (2002). Motivational interviewing and the stages of change. In W. R. Miller & S. Rollnick (Eds.), *Motivational interviewing: Preparing people for change* (2nd ed.). New York: Guilford.

Dingfelder, S. F. (2005). Closing the gap for Latino patients. *APA Monitor on Psychology, 36,* 58–61.

Dobbs, D. (2006, February/March). Mastery of emotions. *Scientific American Mind,* p. 49.

Doctors Without Borders. (N.d.). *About us.* Retrieved September 19, 2008, from http://www.doctorswithoutborders.org/aboutus/index.cfm

Dodd, J. (1971). A retrospective analysis of variables related to duration of treatment in a university psychiatric clinic. *Journal of Nervous and Mental Disease, 151,* 75–85.

Doidge, N. (2007). *The brain that changes itself: Stories of personal triumph from the frontiers of brain science.* New York: Viking.

Dollard, J., & Miller, N. E. (1950). *Personality and psychotherapy: An analysis in terms of learning, thinking, and culture.* New York: McGraw-Hill.

Donahue, C. P., Kosik, K. S., & Shors, T. J. (2006). Growth hormone is produced in the hippocampus where it responds to age, sex and stress. *PNAS, 103,* 6031–6036.

Donato, M. (2006, March). The joy of aging. *Conscious Choice,* pp. 30–33.

Doyle, A. C. (1892/1986). *Sherlock Holmes: The complete novels and stories.* New York: Bantam.

Dreikurs, R. (1973). Private logic. In H. Mosak (Ed.), *Alfred Adler: His influences on psychology today* (pp. 19–32). Park Ridge, NJ: Noyes.

Dreikurs, R., Grunwald, B. B., & Pepper, F. C. (1982). *Maintaining sanity in the classroom.* New York: Harper & Row.

Duncan, B. L., Hubble, M. A., & Miller, S. D. (2000). *The heroic client.* San Francisco: Jossey-Bass.

Duncan, B. L., Miller, S. D., & Sparks, J. A. (2004). *The heroic client: A revolutionary way to improve effectiveness through client-directed, outcome-informed therapy* (rev. ed.). San Francisco: Jossey-Bass.

Eagly, A. H. (1995). The science and politics of comparing women and men. *American Psychologist, 50,* 145–158.

Eckstein, D. (1997). Reframing as a specific interpretive counseling technique. *Individual Psychology, 53,* 418–428.

Edelstein, M. R., & Steele, D. R. (1997). *Three minute therapy: Change your thinking, change your life.* Aurora, CO: Glenbridge.

Egan, G. (2002). *The skilled helper: A systematic approach to effective helping* (7th ed.). Pacific Grove, CA: Brooks/Cole.

Eichenbaum, H. (2001). The long and winding road to memory consolidation. *Nature Neuroscience, 4,* 1057–1058.

Eklund, K. & Johnson, W. B. (2008). Toward cultural competence in child Intake Assessments. *Professional Psychology: Research and Practice, 38,* 356–362.

Ekman, P. (1992). Facial expressions of emotions: New findings, new questions. *Psychological Science, 3,* 34–38.

Ekman, P. (1995). *Telling lies: Clues to deceit in the marketplace, politics, and marriage.* New York: Norton.

Ekman, P. & Friesen, W. V. (1975). *Unmasking the face: A guide to recognizing emotions from facial clues.* Oxford, England: Prentice-Hall.

Ekman, P., Levenson, R. W., & Friesen, W. V. (1983). Autonomic nervous system activity distinguishes among emotions. *Science, 221,* 1208–1210.

Elbaum, P. (2000, August). Personal communication.

Ellis, A. (1955). *New approaches to psychotherapy techniques* (Journal of Clinical Psychology Monograph Supplement, Vol. 2). Brandon, VT: Journal of Clinical Psychology.

Ellis, A. (1962). *Reason and emotion in psychotherapy.* New York: Lyle Stuart.

Ellis, A. (1989). The history of cognition in psychotherapy. In A. Freeman, K. M. Simon, A. S. Elstein, L. S. Shulman, & S. A. Spraafka (Eds.), *Medical problem solving.* Cambridge, MA: Harvard University Press.

Ellis, A., & Dryden, W. (1987). *The practice of rational-emotive therapy.* New York: Springer.

Emerick, J. J. (1997). *Be the person you want to be: Harness the power of neuro-linguistic programming to reach your potential.* Rocklin, CA: Prima.

Eraker, S. A., & Politser, P. (1982). How decisions are reached: Physician and patient. *Annals of Internal Medicine, 97,* 262–268.

Erickson, M. (1959). Further clinical techniques of hypnosis: Utilization techniques. *American Journal of Clinical Hypnosis, 2,* 3–21.

Erickson, M. (1977). Hypnotic approaches to therapy. *American Journal of Clinical Hypnosis, 20,* 20–35.

Erickson, M., & Rossi, E. (1976). *Hypnotic realities: The induction of clinical hypnosis and forms of indirect suggestion.* New York: John Wiley.

Erickson, M., & Rossi, E. (1980). *Hypnotherapy: An exploratory casebook.* New York: Irvington.

Erickson, M., Rossi, E., & Rossi, S. (1976). *Hypnotic realities: The induction of clinical hypnosis and forms of indirect suggestion.* New York: Irvington.

Erikson, M. H. (1980). *The Nature of Hypnosis and Suggestion* (Collected Papers of Milton H. Erickson, Vol 1). New York, NY: Irvington Publishers.

Erwin, C., & McVittie, J. (2005, June 16). Why Adler was right: How new brain science supports Adler's theories of family education and family therapy. Paper presented at the North American Society of Adlerian Psychology 53rd Annual Conference, Tucson, AZ.

Facione, N. C., & Facione, P. A. (1996). Externalizing the critical thinking in clinical judgment. *Nursing Outlook, 44,* 129–136.

Facione, P. (Proj. Dir.). (1990). *Critical thinking: A statement of expert consensus for purposes of educational assessment and instruction. The Delphi Report: Research findings and recommendations prepared for the American Philosophical Association* (ERIC Doc. No. ED315-423). Retrieved September 30, 2008, from http://www.insightassessment.com/pdf_files/DEXadobe.PDF

Farber, B. A. (2003). Self-disclosure in psychotherapy practice and supervision: an introduction. *Journal of Clinical Psychology, 59,* 525–528.

Farber, M. A., Berano, K. C., & Capobianco, J. A. (2004). Clients' perceptions of the process and consequences of self-disclosure in psychotherapy. *Journal of Counseling Psychology, 61,* 340–346.

Farrelly, F., & Brandsma, J. (1974). *Provocative therapy.* Cupertino, CA: Meta Publications.

Feynman, R. P. (1988). *"What do you care what other people think?" Further adventures of a curious character.* New York: Norton.

Fiedler, F. E. (1950). A comparison of therapeutic relationships in psychoanalytic, non-directive and Adlerian therapy. *Journal of Consulting Psychology, 14,* 436–445.

Firestone, R. (1990). Prescription for psychotherapy. *Psychotherapy, 27,* 627–635.

Fisch, R., Weakland, J. H., & Segal, L. (1982). *The tactics of change: Doing therapy briefly.* San Francisco: Jossey-Bass.

Fish, J. M. (1973). *Placebo therapy.* San Francisco: Jossey-Bass.

Fisher, L., Anderson, A., & Jones, J. (1981). Types of paradoxical intervention and indications/contraindications for use in clinical practice. *Family Process, 20,* 26–35.

Flakas, C. (1992). A reframe by any other name: On the process of reframing in strategic, Milan, and analytic therapy. *Journal of Family Therapy, 14,* 145–161.

Flemons, D. (2003). The psychology of the sand-pit: Clinical lessons from Winnie the-Pooh. *Psychotherapy Networker, 21,* 32–37.

Four walls treatment. (1972, October 2). *Time,* p. 101.

Frank, J. D. (1961). *Persuasion and healing.* Baltimore: Johns Hopkins.

Frank, J. D., & Frank, J. B. (1991). *Persuasion and healing: A comparative study of psychotherapy* (3rd ed.). Baltimore: Johns Hopkins University Press.

Frankl, V. (1963). *Man's search for meaning.* New York: Washington Square Press, Simon & Schuster.

Fraser, J. S., & Solovey, A. D. (2007). *Second-order change in psychotherapy: The golden thread that unifies effective treatments.* Washington, DC: American Psychological Association.

Freedman, J., & Combs, G. (1996). *Narrative therapy: The social construction of preferred realities.* New York: Norton.

Freedman, J. H. & Combs, G. (2002). Narrative couple therapy. In Gurman, A. S.; Jacobson, N. S. (Eds). *Clinical handbook of couple therapy (3rd ed.).* (pp. 308–334). New York, NY, US: Guilford Press.

Freud, S. (1943). *A general introduction to psychoanalysis* (rev. ed., J. Riviere, Trans.). New York: Garden City. (Originally published in 1917)

Freud, S. (1924–1950). *Collected papers* (Vols. 1–4). London: Hogarth.

Frija, N. H. (1986). *The emotions.* Cambridge: Cambridge University Press.

Fry, W., & Salameh, W. (1987). *Handbook of humor and psychotherapy.* Sarasota, FL: Professional Resource Exchange.

Fuchs, E., & Flügge, G. (2003). Chronic social stress: Effects on limbic brain structures. *Physiology and Behavior, 79,* 417–427.

Furtmüeller, C. (1964). Alfred Adler: A biographical essay. In , H. L. Ansbacher & R. R. Ansbacher, Eds. *Superiority and social interest: Alfred Adler, a collection of later writings* (3rd rev. ed.). New York: Viking.

Gabbard, G. O. (Ed.). (2000). *Treatments of psychiatric disorders* (Vols 1–2, 3rd ed.). Washington, DC: American Psychiatric Publishing.

Galin, D. (1974). Implications for psychiatry of left and right cerebral specialization. *Archives of General Psychiatry, 31,* 572–583.

Garfield, S. (1994). Research on client variables in psychotherapy. In A. Bergin & S. Garfield (Eds.), *Handbook of psychotherapy and behavior change* (4th ed., pp. 190–228). New York: Wiley.

Garry, M., & Polaschek, D. (2000). Imagination and memory. *Current Directions in Psychological Science, 9*(1), 6–10.

Gazzaniga, H. S. (1972). One brain—two minds. *American Scientist, 60,* 311–317.

Gelso, C. J., & Carter, J. A. (1985). The relationship in counseling and psychotherapy: Components, consequences, and theoretical antecedents. *The Counseling Psychologist, 13,* 155–243.

Gelso, C. J., & Carter, J. A. (1994). Components of the psychotherapy relationship: Their interaction and unfolding during treatment. *Journal of Counseling Psychology, 41*, 296–306.

Gelso, C. J., & Hayes, J. A. (1998). *The psychotherapy relationship: Theory, research, and practice.* New York: Wiley.

Gelso, C. J., Hayes, J. A. (2002). The management of countertransference. In J. C. Norcross (Ed.). *Psychotherapy relationships that work: Therapist contributions and responsiveness to patients.* (pp. 267–283). New York, NY, US: Oxford University Press.

Gendlin, E. (1978). *Focusing.* New York: Everest House.

Gendlin, E. (1996). *Focusing oriented psychotherapy: A manual of the experiential method.* New York: Guilford.

Ghadban, R. (1995). Paradoxical intention. In Mary Ballow (Ed.) *Psychological interventions: A guide to strategies.* Westport, CT: Praeger.

Gibson, L. (2006, April). Mirrored emotion. *University of Chicago Magazine,* pp. 34–39.

Gill, R. E. (2005, September/October). Evidence based psychology gets APA Council approval. *The National Psychologist, 14*, 4.

Gilbert, P. (2002). Evolutionary approaches to psychopathology and cognitive therapy. *Journal of Cognitive Psychotherapy. Special issue on evolution theory and cognitive therapy, 16*(3), 263–294.

Gladwell, M. (2005). *Blink: The power of thinking without thinking.* New York: Little Brown.

Gleser, J., & Brown, P. (1988). Judo principles and practices: Applications to conflict-solving strategies in psychotherapy. *American Journal of Psychotherapy, 42*, 437–447.

Goldberg, C. (1977). *Therapeutic partnership: Ethical concerns in psychotherapy.* New York: Springer.

Goldberg, E. (2001). *The executive brain: Frontal lobes and the civilized mind.* Oxford: Oxford University Press.

Goldfried, M. R. (1989). Foreword. In A. Freeman, K. M. Simon, L. E. Beutler, & H. Arkowitz (Eds.), *Comprehensive handbook of cognitive therapy.* New York: Plenum.

Goldfried, M. R. & Davidson, G. C. (1976). *Clinical Behavior Therapy.* New York, NY: Thomson Learning.

Goldman, A. (1988). *The lives of John Lennon.* Chicago: Bantam.

Goldstein, J. (1973). Rapid elimination of bizarre and delusional behavior. *Psychotherapy: Theory, Research and Practice, 10*, 159–162.

Goleman, D. (1986). *Vital lies, simple truths: The psychology of self-deception.* New York: Simon & Schuster.

Goleman, D. (1992, October 6). Holocaust survivors had skills to proper. *New York Times,* Sec. C, p. 1.

Goleman, D. (1995). *Emotional intelligence: Why it can matter more than IQ.* New York: Bantam.

Goleman, D. (2006). *Social intelligence: The new science of human relations.* New York: Bantam.

Gonsalves, B., & Paller, K. A. (2000). Neural events that underlie remembering something that never happened. *Nature Neuroscience, 3*, 1316–1321.

Gortner, E. T., Gollan, J. K., Dobson, K. S., & Jacobson, N. S. (1998). Cognitive-behavioral treatment for depression: Relapse prevention. *Journal of Consulting and Clinical Psychology, 66*(2), 377–384

Gottman, J. (1974). *How to do psychotherapy and how to evaluate it.* New York: Holt, Rinehart and Winston.

Gottman, J. (1993). *What predicts divorce: The relationship between marital processes and marital outcomes.* Hillsdale, NJ: Erlbaum.

Gottman, J. M. (1995). *Why marriages succeed or fail: And how you can make yours last.* New York: Fireside.

Gottman, J. M., & DeClair, J. (1997). *The heart of parenting: How to raise an emotionally intelligent child.* New York: Simon & Schuster.

Gottman, J. M., & Silver, N. (1999). *The seven principles for making marriage work.* New York: Three Rivers.

Greenberg, L. S. (2004). *Emotion-focused therapy: Coaching clients to work through their feelings.* Washington, DC: American Psychological Association.

Greenberg, L. S., & Paivio, S. C. (1997). *Working with the emotions in psychotherapy.* New York: Guilford.

Greene, D. G., Nystrom, L. E., Engell, A. D., Darley, J. B., & Cohen, J. D. (2004). The neural basis of cognitive conflict and control in moral judgment. *Neuron, 44*, 389–400.

Greenwald, H. (1973). *Decision therapy.* New York: Wyden.

Gross, J. J. (1999). Emotion and emotion regulation. In L. A. Pervin & O. P. John (Eds.), *Handbook of personality theory and research* (pp. 525–552). New York: Guilford.

Gula, R. J. (2002). *Non-sense: A handbook of logical fallacies.* Mount Jackson, VA: Axios.

Hale, A. S. (1997). ABC of mental health: Depression. *British Medical Journal, 315*, 43–46.

Haley, J. (1963). *Strategies of psychotherapy.* New York: Grune and Stratton.

Haley, J. (1973). *Uncommon therapy: The psychiatric techniques of Milton H. Erickson, M.D.* New York: Norton.

Haley, J. (1984). *Ordeal therapy.* San Francisco: Jossey-Bass.

Haley, J. (1993). *Jay Haley on Milton Erickson.* New York: Brunner/Mazel.

Haley, J. (1996). *Learning and teaching therapy.* New York: Guilford.

Halford, W. K., Bernoth-Doolan, S., & Eadie, K. (2002). Schemata as moderators of clinical effectiveness of a comprehensive cognitive behavioral program for patients with depression or anxiety disorders. *Behavior Modification*, 26(5), 571–593.

Hammond, D. C. (1984). Myths about Erickson and Ericksonian hypnosis. *American Journal of Clinical Hypnosis*, 26, 236–245.

Hampton, B. R., & Hulgus Y. F. (1993). The efficacy of paradoxical strategies: A quantitative review of the research. *Psychotherapy in Private Practice*, 12(22), 53–71.

Hanna, F. (2001). *Therapy with difficult clients: Using the precursors model to awaken change.* Washington, DC: American Psychological Association.

Hanna, F. J. (1996). Precursors of change: Pivotal points of involvement and resistance in psychotherapy. *Journal of Psychotherapy Integration*, 6, 227–264.

Hanna, F. J., & Puhakka, K. (1991). When psychotherapy works: Pinpointing an element of change. *Psychotherapy*, 28, 598–607.

Hanna, F. J., & Ritchie, M. H. (1995). Seeking the active ingredients of psychotherapeutic change: Within and outside the context of therapy. *Professional Psychology: Research & Practice*, 26, 176–183.

Hansen, J. (2002). Postmodern implications for theoretical integration of counseling approaches. *Journal of Counseling and Development*, 80, 315–321.

Hansen, J. R. (2005). *First man: The life of Neil A. Armstrong.* New York: Simon & Schuster.

Hayes, J. A., McCracken, J. E., McClanahan, M. K., Hill, C. E., Harp, J. S., & Carozzoni, P (1998). Therapist perspectives on countertransference: Qualitative data in search of a theory. *Journal of Counseling Psychology*, 45(4), pp. 468–482.

Hayes, S. C., Strosahl, K. D., & Wilson, K. G. (1999). *Acceptance and commitment therapy: An experiential approach to behavior change.* New York: Guilford.

Henry, W. P. (1998). Science, politics, and the politics of science: The use and misuse of empirically validated treatment research. *Psychotherapy Research*, 8, 126–140.

Henry, W. P., Strupp, H. H., Butler, S. F., Schacht, T. E., & Binder, J. L. (1993). Effects of training in time-limited dynamic psychotherapy: Changes in therapist behavior. *Journal of Consulting and Clinical Psychology*, 61, 434–440.

Hergenhahn, B. R. (2008). An Introduction to the History of Psychology (6th Ed.). Boston, MA: Wadsworth Publishing.

Hill, C. E., & O'Brien, K. M. (1999). *Helping skills: Facilitating exploration, insight, and action.* Washington, DC: American Psychological Association.

Hill, G. R. (2004, April 13). Emotion-focused therapy and the treatment of trauma. Workshop sponsored by the Academy of Treatment Addictions Professionals, Springfield, IL.

Hill, K. A. (1987). Meta-analysis of paradoxical interventions. *Psychotherapy*, 24, 266–270.

Hinsie, L. E., & Campbell, R. J. (1970). *Psychiatric dictionary* (4th ed.). New York: Oxford University Press.

Hirstein, W., Iversen, P., & Ramachandran, V. S. (2001). Autonomic responses of autistic children to people and objects. *Proceedings of the Royal Society of London*, 268, 1883–1888.

Hobson, J. A., & Leonard, J. A. (2001). *Out of its mind: Psychiatry in crisis: A call for reform.* Boulder, CO: Perseus.

Hollon, S. G., Stewart, M. O., & Strunk, D. (2006). Enduring effects for cognitive and behavior therapy in the treatment of depression and anxiety. *Annual Review of Psychology*, 57, 285–315.

Holmes, T. H., & Rahe R. H. (1967). The social readjustment rating scale. *Journal of Psychosomatic Research*, 11(2), 213–218.

Homer. (1958). *The odyssey: The story of Ulysses* (W. H. D. Rouse, Trans.). New York: Mentor.

Hoorwitz, A. N. (1989). *Hypnotic methods in nonhypnotic therapies.* New York: Irvington.

Horney, K. (1945). *Our inner conflicts.* New York: Grune & Stratton.

Horney, K. (1950). *Neurosis and human growth: The struggle toward self-realization.* New York: Norton.

Horowitz, M. (1983). Psychological response of serious life events. In S. Breznitz (Ed.), *The denial of stress.* New York: International University Press.

Horvath, A. O. (2001). The alliance. *Psychotherapy: Theory, Research, Practice, Training*, 38, 365–372.

Horvath, A. O. (2006). The alliance in context: Accomplishments, challenges, and future directions. *Psychotherapy: Theory, Research, Practice, Training*, 43, 258–263.

Horvath, A. O., & Bedi, R. P. (2002). The alliance. In J. C. Norcross (Ed.), *Psychotherapy relationships that work: Therapist contributions and responsiveness to patient needs.* New York: Oxford University Press.

Horvath, A. O., & Goheen, M. D. (1990). Factors mediating the success of defiance and compliance based interventions. *Journal of Counseling Psychology*, 37, 363–371.

e, J., Landis, K. R., & Umberson, D. (1988). Social relationships and health. *Science*, 241, 540–545.

Howard, K. I., Kopta, S. M., Krause, M. S., & Orlinsky, D. E. (1986). The dose-effect relationship in psychotherapy. *American Psychologist, 41*, 159–164.

Howe, D. (1993–2004). *The free online dictionary*. Retrieved October 2, 2008, from http://www.thefreedictionary.com

Hoyt, M. F. (2002). Solution-focused couple therapy. In A. S. Gurman & N. S. Jacobson (Eds.), *Clinical handbook of couple therapy* (3rd ed., pp. 335–369). New York: Guilford.

Hoyt, M. F. & Berg, I. K. (1998). Solution-focused couple therapy: Helping clients construct self-fulfilling realities. In M. F. Hoyt (Ed.). *The handbook of constructive therapies: Innovative approaches from leading practitioners*. (pp. 314–340). San Francisco, CA, US: Jossey-Bass.

Hubble, M. A., Duncan, B. L., & Miller, S. D. (1999). Introduction. In Hubble, Mark A., Duncan, Barry L., Miller, Scott D. (Eds.). *The heart and soul of change: What works in therapy*. (pp. 1–32). Washington, DC: American Psychological Association.

Hughes, P., & Brecht, G. (1978). *Vicious circles and infinity*. New York: Penguin.

Hull, C. L. (1943). *Principles of Behavior: An introduction to Behavior Therapy*. New York: D. Appleton-Century.

Hull, C. L. (1951). *Essentials of Behavior*. Princeton, NJ: Yale.

Hunsley, J. (2007a). Addressing key challenges in evidence-based practice in psychology. *Professional Psychology: Research and Practice, 38*, 113–121.

Hunsley, J. (2007b). Training psychologists for evidence-based practice. *Canadian Journal of Psychology, 1*, 32–42.

The invisible scars. (2006, November 25). *The Economist*, pp. 41–42.

I think, therefore I am, I think: Consciousness awaits its Einstein. (2007, December 23). *The Economist*, pp. 11–12.

Izard, C. (1977). *Human emotions*. New York: Plenum.

Izard, C. (1979). *Emotions in personality and psychopathology*. New York: Plenum.

Jackson, D. D. (1959). Family interaction, family homeostasis, and some implications for conjoint family psychotherapy. In J. H. Masserman (Ed.), *Individual and familial dynamics* (pp. 122–141). New York: Grune & Stratton.

Jackson, P. L., Brunet, E., Meltzoff, A. N., & Decety, J. (2006). Empathy examined through the neural mechanisms involved in imagining how I feel versus how you feel pain. *Neuropsychologia, 44*, 752–761.

Jackson, P. L., Meltzoff, A. N., & Decety, J. (2005). How do we perceive the pain of others: A window into the neural processes involved in empathy. *NeuroImage, 24*, 771–779.

Jennings, L., & Skovholt, T. M. (1999). The cognitive, emotional, and relational characteristics of master therapists. *Journal of Counseling Psychology, 46*(1), 3–11.

Johnson, L. D. (1995). *Psychotherapy in the age of accountability*. New York: Norton.

Johnson, S., & Greenberg, L. S. (1985). Differential effects of experiential and problem solving interventions in resolving marital conflict. *Journal of Consulting and Clinical Psychology, 53*, 175–184.

Johnson, S. M., & Alevizos, P. (1975). *Strategic therapy: A systematic outline of procedures*. Unpublished manuscript, portions of which were presented at the ninth annual conference of the Association for the Advancement of Behavior Therapy, San Francisco.

Josselson, R. (2000). Stability and change in early memories over 22 years: Themes, variations, and cadenzas. *Bulletin of the Menninger Clinic, 64*, 462–481.

Jung, C. G. (1952). *Symbols of transformation*. New York: Bolingen Foundation.

Kagan, J. (1994). *Galen's prophecy*. New York: Basic Books.

Kahler, C. W., Read, J. P., Stuart, G. L., Ramsey, S. E., McCrady, B. S., & Brown, R. A. (2004). Motivational enhancement for 12-step involvement among patients undergoing alcohol detoxification. *Journal of Consulting and Clinical Psychology, 72*, 736–741.

Kahneman, D., & Tversky, A. (1984). Choices, values and frames. *American Psychologist, 39*, 341–350.

Kahneman, D., & Tversky, A. (1996). On the reality of cognitive illusions. *Psychological Review, 103*, 582–591.

Kandel, E. R. (1999). Biology and the future of psychoanalysis: A new intellectual framework for psychiatry revisited. *American Journal of Psychiatry, 156*(4), 505–524.

Kandel, E. R., Schwartz, J. H., & Jessell, T. M. (2000). *Principles of neural science*. New York: McGraw-Hill.

Kaptchuk, T. J., Kelley, J. M., Conboy, L. A., Davis, R. B., Kerr, C. E., Jacobson, E. E., et al. (2008). Components of placebo effect: Randomized controlled trial in patients with irritable bowel syndrome. *British Medical Journal, 336*, 999–1003.

Katakis, C. D. (1989). Stages of psychotherapy: Progressive reconceptualizations as self organizing process. *Psychotherapy, 26*, 484–493.

Katz, N. (2007, March 15). His brain, her brain. Workshop sponsored by the Institute for Natural Resources, Oak Brook, IL.

Kay C. (2000). *A survivor's perspective: Understanding therapy exploitation: Resources to help you through your recovery from exploitation and negligence by your therapist*. Retrieved September 19, 2008, from http://www.advocateweb.org/hope/bibliographykc/selfdisclosure.asp

Kazdin, A. E. (1986). Comparative outcome studies of psychotherapy: Methodological issues and strategies. *Journal of Consulting and Clinical Psychology*, *54*, 95–105.

Kazdin, A. E. (2008). Evidence-based treatment and practice: New opportunities to bridge clinical research and practice, enhance the knowledge base, and improve patient care. *American Psychologist*, *63*, 146–159.

Kellogg, S. H., & Young, J. E. (2006). Schema therapy for borderline personality disorder. *Journal of Clinical Psychology*, *62*(4), 445–458.

Kelly, G. (1955). *The psychology of personal constructs* (Vols. 1–2). New York: Norton.

Kiecolt-Glaser, J. K., Bane, C., Glaser, R., & Malarkey, W. B. (2003). Love, marriage, and divorce: Newlyweds' stress hormones foreshadow relationship changes. *Journal of Consulting & Clinical Psychology*, *71*(1), 176–188.

Kirmayer, L. J. (1990). Resistance, reactance, and reluctance to change: A cognitive attributional approach to strategic interventions. *Journal of Cognitive Psychotherapy: International Quarterly*, *4*, 83–103.

Kirsch, I. (1990). *Changing expectations: A key to effective psychotherapy*. Pacific Grove, CA: Brooks/Cole.

Kirsch, I., & Lynn, S. J. (1999). Automaticity in clinical psychology. *American Psychologist*, *54*, 504–515.

Kirsch, I., & Sapirstein, G. (1999). Listening to Prozac but hearing placebo: A meta-analysis of antidepressant medication. In I. Kirsch (Ed.), *How expectancies shape experience* (pp. 303–320). Washington, DC: American Psychological Association.

Kiser, D. J., Piercy, F. P., & Lipchik, E. (1993). The integration of emotions in solution-focused therapy. *Journal of Marital and Family Therapy*, *19*, 233–42.

Kleinmuntz, B. (1984). The scientific study of clinical judgment in psychology and medicine. *Clinical Psychology Review*, *4*, 111–126.

Kluger, J. (2006, July 2). *The science of siblings*. Retrieved September 19, 2008, from http://www.time.com/time/magazine/article/0,9171,1209949,00.html

Koizumi, G. (1960). *My study of judo: The principles and the technical fundamentals*. New York: Cornerstone Library.

Koocher, G. (1998). *The science and politics of recovered memories: A special issue of* Ethics and Behavior. New York: Erlbaum.

Kopp, R. (1995). *Metaphor therapy: Using client-generated metaphors in psychotherapy*. New York: Brunner-Routledge.

Kottler, J. A. (1993). *On being a therapist*. San Francisco: Jossey-Bass Social and Behavioral Science Series.

Kotulak, R. (2006, April 30). Gender and the brain. *Chicago Tribune*, pp. 1–10.

Krauss, H. H. (2006). Protoscientific master metaphor for framing violence. *Annals of New York Academy of Sciences*, *1087*, 4–21.

Kroger, W. S., & Fezler, W. D. (1976). *Hypnosis and behavior modification: Imagery conditioning*. Philadelphia: Lippincott.

Kübler-Ross, E. (1969). *On death and dying*. New York: Macmillan.

Kübler-Ross, E. (1975). *Death: The final stage of growth*. New York: Macmillan.

Kübler-Ross, E. (1981). *Living with death and dying*. New York: Macmillan.

Laforge, R. G., Rossi, J. S., Prochaska, J. O., Velicer, W. F., Levesque, D. A., & McHorney, C. A. (1999). Stage of regular exercise and health-related quality of life. *Preventive Medicine*, *28*, 349–360.

Lambert, M. (2004). The effectiveness of psychotherapy. In M. J. Lambert (Ed.), *Handbook of psychotherapy and behavior change* (5th ed.). New York: Wiley.

Lambert, M. (2005). Enhancing psychotherapy through feedback to clinicians. *The Register Report*, *31*, 15–19.

Lambert, M. J. (1992). Psychotherapy outcome research: Implications for integrative and eclectic therapists. In J. C. Norcross & M. R. Goldfried (Eds.), *Handbook of psychotherapy integration* (pp. 9–129). New York: Basic Books.

Lambert, M. J., & Barley, D. E. (2002). Research summary on the therapeutic relationship and psychotherapy outcomes. In J. C. Norcross (Ed.), *Psychotherapy relationships that work: Therapist contributions and responsiveness to patient needs*. New York: Oxford University Press.

Lambert, M. J., & Bergin, A. E. (1994). The effectiveness of psychotherapy. In A. E. Bergin & S. L. Garfield (Eds.), *The handbook of psychotherapy and behavior change* (4th ed., pp. 143–189). New York: Wiley.

Lambert, M. J., DeJulio, S. S., & Stein, D. M. (1978). Therapist interpersonal skills: Process, outcome, methodological considerations, and recommendations for future research. *Psychological Bulletin*, *85*, 467–489.

Lambert, M. J., & Ogles (2002). The efficacy and effectiveness of psychotherapy. In M. J. Lambert (Ed.), *Handbook of psychotherapy and behavior change* (5th ed.). New York: Wiley.

Lambert, M. J., & Okiishi, J. C. (1997). The effects of the individual psychotherapist and implications for future research. *Clinical Psychology: Science and Practice*, *4*, 66–75.

Lankton, S. (2003). An interview with Donald Meichenbaum. *The Milton Erickson Foundation Newsletter*, *23*, 1–24.

Laroche, M. J. & Maxie, A. (2003). Ten considerations in addressing cultural differences in psychotherapy. *Professional Psychology: Research and Practice*, *34*, 180–186.

Lasch, C. (1978). *The culture of narcissism: American life in an age of diminishing expectations*. New York: Norton.

Lave, J. (1988). *Cognition in practice: Mind, mathematics, and culture in everyday life.* Cambridge: Cambridge University Press.

Lave, J., & Wenger, E. (1991). *Situated learning: Legitimate peripheral participation.* Cambridge: Cambridge University Press.

Lazarus, A. A., & Zur, O. (Eds.). (2002). *Dual relationships and psychotherapy.* New York: Springer.

Lazarus, R., & Lazarus, N. (1994). *Passion and reason: Making sense of our emotions.* New York: Oxford University Press.

Lederer, W. J., & Jackson, D. D. (1968). *The mirages of marriage.* New York: Norton.

LeDoux, J. (1998). *The emotional brain: The mysterious underpinnings of emotional life.* New York: Touchstone.

Lefcourt, H. (1966). Internal versus external control of reinforcements: A review. *Psychological Bulletin, 65,* 206–220.

Lekander, M. (2002). Ecological immunology: The role of the immune system in psychology and neuroscience. *European Psychologist, 7*(2), 98–115.

Leonard, G. (1992). *Mastery: The keys to success and long-term fulfillment.* New York: Plume.

Leven, J. (Dir.). (1995). *Don Juan DeMarco.* San Francisco: American Zoetrope.

Levenson, R., Carstenson, L. L., & Gottman, J. M. (1994). The influence of age and gender on affect, physiology, and their interrelations: A study of long-term marriages. *Journal of Personality and Social Psychology, 67,* 56–68.

Levenson, R., & Reuf, A. (1992). Empathy: A physiological substrate. *Journal of Personality and Social Psychology, 63,* 234–246.

Lewin, K. (1935). *The dynamic theory of personality.* New York: McGraw-Hill.

Lewin, K. (1938). The conceptual representation and measurement of psychological forces. *Contributions to Psychological Theory, 1*(4).

Lewin, K. (1948). *Resolving Social Conflicts.* New York. Harper & Row.

Lewin, K. (1951). *Field Theory in Social Science.* New York: Harper & Row. (Original published in 1947).

Lewis, T. F., & Osborn, C. J. (2004). Solution-focused counseling and motivational interviewing: A consideration of confluence. *Journal of Counseling & Development, 82*(1), 38–48.

Lieberman, M. A., Yalom, I. D., & Miles, M. B. (1973). *Encounter groups: First facts.* New York: Basic Books.

Lipsey, M. W., & Wilson, D. B. (1993). The efficacy of psychological, educational, and behavioral treatment: Confirmation from meta-analysis. *American Psychologist, 48,* 1181–1209.

Loftus, E., & Ketcham, K. (1994). *The myth of repressed memory: False memories and allegations of sexual abuse.* New York: St. Martin's.

Loftus, E. F., & Davis, D. (2006). Recovered memories. *Annual Review of Clinical Psychology, 2,* 469–498.

Luborsky, L., Crits-Christoph, P., McLellan, T., Woody, G., Piper, W., Liberman, B., et al. (1986). Do therapists vary much in their success? Findings from four outcome studies. *American Journal of Orthopsychiatry, 51,* 501–512.

Luborsky, L., Diguer, L., Seligman, D. A., Rosenthal, R., Krause, E. D., Johnson, S., et al. (1999). The researcher's own therapy allegiances: A "wild card" in comparisons of treatment efficacy. *Clinical Psychology: Science and Practice, 6,* 95–106.

Lyubomirsky, S. (2001). Why are some people happier than others? The role of cognitive and motivational processes in well-being. *American Psychologist, 56,* 239–249.

Maddi, S. R., & Kobasa, S. C. (1991). The development of hardiness. In A. Monat & R. S. Lazarus (Eds.), *Stress and coping: An anthology* (3rd ed., pp. 245–257). New York: Columbia University Press.

Mandel, H., Weizmann, F., Millan, B., Greenhow, J., & Speirs, D. (1975). Reaching emotionally disturbed children: Judo principles in remedial education. *American Journal of Orthopsychiatry, 45*(5), 867–874.

Maniacci, M., & Manniaci, L. (2002). The use of the *DSM-IV* in treatment planning: An Adlerian view. *Journal of Individual Psychology, 58,* 388–397.

Marci, C. C., Ham, J., Moran, E., & Orr, S. P. (2007). Physiologic correlates of perceived therapist empathy and social-emotional process during psychotherapy. *Journal of Nervous & Mental Disease, 195,* 103–111.

Marshall, R. J. (1972, Summer). The treatment of resistances in psychotherapy of children and adolescents. *Psychotherapy: Theory, Research and Practice, 9,* 143–148.

Marshall, R. J. (1974). Meeting the resistances of delinquents. *Psychoanalytic Review, 61,* 295–304.

Marshall, R. J. (1976). "Joining techniques" in the treatment of resistant children and adolescents: A learning theory rationale. *American Journal of Psychotherapy, 30,* 73–84.

Martin, D. J., Garske, M. P., & Davis, M. K. (2000). Relation of the therapeutic alliance with outcome and other variables: A meta-analytic review. *Journal of Consulting and Clinical Psychology, 68,* 438–450.

Martin, J., Slemon, A. G., Hiebart, B., Hallberg, E. T. & Cummings, A. L. (1989). Conceptualizations of novice and experienced counselors. *Journal of Counseling Psychology, 36,* 395–400.

Martin, R. A. (2001). Humor, laughter, and physical health: Methodological issues and research findings. *Psychological Bulletin, 127*, 504–519.

Masters, W. H., & Johnson, V. E. (1966). *Human sexual response*. Oxford: Little, Brown.

Matthews, W. J., & Langdell, S. (1989). What do clients think about the metaphors they receive? An initial inquiry. *American Journal of Clinical Hypnosis, 31*, 242–251.

Mayer, J. D., & Salovey, P. (1997). What is emotional intelligence? In P. Salovey & D. Sluyter (Eds.), *Emotional development and emotional intelligence* (pp. 3–31). New York: Basic Books.

Mayer, J. D., & Stevens, A. (1993). *An emerging understanding of the reflective (meta) experience of mood*. Unpublished manuscript.

McAdams, D. P., & Pals, J. L. (2006). A new big five: Fundamental principles for an integrative science of personality. *American Psychologist, 45*, 204–217.

McCabe, R., & Priebe, S. (2004). The therapeutic relationship in the treatment of severe mental illness: A review of methods and findings. *International Journal of Social Psychiatry, 50*, 115–128.

McClure, S. M., Laibson, D. I., Loewenstein, G., & Cohen, J. D. (2004). Separate neural systems value immediate and delayed monetary rewards. *Science, 306*, 503–507.

McConnaughy, E. A., DiClemente, C. C., Prochaska, J. O., & Velicer, W. F. (1989). Stages of change in psychotherapy: A follow-up report. *Psychotherapy, 26*, 494–503.

McConnaughy, E. N., Prochaska, J. O., & Velicer, W. F. (1983). Stages of change in psychotherapy: Measurement and sample profiles. *Psychotherapy: Theory, Research and Practice, 20*, 368–375.

McGoldrick, M., Gerson, R., & Shellenberger, S. (1999). *Genograms: Assessment and intervention* (2nd ed.). New York: Norton.

McKie, R. (2005). Chemical kiss turns kids into adolescence. *Observer*. Retrieved September 19, 2008, from http://www.kisspeptin.com

McNair, D., Lorr, M., & Callahan, D. (1963). Patient and therapist influences on quitting psychotherapy. *Journal of Consulting and Clinical Psychology, 27*, 10–17.

Mehrabian, A., & Ferris, S. R. (1967). Inference and attitudes from nonverbal communication in two channels. *Journal of Consulting Psychology, 31*, 248–252.

Mehrabian, A., Young, A. L., & Sato, S. (1988). Emotional empathy and associated individual differences. *Current Psychology Research and Reviews, 7*, 221–240.

Mental health: Does therapy help? (1995, November). *Consumer Reports*, pp. 734–739.

Merriam-Webster's. (2006). *Merriam-Webster's collegiate dictionary* (11th ed., rev. ed.). New York: Author.

Messer, S. B. (2001). Empirically supported treatments: What's a non-behaviorist to do? In B. D. Slife, R. N. Williams, & S. H. Barlow (Eds.), *Critical issues in psychotherapy: Translating new ideas into practice* (pp. 3–19). Thousand Oaks, CA: Sage.

Messer, S. B., & Wampold, B. E. (2002). Let's face facts: Common factors are more potent than specific therapy ingredients. *Clinical Psychology: Science and Practice, 9*, 21–25.

Messer, S. B., & Warren, C. S. (1995). *Models of brief psychodynamic therapy: A comparative approach*. New York: Guilford.

Metcalfe, W., & Mischel, A. (1999). Hot/cool-system analysis of delay of gratification dynamics of willpower. *Psychological Review, 106*, 3–19.

Michenbaum, D. (1977). *Cognitive behavior modification: An integrated approach*. New York: Plenum.

Migneault, J. P., Velicer, W. F., Prochaska, J. O., & Stevenson, J. F. (1999). Decisional balance for immoderate drinking in college students. *Substance Use & Misuse, 34*, 1325–1346.

Miklowitz, D. J., Otto, M. W., Frank, E., Reilly-Harrington, N. A., Wisniewsik, S. R., Kogan, J. N., et al. (2006). A 1-year randomized trial from the systematic treatment enhancement program. *Archives of General Psychiatry, 64*, 419–426.

Mikulincer, M., & Shaver, P. R. (2005). Attachment security, compassion, and altruism. *Current Directions in Psychological Science, 14*(1), 34–38.

Miles, M. B., Marchbank, P., & Neville, P. (1978). *The Beatles in their own words*. New York: Quick Fox.

Miller, E. K., & Cohen, J. D. (2001). An integrative theory of prefrontal cortex function. *Annual Review of Neuroscience, 24*, 167–202.

Miller, G. E., Cohen, S., & Ritchey, K. A. (2002). Chronic psychological stress and the regulation of pro-inflammatory cytokines: A glucocorticoid-resistance model. *Health Psychology, 21*, 531–541.

Miller, N. E. (1971). *Selected Papers on Conflict, Displacement, Learning Drives & Theory Vol.1*; Selected Papers on Learning, Motivation and Their Physiological Mechanisms, Vol. 2. Chicago: Aldine Atherton.

Miller, S. D. (2004). Losing Faith: Arguing for a New Way to Think About Therapy. *Psychotherapy in Australia, 10*(2), 44–51.

Miller, S. D., Duncan, B. L., & Hubble, M. A. (1997a). *Escape from Babel*. New York: Norton.

Miller, S. D., Duncan, B. L., & Hubble, M. A. (1997b, November). Letters. *Social Work, 11*, 619.

Miller, S. D., Mee-Lee, D., Plum, B., & Hubble, M. A. (2005). Making treatment count: Client-directed, outcome-informed clinical work with problem drinkers. *Psychotherapy in Australia, 11*(4), 42–56.

Miller, W. R., Benefield, R. G., & Tonigan, J. S. (1993). Enhancing motivation for change in problem drinking: A controlled comparison of two therapist styles. *Journal of Consulting and Clinical Psychology, 61*, 455–461.

Miller, W. R., & Moyers, T. B. (2004). Motivational interviewing. In G. Koocher, J. C. Norcross, & C. E. Hill (Eds.), *Psychologists' desk reference* (2nd ed., pp. 57–62). New York: Oxford University Press.

Miller, W. R., & Rollnick, S. (1991). Motivational interviewing: Preparing people to change addictive behavior. New York: Guilford Press.

Miller, W. R., & Rollnick, S. (2002). *Motivational interviewing: Preparing people for change* (2nd ed.). New York: Guilford.

Miller, W. R., Taylor, C. A., & West, J. C. (1980). Focused versus broad-spectrum behavior therapy for problem drinkers. *Journal of Consulting and Clinical Psychology, 48*, 590–601.

Miller, W. R., Zweben, A., DiClemente, C. C., & Rychtarik, R. G. (1992). *Motivational enhancement therapy manual: A clinical research guide for therapists treating individuals with alcohol abuse and dependence* (Project MATCH Monograph Series, DHHS Publication No. [ADM] 92-1894). Washington, DC: National Institute on Alcohol Abuse and Alcoholism.

Millon, T. (1996). *Disorders of personality: DSM-IV and beyond* (2nd ed.). New York: John Wiley.

Mineka, S., & Zinbarg, R. (2006). A contemporary learning theory perspective on the etiology of anxiety disorders. *American Psychologist, 61*, 10–26.

Mishne, J. (2002). *Multiculturalism and the therapeutic process*. New York: Guilford Press.

Mosak, H. (1971). Lifestyle. In A. Nikelly (Ed.), *Techniques for behavior change*. Springfield, IL: Charles C Thomas.

Mosak, H., & DiPietro, R. (2006). *Early recollections: Interpretive method and applications*. New York: Brunner-Routledge.

Mosak, H., & Dreikurs, R. (1975). Adlerian psychotherapy. In R. Corsini (Ed.), *Current psychotherapies*. Belmont, CA: Wadsworth.

Mosak, H., & Gushurst, R. (1971). What patients say and what they mean. *American Journal of Psychotherapy, 25*, 428–436.

Mosak, H., & Shulman, B. (1967). Various purposes of symptoms. *Journal of Individual Psychology, 23*, 79–87.

Mozdzierz, G. J. (2002, February 26–28). The use of hypnotic and paradoxical interventions in the treatment of a complex case of Tourette's syndrome. Paper presented at the 42nd annual scientific meeting of the American Society of Clinical Hypnosis, Baltimore.

Mozdzierz, G. J., Elbaum, P., & Houda, A. (1974). Changing patterns in the use of an intake-diagnostic-orientation group. *American Journal of Psychotherapy, 28*, 129–136.

Mozdzierz G. J., Murphy T. J. & Greenblatt R. L. (1986). Private logic and the strategy of psychotherapy. *Individual psychology, 42*(3), 339–349.

Mozdzierz, G., & Friedman, K. (1978). The superiority/inferiority spouses syndrome. *Journal of Individual Psychology, 34*, 232–243.

Mozdzierz, G., & Greenblatt, R. (1992). Clinical paradox and experimental decision making. *Individual Psychology, 48*, 302–312.

Mozdzierz, G., & Greenblatt, R. (1994). Technique in psychotherapy: Cautions and concerns. *Individual Psychology: The Journal of Adlerian Theory, Research and Practice, 50*, 232–249.

Mozdzierz, G. J., Greenblatt, R. L., & Thatcher, A. A. (1985). The kinship and relevance of the double bind to Adlerian theory and practice. *Individual Psychology: The Journal of Adlerian Theory, Research and Practice, 41*(4), 453–460.

Mozdzierz, G., Lisiecki, J., Bitter, J., & Williams, L. (1986). Role-functions for Adlerian therapists. *Individual Psychology: The Journal of Adlerian Theory, Research and Practice, 42*, 154–177.

Mozdzierz, G., Lisiecki, J., & Macchitelli, F. (1989). The mandala of psychotherapy: The universal use of paradox—new understanding and more confusion. *Psychotherapy: Theory, Research and Practice, 26*, 383–388.

Mozdzierz, G., Macchitelli, F., & Lisiecki, J. (1976). The paradox in psychotherapy: An Adlerian perspective. *Journal of Individual Psychology, 32*, 169–184.

Mozdzierz, G. J., Snodgrass, R., & Lottman, T. (1978). Where is he coming from? Where is he at? Contemporary clinical questions and individual psychology. *Individual Psychologist, 15*, 17–19.

Myers, D. (2007). *Psychology* (8th ed.). New York: Worth.

Myers, D. G., & Diener, E. (1995). Who is happy? *Psychological Science, 6*, 10–19.

Napier, A. Y., & Wittaker, C. (1978). *The family crucible*. New York: Harper & Row.

Nathan, P. E., & Gorman, J. M. (Eds.). (2002). *A guide to treatments that work* (2nd ed.). New York: Oxford University Press.

Nathanson, D. L. (1996). *Knowing feeling: Affect, script, and psychotherapy.* New York: Norton.

National Institute on Alcohol Abuse and Alcoholism. (1997, April). Project MATCH: Matching alcoholism treatment to client heterogeneity. *Alcohol Alert/NIAAA, 36.*

National Institutes of Health. (2005). *Depression: What every woman should know.* Retrieved September 30, 2008, from http://www.nimh.nih.gov/publicat/depwomenknows.cfm#sup5

Nay, W. R. (1995). Cognitive-behavioral and short term interventions for anger and aggression. *Innovations in Clinical Practice, 14,* 151–167.

Nesse, R. (1998). Emotional disorders in evolutionary perspective. *British Journal of Medical Psychology. Special Issue: Evolutionary approaches to psychopathology.* Vol 71(4), 397–415.

New Testament: Today's English version. (1966). (2nd ed.). New York: American Bible Society.

Nietzsche, F. (1968). *The Will to Power.* New York: Vintage.

Nigg, C. R., Burbank, P. M., Padula, C., Dufresne, R., Rossi, J. S., Velicer, W. F., et al. (1999). Stages of change across ten health risk behaviors for older adults. *Gerontologist, 39,* 473–482.

Nisbet, R. E., & Ross, L. (1980). *Human inference: Strategies and shortcomings of social judgment.* Englewood Cliffs, NJ: Prentice Hall.

Nolan, C. (Dir.). (2000). *Memento.* Beverly Hills, CA: Newmarket Capital Group.

Noonan, J. (1973). A follow-up of pretherapy dropouts. *Journal of Community Psychology, 40,* 519–528.

Norcross, J. (1997). Emerging breakthroughs in psychotherapy integration: Three predictions and one fantasy. *Psychotherapy, 34,* 86–90.

Norcross, J., Hogan, T. P. & Koocher, G. P. (2008a). Evidence-Based Practice in Psychology. *The Register Report. 34,* Fall, 10–15.

Norcross, J., Hogan, T. Pl. & Koocher, G. P. (2008b). *Clinician's Guide to Evidence-Based Practices: Mental Health and the Addictions.* New York: Oxford University Press.

Norcross, J. C. (1990). Commentary: Eclecticism misrepresented and integration misunderstood. *Psychotherapy, 27,* 297–300.

Norcross, J. C. (2000). Empirically supported therapy relationships: A Division 29 Task force. *Psychotherapy Bulletin, 35,* 2–4.

Norcross, J. C. (Ed.). (2001). Empirically supported therapy relationships: Summary Report of the Division 29 Task Force. *Psychotherapy, 38*(4), 345–356.

Norcross, J. C. (2002a). Empirically supported therapy relationships. In J. C. Norcross (Ed.), *Psychotherapy relationships that work: Therapist contributions and responsiveness to patient needs.* New York: Oxford University Press.

Norcross, J. C. (Ed.). (2002b). *Psychotherapy relationships that work: Therapist contributions and responsiveness to patient needs.* New York: Oxford University Press.

Norcross, J. C., Beutler, L. E., & Levant, R. F. (2005). *Evidence-based practice in mental health: Debated and dialogue on the fundamental questions.* Washington, DC: American Psychological Association.

Norcross, J. C., & Hill, C. E. (2003). Empirically supported (therapy) relationships: ESRs. *The Register Report, 29,* 23–27.

Norcross, J., Koocher, G., & Garofalo, A. (2006). Discredited psychological treatments and tests: A Delphi poll. *Professional Psychology: Research and Practice, 37*(5), 515–522.

Nystul, M. (2006). *Introduction to counseling: An art and science perspective* (3rd ed.). New York: Allyn & Bacon.

O'Connell, W. E. (1975). Humor: The therapeutic impasse. *Action therapy and Adlerian theory.* Chicago: Alfred Adler Institute of Chicago. (Reprinted from *Voices, 5*[2], 1969)

Ofshe, R., & Watters, E. (1994). *Making monsters: False memories, psychotherapy, and sexual hysteria.* New York: Scribner.

Ogles, B. M., Anderson, T., & Lunnen, K. M. (1999). The contribution of models and techniques to therapeutic efficacy: Contradictions between professional trends and clinical research. In M. A. Hubble, B. L. Duncan, & S. D. Miller (Eds.), *The heart and soul of change: What works in therapy* (pp. 201–225). Washington, DC: American Psychological Association.

O'Hanlon, W. H. (2003). *A guide to inclusive therapy: 26 methods of respectful, resistance-resolving therapy.* New York: Norton.

Omer, H. (1981). Paradoxical treatments: A unified concept. *Psychotherapy: Theory, Research and Practice, 18,* 320–324.

Omer, H. (1991). Dialectical interventions and the structure of strategy. *Psychotherapy, 28,* 563–571.

Omer, H. (1994). *Critical interventions in psychotherapy.* New York: Norton.

Orlinsky, D. E. (1989). Researchers' images of psychotherapy: Their origins and influence on research. *Clinical Psychology Review, 9,* 413–441.

Orlinsky, D. E., Grave, K., & Parks, B. K. (1994). Process and outcome in psychotherapy—Noch einmal. In A. E. Bergin & S. L. Garfield (Eds.), *Handbook of psychotherapy and behavior change* (pp. 257–310). New York: Wiley.

Orlinsky, D. E., & Howard, K. I. (1977). The therapist's experience of psychotherapy. In A. S. Gurman & A. M. Razin (Eds.), Effective psychotherapy: A handbook of research (pp. 566–590). Oxford: Pergamon Press.

Orlinsky, D. E., & Howard, K. I. (1980). Gender and psychotherapeutic outcome. In A. M. Brodksy & R. T. Hare-Mustin (Eds.), Women in psychotherapy (pp. 3–34). New York: Guilford.

Othmer, E., & Othmer, S. C. (1989). The clinical interview using DSM-III-R. Washington, DC: American Psychiatric Press.

Othmer, E., & Othmer, S. C. (1994). The clinical interview using DSM-IV: Fundamentals. Washington, DC: American Psychiatric Press.

Ottens, A. J., & Hanna, F. J. (1996). Cognitive and existential therapies: Toward an integration. Psychotherapy: Theory, Research, Practice, Training, 35(3), 312–324.

Ouimette, P. C., Finney, J. W., & Moos, R. H. (1997). Twelve step and cognitive behavioral treatment for substance abuse: A comparison of treatment effectiveness. Journal of Consulting and Clinical Psychology, 65, 230–240.

Overall, B., & Aronson, J. (1963). Expectations of psychotherapy in patients of lower socioeconomic class. American Journal of Orthopsychiatry, 33, 421–430.

Pallonen, U. E., Velicer, W. F., Prochaska, J. O., Rossi, J. S., Bellis, J. M., Tsoh, J. Y., et al. (1998). Computer-based smoking cessation interventions in adolescents: Description, feasibility, and six-month follow-up findings. Substance Use & Misuse, 33, 935–965.

Parsons, T. (1955). Family structure and the socialization of the child. In T. Parsons & R. F. Bales (Eds.), Family: Socialization and interpersonal process. Glencoe, IL: Free Press.

Pascal, E. (1992). Jung to live by. New York: Warner.

Patterson, G. R., & Forgatch, M. S. (1985). Therapist behavior as a determinant for client noncompliance: A paradox for the behavior modifier. Journal of Consulting and Clinical Psychology, 53, 846–851.

Paul, G. L. (1967). Strategy of outcome research in psychotherapy. Journal of Consulting Psychology, 31, 109–118.

Peck, S. (1993). People of the lie. New York: Touchstone.

Peele, S. (2002, June). Motivational interviewing. Workshop sponsored by Haymarket House, Chicago.

Pekarik, G. (1992). Posttreatment adjustment of clients who drop out vs. late in treatment. Journal of Clinical Psychology, 48, 378–387.

Pelusi, N. (2006a, July/August). Jealousy: A voice of possessiveness past. Psychology Today, 64–65. Retrieved September 15, 2008, from http://www.psychologytoday.com/articles/pto-20060721-000004.html

Pelusi, N. (2006b, May/June). The right way to rock the boat. Psychology Today, Retrieved September 15, 2008, from http://www.psychologytoday.com/articles/pto-20060425-000001.html

Peluso, P. R. (2006) The style of life. In Slavik, S. & Carlson, J. (Eds.) Readings in the Theory of Individual Psychology (pp. 294–304). New York: Routledge.

Peluso, P. R. (2007). The ethical and professional practice of couples and family counseling. In L. Sperry (Ed.), The ethical and professional practice of counseling and psychotherapy (pp. 285–351). Boston: Allyn & Bacon.

Peluso, P. R., & Miranda, A. O. (2007). The ethical and professional practice of mental health counseling. In L. Sperry (Ed.), The ethical and professional practice of counseling and psychotherapy (pp. 230–284). Boston: Allyn & Bacon.

Pendergast, M. (1995). Victims of memory: Incest accusations and shattered lives. Hinesburg, VT: Upper Access.

Peng, K., & Nisbett, R. E. (1999). Culture, dialectics, and reasoning about contradiction. American Psychologist, 54, 741–754.

Perls, F. (1969). Gestalt therapy verbatim. New York: Real People Press.

Perls, L. (1970). One gestalt therapist's approach. In J. Fagan & I. L. Shepherd (Eds.), Gestalt therapy now. New York: Harper Colophon.

Persons, J. B. (1989). Cognitive therapy in practice: A case formulation approach. New York: Norton.

Piercy, F. P., Lipchik, E., & Kiser, D. (2000). Miller and de Shazer's article on "Emotions in Solution-Focused Therapy." Family Process, 39(1), 25–28.

Pinker, S. (1999). How the mind works. New York: Norton.

Pinker, S. (2007). The stuff of thought: Language as a window into human nature. New York: Viking.

Pizer, B. (1995). When the analyst is ill: Dimensions of self-disclosure. Psychoanalytic Quarterly, 64, 466–495.

Plutchik, R. (2000). Emotions in the practice of psychotherapy: Clinical implications of affect theories. Washington, DC, US: American Psychological Association.

Polster, E., & Polster, M. (1974). Gestalt theory integrated: Contours of theory and practice. New York: Vintage.

Poon, P., Mozdzierz, G. J., Douglas, S., & Walthers, R. (2007). Confronting patient-initiated boundary crossings: An ethical framework for clinicians. Unpublished manuscript. Western Springs, IL.

Pope, K. S., & Vasquez, M. A. (1998). Ethics in psychotherapy and counseling: A practical guide (2nd ed.). San Francisco: Jossey-Bass.

Powers, R. (1972, April). Adlerian psychology. Lecture sponsored by the Alfred Adler Institute, Chicago.

Presbury, J. H., Echterling, L. G., & McKee, J. E. (2002). *Ideas and tools for brief counseling*. Upper Saddle River, NJ: Merrill, Prentice Hall.

Prochaska, J. O. (1999). How do people change, and how can we change to help many more people? In M. A. Hubble, B. L. Duncan, & S. D. Miller (Eds.), *The heart and soul of change: What works in therapy* (pp. 227–255). Washington, DC: American Psychological Association.

Prochaska, J. O., & DiClemente, C. C. (1982). Transtheoretical therapy: Toward a more integrative model of change. *Psychotherapy: Theory, Research and Practice, 20*, 161–173.

Prochaska, J. O., & DiClemente, C. C. (1984). *The transtheoretical approach: Crossing traditional boundaries of change*. Homewood, IL: Dorsey.

Prochaska, J. O. & DiClemente, C. C. (2005). The Transtheoretical Approach. In J. C. Norcross, & M. R. Goldfried, (Eds). *Handbook of psychotherapy integration (2nd ed.). Oxford series in clinical psychology.* (pp. 147–171). New York, NY: Oxford University Press.

Prochaska, J. O., DiClemente, C. C., & Norcross, J. C. (1992). In search of how people change: Applications to addictive behaviors. *American Psychologist, 47*, 1102–1114,

Prochaska, J. O., Velicer, W. F., Rossi, J. S., Goldstein, M. G. Marcus, B. H., Rakowski, W., et al. (1994). Stages of change and decisional balance for 12 problem behaviors. *Health Psychology, 13*, 39–46.

Project MATCH Research Group. (1997). Matching alcoholism treatments to client heterogeneity: Project MATCH posttreatment drinking outcomes. *Journal of Studies on Alcohol, 58*, 7–29.

Project MATCH Research Group. (1998). Therapist effects in three treatments for alcohol problems. *Psychotherapy Research, 8*, 455–474.

Psychopathology Committee of the Group for the Advancement of Psychiatry. (2001). Reexamination of therapist self disclosure. *Psychiatric Services, 52*, 1489–1493.

Random House American College Dictionary. (2006). New York: Random House.

Raskin, D. E., & Klein, Z. E. (1976). Losing a symptom through keeping it: A review of paradoxical techniques and rationale. *Archives of General Psychiatry, 33*, 548–555.

Rasmussen, P. R., & Dover, G. J. (2006). Purposefulness of anxiety and depression. *Journal of Individual Psychology, 62*, 366–396.

Reis, H. T. (1984). Social interaction and well-being. In S. W. Duck (Ed.), *Personal relationships: Repairing personal relationships* (Vol. 5, pp. 21–46). London: Academic Press.

Reis, H. T., & Patrick, B. C. (1996). Attachment and intimacy: Component processes. In E. T. Higgins & A. W. Kruglanski (Eds.), *Social psychology: Handbook of basic principles* (pp. 523–563). New York: Guilford.

Reynes, R., & Allen, A. (1987). Humor in psychotherapy: A view. *American Journal of Psychotherapy, 41*, 260–269.

Reynolds, D. K. (1976). *Morita therapy*. Berkeley: University of California Press.

Robles, T. F., & Kiecolt-Glaser, J. K. (2003). The physiology of marriage: Pathways to health. *Physiology and Behavior, 79*, 409–416.

Rogers, C. R. (1951). *Client centered therapy*. Boston: Houghton Mifflin.

Rogers, C. R. (1957). The necessary and sufficient conditions of therapeutic personality change. *Journal of Consulting Psychology, 22*, 95–103.

Rogers, R., & Reinhardt, V. R. (1998). Conceptualization and assessment of secondary gain. In G. Koocher, J. C. Norcross, & C. E. Hill (Eds.), *Psychologists' desk reference* (pp. 57–62). New York: Oxford University Press.

Rohrbaugh, M., Tennen, H., Press, S., & White, L. (1981). Compliance, defiance, and therapeutic paradox: Guidelines for strategic use of paradoxical interventions. *American Journal of Orthopsychiatry, 51*, 454–467.

Rohrbaugh, M., Tennen, H., Press, S., White, L., Raskin, P., Pickering, M., et al. (1977, August). *Paradoxical strategies in psychotherapy*. Symposium presented at the annual meeting of the American Psychological Association, San Francisco.

Rollow, C. (1977, February 27). Cooper Rollow sports column. *Chicago Tribune*, Sports Sec., p. 1.

Ronnestad M. H., & Skovholt, T. M. (1993). Supervision of beginning and advanced graduate students of counseling and psychotherapy. *Journal of Counseling & Development, 71*, 396–405.

Rosen, J. (1953). *Direct psychoanalysis* (Vols. 1 and 2). New York: Grune & Stratton.

Rosenweig, S. (1936). Some implicit common factors in diverse methods in psychotherapy. *Journal of Orthopsychiatry, 6*, 412–415.

Rossi, E. (1973). Psychological shocks and creative moments in psychotherapy. *The American Journal of clinical Hypnosis. 16*, 9–22.

Rossi, E. L., & Rossi, K. L. (2007). The neuroscience of observing consciousness and mirror neurons in therapeutic hypnosis. *American Journal of Clinical Hypnosis, 48*, 263–278.

Roth, A. D., & Fonagy, P. (1996). *What works for whom? A critical review of psychotherapy research*. New York: Guilford.

Rotter, J. (1966). Generalized expectancies for internal versus external control of reinforcement. *Psychological Monographs, 80*(609).

Ruggiero, L., Glasgow, R., Dryfoos, J. M., Rossi, J. S., Prochaska, J. O., Orleans, C. T., et al. (1997). Diabetes self-management: Self-reported recommendations and patterns in a large population. *Diabetes Care, 20*, 568–576.

Ruggiero, L., Rossi, J. S., Prochaska, J. O., Glasgow, R. E., de Groot, M., Dryfoos, J. M., Reed, G. R., Orleans, C. T., Prokhorov, A. V., & Kelly, K. (1999). Smoking and diabetes: Readiness for change and provider advice. *Addictive Behaviors, 24*, 573–578.

Rule, W. (2000). Understanding and reframing resistance using angels and devils as a metaphor. *Journal of Individual Psychology, 56*, 184–191.

Rumelhart, D. (1978, December). *Schemata: The building blocks of cognition.* San Diego: Center for Human Information Processing, University of California, San Diego.

Rychtarik, R. G., Connors, G. J., Wirtz, P. W., Whitney, R. B., MiGillicuddy, N. B., & Fitterling, J. M. (2000). Treatment settings for persons with alcoholism: Evidence for matching clients to inpatient versus outpatient care. *Journal of Consulting and Clinical Psychology, 68*, 277–289.

Safran, J. D. & Muran, J. C. (2000). *Negotiating the therapeutic alliance: A relational treatment guide.* New York, NY, US: Guilford Press.

Safran, J. D., Muran, J. C., Samstag, L. W., & Stevens, C. (2002). Repairing alliance ruptures. In J. C. Norcross (Ed.), *Psychotherapy relationships that work: Therapist contributions and responsiveness to patient needs.* New York: Oxford University Press.

Salny, A. F. (2008, February 18). Mensa quiz. *American Way*, p. 78.

Sanders, L. (1981). *The third deadly sin.* New York: Berkley.

Saper, B. (1988). Humor in a psychiatric setting. *Psychiatric Quarterly, 59*, 306–319.

Sapolsky, R. (2004). *Why zebras don't get ulcers* (3rd ed.). New York: Holt.

Saposnek, D. T. (1980). Akido: A model for brief strategic therapy. *Family Process, 19*, 227–238.

Satir, V. (1964). *Conjoint family therapy.* Palo Alto, CA: Science and Behavior Books.

Saunders, S. M., Howard, K. I., & Orlinsky, D. E. (1989). The Therapeutic Bond Scales: Psychometric characteristics and relationship to treatment effectiveness. *Psychological Assessment, 1*, 323–330.

Scarvalone, P., Fox, M., & Safran, J. D. (2005). Interpersonal schemas: Clinical theory, research, and implications. In M. W. Baldwin (Ed.), *Interpersonal cognition* (pp. 359–387). New York: Guilford.

Schnarch, D. (1991). *Constructing the sexual crucible.* New York: Norton.

Schneider, K. J. (1990). *The paradoxical self: Toward an understanding of our paradoxical nature.* New York: Insight Books, Plenum.

Schneider, S. L. (2001). In Search of Realistic Optimism: Meaning, Knowledge, and Warm Fuzziness.

Schwartz, J. M. & Bayette, B. (1997). *Brain Lock: Free yourself from obsessive-compulsive behavior.* New York: Regan Books/Harper Perennial.

Schwartz, J. M., & Begley, S. (2003). *The mind and the brain: Neuroplasticity and the power of mental force.* New York: Harper Perennial.

Schwartz, R. C. (1999). The internal family systems model. In J. Rowan & M. Cooper (Eds.), *The plural self: Multiplicity in everyday life* (pp. 238–253). London: Sage.

Schwartz, R. C., & Johnson, S. M. (2000). Commentary: Does couple and family therapy have emotional intelligence? *Family Process, 39*, 29–33.

Schwartz, S., & Griffin, T. (1986). *Medical thinking.* New York: Springer-Verlag.

Segal, P. (Dir.). (2004). *50 first dates.* Culver City, CA: Columbia Pictures.

Segal, Z. V., Williams, M., & Teasdale, J. D. (2002). *Mindfulness-based cognitive therapy for depression: A new approach to preventing relapse.* New York: Guilford.

Segalowitz, S. J. (1983). *The two sides of the brain: Brain lateralization explored.* Englewood Cliffs, NJ: Prentice Hall.

Seibert, A. (2005). *The resiliency advantage: Master change, thrive under pressure and bounce back from setbacks.* San Francisco: Barrett-Koehler.

Seipp, B. (1991). Anxiety and academic performance: A meta-analysis. *Anxiety, Stress and Coping.* 4, 27–41.

Seligman, M. (1990). *Learned optimism.* New York: Knopf.

Seligman, M. (1994). *What you can change and what you can't.* New York: Knopf.

Seligman, M. (1995). The effectiveness of psychotherapy: The *Consumer Reports* study. *American Psychologist, 50*, 965–974.

Seltzer, L. (1986). *Paradoxical strategies in psychotherapy: A comprehensive overview and guidebook.* New York: John Wiley.

Shacter, D. L. (1996). *Searching for memory.* New York: Basic Books.

Shadyac, T. (Dir.). (1998). *Patch Adams.* San Francisco: Blue Wolf Productions.

Shaver, P., Schwartz, J., Kirson, D., & O'Connor, C. (1987). Emotion knowledge: Further exploration of a prototype approach. *Journal of Personality and Social Psychology, 52*, 1061–1086.

Shepris, C. J., & Shepris, S. F. (2002). *The Matrix* as a bridge to systems thinking. *Family Journal: Counseling and Therapy for Families and Couples, 10*(3), 308–314.

Shoham-Salomon, V., Avner, R., & Neeman, R. (1989). You're changed if you do and changed if you don't: Mechanisms underlying paradoxical interventions. *Journal of Consulting and Clinical Psychology, 57*, 590–598.

Shoham-Salomon, V., & Rosenthal, R. (1987). Paradoxical interventions: A meta-analysis. *Journal of Consulting and Clinical Psychology, 55*, 22–28.

Shore, J. J. (1981). Use of paradox in the treatment of alcoholism. *Health and Social Work, 6*, 11–20.

Shulman, B. (1973). *Contributions to individual psychology.* Chicago: Alfred Adler Institute.

Siegel, D. (2001). Toward an interpersonal neurobiology of the developing mind: Attachment, relationships, "mindsight" and neural integration. *Infant Mental Health Journal, 22*, 67–94.

Situated Learning. (N.d.). Retrieved September 24, 2008, from http://tip.psychology.org/lave.html

Skovholt, T. M., & Jennings, L. (2004). *Master therapists: Exploring expertise in therapy and counseling.* Boston: Allyn & Bacon.

Skovholt, T. M., & Rivers, D. (2004). *Skills and strategies for the helping professions.* Denver, CO: Love.

Skovholt, T. M., & Ronnestad, M. H. (1992). Themes in therapist and counselor development. *Journal of Counseling & Development, 70*(4), 505–515.

Smith, E. E., & Jonides, J. (1999). Storage and executive processes in the frontal lobes. *Science, 283*, 1657–1661.

Smith, M., Glass, G., & Miller, T. (1980). *The benefit of psychotherapy.* Baltimore: Johns Hopkins University Press.

Sneed, J. R., Balestri, M., & Belfri, B. (2003). The use of dialectical behavioral therapy strategies in the psychiatric emergency room. *Psychotherapy: Theory, Research and Practice, 40*, 265–277.

Snyder, D. K., & Schneider, W. J. (2002). Affective reconstruction: A pluralistic, developmental approach. In A. Gurman & N. Jacobson (Eds.), *Handbook of couples therapy.* New York: Guilford.

Sommers-Flanagan, R., Elliott, D., & Sommers-Flanagan, J. (1998). Exploring the edges: Boundaries and breaks. *Ethics & Behavior, 8*(1), 37–48.

Sorenson, R. L., Gorsuch, R. L., & Mintz, J. (1985) Moving targets: Patients' changing complaints during psychotherapy. *Journal of Consulting and Clinical Psychology, 53*(1), 49-54.

Spence, J. T., Deaux, K., & Helmreich, R. L. (1985). Sex roles and contemporary American society. In G. Lindzey & E. Aronson (Eds.), *The handbook of social psychology* (3rd ed., pp. 149–178). New York: Random House.

Sperry, L. (2002a). From psychopathology to transformation: Retrieving the developmental focus in psychotherapy. *Journal of Individual Psychology, 58*, 398–421.

Sperry, L. (2002b). *DSM-IV*: Making it more clinician-friendly. *Journal of Individual Psychology, 58*, 434–442.

Sperry, L., Carlson, J., & Peluso, P. R. (2006). *Couples therapy: Integrating theory, research, and practice* (2nd ed.). Denver, CO: Love.

Sroufe, L. A. Waters, E. (1977). Attachment as an organizational construct. *Child Development, 48*(4) 1184-1199.

Stewart, A. E., & Stewart, E. A. (1995). Trends in birth order research: 1976–1993. *Individual Psychology, 51*, 221–236.

Stewart, A. E., Stewart, E. A., & Campbell, L. F. (2001). The relationship of psychological birth order to the family atmosphere and to personality. *Journal of Individual Psychology, 57*, 363–387.

Stiles, W. B., Honos-Webb, L., & Surko, M. (1998). Responsiveness in psychotherapy. *Clinical Psychology: Science and Practice, 5*, 439–458.

Stiles, W. B., Shapiro, D. A., & Elliot, R. (1986). Are all psychotherapies equivalent? *American Psychologist, 41*(2), 165–180.

Stoltenberg, C. D. (1993). Supervising consultants in training: An application of a model of supervision. *Journal of Counseling and Development, 72*, 131–138.

Stoltenberg, C. D. (1997). The integrated developmental model of supervision: Supervision across levels. *Psychotherapy in Private Practice, 16*(2), 59-69.

Stoltenberg, C. D., & Delworth, U. (1987). *Supervising counselors and therapists: A developmental approach.* San Francisco: Jossey-Bass.

Stoltenberg, C. D., McNeill, B., & Delworth, U. (1998). *IDM supervision: An integrated developmental model for supervising counselors and therapists.* San Francisco: Jossey-Bass.

Styron, W. (1979). *Sophie's choice.* New York: Modern Library.

Sue, D. W., Arrendondo, P., & McDavis, R. J. (1992). Multicultural counseling competencies and standards: A call to the profession. *Journal of Counseling and Development, 70*, 477–486.

Sue, D. W., Bernier, Y., Durran, A., Feinberg, L., Pederson, P. B., Smith, E. J., et al. (1982). Cross-cultural counseling competencies. *The Counseling Psychologist, 10*, 45–52.

Sue, D. W., Carter, R. T., Casas, J. M., Fouad, N. A., Ivey, A. E., Jensen, M., et al. (1998). *Multicultural counseling competencies: Individual and organizational development*. Thousand Oaks, CA: Sage.

Swann, W. B., Chang-Schneider, C., & Larsen McClarty, K. (2007). Do people's self-views matter? Self-concept and self-esteem in everyday life. *American Psychologist, 62*, 84–94.

Swartz, H. A., Zukoff, A., Grote, N. K., Spielvogel, H. N., Bledsoe, S., Shear, M. K., & Frank, E. (2007). Engaging depressed patients in psychotherapy: Integrating techniques from motivational interviewing and ethnographic interviewing to improve treatment participation. *Professional Psychology: Research and Practice, 38*(4), 430–439.

TalkingCure.com. (2005, October 18). "What works" in therapy? Retrieved September 19, 2008, from http://www.talkingcure.com/docs/WhatWorks.doc

Tallman, K., & Bohart, A. C. (1999). The client as a common factor: Clients as self-healers. In M. A. Hubble, B. L. Duncan, & S. D. Miller (Eds.), *The heart and soul of change: What works in therapy* (pp. 91–131). Washington, DC: American Psychological Association.

Tashiro, T., & Mortensen, L. (2006). Translational research: How social psychology can improve psychotherapy. *American Psychologist, 61*, 959–966.

Taylor, S. E. (1982). The availability bias in social perception and interaction. In D. Kahneman, P. Slovic, & A. Tversky (Eds.), *Judgment under uncertainty: Heuristics and biases*. Cambridge: Cambridge University Press.

Teasdale, J. D., Segal, Z. V., Williams, J. M. G., Ridgeway, V. A., Soulsby, J. M., & Lau, M. A. (2000). Prevention of relapse/recurrence in major depression by mindfulness-based cognitive therapy. *Journal of Consulting and Clinical Psychology, 68*, 615–623.

The Economist. (2006). The invisible scars. November 25th, p. 41.

Thornton, J. (2006). A new path to change. *Men's Health*. July/August, p. 156–159.

Tickle-Degnan, L., & Rosenthal, R. (1990). The nature of rapport and its nonverbal correlates. *Psychological Inquiry, 1*, 285–293.

Tolson, J. (2006). Special report: Is there room for the soul? New challenges to our most cherished beliefs about self and the human spirit. *U.S. News & World Report, 141*(15), 57–63.

Tomm, C. (2002). The ethics of dual relationships. In A. A. Lazarus & O. Zur (Eds.), *Dual relationships and psychotherapy* (pp. 44–54). New York: Springer.

Truax, C. B., & Carkhuff, R. R. (1967). *Toward effective counseling and psychotherapy*. Chicago: Aldine.

Tversky, A., & Kahneman, D. (1974). Judgment under uncertainty: Heuristics and biases. *Science, 185*, 1124–1131.

Tversky, A., & Kahneman, D. (1981). The framing of decisions and the psychology of choice. *Science, 211*, 453–458.

U.S. Department of Health and Human Services. (2000). *Mental health: A report of the surgeon general*. Washington, DC: Author. Retrieved September 15, 2008, from http://www.surgeongeneral.gov/library/mentalhealth/toc.html

Valle, S. K. (1981). Interpersonal functioning of alcoholism counselors and treatment outcome. *Journal of Studies on Alcohol, 42*, 783–790.

Van Sant, G. (Dir.). (1997). *Good Will Hunting*. Los Angeles: Be Gentlemen Limited Partnership.

VanWagoner, S. L., Gelso, S. J., Hayes, J. A., & Diemer, R. (1991). Countertransference and the reputedly excellent therapist. *Psychotherapy: Theory, Research, and Practice, 28*, 411–421.

Velicer, W. F., Norman, G. J., Fava, J. L., & Prochaska, J. O. (1999). Testing 40 predictions from the transtheoretical model. *Addictive Behaviors, 24*, 455–469.

Wallach, H., & Maidhof, C. (1999). Is the placebo effect dependent on time? A meta-analysis. In I. Kirsch (Ed.), *How expectancies shape experience* (pp. 321–331). Washington, DC: American Psychological Association.

Waller, G. (1997). Drop-out and failure to engage in individual outpatient cognitive behavior therapy for bulimic disorders. *International Journal of Eating Disorders, 22*, 35–41.

Walt, J. (2005). An interview with Scott Miller. *The Milton H. Erickson Foundation Newsletter, 25*, 1–20.

Walter, J., & Pellar, J. (1992). *Becoming solution-focused in brief therapy*. New York: Brunner/Mazel.

Wampold, B. E. (2001). *The great psychotherapy debate: Models, methods and findings*. Mahwah, NJ: Erlbaum.

Warner, J. (2004, October 14). Battling delayed vs. instant gratification: You brain may be at war over instant gratification and long-term goals (M. Smith, M.D., Rev.). *WebMD*. Retrieved September 30, 2008, from http://forum.psychlinks.ca/showthread.php?t=1073

Watkins, C. W. (1992). Adlerian-oriented early memory research: What does it tell us? *Journal of Personality Assessment, 59*, 248–263.

Watzlawick, P. (1964). *An anthology of human communication*. Palo Alto, CA: Science and Behavior Books.

Watzlawick, P. (1976). *How real is real?* New York: Random House.

Watzlawick, P. (1978). *The language of change: Elements of therapeutic communication*. New York: Basic Books.

Watzlawick, P. (1983). *The situation is hopeless but not serious: The pursuit of unhappiness*. New York: Norton.

Watzlawick, P., & Beavin, J. (1977). Some formal aspects of communication. In *The interactional view: Studies at the Mental Research Institute Palo Alto, 1965–1974* (P. Watzlawick & J. H. Weakland, Eds.). New York: Norton. (Reprinted from *American Behavioral Scientist, 10*[48], 1967)

Watzlawick, P., Beavin, J. J., & Jackson, D. D. (1967). *Pragmatics of human communication: A study of interactional patterns, pathologies and paradoxes*. New York: Norton.

Watzlawick, P., Weakland, J., & Fisch, R. (1974). *Change: Principles of problem formulation and problem resolution*. New York: Norton.

Weeks, G. R., & L'Abate, L. (1982). *Paradoxical psychotherapy: Theory and practice with individuals, couples, and families*. New York: Brunner/Mazel.

Weinberger, J., & Eig, A. (1999). Expectancies: The ignored common factor in psychotherapy. In I. Kirsch (Ed.), *How expectancies shape experience* (pp. 357–382). Washington, DC: American Psychological Association.

Weiner, D. L., & Hefter, G. M. (1999). *Battling the inner dummy: The craziness of apparently normal people*. Amherst, NY: Prometheus.

Weisman, M. M., Bland, R. C., Canino, J. C., Faravelli, C., Greenwald, S., Hwu, H. G., et al. (1996). Cross-national epidemiology of major depression and bi-polar disorder. *Journal of the American Medical Association, 276*, 293–299.

West, J., Main, F., & Zarski, J. (1986). The paradoxical prescription in individual psychology. *Individual Psychology, 43*, 214–224.

Westbrook, A. & Ratti, O. (1974). *Secrets of the samurai: A Survey of the martial arts of feudal Japan*. North Clarendon, VT: Tuttle Publishing.

Westen, D. & Morrison, K. (2001) A multidimensional meta analysis of treatments for depression, Panic and generalized anxiety disorder: An empirical examination of the status of empirically supported therapies. *Journal of Consulting and Clinical Psychology, 69*(6), 875–899.

Whipple, J. L., Lambert, M. J., Vermeersch, D. A., Smart, D. W., Nielsen, S. L., & Hawkins, E. J. (2003). Improving the effects of psychotherapy: The use of early identification of treatment and problem-solving strategies in routine practice. *Journal of Counseling Psychology, 50*(1), 59–68.

White, M., & Epston, D. (1990). *Narrative means to therapeutic ends*. New York: W.W. Norton & Co.

White, M. & Epston, D. (1992). Experience, Contradiction, Narrative & Imagination: Selected Papers of David Epston & Michael White 1989-1991. Dulwich Centre Publications.

Whitehead, A. N., & Russell, B. Principia Mathematica, 3 vols, Cambridge University Press, 1910, 1912, and 1913. Second edition, 1925 (Vol. 1), 1927 (Vols 2, 3). Abridged as Principia Mathematica to *56, Cambridge University Press, 1962.

Whitehead, A. N., & Russell, B. (1910–1913). *Principia mathematica*. Ann Arbor: University of Michigan.

Wickes, R. J. (2003). *Riding the dragon: Ten lessons for inner strength in challenging times*. Notre Dame, IN: Sorin.

Wierzbicki, M., & Pekarik, G. (1993). A meta-analysis of psychotherapy dropout. *Professional Psychology: Research and Practice, 24*, 190–195.

Windle, R. & Samko, M. (1992). Hypnosis, Ericksonian hypnotherapy, and Aidido. *American Journal of Clinical Hypnosis. 34*, 261–270.

Winerman, L. (2006). The culture-cognition connection. *APA Monitor on Psychology, 37*, 64.

Woodworth, R. S. (1947). *Psychology* (2nd ed.). New York: Henry Holt.

Worden, J. W. (1982). *Grief counseling and grief therapy*. New York: Springer.

Wright, J. C. (1960). *Problem solving and search behavior under noncontingent rewards*. Unpublished dissertation, Stanford University.

Wright, J. C. (1962). Consistency and complexity of response sequences as a function of schedules of noncontingent reward. *Journal of Experimental Psychology, 63*, 601–609.

Wright, L. (1994). *Remembering Satan: A case of recovered memory and the shattering of an American family*. New York: Knopf.

Yalom, I. (1970). *The theory and practice of group psychotherapy*. New York: Basic Books.

Yalom, I. (1995). *The theory and practice of group psychotherapy*. New York: Basic Books.

Yapko, M. D. (1997). *Breaking the patterns of depression*. New York: Doubleday.

Young, J. E. (1990). *Cognitive therapy for personality disorders: A schema-focused approach* (Practitioner's Resource Series). Sarasota, FL: Professional Resource Exchange.

Young, J. E. (1999). *Cognitive Therapy for Personality Disorders: A Schema-Focused Approach (Practitioner's Resource Series) (3rd Edition)*. Sarasota, FL: Professional Resource Exchange.

Young, J. E., Beck, A. T., & Weinberger, A. (1993). Depression. In D. H. Barlow (Ed.), *Clinical handbook of psychological disorders: A step-by-step treatment manual* (2nd ed., pp. 240–277). New York: Guilford.

Young, J. E., Zangwill, W. M., & Behary, W. E. (2002). Combining EMDR and schema-focused therapy: The whole may be greater than the sum of the parts. In F. Shapiro (Ed.), *EMDR as an integrative psychotherapy approach: Experts of diverse orientations explore the paradigm prism* (pp. 181–208). Washington, DC: American Psychological Association.

Zaltman, G. (2003). *How customers think: Essential insights into the mind of the market.* Boston: Harvard Business School Press.

Author Index

I

J

H

K

Y

Z

Subject Index

Page references in **bold** refer to tables.
Page references in *italics* refer to information boxes.

A

D

E

F

R

S

T

U

Dear reader:

We sincerely hope that you have found *Principles of Counseling and Psychotherapy: Learning the Essential Domains and Nonlinear Thinking of Master Practitioners* to be useful, enjoyable, and educational. In our efforts to improve upon the book in a future edition, we would welcome your responses to the following brief questions, as well as any additional feedback you would care to offer. Thank you.

Note for Instructors: If you are interested in providing more detailed feedback about the text and its fit within your course, please contact the publisher at **dana.bliss@taylorandfrancis.com** for more information. We welcome all such replies.

School/Institution and mailing address: _____

_____

_____

Department: _____

Instructor's name: _____

Name of the course in which the book was used: _____

1. What I enjoyed most about this book: _____

_____

_____

2. What I liked least about this book: _____

_____

3. My overall reaction to this book: _____

_____

4. Were there specific features of the chapters that you found particularly useful or distracting?_____

_____

_____

_____

5. Were all chapters of the book assigned for you to read, in order? If not, which chapters were omitted from the course readings?_____

_____

_____

6. Compared to other textbooks that you have read for your classes:

    a. how readable (easy to read) was this text?_____

_____

    b. how helpful was this text in understanding the principles of counseling and psychotherapy?_____

_____

    c. how relevant was this text to your learning in this particular class?_____

_____

7. Did the instructor include supplemental readings, presentations, or other materials in the course syllabus? If so, which of these did you find most useful when paired with the book?_____

_____

_____

_____

8. In the space provided, or on an additional sheet of paper if you need more room, please offer any suggestions for improving the book. Please also add any other comments about your experience in using the book._____

_____

_____

_____

_____

_____

_____

_____

Fold here

Optional

Your name: _____

E-mail address: _____

Do we have permission to quote from your comments above in our promotional efforts for *Principles of Counseling and Psychotherapy: Learning the Essential Domains and Nonlinear Thinking of Master Practitioners?*

Yes ❑   No ❑

Sincerely,

Gerald J. Mozdzierz, Paul R. Peluso, & Joseph Lisiecki

Cut here